GLOBAL CIVIL SOCIETY 2004/5

GLOBAL CIVIL SOCIETY 2004/5

Helmut Anheier, Marlies Glasius, Mary Kaldor, editors-in-chief

Fiona Holland, managing editor

First published 2005

SAGE Publications Ltd
55 City Road
1 Oliver's Yard
London EC1Y 1SP

SAGE Publications Inc.
2455 Teller Road
Thousand Oaks, California 91320

SAGE Publications India Pvt Ltd
B-42, Panchsheel Enclave
Post Box 4109
New Delhi 100 017

British Library Cataloguing in Publication data

A catalogue record for this book is available from the British Library

ISBN 1 4129 0306 8
ISBN 1 4129 0307 6 (pbk)

Library of Congress Control Number available

Printed in Great Britain by The Cromwell Press Ltd, Trowbridge, Wiltshire

Mission statement

Global civil society is diverse, creative and chaotic. That's what makes it always interesting, often unpredictable and sometimes very powerful. Studying global civil society is a way of understanding globalisation, which is all too often seen as a predominantly economic phenomenon. The reality of globalisation is more complex. Globalisation is about individual autonomy, responsibility and participation. It embodies a growing global consciousness and emerging sphere of shared values and ideas.

We are interested in how individuals try to take control of global processes rather than being overwhelmed by them. Citizens around the world, their values and identities, communities and forms of political participation, help to shape and, in turn, are shaped by globalisation – in ways that are poorly documented and little understood.

Global Civil Society is an attempt to fill this gap in our knowledge – a gap that could become politically dangerous and socially damaging in a global era full of tensions, anxieties and uncertainties. Bringing together leading thinkers in the social sciences, as well as activists and practitioners in civil societies around the world, the Yearbook seeks to chart and analyse the nature and terrain of global civil society.

The term 'global civil society' is highly contested. Many meanings have been proposed and while some adopt the term enthusiastically, others question the validity of the concept. The ambiguity surrounding global civil society might seem problematic for a Yearbook such as this. But far from being an obstacle, we see the terminological tangle that envelops the concept as an opportunity. Debate about its meaning is part of what global civil society is all about. We offer a simple working definition of global civil society as the realm of non-coercive collective action around shared interests and values that operates beyond the boundaries of nation states.

But this is just one view. As the idea spreads around the globe, is variously manifested and continuously debated, new interpretations will continue to emerge. The Yearbook offers a platform for such debate, the background to key issues and actors, and an exploration of the building blocks of global civil society.

Each edition of *Global Civil Society* is organised as follows:

Part 1 Concepts: is dedicated to ongoing conceptual discussions about the different facets and meanings of global civil society.

Part 2 Issues: explores the role of global civil society in debating and influencing specific global issues. These case studies, built upon original research by experts in relevant fields, offer a different perspective on global issues: 'globalisation from below'.

Part 3 Infrastructure: explores both the political and practical preconditions for global civil society to operate. Political preconditions include, for example, peace and security and freedom of association. Practical considerations include funding, technology, and human resources. Some chapters in this section examine the infrastructure of particular sectors of global civil society, for example the trade union movement or peasants' movements.

Part 4 Records: offers a statistical overview, via tables, maps and diagrams, of global civil society's dimensions and contours. The chronology, gathered by individuals around the world, provides an insight into the myriad protests, conferences and campaigns that are the sinews of global civil society. Integral to this section is a methodological chapter that presents alternative social science approaches and methods of analysis. We believe that conventional nation-state-centred methodology is ill-equipped to understand global civil society and, to that end, we are laying the foundations for a social science 'without borders'.

Global Civil Society is intended for a broad audience: theorists, activists, journalists, policy-makers, students . . . in fact anyone interested in how groups and individuals in civil society are influencing global processes. Perhaps its most important aim is simply this: to stimulate thinking and encourage debate among a range of actors and scholars at global and local levels. In doing so, the Yearbook is part of global civil society itself.

Acknowledgements

The production of the Yearbook depends on the support, input, and contributions of numerous individuals and organisations. We endeavour to acknowledge them all in these pages. The final publication of course remains the responsibility of the editors.

Editorial Committee

Helmut Anheier, David Held, Marlies Glasius, Fiona Holland (managing editor), Jude Howell, Armine Ishkanian, Mary Kaldor, Hagai Katz (data and maps editor), Yahia Said, Hakan Seckinelgin, Sally Stares, Jill Timms (chronology).

Consultations

International Labour Organisations and Global Civil Society seminar, 23 October 2003. Input for chapter 8

Paul Bennett, Philip Bowyer, Jim Catterson, Joabe Cavalcanti, Alana Dave, Steve Davis, Nick Dearden, John Evans, Marlies Glasius, Sarah Glensman, Stuart Hodkinson, Richard Hyman, Dwight Justice, Mary Kaldor, Duncan Pruett, Louise Richards, Yahia Said, Hakan Seckinelgin, Jill Timms, Peter Waterman.

Civil Society: Enriching or By-Passing Democracy: Local, National and Global Levels, Delhi, 7–8 January 2003. Input for chapter 5

Daniele Archibugi, Lois Barber, Neera Chandhoke, Hi-Yeon Cho, Meghnad Desai, Marlies Glasius, Parvez Imroze, Mary Kaldor, Smitu Kothari, Kuldip Mathur, Sudha Mohan, Ranjita Mohanty, Sudha Pai, Praveen Priyadarshi, Usha Ramanathan, Elango Rangasamy, Joel Rocamora, Shanthi Sachithanandam, Satyajit Singh, Meenakshi Thapar, Ivan Vejvoda.

Legal Imperialism versus Cosmopolitan Law: Constructing Global Rules from Above or Below? 29 January 2004. Input for chapter 1

Kenneth Anderson, Law, Ann Barron Law, Chris Brown, Ulrich Beck, David Chandler, Helena Cook, Steve Crawshaw, Helen Duffy, Anthony Dworkin, Pavlos Eleftheriadis, Mient Jan Faber, Marlies Glasius, Christopher Greenwood, Dominick Jenkins. Mary Kaldor, Daniel Levy, David Rieff, John Ryle, Kirsten Sellars Gerry Simpson, Leslie Sklair, Natan Sznaider, Martin Woollacot.

Other input

Special contributions

Olaf Corry (guest box) Ibrahim El-Bayoumi Ghanem (guest box) Wael Khalil (guest box), Marcus Lam (guest box), Maximilian Martin (guest box), Diane Osgood (biotechnology web update), Mario Pianto and Federico Silva (parallel summits), Jill Timms (chronology).

Correspondents: input on chronology

Brian Appelbe, Uri Avnery, Marcelo Batalha, Reine C. Borja, Thierry Brugvin, Joabe Cavalcanti, Hyo-Je Cho, Andrew Davey, Bernard Dreano, Nenad Durdevic, Mary Fischer, Louise Fraser, Iulian Gavril, Nihad Gohar, Anil Gupta, Martin J Gurch, Stuart Hodkinson, Vicky Holland, Zafarullah Khan, Yung Law, Silke Lechner, Maritza Lopez-Quintana, Mukul Mundy, Otilia Mihai, Nuria Molina, Richard Nagle, Alejandro Natal, Beatriz Martin Nieto, Katarina Sehm Patomaki, Mario Pianta, Asthriesslav Rocuts, Marjanie Roose, Thomas Ruddy, Florent Schaeffer, Robert Sommers, Toralf Staud, Vanessa Tang, Kate Townsend, Caroline Walker, Aled Williams.

Others who provided input or support

Daniele Archibugi, David Beckmann, Alexander Beloussov, Amanda Burgess, John Clark, Howard Davies, Jon Deer, Garnett E Foster, Peter Haas, Judith Higgin Anthony Judge, Denisa Kostovicova, Nadia McLaren, John Samuels, Helena Smalikova, Mark Ritchie, Asthriesslav Rocuts, Hakan Seckinelgin, Sabine Selchow, Chris Welzel, Jess Winterstein.

Research and editorial assistance

Mallika Ahluwalia, Rachel Bishop (proof reader), Olaf Corry, Chris Dance (indexer), Michael James (copy editor), Miguel Kanai (data programme), Amarjit Singh, Sally Stares (data programe).

Cover

Paul Lowe (photography), Derek Power (design), *Back cover:* Anthony Giddens, Tim Phillips and Bill Clinton (www.clintonpresidentialcenter.org)

Maps

Hagai Katz (GIS development and analysis), Derek Power (design).

Photography

Martin Adler, Trygve Bolstad, Roberto Brancolini, Morris Carpenter, Nick Cobbing, Howard Davies, John McDermott, Mark Henley, Crispin Hughes, Justin Jin, Paul Lowe, Piotr Malecki, Fernando Moleres, Yola Monakhov, Frederik Naumann, Gary John Norman, Chryssa Panoussiadou, Bruce Paton, Giacomo Pirozzi, Karen Robinson, Marcus Rose, J B Russell, Jacob Silberberg, Irene Slegt, Paul Smith, Chris Stowers, Tacayan, Liba Taylor, Andrew Testa, Jill Timms, J C Tordai, Sven Torfinn, Ami Vitale, Gisele Wulfsohn.

Administrative support

Joanne Hay, Rita Kumar Field, Davina Rodriques, Laurie Spivak.

Participants: Yearbook evaluation conference 25–26 March 2004

Ahmed Mohamed Abdalla, Jeffrey Alexander, Sergio Andreis, Helmut Anheier, Daniele Archibugi, Anthony Barnett, Maria Brant, Bill Burnham, Nicholas Deakin, Nikhil Dey, Nenad Djurdjevic, Marc Edelman, Heba Raouf Ezzat, Richard Fries, Sakiko Fukudo Parr, Tony Giddens, Marlies Glasius, Caspar Henderson, Fiona Holland, Mary Kaldor, Ramin Kaweh, Reetika Khera, Radha Kumar, David Mainwaring, Sumeet Manchanda, Doug Miller, Nuria Molina, Sreedevi Muppirisetty, Robin Murray, Diane Osgood, Vukasin Pavlovic, Jenny Pearce, Liz Philipson, Mario Pianta, Frances Pinter, Gajendran Ranganathan, Lucy Robinson, Peter Sadler, Yahia Said, Philippe Schmitter, Joy Singhal, Sally Stares, Rupert Taylor, Jill Timms, John Urry.

Financial support

We gratefully acknowledge the financial support of the following organisations:

Robert Bosch Foundation
Fondazzione Compania di San Paolo
Ford Foundation
John D and Catherine T MacArthur Foundation
Charles Stuart Mott Foundation
Rockefeller Foundation
The Atlantic Philanthropies
UCLA School of Public Affairs

CONTENTS

Boxes

Figures

Maps

Tables

Records

Contributors

Kenneth Anderson is professor of law at Washington College of Law, American University, Washington DC, and a research fellow of the Hoover Institution, Stanford University. His research and writing interests include international law, the laws of war and human rights, international development, and non-governmental organisations. Prior to becoming a professor, he was general counsel to the Open Society Institute and director of the Human Rights Watch Arms Division

Helmut Anheier is professor at the School of Public Policy and Social Research at the University of California, Los Angeles (UCLA), and director of the Center for Civil Society, and the Center for Globalization and Policy Research at UCLA. He is also a centennial professor at the Department of Social Policy, London School of Economics and Political Science (LSE). His work has focused on civil society, the non-profit sector, organisational studies and policy analysis, and comparative methodology. He is a founding editor of *The Journal of Civil Society* and author of over 250 publications in several languages. His present research examines the emergence of new organisational forms in global civil society, the role of foundations, and methodological aspects of social science research on globalisation.

Siobhan Daly is the research manager of the project 'Visions and Roles of Foundations in Europe' (Centre for Civil Society, LSE/Centre for Civil Society, UCLA). In collaboration with Helmut Anheier, she is conducting a comparative analysis of the roles and policy salience of foundations across Europe, as well as a separate analysis of foundations and the European Union (for publication with Routledge, 2005). Based on her PhD research, which she completed in 2003, she has published on the methodology of comparison, and also on European Social Policy and the Third Sector and the European Union.

Heba Raouf Ezzat teaches political theory at the Department of Political Science, Cairo University. She is coordinator of the Civil Society Program at the Center for Political Research and Studies (CPRS) at Cairo University; and editor of the 'Arabic Version' of the Global Civil Society Yearbook, which will be published by CPRS in conjunction with the Centre for study of Global Governance, LSE. She has published two books in Arabic on women, politics and morality in Islam, and contributed chapters on women, secularism, democracy and human rights, from an Islamic perspective, to a wide variety of English language publications. She is a member of the C-100 initiative by the World Economic Forum for Islamic-Western understanding.

Marlies Glasius is lecturer in NGO management at the Centre for Civil Society, and Coordinator of the Study Group on Europe's Security Capabilities at the Centre for the study of Global Governance, LSE. In 1999 she published *Foreign Policy on Human Rights: Its Influence on Indonesia under Soeharto* (Intersentia). She was managing editor of the Global Civil Society Yearbook 2000–2003, and recently published *Exploring Civil Society: Political and Cultural Contexts* (Routledge, 2004), co-edited with David Lewis and Hakan Seckinelgin. She will publish a sole-authored book entitled *The International Criminal Court: A Global Civil Society Achievement*, with Routledge this year. Her present research interests include global civil society, social forums, the International Criminal Court, and economic and social rights.

Paola Grenier is a PhD student and Dahrendorf scholar at the Centre for Civil Society, LSE. She has researched and written on social entrepreneurship in the UK and internationally, and has been active in the field over the past seven years. Her publications include 'Jubilee 2000: Laying the Foundations for a Social Movement', in John Clark's *Globalising Civic Engagement* (Earthscan 2003); and 'Social capital in Britain: an update and critique of Hall's analysis', CCS International Working Paper 14, with Karen Wright. Grenier's research interests include social entrepreneurship, social capital, and the forms and roles of leadership in civil society.

Mary Kaldor is professor of Global Governance at LSE. She has written widely on security issues and on democracy and civil society. Her recent books include *Global Civil Society: An Answer to War* (Polity Press, 2003) and *New and Old Wars: Organised Violence in a Global Era* (1999). She was a founder member of European Nuclear Disarmament (END), founder and co-chair on the Helsinki Citizens' Assembly, and is currently a governor of the Westminster Foundation for Democracy.

Hagai Katz is a research associate at the UCLA Center for Civil Society, where he recently co-authored a report on the non-profit sector in LA, and a PhD student in Social Welfare at UCLA. He is also special reader in the department of Urban Planning at UCLA, where he teaches Geographic Information Systems. Previously he was deputy director of the Israeli Center for Third-Sector Research at the Ben Gurion University of the Negev, Israel, where he established a national database on non-profit organisations and published extensively on Israel's third sector and civil society.

David Rieff is a widely published author and journalist, covering a variety of subjects including international conflict, disaster, immigration and American politics. He is contributing editor to The New Republic Magazine, and regular contributor to *The New Yorker*, *The New York Review of Books*, *Vanity Fair*, and *The Washington Post*. Currently he is a senior fellow at the World Policy Institute and a fellow at the New York Institute for the Humanities at New York University.

Yahia Said is a research fellow at the Centre for the study of Global Governance, LSE. His experience combines academic research with private sector work and activism. Prior to joining LSE he worked as a corporate finance consultant with Ernst & Young in Russia. He also worked as a project coordinator with the Helsinki Citizens' Assembly in Prague. Yahia Said specialises in issues of economic transition and security in post-communist societies. His publications include 'The New Anti-Capitalist Movement: Money and Global Civil Society', co-authored with Meghnad Desai, in *Global Civil Society 2001* (Oxford University Press, 2001) and Regime Change in Iraq, co-authored with Mary Kaldor (CsGG, 2003).

Mohamed El-Sayed Said is the deputy director of the Center for Political and Strategic Studies at Al-Ahram newspaper. He received his PhD in political science from the University of North Carolina at Chapel Hill, US, in 1983. Since 1985 he has played a key role in the establishment and development of the Egyptian and Arab human rights movement. He is also co-founder and consultant to the Cairo Institute for Human Rights Studies. He established and edited two quarterly journals, *Rowaq Arabi*, focused on the theory and practice of human rights in Arab and Islamic culture, and Egyptian Affairs, devoted to problem solving and promoting creativity in Egyptian society. His publications include *Multinational Corporations and the Future of Nationalism*, *The Future of the Arab Regional System*, and *Businessmen, Democracy and Human Rights*. El-Sayed Said also contributes to a variety of Arab language periodicals and major newspapers in the Arab world.

Jill Timms is a visiting lecturer at Imperial College, London and a research assistant at the Centre for the study of Global Governance, LSE. She teaches a globalisation course in the Department of Sociology, LSE, where she is also completing her PhD on corporate social responsibility. Prior to joining LSE, she taught at the Centre for Labour Market Studies at the University of Leicester. Her current research interests include corporate citizenship, anti-corporate groups, labour activism and social forums.

Hilary Wainwright is editor of *Red Pepper*, the British new left magazine, and research director of the New Politics Project of the Transnational Institute, Amsterdam. She is also a fellow of the Change Centre of the Manchester Business School and of the Centre for the study of Global Governance, LSE. Her most recent book, *Reclaim the State: Experiments in Popular Democracy* (Verso) was published in 2003. Previous publications include *Arguments for a New Left*, (Blackwell, 1993), *Labour: A Tale of Two Parties* (Hogarth Press/Chatto Windus, 1987), and *Beyond the Fragments, Feminism and the Making of Socialism* (Merlin 1981), with Sheila Rowbotham and Lynne Segal. She writes regularly for *The Guardian.*

Peter Waterman is a retired staff member of the Institute of Social Studies, The Hague. He specialises in labour and other internationalisms, old and new, institutional, networked, communicative and cultural. The latest books or collections he has been (co-)responsible for include, *Globalisation, Social Movements and the New Internationalisms*, (London, 2001), and *World Social Forum: Challenging Empires* (New Delhi, 2003).

INTRODUCTION

Mary Kaldor, Helmut Anheier and Marlies Glasius

Iraq today is divided into a 'Green Zone' and a 'Red Zone'. The Green Zone is where the Americans and their coalition partners are housed. It is a suburb of Baghdad, heavily guarded, with fountains and palaces, palm trees and grass. It is there that American and British officials, who are not allowed to leave the zone, busily plan the future of Iraq. Everywhere there are notices, which say: 'What have you done for the Iraqi people today?' The Iraqi government and ministries are housed partly in the green zone and partly in mini-green zones throughout the city – requisitioned buildings that are heavily guarded.

The rest of Iraq is the Red Zone. It is full of activity – people, shops, meetings, kidnappers and bombs. It is a mixture of debate and self-organisation, extremism and crime. In the Red Zone, there is deep mistrust and suspicion of those in the Green Zone. Rightly or wrongly, the Coalition and its Iraqi partners are blamed for everything and many people find it easier to sympathise with the insurgents than with the Coalition forces. But those inside the Green Zone refuse to believe that these views exist.

The Green Zone and the Red Zone can be used as a metaphor to describe the gulf that exists on a global scale between the global green zones, where the political elites live and occasionally meet in summits, and the global red zone – a heterogeneous complex world characterised by what Fred Halliday (2002) calls 'global rancour', the frustration, humiliation and powerlessness experienced by millions of men and women not only in the Middle East but all over the world. The war in Iraq revealed this gulf between the green zone and the red zone, in particular the gulf between those governments that went to war and global public opinion. Indeed, the gap between the global green zone and the global red zone, as we shall argue, overshadows the more publicised cleavages between the West and global Islam and between North and South.

Global civil society can be understood as one mechanism for crossing the divide between the red zone and the green zone. It consists of various channels – groups, movements, organisations – through which people living in the red zone try to influence the elites in the green zones. In 2003–4, the war in Iraq brought global politics into the domestic arena of nearly every country. It led to renewed efforts to overcome the green-red divide through democratic accountability. The debate about Iraq had a powerful impact on domestic debates not only among those countries sending troops, such as the United States, Britain, Spain, Italy, South Korea and Japan, but also in Muslim countries, where conflict between different factions was exacerbated (as in Pakistan or Saudi Arabia), and in countries where the role of the US is hotly debated (as in Latin America). In several countries, its preparation and aftermath actually affected electoral outcomes – the German federal elections of 2002, the Spanish elections of 2004, the European Union parliamentary elections in 2004, and, of course, the US presidential election in November 2004 (although, at the time of writing, we do not know how).

What is happening, in our view, is not a reversal of globalisation but a recasting of sovereignty and democracy in a global context. Globalisation does not mean the end of the state, as many authors point out (Held et al, 1999; Giddens, 2000). What it means is the transformation of the state, the emergence of a new kind of global politics in which the state is one actor among many; and this is in turn has profound consequences for the content and functioning of democracy. Moreover, the state changes in different ways, and at varying paces, in different places and different societies. The war in Iraq, it can be argued, is one of those pivotal events which reveal the contradictory nature of the underlying processes.

In this chapter, we want to show why a focus on global civil society helps us to understand what is happening. It is a way of studying global processes 'from below', from the point of view of individual agency. We start by explaining what we mean by global civil society, and describe current developments with the help of our data collection effort (see Records section). We next consider the implications of the emergence of global civil society for sovereignty and democracy. Finally, we apply these conclusions to the situation in the Middle East and set out two possible future directions for globalisation.

Revisiting global civil society

In *Global Civil Society 2001*, rather than providing a definitive definition, we offered the Yearbook as a continuing platform for an exchange of ideas about the meaning of 'global civil society' (Anheier, Glasius and Kaldor, 2001). We did so because we believe that debating the meaning of the term contributes to an open and self-reflexive global civil society in the end. We defined global civil society, for operational, descriptive purposes only, as a sphere of ideas, values, institutions, organisations, networks, and individuals located *between* the family, the state, and the market, and operating *beyond* the confines of national societies, polities, and economies.

But we were always clear that the concept of global civil society has a normative meaning and that the boundaries of the normative concept are contested. For us, civil society is about managing difference and accommodating diversity and conflict through public debate, non-violent struggle, and advocacy. Historically, civil society was bounded by the state; it was about managing difference within a bounded community and about influencing the state. What we mean by global civil society is not just civil society that spills over borders and that offers a transnational forum for debate and even confrontation; rather, we are concerned about the ways in which civil society influences the framework of global governance – overlapping global, national and local institutions. Some theorists prefer the term 'transnational' to 'global'. But by 'global' we mean more than just 'beyond borders': we refer to the ways in which globalisation has transformed the issues and problems that we face and the role of civil society in confronting them.

One way of understanding this definition is to revive the notion of a social contract. Historically, the concept of civil society referred to those societies which were ruled on the basis of a social contract among its citizens (consent), in contrast to those based on coercion or those without rulers. Civil society could thus be defined as the medium – the various organisations, groups and individuals – through which a social contract is negotiated and renegotiated between individual citizens on the one hand and the centres of power and authority on the other. Up until the middle of the twentieth century, the state was the centre of power and authority. Nowadays, power and authority is dispersed among different layers of governance (see Kaldor, 2003).

This way of understanding civil society helps us to understand its changing meaning over time. In the eighteenth century, civil society referred simply to a society characterised by a social contract; it really referred to a gentlemanly political elite, perhaps elected on limited suffrage, which debated and deliberated about key decisions. In the nineteenth century, Hegel and later Marx defined civil society as the arena between the state and family. The economy was included in this definition because of the growing political role of the newly emerging bourgeois class and the bargaining process that was taking place between state and capital. And in the twentieth century, the Italian Marxist Antonio Gramsci further narrowed the definition to the arena between the economy, the state and the market in recognition of the political role played by workers' movements. For Gramsci (1971), political parties were a part of civil society; he advocated a strategy of conquering the realm of culture and ideology as a way of strengthening the political position of the Communist party.

Nowadays, civil society has come to refer to non-party politics. And this is a reflection of the global nature of civil society in the twenty-first century. The term 'civil society' re-emerged in the last decades of the twentieth century as a reaction against the state and against political parties, which were blocking access to decision-making at state level. The term 'civil society' came to refer to a variety of groups, organisations and individuals who tried to get around the state blockage at local, national and global levels. And this is what we tend to mean today when we use the term.

Understood in this way, the term 'global civil society' can be viewed as a way of recognising how politics has moved beyond the national level. In Chapter 1 of this Yearbook, Anderson and Rieff criticise this understanding and argue that the idea of global civil society is a dangerous fallacy given the absence of representative institutions at a global level. They suggest that the various groups and organisations that call themselves 'global civil society' claim to represent world opinion and to substitute for the functioning of representative democracy at national levels, and that this claim is profoundly anti-democratic. In particular, they suggest that global civil society gets to be equated with a particular group of what might be described as cosmopolitan universalists, standard-bearers of 'environmentalism, feminism, human rights, economic regulation, sustainable development' (p. 29). These 'social movement

Figure I.1: Left and right vs globalisation

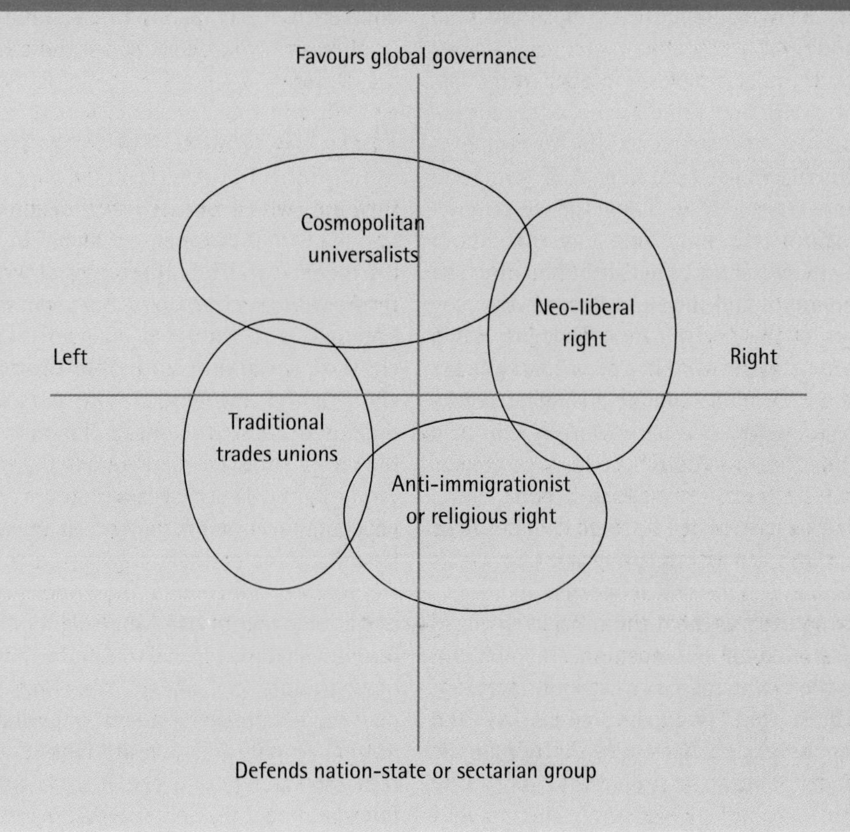

missionaries' have arrogated to themselves a supposed legitimacy that does not and cannot reflect the aspirations of individuals worldwide.

They have a point. Even if we envisage global civil society as a broad arena for political debate, efforts to give substance to the concept (like the Records section of this Yearbook, which measures international non-governmental organisations (INGOs), participation in parallel summits or global meetings, and records global civil society events) do tend to give precedence to the 'nice guys', the new global activists, even though we try to include extremist movements, representatives of political establishments and other kinds of civic institutions as well. What makes our approach different, however, is our emphasis on political positions. What we aim to show, especially in our Issue chapters, is the diverse character of the global political debate, how political stances on specific topics, like oil or democracy, reflect a deeper position on globalisation. In the process of undertaking research for the Yearbook, we have identified four positions on globalisation that appear to run through a number of widely different issues, and which we keep refining, based on our findings.

The first position is the Supporters of globalisation: those who embrace interconnectedness in all fields – economic, political, legal, and cultural – and who believe we are moving towards world government. The second position is the Rejectionists, those who oppose growing interconnectedness in all fields and want to defend the nation-state. What we have discovered is that very few groups or individuals are pure Supporters or Rejectionists; mostly they favour interconnectedness in some fields and not in others. Our last two positions are therefore mixtures. The Regressives support interconnectedness only when it can be used to strengthen particularist interests; generally Regressives also want to defend the nation state. Thus, Regressives may support free trade but not free migration and not the extension of international law. And the final category is the Reformers – these are the people usually identified as making up 'global civil society'. They support interconnectedness and the construction of global governance as a way of benefiting the many rather than the few. They support the extension of international law, especially relating to human rights, for example, but may favour constraints on the movement of capital.

Another way of categorising these positions is in terms of left and right, cosmopolitan and particularist. It is often argued that, under the impact of globalisation, the terms 'left' and 'right' are no longer meaningful. The space for resource choices by governments is constrained by global markets. Policies of 'structural adjustment' and 'transition' or 'convergence criteria' make it difficult for traditional 'left' governments to carry out their commitments to redistribution,. The left become conservatives and the right become the new radicals, pioneers of the global market (Giddens, 1995). The real choices are about whether or not to embrace globalisation, between multilateralism and unilateralism, between cosmopolitanism and particularism. What we are arguing is that these positions have to be combined. 'Left' and 'right' do remain meaningful terms at the global level but they have to be combined with positions on globalisation. This is illustrated in Figure I.1.

The vertical column represents Supporters and Rejectionists, with Supporters at the top and Rejectionists at the bottom. The horizontal axis refers to Left and Right; on the Left are those who favour redistribution and on the Right are those who favour the free market. The Reformers are in the top left-hand square – they are the cosmopolitan universalists, the people who are usually identified with 'global civil society'. They favour individual rights, including economic and social rights, rather than states' rights. All the other squares represent various forms of Regressive position. In the top right-hand corner are those who favour globalisation when it benefits a particular class – global capital. In the lower left-hand corner are those who favour redistribution within a national framework. And in the lower right-hand corner are those who favour a particular national or sectarian class or grouping.

When we discuss global civil society, we refer to the whole range of positions even though, because of our own biases, we tend to emphasise the role of Reformers. In this Yearbook, we discuss those positions in relation to the debate about oil. Thus, Regressives and Rejectionists tend to emphasise the importance of oil: the former are ready to go to war for oil and destroy ecosystems and the latter oppose oil extraction because it leads to war and environmental degradation. Reformers and Supporters, on the other hand, argue that there are better ways to secure energy supplies than through war and environmental degradation, and that alternatives can be found and managed. Chapter 8, on labour movements, describes how trade unions are transforming themselves, in the face of cultural and bureaucratic inertia as well as political differences about North and South, formal and informal, industry and services, from Regressive or Rejectionist to Reformist positions.

The debate about the war in Iraq

How are these positions reflected in the debate about the war in Iraq since it began in 2003? Mazlish (forthcoming) offers three possible frameworks for a future world society. One is American society, or 'Global America', and the deep entrenchment of American political, social and cultural institutions in many key countries of the world as well as in international organisations like the United Nations, the International Monetary Fund, the World Trade Organisation and the World Bank. Mazlish sees a profound paradox: the US, which has been so instrumental in making globalisation possible, is increasingly unwilling to live as a citizen in the very world it created. Thus, falling back into notions of national identity and sovereignty, the US seemingly assumes a quasi-imperial role in the mould of Regressive globalisation.

A second possible framework is what Mazlish labels 'Global Islam', and the attempt of elites and their militant followers in the Islamic world to react to internal modernisation failures by seeking to establish a more global cultural and political presence in the name of religious devotion and tradition. Global Islam is not supported by economic forces, however, but is primarily about the export of internal conflicts and failures to the outside world, including Africa, Asia, and of course Europe and the US. It is another form of Regressive globalisation.

Mazlish's final framework is the victory of multilateralism and what we call the 'reformist' and 'supportive' tendencies in global civil society. This would include a vibrant global civil society, with a loosely coupled international order (for example, a reformed UN system), permeable and multicultural national states with the rise of regional governments such as the EU, and a strong presence of global market institutions and corporations. The problem with such a framework is that it tends to assume the narrow but 'nice' definition of global civil society.

In the run-up to the war in Iraq, the gap between Global America and global civil society overshadowed the conflict between Global America and Global Islam, a conflict which Mohamed El-Sayed Said describes as the 'clash of civilisations' hypothesis. In Chapter 3 he argues that 'the spectacular rise of the anti-war movement during 2002–3 was instrumental in preventing the full triumph of the "clash of civilizations" and "crusade" theories in Arab minds. Furthermore, global civil society offered a brilliant opportunity for voicing Arab protests against injustices seen to be inflicted upon the Arab world by the present international system' (p. 60). As a result, he notes 'a shift in position towards global civil society by a small but growing segment of the Islamic movement' (p. 61). In effect, the West was no longer seen as monolithic – the involvement of Muslims along with Western peace activists offered a political space where it was possible to oppose both American neo-conservatism and fundamentalist Islam.

The simple-mindedness and instrumentalism of the Bush vision of spreading democracy may be ridiculed, but the anti-war movement has offered no alternative

Nevertheless, it would be wrong to romanticise the anti-war movement and to make the kind of claims that Andersen and Rieff criticise. The anti-war movement has tended to be one-sided, to put more emphasis on its opposition to American policy than on opposition to terror and dictatorships. The Middle East has, up to now, been untouched by the wave of democratisation experienced in other parts of the world. The Bush administration claims that its goal is to democratise the Middle East. Because the anti-war movement opposes the US, it has allowed the Bush administration to get away with the rhetoric of democratisation. The simple-mindedness and instrumentalism of the Bush vision of spreading democracy may be ridiculed, but the anti-war movement has offered no alternative – in fact, the lack of democracy in the Middle East hardly seems to be recognised as a problem in these circles.

The continuing war in Iraq is played out as a conflict between two forms of Regressive globalisation. On the one side are the supporters of Global America. On the other side is a mixture of militants from the former Iraqi regime and from extreme Islamic groups, who are beginning to coalesce around a kind of new Islamic nationalism. There is sometimes a tendency among those who opposed the war to gloat over the tragedies in Iraq because they mean failure for the US. Some parts of the anti-war movement have even been collecting money to support the so-called 'armed resistance' in Iraq. Far from being Reformist, as Mazlish suggests, the anti-war movement could also join the ranks of Regressive globalisers by contributing to the polarisation of world views.

Yet there is an emerging civil society in Iraq. There are groups and individuals, both religious and secular, who are trying to build a democratic Iraq (see Box I.1). Many of these people operated underground in the Saddam years and argued that a strategy similar to that adopted in eastern Europe and Latin America during the 1970s and 1980s could have been a better way to undermine the regime. The last years of Saddam's reign were post-totalitarian; it was no longer possible to insulate Iraqi society from outside pressure. Civil society groups argue that they knew a coup was impossible; but a slow strategy of eroding or strangling the regime from within with outside support might have achieved a more peaceful and therefore more secure transition to an open society. Some supported the war because they believed it was the only way to topple Saddam Hussein. But, at the time of writing, when Coalition and its Iraqi allies have lost all credibility, many of them are beginning to see Global Islam as their protector (Kaldor and Said, 2004). There is a real risk that the polarisation between Global America and Global Islam will squeeze out the space for these groups – which is why the role of the anti-war movement in supporting peaceful change could be so important.

Beyond Iraq, the chapters by Arab authors in this Yearbook do suggest ways in which global civil society could help to expand what El-Sayed Said calls the 'associative space' and start opening up societies in the Middle East. In Chapter 2 Heba Raouf Ezzat argues that this requires a reconceptualisation of civil society so as to encompass multicultural perspectives. Indeed, she echoes Anderson and Rieff in her criticism of the dominance of Western universalising ideas. She insists that the religious and the civil must be integrated. And she points to historic Islamic entities like the *Waqf* (endowments) as modern and non-secular institutions that need to be considered as manifestations of civil society in an Islamic context.

At the same time, the description by Mohamed El-Sayed Said of the human rights movement in the region, strengthened by defections from the left and networked across and beyond the region, is reminiscent of developments in Latin America and central Europe 15 years ago. This suggests that, as in Iraq, similar strategies for opening up society might be more likely to initiate a democratisation process than the methods proposed by the Bush

Box I.1: Civil society in Iraq

Very little was known about Iraqi society under Saddam Hussein; two loud voices tended to dominate – the regime and the exiled opposition. Ironically, they were both broadcasting the same message: any act of dissent was liable to be discovered and brutally punished. The aftermath of the war revealed a different picture. In its waning years Saddam's regime was post-totalitarian. Along with other state institutions, its repressive apparatus had decayed, rather like that of the Communist regimes of eastern Europe in the 1970s and 1980s. This allowed some to explore spaces vacated by the regime for various expressions of civil society – including dissent.

There were, for example, informal groups gathered around disillusioned ex-Baathists. The Hewar (dialogue) Gallery was established by Qasim Al-Sabti, an artist and committed Baathist until he resigned in protest over the invasion of Kuwait. The gallery was a place where artists could exhibit their work and find foreign buyers. It also featured a cafe where they met to talk. Some of those who frequented Hewar were more openly opposed to the regime than others. The Najeen (survivors) group, for example, was comprised of young artists who did not conceal their disgust with the regime. Their leader, Basim Al-Hajjar, was expelled from the final year at the Academy of Visual Arts for refusing to make a sculpture of Saddam Hussein for his graduation project. Hewar enabled Najeen and others like them to appear in public, voice their opinions and exhibit their work. Hewar is still a favourite meeting place for Iraqi artists. After the war Najeen went on to stage the first play in the still-smouldering building of the Al-Rasheed Theatre.

Another example is the group which met every Wednesday at the house of Ali Al-Dabbagh, a former mid-level Baath party official. The group was comprised of both current and ex-Baathists and would debate political and theoretical issues. One member of the group was arrested and executed, but they continued nevertheless to meet. The main point of Hewar and the Wednesday group was not so much the level of their opposition but the fact that they offered a public space that was outside the regime's discourse.

Mosques and seminaries offered similar spaces. Shia clerics continued to feel the full force of the regime's repression until its last days. That did not prevent them from emerging as the main source of moral authority among the Shia; Grand Ayatollah Ali-Sistani, the spiritual leader of the Iraqi Shia, is arguably the most influential person in Iraqi politics today. Sunni clergy, too, were active in building an independent public sphere. Abdul Al-Salam Al-Kubaisi, who runs a seminary in the Baghdad district of Al-Aadhamiya, describes a strategy that was aimed at isolating the regime rather than confronting it head-on. He says this strategy was working and that the regime was on the verge of collapse before the war. Today, Al-Kubaisi is a leading member of the Council of Muslim Clerics, a group that aspires to be the political wing of the insurgency in the Sunni areas.

The existence of these spaces suggests that fear of repression is not sufficient to explain the lack of a more visible opposition in Iraqi society under Saddam. Most Iraqi elites, including intellectuals and professionals, supported the regime implicitly or explicitly. Some kept a low profile and stayed out of politics. Others played along in anticipation of handouts or career advancement. At times, it seems that the regime tried to bribe the entire middle class. Some refrained from attacking the regime out of nationalist motives, fearing that its collapse would jeopardise the country's integrity and independence. Some Iraqi intellectuals speak about feeling guilty for not doing more to topple the dictator.

People like 'Salam Pax' – who became known worldwide as the Baghdad Blogger – were, perhaps unsurprisingly, rare. In September 2002 this anonymous young Iraqi began posting accounts of daily life in Baghdad on the Internet, a web diary that, being critical of Saddam's regime, could have cost him his life.

Whatever Iraqis felt about the regime, they were not ready to fight for it, as the lack of Iraqi resistance to the invading Coalition forces revealed. The Iraqi military did exactly as instructed by the Coalition: they laid down their arms and went home. Something similar happened to the entire state apparatus. In many ways the Iraqi state ceased to exist on 9 April 2003. But Coalition troops were not prepared to fill the resulting security and political vacuum. Initially, they were not even willing to do so. Chaos ensued with mobs stripping, dismantling and burning almost every state and public building. Iraq teetered on the brink of primordial chaos.

Even in the depths of that moment, which many described as the darkest in the country's troubled history, there were civic initiatives: workers stayed in their factories to prevent looting; museum employees took valuable artefacts home to protect them; local youths organised neighbourhood-watch groups; imams organised search parties to collect and return looted medicine and equipment to hospitals. Indeed, this is how firebrand cleric Muqtada Al-Sadr, who later launched an armed insurgency against the occupation, started his activity in post-Saddam Iraq.

Eventually the worst of the criminal chaos died down. The relative stability may well have been the cumulative result of the various initiatives that Iraqis undertook to step back from the brink. However, many came to the conclusion that Coalition troops were all that stood between a semblance of peace and total anarchy.

Despite continuing unrest, today Iraq is bustling with self-organised groups and political debates. Initially, exile parties that had organised clandestine activities under the regime were the most visible. The Iraqi Communist Party newspaper, *Tariq Al-Shaab*, was the first to be distributed in Baghdad, days after the fall of Saddam. It has since been followed by an estimated 200 titles. Secular groups and parties are strongest at the national level and within new government structures. Since they are largely composed of exiles and have little capacity for mobilisation, and because they are seen to be too close to the Coalition forces, they are increasingly disconnected from society. Religious groups, especially those with a nationalist agenda like Al-Sadr and the Council of Muslim Clerics, are gaining ground.

Although officially disbanded, the Baath Party and the former regime are omnipresent. Thousands of followers and recipients of favours, not to mention the regime's henchmen, would find it difficult to admit they have been wrong all these years, or they feel nostalgic. Many ex-Baathists have joined radical Islamic parties and groups that are associated with the insurgency in one way or another. Others are seeking to re-enter the political mainstream. An example of the latter is the Beit Al-Hikma (house of wisdom) think tank. Under Saddam it manufactured ideology on both domestic and international issues for the regime. Today, with its former managers in exile, it is trying to forge a new role, relying on the intellectual potential of its members who represent some of Iraq's leading political and social scientists.

There is a plethora of old and new democratic and civic initiatives. Among students, for example, there is the General Union of Students (GUSIR), which was founded in 1948 and existed underground in the Saddam years. They are campaigning to restore Iraqi schools and universities, correct the injustices of the regime and protect students' rights vis-à-vis the new authorities. For example, they campaigned for the return of student hostels occupied by Coalition troops while arranging alternative accommodation for out-of-town students. They also succeeded in forcing the Minister for Higher Education to recognise students' right to organise.

There are several human rights groups in Iraq today. Some, like the Organization of Free Political Prisoners, have moved from cataloguing the regime's crimes and accounting for its victims to investigating human rights violations by Coalition troops. The Municipal Council in Ammara is tracking down the regime's henchmen, who moved at the end of the war, to make sure they do not disappear into society. The council is also monitoring local government and organising clean-up and neighbourhood-watch initiatives.

Women are probably the best-organised segment of Iraqi society. One consequence of Saddam's war adventures and brutality is that women constitute 60 per cent of Iraq's adult population. Many women feel empowered by the opportunity to influence their country's future. They have also benefited from the Coalition's policy of paying all public sector employees salaries, which exceed their pre-war levels by a factor of thirty. Women are heavily represented in this sector. This is creating a new dynamic in society, since many men have lost their source of income in the private sector and the military. At the same time, women are threatened by terrorist and criminal violence, forcing many to stay at home. Some religious activists who have gained prominence since the collapse of the regime are promoting policies that would circumscribe women's freedoms. For example, there was an attempt to refer family matters to religious Sharia Courts. A coalition of women's groups, led among others by Hana Edward of the Iraqi Al-Amal Association, campaigned successfully against this. Women's groups also succeeded in inserting a clause into the interim constitution mandating that women constitute 25 per cent of all governing bodies – six out of 30 ministers in the current government are women. On 16–17 June 2004, Al-Amal gathered some 360 women activists from across the country to devise a strategy for their engagement in the political process.

If the continuing violence is to be stopped, civil society needs to fill the political vacuum left by the regime and build a legitimate alternative both to the occupation and to the perpetrators of terror.

Yahia Said, Centre for the study of Global Governance, London School of Economics

administration. Indeed, it is the job of global civil society as much as governments to engage in such a process. Both Raouf Ezzat and El-Sayed Said stress the importance of cyberspace – electronic publications, chatrooms and weblogs – in opening up links with global civil society. Raouf Ezzat's argument underlines the methodological importance of recording those elements of civil society that cannot easily be counted. Illustrating this empirically, El-Sayed Said describes the emergence of an Egyptian anti-globalisation movement as well as an array of formal and informal networks and individuals that are components of this common campaign.

The other side of the supposed divide, Global America, can also do with opening up. This may seem a peculiar assertion, as the US is a functioning democracy, with a free media and a high percentage of the population with Internet access. However, although the US is a nation of immigrants, parts of it remain curiously isolated and ignorant about the lives, world views and dilemmas of non-Americans. Of course, as Karl W Deutsch's adage reminds us somewhat humorously, the true test of power is one's capacity of being able to ignore information. In this sense, the relative isolation of parts of US society outside elite academic and policy circles may well be a function of its dominance. Indeed, what little information the US population gets about the outside world derives mainly from a narrow band of 'Regressive' news sources: 22 per cent of Americans now receive their daily news from talk radio, a mix of interviews and commentary by right-wing talk-show hosts, who make no pretence of presenting unbiased information (*NOW with Bill Moyers*, 2004). An equal percentage gets most of its news from the conservative Fox News Channel. Not surprisingly, there is a large overlap between Fox viewers and Republican voters (Pew Research Center, 2003). Whether these people would vote differently, or change their minds on unilateralism and the war on terror, if they were more exposed to views from the outside world is an open question. The fact is that they are not so exposed.

Some of those who opposed the war in Iraq, especially among the American churches, do make a concrete effort to expose middle Americans to different information and views, with speaking tours and conferences. Moreover Fahrenheit 9/11, Michael Moore's provocative film, is widely showing in the mid-West. These efforts need to be supported by groups and individuals in other parts of the world. Perhaps because the United States is seen as the global hegemon, there is a tendency to treat it differently from other parts of the world. Liberals and radicals are, it seems, willing to interfere and 'strengthen' civil society everywhere except in the United States. Unlike Islamists, conservative unilateralists in the US are given up as lost causes. In order to really meet the challenge of averting the 'clash of civilizations' that Regressive globalisers believe in and long for, global civil society should attempt to include and persuade middle Americans as much as Islamists. This is all the more important because in an age of global hegemony all world citizens have a stake in the US elections, but only Americans have a vote in them.

Individuals and identities

In order to deal with the complexity and multi-faceted nature of global civil society, most scholars focus either on a specific thematic field or on a particular organisational form. Some, particularly those oriented towards data-gathering and quantitative research, have focused on international NGOs (for example, Anheier and Themudo, 2002). Others, mainly on the left, have focused on global social movements (Della Porta, Kriesi and Rucht, 1999; Cohen and Rai, 2000; Hamel et al. 2001; Buttel and Gould, 2004). Yet others focus on networks (Keck and Sikkink, 1998; Diani and McAdam, 2003; see also the chapter on networks by Anheier and Katz in Part 4 of this Yearbook).

We have tried in this Yearbook to give space to all three approaches. However, each of them, even in combination, tends to see global civil society through an organisational lens, thereby giving short shrift to individuals, their attitudes and actions. Therefore, we try in this edition to give more explicit attention to the role of the individual in global civil society, with Chapter 6 on 'pioneers' of global civil society by Paola Grenier, and some analysis here and in Chapter 2 by Raouf Ezzat of the identity and role of the individual. For, as Raouf Ezzat puts it, 'it is, after all, the individual who decides to communicate, network, act and move, travel and demonstrate, and embrace notions of moral responsibility on a global scale. She or he transcends national boundaries, and bridges different public spaces – domestically and globally' (p. 46).

Geographical identities

Few terms have been used and misused more in the globalisation literature than 'individual' and 'cultural identity'. Huntington's thesis of multicultural erosion of America's cultural core refers to identity, as does Mazlish's Global Islam, and so do major theorists like Appadurai, Beck, Giddens and Held. While commentators like Huntington (2004) paint the image of an erosion of

Table I.1: Geographic identities 1981–1999/2000

Region	N*	1981 Local	1981 National	1981 Supra-national	1990 Local	1990 National	1990 Supra-national	1999/2000 Local	1999/2000 National	1999/2000 Supra-national
Sub-Saharan Africa	2				53	32	16	52	38	11
Middle East and North Africa	1				45	46	9	42	45	12
South Asia	1				52	39	9	42	53	5
East Asia and Pacific	3				51	46	4	58	37	5
Latin America and the Caribbean	3				44	42	14	45	39	16
North America	2	67	7	27	49	36	16	47	35	18
Western Europe	18	63	28	9	61	28	10	63	28	9

World Bank income groups	N*	1981 Local	1981 National	1981 Supra-national	1990 Local	1990 National	1990 Supra-national	1999/2000 Local	1999/2000 National	1999/2000 Supra-national
High-income	22	64	25	11	59	31	10	62	28	9
Upper-middle-income	3				56	33	11	57	33	10
Lower-middle-income	3				53	39	8	41	48	11
Low-income	2				51	35	15	50	42	8

Note: Figures indicate percentages of respondents self-identifying as local, national, and supranational.
* Denotes number of countries surveyed.

Sources: EVS 1981,1990, 1999; WVS 1990/1, 2000 (European Values Surveys and World Values Surveys, URL).

national identities, others like Saul (2004) see a rebirth of nationalism, also suggested by Kaldor and Muro (2003), who have pointed to an increase in religious and nationalist militant activity in nearly all parts of the world. The image evoked is one a fragility and uneasy change. But are geographic identities indeed on the move and, if so in what direction?

Two long-standing strands of social science theory shape today's understanding of individual identity. One is rooted in developmental psychology and sees identity as the result of 'deep socialisation', that is, early value-forming experiences and learning processes that make up the core personality traits and character dispositions. This psychological understanding is close to what could be called the 'hard-wired' aspect of identity as a sense of self – once formed, it is fairly stable throughout the life course and relatively resistant to political, cultural and social changes.

The other understanding of identity is more sociological and cultural in nature and sees it as the outcome of ongoing search processes. Individuals try to forge, negotiate and reconcile their own world views and notions of self with that of society. Given the multiple roles people perform in modern, diverse societies, this more 'soft-wired' form of identity is not only evolving, it is also precarious and precious. It refers less to identity as 'self' than to identity in relation to categories such as nation, religion, place, or belonging.

Research on identity and globalisation is conducted within these two traditions, with the general assumption that 'individuals increasingly have complex loyalties and multilayered identities, corresponding to the globalization of economic and cultural forces and the reconfiguration of political power' (Held and McGrew, 2000: 35). Cultural anthropologists and psychologists have explored the 'deeper' facets of identity formation, but usually in respect of one specific place or culture. Such research, of which Appadurai (1996) is exemplary, suggests that indeed globalisation is having an impact on self-formation, largely by increasing dissonances between cultural 'similarities' and 'difference' that are separated from territorial units. The equation of space, community and meaning is being eroded and can serve ever less as an anchor between primary and secondary socialisation, that is, between hard- and soft-wired facets of identity. Subject to a barrage of media, advertising and other images, people learn to confront such dissonances by creating imagined worlds that offer 'a series of elements (characters, plots, and textual forms) out of which scripts can be formed of imagined lives, their own as well as those of others living in other places' (Appadurai, 1990: 299). Similarly, Beck (2000: 54) suggests that 'more people in more parts of the world dream of and consider a greater range of possible lives than they have ever done before', thereby dissociating their identity from territorial communities.

To what extent do survey results support the changing notion and relationships of identity? To approach these questions, we assessed available survey research from a wide range of sources in an effort to identify data-sets that allow for the greatest number of comparisons both cross-nationally and longitudinally[1]. Among the surprising findings about changes in identities is first and foremost the stability of responses to identity-related questions over time, at the regional level and for income groups. This is in contrast to the more fluid picture suggested by analysts such as Beck or Appadurai. As Table I.1 shows, 63 per cent of the population in western Europe expressed local identities in 1981, 61 per cent in 1990, and 63 per cent in 1999/2000. Likewise, the relative shares for national and supranational identities have remained stable over the last 30 years. For Turkey, Latin America and the Caribbean, and North America, the same stability prevails over the last 20 years, as it does for the group of high-income and middle-income countries.

At the same time, there are indications that identities are shifting, yet at different rates and directions, and by no means in any dramatic way. As Table I.1 indicates, South Asia (India) saw an increase in national identity and a decrease of local identity, as did Sub-Saharan Africa (Nigeria, South Africa), but with a decline in supranational identity. What is more, both lower middle-income and low-income countries see an increase in national identity. Taken together, the findings suggest the absence rather than presence of a general shift in identity as a result of globalisation. Where shifts have taken place, they are more likely the result of national political developments (South Africa) or continued nation-building (Nigeria, India).

Within Europe (Table I.2), we see the emergence of a dual identity whereby over half of the respondents state 'national and European' or 'European and national' as opposed to national identities only. What is more, the dual identity is more pronounced among the younger cohorts (51 per cent) than Europeans aged 55 and above (42 per cent); among the well-educated (57 per cent) than less well-educated (39 per cent); and higher among the self-employed, managers and professionals than among the unemployed and retirees. This would support our controversial finding, in *Global Civil Society 2001*, that global civil society is most developed in Europe: Europe, it would seem, with dramatic exceptions such as the Balkans throughout the 1990s, is rich in 'rooted cosmopolitans' who are comfortable with multiple identities.

In terms of identification as 'Global Citizen' (Table I.3), respondents in the Environics study were split between one-quarter who regarded themselves as global citizens and three-quarters who did not. Global citizens are most frequent in Germany, Canada, Russia, the UK, Italy, Sweden, and South Korea, with about one-third of respondents, and least frequent in Indonesia, Brazil and Chile, with about one in ten. Of course, there is much more to the question of identity than can be suggested with the help of survey data. Nonetheless, two closely related conclusions emerge. The results do not suggest a significant shift in national versus global

---

1 *'To which of these geographical groups would you say you belong first of all? [locality or town; state, region or province; country as a whole; continent; world]'. (European Values Surveys and World Values Surveys [URL], 1980–2000).*
'Do you regard yourself as a "Global Citizen"' [local neighbourhood; religious community; professional community, colleagues; voluntary associations, clubs; nation or national culture]. (Environics, 2001, 2002).
'Do you regard yourself as a "Global Citizen"' [yes, no]. (Environics, 2001, 2002).

Table I.2: National and regional identities, European Union, Autumn 2003

		Nationality only	Nationality and European	European and nationality	European only
Sex	Male	35	49	9	5
	Female	44	45	5	2
Age	15–24	33	48	10	4
	25–39	33	51	9	4
	40–54	39	49	7	4
	55+	49	42	4	3
Employment	Self-employed	32	52	8	5
	Managers	24	57	12	4
	Other white collars	31	56	7	3
	Manual workers	44	44	6	4
	House persons	49	42	4	2
	Unemployed	44	40	8	3
	Retired	49	41	5	3
Education	Below high-school	53	39	4	2
	High-school	42	45	6	3
	Post-secondary	25	57	10	5
TOTAL		40	47	7	3

Note: Figures show percentages of respondents self-identifying as national and European.

Source: European Opinion Research Group (2004)

identities across the board; rather, they point to a slower and more diverse process that varies between as well as within countries. Moreover, national identities seem stronger in weaker economies and more peripheral countries, as well as among poorer population groups generally, which opens opportunities for Regressive globalises such as Global Islam or nationalism in the US. By contrast, local and supranational identities seem more pronounced in richer, more developed countries, and among the educated and well-to-do.

Secularisation or a revival of religion?

Islamic authors (Raouf Ezzat; AnNa'im, 2002) have argued that mainstream research on global civil society, including this Yearbook, has been too secular in its orientation, missing the importance of religious motivation and religious concepts in global civil society, even in ostensibly secular movements. In order to judge the exigency of the question of religion in global civil society, we need to assess whether the world at large is becoming more or less religious. It turns out that both are happening, but greater emphasis on religion affects more people around the world than secularisation does. There is greater importance attached to religion in

Table I.3: Identification as global citizen

	Yes	No
Argentina	21	79
Brazil	13	87
Canada	34	66
Chile	15	85
France	23	77
Germany	36	64
India	28	72
Indonesia	11	89
Italy	41	59
Japan	25	75
Korea, Rep. of	30	70
Mexico	27	73
Nigeria	23	77
Russia	31	69
Spain	19	81
Sweden	30	70
Turkey	18	82
United Kingdom	31	69
United States	28	72

Note: Figures show percentages of respondents identifying (or not) as global citizen.

Source: Environics International (2002)

Table I.4: Changes in imortance of cultural elements

Region	N*	Work 1990	Work 1999	Family 1990	Family 1999	Leisure 1990	Leisure 1999	Religion 1990	Religion 1999
Sub-Saharan Africa	2	87	82	92	97	49	44	76	83
Middle East and North Africa	1	59	69	87	97	24	41	61	77
South Asia	1	86	78	77	93	17	29	49	57
East Asia and Pacific	3	58	54	78	81	21	25	11	11
East and Central Europe	11	54	61	79	80	29	23	19	19
Western Europe	15	56	54	84	87	40	40	20	18
Latin America and the Caribbean	3	73	79	87	94	34	47	42	53
North America	2	61	53	92	95	43	41	42	46
Grand Total	38	60	60	83	86	34	34	27	28

Note: Figures show percentages of respondents identifying cultural elements as important.
*Denotes number of countries surveyed.

Source: Environics International (2002).

Nigeria, South Africa, India, and Mexico (Table I.4). Such a rise in religiosity is much less evident in most of Central and eastern Europe. Slight increases in religiosity are detectable in the US. The growth of religion in Asia, the Middle East and Africa is less along highly institutional structures (eg the Catholic Church hierarchy), but within less institutional religions like Protestantism and Islam. The former emphasises local community and individualism, the latter, similar to social movements, the notions of brotherhood and communal suffering, particularly in the Middle East and Central Asia. In western Europe, by contrast, the importance of religion dropped in twelve out of fourteen countries, with only Portugal showing an increase, and Sweden basically steady. Thus, the world is drifting apart on the issue of religion. Most critically, the countries of north west Europe we identified as centres of global civil society are moving in an opposite direction to the rest of the world. The success of discussions and accommodations between secular and religious worldviews may therefore be pivotal to the success of global civil society as a normative idea in coming years.

Democracy and Sovereignty

A major theme of *Global Civil Society 2004/5* is democracy. There is a tendency in popular usage to assume that civil society and democracy are the same thing. But is this true? Contemporary civil society is global. But democracy, if by this we mean the establishment of representative institutions, is necessarily bounded at national and local levels. So does the global character of twenty-first century civil society help or hinder democracy?

In political theory, a distinction is often drawn between the *procedures* and the *substance* of democracy. Procedural democracy includes elections, parliaments, separation of powers, rule of law, and so on. As Hilary Wainwright points out in Chapter 5, substantive democracy is about political equality – the extent to which individual citizens can influence the decisions that affect their lives. Most theorists would argue that procedural democracy is a precondition for substantive democracy – claims that substantive democracy can be achieved without procedures are typical of totalitarian regimes.

Procedural democracy is territorially bounded. Democracy is based on group of citizens who are generally defined in territorial terms. The citizens who live in a particular territory vote for their representative institutions. These institutions have the responsibility for rule-making. The big problem associated with globalisation is that, with the possible exception of the US, fewer and fewer rules are made by national parliaments. Parliaments no longer represent the main centres of decision-making. Power, as we have argued, is increasingly dispersed among different levels of governance. Thus, even if procedures are perfect, substantive democracy – the ability of citizens to influence the decisions that affect their lives – is necessarily limited at the national level because fewer significant decisions are taken at the national level.

Substantive democracy requires an active civil society, an arena where people can express themselves freely, organise associations, and try to influence decision-makers. Civil society is a 'voice not a vote' (Edwards, 2003). Civil society increasingly spills over borders and reacts to, feeds on and contributes to the process of globalisation. In other words, the simple linear relationship between civil society and democracy is broken. What does this break imply for the future of democracy?

In Chapter 1, Anderson and Rieff (p. 30) argue that civil society organisations are the 'glory of democratic societies, but they are not the electoral institutions of democracy'. The various groups, networks, institutions and organisations that compose civil society offer individuals a chance to express their opinions, however extreme, and to speak and act according to their consciences, without concern for the realities of power or the compromises and adjustments that inevitably have to be made in elected assemblies. At a global level there are no representative institutions, nor should there be, since it would not be possible to represent the peoples of the world in one parliament. Therefore, say Anderson and Rieff, the term 'global civil society' is dangerously misleading; it suggests that a particular section of world opinion, the Western universalising section, has arrogated to itself the claim to represent the world's people.

How might we unpack these issues at different levels of governance?

National democracy

The paradox of the current epoch is that, at the very moment when procedural democracy is spreading, decision-making at a national level is being 'hollowed out'. The last two decades have witnessed the fall of Communist regimes and the spread of democracy, in particular the decline of military governments, in Asia, Latin America and Africa. This phenomenon, it can be argued, is linked to globalisation and, indeed, to global civil society. It has become increasingly difficult to insulate societies from the outside world; pressure of trade, travel, indebtedness, as well as increased communication, have made closed authoritarian states much harder to sustain. Pressure for democratisation has been partly a result of pressures from above; international financial institutions, outside governments, and international donors have demanded political reform alongside market reform. More importantly, pressure for democratisation has come from below, from civil society groups that have been able to expand the space for their activities through links with the outside world. Keck and Sikkink (1998) talk about the 'boomerang effect' whereby civil society groups can use their links with the outside world to put pressure on their own governments.

At the same time, however, we can also observe growing apathy in many countries, in the form of a decline in voter turnouts or in political party membership as well as pervasive distrust in elected officials. This phenomenon too can be linked to globalisation. It may have something to do with the limited powers of elected representatives at the national level and the disappointment of voters with politicians who often do not or cannot carry out electoral promises because their freedom of manoeuvre is narrowed. It also may have something to do with global civil society, since many activists who feel blocked at the national level by traditional political parties or by the constraints of power at the national level, choose to focus their energies on local and global issues, thus reducing the level of public debate and action at the national level. The growing tendency for populist parties and movements to form around national or religious issues may also be linked to the decline of substantive democracy since national or religious issues may make it possible to mark out political difference in societies where socio-economic political difference are circumscribed by the global economy. A typical phenomenon in many parts of the world is 'illiberal' or 'cosmetic' democracy, where formal procedures have been introduced but where substantive democracy is extremely weak.

However, a new phenomenon has been the mobilisation of global civil society to influence elections. Even if parties are weak, activists in various movements and NGOs have increasingly organised themselves to invigorate voting behaviour. This phenomenon was first noticed in the Rock the Vote campaign in Slovakia, when civil society activists with international support campaigned to get people to vote in the 1994 elections, in order to remove the nationalist elected dictator Meciar. This experience was copied in Croatia and led to the defeat of the Croatian extreme nationalist Party, HDZ; and later it was copied in Serbia through the young people's resistance campaign Otpur. During 2003/4, as shown in Box I.2, we can observe increasing examples of civil society groups mobilising in elections. Thus, the Otpor activists from Serbia, with financial support from George Soros, introduced their tactics in Georgia and this led to the removal of Edward Shevardnadze. Likewise in India's 2004 elections, a coalition of social

Box I.2: Protest voters

In an era of voter apathy, particularly in many industrialised countries, a funny thing happened in 2003/4. Voters realised, as if for the first time, that power lay in their hands. Around the world hundreds of thousands raised placards in protest and millions marked crosses on ballot papers. What galvanised them into action? A new crop of citizens and advocacy organisations, often technologically smart and with global reach, are using the Internet, email and mobile phones to mobilise ordinary people to exercise their rights – at the ballot box, on the streets, or face-to-face with their political representatives.

During 2003–4, Georgians took to the streets in the 'Rose Revolution' that forced out their president; India's marginalised groups helped the Congress Party to victory; angry Spaniards ousted the government that had led them into war in Iraq; Britons dealt the Labour administration a bloody nose in local elections. Even Argentines, who in recent years have expressed their hostility to political authority in a wave of protests, expressed renewed faith in elections in 2003. This was a year when, around the world, voters – frustrated, volatile and increasingly mobilised – spoke truth to power.

The results of many elections and opinion polls around the world suggest that voting behaviour was influenced by several factors: the US/UK war in Iraq, its messy aftermath and the spectre of ongoing terrorist attacks. If, in 2003, opposition to the war on Iraq emerged as a unifying force, in 2004 it became a global issue, mobilising people not only to demonstrate but also to change their political preferences, or simply cast a vote they might not have done otherwise. In the British local elections, which the incumbent Labour government argued were more about rubbish collection, policing and street lighting, Iraq was a key concern for many voters. On 10 June they dealt Labour a sharp rebuke. Labour received 26 per cent of the vote, trailing third after the Conservatives and Liberal Democrats. It was their lowest share of a local election vote for decades – in an election when turnout went up (*BBC News*, 2004).

The Spanish parliamentary elections in March 2004 provided more dramatic evidence of how Iraq was influencing voter behaviour. Almost 90 per cent of Spaniards had opposed the war on Iraq. Then came a series of bomb blasts that ripped through crowded commuter trains in Madrid's rush hour, killing 190 people and injuring 1,500. In the immediate aftermath of the bombings, premier José Maria Aznar blamed ETA, the Basque separatist organisation, while dismissing the possibility of Al-Qaeda involvement. When it was revealed that, in fact, the bombers did have links to Al-Qaeda, many Spaniards accused the government of suppressing the information to avoid an anti-war backlash at the polls (Richburg, 2004). On 13 March, a 'day of reflection' preceding the election, more than 11 million people thronged the streets of Spain's major cities to mourn the victims and protest against the terrorist attacks. That evening, hundreds of people gathered outside the governing Popular Party's headquarters in Madrid, accusing the government of covering up the investigation into the bombing. Political protest had been forbidden on this 'day of reflection', with punishment threatened for any demonstrations. As one demonstrator said:

> *But what if it is just the result of a spontaneous crush of SMS messages? The use of big media, which have been greatly tendentious in some cases, has not been as powerful as text messaging to spread the news and ask for the truth in the most intensive days of democracy in Spain. (Dominguez, 2004)*

Mobile phone traffic increased 40 per cent that weekend, a rise attributed to the text-led protest (Castells, 2004). Rallying via SMS – called 'smart mobs' by Howard Rheingold (2002) – has significant precedents. In 2000 a million Filipinos, galvanised by a deluge of text messages, gathered in the capital, Manila, to demonstrate against then president Joseph Estrada. And the year before, in Seattle, mobile phones and the Internet played a key role in the protests against the World Trade Organisation by the nascent anti-capitalist movement. On 14 March 2004, the day after their mass mobilisation, Spaniards voted Aznar out of office and elected the Socialist Party, led by José Luis Rodriquez Zapatero. At 77 per cent, turnout was 8.5 per cent higher than in the 2000 general election.

Spain's election will have been closely watched in America by a new crop of citizen and voter associations that are mobilising voters in the run-up to the presidential election in November 2004. These civil society groups are targeting two constituencies that they believe can swing the vote: the young and politically disaffected; and all of those who, such is their frustration with government policies or politics generally, would be reluctant to vote. MoveOn.org, a web-based advocacy group, is using the Internet to mobilise and coordinate people who want to volunteer, donate, lobby their representatives and vote in the forthcoming US election. Created in 1998 by Silicon Valley entrepreneurs, Wes Boyd and Joan Blades, MoveOn.org grew out of public frustration with the impeachment process; after the impeachment of president Clinton it turned to electoral action. Under the strapline 'citizens making a difference', MoveOn.org used word-of-mouth emailing to mobilise voters and donors. To date, more than 1.7 million people have signed up and, through a secure website, donated US$8,880,000 in campaign contributions.

> *MoveOn PAC's campaign contributions provide financial assistance to support congressional candidates who embrace moderate to progressive principles of national government. Our intention is to encourage and facilitate smaller donations to offset the influence of wealthy and corporate donors . . . MoveOn.org's intention is to provide individuals, who normally have little political power, to aggregate their contributions with others to gain a greater voice in the political process. (MoveOn PAC, URL)*

The League of Pissed Off Voters (URL) is another web-based American organisation, which aims to engage 17–35-year-olds in the democratic process in order 'to bring about a progressive governing majority in our lifetime'. Via an online network, the League offers virtual and physical resources, including voter guides and conventions for 'voter organisers', who will in turn educate their peers on why they should vote.

Opinion polls show that American disenchantment with the Iraq war and its aftermath is growing. How far it will influence the presidential election remains to be seen. It is not the only issue attracting global solidarity.

International support bolstered Georgians who were struggling against a corrupt and undemocratic regime. Parliamentary elections in November 2003 returned President Eduard Shevardnadze to power but voting irregularities were so widespread that even the main opposition candidate, Mikhail Saakashvili, was unable to vote. More than 100,000 people camped out on Tblisi's streets, listening to speeches by the Saakashvili and other opposition figures, refusing to move, and putting flowers in the barrels of soldiers' guns. The 'Rose Revolution' forced Shevardnadze to resign, the election result was annulled, and in the January 2004 rerun of the elections Saakashvili secured more than 96 per cent of the vote (Mikhail Saakashvili, URL).

Argentines also succeeded in changing the balance of power in their 2003 elections. Since 2001 Argentina has experienced a wave of demonstrations against an economic crisis that has left 50 per cent of people below the poverty line and more than 20 per cent unemployed. Around the country workers have taken over factories declared bankrupt by their owners. It was at one of these factories, just days before the election in 2003, that police attempted to evict women textile workers. The confrontation ended in violence but far from being deterred, some 25,000 protesters regrouped the following day (Vann, 2003). This was the context in which Argentines voted in the presidential election of May 2003. They are required by law to go to the polls and in recent years disenchantment with politics has led millions to cast spoiled or blank votes. However, in 2003 only 500,000 blank or contested ballots were cast compared with four million in the 2001 legislative elections. Nestor Kirchner won the presidential election by default after Carlos Saul Menem, the former president, withdrew.

Mobilisation of voters by a range of civil society groups and political parties was influential in the 2004 Indian election. Turnout was 56 per cent, defying predictions of significant voter decline. As Hilary Wainwright points out in Chapter 5, global civil society played a role, albeit an indirect one. The Fourth World Social Forum, held in Mumbai in 2004, brought formal parties on the left together with civil society groups and social movements, including Dalit organisations. Parties on the left went on to play an influential role in the May 2004 elections, campaigning against communalism and convincing a diverse range of parties of the need for a secular government. The Congress Party's surprise victory would have been impossible without strategic alliances with various political parties and a groundswell of support from those marginalised and alienated by the BJP's policies (Chandrasekhar, 2004). The BJP's 'India Shining' campaign backfired badly; for the rural poor, farmers and people of low caste and class it served as a painful reminder of how the government's economic policies had failed them. Their reaction to this ill thought-out campaign and the BJP's perceived support for the massacre of Muslims at Gujarat heralded the unexpected victory of the Congress Party.

Fiona Holland, Centre for the study of Global Governance, London School of Economics

forces, including Muslims and people of low caste and class, rejected the Bharatiya Janata Party's neo-liberal economic policies and voted in the Congress Party. The war in Iraq also influenced election behaviour, with civil society groups organising to oppose pro-war governments in Spain, Italy, the UK and the US.

What this experience suggests is a recasting of national democracy. Sovereignty is not being eroded so much as transformed. Civil society is beginning to understand that the framework of global governance is composed of states and that who is elected matters at a global level. On the other hand, it is also learning how to make use of global networks to enhance democracy at the national level. Table I.5 based on our Records section presents data for a purposive sample of high-, medium- and low-ranking countries on a World Bank measure of voice and accountability. Taking this as a rough measure of democracy, it is clear from the table that this is positively linked to globalisation, measured in terms of Internet usage and air travel, and to global civil society if a surrogate measure of membership of INGOs is used. The linear correlation between the World Bank's ranking of voice and accountability and Internet use per 100,000 population is 0.84 at the country level, and 0.56 for the relationship between Internet use and membership in INGOs. Figure I.2 demonstrates the positive relationship between these indicators graphically.

Local democracy

Many democracy theorists argue that an important way to reinvigorate democracy is greater devolution to the local level. Nation states are centralising institutions and increased public participation can best be achieved at a local level. While it is true that many decisions are now taken at the global level, it is also the case that the increased complexity of decision-making allows for greater 'subsidiarity', that is to say, allowing as many decisions as possible to be taken at the level closest to the citizen. Membership of the European Union has allowed regions like Scotland, Flanders and Catalonia to pursue fairly autonomous policies within a framework that allows sovereignty and national self-determination to operate as more fluid, less all-or-nothing concepts.

In Chapter 5, Hilary Wainwright asks whether global civil society enhances or undermines democracy at a local level. As at the national level, the conclusion is double. On the one hand, many local civil society groups that have been able to improve the substantive democratic conditions of local government through global links: ranging from parts of China where global links provided activists with a higher profile, allowing them to open public debates that would otherwise have remained closed, to the successful export of the 'participatory budget' model from Porto Alegre to 18 other countries, partly through the mediation of the World Social Forum. Other municipalities have been able to strengthen their positions vis-à-vis national governments and to respond to the needs of their citizens through global links – fair trade arrangements, twinnings, appeals to global public pressure, direct relations to donors. On the other hand, the influx of INGOs and the conditions attached to aid may seduce local civil society groups into prioritising donor concerns above local needs, or they may smother local initiatives.

Democracy at a global level?

We share Anderson and Rieff's scepticism about a world parliament and about the possibility of procedural democracy at a global level. But we disagree with Anderson and Rieff's implicit assumption that the clock can be turned back, that civil society can become national again and the simple world of national sovereignty and democracy at the national level restored. Herein lies the case for global civil society. If key decisions are taken at the global level, there have to be mechanisms for increasing the responsiveness of global institutions to the demands of individual citizens. Procedural democracy at the global level could not achieve that because the world is too complex to be represented by a world parliament. Dialogue and deliberation, which are in principle open to all civil society groups and which take place at many levels, are the next best option. Global civil society is not representative. It is not the same as democracy. But it could be considered what has been called a 'functional equivalent' (Rosenau, 1998: 40–1) or an 'alternative mechanism' (Scholte, 2001: 15) for democratising global governance. Moreover, if global civil society was to be combined with subsidiarity – more decision-making at a local level – it could enhance the participatory role of the individual citizen.

The problem with Anderson and Rieff is that they are nostalgic for an era of national simplicities. It is a world that no longer exists, probably for the better. The price that was paid for national sovereignty was the existence of repressive undemocratic governments. The erosion of democracy at the national level has meant the erosion of authoritarianism at the national level too. The choice, as in Iraq, for post-authoritarian states is between democracy and failure, that is to say, lawlessness, lack of legitimacy and pervasive violence. It may be that it is only through global links that democracy can be strengthened at the national level, albeit imperfectly.

Thus, the issue now is, how to choose national representatives at the global level through elections and how to maximise the possibilities for individuals to debate and influence significant decisions through a combination of subsidiarity and dialogue.

What the past year has exposed is the way that global debates can be domesticated and domestic debates globalised. To the extent that democracy is recast as a contribution to global debate and deliberation, there are real possibilities for constructing an effective framework for global governance, for closing the gap between the green zone and the red zone. To the extent that civil society remains wedded to old-fashioned notions of sovereignty, the end result may not be democracy but continuing insecurity; terrorism rather than global civil society may be crossing the red-green divide.

If key decisions are taken at the global level, there have to be mechanisms for increasing the responsiveness of global institutions to the demands of individual citizens

Conclusion

The war in Iraq may turn out to be one of those moments that change the way people perceive power and the politics of power. Global civil society, in all its political and cultural variety and manifestations, has a central role to play in influencing those perceptions. The Bush administration, supposedly the most powerful actor in the world, believed that it could impose democracy on Iraq through military power and that the example of Iraq would help to topple authoritarian regimes in the region as a whole. Although many Iraqis were initially grateful for their liberation, the US rapidly lost Iraqi goodwill through its arbitrary and excessive use of military power. Military power became the primary obstacle rather than the means to achieve the administration's objective.

Moreover, the unilateral use of power contributed to the gap between the green and the red zones; it exacerbated 'global rancour'. Global terror, far from abating, has increased in 2003/4 with incidents in Casablanca, Istanbul, Riyadh, and Madrid. And in the Middle East, the continuing violence in Palestine and the attacks on locals and Westerners in Saudi Arabia suggest that the war has brought, not democracy, but even more insecurity.

All the same, Europe and Africa do seem to be making further strides in building multilateralist structures. The EU has finally achieved its enlargement from 15 to 25 states, although its constitution will still be subject to national referendums, and the rise of anti-Europe parties may slow down further integration. Two important new organs of the African Union, the Peace and Security Council and the African Court of Human and Peoples' Rights, have come into force in 2004. The former is actively involved in trying to resolve the Darfur crisis in Sudan. At the time of writing, it has sent military observers and alluded to the possibility of military intervention under a United Nations mandate.

The question is, which of these developments will turn out to have been more important in the long run. While the limitations of unilateralist military power are making themselves felt, the power of multilateralist institutions to resolve crises is by no means indisputable. The failure to prevent the 1994 genocide in Rwanda is the most vivid reminder, but the weakness of their response to the HIV/AIDS pandemic is no less dramatic.

In the 2001 and 2003 Yearbooks, we described four possible scenarios: unilateralist, bargain, division and utopian (Anheier, Glasius and Kaldor, 2001; Kaldor, Anheier and Glasius, 2003). The two extremes, unilateralist and utopian, continue to be the most relevant. The nightmare scenario is one in which Iraq becomes the theatre of the conflict between Global America and Global Islam, violence spreads throughout the Islamic world (compounded by tribal ethnic and religious cleavages that are exploited by the entrepreneurs of violence), and terror rather than global debate enters the domestic arena in many Western countries. In such a situation, the result could also be a strengthening of extremists in the West, and a test of global civil society, perhaps beyond its limits, for the reasons we outlined above.

There is, of course, a more positive scenario. This is one in which the United States and its coalition partners come to recognise that democracy in Iraq, stability in the Middle East, and security for their own citizens can be achieved only through a return to multilateralism and through an intensive dialogue with global and local civil society. In this scenario, the US joins the UN, the EU and the African Union in finding solutions for Sudan, Iraq, Afghanistan and Palestine by supporting civil society and dealing with human rights violations through international law. At the time of writing, there are some signs of a shift towards such a scenario. The UN Special Representative, Lakshmi Brahimi, did engage

Table I.5: Democracy, globalisation and global civil society

Country	Voice and accountability 2002	Air transport* 2001
Korea, Dem. Rep.	0.0	0.00
Iraq	0.5	
Eritrea	1.0	
Myanmar	1.5	0.01
Congo, Dem. Rep.	2.0	0.00
Turkmenistan	2.5	0.31
Cuba	3.0	0.08
Laos	3.5	0.04
Sudan	4.0	0.01
Libya	4.5	0.11
Sri Lanka	48.0	0.09
Fiji	48.5	0.73
Madagascar	49.0	0.04
Albania	49.5	0.04
Bolivia	50.0	0.19
Ghana	50.5	0.02
Benin	51.0	0.01
El Salvador	51.5	0.27
Nicaragua	52.0	*0.01*
Germany	95.5	0.69
Iceland	96.5	4.89
New Zealand	97.0	2.97
Switzerland	97.5	2.31
Netherlands	98.0	1.25
Norway	98.5	3.22
Sweden	99.0	1.47
Finland	99.5	1.29
Denmark	100.0	1.19

*number of passengers carried, per capita

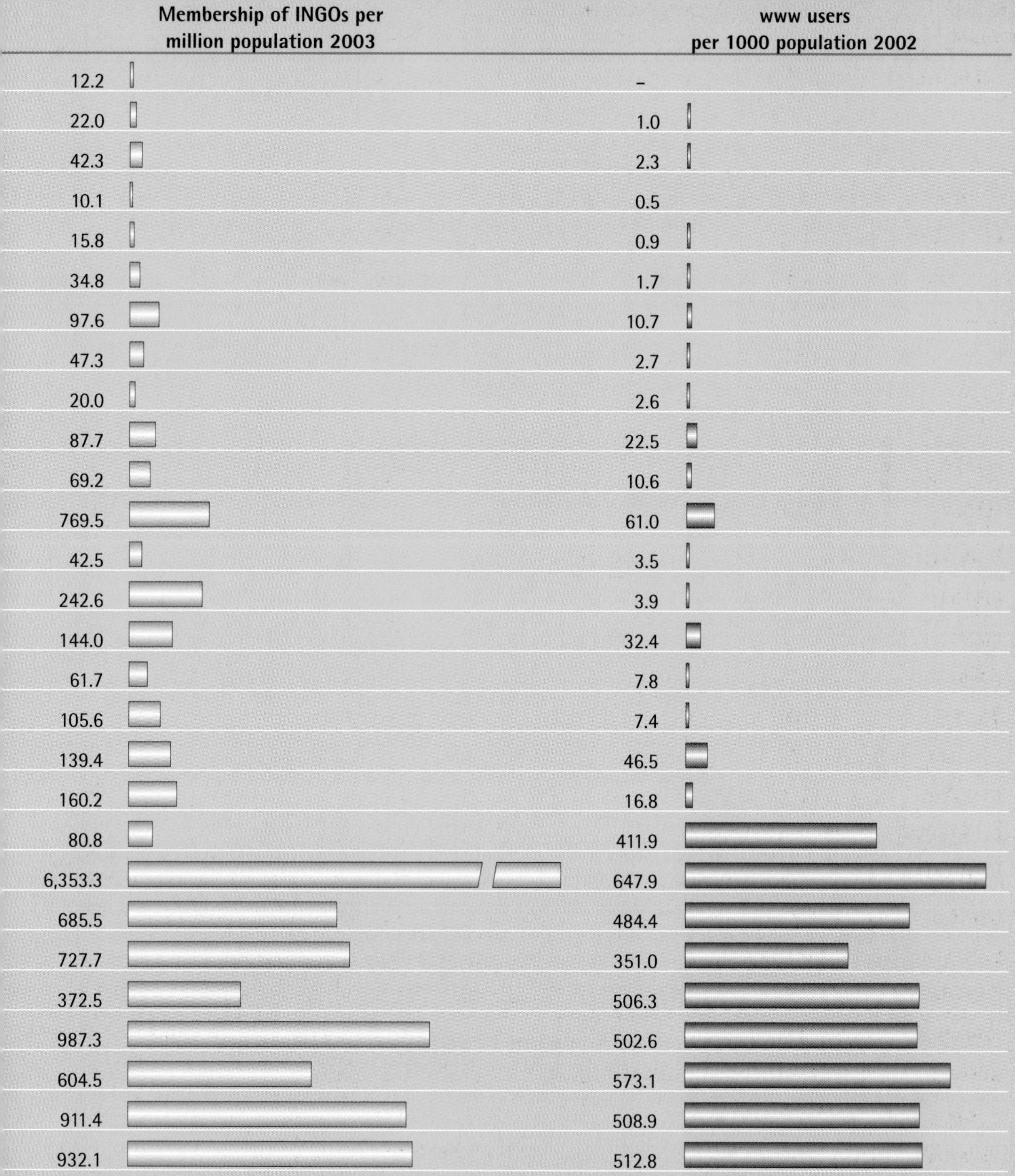

Membership of INGOs per million population 2003	www users per 1000 population 2002
12.2	–
22.0	1.0
42.3	2.3
10.1	0.5
15.8	0.9
34.8	1.7
97.6	10.7
47.3	2.7
20.0	2.6
87.7	22.5
69.2	10.6
769.5	61.0
42.5	3.5
242.6	3.9
144.0	32.4
61.7	7.8
105.6	7.4
139.4	46.5
160.2	16.8
80.8	411.9
6,353.3	647.9
685.5	484.4
727.7	351.0
372.5	506.3
987.3	502.6
604.5	573.1
911.4	508.9
932.1	512.8

Figure I.2: Democracy, globalisation and global civil society

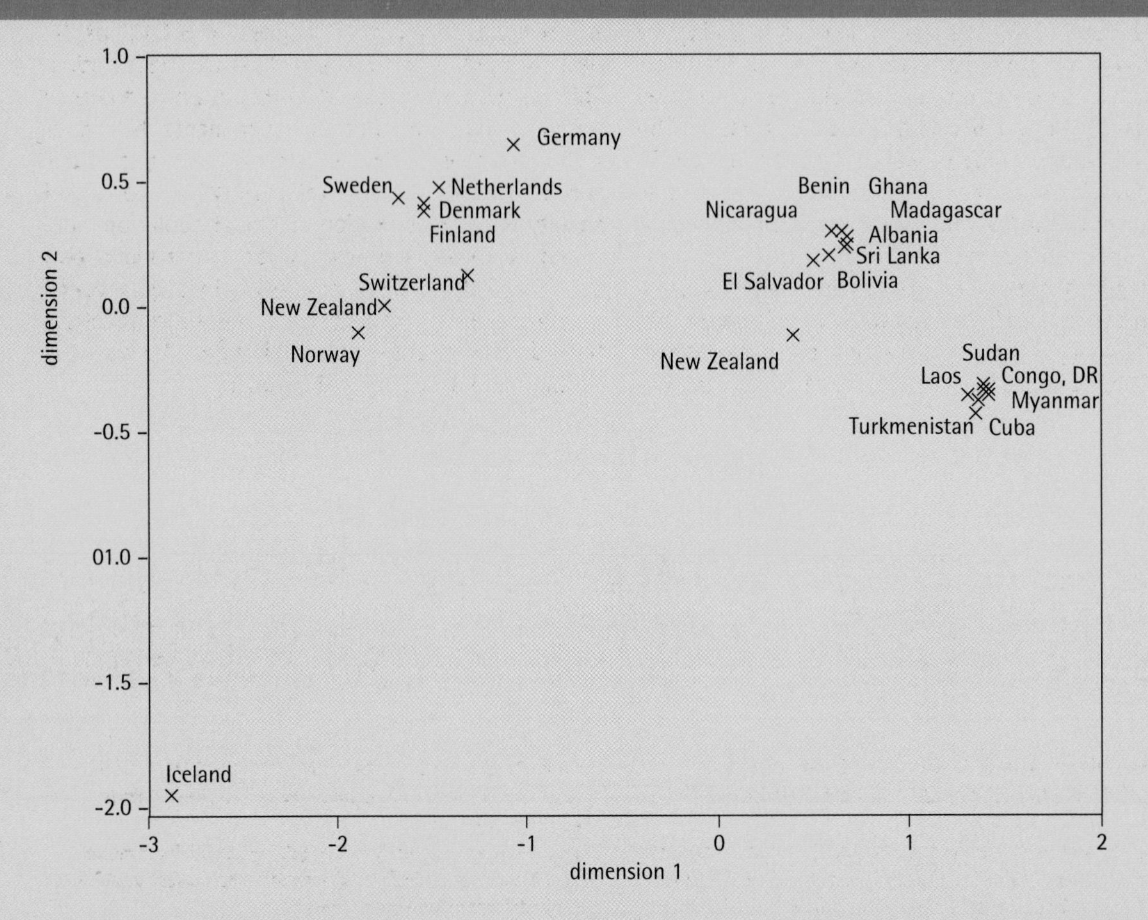

Figure I.2 shows the results of a multidimensional scaling analysis, which aims to depict the similarities and differences between the countries in Table I.5 on their values for measures of democracy, globalisation and global civil society (for technical details please see the glossary). The three clusters of countries reflect the purposive sampling used, so that we can identify high-, mid- and low-scoring countries on voice and accountability as we move from left to right hand side. An interesting feature of the plot is that the inclusion of three other indicators in the analysis does not reduce this clustering effect to any great degree: that is, the rankings for voice and accountability are reflected in similar patterns for the other variables. This demonstrates the positive associations between the indicators. However, the plot adds a little more detail to our understanding of the nature of the patterns among these measures.

The group of seven countries on the far right hand side of the plot (Turkmenistan, Cuba, Libya, Myanmar, Laos, Democratic Republic of Congo and Sudan) are very tightly clustered: they tend to have very similar and relatively low values on all four indicators. The eight countries in the middle of the plot (Fiji, El Salvador, Bolivia, Sri Lanka, Albania, Nicaragua, Madagascar, Benin and Ghana) tend to have slightly higher but also very similar scores on all four variables. Fiji is the exception, being set apart a little due to its unusually high rate of INGO membership per million of the population. Whilst a very useful indicator, INGO membership needs to be interpreted with some caution with respect to population size, since the per capita measure is often very large for countries with small populations. A similar effect is seen for Iceland, which is set apart from the other high-scoring countries because of its very high rate of INGO membership. The eight other countries (Germany, Netherlands, Sweden, Denmark, Finland, Switzerland, New Zealand and Norway), with high values on each of the four indicators, are markedly less tightly clustered than the other two groups. This is due to the fact that, relative to the countries in the other two groups, they cover a broader range of scores on the indicators for air transport, INGO membership and Internet use. The order in which they appear on the vertical axis reflects most strongly their rankings on air transport (with increasing scores as one moves from the top downwards).

in wide-ranging consultations inside Iraq, and the latest (at the time of writing) Security Council resolution does give the United Nations a key role in constraining the behaviour of American troops. The international community's response to Darfur will provide another key test of the viability of the 'utopian scenario'. This scenario would require global civil society to shed the anti-Americanism of some of its proponents and to engage both the US and the Islamic world on equally critical but constructive grounds.

In these senses, global civil society cannot be, and has not been, a helpless bystander at this crossroads. Our chronology of global civil society events shows that, after the war began, the protests and demonstrations about Iraq died down; but a continuation can be observed of what have become bread-and-butter global meetings, testifying to the continuing vitality of the underlying global process of debate and deliberation. This has been accompanied by the return to domestic politics in order to influence governmental behaviour at the global level; the most dramatic example of this was perhaps the Spanish elections of 2004. Global civil society is the mobilisation of global public opinion. Therefore, the debates and positions within global civil society can affect the framework of global governance and cross the red-green divide in a positive direction, both directly at the global level and in the way it is beginning to recast domestic politics.

References

Anheier, Helmut, Glasius, Marlies, and Kaldor, Mary (eds) (2001) *Global Civil Society 2001*. Oxford: Oxford University Press.

Anheier, Helmut and Themudo, Nuno (2002) 'Organisational Forms of Global Civil Society: Implications of Going Global', ch. 7 in Marlies Glasius, Mary Kaldor and Helmut Anheier (eds), *Global Civil Society 2002*. Oxford: Oxford University Press.

Appadurai, Arjun (1990). 'Disjuncture and Difference in the Global Cultural Economy' *Public Culture*, 2(2): 1–24.

– (1996) *Modernity at Large: Cultural Dimensions of Globalization*. Minneapolis: University of Minnesota Press.

BBC News (2004) 'Iraq "shadow" hits Labour's vote' (11 June). www.news.bbc.co.uk/1/hi/uk_politics/3796267.stm

Beck, Ulrich (2000) *What is Globalization?* Cambridge: Polity Press.

Buttel, Frederick H. and Gould, Kenneth A. (2004) 'Global Social Movement(s) at the Crossroads: Some Observations on the Trajectory of the Anti-Corporate Globalization Movement', *Journal of World Systems Research*, 10(1): 37–66.

Castells, Manuel (2004) 'Politics and Power in the Network Society' (Miliband Lecture, 18 March). London: London School of Economics.

Chandrasekhar, C. (2004) 'The Verdict and the Way Ahead', *Frontline*, 21(12).
www.flonnet.com/fl2112/stories/20040618003911700.htm

Cohen, Robin and Rai, Shirin (eds) (2000) *Global Social Movements*. London: The Athlone Press.

Della Porta, Donatella, Kriesi, Hans-Peter and Rucht, Dieter (eds) (1999) *Social Movements in a Globalizing World*. London: Palgrave.

Diani, Mario and McAdam, Doug (2003) *Social Movements and Networks: Relational Approaches to Collective Action*. Oxford: Oxford University Press.

Dominguez, Eva (2004) 'SMS, the Star Media of the Spanish Elections', *Poynteronline* (16 March). www.poynter.org/column.asp?id=31&aid=62558

Edwards, Michael (2003) 'NGO Legitimacy - Voice or Vote?'. Global Policy Forum (February). www.globalpolicy.org/ngos/credib/2003/0202rep.htm

Environics International (2001) *Global Issues Monitor*. Toronto: Environics International.

– (2002) *Global Issues Monitor*. Toronto: Environics International.

European Opinion Research Group (2000–2003) *Standard Eurobarometer 54–60*. Brussels: European Commission. http:/europa.eu.int/comm/public_opinion/standard_en.htm

– (2004) *Standard Eurobarometer 60 (Fieldwork: October–November 2003)*. Brussels: European Commission. http:/europa.eu.int/comm/public_opinion/archives/eb/eb60/eb60_rapport_standard_en.pdf

European Values Surveys (EVS) and World Values Surveys (WVS) (URL) www.sscnet.ucla.edu/issr/da/index/techinfo/M9911.HTM (consulted 23 July 2004).

Giddens, Anthony (1995) *Beyond Left and Right: The Future of Radical Politics*. Palo Alto, CA: Stanford University Press.

– (2000) *The Runaway World: How Globalization Is Reshaping Our Lives*. London: Routledge.
Gramsci, Antonio (1971) *Selections from the Prison Notebooks*. London: Laurence and Wishart.
Halliday, Fred (2002) *Two Hours That Shook the World. September 11, 2001: Causes and Consequences*. London: Saqi Books.
Hamel, P., Lustiger-Thaler, H., Pieterse, J. and Roseneil, S. (eds) (2001) *Globalisation and Social Movements*. London: Palgrave.
Held, David and McCrew, Anthony (eds) (2000) *The Global Transformation Reader*. Cambridge: Polity Press.
Held, David, McGrew, Anthony, Goldblatt, David, and Perraton, Jonathan (1999) *Global Transformations: Politics, Economics and Culture*. Cambridge: Polity Press.
Huntington, Samuel (2004) *Who Are We? The Challenge of America's National Identity*. New York: Simon and Schuster.
Kaldor, Mary (2003) *Global Civil Society: An Answer to War*. Cambridge: Polity Press.
–, Anheier, Helmut, and Glasius, Marlies (2003) *Global Civil Society 2003*. Oxford: Oxford University Press.
– and Muro, Diego (2003) 'Religious and Nationalist Militant Groups', ch. 7 in Mary Kaldor, Helmut Anheier and Marlies Glasius (eds), *Global Civil Society 2003*. Oxford: Oxford University Press.
– and Said, Yahia (2004) *Impressions from a Visit to Iraq April 28–May 10 2004*. London: Centre for the Study of Global Governance, London School of Economics.
Keck, Margaret E. and Sikkink, Kathryn (1998) *Activists Beyond Borders: Advocacy Networks in International Politics*. Ithaca: Cornell University Press.
League of Independent Voters (URL) http://indyvoter.org/article.php?id=28 (consulted 16 July 2004).
Mazlish, Bruce (forthcoming) 'The Hi-jacking of Global Society?', *Journal of Civil Society*, 1(1).
Meyer, John W., Boli, John, Thomas, George M. and Ramirez, Francisco O. (1997) 'World Society and the Nation-State', *American Journal of Sociology*, 103(1): 144–81.
Mikhail Saakashvili (URL) www.fact-index.com/m/mi/mikhail_saakashvili.html (consulted 16 July 2004).
MoveOn PAC (URL) www.moveonpac.org/whoweare.html (consulted 16 July 2004).
NOW with Bill Moyers (2004). 'Talk Radio', PBS (13 February). www.pbs.org/now/politics/talkradio.html
Pew Research Center (2003) 'Strong Opposition to Media Cross-Ownership Emerges' (13 July). http://people-press.org/reports/display.php3?ReportID=188
Rheingold, Howard (2002) *Smart Mobs: The Next Social Revolution*. Cambridge, MA: Perseus Publishing.
Richburg, Keith (2004) 'Spanish Socialists Oust Party of U.S. War Ally', *Washington Post* (15 March). www.washingtonpost.com/wp-dyn/articles/A57707-2004Mar14.html
Rosenau, James (1988) 'Governance and Democracy in a Globalising World', in Archibugi, Daniele, Held, David and Kohler, Martin, *Reimagining Political Community*. Cambridge: Polity Press.
Saul, John R. (2004) 'The Collapse of Globalism and the Rebirth of Nationalism', *Harper's Magazine*, March: 33–44.
Scholte, J. A. (2001) 'The Globalization of World Politics', in J. Baylis and S. Smith (eds), *The Globalization of World Politics: An Introduction to International Relations*. Oxford: Oxford University Press.
Smart Mobs (2004) 'Spain Smartmob Report en Espanol' (1 April). www.smartmobs.com/archives/002935.html
Vann, Bill (2003) 'Argentine police attack workers protest', *World Socialist Web Site* (23 April). www.wsws.org/articles/2003/apr2003/arg-a23.shtml

CONCEPTS OF GLOBAL CIVIL SOCIETY

CHAPTER 1

'Global Civil Society': A Sceptical View

Kenneth Anderson and David Rieff

Introduction

This chapter aims to raise scepticism about both the conceptual and the practical foundations of 'global civil society'. We describe, and then challenge, a widely received, standard account of what it means for international non-governmental organisations (NGOs) and international social movements to be described as constituting 'global civil society'. In particular, we are dubious about the very application of the term 'global civil society' to the international NGOs and new social movements said to comprise it.

We are sceptical, first, of the claim that transnational or international NGOs constitute 'global civil society', at least if this term is intended to draw upon on the conceptual machinery of 'civil society' as understood to apply in a settled domestic democratic society. This claim, in our view, is misplaced; indeed, we find the term 'global civil society' conceptually incoherent. Our argument goes on to consider why, however, if our scepticism is indeed justified, such inflated ideological claims are made so as to convert international NGOs conceptually into 'global civil society'. We also consider other, better, ways of viewing the rise of transnational and international NGOs, including as a quasi-religious movement and as a revival of the post-religious of the earlier European and American missionary movements. Alternatively, we suggest, the global civil society movement might better be understood as imagining itself as the bearer of universal values, both operating in the teeth of globalisation and yet simultaneously using globalisation as its vehicle for disseminating universal values. It may be even better understood as a movement seeking to universalise the ultimately parochial model of European Union integration.

We are sceptical, second, about whether the values that the global civil society movement embodies are, indeed, as desirable as the movement's supporters would claim. Specifically, the fundamental moral values of the global civil society movement appear to be about human rights rather than democracy. Despite valiant theoretical attempts by global civil society theorists to find ways to satisfy the requirements of democracy while recognising the limits of electoral participation in something intended to encompass the whole world, we argue that the 'democracy deficit' of the international system is buttressed rather than challenged by the global civil society movement, despite its commitment to human rights. Indeed, we argue, the global civil society movement seems to present human rights as a set of transcendental values and as a substitute for democracy, whereas, we would have thought, each ought to be considered indispensable. But, if this is the case, why is it so? We argue that it is best understood as intertwined quests for legitimacy both by the NGOs said to make up global civil society and by public international organisations such as the UN. We suggest that each legitimises the other in a system that is not only undemocratic but also ultimately incapable of becoming democratic. This, we argue, is what drives the severe inflation of ideological rhetoric surrounding claims about 'global civil society'.

The final question addressed in this discussion is deliberately speculative, and we do not pretend to finality in our responses. Nonetheless, we pose the question: what does the discourse of 'global civil society' mean post-September 11 and in the midst of conflicts in Iraq and Afghanistan and the war on terror? We tentatively suggest that, following September 11, sovereignty and democratic sovereignty are back at the centre stage of political discourse. This, we suggest, is as true for states as it is for international organisations such as the UN. One consequence is, perhaps, that since September 11 attention has shifted away from 'global civil society', considered as a marker of international legitimacy, and back towards relations between powerful states, the superpower, and the UN Security Council. Global civil society, both as a concept and as a practice, might be seen by future historians as essentially a 1990s discourse, which reached its apogee with the 1999 Seattle protests and the 2000 Millennium Summit, but which is frankly much less important in 2004 than it was in 2000.

The standard account of global civil society

The standard account of the meaning of 'global civil society' (and this is deliberately the simple, unsophisticated analysis written for broad consumption which, while running the risk of caricature, nonetheless highlights some salient features) runs as follows.

Globalisation, it is said, is gradually eroding the authority of sovereign states, which traditionally have exercised control over actions, events, and persons within their borders and, in the case of powerful states, touching their vital interests abroad (Waters, 1995). The processes of economic globalisation are instead transferring unprecedented power to a variety of transnational actors, including transnational business and financial interests. Many of these transnational business actors are familiar Western transnational corporations, such as Shell Oil or Proctor & Gamble; others, however, are much less 'brand-visible' to Western consumers and include the movement of ethnically based diaspora capital across borders, such as the circulation of ethnic Chinese capital around the markets of the Pacific Rim (Chua, 2003). These actors are able to take advantage of the increasingly global nature of economic and many other activities, whereas economic regulation remains fundamentally national because the principle of national sovereignty remains, well, sovereign.

In addition to transnational economic actors, a wide variety of other actors also flourish in an environment in which economic transactions, transportation and, above all, communications are both transnational and inexpensive (Rugman, 2001). These other actors include NGOs of every variety and purpose, leveraging their influence globally through global media and new technologies such as the Internet (Gamble, King and Ku, 2000). The falling cost of worldwide communications, however, has especially favoured the development of transnational social movements. These include not just international NGOs but transnational social movements at a mass and not simply an organisational or institutional level, including the growth of transnational religious movements such as Islam, new social movements such as Falun Gong, as well as a globalised popular culture. Unsurprisingly, too, these actors also include transnational organised crime, which takes advantage of gaps between state jurisdictions to set up transnational operations in drug trafficking, weapons smuggling, illegal immigration, trafficking in persons, prostitution and the exploitation of child sex workers, and other illegal activities. Finally, of course, there are transnational terrorist organisations, such as al-Qaeda, that rely on a web of globalised economic transactions to finance themselves (including cross-border crime such as drug trafficking), international social movements that provide a base of social support that transcends borders, and cross-border acts of terrorism; transnational terrorism acts, in effect, as a kind of perverse NGO.

One important source of the presumed erosion of sovereignty is the loss of regulatory control over cross-border actions, which produces situations for which regulation is urgently needed, such as cross-border protection of the natural environment (pollution knows no borders). Still, the erosion of sovereignty generally is understood, on the standard account, to be a good and worthy thing (Held et al, 1999). Sovereignty is at best an impediment to the universal good governance of human beings, whose fundamental rights and needs know no borders, and to the ideal of political progress which, in a long intellectual tradition, has been understood to lead to universal political governance for the protection of universal human rights and the provision for universal human needs. At worst, sovereignty has served, on the standard account, to protect regimes that oppress their own people and, perhaps worst of all, that wage war (the right to wage war, after all, was long seen as the defining attribute of sovereignty). A globalising world stands in need of a globalising political authority to regulate it, according to the standard account, less because of the failures of sovereign states to regulate adequately the transactions of the global world than because of the moral deficiencies of the very idea of sovereignty (Beck, 2003).

What is needed instead, therefore, is global governance, ideally exercised by a reformed and transformed United Nations, in order to protect the poor and global labour, promote the global distribution of wealth and the equity of trade, and safeguard the environment, health, human rights, gender equity and many other things. The just claims of global governance are impeded, however, by the residue of sovereignty, and above all by the sovereignty of the world's superpower, the United States, which sees much to lose and little to gain from global governance because of the authority it would have to yield to others over how it uses its

Voice of the people: but post 9/11 how powerful is it?

power. (Although all states would have to cede authority, the more powerful the state, the more power is ceded; and the US, the most powerful state of all, would have to cede the most power.) This is indeed vexing, on the standard account. And yet the growth of transnational global governance is understood as historically inevitable. It is as natural a process as the consolidation that the US experienced in the nineteenth century, or the consolidation that the EU is heroically undergoing today (Giddens, 2000). It cannot help but occur, eventually, for it is not merely a matter of ideology but is materially driven by essentially the same forces that today benefit from an economy that is global in effect but nationally controlled – technology, communications, and transportation especially – and that tomorrow will benefit from markets that are both globally open and globally regulated rather than regulated piecemeal by conflicting and counter-efficient national regulators. Be of good cheer, for, on the standard account, the material conditions of history drive forward both the erosion of sovereignty and the final triumph of global governance.

We are, however, at a dangerous historical moment: transnational economic forces are taking advantage of the current vacuum in which national sovereignty is being eroded but is not definitively being replaced by global governance. Much of the burden of sustaining the dream has fallen, ideologically at least, not just upon the existing organs of international governance such as the UN (which is understood even by its friends to be, however noble in original intent, inefficient and weak at best, and venal and lacking in legitimacy at worst), but also upon transnational NGOs (Kaldor, Anheier and Glasius, 2003). This may appear, on the standard account, initially somewhat surprising; who are these self-appointed NGOs to be the bearers of anything besides their own interests and values? Yet international NGOs have gradually taken a leading role in providing what is declared to be the legitimate, and politically legitimising, input of the world's peoples across a myriad of issues and causes (Tyler, 2003). International NGOs come together to advocate for the peoples of the world, those who would otherwise have no voice, given that the actors they seek to influence, which include both economic actors and the world's superpower, are globally unregulated.

It is conceptually appropriate, on the standard account, to describe this conglomeration of transnational NGOs and associated social movements as 'global civil society' (or 'international civil society' or 'transnational civil society') because they are civil society organisations that operate on a transnational or international rather than a domestic scale (Keane, 2003). Yet their advocacy function is really analogous, on a global scale, to that of their domestic society homologues. And given that the international arena is far from democratic, their advocacy is all the more necessary because international civil society provides the only voice the 'peoples' of the world have to intermediate on their behalf with transnational actors or international institutions (*The Economist*, 1999).

Nonetheless, it is essential to be clear, even in the midst of delivering this standard account, that those who speak with enthusiasm about global civil society in fact have a specifically value-laden view of it. It is, in effect, institutionalised 'new social movements' – promoting environmentalism, feminism, human rights, economic regulation, sustainable development, and so on – that count (Carothers, 1999a). Yet the Roman Catholic Church and many far more politically conservative Christian denominations, for example, are in fact transnational NGOs of great size, resources, members and energy. But for their politics, they surely would be included as part of 'global civil society' on any politically neutral interpretation of that term. But 'global civil society' is understood by its advocates to be a 'progressive' movement, and thus it contains only certain politically progressive NGOs and social movements (Rieff, 1998).

With that caveat to the standard account, therefore, global civil society is thus perceived as the logical continuation of the growth of civil society (or at least of 'progressive' civil society), elevated from the level of merely domestic democratic society. Global civil society is the advocate and intermediary for the people of the world both in the nascent institutions of global governance as well as against those transnational actors – transnational economic actors and the US, principally – that impede the emergence of global governance that reflects 'progressive' values. Without global civil society, the people of the world have no voice and no representation to advocate for 'correct' values before the world's transnational institutions. These transnational NGOs are properly called 'global civil society' and not merely 'advocacy NGOs' for the fundamental reason that they are perceived, on the standard account, to speak for the people of the world (Williams, 1997).

Why 'global civil society' is a misnomer

The claim to be 'global civil society' is at its heart a claim to be something more than merely a collection of advocacy NGOs and social movements with visions and axes to grind on any number of particular topics. Global civil society is claimed to be the international, transnational analogue of that which is called 'civil society' in a settled domestic democratic society. This claim rests, however, on two alleged analogies: between 'civil society' and 'global civil society' and between a settled domestic democratic society (in which civil society is a part of the fabric of domestic society) and an 'international society' or, if one likes, 'international community'. These analogies seem to us flawed, in closely related ways.

The analogy between civil society and global civil society rests on the assumption that the NGOs bearing these conceptual labels can and do play similar roles in very different settings. Civil society institutions that are part of the social fabric of a settled domestic democratic society are able to play the role of single-minded advocates – organisations with an axe to grind and a social mission to accomplish – precisely because they are not, and are not seen as being, 'representative' in the sense of democratic representation (Anderson, 2000). They do not stand for office. Citizens do not vote for this or that civil society organisation as their representatives because, in the end, NGOs exist to reflect their own principles, not to represent a constituency to whose interests and desires they must respond. NGOs, in their most exalted form, (and there are many hybrid exceptions) exist to convince people of the rightness of their ideals and invite people to become constituents of those ideals, not to advocate for whatever ideals people already happen to have. Thus, voters may listen to what NGOs tell them as lobbyists and advocates but, in the end, NGOs are separate from the ballot box.

True, voters do vote for political parties, which are, in some sense, civil society organisations. Yet political parties, like labour unions, while non-governmental in certain ways, are historically separate from the NGOs that serve as the touchstones of the global civil society analogy – the crusading or do-gooding organisations that see themselves as bearers of values far more universal than the agglomerated interest groups that are political parties. Certainly, those who draw an analogy between global civil society and domestic civil society are thinking not of political parties but rather of such examples as the American Civil Liberties Union in the US or the Grupo de Apoyo Mutuo of Guatemala (supporting families of the disappeared), or the Grameen Bank in Bangladesh (providing micro-credit and organising development projects among the poor) (Otto, 1996). This partly reflects the view, often justified, among civil society advocates that political parties, when not merely venal and despite their rhetoric to the contrary at party congresses and conventions, are bearers of interests, not of the universal values disinterestedly held on which civil society organisations pride themselves: global civil society advocates would not necessarily *want* to assimilate themselves by analogy to political parties.

At the same time, it has also been observed that in democratic transitions there is an indispensable point when talented and virtuous people, committed to the democratic process, must invigorate the political party process precisely because, responding to multiple interests of multiple groups, it serves a vital social and political integrating function in a way that civil society organisations, remaining isolated in their purity of principle, cannot do (Carothers, 1999a). Civil society organisations are therefore the glory of democratic societies, but they are not the electoral institutions of democracy. And because they are not electoral institutions, (not representative in the electoral sense) they are free to be pure, unabashed advocates of a point of view; free to ignore all the contradictory impulses that democratic politics requires and the compromises and adjustments and departures from principled purity that democratic politicians must make; and free to ignore entirely what everyone else, the great democratic masses and their leaders, might think in favour of what they themselves believe is the right, the true, and the good (Anderson, 2001).

International NGOs may believe that they play this same role in the international realm but, in so far as they aspire to the legitimacy of 'global civil society', they cannot and do not. The reason is beyond their control: the system in which they purport to advocate is not democratic. And because it is not, their advocacy role cannot be and is not the same; the analogy fails. The difference lies in the claim of 'representativeness' (Annan, 1999a). In a settled domestic democratic society, civil society advocacy claims to represent no one other than itself, and stakes its legitimacy, first, on the right and value of free expression and, second, on the ability to persuade others to adopt its views. In some cases, it might organise itself as a voting bloc, an electoral interest group, but it is striking that within democratic societies the most effective civil society advocacy organisations have no electoral constituencies of their own, but rely on their rational persuasiveness; if they have a constituency, it is the media. International civil society, when it sees itself as global civil society, aspires to a quite different, and much more inflated, set of roles: first, to 'representativeness', and second, to 'intermediation' – to stand between the people of the world and various transnational institutions (Annan, 2000). Civil society organisations in domestic democratic societies do not claim either to represent or to intermediate; they do not stand between the people and their elected representatives, because the ballot box does.

Obviously, this scepticism about the analogy between civil society in a domestic democratic society and global civil society in an undemocratic global system is closely related to the second grounds for scepticism, about the analogy between a settled domestic democratic society and what is inappositely (begging the question, as it were) called 'international society' or the 'international community' (Rieff, 1999). Because, plainly, international society is not democratic, international NGOs are deprived of the democratic context in which their (disanalogous) domestic counterparts act. That democratic context, peculiarly, allows domestic civil society organisations to be what we understand as 'civil society' by relieving them of the possibility, the obligation, and indeed the temptation to regard themselves as representatives or intermediaries.

Scepticism about the claims of 'global civil society', therefore, rests on scepticism about its analogy with domestic civil society and about the analogy between domestic democratic society and international society. In each case, the touchstone is the problem of democracy. The claim of global civil society is that it plays the same role as domestic civil society but, because the environment in which it acts is not democratic, it aspires, perversely, to roles that domestic civil society does *not* claim, namely, representation and intermediation. The claim of global civil society elevates the status and reach and importance of what are otherwise merely international NGOs advocating and acting for what they see as the right and the good. It elevates them, however, supposedly to the equivalent level of civil society but by claiming precisely what civil society eschews, because it operates in a democratic

NGOs apolitical

© TACAYAN/PANOS PICTURES

International NGOs: advocacy organisations or representatives of the world's peoples?

environment. But the key in these ironies is always the democratic deficit of the international system, and the question whether it can be made up.

Before turning to those issues, however, we should acknowledge the two principal objections to this scepticism about the claims of global civil society. The first objection (which will be taken up later as one of the normative concerns about democracy) is that this account makes too much of democracy and electoral democracy in particular (Held et al, 1999). Domestic democratic systems, it might be said, are not so democratic as all that, and the ballot box is overrated and fetishised in what is really better understood as an agglomeration of interest groups in which NGOs indeed serve as representatives and intermediaries. Democracy is not all that it is made out to be, and our scepticism sets too high a bar by invoking it.

The second objection is a practical one. Even if this scepticism, this lack of anology, should be acknowledged in some way as true, then is that really a reason for NGOs to pack up their tents, so to speak, and go home? Isn't the proper response to press on for the sake of both their causes and the democratisation of the international system, so that the scepticism is defanged by making the system democratic and the NGOs genuinely a global civil society? The short answer is that our scepticism is a basis for giving up the ideological pretensions of global civil society in order to focus on accomplishing specific social missions, but this objection will likewise be taken up at greater length below, under the normative discussion of democracy.

Other ways of understanding international NGOs

It is worth noting that international NGOs can be understood as a social movement on very different models from that of global civil society. One or another of these might be thought frankly more powerful in explaining the international NGO movement. One model is simply that of a contemporary secular, post-religious missionary movement (Anderson, 1998).

On this view, the NGO movement, rather than being global civil society in the contradictory sense discussed earlier, is simply the analogue of the Western missionary movements of the past, which carried the gospel to the rest of the world and sought in this way to promote truth, salvation, and goodness. It is a weak sense of religious movement because it claims a connection to earlier religious missionary movements only by analogy, rather than through a genuinely historical inheritance. Yet even by analogy alone it remains a powerful way of explaining the international NGO movement. It is a movement with transcendental goals and beliefs. It is self-sacrificing and altruistic. It asserts a form of universalism and builds it into its transcendentalism. It appeals to universal, transcendental, but ultimately mystical values – the values of the human rights movement and the 'innate' dignity of the person – rather than to the values of democracy and the multiple conceptions of the good that, as a value, it spawns. Most notably, its personnel do indeed resemble missionary orders – the human rights organisations, for example, might be thought of as the Jesuits of the movement, or perhaps Opus Dei, keepers of the true doctrines, the true universals, while the development organisations might be thought of as the equivalent of the Maryknoll Order, one of the Catholic missionary orders devoted to human development among the world's poor. (If this be thought offensive as a caricature, no offence is intended, as it is proposed as an aid to thinking beyond the categories of liberalism writ into liberal internationalism; if, on the other hand, this characterisation is thought offensive because sacrilegious to the NGO movement – what, nineteenth-century foreign missionaries in modern dress? – well, that is just the point.)

Why does this matter? Because, in so far as the NGO movement, especially in aspiring to the status of global civil society, actually elevates itself into a religious movement, it underscores that the universal claims it makes are so only in the sense that each religion makes its own universal claims. That is, each religion makes a claim of universality, but – seen severally from the outside – each is just one among many such religions. Seen as a religion, seen as missionary work, global civil society's (fundamentally human rights) claims are just one set of universal claims amid all the others that religions and transcendental philosophies make. There is no obvious sense in which any one of them has special authority. This, obviously, threatens the moral hegemony that the NGO movement claims through its morality of human rights, and so has been a reason for resisting the analogy to religious missionary movements and for preferring the much more accommodating ideology of global civil society.

A second way of seeing the international NGO movement and its claims about the need for global governance – the presumed obviousness of the good of overcoming sovereignty – is that it universalises and claims as the path of history the ideal of creating larger and larger political entities. The narrow motivation for doing so is perfecting the regulation of transnational actors. The broad motivation is that it is thought to be the historically progressive thing to do. But it might be thought that this universalising of size and number in fact represents the fetishising of a parochial model – that of the EU (Giddens, 2000). One may admire the accomplishments of the EU without believing that it represents a universal model for humankind at the planetary level. One may understand European grandees whose experience has taught them that integration works – works in Europe and can create peace, prosperity, and respect for human rights – without actually believing the corollary, not just that it can work elsewhere, but that it can work on a planetary level (Carothers, 1999b). Why does this matter? Because it raises the possibility that what has been urged with such grandiosity as the universal condition of liberal internationalism is, instead, simply the unjustified universalising of a particular historical and cultural experience, EU integration – a project, moreover, whose ultimate outcome is far from clear.

Its personnel do indeed resemble missionary orders – the human rights organisations, for example, might be thought of as the Jesuits of the movement . . . while the development organisations might be thought of as the equivalent of the Maryknoll Order

What is common among these alternative views is that they challenge a key moral assumption built into the ideology of global civil society: the universality and transcendence and *completeness* of its moral system, which is that of universal human rights. They question whether leaving democracy out of account can give a complete moral system in the way that the ideology of human rights claims to – while not coincidentally leaving the interpretation and authority of that ideology in the hands of global civil society itself. In invoking either religious models or EU parochialism, alternative explanations of the international NGO movement challenge the movement's universal claims. Thus, by extension, they challenge a key reason for which the claim to be 'global civil society' was invoked in the first place namely, its claim to be universal, representative, and an intermediary for the peoples of the world. Each alternative explanation in its own way threatens the authority that the international NGO movement claimed for itself when it appropriated the elevated, ideologically extravagant language of global civil society.

The value of democracy

A further ground for scepticism about global civil society is that the universalist values that it espouses may not be so good, or at least so *complete*, as it implies. The key issue, once again, is the question of democracy or, more precisely, democratic legitimacy and the lack thereof – the much discussed 'democratic deficit' (Diamond, 2003). Against our moral complaint that the international system lacks democratic legitimacy, and that this is a major problem for advocates of global civil society who are inclined to substitute human rights for democracy, there are perhaps five principal responses. We will set them out and offer a reply to each of them.

First, it can simply be said that global democratic legitimacy is not as necessary, or at least not as important, as our moral claim makes it out to be. It can be said, for example, that the claim that the international system lacks democratic legitimacy ignores the fact that most so-called national democracies are not really democratic, but are really just collections of colliding interest groups, in which the ballot box plays a relatively small role in how political decisions are reached. Our account fetishises the ballot over actual political relations in democratic states. We have, it can be said, raised the bar for the democratic legitimacy of the international system far higher than it is in so-called democracies. Democratic legitimacy is mostly an illusion in democratic states, not the fact of the matter; what matters is instead the perception of their legitimacy. And that perception is less a function of actual, successful democratic process than the fulfillment – through the performance of efficient government, bureaucracies, and economies – of the material expectations of the citizenry. The citizenry's material expectations trump its expectations of democratic perfectionism (Alvarez, 2000).

The difficulty with this response is that, despite the many failings of democratic sovereign states, and however imperfect their democratic systems, the fact remains that democratic legitimacy – of the kind obtained only at the ballot box – *does* matter. It is simply a fact of contemporary life. Modern nation-state constitutionalism is right about that – a legitimate state is one that is democratic, respects basic human rights and the rule of law, and looks after the common good. In that, the ballot box is indispensable. This is true both in fact and as a matter of perception; in the contemporary world, states that seek legitimacy without elections have serious difficulties in reality as well as perception (Annan, 1999b).

This reply, that the ballot box is indispensable, anticipates the second response. Even granted that democratic legitimacy is a requirement of legitimacy in the world today, for nation states as well as for an international system, it is *not* the case that democratic legitimacy requires the actual ballot box (Held, 1991). There are methods of participation other than elections that can supply democratic legitimacy – after all, representative democracy is itself a modification of the 'purest' form of democracy, so why not others? These others include participation through intermediaries, such as NGOs and other 'organic' sites of people's actual lives, rather than through the formality of universal suffrage. And so, for example, we have suggestions for a new upper chamber of the UN General Assembly, to be filled by representatives of NGOs, and many other proposals that would deal with the fact that even representative, quasi-parliamentary democracy at the level of the whole planet is not realistic (Held et al, 1999).

The effect of these other mechanisms for achieving democratic legitimacy is, notably, to restore international NGOs to precisely the position of intermediation and representation that we earlier denied them on the grounds that they are not a replacement for the ballot box. And we remain as unenthusiastic as before. This form of global civil society, and this ballot-free representation and intermediation, is *not* civil society as we have so far understood it. It is *not* democracy as we have understood it because, however imperfect its implementation, it does include the mystery of the ballot box. And it is, moreover, morally wrong to the extent that it indulges in a sleight of hand over what the world generally understands democracy to mean, which does include the ballot box.

The third response acknowledges the force of this reply, and accepts that democracy means ballot boxes, parliamentary elections, and the associated apparatus. These are necessities that cannot be wished away by means of new social movements, intermediation through NGOs or labour unions or peasant assemblies or UN conferences or anything else. Therefore, let us straightforwardly create a world parliamentary system; the role of international NGOs is merely to advocate for that system, and it is mistaken to accuse NGOs of having a role other than temporary midwife to a democratic system. Let us have elections and make planetary democracy a reality (Commission on Global Governance, 1995).

This response is admirable in confronting the issue directly, without any sleight of hand whatsoever.

Unfortunately, it confronts a profoundly practical problem, which is that it is unlikely that planetary parliamentary democracy is possible. Democracy is a system of government that rapidly bumps up against human problems of space and numbers. It is not, in our understanding, infinitely upwardly scalable, and certainly not scalable up to the level of the whole planet (Diamond, 1999).

On the contrary, what we refer to as the world's large democracies, with their tens of millions or hundreds of millions of people, are really compromises between the requirements of democracy, which tends towards the smaller, and the wealth of the common market, which, being a network, *does* benefit from growing larger and larger. Democracy and the common market are frequently confused, particularly by economists of a conservative persuasion, but it is important to understand that, although the large, wealthy democracies have compromised their democracies significantly in a shifting trade-off between democracy and wealth, size and numbers take a severe toll upon the purity of democracy. The large democratic states are helped in various instances by common languages, common cultures, common ethnicities and common religions, none of which are present at the level of the whole planet (Harrison, 2000). It is simply not the case that parliamentary democracy can be projected and scaled upwards from the nation state to the whole planet.

The same problem afflicts the closely related claim that the international system already *has* democratic legitimacy, through the legitimacy of the nation states that make it up (which ignores the question of how many of those states are democratic); nation states pass their legitimacy upwards to endow the international system with legitimacy. No doubt for many purposes – the setting of international postal rates, for example – such legitimacy is sufficient (Slaughter, 2004). But, as the international system both tasks itself with more and more intrusive tasks and, it must be said, is assigned more and more intrusive tasks by leading states, including the US, the ever more diluted legitimacy that passes upwards from nation state to international system is inevitably far too attenuated to satisfy the requirements of those new tasks.

The fourth response likewise confronts the issue head-on. It says that democratic legitimacy is not really the issue; the international system, through the tutelage of global civil society, has another, different, moral basis and legitimacy. It is the moral foundation of human rights. Democracy is a lovely thing, if you can have it, but although it is sometimes thought of as the moral exercise of ordered liberty, really it is just a way, in the language of economics, of sorting mass preferences, a sort of market in politics, nothing more. It is not a fundamental moral principle. Human rights, on the other hand, *is* about fundamental moral principle. And what global civil society brings to the international system, infuses it with and advocates for, is human rights. It, rather than democracy, is what gives moral and political legitimacy.

This response puts squarely on the table what is often an occult move by human rights advocates. Noting correctly that somewhere, higher or lower, in the canon of human rights one can find many references to the value of democracy, they claim that they, too, favour democracy. Yet, in fact, it would be more accurate to say that, seeing the insuperable difficulties in creating a genuinely democratic international system, they opt for substituting the ideology of human rights for the ideology of democracy (Casey and Rivkin, 2001). But this substitution likewise fails the test of civil society in a liberal, democratic, constitutional order, consisting of democracy, human rights and individual guarantees, the rule of law, and the common good. It dispenses with one but says that it does not ultimately matter so long as the other is available. But it does matter.

Moreover, the top-down nature of human rights norms, and the fact that they are held, formed, fomented and determined by what might appear, for example, in a UN conference on women or the environment or race to be a vast agglomeration of groups and people, is in fact a tiny collection of transnational activists responding to the sometimes downright peculiar cultural characteristics of these groups. Like other religionists, they imagine that they carry forth moral universals that they have somehow discerned. As they fly effortlessly from place to place, continent to continent, capital to capital, they cannot imagine that they are less than a universal class, pure and disinterested, beyond geography and the parochialism of place. They cannot grasp that 'international' is not the same as 'universal', and that even those who have apparently abandoned fidelity to location might still have interests, class interests to defend, the interests of, well, the interests of those who live in the jet stream. Nor can they grasp that there are those at the bottom who, without being moral relativists, nonetheless believe that they are just as capable of discerning the true universals, just as capable of identifying universal values, as those who take the overnight flight business class from New York to Geneva.

The fifth and final response is an intensely practical

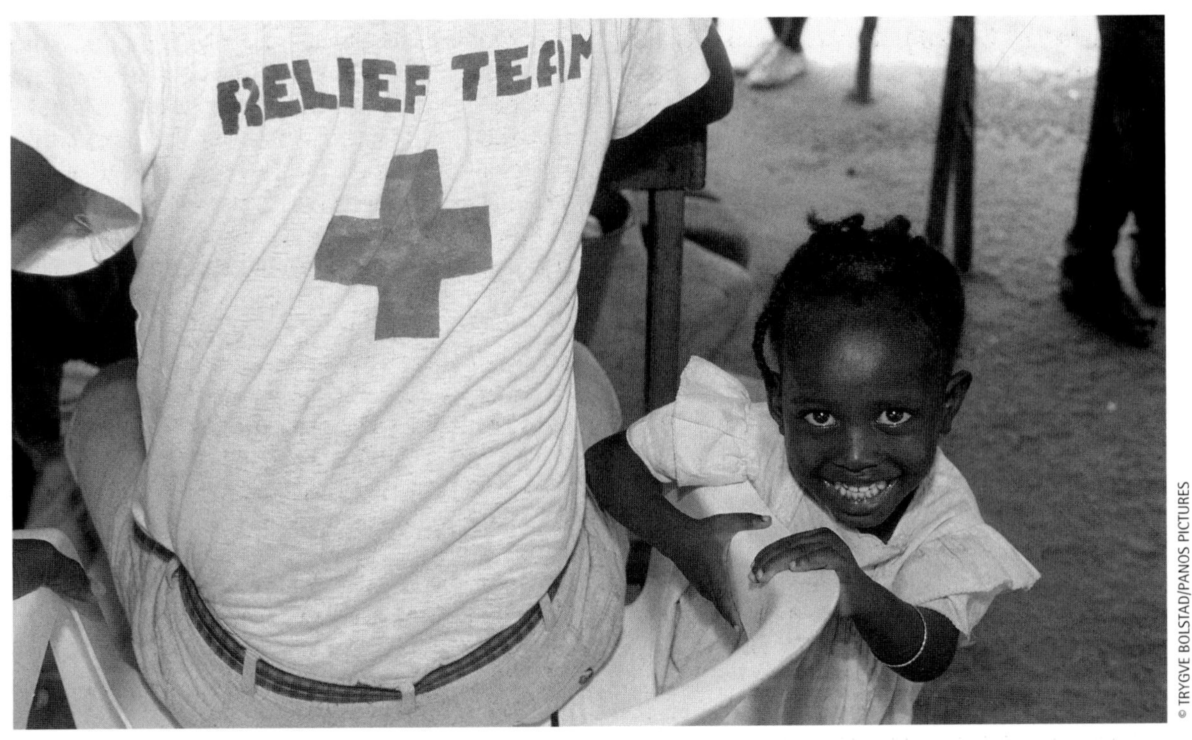

© TRYGVE BOLSTAD/PANOS PICTURES

Should NGOs 'pack up and go home'?

one. Is not the effect of this corrosive scepticism merely a call for the NGOs to pack up their tents and go home? Of what possible value could that be? If the fundamental complaint is that the international system is undemocratic, how would it help if the NGOs were to leave the scene, especially since our claim is that the international system not merely is undemocratic but can never become democratic? The question is an important one because it highlights what we do *not* ask international NGOs to do, that is, to pack up and go home – far from it. The original claim of international NGOs was that they merited being respectfully heard by those engaged in international planning and execution of policy, as well as receiving a share of the budget because of their expertise and their competence. That is what should indeed command respect.

But the claim to constitute 'global civil society' asserts a sharply different claim and role – that of intermediary and representative of the world's peoples. This is a claim for a legitimate place that at once elevates the role of NGOs and, significantly, dispenses with the need for NGOs to prove their expertise and competence, whether in development, humanitarian relief, health, or whatever. After all, if they represent someone, especially a 'someone' who is so vague as to be entirely malleable, then what matters is their representation, not their competence at any actual skill. This is a seductive position for any NGO because it places it permanently beyond the bounds of serious accountability. But it is also a recipe for failing to serve those who most need the help of international NGOs. Our call, therefore, is not for international NGOs to retire from the field, but instead to assert themselves on the basis of their expertise and competence and, concomitantly, to give up their claims to intermediation and representation – that is, to give up the claim to constitute global civil society.

A 1990s discourse in a post-9/11 world?

And yet there is a whiff of tiredness about this whole discussion – both the claims and our responses. It all feels very much like a discussion from the late 1990s rather than 2004, a discussion from pre-September 11. The question is, what remains of this kind of discourse in a world in which security is back on the table, and with it the value of sovereignty. The love affair between global civil society and international organisations, each legitimising the other, during the 1990s, has given way to an international system under a specific challenge

Targeting aid: the world has become a more dangerous place for humanitarian NGOs

from the world's superpower: make yourself relevant or see yourself disappear. Time was when the UN Secretary General could go and address the Millennium Forum of NGOs in 2000 and describe in ecstatic terms how they represented the world's peoples (Annan, 2000). Today, Annan has, and must have, his eye on the White House and a handful of other capitals; and NGOs, whether styling themselves as global civil society or anything else, appear frankly irrelevant as the grown-ups, nation states, confer among themselves, sometimes with international organisations and sometimes not.

In some respects, therefore, the ideal of a love affair, the mutual legitimisation, between the nascent organs of global governance and their loyal, if sometimes critical, constituency, global civil society, appears to have led the NGOs astray. There is a marriage, loveless and probably childless, to be sure, and, moreover, one that is in serious danger of ending in divorce. But it is not between international institutions and the NGOs: it is between the leading nation states, particularly the superpower, and the UN. The love affair between international organisations and global civil society was never more than a minor affair with a minor mistress; when push came to shove, as it did on September 11 and again in the war in Iraq, what mattered was the marriage (including the potential divorce), not the affair. The NGOs promised that they would, on behalf of the people of the world, confer legitimacy on the nascent organisations of global governance. It has turned out that what matters to the Secretary General, when the stakes are genuinely high, is the legitimacy that comes from the capitals of important nation states. The legitimacy of the 'world's peoples', at least as conveyed by global civil society, is merely icing on that cake, dispensable as and when necessary. If that is the case, then perhaps it is the strongest, least theoretical reason of all why the international NGOs should give up their claims to constitute global civil society, give up their dreams of representing the people of the world – indeed, devote fewer of their resources to advocacy and to creating a system of global governance and more time and care to the actual needs of their actual constituencies, and re-establish their claims of expertise and competence.

That is our advice. Nevertheless, the complications and convulsions of the world in circumstances of terror, the war on terror, September 11 and March 11, and the wars in Iraq and Afghanistan all raise questions about the proper roles of international NGOs, *even if* they give up the pretence of representativeness and intermediation. For example, the bombings of the UN and the international Red Cross headquarters in Iraq, and the kidnap and murder of NGO representatives as a strategy of asymmetric fighting in Iraq and Afghanistan, raise questions about the role international NGOs can hope to play in the world's most difficult circumstances (Anderson, 2004). Of course, at one level, this is the wrong question; the whole world is not at war, and while international NGOs that operate in dangerous zones are the most visible in the media, the overwhelming majority of international NGOs work in quite different circumstances; their personnel are not being kidnapped nor are their headquarters being blown up. It would be a mistake to generalise on the basis of the visible minority of NGOs that work in conflict situations.

Nevertheless, even with that caveat, it is also true that, even where conflicts are not occurring, international NGO work has become much more difficult and significantly more dangerous. The problem is compounded by a confusion indulged in by both the UN and its agencies on the one hand and by many international NGOs on the other. This is the fiction of neutrality in the work of international NGOs. There are moments of crisis and disaster in which basic human needs take precedence over other considerations, moments of humanitarian emergency in which, arguably, humanitarian aid can be thought to be genuinely neutral, in the sense that it responds only to need. The organisations, including NGOs, that work in such circumstances have traditionally benefited from a doctrine of humanitarian inviolability based on the belief that no one could oppose activities aimed at relieving dire human suffering. That doctrine of humanitarian inviolability is in crisis and under attack today from fighters who have discovered in Western aid workers an easy means of leverage, another form of asymmetric warfare (Anderson, 2003). But it is also in crisis because the aid agencies themselves have sought to extend the concept of humanitarian inviolability to cover a series of NGO and international agency activities that cannot properly be regarded as neutral.

Nation building is not a politically neutral activity. On the contrary, it is an activity that requires the assistance of many outside agencies, whether governmental or non-governmental, if it is to work at all (itself an open question), whose interventions, however tactful, cannot be considered neutral (Rieff, 2002). The commitment to democracy is not neutral; there are many in the world who are opposed to it. The commitment to basic human rights, including the rights of women, is not neutral; it is the object of intense opposition, and not merely from the Taliban and Saudi Arabia. The list of matters that are essential to remaking a political society and yet on which outside aid agencies, including NGOs, cannot remain purely neutral (in the sense of viewing any outcome as morally and politically acceptable) is very long. It follows that the claim of humanitarian inviolability for the activities of agencies involved in nation building is unsound. Such agencies have a claim to inviolability; however, it is not based on the humanitarian nature of their work but rather on the democratic rule of law. The confusion of these two kinds of activity, and the respective bases on which they operate, is potentially a fertile source of tragedy in many sites of nation building today – not just in Iraq or Afghanistan, but also in Kosovo, East Timor, and other places. The confusion places genuinely neutral humanitarian relief in a situation of dire risk, and suggests, incorrectly, that nation building is a value-neutral enterprise.

The circumstances of the post-September 11 world have altered the relationship between global civil society and public international organisations such as the UN. They have altered the relationship of mutual legitimisation in which global civil society organisations provided legitimacy to public international organisations that substituted for the democratic legitimacy that one might otherwise have thought was required. For their part, public international organisations gave to international NGOs an unprecedented legitimacy based not on competence or expertise but on the presumption of representativeness. That cosy embrace of mutual legitimisation is no longer at the heart of international organisations, which today look directly to the most powerful nation states.

No strings attached? Humanitarian work is rarely neutral

This means, however, that international NGOs must also redefine their relationships and their conception of their legitimacy. For many, it means, too, defining the relationship between them and the superpower, the US. Global civil society (in the progressive, left-wing, normative sense that advocates of the concept ordinarily mean) faces something of an identity crisis not only with respect to the US but necessarily as well with respect to its self-conception. Actions of the US, whether one agrees with them or not, have taken centre stage in the world in a way not true for a long time; and, particularly, at a moment in which international NGOs cannot simply seek their identity in an idealised relationship with international global governance, they must determine where they stand in relation to the US. Belief in a strong form of liberal internationalism as the only acceptable basis of global governance leads, at the present moment, to principled opposition to the Bush administration, which is committed to a strong form of democratic sovereignty as the foundation of (limited) global governance. Equally plainly, much of the global civil society movement has simply defined global civil society to be anti-Americanism, a sort of countercultural ideology based on mere opposition, intellectually sterile where not outright self-contradictory, and morally uninteresting. If the intellectuals of the global civil society movement wish to guarantee its irrelevance to future political debates, this is surely the way to do it, but the loss to the discourse of the morality of globalisation and its future directions would be immense.

This is partly what the debate over the reconstruction in Iraq is about for international NGOs. The US government has had mixed views – on this as on many things – about the role of NGOs in occupied Iraq. Drawing on a sort of 'compassionate conservativism' rhetoric grounded in certain self-help and limited government ideologies within the US and its unquestionably robust civil society, the Bush administration believed that international NGOs could take a lead in reconstruction. But such a lead was in fact far beyond the capacities of the NGOs. Irrespective of what one thinks of Halliburton or Bechtel, it was always some international corporation that would have to rebuild the oil facilities, for example, obviously not an NGO; and the question was simply, would it be American, British Russian or French? In part, of course, underestimating what kind of rebuilding would be required and what kind of opposition would be faced, but also underestimating the visceral hatred of many of the international NGOs for the US, the Bush administration assumed that international NGOs would be – well, what? partners? grantees? contractors? – *present*, at least, in occupied Iraq. Global civil society, with its set of ideological blinkers, has never really understood that, for reasons grounded in a very American ideology, a sizeable part of the Bush administration has always been receptive and, indeed, overly receptive, to the work of NGOs.

The reasons for the non-presence of the international NGOs in Iraq are overdetermined. On the one hand, the levels of violence and risk certainly deterred many organisations. But on the other hand, attitudes ranging from the refusal to be 'tainted', as it were, by the occupation to a straightforward desire that the occupation would break down altogether, despite the obvious disaster that would mean for the Iraqis, have also been a decisive reason for the absence of the usual collection of international NGOs from Iraq (Anderson, 2004). At the same time, another part of the Bush administration, taking careful note of the aftermath of the bombings of the UN and Red Cross headquarters in 2003, and the subsequent mass exodus of organisations, has questioned whether the NGOs and UN agencies really mattered very much in the actual reconstruction efforts, as opposed to providing icing on the cake of a legitimacy that mattered more to outsiders than to ordinary Iraqis. It was not so clear that the exit of the aid agencies mattered very much to concrete material facts of reconstruction – electricity, security, and so on. The convulsions at the time of writing (May 2004), with sharply increased levels of fighting in Iraq, hostage taking and executions of Western NGO workers, and the scandals of the prison abuses, leave it unclear whether it is true that international legitimacy of the kind offered by UN and NGO agencies, even if it did not contribute directly to material conditions such as electricity and potable water, would have contained the present violence. It is not possible to know how things will turn out as of this moment, and we will not speculate further about current events.

What is clear, however, is that the coin that many NGOs, like the UN agencies, offer is now not necessarily their competence or expertise. What they offer is legitimacy and cover – a sort of branding process whereby money from various national sources, particularly from the US, is 're-branded' with the logos of some NGO, or UN agency, or both. Legitimacy is not to be sneered at, to be sure; it is an invaluable, if intangible, element of political stability, in Iraq as elsewhere. But the entitlement of international NGOs to offer legitimacy, and to receive legitimacy, which is among the ideologically extravagant claims of global civil society, is suspect. Nor is it merely an academic question, a question of the success or failure of this or that intellectual analogy. The stakes are much, much higher. Organisations that have legitimacy based on representativeness have less necessity, frankly, to be either expert or competent. It is a recipe for rot and utter lack of accountability.

Unmoved by the claims of representativeness, and disbelieving that the assent of NGOs to this or that is a substitute for ballot-box democracy, we believe that the value and the salvation of the international NGO movement lie in giving up the pretensions, however seductive, of the ideology of global civil society and making its case to be heard on the basis of undeniable expertise and competence.

REFERENCES

Alvarez, Jose (2000) 'Multilateralism and its Discontents', *European Journal of International Law*, 11, March.

Anderson, Kenneth (1998) 'Secular Eschatologies of the Internationalized New Class', in Peter Juviler and Carrie Gustafson (eds), *Religion and Human Rights: Competing Claims?* New York: ME Sharpe.

– (2000) 'The Ottawa Convention Banning Landmines, the Role of International Non-Governmental Organizations and the Idea of International Civil Society', *European Journal of International Law*, 11(1): 91–120.

– (2001) 'The Limits of Pragmatism in American Foreign Policy: Unsolicited Advice to the Bush Administration on Relations With International Non-Governmental Organizations', *Chicago Journal of International Law*, 2: 371–88. www.ssrn.com

– (2003) 'Who Owns the Rules of War?', *New York Times Magazine*, 13 April. www.ssrn.com

– (2004) 'Humanitarian Inviolability in Crisis: The Meaning of Impartiality and Neutrality for UN and NGO Agencies Following the Afghanistan and Iraq Conflicts', *Harvard Human Rights Journal*, 17 (Spring): 41–74. www.ssrn.com

Annan, Kofi (1999a) 'Secretary General says "global people power" best thing for the United Nations in long time' (Secretary General to World Civil Society Conference, 8 December 1999), M2 Presswire, 9 December.

– (1999b) 'Two Concepts of Sovereignty', *The Economist*, 18 September.

– (2000) 'Secretary General, addressing participants at Millennium Forum, calls for intensified "NGO revolution"', M2 Presswire, 23 May.

Beck, Ulrich (2003) 'The Analysis of Global Inequality: From National to Cosmopolitan Perspective', in Mary Kaldor, Helmut Anheier and Marlies Glasius (eds), *Global Civil Society 2003*. Oxford: Oxford University Press.

Carothers, Thomas (1999a) *Aiding Democracy Abroad: The Learning Curve*. Washington, DC: Carnegie Endowment.

– (1999b) 'Civil Society: Think Again', *Foreign Affairs*, 22 (Winter): 18–29.

Casey, Lee A. and Rivkin, David B. (2001) 'Europe in the Balance: The Alarmingly Undemocratic Drift of the European Union', *Policy Review*, 107. www.policyreview.org

Chua, Amy (2003) *World on Fire: How Exporting Free Market Democracy Breeds Ethnic Hatred and Global Instability*. New York: Doubleday.

Commission on Global Governance (1995) *Our Global Neighbourhood*. NY: Oxford University Press.

Diamond, Larry (1999) *Developing Democracy: Towards Consolidation*. Baltimore, MD: Johns Hopkins University Press.

– (2003) 'Universal Democracy?', *Policy Review*, 119. www.policyreview.org

The Economist (1999) 'Special: Citizens Groups: The non-governmental order: Will NGOs democratise, or merely disrupt, global governance?', 11 December.

Gamble, John, King, John and Ku, Charlotte (2000) 'International Law – New Actors and New Technologies: Center Stage for NGOs?' *Law and Policy in International Business*, 31: 221–62.

Giddens, Anthony (2000) *Runaway World: How Globalization is Reshaping Our Lives*. New York: Routledge.

Harrison, Lawrence E. (2000) 'Culture Matters', *The National Interest*, 60 (Summer): 55–65.

Held, David (1991) 'Democracy and the Global System', in David Held (ed), *Political Theory Today*. Cambridge: Polity Press.

– McGrew, Anthony, Goldblatt, David and Perraton, Jonathan (1999) *Global Transformations: Politics, Economics and Culture*. Stanford, CA: Stanford University Press.

Kaldor, Mary, Anheier, Helmut and Glasius, Marlies (2003) 'Global Civil Society in an Era of Regressive Globalization', in Mary Kaldor, Helmut Anheier and Marlies Glasius (eds), *Global Civil Society 2003*. Oxford: Oxford University Press.

Keane, John (2003) *Global Civil Society?* Cambridge: Cambridge University Press.

Otto, Dianne (1996) 'Nongovernmental Organizations in the United Nations System: The Emerging Role of Civil Society', *Human Rights Quarterly*, 18: 107–41.

Rieff, David (1998) 'The False Dawn of Civil Society', *The Nation*, 22 February.

– (1999) 'The Precarious Triumph of Human Rights', *New York Times Magazine*, 8 August.

– (2002) *A Bed for the Night: Humanitarianism in Crisis*. New York: Simon & Schuster.

Rugman, Alan (2001) *The End of Globalization: Why Global Strategy Is a Myth & How to Profit from the Realities of Regional Markets*. New York: Random House.

Slaughter, Anne-Marie (2004) *A New World Order*. New Jersey: Princeton University Press.

Tyler, Patrick (2003) 'Threats and Responses: News Analysis: A New Power in the Streets', *New York Times*, 17 February.

Waters, Malcolm (1995) *Globalization*. New York: Routledge.

Williams, Jody (1997) Acceptance Speech for 1997 Nobel Peace Prize, 10 December. www.foreignaffairs.org/envoy/documents/v8n6_nobel.html

CHAPTER 2

BEYOND METHODOLOGICAL MODERNISM: TOWARDS A MULTICULTURAL PARADIGM SHIFT IN THE SOCIAL SCIENCES

Heba Raouf Ezzat

Social sciences and the global: new régime or new raison d'être?

The idea of 'methodological nationalism' as a fundamental obstacle to a deeper understanding of global civil society is one of the major concerns of the Global Civil Society Yearbook (Anheier, Glasius and Kaldor, 2001: 17–18; Kaldor, Anheier and Glasius, 2003: 4–5). This is assumed to be the major challenge facing the social sciences, preventing us from grasping the complexity and significance of the emerging global civil society. The argument is that, due to the loss of the centrality of the nation state as an actor in international relations as a result of globalisation, there is an urgent need to rethink, at the theoretical level, its power and role.

In *Global Civil Society 2003*, Martin Shaw (2003: 37) wrote that, to date, the methodology in the 'ancien régime' was very much 'domesticated', and this obscured different aspects of global civil society. Ulrich Beck's contribution (2003: 46–7) to the same volume mirrored this concern. He focused on the need for a new approach to the social sciences. One can describe the rationale of, and the concern behind, these arguments as fundamentally 'spatial'. The implication is that we simply need to 'expand' the methodology and conceptualisation of the social and human sciences in order to match the cosmopolitan scale of civil activity.

My argument here is that this paradigmatic shift cannot take place without going beyond modernism and the assumptions that formed the fundamental philosophical underpinning of social sciences. To go beyond methodological nationalism would mean seeing modernism not only in terms of the way in which socio-political and economic structures are rapidly transcending the boundaries of the nation state, but also in terms of the essence and nature of that change and its theoretical implications.

In addition, it is essential to see modernism as a 'rational mood' (Rengger, 1995: 110–11), which has defined 'reason' in a very limited, utilitarian manner, according to which the rational individual is not influenced by emotions, metaphysical notions, inherited culture or ideological doctrines. Beyond the nation state as a locale that compartmentalised social science methodology, modernity has retained its grip on the social sciences even though it has lost its hold on the real world. The process of global change demonstrates that human beings do not always focus on a narrow understanding of self-interest but are influenced by such considerations as communal, national and universal solidarity. In other words, human beings are compassionate and are prepared to devote effort, time and money to worthy causes. Indeed, some global civil society activists are prepared to risk their lives for such causes.

The narrow rational mood that dominated thinking about international relations dramatically changed in the 1990s with the striking rise of global civil society as a key actor on the transnational scene. The morphology and genealogy of global social movements challenges the idea of 'rational choice', upon which realpolitik approaches in political science, international relations and other social sciences were based. The new transnational movements build their causes on more emotional, humane and a-rational choices: they give environmental causes priority over economic profit, defy narcissistic individualism and transform urban spaces. Global civil transactions have a philosophical dimension and represent for many activists a search for meaning and identity that goes beyond the modernist philosophical notions of individualism, as well as beyond modernity's central socio-political structure, namely, the nation state.

Those who study globalisation have tended to focus on socio-political-economic manifestations of global change. The ontological and philosophical dimensions, so far overlooked, have to be brought back in to the construction of the global social sciences and their theoretical framework. Not only do we need to reflect on the theoretical problems raised by global social movements, but they should become the focus of a new philosophical anthropology, combining abstract concepts with concrete empirical indicators.

Bridging the gap between theory and philosophy on the one hand and day-to-day reality on the other would add dynamism to the approaches and tools of analysis, and allow researchers to see more clearly and profoundly the depth, as well as scope, of change (Heller, 1978; Geertz, 2000). Hence, it is important to investigate not only the factor of space in globality but its shifting logic; (by the term 'globality' I mean the scale and nature of the new phenomena that emerge from the process of globalisation).

The geographies of globality are re-mapping the topographies of the individual and collective self. There is a new appreciation of the individual and his or her universal moral obligation, as well as a new understanding of individual capacity, not only to achieve self-fulfilment, but to go beyond that in the search for the global common good. It was mainly Heidegger (1992; 1997) who wrote in Western modern philosophy about the relations between the self, place and time. The global transformation of the meaning of these three concepts necessitates some new reflections. Combining neo-Marxist ideas of anti-capitalism with existential ideas of the individual activist would represent a remarkable shift in our analytical capacity (Harvey 1989;1993; Heidegger 1992; 1997).

Global civil society should not be investigated only at the macro level of movements, networks and collective strategies of resistance, but also at the micro, individual level of changing perceptions and concepts, and emerging images of the self and the world. Only by grasping global civil society as a multi-layered phenomenon can we start to imagine how a new map of the social sciences could be drawn.

Modernity 'at large' (Appadurai, 1996) does not simply require that the categories and concepts of the social sciences be stretched and expanded, but also revisited, restructured and reformed.

I also want to reassert that the rise of global civil society reflects not merely a tendency to become 'anti' (anti-capitalist, anti-war, anti-violence, and so on) but that it is ontologically different, and introduces what can be seen as a new 'a-modern' logic. 'Refusing to be modern', as Albrow (1996: 11) described some aspects of global movements, revisiting notions of modernity and reforming them – including capitalism – does not necessarily mean being anti-modern or the antithesis of modernity. Rather, it opens up the possibility of transcending modernity altogether and embarking on a genuine search for comprehensive alternative visions and new civil strategies of global democratic governance in every domain and at all levels.

A-modernism attempts to recapture the humanist essence of the Enlightenment and the notion of a democracy of civil presence: it seeks to soften rationality, revise unilinear conceptions of history and theories of progress; confront the consequences of the 'privatisation' of morality and the trivialisation of religion as a social and progressive force. One can argue that, although the 'condition' and the platforms might be 'postmodern', the essence of social movements need not necessarily be so.

Civil movements benefit from the atmosphere engendered by the deconstruction of modernist myths by postmodern culture, but not all of them embrace postmodernist ultra-relativism or extreme nihilist views. Only a truly a-modern as well as multicultural paradigm can capture the complexity of these dimensions, by exploring the mosaic narratives of parallel, overlapping and/or clashing global movements, and listening carefully to their respective voices and arguments.

To achieve that, the new global social sciences first need go beyond the ethno-centric bias of the Western imagination, recognising the historical experience of other regions, and exploring the institutions and strategies that facilitate social empowerment and social justice within different multicultural contexts. One example would be the Islamic endowments (*Waqf*) that can be found in many Islamic societies across regions and sub-cultures. They performed what could be called, in contemporary terminology, anti-capitalist functions, and were also vehicles for social welfare that were independent of – and a challenge to – state authority (see Box 2.1). Second, the new global social sciences should go beyond the 'liberal' bias of notions and institutional forms usually acknowledged by modernist models. The fact that the civil society is now seen through liberal lenses should not lessen the importance of past civil society endeavours that were rooted in different notions of socialism.

Global civil society began to emerge as a topic in social sciences in the same period as the fall of the Soviet Union. It was somehow assumed that no lessons could be drawn from traditional or socialist welfare systems. The claim that the world had reached the 'end of history' enhanced the hold of the liberal perspective on the academic mind even further (Box 2.1).

In order for the social sciences to become genuinely

Box 2.1: Islamic Waqf: recapturing the spirit of the common good

Methodological nationalism, or rather modernism, fails to take into account the historical concepts and institutions of civil societies with non-Western experiences. Yet the roles, efficiency and relevance of many non-Western social welfare institutions have the potential to fulfill current socio-civic functions.

Waqf, the Islamic endowments system, is a good example of a socio-economic apparatus that could cross the boundaries between the civil, the social, the economic and the political in different Islamic contexts. Literally, Waqf means money restricted to specific purposes, so it cannot be redirected by a governmental authority for any other use. Until the mid-twentieth century, Waqf, which dates back to the rise of Islam, was a major civil society institution in the Arab region. It represents an individual's donation for public purposes. Islamic jurisprudence gave this money full civil, legal and political protection. Endowments mushroomed to serve the needs of society and provide it with capital that would keep it empowered vis-à-vis the state.

Waqf is rooted in the teachings of the Prophet Muhammad, who said that the dead can still be rewarded by Allah in numerous ways; for example, if their pious children prayed for them, or the dead person bequeathed knowledge of benefit to humankind, or she or he allocated money to serve public purposes. It became common to dedicate Waqfs to the memory of one's parents, a practice that helped turn death into a constructive force for civil action. These funds were directed to all spheres of social welfare and addressed the needs of society in every domain.

In the West, the property of the church was originally paid for by the people and manipulated by the church, which resulted in the latter's growing role in the political domain. This led to the secularisation of the public sphere, and the separation between church and state in order to empower citizens and democratise power. The Islamic model was very different. Waqfs were the result of individual will, which turned metaphysical notions of life after death into a motivation for civil action, initiated and implemented by the people.

Islamic jurists and courts maintained the independence of Waqfs from the state-dominated political sphere. This in turn, helped the balance of power, because the judiciary was funded by the Waqf and therefore remained independent from the state.

Waqf supported progressive social and environmental causes, including, for example, shelters for women subjected to domestic violence, building of schools and hospitals, assistance to the poor, orphans and elderly, the provision of clean water, cleaning of streets, care for abandoned animals and seed for birds in public squares. Waqf institutions supported Muslim civil society from Morocco to India and Indonesia, offering a model of combined religious and civil associations, which was adopted by Christian and Jewish communities within the Muslim world. By the beginning of the twentieth century, 30–50 per cent of land and real estate in the Arab region consisted of Waqf endowments.

After independence, Egypt began legislating to manipulate assets and control all civil activities, claiming that it was 'modernising' religious institutions. Ministries of Waqf were established in Egypt and many other Arab countries, even though these amounted to a contradiction in terms. Civil society lost a major source of funding, as well as power and independence.

In recent years there have been attempts to revive Waqf, combining the tradition with modern rules of accounting, management and transparency. In Kuwait, Morocco and other parts of the Muslim world, Ministries of Waqf are creating independent tax-free Waqf units that would be accountable to the legal system, yet have their assets protected from government bodies. If Waqf can regain its original non-governmental logic it could help civil society overcome the many challenges it faces, and provide funding to enable civic institutions to network regionally and globally.

Ibrahim El-Bayoumi Ghanem, National Center for Social and Criminal Research, Egypt

© KAREN ROBINSON/PANOS PICTURES

global, it would be necessary to invent new approaches, functions and institutions, or develop unprecedented forms of civil association. Yet we could also find a wealth of concepts, strategies, institutions and networks in the past, which by their existence mitigated against the misuse of power by the state. To date these have been overlooked by researchers. Hence, a new paradigm shift needs to be built on multicultural visions. We need to adopt a highly pluralistic and diverse approach in our attempt to construct a multicultural paradigm, if we are to ensure its relevance and explanatory capacity. Unless we include different regional historical and cultural experiences in the debate about the nature and meaning of globality, our vision will remain 'flat' while the reality is multi-dimensional.

Paradigm shifts do not occur by simply recognising their necessity and urgency. They develop mainly through three processes: first, the revision of the meaning of concepts, combined with a change in the topography of conceptual systems; second, the rise of issues and circles of research within or among disciplines; and third, networking debates previously too encapsulated and isolated to move the issues to a new plateau. In the following sections I will suggest how the global dimension of these three processes might attain the desired paradigm shift in the social sciences.

Mapping global civil society: the topography of a concept

Three major issues need to be addressed when debating global civil society as a cluster concept. Together they form the controversial semantic spaces of the concept and formulate its complex shifting and contested meaning.

1. The global and the trans-local

The distinction between the global dimension of the concept and mere trans-local interactions is an important factor in defining the relations and networks that should be included in research and study.

Trans-locality means connectedness across nation-state boundaries. This is a characteristic of organised crime, diasporic networks and religious missionaries – activities that take place beyond the nation state but do not necessarily reflect a global tendency. To belong to 'global' civil society requires the ability to build coalitions across religious, ethnic and ideological boundaries. Militant extremist transnational networks are neither civil nor global in that sense, although they are trans-local and transnational. Likewise, transnational Muslim campaigns against banning the veil in French schools and public offices reflect a trans-local solidarity. They do not, as such, foster an Islamic 'global' imagination that would galvanise the same networks in support of a non-Muslim minority's right to its own dress codes. Only when trans-local networks can transcend the narrow concept of identity, which arises from specific and 'thick' differences, towards a shared – even if 'thin' and minimal – humanist and universal horizon, can one then classify the interaction as globally civil.

In this context we also need to remember that the cosmopolitanism of global civil society's domains and networks is a predominantly urban phenomenon. Urbanisation is an inseparable component of their 'modern' nature. If the nation state was the creation of modernity, cities were the space within which modern ideas were realised. Urban spaces were the locale of individuality, citizenship and social mobility – as well as mobilisation. The urban ideal has been transformed as a result of dramatic changes to its socio-economic spaces and cultural maps. The image of modern urban spaces was framed by nationalism and the homogenous culture of modern citizenship and was usually 'enforced' by the nation state, which was in a continuous dialectical relationship with notions of ultra-individualist self-fulfilment.

The rise of awareness and defence of the vernacular dimension of identity marked a shift to the current 'multicultural' moment in the history of capitalist urban spaces. Local and global civil societies are the product of capitalism, a factory of cultural fragmentation that changed the nature of civil society, making it increasingly mosaic and hybrid, while at the same time the state was advocating a coherent notion of nationhood and citizenship. This dialectical relationship is one of the major paradoxes of modernity (Harvey, 2001: 121–7; Kymlicka, 2001: 45–66; AlSayyad, 2001: 1–16). The challenge facing global civil society, then, is how to maintain the vernacular without losing the universal, and how to 'tame' modernism and capitalism without losing some of modernity's undisputed gains at the scientific and intellectual, as well as individual and social, levels.

Although urban in origin, global civil society challenges 'modern' atomistic individuality and attempts to transcend locality and nationalism, striving towards an original and unprecedented blend of globality on the one hand and the politics of cultural identity on the other. The bodily is mixed with the environmental, the specific with the universal, and the individual with the collective in an extremely complex matrix that will be explored shortly.

Cyberspace, likewise, cannot escape being an urban space, although 'not as we know it'. 'E-topia' has many 'modernist' qualities, and the individual is the major social agent (Mitchell, 1999: 3, 82). It is overwhelmingly dependent on technology that is usually available in cities, and depends on individual initiative rather than inherited traditional bonds and identities. Social theory needs to develop theoretical tools suited to the virtual space as a neo-urban domain that transcends the local-global dichotomy.

2. The civil and the uncivil

While globality has been explored and debated, civility does not have a clear definition. On the one hand we should not mix form with content, as Janet Abu-Lughd (1998: 227–38) reminds us. Many associations and NGOs are situated in the 'civil' local or global public sphere, advocating rights or representing groups, but how can we assess the extent of their 'civility?'

If we revise the nature, role and boundaries of the nation state, we should remember that a major 'modern' compromise was the nation state's monopoly of the use of force. As a result, the 'civility' of civil society was determined by its commitment to abstain from the use of force. If we go beyond the nation state paradigm how far should this compromise be rethought? In addition, the nation state represented a civil and rational (secular) apparatus, which supplanted religious (supposedly irrational) bodies. Civility was linked to notions of secular rationalism and measured in daily life by European cultural values that were heavily ethno-centric in this respect.

The religious factor was hence excluded (or rather expelled) from the semantic field and marginalised in academic debates. Revisiting the assumptions of modernist social theory on religion, philosophy and social sciences (De Vries, 1999; Taylor, 2002) necessitates a redefinition of the notion of civility that does not insist on secularity. Indeed the active presence of religious associations in 'civil' societies worldwide invites the de-secularisation of civility. Therefore, I would argue that the religious element in civility should be re-contextualised and reconstructed, challenging both the faltering modernist assumption that religious devotion fades with increasing modernisation, and post-modern images of anti-civil fundamentalism.

We notice also that many secular social movements draw heavily on religious notions of justice and equality; and different faiths are an inspiring source of a liberation theology that accommodates some ideologically radical conceptions of democracy. On the other hand, in many Islamic countries after independence, secularism has been a force for totalitarianism, not democratisation and progress, as in the European historical experience (Esposito, 2000: 10–12; Keane, 2000: 36–7).

After 9/11 those interested in the world of Islam engaged in a major search for a 'liberal' Islam to combat extremism and terrorism. In the present context, one can also trace serious efforts to construct a radically democratic global and progressive Islam. The emergence of a political movement out of the anti-war coalition in the UK, where Muslims have a strong presence, or the solidarity between different ethnic, religious and political groups in defence of civil liberties in the US, indicates a substantial change in the nature of the 'civil' in the global society we are examining.

There is no way we can understand the logic, strategies and dynamics of civil society anywhere in the Third World unless we bring the transcendental dimension back into our analysis. Religious devotion is a fundamental motive for many social movements in the South, from Latin America to Africa and South Asia. In many of these countries, grassroots politics, whether local or global, depend heavily on sacred notions, images and principles, and the religious dimension is mixed with public mobilisation. This is not the case in global civil society networks in the North, at least not with the same weight or vigour.

In *Global Civil Society 2002*, Abdullahi An-Naim (2002) suggested appropriating social theory to include and integrate religious organisations. He also pointed out that the fundamentalist threat could be religious as well as nationalist, a point elaborated by Mary Kaldor and Marlies Glasius (2002) in the same volume, and re-examined by Mary Kaldor and Diego Muro (2003) in *Global Civil Society 2003*.

I argue that the retreat of secularism would require more than just the simple 'appropriation' of social theory. The religious and transcendental dimensions need to become a genuine variable in the new paradigm. The fact that religious actors are present in the global arena, including the World Social Forum, confirms that the 'religious' can no longer remain rigidly contrasted with the 'civil'. An important area for future examination would be how different global agents 'negotiate' across the secular-religious divide and how they achieve an 'overlapping consensus'.

Norwegians protest against the war on Iraq

In this context we should differentiate between the two manifestations of religious devotion: its potentially negative role as a threat to civility, if it is used to exclude others and resorts to violence, which might have a devastating impact on global civil society; and its role as a strong motivation for civil engagement that can contribute to a global 'conversation' and encourage a sense of global citizenship (Casanova, 1994: 1–39; Smart, 1997: 289–95). If the 9/11 attacks were a result of the former, they triggered the latter – inter-religious solidarity to bring about reconciliation in local multi-ethnic communities in the US, as well as the global campaign against the wars on Afghanistan and Iraq, which was initiated by both Christian networks and Islamic organisations.

If the role of religion is re-established against modernist assumptions about secularism and positivist rationalism, social sciences based on European modernism will prove inadequate and in need of reform. Alongside anti-capitalist and anti-consumerist movements, different religious traditions and notions of justice and equality can become a source of ideas for philosophising on the global condition. This would contribute to the alternative world that global civil society is engaged in formulating, especially on issues such as human rights, environmental politics, global economic justice and equity between women and men.

3. The societal and the individual

The third semantic space of global civil society is the societal. Social theory was built upon the communal notion of society bound by place and originating in kinship relations and their contexts (tribal, ethnic, religious, and so on). When modernity attempted to 'overcome' pre-modern identities that were based on pre-capitalist social and cultural structures, the 'civil' bond was the substitute and national citizenship became central.

Here we should remember that the birth of civil society carried a genetic paradox. Modernity focused on individualism, a self-centred conception of the human self, and a liberation of the citizen from primordial identities. Yet, in order to defend him- or herself from the market and the state, the citizen had to enter the public sphere, joining with others in socio-political endeavours, pressure groups, civil associations, trade unions and, more recently, global networks too. The modernist condition of individuality described as the 'end of the public man' (Sennett, 1976: 3–24) was coupled with a structural inevitability of public engagement. During the last three decades this paradox has been bridged by social movements that declare that the private is public, and further by the global social movement, which asserts that the local and the global overlap (Hannerz, 1996: 44–55). The modern social bond developed historically as a mix of communitarian (*Gemeinschaft*) and contractarian (*Gesellschaft*) relationships. Gradually, individual and contractual associations became the dominant forms, while organic communitarian societal bonds diminished. One of the human consequences of globalisation is the decline of 'society', the transformation of community and the emergence of different spaces of 'togetherness'. Alongside this developed the distinction between 'being aside', 'being with' and 'being for' (Bauman, 1995: 45–5; 2001: 39–49). These changes are very relevant to our analysis of the societal nature of global civil society.

While society as an entity is based on bonds of collective identity, rooted in history and shared by memories, language, moral commitments, established norms and common aspirations, these depend heavily on space as 'common ground', which in an age of globalisation and mobility is in flux. The question would then be: is global civil society a real 'society' or is it rather a 'togetherness', which brings to the same spaces of globality movements and organisations that in essence share very little?

The second important issue in investigating this dimension of globality is the search for the 'global agent', the central analytical category of global social sciences. Is it the movement or the collective body (NGO), or should it be conceptualised primarily as the individual who is the actor on the global scene? As a discipline, sociology has turned to the study of collective units of analysis, giving attention to groups and movements even during the behavioural era when the individual, conceived as an abstract entity or metaphor for the masses, was studied to explain collective behaviour. The return of the individual/individual in social theory supports the call for the individual to be the focal point of departure in any analysis of global civil society. If this society is mainly described as the 'network society', born in the information technology age, it is, after all, the individual who decides to communicate, network, act and move, travel and demonstrate, and embrace notions of moral responsibility on a global scale. She or he transcends national boundaries and bridges different public spaces –domestically and globally.

If the role of the individual is often overlooked in research, this is due to the image of global civil society as a counter-Leviathan resisting the Leviathan of the state, as Hobbes described it, expanding across national boundaries and challenging sovereignty as well as the modernist legacy of the nation state. This notion depends on how we perceive global civil society – as counter-hegemony, counter movement or infra-politics, ie, a search for meaning and counter-discourse (Mittelman, 2000: 165–78). The more we approach it as a counter-narrative, the more we can re-capture the individual dimension of global civil society. Currently the individual is marginalised by the focus on the 'societal' nature of global civil action, 'social movements' as frames of mobilisation, and 'networks' as modes of connection and communication. Looking at global civil society through the prism of individual agency can help distinguish between movements and organisations. Within global civil society, movements differ from organisations in their 'power rationale', a difference measured by the nature of affiliation, the role of the individual, and the logic and form of organising action and its direction.

Box 2.2: The socialist legacy of the Nasser Bank in Egypt

While the Grameen Bank in Bangladesh has been widely celebrated as a model means of empowering women, the Nasser Bank, which has been fulfilling a similar role in Egypt, has received little attention.

The Nasser Bank was established 1972. Although set up during the second year of the rule of President Anwar Sadat, it was run according to the socialist principles of the Nasser era before Egypt adopted open market policies. The Bank attempted to combine modern rules of administration with traditions of Islamic charity. The Bank collects Zakat (alms), which is calculated by each person according to his or her income, via a voluntary system of committees based in the mosques. In 2000 there were 6,000 such committees. The collection system has built-in accounting and accountability measures.

The Bank upholds a socialist policy, using donations to address the charitable needs of lower-class, self-employed men and women, students and female-headed households. There are an estimated 96 branches, covering all parts of the country, which run microcredit schemes with a total budget of 400 million Egyptian pounds.

Recently the government has stepped in, pressuring the Nasser Bank to hand over supervision of the voluntary collection committees to the Ministry of Social Affairs. Lately the state has been attempting to control the Zakat money, which is estimated to amount to billions of pounds, of which only a fraction is handed to Zakat committees and the remainder distributed individually through kinship and informal social networks.

While NGOs tend to professionalise and adopt corporate strategies (Kaldor, Anheier and Glasius, 2003: 9), movements tend to influence corporate bodies to humanise, to become less rigid and more responsive to moral and environmental causes. Here one should distinguish between movements and organisations on the basis of their mission and degree of utopianism. Within global civil society there is, of course, a rainbow of movements and organisations; some have a dual nature, while others present only one face.

These different dimensions include many variables, which need to be ordered into a meaningful picture. The following section will attempt to sketch some of the variables out of which we can construct a new theory of globality to contribute to the aspired paradigmatic shift.

Matrixing the global spheres of the 'public'

The emergence of global civil society created a global public sphere. Variously described as post-national, transnational or intra-national, this sphere is somehow assumed to be a spatial extension of the domestic arena. 'Out there', various NGOs and movements 'network', build coalitions and 'virtually network' to organise events, issue statements, exchange information, and hold simultaneous events, such as the anti-war demonstrations of 15 February 2003. How then should we conceive of the global public sphere?

In *Spheres of Justice*, Michael Walzer (1983) explored the concept of justice as a spherical notion, identifying various measures and criteria in each domain that form the meaning of justice. We can apply that complex and visionary approach here.

Global civil society is best understood not as being located in a single global public sphere but rather as existing within a matrix of spheres, which are interlinked but can develop asymmetrically; and which prove sometimes to be inconsistent and even contradictory in their content, direction and normative orientation. The local and the global overlap and are sometimes difficult to differentiate. Paradoxically, this is the source of, as well as a challenge to, an alternative kind of globalisation. A fundamental shift in the social science approach to global civil society can happen only through interdisciplinary research on the different spheres, their shifting nature and hybrid relations.

The shared, overlapping and converging spaces are many, but there is divergence too. Contradictions can emerge between the national public sphere and the 'cosmopolitan public sphere'. Diverse cultural, economic and political differences, and contexts and histories, cannot be overcome simply by networking and mobilisation. An understanding of these differences should enable activists and organisations to avoid weaknesses inherent in global civil society as well as locate them in the hegemonic structures they are struggling against.

I would like to suggest a number of variables/spheres (six 'v's) that could be the subject of interdisciplinary research, which is designed to develop approaches and conceptual maps that would lead to the emergence of the new paradigm of global social science.

1. The virtual

Global civil society is embedded in the notion of the network society. The emergence of global civil society was facilitated by communications technology, in particular the Internet. Yet many questions can be raised across disciplines regarding the dialectic relationship between global civil society and cyberspace.

Beyond information and communication, cyberspace is a realm of virtual realities. It introduces a notion of time and space that is relatively new. Heidegger predicted that there might come a moment in history when time and place could be separated (Casey, 1997: 243). While virtual reality fosters the individuality of the Internet user, global agency promotes the logic of globality, the search for a universal common good and the sense of 'being for' peace, equality, and justice and against war, capitalism, violence, and so forth. So how can we examine this complicated relationship and its different dimensions?

Castells (1998: 376–468) describes cyberspace as a space of flows, a placeless place where there is timeless time. He notes that the Internet is more than just a tool, it fits with the basic features of the kind of social movements emerging in the information age (Castells, 2001: 139). Interdisciplinary research that explores the ontological and sociological implications of these developments could help build a new theory of the virtual as much as it can help us develop global social sciences.

Anarchy might be a useful analytical frame in this context. This point will be clarified shortly when we tackle the issue of the virtuous and utopian. Here we would like only to underline the conflicting relationship between the virtual and the historical. While the time factor is conceived of in terms of 'the politics of everyday life', which is a distinctive aspect of global civil society, we should consider time in terms of the longue durée too.

It is difficult to understand global civil society, its shortcomings and paradoxes, without understanding the diverse trajectories of movements and civil societies in different regions, which have joined a global cause and in doing so reformulated their constituencies, strategies and actions. As much as they were transformed by going global, they cannot easily escape their cultural and socio-historical context, which in turn has an impact on the changing nature of the concept of global civil society.

Virtuality should not obscure the fact that activists often meet, and that place in the global public sphere has diverse historical genealogies. The virtual, the real and the historical are interwoven and dialectic. In this context a multicultural conception of global civil society defies the claim of the 'end of history'. It challenges the modernist narrative on history, resurrects cultural histories and identities, and reforms them dramatically. It recaptures hope and confirms that 'another world is possible'. Virtuality, which is usually conceived as being instant and of the present, does not nullify the historical. This is not a theoretical assumption, but is clear from the slogans of the movement, such as: 'We are the stubborn history that repeats itself in order no longer to repeat itself'; 'We are the end, the continuation and the beginning' (Ainger, 2003: 387, 522, 525). Issues at the heart of anti-capitalism, like the debt burden of the South or the digital divide, cannot be understood outside their historical dimension.

These remarks may seem puzzling and even confusing, but that is the point. This is exactly why we need to develop a new theory, which will require deep reflection on the philosophical and theoretical implications of globality.

2. The visual

A new dimension of the social scene locally and globally is the rise of the 'spectacle'. Visual messages and signals, pictures and images are increasingly becoming icons. They constitute the new vocabulary of the global age, transcending the barriers of language and culture.

On the Internet the visual is the instant medium of communication. In the broadcast and print media film and photographs summarise global shifts, reflect the scale of disasters and convey people's suffering, as well as their aspirations. Social movements are often triggered by an image that can catalyse action and social change – often more effectively than dutiful NGO campaigns (Castells, 2001: 141). Sympathy for the victims of 9/11 was based on 'seeing' the catastrophe on screen, and solidarity with the second Intifada in Palestine emerged after Agence France-Presse released footage of the assassination of the child Mohamed Al-Dorra by Israeli soldiers.

Environmental disasters, campaigning for relief and solidarity with their victims, and campaigns against HIV/AIDS, depend on shocking images to enhance global compassion. The 'image' of the US as the model of liberal democracy and land of civil liberties was strongly damaged (arguably beyond repair) by the pictures of caged prisoners of war in Guantanamo Bay and the appalling images of American atrocities against imprisoned Iraqis. The global circulation of such images via the Internet shows how the virtual overlaps with the physical, and how the imagination is triggered by the visual. Cognitive impressions are increasingly dependant on visual factors.

The media play a powerful role, not only as vehicles for disseminating images but as arbiters of how they should be perceived. The media can create a spectacle out of an image or trivialise its significance. Civil society activists need media coverage in order to attract attention to, and support for, their cause, particularly, for example, international anti-war and anti-capitalism campaigns. When the mainstream media distort the 'image' of global civil society's agents, activists often seek to assert their 'presence' by creating alternative platforms or seeking different avenues. Cyberspace offers a major public platform and access to a significant targeted audience. Increasingly, global civil society actors are using alternative media platforms, often web-based, which rely heavily on the visual, in order to mobilise support.

In this context the human body becomes a liberated space and a central platform for visual signs and signals. The physical appearance – as well as body language – of an aboriginal activist in traditional clothes, a masked demonstrator against nuclear weapons, or a veiled French Muslim with the symbols of all religions drawn on her face, is a powerful medium of communication. The problem here is the focus on the spectacle rather than the action (Bauman, 1999: 70–1), which creates a false sense of achievement but does not change the structural relations that lead to global injustice (Harvey, 2000: 130).

This preoccupation with the visual also risks strengthening the modernist centrality of physicality (place and body) at the expense of reason and intellect (developing theories and polishing discourses). This aspect of modernity has been neglected by critics, who often assume modernity is about reason only. Their perspective ignores the inevitable shift to physicality if reason is defined solely in terms of secularity and temporality, and any transcendental or historical dimensions are rejected (Segel, 1998: 1–13).

Jordanians who support Saddam Hussein demonstrate against the war on Iraq

3. The vocal

Global civil society manages difference and diversity by democratic conversations. These discussions do not aim necessarily to reach a consensus but to accommodate diversity in a soft and flexible manner. In different forums and parallel summits, where activists and NGOs come together from different countries, there is a 'fusion of horizons of meaning' (Gadamer, 1990: 350). Coming from different cultural and linguistic backgrounds, global agents engage in a process of 'negotiation' to reach agreement and debate mutual concerns. In this context 'translation' and 'interpretation' in the deep sense are inevitable (Bhabha, 1995: 236–56; Harvey, 2000: 190).

One can raise many questions, such as how language is used and how it can be manipulated. If different actors resort to the 'global' language of, let us say, English, how far does that affect their power to express themselves in their respective native languages; and to what extent does that inhibit their ability to challenge globalism and to genuinely express an alternative model or conceptual framework? Also, what are the implications for the dominance of English on the Internet? How much is cyber-networking influenced by the dominant language, terminologies and cultural perceptions of the West?

4. The virtuous

If modernity is to be revisited and methodological nationalism challenged, this would return the question of virtues, values and morality to mainstream theoretical and methodological debates in the social sciences. If global civil society is civil, what are the civic virtues it regards as essential, and how are they negotiated among different actors and reflected in strategies of action and circles of interest?

The nation state was not only a political apparatus but, it was argued, a moral agent as well, moral accountability shifting from the individual and community to the state, with its legal framework and educational institutions. Milgram's classic study (1974) of obedience to authority and Bauman's investigation (1993) of post-modern ethics suggest that rationality was gradually superseding morality; the result was a morality without ethics, subject to interpretations of national interest that had little to do with classic notions of ethics or morals.

The condition of globality is paralleled by multiple and overlapping moralities. Causes that try to bridge different cultural values and synthesise moralities into a humanist layer that is shared by all (yet retains distinct value systems) usually acquire moral legitimacy. Whether the cause is humanitarian, egalitarian or environmental, diverse moral codes provide it with their respective ethical underpinnings. Muslims, Christians, and Hindus use their religious/spiritual discourse, and neo-Marxists their anti-capitalist ideological analysis, but they are united in their condemnation of human rights violations in areas of conflict or the degradation of the environment. The human being and nature are shared abstract entities with moral value, even if conceptions of the sacred and the profane are different.

Global civil society includes webs of normative meaning. It is mobilised around values, identity and culture, and the investment of this 'moral capital' (Castells, 2001: 140; Kane, 2001; Keane, 2003: 194–6). We should identify the spaces where the different social science disciplines can meet to investigate the moral questions raised by global civil society. How are civic virtues within the global public sphere formed and 'transformed' through direct contact and negotiated public interests? And then how are they synthesised and advocated on the basis of moral and ethical values? In its resistance to capitalism, war, abuse of natural resources, its keen attempts to end violence against women, bring criminals of war to justice, and advocate corporate transparency, we can see how global civil society draws on a rich moral discourse that is more relevant to the masses than ideological rhetoric.

This moral question deserves more examination. Here it is also important to consider the relationship between the virtuous and the virtual. How much cyber-networking is devoted to global civil causes compared with uncivil causes? Do Internet users recognise the importance of the web for global endeavours as opposed to individual communication or pleasure-oriented uses?

The problematic relation between the individual and the collective conception of the self mentioned above has ultimately moral implications as well. How can the absolute be advocated on a cyber medium that is essentially and existentially relative? And do civil virtues change when they become 'virtualised' (Schultze, Q. 2002)?

5. The violent

After 9/11, when the 'war on terrorism' was used as an excuse to tighten the legal constraints on civil society organisations and especially Islamic NGOs suspected of being pro-terrorist, basic rules of international law and human rights were violated. The blunt violence of some militant groups against civilian targets was met with uncivil actions, which violated the civil liberties of many people; and with the use of the law to exercise hege-

Arabs and Israelis unite in protest against the 'separation' wall

mony, and even violence, against civil bodies, which lacked protection under the obscure rules of the war on terrorism.

Although one of the promises of modernity was reaching civil peace after prolonged urban unrest and religious war, violence did not vanish. The monopoly over the use of force by the nation state did not lessen the rate and scale of violence but rather expanded it beyond any limitations and against the boundaries of any moral legitimacy (Keane, 1996; Bauman, 1989). The question of violence is hence very much related to modernist arrangements of the 'nation state deal'. If the nation state is challenged, these arrangements should be revisited. This does not mean that the use of force should become the right of everyone, or that we should shift to a state of violent anarchy. It simply means that the issue of the use of force, in varying degrees, by global civil society actors should be open to debate.

This has implications for the legal framework of global civil society, an issue that has been discussed in previous Yearbooks (Glasius, 2002; Fries, 2003). Global civil society needs to discuss this sensitive issue openly and make clear the difference between the legitimate use of force by, for example, civil actors acting in self-defence against forces of military occupation, and the immoral targeting of unarmed civilians by such forces. It also needs a more concerted mobilisation when activists, who lack protection under international law, are subject to violence or become the targets of military action. This is an issue for movements such as Solidarity International, whose activists have been subject to deliberate military attack by the Israeli army in the Palestinian Occupied Territories. Such violence resulted in the deaths of two foreign 'human shields' in 2003, one American and one British.

Violence used unilaterally by a superpower does not necessarily require a violent retaliation by global civil society activists. Many adopt a pacifist response. But, if we are revising methodological nationalism, the issue of violence and the legitimate resort to more assertive strategies of resistance should become a moral, as well as an analytical concern. I should stress again that this is not a call for global civil society to become violent. On the contrary, this is an attempt to investigate avenues of expression and resistance that would allow a range of options, potential strategies and tactics beyond the bitter choice, enforced by an increasingly violent and anti-civil hegemony, between pacifism

Box 2.3: The Anti-Globalization Egyptian Group

The Anti-Globalization Egyptian Group (AGEG) emerged in May 2002 as the antithesis of Egyptian politics. Representing a new form of political activism, it emerged as a result of a combination of factors: the stagnation of democratisation, the failure of political parties to address the challenge of authoritarianism, capitalist economic and political globalisation, and antagonism among political parties.

How do democrats remain active in an authoritarian context? Can a vibrant civil society survive without a legal presence? When official intervention under the pretext of 'emergency laws' makes it increasingly difficult for citizens to engage politically or to form political parties or even professional unions, how can activists remain active? These were the questions a group of young and middle-aged leftist democrats had been asking themselves. In summer 2000, when the government issued Law No 100 for Syndicates and Law No 153 for NGOs, and with the outbreak of the Palestinian Intifada in September, the political atmosphere changed. Sporadic and populist grassroots demonstrations took many people by surprise. For the first time in decades there were student protests in universities and schools. A new generation of student activists were chanting songs from the Nasser era, expressing pan-Arab nationalism and Egypt's responsibilities towards Palestine. Ultimately, however, these protests failed to strengthen the student movement, which has been shrinking since the 1970s.

In October 2000 the Egyptian Popular Committee for Support of Palestine (EPCSP), formed by a group of leftist veterans, attracted a wider audience, offering as it did a practical alternative to silent anger and sympathy. EPCSP aid 'caravans', which carried food to the Palestinians, became political events in themselves as they passed through cities on route to the border. Although the EPCSP lacked legal standing, and never attempted to become an NGO, it was not suppressed by the security forces.

The invasion of the West Bank between March and April 2002 strengthened the EPCSP's hand; popular anger against Israel had found a focus and a network. Some 20,000 people demonstrated for five hours outside Cairo University, the first of such a size for years, until security forces scattered protestors with tear gas and batons. At the same time, anti-capitalist discourse rose to the surface, starting with young leftists and gaining momentum among a broader circle of political activists. Many Egyptians from different backgrounds joined the campaign to boycott British and American products. The public mood had changed, and a commitment was made to developing a 'Third Place' between that of a legal NGO movement (which was politically impossible) and that of an old-fashioned underground cell.

Local activism and global networking

At the founding conference of AGEG in May 2002, 200 people exchanged ideas about how to move forward. The two-day event was held at the Syndicate for Accountants and was attended by leading socialists, including Samir Amin. The first major event AGEG organised that year was a rally against the visit of World Bank Group president James Wolfensohn. This event, which included speeches by speakers from the international anti-capitalist movement, attracted more than 300 people and marked AGEG's first link with the global movement. The small number of participants should not detract from the event's significance – particularly with the usual exaggerated presence of security forces and riot police.

As the clouds of war were gathering in the region, AGEG was one of the key civil actors forming the anti-war movement in Egypt. In the run-up to the first US attack on Iraq on 20 March 2003, this movement attracted the support of a range of political persuasions and forces. The demonstrations in Cairo on 15 February were fairly small, but again significant. After the invasion, there were larger protests in Cairo's biggest square, Tahrir. People spent the night on street, protesting against the first wave of attacks on Iraq but ending up discussing domestic concerns and shouting for democratisation. The result was the arrest of nearly 1,500 people, activists and non-activists alike. Five anti-war activists, including three from the AGEG founding committee, were prosecuted by the state for illegal political activity. Two opposition MPs were beaten up. One was arrested and detained for a couple of weeks, and the other was hospitalised with serious head injuries inflicted by the security forces.

Since the war on Iraq, AGEG has been going through a period of reflection. One particular issue is the development of a more regular (and patient) mode of operation. Currently our website provides the space for that discussion, as well as information about meetings and seminars. Our other concern is how to relate anti-capitalist discourse to the language of daily life, and to connect it to the suffering of ordinary Egyptians. We want show people how rising costs of living, increasing unemployment and deteriorating basic services are linked to the structural adjustment programmes dictated by the IMF and World Bank. Networking with independent solidarity committees and global anti-war and anti-capitalist activists is a priority. Parallel attention is given to supporting grassroots community leaders in their struggles, which are inseparable from the globalisation of capital.

The activities of AGEG and the responses we receive – from journalists, academics and ordinary people – show how the local is very much linked to the global. Supporting the Iraqis and Palestinians did not prevent AGEG from simultaneously campaigning against a European multinational company that was brought in to replace the system of indigenous garbage collection in greater Cairo. This devastated the lives of Egyptian garbage collectors, as well as imposing much higher charges on householders. Campaigners pursued the case in court, arguing that charging such fees would be unconstitutional. Lay people joined the lawsuit and victory helped raise awareness of citizens' power. The court ruling was distributed during an anti-war event designed to express solidarity with Iraqis; a local victory for civil society celebrated in a global space.

A new political space

AGEG has no official legal status. It operates flexibly with respect to networks and uses cyberspace to share its passion for social justice and a humane globalisation. This approach allows news of events to be spread rapidly, resulting in actions that are almost instant and temporary, but which can catalyse change. In this way we operate in a new social space that is closely watched by the state. No single group or network can claim all the credit or bear full responsibility for events and their consequences. This new form of civil action, which differs from established political and civil bodies, is constantly evolving. It is hard to predict how it will develop – something we see as a positive trend, allowing us to debate and innovate. It also makes state suppression or control difficult. Still, we have been subject to political harassment. A founding member was arrested by the security forces for a few weeks without charge, and another was accused of forming a Communist cell to overthrow the regime. This latter charge was rejected by the court.

Despite these challenges the Egyptian anti-war movement has grown, establishing links with the world movement and taking part in the global anti-war demonstrations of 15 February 2003. In December 2003, Cairo hosted the Second International Conference against Capitalist Globalisation and US Hegemony, in which activists from across the political spectrum participated. The conference attracted nearly 700 local and 200 international and Arab activists. It was run on a voluntary basis, with Egyptian participants hosting international comrades.

Despite the stagnation of formal political democratisation, there is much going on beneath the surface, emerging in various forms and networking with global civil society.

Wael Khalil, IT engineer, co-founder of AGEG

(which by its nature often emasculates protagonists who lack any tactic except 'turning the other cheek') and radical militancy. This should not be the concern only of peace and anti-capitalist movements but also a matter for socio-political comparative research that would contribute to the paradigmatic shift under discussion.

6. The visionary

Global civil society brought back the spirit of utopia. Movements do not want to give in to the ugly reality and many global activists genuinely dream of a more virtuous world where values and morals, in their diverse global and civil definitions, would become reality. Compared with the social movements of the 1960s, there is now a more utopian aspiration, a more public-oriented tendency, and a more universal and culturally sensitive awareness. Global civil society is not merely a manifestation of resistance but embodies a utopian world view as well (Keane, 2001: 23).

In our context, we should stress that utopias are not merely simple-minded dreams or naive aspirations, but are conceptual systems and have an ideological strength. They can also have methodological implications. Anarchy is one of the major ideas that can help us explain the global scene: the goal of many movements is not to restore order but rather to use the dominant anarchical dimension of international relations (Bull, 1995) to engage with the hegemony of the rising uni-polar empire, in order to strive for justice and equality, challenging at the same time – and on a global scale – the authority of the nation state and its moral credibility. This will have far-reaching implications for theory and methodology if researchers take seriously different classical and contemporary ideas of anarchism, its theoretical notions and debates, and how they can reshape the structure and content of social theory.

Utopia is far more relevant to the paradigm shift and its theoretical and conceptual structure than the 'utopian scenario' that Marlies Glasius and Mary Kaldor (2002: 29) have sketched. The utopian factor in its more theoretical dimension can contribute to the transformation of the social sciences. Researchers can become agents of change and not mere observers of a major historical transformation in the course of humanity, as much as activists can become a source of theoretical ideas of extreme importance for academia. Through networks, mobilisation, fair trade, alternative media and grassroots sustainable development projects, global civil society can create spaces where utopia comes close to realisation. Although this is only on a small scale, the potential for the networks to grow and really make a difference in the long run is huge.

From debating networks to networking debates

There are currently many heated debates within the social sciences that are highly relevant to transforming the paradigm; lack of progress to date is probably due to the absence of theoretical and academic networking. The importance of a project like the Global Civil Society Yearbook is that it can become the platform for such efforts. To develop a new theoretical framework, social scientists, who are already investigating global transformations, coalition building and fragmentations, should pursue genuinely comparative multicultural research on global civil society. To create a 'road map' for cross-disciplinary research, we need to bridge the boundaries that exist on many levels.

Bridging the boundaries between ideology and social theory

Fukuyama's theory of the end of history, by which he meant the end of ideology and the ultimate triumph of capitalist liberalism, has proved to be false (Fukuyama, 1992: 45,205; Jacoby, 1999). Ideologies – as well as utopias – are conceptual systems that address issues of human nature, social goods, and notions of freedom and justice. Our aim is not only to redefine contested concepts (Gaus, 2000: 26–32; Freeden, 1996), but also to challenge the boundaries of different disciplines, create new spaces for research and develop innovative methodologies that can help us interpret new realities.

If core concepts, such as the nation state, are revisited, ideologies that have theorised about a post-state political society (mainly anarchism and Marxism) need to be revisited too. They have never been more relevant.

The new dimension in emerging approaches is that different concepts can be seen as variables in shifting conceptual systems. In the 1960s Nettle (1968) called the state a central 'conceptual variable' in the paradigm of the social sciences. It is remarkable how, 30 years later, Manuel Castells used a similar description, stressing that the relations between the self, the net, the state and capitalism are similar to a system of variable geometry (Castells, 1998: 1). Similarly, Michael Freeden (1998) sees ideologies, old and new, as conceptual systems with shifting meanings and open boundaries.

These perspectives allow us to see the relations, transformation and cross-fertilisation of various ideologies and conceptual systems. More importantly, we can foresee potential matrixes and envisage different scenarios, as the editors of this Yearbook attempt to do in their Introduction.

Bridging the boundaries between different philosophical traditions

If a philosophical approach is applied to research on global civil society, we need to develop a blend of various such traditions. Anglo-American and French schools of thought have dominated the formulation of theories of concepts and approaches, partly because of the lack of democracy that inhibits social science research in many parts of the world, not to mention the dominance of the North-South divide within academia. Recapturing the transcendental spirit of German and eastern European – as well as non-Western – philosophies would be important in shaping the paradigm shift. Multiculturalism is not only necessary on the existential, practical and civil levels, but on the philosophical-epistemological level too.

A pro-Islam, anti-capitalism demonstration in Indonesia

Increasingly, there is a fusion of different ideologies in the major debates about social theory. The focus on the rights of the person, or the socio-political agent, and how to create a sense of identity that would hold society together, is at the heart of the individualist-communitarian debates within liberal theory. Even here critics perceive elements of conservatism.

There are also the liberal-radical debates within democratic theory, the national versus the global in political science and sociology, and the secular versus the religious in philosophy and sociology of religion. Other controversial discussions that should not be overlooked include: the vocal versus the physical, language versus the body, the biological versus the cultural, the scientific versus the moral and, last but not least, nature versus reason.

Emerging 'chosen' identities and 'invented' moralities have influenced the definition of community. Identity in an age of globalisation is becoming increasingly hybrid, constantly affecting the structure of ideological conceptual systems. Individuals belong to different communities that overlap and sometimes conflict. In many cases the sociological is very much affected by the technical and the scientific; hence the different sciences can not afford to remain isolated.

Bridging the boundaries between the social and natural sciences

It is noteworthy that global civil society is heavily engaged in campaigns that challenge the absolute authority of science over human destiny and over nature, alongside more conventional challenges to the market and the state. Yet little attention has been paid to scientific discoveries about the logic of the universe that have implications for social theory, which might be relevant to our understanding of the development and transformation of global movements.

Johnson's book *Emergence: The Connected Lives of Ants, Brains, Cities and Software*, encourages reflection on how movements alternate between a togetherness that celebrates independence, and the gradual and deliberate formation of a 'society' that clusters together (Johnson, 2001: 11–23). One might then ask how far parallels can be drawn between new discoveries in microbiology and entomology about the nature and mechanisms of clustering, and the behaviour of human beings in the global sphere. This necessitates a new understanding of the increasing interdependency of science, social theory and moral philosophy.

© JC TORDAI/PANOS PICTURES

Multiculturalism and diversity needs to be mirrored in social theory

This is not an easy task. Previous attempts at interdisciplinary research led social scientists to adopt some of the methodological approaches of their natural science colleagues. Now it is the turn of natural scientists to recapture their humanist ideals of bettering lives around the world, in order to understand holistically the complexity and interdependence of the universe. Moral and social concerns should be shared across all scientific disciplines.

Beyond current indicators of global civil society

Until the paradigm shift takes place, we have to rely on inadequate indicators to measure global civil society. Typically, these indicators are based on aggregate statistics, which overlook cultural and societal differences in defining the boundaries of the public and the civil spheres. As a result, many civil actions in the South are overlooked because they do not fit the criteria of standard indicators, which are based on the experience of civil society in the North. For example, there is an increasing number of NGOs in the Arab world but at the same time a dramatic shrinking of the public space available for democratic debate. The process of gradual democratic transformation experienced by the Arab world in the 1980s is now stagnant, and it seems as if pressures from abroad to reform succeed only in triggering nationalistic opposition because of hostility towards Western policies in the region, especially in Palestine and Iraq. Local civil society activists who encourage reform are often accused of pursuing foreign agendas, especially when it comes to human rights. This is a paradox and a dilemma that many civil activists in the region struggle with.

The 2002 Report of the Arab Network of NGOs (Qandil, 2003: 1–10) showed that, after just one year of relative freedom and changes to the law, thousands of NGOs had registered in Egypt and Morocco. Hitherto, this large informal civil sector had been ignored.

Indicators can also signal the absence of some spheres of civil society in some regions. We need to ask why. A strong peasant movement is almost absent in the Arab world, and the student movement is rapidly withering away. How do such regional or national differences affect perceptions and evaluations of global civil society's connectedness in certain spheres? Women's empowerment in the Arab world is a good example.

While there is increasing interest among civil society groups in women's rights, the wider democratic process is lagging behind. How far should official indicators of gender equality be seen as a positive sign? Would such developments be seen as empowering women or merely 'feminising despotism' by masking authoritarianism with deceptive statistics that show an increase in the presence of women in this or that sector?

Furthermore if this development is supported by the global women's movement, how can this asymmetric relationship between domestic and global civil society be evaluated, especially when it strengthens elites that would not – at least in the short run – initiate real democratic change? Indeed, instead of remaining at the forefront of the democratic struggle, many Arab feminists are co-opted by the state apparatus, while at the same time maintaining strong links with the global women's movement.

The diverse and asymmetric levels of development and structural-financial power within the global public sphere, and between activists and bodies in the North and the South, must also to be kept in mind if we want to achieve genuine social justice and global democracy (and equality) in the future.

REFERENCES

Abu-Lughd, J. (1998) 'Civil/Uncivil Society: Confusing Form with Content', in M. Douglas and J. Friedman (eds*), Cities for Citizens: Planning and the Rise of Civil Society in a Global Age*. New York: John Wiley.

Ainger, K. et al (eds) (2003) *We Are Everywhere: The Irresistible Rise of Global Capitalism*. London: Verso.

Albrow, M. (1996) *The Global Age*. Cambridge: Polity Press.

AlSayyad, N. (ed) (2001) *Hybrid Urbanism: On the Identity Discourse and the Built Environment*. London: Praeger.

Anheier, H, Glasius, M. and Kaldor, M. (2001) 'Introducing Global Civil Society', ch 1 in H. Anheier, M. Glasius and M. Kaldor (eds), *Global Civil Society 2001*. Oxford: Oxford University Press.

An-Na'im, A. (2002). 'Religion and Global Civil Society: Inherent Incompatibility or Synergy and Interdependence?', ch 3 in M. Glasius, M. Kaldor and H. Anheier (eds), *Global Civil Society 2002*. Oxford: Oxford University Press.

Appadurai, A. (1996) *Modernity at Large: Cultural Dimensions Of Globalization*. Minneapolis: University of Minnesota Press.

Bauman, Z. (1989) *Modernity and the Holocaust*. Cambridge: Polity Press.

– (1993) *Postmodern Ethics*. Oxford: Blackwell

– (1995) *Life in Fragments: Ethics in Postmodern Morality*. Oxford: Blackwell.

– (1999) *In Search of Politics*. California: Stanford University Press.

– (2001) *Seeking Safety in an Insecure World*. Cambridge: Polity Press.

Beck, U. (2003) 'The Analysis of Global Inequality: From National to Cosmopolitan Perspective', ch 3 in M. Kaldor, H. Anheier and M. Glasius (eds), *Global Civil Society 2003*. Oxford: Oxford University Press.

Bhabha, H.(1995) *The Location of Culture*. London: Routledge.

Bull, H. (1995) *The Anarchical Society: A Study of Order in World Politics*. London: Macmillan.

Casanova, J. (1994) *Public Religions in the Modern World*. Chicago: University of Chicago Press.

Casey, E. (1997) *The Fate of Place*. California: University of California Press.

Castells, M. (1998) *The Rise of the Network Society*. Oxford: Blackwell.

– (2001) *The Internet Galaxy: Reflections on the Internet, Business and Society*. Oxford: Oxford University Press.

De Vries, H. (1999) *Philosophy and the Turn to Religion*. Baltimore, MD: Johns Hopkins University Press.

Esposito, J. (2000) 'Islam in the Twenty First Century', in J. Esposito and A. Tamimi (eds), *Islam and Secularism in the Middle East*. London: Hurst and Company.

Freeden, M. (1996) *Ideologies and Political Theory: A Conceptual Approach*. Oxford: Oxford University Press.

Fries, F. (2003) 'The Legal Environment of Civil Society', ch 9 in M. Kaldor, H. Anheier and M. Glasius (eds), *Global Civil Society 2003*. Oxford: Oxford University Press.

Fukuyama, F. (1992) *The End of History and the Last Man*. London: Penguin Books.

Gadamer, H. (1990) *Gesammelte Werke, Band 1: Wahrheit und Methode (Hermeneutik I: Grundzüge einer philosophichen Hermeneutik)*. Tübingen: J. C. B Möhr.

Gaus, G. (2000) *Political Concepts and Political Theories*. Oxford: Westview Press.

Geertz, C. (2000) *Available Light: Anthropological Reflections on Philosophical Topics*. New Jersey: Princeton University Press.

Glasius, M. (2002) 'Expertise in the Cause of Justice: Global Civil Society Influence on the Statute for an International Criminal Court', ch 7 in M. Glasius, M. Kaldor and H.

Anheier (eds), *Global Civil Society 2002*. Oxford: Oxford University Press.
– and Kaldor, M. (2002) 'The State of Global Civil Society: Before and After September 11', ch 1 in M. Glasius, M. Kaldor and H. Anheier (eds), *Global Civil Society 2002*. Oxford: Oxford University Press.
Harvey, D. (1989) *The Condition of Postmodernity*. Oxford: Blackwell.
– (1993) 'From Space to Place and Back Again: Reflections on the Condition of Postmodernity', in J. Bird et al (eds), *Mapping the Futures: Local Cultures , Global Change*. New York: Routledge.
– (2000) *Spaces of Hope*. California: University of California Press.
– (2001) *Spaces of Capital: Towards a Critical Geography*. New York: Routledge.
Hannerz, U. (1996) *Transnational Connections: Culture, People, Places*. New York: Routledge.
Heidegger, M. (1997). *Gesamtaugabe*, Vol. 66 *(Besinnung): Sein und Zeit*. Frankfurt am Main: Vittorio Klostermann.
– (1992) *The Concept of Time* (English-German edn, trans. William McNeill). Oxford: Blackwell.
Heller, A. (1978) *The Renaissance Man* (trans. Richard E. Allen). London: Routledge and Kegan Paul.
– (1995) 'The Concept of the Political Revisited', in David Held (ed), *Political Theory Today*. Oxford: Polity Press.
Jacoby, R. (1999) *The End of Utopia: Politics and Culture in an Age of Apathy*. New York: Basic Books.
Johnson, S. (2001) *Emergence: The Connected Lives of Ants, Brains, Cities and Software*. London: Penguin Books.
Kaldor, M, Anheier, H, and Glasius, M. (eds) (2003) 'Global Civil Society in an Era of Regressive Globalisation', ch 1 in M. Kaldor, H. Anheier and M. Glasius (eds), *Global Civil Society 2003*. Oxford: Oxford University Press.
Kaldor, M. and Muro, D. (2003) 'Religious and Nationalist Militant Groups', ch 7 in M. Kaldor, H. Anheier and M. Glasius (eds), *Global Civil Society 2003*. Oxford: Oxford University Press.
Kane, J. (2001) *The Politics of Moral Capital*. Cambridge: Cambridge University Press.
Keane, J. (1996) *Reflections on Violence*. London: Verso.
– (2000) 'The Limits of Secularism', in J. Esposito and A. Tamimi (eds), *Islam and Secularism in the Middle East*. London: Hurst and Company.
– (2001). 'Global Civil Society', ch 2 in H. Anheier, M. Glasius and M. Kaldor (eds), *Global Civil Society 2001*. Oxford: Oxford University Press.
– (2003) *Global Civil Society*. Cambridge: Cambridge University Press.
Kymlicka, W. (2001) *Politics in the Vernacular: Nationalism, Multiculturalism, and Citizenship*. Oxford: Oxford University Press.
Milgram, S. (1974) *Obedience to Authority: An Experimental View*. London: Tavistock.
Mitchell, W. (1999) *E-topia*. Cambridge, MA: MIT Press.
Mittelman, J. (2000) *The Globalization Syndrome: Transformation and Resistance*. New Jersey: Princeton University Press.
Nettle, J. (1968) 'State as a Conceptual Variable', *World Politics*, 20(4): 559–92.
Qandil, A. (ed) (2003) *The Arab Network of NGOs Annual Report 2002*. Cairo: the Arab Network of NGOs Publications.
Rengger, N. (1995) *Political Theory, Modernity, and Postmodernity: Beyond Enlightenment and Critique*. Oxford: Blackwell.
Schultze, Q. (2002) *Habits of the High-Tech Heart: Living Virtuously in the Information Age*. Michigan: Baker Academic Books.
Segel, H. (1998) *Body Ascendant: Modernism and the Physical Imperative*. Baltimore, MD: Johns Hopkins University Press.
Sennett, R. (1976) *The Fall of Public*. New York: Norton.
Shaw, M. (2003) 'The Global Transformation of the Social Sciences', ch 2 in M. Kaldor, H. Anheier and M. Glasius (eds), *Global Civil Society 2003*. Oxford: Oxford University Press.
Smart, N. (1997) *Dimensions of the Sacred: An Anatomy of the World's Beliefs*. London: Fontana Press.
Taylor, C. (2002) *Varieties of Religion Today*. Cambridge, MA: Harvard University Press.
Walzer, M. (1983) *Spheres of Justice*. New York: Basic Books.

CHAPTER 3

GLOBAL CIVIL SOCIETY: AN ARAB PERSPECTIVE

Mohamed El-Sayed Said

Introduction

In this chapter I argue that the spectacular rise of the anti-war movement during 2002–3 was instrumental in preventing the full triumph of the 'clash of civilizations' and 'crusade' theories in Arab minds. Furthermore, global civil society offered a brilliant opportunity for voicing Arab protests against injustices seen to be inflicted upon the Arab world by the present international system. The huge expanse and great diversity of the global civil universe should allow for the promotion and gradual engagement of Arab civic activism within this arena. However, this process has only begun. Ultimately, it may present an alternative to, and a dialectical negation of, terrorism and other forms of alienated ideological and practical opposition by Arabs and non-Arabs alike to the hegemonic practices within the global system. But there are many obstacles to the involvement of various forms of Arab civic protest in global civil society and these will be discussed below.

Selective perceptions of global civil society

Perceptions of global civil society in the Arab world are highly influenced by a sense of alienation, which is rooted in Arab relationships with the present international system. As a result of this alienation, Arab political development has been relatively isolated from non-governmental civic and cultural life at the global level (Yassin, 1998). Knowledge of, and interactions with, global civil society have long been minimal. Relative isolation was reinforced by the prevalence of despotic regimes that drastically curbed the vitality of Arab civil and political life and its incorporation at the global level.

It is natural, therefore, that various streams of thought and practice in the Arab world adopted different positions in relation to the world at large. These positions focused more on the role of global civil society relative to the collective concerns of Arabs than on the global historical project implied in the concept itself. In this sense, Arab perceptions of global civil society are selective. However, they all share a deep sense of grievance caused by chronic internal crises and what is commonly seen as hegemonic injustice within the formal system of international relations (Amin, 1998). Long before global civil society captured people's attention, Arab political thought was dominated by an intense rejection of globalisation and hegemony (Qandil, 2002: 191). The rise of the anti-globalisation movement came, therefore, as a pleasant surprise and was immediately met with enthusiasm by many in the Arab world (Ghalioun, 1999). In brief, political motives, particularly those related to the Palestinian national struggle, provided the main impetus for the celebration in the Arab world of the anti-globalisation movement and accordingly of global civil society. According to an Arab activist who attended the first Arab anti-globalisation conference in Beirut: 'The Palestinian tragedy is the consequence of the imperial globalisation policy' (Ibrahim and Nasser, 2004).

However, attitudes towards global civil society continued to be shaped by the particular ideologies and political outlook of various streams of thought. Liberals and humanists welcomed the rise of global civil society as a promise of liberation from both the suffocating domestic environment and external pressures (An-Na'im, 2002; Al-Bassam, 1997). Nationalists and radicals conceived of it as a dialectical antithesis to the hegemony of Western civilisation (Al-Gabry, 1998) and, because they are more concerned with national identity, they could not share the high hopes placed on global civil society by liberals and democrats (Abdalla, 1999). Globalisation is conceived of as yet another cycle of the constant imposition and expansion of Western civilisation. Radical Islamists – particularly the Jihadis, including Al-Qaeda – almost totally ignored the phenomenon, simply because

The rise of the anti-globalisation movement was welcomed by many in the Arab world

of their intrinsic hostility to all non-Muslims. The phenomenon also disturbs their call for a religious war against a monolithic 'West', dominated, in their view, by an alliance of Jews and crusaders. Nevertheless, even they couldn't ignore the massive opposition to the war on Iraq. Osama Bin Laden, with all his prejudices about the West, described these reactions as 'positive', in return for which he promised a ceasefire in Europe (Al-Jazeera, 2004b).

Conversely, a nascent and fast-growing Islamic political and cultural movement has started to interact and work closely with global civil society, seeing it as a hopeful alternative to both isolation and alienation. Al-Wahda al-Islamiya (2003) notes the increasing popularity of the anti-globalisation movement, especially in Europe. Moderate Islamists writing in Moheet.net (URL), a major electronic Arabic journal, even revised traditional Islamist views on Hollywood as an icon of Western decadence when many film stars protested against the war on Iraq. The shift in position towards global civil society by a small but growing segment of the Islamic movement is a significant development in the way the Arab world interacts with social movements originating in other regions. To those who followed the anti-war rallies in the Western world, this change was obvious. Islamists, shouting their religious slogans, marched for the first time alongside anarchists, Trotskyites and other socialists, members of various Christian congregations, and peace activists of all persuasions, including representatives of the gay movements. Through their participation, many Islamists negotiated the building of anti-war coalitions and actions. To many, this mixing seemed exotic or odd, particularly in comparison with earlier cooperation between Islamic and global organisations in the field of international relief, for example in Bosnia and Kosovo.

The position taken by global civil society on Iraq and other issues has encouraged mainstream Muslim organisations to establish not only temporary partnerships but long-term arrangements based on mutual understanding and shared values. A variety of interfaith dialogues has been born in the context of collaborative operations beyond Bosnia, Kosovo and other places (Al-Berkalay, 2002). In fact, the quest for better under-

British Muslims protest against the Iraq war

standing and the growing interest in dialogue among sections of mainstream and radical Islamists are some of the most inspiring and promising trends in Arab interactions with global civil society. While hard to assess in terms of magnitude and precise impact, the sheer size of this sector in Arab NGOs and in the associative space, promises significant change. One can only compare this situation with views and forms of interaction in the past, which were filled with suspicion, futile theological debates, and even hostility. Working together in the civic arena is itself a gigantic step forward, in terms of mutual understanding and convergence on what religious practice should be about in a world replete with poverty, war and social maladies (Commission on Global Governance, 1999: 48–9)

Another interesting feature of Arab engagement in global activism pertains to the awakening of Arab immigrant communities in North America, western Europe, and many other parts of the world, particularly after 9/11. Having been reared in the suffocating environment of Arab authoritarian politics, the first generation of Arab migrants had little faith in, and limited incentive for engagement with, the civil and political life of host democratic countries. Their ordeal in the wake of 9/11 encouraged many to begin to participate in defending their civil rights alongside their newly discovered comrades in national and global civil society. Arab migrant communities are also exploring their potential role as a bridge between their country of origin and their new homeland (Bayoumi, 2003). All of these factors are bringing about diverse forms of Arab articulation and engagement in global civil society, perhaps for the first time.

While generally promising, vigorous Arab activism in global civil society depends mainly on the future course of Arab political and cultural development. Until recently, the most powerful trend of thought in Arab politics and culture was striving for a strong state rather than a vital civil society. In fact, many Arabs still reject the very notion of civil society as a 'Western fabrication' designed to distract Arabs from their heritage and true aspirations (Shafeeq, 2004). Others doubt the ability of Arab civil society organisations to engage effectively with global civil society. The actual experience of engagement has met varying degrees of success. As Amani Qandil (2000: 177) points out, the negotiating capabilities of Arab NGOs as compared with global NGOs, are still limited.

> *Previous UN-sponsored conferences at the global scale which determined the agenda of action for the 21st century revealed these limits quite clearly. . . . in the last document published by the UN in 1998, on international NGOs with consultative status, we find 964 registered organisations, only 27 of which are Arab. This reality restricts the effectiveness of Arabs in the global assembly known as CONGO.*

Old memories

Despite long isolation, the notion of global civil society may not be entirely new to the region. The term is familiar to those who lived through the struggle for national independence. One of the main dimensions in the 'national liberation' discourse was international public opinion. Addressing international public opinion was one of the main weapons in the struggle for national liberation because it proved instrumental in pressuring the governments of colonial powers to end occupation and colonisation.

In fact, the institutional memories of present regimes in the Middle East still contain instances when civic and political protest in the Western world contributed to the demise of classic colonialism or the defeat of colonial aggression. The failure of the British, French, and Israeli aggression against Egypt in 1956 owes a great deal to popular opposition in the Western world, including the UK and France. The granting of independence to Algeria in 1962, after 130 years of colonial incorporation, was forced by several years of brutal war, as well as a complete change of mood in France due to intellectual opposition to colonisation. In the Arab region, as elsewhere in the colonial world, the struggle for independence triumphed more easily when coupled with a change of outlook within the civil and political societies of colonial powers (Duare, 2004). Interestingly, some theorists of global civil society have traced the origins of the concept to the legacy of national liberation struggles (Korten, Perlas, and Shiva, 2002).

The passage of time since independence could have undermined the importance of international public opinion were it not for the fact that Arabs continued to feel the primacy of national concerns, such as the Palestine question and the question of Iraq, for which they needed the support of peoples and individuals in the outside world (Khashan, 2000). And international public opinion was not always so sympathetic; it failed to come to their rescue in times of great need, such as the occupation by Israel of all-mandate Palestine as well as the territories of a number of Arab states, since 1967. Arabs blamed themselves for failing to address international public opinion, explaining it not by failures embedded in Arab authoritarianism but by technical factors, such as the lack of a developed media.

Global civil society, as opposed to the amorphous nature of 'international public opinion', is a material and durable body of organisations and institutions, well connected across borders and cultures. Therefore, traditional ways of addressing international public opinion were inappropriate for engaging with global civil society. This accounts for the cyclical nature of interest in international public opinion on the part of state and non-state actors in the Arab world. Periodically, Arab governments would decide to establish media institutions dedicated to communicating with the public in Western countries. These decisions were widely publicised. With the discovery that these institutions existed only on paper, the issue slipped away from public consciousness, only to re-emerge when frustration mounted with the triumph of Zionist propaganda in the Western world and with the disappointing responses by international public opinion.

The plight of the Palestinian people has galvanised Arab civil society

The anti-globalisation movement

Arab culture started to recognise global civil society only when the anti-globalisation movement took centre stage in Seattle in 1999. Arab intellectuals were attracted to this movement for a number of reasons, the most important being its resonance with their own frustration over US policy in the region. Globalisation was rejected by Arab intellectuals simply because it was characterised as Americanisation and because Arabs were angry with the US for its insensitivity towards their cause and its bias towards Israel. Another reason for intellectual interest in the anti-globalisation movement was the revival of the search for alternatives to unilateral hegemony. In this sense, the anti-globalisation movement, and global civil society at large, was seen as the 'second superpower'. The quest for justice and sympathy for the world's poor was also admired, even by Islamists (Islam On Line, 2002).

Interest in discussing the nature and relevance of the ideologies professed by various strands of the international anti-globalisation movement, and awareness of its historical significance, are restricted to intellectuals, activists, and offshoot local organisations. Most Arab intellectuals do not approve of the anarchist and ultra-radical ideologies that dominate this movement. They agree only with the movement's protest against globalisation-cum-Americanisation. That said, the anti-globalisation rallies have met with great enthusiasm in the Arab world, and global civil society has been recognised first in the unfolding of global protest against unjust globalisation. It goes without saying that for most Arab intellectuals, globalisation revives the frightening legacy of European colonialism, which brought the world together by the power of arms (Al-Senousy, 2003: 145–6). Young Arab radicals have started to construct their own anti-globalisation movement.

Iraq: the sudden rediscovery

While interest in fighting hegemonic globalisation is limited to small circles of the politically minded public, the massive rallies against the war on Iraq brought global civil society home to almost every family in the Arab world. The anti-war movement had another, more constructive, impact. For some time, Arab political culture has been drifting towards a theory that characterises American policy in the region, including the 'war on terrorism', as a new 'crusade' or religious war against Islam and the Muslim world (Hussein, 2002). The overwhelming majority of Arabs believe that their societies and cultures have been targeted for destruction by the US and possibly by the West at large. These concerns were systematically voiced in the Arab media. When Iraq was invaded in March 2003, the common cry among almost all Islamist and nationalist forums in the Arab world was:

> *Oh Muslims, brethren of faith everywhere, Drums of the Crusaders' war are newly sounding loud again. (Al-Minbar, 2003)*

In fact, Arab perceptions of American and Western policies in the region are strongly motivated by alienation and fear. Long after the war ended, on the popular Al-Jazeera talk show, *The Opposite Current*, 80 per cent of viewers who voted gave a positive answer to the question: 'Is the war on Iraq a new Crusade?' And as recently as March 2004, 80 per cent of respondents to another poll by Al-Jazeera.net believed that the aim of US policy in the Middle East was to obliterate Arab identity (Al-Jazeera, 2004a). However, this view receded

Box 3.1: The first pan-Arab gathering against globalisation, Beirut, November 2001

A group of Arab activists and intellectuals who took part in the global anti-globalisation movement called for an assembly or gathering of like-minded young Arabs to convene in Beirut on 3–4 November 2001. A number of eminent figures in anti-globalisation movements, such as Jose Bove of the French agricultural union, Christophe Aguitton from ATTAC, and Jean Claude Amara of Droits Devan, took part in deliberations. The gathering aimed to achieve the following:

- to monitor the latest developments and 'the war on terrorism'
- to encourage debates on various issues related to globalisation
- to create space and opportunities for the exchange of relevant experiences and exploration of alternatives.

The gathering proved instrumental in encouraging the formation of anti-globalisation activism at the national level in a number of Arab countries, some of which have emerged as important partners in the anti-war rallies, such as the Egyptian Anti-globalisation Group.

significantly in Arab newspapers and among the general public. In the Islamic media too, the theme became less frequent.

In the period before the actual invasion of Iraq, the stress on the Arab psyche was enormous, due to the deterioration of the Palestinian–Israeli conflict and the sanctions imposed on a number of Arab states, including Iraq. Arabs felt that their destiny was at stake. The sense of crisis was all encompassing, pervasive, and shattering. Purely religious and cultural explanations of (American) war plans could have swayed the overwhelming majority of Arabs towards a complete (moral and cultural) rupture with the international system, and led them to ally themselves in principle with the militant fundamentalist fringe in Arab and Muslim politics. In fact, sympathy with the fundamentalist worldview had been growing since 2000, which saw the collapse of Palestinian–Israeli negotiations in Camp David-2 and the brutal suppression of the Palestinian Intifada.

It was mainly due to the remarkable intervention of global civil society against the war on Iraq that major radical nationalist and Islamist parties or political figures could advance solid counter-arguments to religious and cultural theories of the war. First, radical activist George Hwatmeh argued that the anti-war rallies were evidence of the obsolescence of the 'clash of civilizations' theory (Hwatmeh, 2003). In Lebanon, Hezbollah appealed for an end to the 'crusade' explanation of the Anglo-American war on Iraq (Al-Hoda, 2003). To ordinary Arabs it was evident that large sections – and often majorities of Western societies opposed the war on Iraq as unwarranted and unjust. Second, the involvement of followers of almost all major Christian congregations in anti-war rallies worldwide belied any claims that the war had a religious motive or mandate. Third, opposition to the war was not limited to global civil society activists. The majority of leaders of western European states, including the Vatican, were opposed to the war. These aspects of the struggle against the war were followed closely and admired by almost the entire Arab population, something that contributed significantly to the partial retreat of the 'religious war' theory (Al-Shobky, 2003).

© ANDREW TESTA/PANOS PICTURES

Anti-war marches in Europe dampened the 'clash of civilizations' theory

A lonely revolution no more!

The suffering of the Palestinian people under Israeli occupation, as well as in refugee camps constructed since 1948 in Lebanon, Syria, Jordan, and inside the Occupied Territories, is the greatest source of Arabs' alienation from, and disenchantment with, the West, and the system of international relations generally (Korany and Dessouki, 1991). For a long time, the struggle of the Palestinian people for their historical and political rights found little understanding at the grassroots level in the Western world. Palestinians felt they were alone in their struggle for national rights, particularly after the signing of the Camp David Accords in the US in 1978, which symbolised the rise of a new environment in the Arab region. To the Palestinians, Egyptian President Sadat's visit to Jerusalem in 1977 and the signing of the Camp David Accords undermined the theory that all Arabs were bound to the struggle against Israel. Egypt's stance signalled the exhaustion of some Arab countries by the continuous conflict with Israel and its supporters in the Western world. And, as Israel's rejection of their national rights continued, Palestinians felt they had to take matters into their own hands rather than rely on the rest of the Arab world for salvation. Launching the struggle alone, without much help from other Arabs or the world at large, deepened their sense of loneliness.

This sense of isolation has changed over time, particularly during the first Intifada (1987–90), when not only NGOs but the mainstream media and western European governments openly sympathised with the right of the Palestinian people to self-determination. This shift in the international handling of the Palestinian issue has influenced Israel's attitude towards the recognition of some rights. Many major INGOs have promoted Palestinian rights by establishing a direct or indirect presence in the Occupied Territories, particularly in the wake of the Oslo Accord in 1993. Almost 1,000 NGOs have a direct or indirect presence in the Palestinian Occupied Territories (Palestine Center, 2001; United Nations Information Report, 2002).

The outbreak of the second Palestinian Intifada, which began in 2000, found a somewhat different environment. The blowback from the peace process frustrated and confused state and non-state actors worldwide. The extraordinarily brutal turn of the conflict may have also demoralised global activists for peace in Palestine, as it certainly did many Jewish and Israeli peace activists. The events of 9/11 only made matters worse for the Palestinian people. Pro-Israeli groups in the Western world launched a massive propaganda campaign that sought to establish similarities or links between Palestinian and Al-Qaeda violence. This propaganda had little impact on public opinion, even in the US, because the Palestinian cause was seen as a national struggle. But confusion and, consequently, inaction, prevailed.

In fact, the first year of the Intifada witnessed few attempts on the part of global civil society to stop the violence and put the peace process back on track. Repeated Palestinian and Arab calls for international protection were heeded only by a small fringe within global civil society, including the international human rights movement, until the massive reinvasion, by the Israeli government of Prime Minister Sharon, of the Occupied Territories in March and April 2002. And as the international community and global civil society utterly failed to stop some of the most brutal forms of collective oppression, such as house demolition, the destruction of agricultural fields and public utilities, harassment at checkpoints, assassinations, economic blockade, and detention of thousands, Palestinians felt on their own again. This sense of isolation contributed to the rise of suicide bombing, as it was seen by many Palestinians as their only option. In my view, if the early forms of civil protest had met with greater understanding globally, the Palestinians would have resisted the drift towards the militarisation of the Intifada.

Since March 2002, the situation has improved, with activists devising more tangible forms of support, such as human protection shields. However, the degree of solidarity given to Palestinians by global civil society organisations remains much less than is needed to end the Palestinians' sense of isolation (Wood, 2004). In fact, global opposition to the war on Iraq provided the opportunity for a more forceful show of sympathy with the Palestinians' plight. It is noteworthy that nothing similar to the movement against the war on Iraq has ever emerged against the war on the Palestinians, even at its height. Therefore, the magnitude of opposition to the war on Iraq offered pro-Palestinian groups an exceptional opportunity to make their voices heard. A number of global civil activists were thus motivated to take up the Palestinian cause of ending the Israeli occupation as an important goal. Neither Palestinians nor other Arabs appreciated the immense sacrifices made by some global peace heroes (*Electronic Intifada*, 2004). In June 2003, Al-Awada, a major coalition of Palestinian NGOs, instituted the Rachele Corrie award for non-Palestinian individuals or groups who demonstrate exceptional dedication to the cause of Palestinian rights. This award was granted for the first time in Toronto to the international solidarity movement with which Rachele had been associated. Rachele, a 23-year-old American college student, was the first non-Palestinian activist to be killed in the Occupied Territories by the Israeli Defence Force (IDF), on 16 March 2003. Rachele interposed herself between a Palestinian family house in Rafah/Gaza, which was about to be razed, and an IDF bulldozer.

> *The massive machine rolled over her and then back again. (Palestine Monitor, June 2003)*

Human rights versus regime interests

The image of global civil society in the Arab world is shaped by its contradictory impact on Arab regimes and Arab strategic elites. In the post-colonial era, global civil

© MARK HENLEY/PANOS PICTURES

society struggles against Western imperialism and militarism worked, by default, in favour of Third World regimes. For this reason, the spectacular show of global opposition to the war on Iraq was warmly welcomed by Arab regimes whose very survival was seen to be at stake. Some regimes that prevent all forms of popular protest in their own countries were so impressed that they orchestrated similar spectacles by organising big anti-war rallies. For example, the Egyptian ruling party organised a rally of a million people in a distant and relatively calm neighbourhood of Cairo to coincide with the flood of demonstrations around the world in February 2003. At the same time, smaller demonstrations organised by independent activists were denied a licence. Rallies that emerged spontaneously were brutally suppressed. Similar events took place in many other Arab countries.

The contrast between the enormous and open opposition to the war in many countries and the failure of Arab civil societies to display similar opposition was attributed to the authoritarian nature of the state in the region. Having global civil society on their side in times of major crises, such as the war on Iraq, was never more than a passing 'convergence of interests' for such states. It did not imply a new openness towards global or local civil societies. In fact, the very notion of civil society causes an allergic reaction in these regimes, which see civil society's intervention in 'high politics' as a threat to their monopoly of power (Gilbraith, 1996). Their ideology and reasoning are founded on the belief that 'the state knows better' and that peoples' intervention in the field of politics generally, and strategic affairs specifically, disturbs, and creates chaos in, the 'natural order' of things. Accordingly, these regimes have an ambivalent attitude towards global civil society. They both welcome it and deny its ability to influence strategic political decisions, even in democratic societies. This is why regimes in the Middle East highlighted the refusal of a number of western European leaders to heed their own public opinion when it came to the war on Iraq.

Two more factors weigh negatively in authoritarian regimes' view of global civil society. The first is the tendency of global civil society to disregard sovereignty and the principle of non-interference in domestic affairs of the nation state (Keane, 2004). For example, highlighting human rights abuses can cause problems for authoritarian regimes in terms of their image abroad.

The second reason for ambivalence and distrust is that, typically, global civil society works by engaging local allies. The very notion of global civil society implies that domestic civil societies will evolve and eventually gather the needed strength to hold leaders and regimes accountable. Arab human rights organisations, for their part, took full advantage of the space created by global civil society to promote their cause and pressure their governments for a complete overhaul of the legal system and legal practice relevant to the protection of human rights. Against the active alliance of local and global human rights organisations, authoritarian regimes use 'the nationalist discourse' to deter the growth of home-grown movements. Periodically, regimes use massive media and propaganda campaigns to portray local civic activists as traitors or conspirators. In many trials of local democracy and human rights activists, the main charges have focused on 'polluting the image of the nation abroad'. These charges betray the nature of the authoritarian client state in the region (Anderson, 1987; S Ibrahim, 2001).

The agonising evolution

The relative success of Arab authoritarian regimes in evading international and national accountability for human rights abuses is partly explained by their 'organic links' with the hegemonic powers in the present world system. For the US, in particular, the region has been important only for its oil and Israel. To this list, we might as well add a third, and in some cases more important, consideration, namely, strategic services that were delivered by allied Arab states both during and after the cold war. One of the main legacies of regional and international politics during the cold war was the systematic use of Islam by hegemonic Western powers, in conjunction with local allies, to check the advances of Soviet communism and local nationalism (Heikal, 1986). In the 1980s, massive numbers of young men from almost all Arab countries were jointly mobilised by several Arab regimes and the US to fight the Soviet Union in Afghanistan. The birth of Al-Qaeda and other fanatical Islamist organisations is rooted in the legacy of such opportunistic use of religion for political purposes. Prince Saud Al-Faisal, the foreign minister of Saudi Arabia, openly confessed of Saudi-American responsibility for the consolidation of Bin Laden and company, in a speech delivered in the US as recently as April 2004 (*Asharq Al-Awsat*, 27 April 2004). The anti-Soviet campaign in Afghanistan, which was jointly operated by Muslim countries and the US under the rubric of 'Jihad', constituted only one source of the fantastic growth of fundamentalism and religious fanaticism in Arab countries. Many other factors also contributed to it, among them the use of Islam by authoritarian Arab states against radical dissent during the 1970s; the dismal social and economic performance during the last 25 years; the breakdown of old social structures due to the impact of the oil economy; and the identity crisis resulting from humiliating defeats in successive military and diplomatic encounters with Israel.

All these factors contributed to the painful evolution of Arab civil societies. The rise of Islamic fundamentalism brought with it a general suspicion of foreign cultures. The terrorist fringe within the political Islamic current based its strategy on unleashing a spiral of violence and religious wars in which it would be seen as the 'natural leadership' of Muslim societies (Said, 2000). The attacks of 9/11 fitted this strategy perfectly. Given the extreme frustration with the US bias towards Israel in the region, it was thought that engaging Americans in a spiral of violence would push all societies towards fanaticism. The spectre of 'international terrorism', represented by Al-Qaeda, has thus complicated already strained relations between Arabs and other major cultures around the world. Mutual fears and suspicions have deepened doubts on both sides about the commitment to basic human values. Arabs maintain their condemnation of the 'double standards' applied by major Western powers, especially the US, in the region. In return, many in the Western world question the compatibility of Arab culture and Islam with democracy and human rights (Hefner, 2001; Dalacoura, 1993).

In this context, global civil society seems to constitute the main bridge across an artificial divide. However, remarkable efforts have to be made in order to overcome the doubts and distrust that exist not only between states but deep within societies. The French government's recent ban on the wearing of overt religious garb, in particular the *hijab*, in schools demonstrates the dilemma (Bayoumi, 2004).

Fundamentalism and fanaticism contributed significantly to the expansion of the mandate given to the security apparatus by authoritarian Arab regimes. Hence, the partial liberalisation declared by these regimes during the 1970s and early 1980s was practically halted, causing stagnation in some cases and internal strife in others (Ibrahim and Karim, 1999). This reality is consuming the energy of many Arab civil societies. These agonising developments in Arab politics and culture during the last two decades have had a very negative impact on Arab societies' relationships with the outside world. The growth of religious fundamentalism and fanaticism in the Arab world in the last 25 years has left only a small space for the evolution of other traditions and trends of thought. In the majority of Arab countries the rise of fundamentalism has had negative effects on both civic and political arenas.

Other factors have also contributed to political and civil stagnation. Progressive forces were shattered by the collapse of the Soviet Union and the socialist bloc. The potential growth of the liberal and democratic trends was severely restricted by popular disgust with the West for being so thoroughly allied to Israel, or for failing to bring it into line with international law and rules of justice. The breakdown of labour and popular movements, due to economic decay, deprived all secular and progressive trends of the broad social support needed to construct vibrant and effective civil societies (Ismael and Ismael, 1997).

While people hold positive views on democracy and social activism, they are unwilling to pursue these goals actively by joining political parties or advocacy organisations themselves

Young Arab generations are inclined to think in terms of religion, politically and culturally. The remaining and relatively ageing activists are spread thinly across a massive political and civic agenda, with limited resources and sometimes a legacy of divisions. It was only natural that local civil societies and civic culture were slow to grow, and they are still limited to only a few fields of action. One should also indicate the presence of a certain level of shallowness that results from a lack of adequate rootedness throughout society (Bin Nfissa and Qandil, 1997). Many activists cite the negative impact of foreign funding on civil society, arguing that advocacy organisations have been alienated from their national environment by the quasi-business mentality that this funding encourages (Corpacio, 1998: 28). Hence, the associative space, and in particular advocacy organisations in Egypt, Syria, and several other Arab countries, are often accused of elitism. This accusation is true in the sense that mass mobilisation is limited and mass response is weak, or even absent. According to recent public opinion polls in Egypt, while people hold positive views on democracy and social activism, they are unwilling to pursue these goals actively by joining political parties or advocacy organisations themselves. Accordingly, no more than seven per cent of Egyptians are members of NGOs and no more than two per cent are members of political parties (Al-Ahram CPSS, 2000). All these problems are reflected in the belated and narrowly based encounter with global civil society.

However, certain exceptions to this bleak canvas are noteworthy. Human rights advocacy seems the most articulate and sophisticated realm of civic struggle in the Arab world. Human rights organisations in various Arab countries occupy a commanding position in the struggle against oppression and for fundamental liberties and legal reform. For example, the Tunisian League has pioneered this trend at the national level. Today, organised civic action in the field of human rights is well developed in Egypt, Morocco, Sudan, Yemen, Syria, and Algeria. At the pan-Arab level, the Arab Organisation for Human Rights started the trend in 1982. Today, a younger and more militant generation of human rights activists prefers networking at the Arab regional level to forming centralised pan-Arab organisations. Coordination and joint action in the field of human rights is led by the Cairo Institute for Human Rights. Networking with international, and specifically Mediterranean, human rights NGOs has already established a powerful legacy. The remarkable momentum acquired by human rights advocacy in the Arab world since the mid-1980s can be explained partly by the decline of radical political formations. Stagnation and crises within leftist groups has forced a great number of radical and democratically oriented intellectuals to channel their energies into the human rights field. This trend is apparent in Egypt and Palestine. The Egyptian Organisation for Human Rights was created in 1985, when hopes for a swift democratic transition vanished and leftist parties, both official and underground, were deserted. In Palestine, human rights groups benefited from the release of many activists by leftist factions. The relative success and increasing professionalism of human rights work encouraged this trend.

On the other hand, Palestinian civil society has grown simply because it has been the main provider of leadership and social services for a nation deprived of its own state and government (Amr, 1995). Many Palestinian NGOs have been formed in the last 25 years. Organisations whose mandate is to monitor human rights abuses led the way and continue to be the most developed aspect of Palestinian civil society. Haq has pioneered this trend since its foundation in 1979. More recently, human rights advocacy has become specialised,

Box 3.2: The Sudanese women's movement

The women's movement in Sudan was one of the earliest and most powerful manifestations of women's struggle against discrimination in the Arab world. It gained great momentum in the 1960s and 1970s. However, the movement was forced into retreat by the military Islamist government, which was established by a coup in 1989. The leading women's organisation, the Sudanese Women's Union, had to work from abroad, in exile, to escape repression. The military government enacted a number of laws, such as the public order code and personal status law, which stripped women of their basic human rights. However, recent peace talks have enabled women activists to prepare for the building of a unified movement inside a future democratic Sudan. Hence the call for an all-Sudanese national democratic convention, which would bring together a variety of organisations struggling for equality. The convention demands that Sudanese legislation be harmonised with international standards on women's rights, including social and political rights, the rights of displaced and refugee women, cultural rights and freedom of expression, health rights, and the elimination of female genital mutilation. The Sudanese women's movement has been assisted by various international governmental and non-governmental organisations, and continues to engage a wide variety of global civil society actors.

with NGOs focusing on land, right of return, legal aid, and health services. Human rights activism seems to have also compensated for the declining role of professional syndicates in defending public liberties, particularly in Egypt, Syria, and Sudan. However, these syndicates continue to play a part in those Arab countries where social movements are rather weak.

In other Arab countries, women's organisations have played an important role in the development of civil society. In Palestine, women's activism and networks have shouldered the great burden of civic struggle in terms of social cohesion, service provision, and resistance, particularly during the first Intifada (1987–90).

In the case of the Sudanese women's movement, the national struggle gained priority over the specifically feminist aspects of the movement. In Morocco, long traditions of civic and political pluralism and activism greatly helped the process of democratisation (Koronfol, 2000: 179–90). The women's movement in Morocco is the most highly developed in the region. Its focus on gender issues further enriches its standing in the civic and political arena. The relentless struggle for women's rights was eventually rewarded by the introduction in 2003 of the most progressive legislation on family status issues in the Islamic world. It is also in Morocco that we find human rights struggles most successful in linking with masses and bringing better legislation (Layachi, 1998; Reuters, 2003). In Sudan, the movement is respected for its heroic struggle against periodic military coups, including the present regime. The resilience of the Sudanese women's movement is testimony to the Arab tradition of sacrifice for the public good. The human rights and women's movements have been more successful in raising public awareness than the NGOs that focus on environmental issues, health, education, and urban politics. These philanthropic, religious, and development organisations represent the overwhelming majority of NGOs in every Arab country. In Egypt alone there are 15,000 NGOs of this type and in Morocco the number of NGOs has grown from several hundred to almost 45,000. Often these organisations have a close relationship with government officials and ruling elites, which makes criticism of official policies more difficult.

However, those NGOs in the field of development are beginning to challenge the formal development strategies pursued by Arab governments. The Arab NGO Network for Development is a good example of this, operating as it does at the pan-Arab level and collaborating with similar interests globally. Founded in June 1996, with a membership of 55 NGOs from 12 Arab countries, the network emerged from the regional preparatory process for the World Summit for Social Development. It consists of a general assembly and a coordination committee elected every two years. The network's vision is rooted in the concepts of democracy, human rights, and sustainable development as the foundations for just social relations across the Arab world. The network considers that structural adjustment programmes and the imposition of a single economic model contradict the principles of democracy and diversity, and violate the fundamentals of human rights, especially those related to self-determination. The network's short-term objectives focus on building an efficient and strong Arab NGO sector and include reviewing legislation, strengthening solidarity with member organisations in times of crisis, and developing links with other networks and committees, and with UN and international governmental and non-governmental agencies.

British Muslims, Oldham, UK

Arab advocacy organisations have much stronger connections with global civil society than their counterparts in traditional fields of philanthropy, religion, and development. Such advocacy groups share with global civil society the desire to make democracy and the rule of law more meaningful to ordinary people. Empowerment in the context of democratisation is the key philosophy of many of these organisations. Networking, mutual assistance and coordination, and implementation of joint programmes of action are growing. Today, the extent of Arab participation in global civic life is unprecedented. The achievements of advocacy and public activism in the Arab world are not observed in actual legislation or public policy but rather in public consciousness and mood. In other words, while material gains are meagre, advocacy has resulted in building consensus on an impressive agenda for the transformation of Arab political and civic frames.

We cannot leave this discussion without briefly highlighting the unique feature of contemporary Arab civic life, which is linked to migration to western Europe, Australia, and North America. The relative maturation of such Arab migrant communities eventually gave birth to unique civil societies that strove to connect with their counterparts at home (Noakes, 1995). The crisis that followed 9/11 further galvanised these communities into participation with global civil society.

The associative space in many Arab countries has grown in leaps and bounds during the last decade. Authoritarian controls are losing their grip on societies and becoming increasingly obsolete. NGOs are acting with greater courage and sense of responsibility. Arab printed, electronic, and satellite television journalism is also contributing to what seem to be exceptionally rich and active debates. These factors are contributing to the mushrooming of contacts and networking between local Arab civil societies and global civil society

It remains the case that the real burden of promoting Arab participation and incorporation in global civil society rests on the shoulders of the humanist and progressive trends on both sides. And prospects for a qualitative leap in the process still await the transformation and democratisation of Arab politics.

REFERENCES

Abdalla, A. (1999) *Globalisation: Roots, Off-shoots and How to Deal With It.* Kuwait: Alam El Fekr.

Al-Ahram CPSS (Center for Political and Strategic Studies) (2000) A Summary of the Results of the Opinion Survey on People's Attitude on Democracy and Other Related Issues in Egypt. Memo. Cairo.

Al-Bassam, D. (1997) 'Arab Joint NGOs Action'. A paper presented to the Second NGOs Network conference. Cairo.

Al-Berkalay, M. H. (2002) 'Islamic Organisations: Positive partnership with Global Organisations', *Al-Alamyiah*, 147.

Al-Faisal, Saud, Prince (2004) 'The United States and Saudi Arabia: A Relationship Threatened by Misconceptions.' *Asharq Al-Awsat*, 27 November 2004. www.asharqalawsat.com

Al-Gabry, M. A. (1998) 'Globalisation and Cultural Identity'. *El Mostakbal El Arabi*, 228 (February).

Al-Hoda (2003) 'Hizbullah salutes demonstrations in the West and calls for ending the discourse on Crusade wars'. Al-Hoda on Line. Com/akhbar (15-12-1423h).

Al-Jazeera (2004a) 'Does the greater Middle East project aim at obliterating Arab Identity?' 18 March. www.aljazeera.com

– (2004b). 15 April.

Al-Minbar (2003) www.alminbar.net/alkhutab (23-10-1423h).

Al-Senousy, S. (2003) *Globalization: An Open Horizon and a Frightening Legacy.* Cairo: Meritt Publications.

Al-Shobky, A. (2003) 'Religious war? A call for confrontation or withdrawal?' *Al-Ahram*, 10 June.

Al-Wahda al-Islamiya (2003) 'Tyranny on earth and sisters'. Vol 16, March.

Amin, Galal (1998) 'Globalisation and the State'. *El Mostakbal El Arabi*, 228 (February).

Amr, Ziad A. (1995) *Civil Society and Democratic Transition in Palestine.* Cairo: Ibn Khaldoun Center.

Anderson, Lisa (1987) 'The State in the Middle East and North Africa', *Comparative Politics*, 20(1): 1–18.

An-Na'im, A. (2002) 'Religion and Global Civil Society: Inherent Incompatibility or Synergy and Interdependence?', in Marlies Glasius, Mary Kaldor, and Helmut Anheir (eds), *Global Civil Society 2002.* Oxford: Oxford University Press, pp 55–73.

Bayoumi, A. (2003) *American Muslim Experience in the Political and Legal Fields Two Years After September Events.* CAIR Report. Washington DC.

– (2004) 'European Approaches to Integrate Muslims', *Seattle Post-Intelligencer*, 3 October.

Bin Nfissa, Sara and Qandil, Amani (1997) 'NGOs in Egypt'. Cairo: Al-Ahram CPSS.

Commission on Global Governance (1999) *Our Global Neighbourhood.* New York: Commission on Global Governance.

Corpacio, Shella (1998) *Civil Society in Yemen: the Political Economy of Activism in Modern Arabia.* Cambridge: Cambridge University Press.

Dalacoura, K. (1993) *Islam, Liberalization and Human Rights: Implications for International Relations.* London: I. B. Tauris.

Duare, Parsenjit (ed) (2004) *Decolonization.* New York: Taylor & Francis Inc.

Electronic Intifada (2004) 'Rachele Corrie 1979–2003: One Year Later'. 16 March.

Ghalioun, B. (1999) *Bids on Globalisation.* Mafhoum.com. pressr/

Gilbraith, M. (1996) 'Civil Society in the Arab World, the Promise and Peril of Democratization and Prospects for the Arab World', *Civil Society: Democratic Transformation in the Arab World*, 5 (October): 11–15.

Hefner, R. (2001) 'Public Islam and the Problem of Democratization', *Sociology of Religion: A Quarterly Review*, 62: 491–514.

Heikal, M. H. (1986) *Suez Files.* Cairo: Al-Ahram.

Hussein, Magdy (2002) *A Religious War Against Islam.* www-alshaab.com/Gif. 23 August.

Hwatmeh, N. (2003) *The Collapse of the 'Clash of Civilizations' and 'Conflict of Religions'.* Mafhoum.com/press 5

Ibrahim, N. and Nasser, M. (2004) 'The First Pan-Arab Gathering Against Globalisation', *Greneleos.* 8 April.

Ibrahim, S. (2001) 'A Statement on the Charges of "Polluting Egypt's Reputations Abroad". 24 May.

Ibrahim, S. and Karim, S. (1999) *Civil Society and Democratic Transition in the Arab Homeland.* Annual report 1999. Ibn khadoun center, Cairo.

Islam On Line (2002) 'Capitalism sucks peoples' blood'. www islam-online.net 17 January.

Ismael, T. and Ismael, J. (1997) 'Civil Society in the Arab World: Historical Traces and Contemporary Vestiges', *Arab Studies Quarterly*, 19 (Winter).

Keane, John (2004) *Global Civil Society?* Cambridge: Cambridge University Press.

Khashan, H. (2000) 'Revitalizing Arab Nationalism', *Middle East Quarterly*, 7 (March).

Korany, Bahgat and Dessouki, Ali H. (1991) *The Foreign Policies of Arab States.* Boulder, CO: Westview Press.

Koronfol, H. (2000) *Civil Society and Political Elites: Exclusion or Integration.* Casablanca: Orient Africa.

Korten, D., Perlas, N. and Shiva, Vandana (2002) *Global Civil Society: The Path Ahead.* www.pcaf.org/civilsociety/path

Layachi, Azzedine (1998) *State, Society and Democracy in Morocco: The Limits of the Associative Life.* Washington, DC: Center for Contemporary Arab Studies, Georgetown University.

Moheet.net (2002) http://us.moheet.com/asp.show (13 March)

Noakes, Greg (1995) 'American Muslim Activism', *Washington Report on Middle Eastern Affairs*. April/May: 73–5
Palestine Center (2001) 'Activists Pursue Peace through International Grass-roots Initiatives.' A report on a conference held by the Centre for Policy Analysis and Studies, November (Washington, DC) http://www.Palestinecenter.org
Qandil, Amani (2000) *Civil Society in Egypt*. Cairo: Al-Ahram Foundation.
– (2002) *Global Civil Society*. Cairo: Al-Ahram Foundation
Reuters (2003) 'Moroccan King boosts women's rights', 10 October.
Said, M. E. (2000) 'Islam and Social Conflict', in Mary Kaldor and Basker Vashee (eds), *Restructuring the Global Military Sector. Vol 1: New Wars*. London and Washington: Pinter. pp 78–107.
Shafeeq, M. (2004) 'Global Strategies and the Invention of Civil Society', *Al-Hayat*, 29 February.
United Nations Information Report (2002) 'The United Nations and Non-governmental Organizations on the Question of Palestine.' No 6 (September).
Wood, B. (2004) 'Where Are International Aid Organisations?' PalestineChronicle.com./article, 16 March.
Yassin, S. (1998) *Arab 'Time' and Global Future*. Cairo: Dar El Mostakbal El Arabi.

PART 2

ISSUES IN GLOBAL CIVIL SOCIETY

CHAPTER 4

GLOBAL CIVIL SOCIETY: OIL AND ACTIVISM

Yahia Said

Ngalba, Chad: As night fell and the bright lights of the brand new oil field wrapped this hamlet in their golden glow, Neurmbaye Elie, a local farmer, pointed across the field before him. There, Mr. Elie said, just left of the blazing gas flare, under the streetlight, once stood the village initiation site. Animals were sacrificed there, spirits were supplicated, and the village boys became men. Then it became part of the oil complex, fenced in, a patch of earth not unlike the rest; the village got about $130 for it. Now, he worries. What if the spirits, displeased, sprang from that sacred ground and spread willy-nilly across the land? (Sengupta, 2004)

Oil's promise of fabulous riches has an irresistible lure for governments, corporations and ordinary people. They should know better, as oil fortunes are usually laced with a heavy dose of misery. Opulent Parisian boulevards in early twentieth-century Baku, universal health and education in 1970s Iraq, and lush golf courses in the desert emirate of Dubai are matched by oil-fuelled killing fields in Chechnya and Angola and the ominously melting polar ice caps. These contradictions have made oil the focus of confrontations between governments, companies and activists. Front lines, real and imaginary, run across every oilfield and pipeline from Aceh to Alaska.

Oil has two characteristics that make it of particular interest from a global civil society perspective. First, oil is a global commodity in as much as it has been traded on the global market for decades. Both exporters and importers of oil have experienced the forces of globalisation, from interdependence to loss of sovereignty, before it became a pervasive phenomenon. Second, oil brings together concerns as diverse as war and human rights, development and environmental sustainability, governance and corporate responsibility. Therefore, oil campaigns involve the building of cross-border and cross-disciplinary activist networks and alliances.

This chapter first considers the character of oil as a global commodity, then looks at the groups, networks, and individuals engaged in this debate with the aim of identifying the main arguments. Finally, it examines the relationship between these arguments and our positions on globalisation (Kaldor, Anheier and Glasius, 2003).

Oil as a global commodity

Oil has certain unique characteristics that have profound implications for development, human rights, conflict and the environment – some of the main areas of civil society contestation.

Oil is still the most important source of energy, and the demand for oil increases more or less in line with global economic growth. Although advanced 'post-industrial' economies have improved energy conservation and are also investing in alternative energy sources, countries like China and India, which are catching up, are becoming increasingly dependent on oil.

The supply of oil depends on natural endowment and not on the productivity of labour. Hence, the income accruing to the suppliers of oil takes the form of rent rather than profits and wages. As a form of income, rent depends on ownership or control of a natural resource, in particular the territory where the oil is located, rather than on ownership or control of capital and labour.

Oil is a finite resource. Although predictions of global shortage have been persistently exaggerated over time (see Box 4.1), sources of oil have become increasingly difficult to extract, either for technical reasons (deep-sea drilling) or for social reasons, as many oil reserves are based in regions of instability – the 'social equivalent of deep-sea drilling', according to one oil executive.

Oil is a capital-intensive commodity requiring large, fixed long-term investments. Capital requirements grow as oil is tapped in increasingly remote areas and transported over longer distances. This, combined with the commodity's geostrategic legacy, has left its mark

Box 4.1: Twin peaks: Hubbert's Peak vs the Resource Pyramid

The scenario described above is a variation of Hubbert's Peak, named after M King Hubbert, the American geophysicist who worked for Shell and the US Geological Survey. In 1956, Hubbert predicted that global oil output would peak around 1995 and thereafter gradually decline. As with most Malthusian prophecies, the cataclysmic oil shortage seems to be always just around the corner. By Hubbert's reckoning we should now be in the midst of an oil crisis. His proponents continue to shift the crisis point forward every couple of years.

Moving Hubbert's Peak

Conventional oil (billions of barrels)	1989	1990	1992	1993	1995	1996	1997	1999
Produced	600	628	697	718	761	784	785	820
Reserves	725	806	725	722	800	836	823	827
Discovered	1,325	1,434	1,422	1,440	1,561	1,620	1,618	1,647
Yet to find	250	216	228	210	189	180	182	153
Yet to produce	975	1,022	953	932	989	1,016	1,005	980
Ultimate	1,575	1,650	1,650	1,650	1,750	1,800	1,800	1,800
Annual depletion rate (%)	2.3	2.1	2.3	2.3	2.6	2.6	2.6	2.2
Depletion mid-point (year)		**1998**	**1998**	**1998**	**2000**	**2001**	**2001**	**2003**

Source: The Coming Global Oil Crisis (URL)

Opponents of Hubbert's Peak employ the Resource Pyramid theory (Ahlbrandt and McCabe, 2002). According to this approach, the amount of available oil reserves is not fixed but varies according to economic, political and technology parameters at any given historical moment. At the top of the pyramid are high-quality resources that are easy to extract. As one moves towards the bottom, resources become harder and more expensive to extract and transport. The reserve estimate depends on the 'assessment slice', a point across the pyramid that depends on the point of economic feasibility. At any point in time, the slice divides the pyramid into the part of oil reserves that are economically feasible to develop (above the slice) and those that are out of reach. As technology improves and access to remote regions becomes easier, the slice can move down the pyramid, thus enlarging the amount of available resources. Opponents of Hubbert's Peak do not deny that one day oil resources will dry up, but they expect the peak to occur at a much later date and the decline to be more gradual (Yergin, 2004).

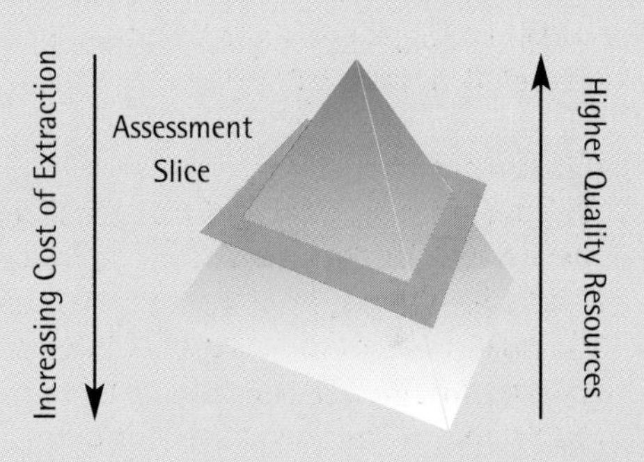

on the corporations involved in oil exploration and development. Oil production is concentrated in a handful of vertically integrated multinationals with vast resources. Their highly paid engineers, managers and lawyers pride themselves on being able to keep oil flowing under any circumstances. Executives are used to manipulating small governments and communities, just as they are comfortable working hand in glove with their domicile governments, the classic example being the role played by oil companies in helping the Shah of Iran, Mohammed Reza Pahlawi, topple the Musaddaq government in Iran in 1949, at the behest of Western powers (Yergin, 1991).

At every stage of the process – production (disturbance of natural habitats), transportation (oil spills) and use (release of carbon dioxide and other pollutants) – oil has serious environmental consequences.

While civil society contestations in areas where oil

© AMI VITALE/PANOS PICTURES

has a direct impact are relatively straightforward, there is significant disagreement over its indirect impact, what has been called the 'oil curse'. This refers to the paradoxical failure of oil-rich countries to translate their comparative advantage into better economic and social performance than their less well-endowed peers. Far from it: they seem to be prone to underdevelopment, predatory government, state collapse and war.

A majority of analysts perceive a correlation, both anecdotal and empirical, between resource dependence, underdevelopment and social and political instability (Auty, 1990; Gelb, 1988; Karl, 1997; Sachs and Warner, 1997). The debate over the oil curse is a subset of the broader resource curse debate. It traces its roots all the way back to the Greek legend of King Midas, whose ability to turn everything he touched to gold brought him nothing but misery and ruin. Medieval thinkers blamed easy riches for human sloth and Adam Smith warned of 'the income of men who love to reap where they never sowed' (Smith, 1776/1937: 399).

One version of the resource curse argument is the 'Dutch disease'. This is the argument that increasing oil dependence leads to appreciation of the currency and decline in competitiveness of other more labour-intensive sectors, both manufacturing and agricultural. Often oil-dependent governments invest in new industrial sectors that turn out to be unsustainable. When the oil price falls or when resources are depleted, such economies face severe problems. The 1980s debt crises started with oil-dependent countries before rippling through the rest of the Third World. It was triggered by a crash in oil prices. Of course, the economic and development literature offers many policy prescriptions for the adverse economic consequences of oil export dependence and for preparing an alternative development base for when oil runs out. Yet most oil-producing nations – the big exception is Norway – seem to have failed to live up to these challenges.

This gives rise to a second version of the oil curse argument: the predatory state. This argument builds on the Weberian notion that states are shaped by their main source of income (Weber, 1914/1979). In democratic societies, taxation is the main source of state revenue and rulers depend on public consent. Citizens recognise the necessity of paying taxes by accepting the state's legitimacy and the benefits derived from government expenditures. In the former Communist states, taxation was also important as a source of revenue; compliance was achieved through a mixture of ideology and repression. An oil-dependent state is one in which the primary source of revenue is oil rents. Typically, rentier states are predatory. They do not need to bargain with their citizens because they do not depend on their citizens for taxation. They merely need to remain in power, which they do through a mixture of patronage and repression. They create loyal networks of support through patronage and they combine this with repression. A position in government is an opportunity for rent-seeking rather than for public service. Hence, oil states are too dependent on this predatory behaviour to be able to break the cycle of oil dependence and, at the same time, they have sufficient resources to carry out coercive functions.

Nowadays, however, rentier states are often failing states. It is much more difficult to retain control through coercion because of globalisation. Even in the most closed authoritarian states, dissidents can gain access to the outside world through the Internet. The spread of small arms and organised crime also means that without democratic legitimacy, it is much more difficult for a state to maintain a monopoly of organised violence, and thus to control territory through purely military means. Even rich oil countries like Saudi Arabia have become sites of instability and low-level violence. Thus, if the Dutch disease argument explains continued poverty and underdevelopment, the predatory state argument explains why so many governments have failed to reverse Dutch disease and why oil states tend to violate human rights.

Yet a third argument has to do with the relationship between oil dependence and conflict. Collier and Höffler (2001), analysing data on 1,167 conflicts between 1960 and 1990, find a strong correlation between dependence on primary commodity exports and the risk of conflict. Analysts disagree whether this correlation is causal in nature and through which avenues it occurs.

The most common explanation of the link between oil and conflict stresses oil's geostrategic importance. According to this argument, oil was and remains an essential ingredient of capitalism and superpower status. Without secure access to cheap oil, neither can survive. Secure access to oil means control over territory, and this can be achieved either directly through military conquest or indirectly through influence over oil states. There is ample historical evidence to support this argument. Daniel Yergin's popular monograph (1991), *The Prize*, interprets the entire history of the twentieth century as a quest for oil, with superpowers and corporations collaborating to secure profits and dominance. In both First and Second World Wars, control of oilfields shaped strategies on all sides. The geo-strategic argument is quite popular among activists, many of whom extend it into the twenty-first century:

> *US control of oil and the guaranteeing of access to it was the cause of the Gulf War in 1991, and is also the cause of an imminent war against Iraq, since the world's most important oil reserves lie in that region. Access to this resource led to the intervention in Afghanistan, an important gas pipeline route that connects the Caspian region with Europe. Similarly, the objective of the war declared in Colombia is the control of oil production in that country and also improving its presence in the region. Specifically, to avoid losing control over the crude oil coming primarily from Venezuela. Plan Puebla Panama and the 'New Horizons' military initiative include the construction of pipelines directed toward the United States. (Oilwatch, 2003)*

This argument is reinforced by the rhetoric emanating from Washington on the need to secure oil supplies as a matter of national security and by the incestuous relationship between the Bush administration and several energy companies.

Opponents of the geopolitical narrative argue that, rather than dictating US policy, concerns over energy security are being used as pretext for geopolitics. If Iraqi oil were to come on stream fully as a result of US involvement in that country, it could depress oil prices to the point of making oil in Russia, the Caspian, West Africa and the Gulf of Mexico economically less viable, thus devaluing billions of dollars of investments in these regions and hurting most multinational oil companies. It would also weaken the argument for opening the Alaska National Wildlife Refuge and the Rockies to oil exploration, one of the main planks of US Vice-President Dick Cheney's energy policy (Cable, 2003). The lower oil prices would also eat into the revenues that US oil corporations could hypothetically gain from controlling Iraqi oil resources. It is not even a given that US oil companies could emerge as the main 'owners' of Iraqi oil wealth. They would have to compete with the new Iraqi government as well as other multinationals. An analysis of the benefits to the US from controlling Iraq's oil resources should take into consideration the total cost to the US, including the war. Table 4.1 provides a hypothetical analysis of the war in Iraq as an investment aimed at controlling Iraqi oil wealth. It shows that US-Iraq Oil Inc would be a loss-making enterprise.

Likewise, it is argued that the jockeying over Caspian oil and export routes is not about safeguarding access to oil from Russia and Iran but using oil to marginalise them politically. In an informal conversation, an oil executive complained about the Clinton administration's efforts to promote the Baku-Tbilisi-Ceyhan pipeline and the pressure it was exerting on oil companies. He accused the administration of trying to compel oil companies to finance its foreign policy.

Even if the premise is accepted that oil is essential for the functioning of capitalism, it is not at all clear that the traditional geostrategic approach is the best way to secure oil supplies. Given that it is much more difficult to control territory through military means, geopolitical approaches can compound the instability that is increasingly typical of predatory states, tipping the balance towards state collapse. The war in Iraq, the associated collapse of the Iraqi state and the ongoing insurgency have, at least for the time being, reduced the security of supply coming from that country. The insurgency, which is attracting Islamic terrorists from all over the world, has created an added threat to oil supplies from Saudi Arabia and the region as a whole. This is reflected in the current surge in oil prices, which have at times reached record highs.

There is plenty of evidence to show that oil fuels war economies in many regions. Oil revenues are tapped to sustain conflict either directly, as by the Angolan or Sudanese governments, or indirectly though extortion of oil companies and workers, kidnapping and check-points as by the Russian Army and the rebels in Chechnya, the Revolutionary Forces of Colombia (FARC) leftist guerrilla group, and the secessionist Free Aceh Movement (GAM) in Indonesia. Indeed, the role of oil in many of today's conflicts is more direct in this respect, and even small reserves are sufficient to fuel brutal conflicts for many years.

Authoritarianism and war in oil-dependent countries is a combined product of oil dependence and geopolitics. In the past, this combination was compatible with ensuring secure oil supplies for the developed world, profits for multinational oil companies and even some modicum of development in oil-dependent economies. Today, it is no longer possible to combine these competing demands. With globalisation the main result of oil dependence and geopolitics seems to be state collapse, which is not only a threat to oil supplies but a source of global insecurity.

Table 4.1: The war in Iraq as an investment in controlling Iraqi oil wealth

US$ millions, unless stated otherwise

1) Year	**2003**	**2004**	**2005**	**2006**	**2007**	**2008**	**2009**	**2010**	**2011**	**...2027**
2) Daily export (millions of barrels)	0.5	1.5	2	3	4	4	5	5	6	6
3) Price ($ per barrel)	30	35	35	33	33	30	30	28	28	28
4) Revenue (2x3x360)	5,400	18,900	25,200	35,640	47,520	43,200	54,000	50,400	60,480	60,480
5) Iraq's share	5,400	18,900	25,200	30,000	35,940	35,400	40,800	40,080	45,120	45,120
6) US share (4 minus 5)	-	-	-	5,640	11,580	7,800	13,200	10,320	15,360	15,360
7) US outlays	70,000	70,000	35,000	10,000	10,000	10,000	10,000	10,000		
8) Net US revenue (6 minus 7)	**–70,000**	**–70,000**	**–35,000**	**–4,360**	**1,580**	**–2,200**	**3,200**	**320**	**15,360**	**15,360**
9) Discount rate	5.5%									
10) Net present value	–$51,808									

Assumptions:

1 25 years typical investment horizon for oil projects

2 Projected ramp-up to six million barrels per day – the most optimistic forecast

3 Prices to ease gradually from current levels to $28 per barrel after Iraqi ramp-up – an optimistic assumption given likely impact of additional Iraqi oil on prices, as well as expected additional output from other regions

5 Based on Iraqi government budget until 2006 (CPA, URL) then assuming that the US will keep 50 per cent of new oil revenue – optimistic since national governments customarily keep up to 88 per cent (Yergin, 2002)

7 Outlays: 2003 and 2004 based on additional congressional appropriations for war (Cost of War, URL); 2005 assuming half that level. Investment in oil infrastructure of $50 billion. Estimates range from $20 billion (Yergin, 2002) to $100 (Heritage, URL) of investments necessary to ramp-up production to six million barrels per day over five years. This assumes no US troops in Iraq after 2005.

9 US government cost of borrowing based on 20-year US Treasury bond – a conservative assumption for a project with such high risks, including the possibility of lower output, political unrest, nationalisation and lower oil prices

10 In reality, the net present value would be even lower since the above calculation is based on revenue rather than net income. It does not account for extraction and transportation costs.

Campaigns and groups

The oil curse framework has significant implications for activists who contributed to its development by highlighting the interconnectedness of the various consequences of oil dependence. The framework has inspired the creation of integrated campaigns that unite peace, human rights, environmental and social justice activists. This has not always been the case. Traditionally, and up until the 1980s, anti-colonial Southern activists and their Northern supporters from the left campaigned for the establishment of national sovereignty over oil resources, as opposed to Western control via the multinationals. At times, this brought them into conflict both with environmental activists, who opposed oil development regardless of who controlled it, and with human rights campaigners, who saw no reason to trust nationalist leaders any more than the client regimes they opposed.

The oil curse framework clarifies the relationship between the various campaign targets: Western powers, multinational corporations, predatory Southern governments, oil dependence and oil itself. The struggle of the Ogoni people in the Niger Delta since 1993 represented a watershed in this context. There, Southern activists confronted both a predatory national government and the oil multinationals, with the full support of a broad spectrum of international groups (see Box 4.2).

Many activists use the oil curse as an argument for opposing any form of oil development since, by its nature, the industry is a harbinger not only of environmental degradation but also of social injustice, political oppression and war. Environmental groups espousing such positions are the most visible campaigners on oil issues today. Greenpeace, Friends of the Earth and the World Wide Fund for Nature feature prominently in global networks and campaigns surrounding, for example, the Kyoto Protocol on Climate Change, the World Summit on Sustainable Development and the World Bank's Extractive Industries Review. They are also active in regional campaigns that target specific oil and gas projects, from Alaska to Chad and from Azerbaijan to Ecuador. Often such regional campaigns have been the springboard for INGOS to expand their campaigning in order to encompass issues of indigenous people's rights, human rights, development and corporate responsibility. For example, Greenpeace played a leading role in the international solidarity campaign in support of the Ogoni people (see Box 4.2). Friends of the Earth is working with the Kurdish Human Rights project in the campaign against the Baku-Tbilisi-Ceyhan pipeline (see Box 4.3).

Fuelled by oil: Indonesian GAM fighters

There is insufficient space in this chapter to enumerate the environmental aspects of oil development and consumption. In general, the environmental impact of oil can be separated into two broad categories: environmental and biodiversity issues, which are associated with oil and other industrial activities; and climate change, which is associated specifically with the consumption of fossil fuels. While it is possible to reduce the impact on biodiversity through diligence and technological innovation, climate change is an inherent consequence of using oil and other fossil fuels. It can be avoided only by switching to other, more sustainable sources of energy. Over the past decade, climate change has become the central issue for environmental activism on oil (see Box 4.4).

The protection of indigenous people's rights provides a bridge between environmental and human rights issues. This combination has been the model for many regional oil campaigns since the Niger Delta campaign, in which the protection of the Ogoni People and their habitat against abuse by Shell and the Nigerian government was the central issue (see Box 4.2). International environmental groups are often criticised for being oblivious to Southern needs, especially in the social and economic spheres. By supporting local indigenous groups, environmental campaigns acquire both a human face and a local constituency which helps them pre-empt such attacks. Human rights activists and other groups can acquire broader appeal and appear less controversial by espousing indigenous rights issues. Indigenous people's issues are therefore some of the most prominent in campaigns against oil development. Groups in the Amazon basin

Box 4.2: Shell in Nigeria

> *By the time I finish, Nigeria is going to be ashamed standing before the council of the world. (Ibeanu, 1999: 21)*

© JACOB SILBERBERG/PANOS PICTURES

Nigeria provides one of the most tragic examples of the oil curse. Since the beginning of large scale commercial development in the 1950s, tens of billions of dollars from oil exports have translated into a net deterioration in the economy, human development and the environment throughout the country. From the end of the 1967–70 civil war, Shell, the largest oil producer in Nigeria, was closely associated with the military dictatorships that ruled the country until 1998. Both share the responsibility for Nigeria's plight. Nowhere is this more manifest than in the Niger Delta, Nigeria's main oil-producing region. Here, the equally fragile ecosystem and indigenous population have been severely damaged by decades of reckless exploration and production, economic mismanagement and political oppression.

In 1993, the Movement for the Survival of the Ogoni People (MOSOP) was established, making environmental as well as emancipatory demands. Its peaceful campaign was met with brutal repression, culminating in the execution of Ken Saro-Wiwa and eight other MOSOP leaders in 1995. The struggle of the Ogoni people – one of the smaller indigenous groups inhabiting the Delta – had major repercussions throughout Nigeria. It also inspired the anti-capitalist movement worldwide. Activists in Global Exchange and the Ruckus Society, who went on to lead riots in Seattle and Prague, started out campaigning with and for Ken Saro-Wiwa and his followers. Leveraging support from global civil society was integral to Ogoni strategy. Its appeal to activists worldwide lay in its holistic approach, which linked environmental demands with the struggle for indigenous rights, social justice and human rights. Ogoni activists succeeded in 'globalising' their struggle by holding the multinational corporations to account alongside the military dictatorship, and linking local demands with global issues of the environment and corporate responsibility. Their success inspired indigenous rights movements and local activists elsewhere, most notably the Zapatistas in Mexico.

> *I and my colleagues are not the only ones on trial. Shell is here on trial and it is as well that it is represented by counsel said to be holding a watching brief. The Company has, indeed, ducked this particular trial, but its day will surely come and the lessons learnt here may prove useful to it for there is no doubt in my mind that the ecological war that the Company has waged in the Delta will be called to question sooner than later and the crimes of that war be duly punished. The crime of the Company's dirty wars against the Ogoni people will also be punished. (Saro-Wiwa, 1995)*

Shell was caught completely off guard by the global resonance of the Ogoni movement and attacks on its installations. As a result, it was forced to suspend oil production in Ogoniland in 1993. Shell had to move quickly from tacit support of the dictatorship to public relations damage control, before fully reassessing its policies in countries of operations and its relationships with host communities. In 1997, the company published its *Statement of General Business Principles* (Royal Dutch/Shell Group of Companies, 1997), which – a first for a multinational – referred to human rights. Its subsidiary in the Niger Delta began publishing annual People and the Environment reports, organising stakeholder meetings, replacing community outreach with a broader development programme, and reviewing its environmental assessment procedures. This raised the bar for corporate social responsibility across the sector.

Box 4.3: Baku-Tbilisi-Ceyhan Campaign

There is a construction project being planned involving UK multinationals which is condemned by Amnesty International and 78 environmental and human rights groups around the world. If it goes ahead, the project will hasten global warming, destroy democracy, increase corporate power, stifle dissent, cause human rights abuses and create refugees. (Thomas, 2003)

The Baku-Tbilisi-Ceyhan (BTC) Campaign is a coalition of environmental and human rights groups opposed to the construction of a 1,000-mile pipeline to transport a million barrels of Caspian oil a day from Baku in Azerbaijan to the Turkish Mediterranean port of Ceyhan, via Tbilisi, Georgia.

The campaign works through public education and advocacy in the UK, the EU and the pipeline countries. It issues regular press releases and organises lectures, round tables and protests. It lobbies parliamentarians, government officials, and private and public lenders. A major thrust of the campaign is to block public funding for the pipeline by bilateral and multilateral organisations. It is also challenging the legality of the pipeline and the governing agreements in Turkey, the UK and the EU. The coalition, which comprises several groups from the region through which the pipeline will pass, is dominated by three British groups: the Kurdish Human Rights Project, Corner House and Friends of the Earth.

There is hardly any aspect of the pipeline that the campaign does not attack. Activists argue that, when completed, the pipeline will contribute to the release of greenhouse gases equivalent to the output of all UK power stations, and will threaten marine life at the port of Ceyhan and precious mineral water sources in Georgia. The risk of environmental damage is exacerbated by the route of the pipeline, which runs through an earthquake zone in Turkey. Economically, the campaign prophesies that the pipeline will cause increased dependence on oil exports in the countries it passes through, without meeting their development and poverty reduction needs. Moreover, it will cause loss of property and livelihoods for people living along its route. Politically, the pipeline passes through a fragile region rife with geopolitical and ethnic tensions, frozen and active conflicts, and human and minority rights violations. Campaigners say the pipeline will exacerbate all of these. The BTC pipeline is also attacked as another example of how an alliance of multinational oil corporations, superpowers and international finance can infringe sovereignty and self-determination in the South. The campaign singles out Host Country Agreements, which are designed to protect BP and other members of the consortium against confiscation and unfavourable legislation after the project has begun, as a violation of sovereignty, the constitution and international norms.

Proponents of the pipeline have tried to address some of these concerns, with varying degrees of success. Environmental and Social Impact Assessments (ESIAs) were conducted in the route countries and consultation held with the various stakeholders. The consortium has also planned various projects throughout the life of the pipeline under a Community Investment Programme. The campaigners question the rigour of ESIAs and the validity of some of the community consultations. The BTC Campaign alleges that some of the consortium's consultations in Kurdish villages in Turkey never actually took place (BTC Campaign, 2003). It also questions the efficacy and sustainability of the proposed community investment programme if the same top-down approach as in the rest of the project is adopted.

One of the most persistent criticisms of the pipeline is that it was borne out of geopolitical rather than economic considerations. For many observers, BTC is also known as the 'no Russia, no Iran pipeline'. The US has made the BTC pipeline a major plank of its foreign policy. The administration hopes the pipeline will help contain Iran, strengthen Turkey and limit what it views as Russian encroachments on the newly independent 'democracies' of Georgia and Azerbaijan. Turkey is going along with the project in the hope of carving out its own sphere of influence in the region. By supporting the Western pipeline route, Azerbaijan and Georgia hope to secure the support of US and Turkey in the face of external threats (from Russia, Iran and Armenia, for example) and against domestic enemies. They are forging ahead with attempts to strengthen their ties to the West including, for example, Azerbaijan's recent bid to join NATO. Predictably, this has drawn the ire of both Russia and Iran.

The results of this 'Great Game' have so far been a net loss to everyone involved. Geopolitical considerations have become an obstacle to finding the most economically viable option for the development of the region's oil resources. The wrangling has marked a new low in US-Russian relations and, as such, has resuscitated Cold Warriors

Box 4.3: continued

on both sides. It is endangering the fragile détente between Iran and the West, and weakening supporters of the latter within the Islamic republic. The geopolitical rivalry has maintained and sometimes intensified the region's myriad conflicts. Finally, the Azeri government is exploiting regional and global power rivalries to strengthen its hold on power at home. It hopes that an alliance with the West will let it get away with undemocratic practices and human rights violations.

Apart from the geopolitics, it is difficult to accept the outright condemnation of the BTC campaign. Activists' demands that the pipeline should not proceed unless it eliminates poverty, solves conflict, improves governance and ends human rights violations sound a lot like rent-seeking – the greedy scramble for oil riches that is ignited whenever new oil is discovered. The BTC Campaign did not succeeded in preventing the construction of the pipeline, which is currently under way. By keeping the spotlight on the parties involved, it may succeed in mitigating some of its worst repercussions.

involved in AmazonWatch and other networks have been successful in blocking oil and gas projects. A coalition involving AmazonWatch, Friends of the Earth, Bank Information Center, Environmental Defense, Amazon Alliance and the Institute for Policy Studies succeeded in dissuading the US Export Import Bank from providing funding for a the controversial Camisea Project in Peru in 2003. In 2002, U'wa activists succeeded in forcing Occidental to shelve plans to explore for oil on their lands in Colombia (AmazonWatch, 2002).

Human rights activists have been pursuing violations committed either directly by the security services of oil multinationals or by paramilitary groups and national security services acting on behalf of those companies. Amnesty International and Human Rights Watch, among others, have campaigned against paramilitary violence and attacks on trade union activists in the oilfields of Colombia, where BP, Occidential and Talisman Energy, among other companies, are operating. Groups have also protested against widespread human rights violations by the Indonesian military in the oil-rich regions of Aceh and Kalamntan. In the case of Aceh, ExxonMobil was accused of providing logistical support to the military (Schultze, forthcoming).

Increasingly, human rights groups have been campaigning against oil and gas projects in zones of conflict

© SVEN TORFINN/PANOS PICTURES

Box 4.4: The Kyoto Protocol to the United Nations Framework Convention on Climate Change

The history of the Kyoto Protocol brings together the entire spectrum of civil society positions on oil and energy. Rejectionist environmental groups succeeded in putting the issue on the public agenda, and continued to campaign until policy-makers were forced to take notice. The protocol was the result of collaboration between Reformers and Supporters. It combines regulatory intervention through a multilateral process, redistribution from rich to poor countries and cooperation between government, civil society and corporations on the one hand with the use of market mechanisms on the other. In the end, Kyoto was all but abandoned by the Rejectionists as too little, too late. Today, it is being blocked by Regressives in the US and Russia, who see it as a threat to their national interests.

The 1992 UN Framework Convention on Climate Change, which has been ratified by 188 states and has been in effect since 1994, recognises the problem of human-induced global warming and commits signatories to work towards the ultimate goal of reducing the production of the greenhouse gases that cause it. The convention is a framework for future action that recognises the different responsibilities of rich and poor countries but does not specify any concrete measures. The 1997 Kyoto Protocol is meant to do just that. Most importantly, it sets a quantitative target for developed countries of a five per cent reduction by 2012 of the 1990 level of emissions. The protocol imposes no requirements on developing countries. The average reduction target is distributed among developed countries in various proportions. For example, the EU is expected to achieve a reduction of eight per cent, while Australia (which is refusing to sign the protocol) can increase emissions by eight per cent. The protocol commits developed non-transition countries to providing additional financial resources and technology transfers to developing countries in order to promote sustainable development.

It offers several market mechanisms to reduce emissions. Through the Clean Development Mechanism (CDM), developed countries can offset emissions against absorption by, for example, planting new forests, or sinks. They can obtain credits for helping reduce emissions in other countries or for financing sustainable energy in developing countries that achieve better reductions than required by the protocol. They can sell emission credits to others ('carbon trading').

The Kyoto Protocol will come into force only if ratified by 55 countries, including developed nations that account for at least 55 per cent of total carbon dioxide emissions, as measured in 1990. This goal is not achievable if both Russia (17.4 per cent) and the US (36.1 per cent) continue to balk at ratifying it (UNFCCC, 2002).

A broad network of environmental and other groups campaigned for the adoption of the protocol and for strengthening its provisions. However, many groups, such as Greenpeace, have become disillusioned with the outcome. Far from making a total break with the economic model of the Industrial Revolution era, which is predicated on the use of fossil fuels, Kyoto only offers minor adjustments to the margins. The process itself was hijacked by a bureaucratic elite that is deficient in terms of both scientific rigour and democratic accountability (Lohman, 2001). The activists direct most of their scorn at the market mechanisms, which they argue provide loopholes to developed countries, assign them ownership over the world's climate and encourage other forms of environmental damage through the promotion of monocultures (Greenpeace, 1998).

One of the main bodies associated with the convention is, in essence, a 'transnational advocacy network', inappropriately named the Intergovernmental Panel on Climate Change (IPCC). The IPCC, which comprises 3,000 scientists from around the world, has argued convincingly that climate change is induced by human activity. Thanks to the IPCC, and despite vociferous early denials, today most oil and automotive manufacturers, with the notable exception of ExxonMobil, accept the main premise of Kyoto.

Another set of civil society actors that has campaigned against Kyoto has had some success, not in winning over public opinion, but in scuppering the agreement at governmental level. The Global Climate Coalition (GCC) was established in 1989 to 'coordinate business participation in the international policy debate on the issue of global climate change and global warming' (Global Climate Coalition, URLa). The campaign, spearheaded by ExxonMobil, was dedicated to undermining the science of global warming and the Kyoto Protocol by, among other things, lobbying the US government. The GCC claimed to represent over six million US companies. With the exception of ExxonMobil, most multinational oil companies left the GCC as the reputational costs of denying global warming soared. These included BP, Shell and Texaco. However, together with the American Petroleum

Box 4.4: continued

Institute and the Competitive Enterprise Institute (CEI), the GCC played a vital role in shaping the US position on climate change. On its website, the GCC, which ceased its operations in 2002, proudly proclaims its mission accomplished:

> *The Global Climate Coalition has been deactivated. The industry voice on climate change has served its purpose by contributing to a new national approach to global warming. (Global Climate Coalition, URLb)*

Indeed, with the Bush administration, hardly any convincing was required. Parts of the administration used groups such as the GCC to promote their anti-Kyoto policy. The Stop Esso campaign, which comprised Greenpeace, Friends of the Earth and People's Planet, argues that the White House encouraged the CEI to sue the US Environmental Protection Agency over the science of climate change (Stop Esso, URL).

and in countries ruled by authoritarian regimes, such as Sudan and Burma. Global campaigning against Talisman Energy's work in Sudan, which activists argued was contributing to the country's civil war, was among the factors leading to the company's ultimate departure in 1999. The Presbyterian Church played a key role in these efforts. Arco and Texaco were forced by the US Campaign for Burma, and other activists, to abandon projects in the country.

One approach that has been employed with increasing efficiency is litigation in the US via the Alien Tort Claims Act (ATCA) of 1789, which was originally designed to combat piracy. This Act grants jurisdiction to US Federal Courts over 'any civil action by an alien for a tort only, committed in violation of the law of nations or a treaty of the United States' (Global Policy Forum, URL). Groups like Earthrights International, which combines human rights and environmental demands, and International Labour Rights Fund have used ATCA to file suits against Unocal in Burma, Shell and Chevron in Nigeria, Talisman Energy in Sudan, ExxonMobil in Indonesia and Texaco in Ecuador and Peru. The case against Unocal in Burma has proceeded furthest, with hearings pending both before Federal and California State Courts.

> *The Superior Court of California's decision makes the case against Unocal the first in U.S. history in which a corporation will stand trial for human rights abuses committed abroad. (Earthrights International, URL)*

The case against Texaco in Ecuador was dismissed but has now been taken on by an Ecuadorian court.

Multinational oil companies have always been the main target of oil activists. The breakdown of the link between authoritarianism and stability and the explosion of cross-border activism in the 1990s has left the once unassailable oil multinationals more exposed than ever. BP in Columbia, Shell in Nigeria, ExxonMobil in Indonesia, Total in Angola and Unocal in Burma, to name a few, faced serious reputational problems as a result of their association with conflict, human rights violations, and environmental degradation. The reaction in the industry to this new vulnerability was diverse. Smaller, privately held or state-owned companies, as well as those with little downstream exposure, which could not be affected by consumer boycotts, were prepared to shrug it off as long as there were profits to be made. Larger, publicly held companies exposed to both investor and consumer actions, as well as the threat of litigation, responded in a variety of ways, from cosmetic public relations and community outreach to attempts at fundamentally rethinking the way oil companies do business and their relations to the various stakeholders and the environment. At this stage, it remains unclear whether this new awareness of their broader responsibilities is sustainable in the long term, or whether it is a passing fad, a reaction to outside pressure that will subside as soon as the pressure eases (Oliviero and Simmons, 2002). The diversity of responses to public pressure suggests that some companies are prepared to extract oil regardless of the consequences.

The need for a binding multilateral mechanism governing the oil industry and the rights and responsibilities of multinational oil companies seems obvious if tragedies like those of Nigeria are not to be repeated in the future. Yet most companies are reluctant to submit

Box 4.5: Multilateral initiatives

Over the past four years, a number of multilateral initiatives have addressed the role of oil and other extractive industries in underdevelopment, authoritarian rule and conflict. In most cases, these initiatives were a direct consequence of successful campaigning by INGOs and networks. The Voluntary Principles on Security and Human Rights (US Department of State, 2000), signed in December 2000, was initiated by the US Department of State, the British Foreign Office and a number of multinationals domiciled in these two countries. Human Rights Watch and Amnesty International participated in this initiative. But it was persistent campaigning by NGOs against human rights abuses, which they alleged were committed by security forces guarding oil installations, that led to the Voluntary Principles on Security and Human Rights. The document sets standards for security at oil installations, which are compatible with human rights. As such, these principles represent a minimalist approach, combining do-no-harm and voluntarism.

The Extractive Industries Transparency Initiative (EITI, URL) was launched by Britain at the Johannesburg Summit in 2002 with the aim of tackling one of the main sources of the oil curse: the lack of transparency about payments by oil companies to governments, and the misuse of these payments by governments. The initiative aims to address some of the shortcomings of previous arrangements by targeting all companies and by aiming to include mandatory measures. One example of such measures is to demand the disclosure of payments by corporations to governments as part of stock exchange listing procedures and other official filings.

The EITI is a direct consequence of the Publish What You Pay campaign, which was launched by Global Witness and international financier George Soros in 2002. Global Witness is a small London-based group that has taken a lead in investigating the misuse of natural resource revenues by corrupt governments and the role of these resources in fuelling conflict (Global Witness, 1999). Publish What You Pay (URL) calls 'for mandatory disclosure of payments to and transactions with governments by multinational natural resource companies, their subsidiaries and business partners'. It brings together 200 groups from across the globe.

The World Bank, stung by a myriad of campaigns targeting its extensive oil and gas portfolio, launched the Extractive Industries Review (EIR) in 2001, inviting a wide range of experts and stakeholders to discuss the future of the Bank's involvement in such projects. The final report (EIR, 2003) recommends that any future involvement by the World Bank in the oil, gas and coal sectors should be conditional upon putting in place mechanisms that ensure poverty reduction and environmental sustainability. It also calls for a rebalancing of the economic, social and environmental considerations of the Bank's lending. The report, which essentially proposes a moratorium on the Bank's lending in this sector, unleashed a heated debate within the Bank and beyond. The Bank's management has rejected this recommendation and, in August 2004, the board agreed with them, arguing that oil and gas development in developing countries is essental if they are to meet the Millennium Development Goals (IBRD, 2004).

Apart from the initiatives mentioned above, a number of smaller multilateral and unilateral arrangements aim to bring greater transparency and accountability to the use of oil revenues. These include arrangements to monitor the use of Azerbaijan's and Angola's oil revenues, as well as those of Chad and Cameroon. African states associated with New Partnership for Africa's Development (NEPAD) have given similar undertakings.

to anything beyond voluntary arrangements. Even those that have wholeheartedly embraced greater responsibility, sensing a competitive advantage in their approach, are resisting arrangements that would create a more level playing field.

Activists have been divided in their approach to multinational oil companies. Anti-corporate groups, such as CorpWatch and Global Exchange, have been consistent and uncompromising in their pursuit of multinationals. They reject any notion of corporate responsibility as whitewash and set out to expose it as such, not without success. The approach of prominent environmental groups like Greenpeace and Friends of the Earth is not dissimilar, as demonstrated by the Stop Esso campaign (Stop Esso, URL). ExxonMobil has been singled out by activists for its leading role in denying global warming and attempts to derail the Kyoto Protocol on climate change.

Other groups have been more forgiving, at times drawing the ire of CorpWatch and other radical groups.

Conservancy International and other NGOs joined with BP, Shell and Chevron, among other companies, in the Energy Biodiversity Initiative, which was launched in 2002 with the aim of developing technologies to integrate biodiversity concerns into upstream oil development (EBI, URL). A similar approach was adopted by Human Rights Watch and Amnesty International with the Voluntary Principles on Security and Human Rights (see Box 4.5).

Watchdogs like Global Witness and Transparency International have combined the two approaches. They do not shy away from supporting initiatives such as the Extractive Industries Transparency Initiative but keep a watchful eye on corporate transgressions in their financial dealings with corrupt governments.

Positions on globalisation

In previous chapters on the anti-capitalist movement, and finance and trade, we have tried to show how positions on globalisation shape the debates in which global civil society is engaged. The same framework can be applied to the oil debate.

Positions on oil can be mapped between two polar approaches: 'its all about oil' and 'oil has nothing to do with it'. Rejectionists and Regressives tend to take the first position while Supporters and Reformers are more sceptical.

Rejectionists

According to Rejectionists, who espouse the 'it's all about oil' position, there is a direct causal relationship between oil, environmental degradation, uneven development, human rights violations and war. Reverend Desmond Tutu, together with six other Nobel Peace Prize laureates, wrote to World Bank President James D Wolfensohn, urging him to phase out funding for oil and coal projects:

> *War, poverty, climate change, greed, corruption, and ongoing violations of human rights – all of these scourges are all too often linked to the oil and mining industries. (Nobel Laureates, 2004)*

According to this line of thinking, an unholy alliance of multinationals, international finance institutions and Northern governments is perpetuating oil dependence at the expense of the environment and the poor, especially in the South. Thirst for oil is fuelling wars of aggression and Great Game confrontations. One of the main slogans of the 15 February 2003 demonstration against the war in Iraq, the biggest in British history, was 'No Blood for Oil', suggesting that oil was the main motive behind the war.

According to this position, conflicts over oil will intensify because of the growing tension between global dependence on this source of energy and its gradual depletion. In order to quench an insatiable demand for profits and energy, superpowers and their oil companies are pursuing dwindling resources in all corners of the globe through increasingly aggressive methods. At the same time, energy-intensive models of development are drawing more and more developing nations into the fray, either as oil-dependent exporters such as Chad or as major oil importers such as China. Rejectionists argue that this struggle will come to a head in the next five years as oil production peaks while demand continues to spin out of control.

The proponents of the 'it's all about oil' arguments warn that current levels of oil production and consumption are bound to have cataclysmic environmental consequences, such as global warming, even before oil reserves are exhausted. As former British environment minister Michael Meacher wrote recently:

> *If we do not immediately plan to make the switch to renewable energy – faster, and backed by far greater investment than currently envisaged – then civilisation faces the sharpest and perhaps most violent dislocation in recent history. (Meacher, 2004)*

This position is usually espoused by Rejectionists, who, according to a definition we developed in previous Global Civil Society yearbooks (Said and Desai, 2003), are civil society actors who equate globalisation with global capitalism, and reject both. At the heart of the Rejectionist argument is an inherent mistrust of markets, especially when it comes to public goods such as energy and the environment.

The Rejectionists oppose almost any form of oil development, whether it is a project, tanker or pipeline. In an echo of their demands in the areas of finance and trade, they call for 'energy sovereignty' and self-reliance. According to Rejectionists, access to energy is a human right that should be democratised and decentralised. It should be removed from the market to avoid economic forces that lead, inevitably, to injustice and environmental degradation (OilWatch, 2002).

The majority of activists on oil issues, especially environmental and indigenous people's groups that seek to block oil projects, can by classified as Rejectionists.

Table 4.2: Positions on globalisation and oil

	Globalisation is:	Position on globalisation	Position on oil
Supporters	Capitalism minus the state	Should be defended at all cost: the alternative is fascism	Oil has nothing to do with conflict, authoritarianism and state failure; market mechanisms can address oil shortage and global warming
Regressives	Capitalism plus the state	San work only under superpower hegemony	Securing oil supplies is a matter of national interest justifying extreme measures
Isolationists	Capitalism minus the state	Should be reversed – deglobalisation, localisation	Same as Regressives and therefore oil causes conflict, authoritarianism and state failure
Reformers	Capitalism plus transformed state	Should be humanised	Tension due to the anachronism of oil creates conflict – needs to be addressed with global warming through multilateral intervention

The polarisation which followed 9/11 and the war in Iraq meant that many activists have adopted Rejectionist positions.

© JOHN MCDERMOTT/PANOS PICTURES

Supporters

At the other end of the spectrum are those who argue that 'oil has nothing to do with it'. Regardless of the accuracy of the doomsayers' predictions, Supporters believe that market forces are perfectly capably of balancing the demand and supply of energy without recourse to war. If oil indeed becomes scarce, its price will rise, making alternative sources of energy more lucrative and encouraging investments in these areas. As Ahmad Zaki Yamani, the former Saudi oil minister, put it, 'The Stone Age did not end because the world ran out of stones, and the oil age will end long before the world runs out of oil' (Lovins and Lovins, 2002: page xx).

Proponents of this approach either reject doomsday scenarios related to global warming or suggest that environmental damage caused by oil consumption can be mitigated by creating a market where oil consumers can trade the right to pollute. If global warming is an established fact, pollution rights will become so expensive that they significantly depress consumption.

Supporters reject the link between oil, under-development, human rights violations and wars, which they attribute entirely to human factors. They attack those who see a link between oil, underdevelopment and conflict for lack of rigour and improper use of data (Lewis, 1989).

The proponents of 'oil has nothing to do with it' approach are mostly Supporters, people who according to our prior definition equate globalisation with global capitalism and support it. Supporters have unlimited faith in the power of the invisible hand, especially if liberated from human meddling. Therefore, most of their policy prescriptions call for the removal of market-distorting policies, institutions, excessive fuel taxes and economically unjustifiable/premature government investment in oil alternatives. Likewise, they argue against the politicisation of oil and oil companies and their use as instruments for geopolitical and strategic interests. Supporters call for the reduction of transaction costs and creation of new markets to deal in oil externalities and uncertainties: for example, better information on proven reserves, larger strategic reserves and trading in greenhouse emissions (Coon, 2002). Supporters are a minority. They are concentrated in free-market think-tanks, academia and the liberal media. They include such personalities as Yamani and Yergin as well as the Heritage Foundation and The Economist.

Regressives and Reformers

Between the two extremes are the Regressives and the Reformers of our previous definitions. Regressives support a hegemonic, superpower-centred approach to globalisation. Despite their declared faith and commitment to free markets, they are prepared to interfere in their workings to produce a better outcome from a national interest point of view. Reformers believe in globalisation with a human face, democratic global governance and civil society. They openly doubt the ability of markets to deliver optimal outcomes and call for state intervention at national and global levels. In contrast to Regressives, however, they have in mind a transformed state working through multilateral organisations and in cooperation with civil society.

Both go some way towards accepting the notion of an impending crisis, but they differ in its explanation as well as in the emphasis they place on its aspects. Thus, Regressives are more concerned with the oncoming supply shortfall and the increased dependence on Middle East oil, while downplaying the environmental consequences of continued oil consumption. They use this analysis to embrace a more aggressive posture, justifying the accusations levelled against them by the Rejectionists.

> *Energy security must be a priority of US trade and foreign policy. We must look beyond our borders and restore America's credibility with overseas suppliers. (NEP Development Group, 2001)*

Like Supporters, they reject as excessive and market-distorting high fuel taxes and environmental regulation aimed at curbing oil production and consumption at home. By doing so, they implicitly shift the burden from oil consumers to producers. The largest demonstration in British history was organised by Rejectionists to protest the war in Iraq on 15 February 2003. In the autumn of 2000, mass protesters against fuel taxes brought Britain to a virtual standstill. These protestors adopted a Regressive position.

Regressives include conservative and neo-conservative think-tanks and groups, mostly concentrated in rich countries. The American Petroleum Institute and the Global Climate Coalition (see Box 4.4) represent Regressive positions.

Reformers are concerned with the anachronism of oil dependence and the political, economic and environmental dislocations that this continued dependence is likely to generate in the future. Unlike the Regressives, Reformers do not view physical shortage, market distortions and authoritarian Middle Eastern governments as the main source of future oil conflicts. They believe the problem emanates from the disconnection between oil dependence and the new technological and economic paradigm.

For Reformers, scarcity of oil is not a geological fact but rather a function of complex economic, political, technological and human factors.

> *The terms petroleum, crude oil, natural gas and natural gas liquids each have precise scientific definitions. But appending the word resource to any of them creates a term that crosses the boundary between science and social science and includes economics. Many geologists begin to feel uncomfortable in this area between science and social science. (Ahlbrandt and McCabe, 2002)*

Reformers believe that market mechanisms alone are insufficient to encourage more sustainable sources of energy, and that regulation at national and global levels is needed to forestall impending crises and provide a more equitable outcome.

Reformers include many human rights groups such as Human Rights Watch, Amnesty International and other NGOs working with governments and corporations to devise multilateral mechanisms to mitigate the impact of oil developments.

Conclusions

There is a contradiction between post-industrial, information-centred, weightless economies and a world economy still dependent on oil. Oil continues to fuel conflict in a variety of ways, but it is no longer the decisive factor in battle. Territorial conquest and authoritarian rule, once the main methods of securing oil supplies, are much more difficult nowadays.

Activists have played a significant role in ending the reign of oil as the engine of history. They can look at the past decade with pride. Human-induced global warming is now a broadly accepted fact. From Sudan to Colombia, activists have forced oil companies and governments to do the unthinkable – abandon oil development altogether or fundamentally revise projects to take activists' demands into consideration. Oil can no longer be delivered at any cost.

Yet many activists still espouse positions on oil coloured by nineteenth- and twentieth-century approaches. Doomsday prophesies of impending shortage and environmental cataclysm go hand in hand with new Great Game theories and other geopolitical scenarios of world domination through the control of oil supplies.

Oil's continued domination of the world economy is in part a consequence of conscious effort by powerful social forces to retain their privileges. Some multinational oil companies and associated industries have a vested interest in perpetuating the reign of oil, regardless of the mounting environmental, social and political costs. Their allies are politicians who still harbour imperial ambitions based on military power and client regimes. Together, they are trying to keep oil at centre stage using the rhetoric of securing strategic supplies. Yet through their very actions, they are exacerbating conflict and destabilising oil markets.

Activists who insist that 'it's all about oil' may play unwittingly into the hands of their worst enemies by perpetuating their narrative. The question is: can this dynamic lead to deglobalisation by promoting imperial hegemony on one side and nationalist reaction on the other? And can deglobalisation prolong the reign of oil as a major strategic commodity? In other words, can the mutually reinforcing 'it's-all-about-oil' narrative become self-fulfilling?

REFERENCES

Ahlbrandt, Thomas S. and McCabe, Peter J. (2002) 'Global Petroleum Resources: A View to the Future'. *Geotimes*. 7(11): 14–18.

AmazonWatch (2002) 'Newsroom Report: Civil Conflict and Indigenous Peoples in Colombia' (1 March). www.amazonwatch.org/newsroom/view_news.php?id=638

Auty, R. (1990) *Resource Based Industrialization: Sowing the Seeds in Eight Developing Countries*. Oxford: Clarendon Press.

BTC (Baku-Tbilisi-Ceyhan) Campaign (2003) *Environmental and Human Rights Fact Finding Mission, Baku-Tbilisi-Ceyhan Pipeline – Turkey Section*. www.bankwatch.org/issues/oilclima/baku-ceyhan/downloads/ffm_turkey_all_03-03.pdf

Cable, Vincent (2003) 'Saddam's Other Weapon of Mass Destruction: The Potential Economic Fallout from a War in Iraq', Global Dimensions Seminar, 10 February. www.globaldimensions.net

Collier, P. and Höffler, A. (2001) *Greed and Grievance in Civil War*. Washington, DC: World Bank.

Coon, Charli E. (2002) *Side-by-Side Analysis of H.R. 4* (WebMemo #145). Washinton, DC: Heritage Foundation, 16 September. www.heritage.org/Research/EnergyandEnvironment/WM145.cfm

Cost of War (URL) http://costofwar.com (consulted 27 June 2004).

CPA (URL) www.cpa-iraq.org (consulted 27 June 2004).

Earthrights International (URL). www.earthrights.org/unocal/index.shtml (consulted 23 June 2004)

EBI (Energy Biodiversity Initiative) (URL)

EITI (Extractive Industries Transparency Initiative) (URL) www.dfid.gov.uk/News/News/files/eiti_statement.htm (consulted 24 June 2004).

Gelb, A. (1988) *Oil Windfalls: Blessing or Curse?* New York: Oxford University Press.

Global Climate Coalition (URLa) www.globalclimate.org/aboutus.htm (consulted 24 June 2004).

– (URLb) www.globalclimate.org (consulted 24 June 2004)

Table 4.3: Global civil society responses to oil

	Organisation					Activity					Position			
	Individual	NGO/group	Movement/network	Think-tank/academia	Media/website	Inform/educate	Lobby	Mobilise	Serve	Riot/celebrate	Rejectionist	Supportive	Reformer	Regressive
AfricaFiles			●		◐	◐		○	●		◐		●	
AmazonWatch			◐			●	◐	○			◐		●	
American Petroleum Institute		◐		●		●	◐		○			●		◐
Amnesty International		●	◐			◐	●	○					◐	
CEE Bankwatch		◐	●		●	◐	○				◐		●	
Christian Aid		◐				○	●		◐				◐	
Corner House		◐		●		●	◐	○			◐		●	
CorpWatch		◐				●		◐		◐				
EarthRights		◐				●	◐			◐				
EBI (Energy Biodiversity Initiative)			◐			◐	○		●			●	◐	
Economist, The					◐	◐	○		●			◐	●	
Environmental Defence		◐	●			●	◐	○			◐		●	
Extractive Industries Review[a]						●	○		◐				◐	
Financial Times					◐	◐	●					●	◐	
Friends of the Earth		●	◐			○	●	◐			◐			
Global Climate Campaign			◐			●	◐	○				●		◐
Global Exchange		◐			○	●	◐		○	◐				
Global Witness		◐				●	◐				●		◐	
Greenpeace		●	◐			○	●	◐		●	◐		●	
Human Rights Watch		◐				◐	●						◐	
IBLF[b]		◐				●	◐		○			●	◐	
Institute for Policy Studies				◐		◐	●	○			●		◐	
Kurdish Human Rights Project		◐				●	◐	○			◐		●	
MOSOP[c]			◐			○	●	◐		○	◐			
Oil Watch			◐				●	◐			◐			
Open Society Institute		◐				●	◐	○					◐	
Sierra Club		◐				●	◐	○			●		◐	
Transparency International		◐				●	◐		○				◐	
Wall Street Journal				◐	◐	●				●	◐			
Wolfenson, James	◐				○	●		◐				●	◐	
Yamani, Ahmad Zaki	◐				◐	●		●				◐		

a Commission
b International Business Leaders' Forum
c Movement for the Survival of the Ogoni People

◐ Predominant
● Significant
○ To some degree

Global Policy Forum (URL)
www.globalpolicy.org/intljustice/atca/atcaindx.htm
(consulted 23 June 2004).

Global Witness (1999) *A Crude Awakening: The Role of Oil and Banking Industries in Angola's Civil War and the Plunder of State Assets*.
www.globalwitness.org/reports/show.php/en.00016.html

Greenpeace (1998) *Greenpeace Analysis of the Kyoto Protocol* (Greenpeace Briefing Paper). Bonn: UNFCCC Sessions of the subsidiary bodies Bonn, 2–12 June.
http://archive.greenpeace.org/climate/politics/reports/kyoto.pdf

Heritage (URL) www.heritage.org (consulted 27 June 2004).

Ibeanu, Okechukwu (1999) 'Ogoni – Oil, Resource Flow and Conflict', in T. Granfelt (ed.), *Managing the Globalized Environment*. London: Intermediate Technology Publications.

IBRD (2003) *Striking a Better Balance – The World Bank Group and Extractive Industries*: 'The Final Report of the Extractive Industries Review'. Washington, DC: World Bank.

– (2004) 'World Bank Group Board Agrees Way Forward on Extractive Industies Review', News Release, 3 August.

Kaldor, M., Anheier, H. and Glasius, M. (2003) 'Global Civil Society in an Era of Regressive Globalization' in Anheier et al. (eds) *Global Civil Society 2003*, London OUP

Karl, T. L. (1997) *The Paradox of Plenty: Oil Booms and Petro-States*. Berkeley: University of California Press.

Lewis, S. R. J. (1989). 'Primary Exporting Countries', Ch. 29 in Hollis Chenery and T. N. Srinivasan (eds), *Handbook of Development Economics*, ii. Amsterdam: Elsiver.

Lohman, Larry (2001) *Democracy or Carbocracy? Intellectual Corruption and the Future of the Climate Change Debate* (Briefing Paper 24). Sturminister Newton, UK: The Corner House.
www.thecornerhouse.org.uk/pdf/briefing/24carboc.pdf

Lovins, Amory B. and Lovins, L. Hunter (2002) 'Energy Forever', *The American Prospect*, 2 November.
www.prospect.org/print/V13/3/lovins-a.html

Meacher, Michael (2004) 'Plan Now for a World Without Oil', *Financial Times*, 5 January

NEP Development Group (2001) *National Energy Policy: Report of the National Energy Policy Development Group*. Washington, DC: US Government Printing Office.

Nobel Laureates (2004) Letter to James Wolfensohn, 9 February.
www.eireview.info/doc/EIR%20Nobel%20Letter%20-%20New.pdf

Oilwatch (2002) 'Position Paper on Energy Sovereignty', The Eighth Conference of Parties to the Framework Convention on Climate Change, New Delhi.
www.wrm.org.uy/actors/CCC/energy.html

– (2003) Oilwatch declaration. World Social Forum 2003. Security vs. Sovereignty.
www.wrm.org.uy/actors/WSF/oilwatch.html

Oliviero, M. and Simmons, A. (2002) 'Who's Minding the Store? Global Civil Society and Corporate Responsibility', in Marlies Glasius, Mary Kaldor and Helmut Anheier (eds), *Global Civil Society 2002*. Oxford: Oxford University Press.

Publish What You Pay (URL)
www.publishwhatyoupay.org/resources/leaflet.pdf
(consulted 24 June 2004).

Royal Dutch/Shell Group of Companies (1997) *Statement of General Business Principles*. www.fbk.eur.nl/DPT/VG8/ETHICSMANAGEMENT/shell_code.pdf

Sachs, J. and Warner, A. (1997) *Natural Resource Abundance and Economic Growth*. Cambridge, MA: CID, Harvard University.

Said, Y. and Desai, M. 'Trade and Global Civil Society: The Anti-Capitalist Movement Revisited', in Mary Kaldor, Hemlut Anheier and Marlies Glasius (eds), *Global Civil Society 2003*. Oxford: Oxford University Press.

Saro-Wiwa, Ken (1995) Closing Statement to the Military Appointed Tribunal.
http://archive.greenpeace.org/comms/ken/state.html#shell

Schultze, Kirsten (forthcoming) 'The Conflict over Aceh: Struggle for Oil' in Kaldor, Mary and Said, Yahia eds. *New and Old Oil Wars*, London: Routledge

Sengupta, Somini (2004) 'The Making of an African Petro State', *New York Times*, 18 February.

Smith, A. (1776/1937). *An Inquiry into the Nature and Causes of the Wealth of Nations*. New York, Modern Library.

Stop Esso (URL) www.stopesso.org (consulted 24 June 2004).

The Coming Global Oil Crisis (URL) www.oilcrisis.com (consulted 24 June 2004).

Thomas, Mark (2003) 'If a British company proposed to upgrade and relocate Hell to Ethiopia, new Labour ministers would talk of creating jobs and having a constructive dialogue with Satan', *New Statesman*, 14 July.

UNFCCC (United Nations Framework Convention on Climate Change) (2002) *A Guide to the Climate Change Convention and its Kyoto Protocol*. Bonn: Climate Change Secretariat.
http://unfccc.int/resource/guideconvkp-p.pdf

US Department of State (2000) Voluntary Principles on Security and Human Rights.
www.state.gov/www/global/human_rights/001220_fsdrl_principles.html

Weber, M. (1914/1979) *Economy and Society*. Berkeley: University of California Press.

Yergin, Daniel (1991) *The Prize: The Epic Quest for Oil, Money and Power*. New York: Simon & Schuster.

– (2002) 'A Crude View of the Crisis in Iraq', *Washington Post*, 8 December.

– (2004) 'Imagining a $7-a-Gallon Future', *New York Times*, 4 April.

CHAPTER 5

Civil Society, Democracy and Power: Global Connections

Hilary Wainwright

When commentators with very different political views converge in their dismissal of civil society as of little value for democracy, it is worth looking at what lies behind their consensus. Thomas Carothers of the Carnegie Endowment Trust sees the US government as the main hope for democracy, although he is critical of some of its policies (Carothers, 2004). Tariq Ali of *New Left Review* and a leader of the 1960s movement against the US war in Vietnam sees the US presence in Iraq as a disaster for democracy (Ali, 2002). Both writers question the common presumption that support for civil society makes a significant contribution to democracy; indeed, both maintain that such support often defuses opposition and falsely legitimises undemocratic regimes.

The arguments of Carothers and Ali share the premise that support for civil society rarely steps on the toes of those in power, and so at best leads to liberalisation in terms of cultural and social rights but not necessarily to the democratisation of a political regime. In fact, argues Carothers:

> *Support for civil society might help strengthen semi-authoritarian regimes by giving frustrated citizens the impression that important reforms are taking place, thereby bleeding off a certain amount of accumulated internal pressure for change . . .*

He puts it bluntly:

> *It is very possible that outside democracy promoters can work for years helping to . . . nourish civic advocacy, foster greater women's rights, and promote more democratic civic education without contributing to a basic change of regime type. (Carothers, 2003: 11)*

His own proposals for supporting democracy are concentrated on direct aid for a plurality of political parties, elections, rights of political association and other aspects of representative democracy. Tariq Ali's conclusions are similar, though without particular recommendations:

> *NGOs will descend on Iraq like a swarm of locusts . . . Intellectuals and activists of every stripe will be bought off and put to work producing bad pamphlets on subjects of purely academic interest. This has the effect of neutering potential opposition, or to be more precise, of confiscating dissent in order to channel it in a safe direction. Some NGOs do buck the trend and are involved in serious projects, but these are an exception. (Ali, 2003: 03)*

For Ali, the main problem is that civil society is separated from politics (except among religious groups that move in to fill the political vacuum, with undemocratic results). But this weakness in the ability of civil society to influence political power is not inherent in the character of organisations in civil society, as Ali and Carothers tend to imply. I will argue that they are probably right about many of the organisations receiving international funds, mainly American, as do civil society organisations in Iraq. There are good reasons for questioning assumptions of an automatic flow between civil society organisations that are (or claim to be) democratic, and the process of democratising state power. This chapter will explore several of them. I will also contrast the situations where civil society organisations fail to make an impact on political power with contexts in which civil society has been a unique source of power, exercised autonomously from the state, for democratic change. I will ask what conditions make this possible and what role global organisations and networks of civil society have played in the process. Finally, I will return to Iraq and illustrate my argument with references to organisations struggling for democracy that have emerged in civil society independent of, indeed out of resistance to, the occupying powers.

My purpose is not to defend some abstract or universal connection between civil society and democracy. Rather, I start from an analysis of democracy which points to civil society as a *potential* source of power for democracy. I then try to understand through

© SVEN TORFIN/PANOS PICTURES

Democracy is not only about the vote

several examples – some positive, some negative – the conditions under which, and the ways in which, this potential is realised.

Defining democracy

In this discussion of civil society and democracy, I am assuming the root definition of democracy: the people in power; 'demos' meaning 'people' and 'kratos' meaning 'power'. Democracy cannot be equated with particular institutions – free elections, a plurality of parties, for example – important though these institutions might be as a means of achieving the fundamental goal of democracy. There must be a definition of democracy based on principles against which it can be judged how far institutions are meeting the goals for which they were created. Rule by the people rather than an elite, a monarch or an aristocracy implies control of the decisions of the polity by all the people in that polity. Access to decision-making has to be on the basis of equality – anything less would produce rule by an elite. I therefore take popular control and political equality to be the fundamental principles of democracy (Beetham, 1999).

Control will, of course, often be mediated rather than direct but the means of mediation and representation must be assessed in terms of the extent of popular control they afford, along with equality of access to them: how far do nominally democratic institutions enable people to control the decision-making process? The institutions of democracy vary historically and culturally, although clearly some almost have the status of a universal principle: the universal franchise, for instance. There has, however, to be a process of ongoing testing and experiment to discover improved mechanisms for popular control and political equality, which build on the foundation of the franchise. Decades of the vote have taught us that even the most transparent and direct forms of representation can be undermined by undemocratic institutions that flourish beyond the reach of elected representatives: *within* the state, bureaucracy and vested interests; *outside* it, pressure from private business and unaccountable international institutions. These principles keep democracy vigilant, since they make it clear that institutions are more or less democratic; they are never perfectly democratic. The democratic power of civil society becomes relevant at both these points of vigilance: first as a means of resisting tyranny within the state and laying the foundations of political equality and popular control, and second as a means of building democratic counter-power to the anti-democratic sources of power outside the state, which have long been eroding the power of the franchise.

Recent highs and lows of civil society and democracy

The history of civil society's ability to play these roles has been varied. Indeed, in western and eastern Europe, the last 30 years have seen both the high point of this connection and, more recently, its almost complete severance. The high point of connection between civil society and democracy included the emergence in the 1970s in western Europe of sustained social movements rooted in civil society, and in the 1980s in the east the dissident networks building up to the 'Velvet Revolution' of Wenceslas Square in Prague and the fall of the Berlin Wall. A common feature of both these contexts was a conception of civil society not simply as a 'sphere' but as a source of power for democratic change. There are signs that we are seeing a revival – in new, more international forms – of this awareness of civil society as a source of power, including power to bring about political change. The victory in March 2004 of the Socialist Party in Spain, for example, against the pro-Iraq war People's Party of Aznar cannot be explained in terms primarily of party activity or psephological trends. The change of government was also the result of the anti-war movement's ability to mobilise a popular and, at least at that moment, hegemonic countervailing power far beyond the capacities of a traditional political party.

Sources of optimism and their collapse

As for civil society strengthening democracy, the distinctive feature of the movements of the 1970s is that they saw sites for social change beyond the state, for example in family and personal relationships, in culture, at work, with neighbours – wherever there were relationships between people, including internationally, and even spanning relations between humans and the physical environment. The feminist movement is perhaps the classic example, but the same methodology – 'change starts at where you are' – permeated most of the movements, including the peace movement of that period. People refused to reproduce consciously the relationships of injustice or oppression in which they were complicit, including, in the case of women, relations which caused them to suffer, but in which they acquiesced. The actions taken to break out of daily acquiescence, whether by organising collective childcare, or by marching off to surround a missile base, or by refusing to work in unsafe conditions, became an independent base from which they tried to change government or municipal policies: to get public funding for childcare, to force a withdrawal of missiles, or to win legislation to give workers the power to veto unsafe conditions. Civil society at this point had the power to transform the state. In many situations, it used this power to ensure that elected governments implemented their election promises. In these historical examples, civil society directly strengthened democracy in the sense of its core meaning: 'government by the people'. They made the link between the people and their representatives more direct, more actively accountable.

In central and eastern Europe, too, the thinking and the activity of the 1980s networks of dissent went beyond classical understandings (Tocqueville, 1835/1988; Kaldor and Vejvoda, 2002) of the relation between civil society and democracy. In the classic Tocquevillean view, the very existence of civil society – understood basically as social associations and relationships of all kinds independent of the state – was a protection against abuses of state power. In the thinking and language of the 1980s, central and eastern European dissident networks composing 'civil society' moved from this defensive role to something more proactive. Increasingly, the term was used to refer to a diffuse agency for change with an emphasis on self-organisation, mutual support and autonomy, which, not necessarily intentionally, increasingly became a de facto challenge to authority. Under almost total state domination, as Solidarity founder Lech Walensa put it, 'to laugh is to become political'. Jazz clubs in the beer cellars of Prague, informal gatherings in the baths of Budapest and 'networks of sympathy' across central Europe all nurtured political revolt. Such civil society initiatives formed, partly through the repressive reaction of the state, partly through their own persistence and moral integrity, the foundations of a struggle for democracy in eastern Europe. It was an experience which, like the social movements in the West, reinforced the idea of a natural spillover from democratic initiatives in civil society to the democratisation of political power.

Both these experiences of connection between civil society and democracy depended on conditions that were taken for granted at the time and even treated with contempt in the West, but which now have been all but devastated by unregulated market economics. In western Europe, the pressure civil society could apply to bring about democratisation of the state depended on already existing social democratic institutions at national and local levels, and a powerful mainstream party publicly committed to social justice and dependent in part on the support of civil society networks, including trade unions. These social democratic institutions provided connections and wiring – sometimes tangled and blocked – through which currents of democratic energy could flow, from civil society through to political power. In eastern Europe, the idea of civil society as a source of democratic agency depended on loose forms of solidarity, values of mutual support and a subculture of social relationships that rejected both the bureaucratic collectivism of official Communism and the commercial, uncaring individualism encouraged by corporate capitalism.

In western Europe, privatisation, deregulation and a generalised onslaught on state provision has weakened the leverage of civil society on political institutions

In western Europe, privatisation, deregulation and a generalised onslaught on state provision has weakened the leverage of civil society on political institutions. In contexts of thoroughgoing privatisation, the absence or weakness of a partner or means of dialogue within the state has led to a separation, locally, of civil society from political power. This has led to the marginalisation of civil society as a source of power, sometimes paralleled by its elevation as a source of legitimacy for an increasingly undemocratic state. In central and eastern Europe, the rampant character of the market has made it difficult for the velvet revolution networks to sustain themselves as lasting pressures for democracy. Autonomous civil society activity continues, but with little purchase on political power.

New connections, local and global

There are exceptions, often local, that prove the rule. One that is explored in this chapter is the experience of certain Brazilian cities where neo-liberalism has not yet wreaked its havoc. In several cities, a powerful alliance between civil society and a political party elected to municipal office (the Workers' Party or Partido Trabhalidores, PT), with a commitment to sharing power with civil society, was able to develop an impressive and now infectious process of popular participation in the decisions about the city's budget.

Such local initiatives have a new significance now, as a new relationship between civil society and democracy is being forged at the international level. One aspect of this is the rapid learning and creative imitation of local initiatives across the world. We therefore face a contradictory situation, which will be reflected in this chapter. In countries most acutely at the receiving end of the unregulated market – whether by legislation or by military force – the local connections between civil society and democracy have been weakened or have hardly emerged. At the international level, however, there is a new impetus to build organisations of civil society as a force for achieving and deepening democracy or rebuilding it in a radically new context.

The changing international relations of civil society

There has long been a tradition of international action by civil society to win or to defend democracy. Several factors in the past 20 years or so have enhanced and qualitatively changed the power of democratic civil society in this process. First, the global interdependence of nation states is now both far greater than ever and matched by an awareness of this interdependence: to adapt John Donne, 'no regime is an island, sufficient unto itself'. Even the most determinedly autarchic regime now depends on international institutions and relations, especially economic relations, with other countries. North Korea's Kim Il Sung has had to acknowledge this when faced with a major disaster. Sometimes, it is financial markets which provide life-support systems to dictatorial regimes – Iraq's Saddam Hussein and his elite benefited to the end from international financial flows. Sometimes, international investment facilitates oppression of minority peoples like the Ogoni: the Nigerian regime depended on international oil corporations. Sometimes, it is aid and trade: Israel's government would find it difficult to persist with its denial of Palestinian rights if the US refused to provide finance, and if the Europeans used Israel's dependence on their markets to back up their weak opposition to its policies. China too

Box 5.1: Funding democracy

A wide range of international NGOs, government aid agencies, intergovernmental organisations, private philanthropic foundations, and some religiously motivated interest groups are involved in the promotion of democracy. One general pattern is that democratic nation states figure prominently in this field, often as providers of overseas development aid but also as major sources of funding for NGOs that promote democracy. Private philanthropists also fund democratisation, whereas religious NGOs are much less likely to operate explicitly in terms of democracy.

NGOs and the promotion of democracy

The National Endowment for Democracy (NED) in the United States is a non-governmental grant-making body, with organisational independence but significant funding from the US government. Since 1983, it has given grants to projects designed to promote democracy, currently funding programmes in over 85 countries. The diversity of projects funded can be illustrated by listing some recent grant recipients. These include:

- *The Welfare Association for Development of Afghanistan* (WADAN), a body encouraging democratic practices among Maliks (regional traditional leaders), now expanding its project to 20 additional districts. WADAN is to set up regional offices in Kandahar and Kunduz to train 1,000 Maliks in peace-building, conflict resolution, democracy, and women's rights in ten districts each in the southern and northern provinces of the country
- *Poder Ciudadano* in Argentina. Its grant will support local community organisations working to increase citizen participation, civic education and advocacy in six provinces of Argentina.
- *Civic Exchange* in Hong Kong, which will receive a grant to conduct a programme to explore options for the post-2007 political system in Hong Kong
- *The Center for Sustainable Human Development*, Inc. (CESHUD) in Liberia, which is to provide civic education through its community radio station, aiming to stimulate public debate
- *Medienhilfe* in Serbia, which will work to support local independent media by covering the operating costs of nine independent electronic media sources in the so-called Association of Independent Electronic Media (ANEM) network.

The NED also started the World Movement for Democracy, a global network designed to bring 'democrats, including activists, practitioners, academics, policymakers and funders' together to cooperate in the promotion of democracy. Similarly, the Westminster Foundation for Democracy (WFD) in the UK receives significant UK government funding 'to provide assistance in building and strengthening pluralist democratic institutions overseas', which it does mainly by funding projects aimed at building pluralist democratic institutions outside the UK. The total annual value of grants made has recently averaged from £3 million to £4 million. A majority of these grants were for relatively small-scale projects with budgets under £11,000. Projects range from human rights education, training for political parties, political NGOs, journalists and trade unions, and leadership training for women, to equipment for parliaments. Since its creation in 1992, WFD has funded parliamentary strengthening projects in countries and entities as diverse as Armenia, Cuba, Ghana, Kazakhstan, Malawi, the Occupied Territories, Russia and Yemen. Support for NGOs concentrates on advocacy organisations and NGO networks and resource centres in central and eastern Europe and the Commonwealth of Independent States.

States funding democracy

Apart from funding NGOs like NED and WFD, democratic states promote democracy directly by supporting civil society organisations pushing for (or considered a part of) democracy, often though overseas aid programmes. Although donors increasingly focus on institutions and good governance (Öniş and Şenses, 2003), only some major overseas aid donors like the US, Canada and Sweden focus explicitly on promoting democracy. The Swedish International Development Agency (SIDA) in 2002 spent over 15 per cent of its budget (Kr1,726 million, US$233 million) on human rights and democracy. This included contributions for legislation, public administration, support to the mass media, conflict management and peace promotion. In comparison, the US Agency for International Development (USAID) in 2002 spent 13 per cent (US$990.6 million) of its budget on 'democracy and governance/conflict'.

An example of an intergovernmental agency supporting democratisation is the European Union's European Initiative for Democracy and Human Rights (EIDHR), which aims to 'strengthen democratisation, good governance and the rule of law'. The European Commission has recently raised the budget of the EIDHR for 2004 by over €26 million to €132.6 million ($163.2 million).

Private philanthropy and democracy

Many private philanthropic foundations work for democratisation in some way. Among them are the Mott Foundation, the William and Flora Hewlett Foundation, the David and Lucile Packard Foundation, and the Saskawa Peace Foundation. Some are very specific about their support for democratisation, however. The Democracy Coalition Project (DCP), for instance, was started in June 2001 as an initiative of the Open Society Institute (started by the financier George Soros). The DCP conducts research and advocacy relating to democracy promotion policies at the national, regional and global levels. It relies on an international network of civil society organisations, scholars, foreign policy experts and politicians committed to democracy promotion. The formation of the DCP was inspired by the signing by over 100 states of the Warsaw Convention, in which the signatories recognise, among other things, 'the universality of democratic values' creating a 'Community of Democracies'. Similarly, the Starr Foundation, set up by the insurance entrepreneur Cornelius Vander Starr, has concentrated some of its considerable funds, which total approximately US$3.5 billion, in the area of 'public policy on international relations and the promotion of democratic institutions around the world'.

Religious organisations and democracy

Although there is some overlap, religious NGOs are less likely than states or independent human rights groups, for example, to frame their efforts in terms of democratic governance, preferring notions such as 'justice' or 'peace' instead. The otherwise politically engaged Quakers are a good illustration of this tendency. A recent development in this area, however, is the Congress of Democrats from the Islamic World, which convened in Istanbul, Turkey, in April 2004. The initiative was sponsored by a mixture of governmental, intergovernmental and non-governmental bodies: the National Democratic Institute, the United Nations Development Programme, the Turkish Democracy Foundation, and 16 governments and foundations from the US, Europe, and the Middle East. Delegates in the congress included current or former government officials, parliamentarians, and political leaders from ruling and opposition parties who had 'a proven individual record of democratic commitment and achievement'. They met to discuss 'their personal experiences with democratic governance, highlight progress made in many predominately Muslim countries, and address challenges that face the movement toward democratic reform'.

- European Initiative for Democracy and Human Rights (EIDHR) www.europa.eu.int/comm/external_relations/human_rights/doc/com01_252_en.pdf
- Open Society Institute: www.soros.org
- Quakers (American Friends Service Committee): www.afsc.org
- The Congress of Democrats from the Islamic World: www.cdiw.org
- The Democracy Coalition Project: www.demcoalition.org/html/home.html
- The Starr Foundation: http://fdncenter.org/grantmaker/starr/#prog
- Rowntree Charitable Trust: www.jrct.org
- USAID civil society programme: www.usaid.gov/our_work/democracy_and_governance/technical_areas/dg_office/civ.html
- Westminster Foundation for Democracy: www.wfd.org
- World Movement for Democracy: www.wmd.org/information.html

Olaf Corry, University of Copenhagen

Note: *The Guide to Sources of Funding in International Democratic Development*, 2002, compiled by the National Endowment for Democracy Resource Center, contains information on and links to over 100 organisations that provide funding for groups working in the area of international democratic development: www.ned.org/research/funding/democracyfunding.html

© NICK COBBING/PANOS PICTURES

gets away with flagrant abuse of human rights because its Western trading partners turn a blind eye to it. Boycott is not necessarily the most effective tactic; its relevance depends to a significant degree on whether movements for democracy in these countries ask for it, as they did, for example, in South Africa. The intensifying global integration of international markets has increased immeasurably the scope for the kind of international civic action that helped to bring down apartheid in South Africa.

The second related reason for the new impetus towards creating civil society organisations across national boundaries is that many of the main threats to humanity are international in character, leading people to think and act beyond their national borders. The threat of nuclear war, coming from East and West, was one factor that stimulated the birth of an East–West citizens' movement against nuclear war and the institutions of the cold war in the 1980s. The international character of this movement changed the political imagination of a generation across Europe, making international organising and networking as natural as making a banner or writing a leaflet. By the late 1990s, it was issues of economic authoritarianism – the outlawing, for example, of social, environmental or cultural regulation of trade, investment or subsidy – that posed the need for international action. The World Trade Organisation (WTO) provided an international focal point for the struggle for democratic control over these 'economic' machinations.

Third, the threatened damage to the ozone layer and the disastrous consequences of climate change make the world not only a more precarious place but also politically a smaller one – or at least a more cohesive place across which people feel they have no option but to get organised. Finally, new technology has provided not only tools of communication with which civil society can organise itself increasingly easily at a global level, but also tools which can be used – it is not an automatic technical fix – to extend openness, transparency, and the spread of information and debate across national borders and through many cultural and political barriers.

There is one consequence of these changing global circumstances, whose character is now only is now coming into view. My perception of it is probably little more than a tentative hypothesis, namely, that in the past ten years or so, the relations between civil society organisations and movements North and South have become more egalitarian, based more on a sense of a common struggle and a common search for democratic and economically just alternatives. In the past, sympathetic people in the North have related to movements for justice and democracy in the South through solidarity: raising political and financial support, explaining the movements' case to the public, putting pressure on Northern governments, perhaps volunteering to help the Southern struggle directly. Now, for a start, solidarity is increasingly about finding the common points of leverage in the international system through which together we can focus our power: for example, the WTO negotiations over the agreement to open up public services to international corporations. Second, movements in the North are finding themselves increasingly needing to go beyond solidarity and *to learn* from social and political innovations coming from the South for the development of alternatives.

As we shall see later in this chapter, this creates new possibilities for democratic civil society to realise its potential as a source of power to democratise political power. Despite good motives, however, the support of international groups – notably civil society groups in the North for civil society organisations in the South – can sometimes weaken the power of local civil society. This chapter will consider the case of Guatemala immediately after the end of the dictatorship, where the consequences of (mainly) financial support from European organisations for democracy were, to say the least, ambiguous. One reason for the problems was an unequal power relationship between international sources of funds and other supports and local groups. Northern civil society funders insisted on their own criteria and objectives at the expense of precarious local needs and dynamics.

My suggestion is that, although the Guatemalan experience is still common, there is a greater alertness to inequalities of power on the part of organisations in the South (and the East) at the receiving end of Northern and Western support. Second, the connection between international civil society and local democracy is now less one of patronage (from a powerful Northern funding body to a local initiative, as in Guatemala) and more one of local initiatives spreading innovations, building campaigning networks that join together groups from many different countries. Towards the end of this chapter, I assess the significance of the emergence of the World Social Forum (WSF), a self-organised space that aims to nurture this process. The WSF, held for the first time in Pôrto Alegre in 2001, is an extraordinary, perhaps precarious, development in global civil society. It emerged out of movements that challenged (and began to fill) the democratic vacuum surrounding global economic institutions such as the WTO, the IMF and the Round Tables of global corporations. Its fourth 'edition' in 2004 in Mumbai brought together over 130,000 civil society activists. The WSF and the regional, national and local social forums that it has generated aim to create space for global civil society debate and networking, around the conviction that 'another world is possible'. Is it fulfilling its promise? Can it create a means of global self-help in the struggle for democracy everywhere? What is its role in the interconnected struggle against not only political repression but also the authoritarianism of the economic institutions that now dominate the world market?

The democratic force of civil society: a local example

A useful case study to start with is one that shows civil society strengthening popular control and achieving greater political equality, and in so doing reinvigorating corrupt representative institutions. The increasingly well-known, almost emblematic, experience of the participatory budget in Pôrto Alegre, the site of the first three WSFs, though local in origin, has become influential internationally, spreading the principles of civil society as a means of deepening democracy.

While the movements for democracy in central and eastern Europe emphasised the democratic power of civil society through *autonomy from* the state, the Brazilian initiatives illustrate the democratic impact of civil society as a source of power, based on this autonomy, *over* the state. From the late 1980s and early 1990s, when the Brazilian Workers' Party (PT) won electoral victories in significant cities like Pôrto Alegre, the capital of the southern region of Rio Grande Do Sul, Brazilian civic movements and NGOs working closely with the PT pioneered participatory budgeting (PB), a form of municipal government through which democratically organised civil society strengthened popular control over local state institutions. Through a process of direct popular participation in determining the priorities of the city council's budget, and then in monitoring how these priorities were carried out, direct and delegated forms of democracy provided a means of democratic control over the state apparatus, and also corporate investors, which complemented the relatively weak control of elected representatives. An open process of negotiation replaced a more hidden decision-making process, which, though accountable to the mayor, had involved public officials exclusively.

The historical origins of PT are distinctive to Brazil, though international experiences of exile and continent-wide influences, such as liberation theology, have been important. Formative influences on the PT lie in the popular movements: militant trade unions from the industrial hinterland of São Paolo; radical Catholic cells, rural and urban; the landless movement; committed intellectuals and students. The end product, the Partido Trabhalidores, has been uniquely influenced by and dependent on grassroots civil society organisations. In resisting the dictatorship, these organisations created their own kinds of participatory democracy at the same time as they campaigned for liberal democratic rights and the democratic rule of law. These two kinds of democracy have been fundamental to the PT ever since. They are glued together by, among other influences, the cultural egalitarianism of Paulo Freire.

Freire's approach illustrates what has been distinctive about the PT. Known in the West primarily as a theorist of education, he was also a theorist of power, observing the way we imitate traditional patterns of power and reproduce them when we ourselves gain any power. The goal of his approach to education was to break these patterns and so obstruct the reproduction of established power relations. The PT's participatory

© PAUL SMITH/PANOS PICTURES

Some Brazilian citizens share control of their cities' financial planning

methods of government carry through to politics Freire's emphasis on cultural as well as political and economic transformation.

This leads to an unusual modesty for a political party, which could account for the longevity and self-correcting mechanisms of the experiment. Celso Daniel, a founder of the PT and former mayor of Santo Andre, expressed this awareness of the limitations of political office. 'We believed in taking with us into office the principles of democracy from the movements from which we came', he said. 'That meant sharing political power, the management of the city, with the community.' 'Finance is power', declared Daniel. So the first test of sharing power was to open up the process of setting the budget (Wainwright, 2003: 31).

The invention in Pôrto Alegre of what has since become an elaborate, law-governed, transparent process of popular negotiation across neighbourhoods and between participatory and municipal representatives began with a practical problem. When the newly elected PT mayor in 1989 looked at Pôrto Alegre's finances, he found the city virtually bankrupt, with evidence of rampant corruption. Instead of presuming to sort the problem out within the town hall, the PT called a meeting of residents and community organisations in the city. Together, they worked out a system not only for direct popular involvement in setting priorities but also for democratic monitoring of spending. The consequences in terms of democracy were not consciously planned, but what began as a precarious experiment produced a new kind of public institution. In practice, if not yet in theory, elements of a new paradigm of relations between civil society and political democracy came into being. There is a tendency to make an icon of Pôrto Alegre whereas, like any experiment with democracy, it is a messy, uncertain process, now with 15 years' hindsight to learn from its mistakes. Some achievements, however, can be summarised for their wider relevance.

First, over time, it led to the creation of an autonomous, transparent and generally accountable public sphere, which acted as a permanent watchdog over state institutions, supplementing the weaker but formally more legitimate role of elected politicians. This watchdog ensured the effective delivery of the mayoral mandate, in particular the reduction of inequalities of income and access to services (Wainwright, 2003: 66)[1]. Second, it established transparency and accountability over municipal state departments that had become a law, and a little empire, unto themselves, moving into orbit beyond the effective control of elected politicians, who were often preoccupied with their careers. Finally, the combination of a participatory process honed by years of experiment and self-correction, and a representative system shaken into vigilance by this new citizens' watchdog, increased the overall legitimacy of local democracy. This, in turn, increased the city's bargaining power with international organisations such as multinational corporations, the World Bank and the Inter-American Development Bank.

The case of Pôrto Alegre – and of the other Brazilian cities that have followed it, including parts of São Paulo – does not *prove* the democratic impact of civil society. Possibly, this cannot ever be proved in a general way. It does, however, illustrate the strengthening of democracy through the sharing of important decisions, often the outcome of tough negotiation between elected politicians and democratic civil society. The mayor, whose power derives from votes, has the final say, but without the effective participation of civil society, the mayor will not be able to carry through the policies for which he or she was elected. Hence the quality of life in the city will suffer and the mayor might well lose his or her position. Mutual dependence, therefore, underpins the process of negotiation, which needs two preconditions: first, that civil society mobilises sources of popular power (including knowledge) unavailable to the state and lets them speak, and second, that the political representatives of the state listen and act.

The local and global flows of civil society

The Brazilian practice has generated much thinking. A constant stream of would-be participatory municipal representatives, students, journalists and others contact the mayor's office in Pôrto Alegre to arrange a visit or gather information; the city council has set aside cheap apartments especially to house them. There is regular contact with other Latin American movements and parties already experimenting or intending to experiment with similar ideas. In Montevideo, for example, local movements and the radical political coalition, Frente Amplio, have been working on a slightly different model. There is an interesting reversal here of the usual flow of knowledge within international civil society. All too often, technical and intellectual support flows North to South. This time it is South to North. Similarly, the chain of influence is not from global civil society to a local struggle for democracy but from a local innovation – the product of unique historical circumstances – to an increasingly international web of innovative political actors, who then spread different interpretations of the local experiment.

Some of the greatest interest in PB comes from countries in the North struggling to control their public sectors, keep them public, or stop corruption. A French-based network, Democratiser radicalement la démocratie (DRD), was set up in 1998 to spread the practice of participatory budgeting and administration through a process of mutual learning and exchange. Experiments in participatory administration have since spread to 18 countries, partly through the organisation of seminars at the WSF, each attended by several hundred people. Another group, Association of the New Municipality, was set up in 2002 in Italy following a visit by several Italian mayors to Pôrto Alegre. It brings together mayors, NGOs, unions and local social forums to work on the issue of participatory budgets and administration. There is growing interest in central and eastern Europe even as far as Nirilsk, a rich isolated Russian town near the Arctic circle, where a recently elected radical mayor plans to learn from the Pôrto Alegre model.

The most developed application of the idea is in Italy, where municipalities large and small have not only applied similar principles of administration but also passed the ideas on to towns and cities with which they have international connections.

The seaside town of Grottamare illustrates this combination of the local and the ambitiously international. In the mid-1980s, it saw popular resistance to an attempt, driven by a group of international financiers, to turn its harbour into a marina and complex of swimming pools and large hotels, creating a centre for 'global tourism' and relegating the medieval town centre to a residual curiosity. This followed years of neglect by the local Christian Democrat and Socialist political elite.

1 *The statistical evidence backs up this conclusion. Progress towards social equality is far more advanced in Pôrto Alegre than in other cities. Nine thousand families who, 12 years ago, lived in shacks now have regularised brick housing; nearly the whole population (99%) have treated water; the sewerage system serves 86% of the city compared with 46% in 1989. A detailed analysis of the municipal budget after 1989 shows that the lower the average income of the participatory budget region, the greater the volume of public investment per head (CIDADE/PMPA, 2000).*

The 'No' campaign was successful and its leadership – a coalition named Participation and Democracy, made up of people from within parties and outside them – won the municipal elections. After the election, the coalition convened public meetings for every citizen, leading to the creation of self-organised neighbourhood committees that became an independent monitor of, and pressure on, the municipality's ability to enact its promises. Thus began a process of shared decision-making about the content of a new urban plan, whose aim, as far as the tourism of the town was concerned was, in the words of the first radical mayor, Massimo Rossi, 'a tranquil tourism that was about nature, culture and human relationships – not consumerism'. The new administration soon made international contacts. It has been engaged for many years in work with Itiuba, a village in northeast Brazil, with a village in Guinea Bissau and a town in the Ukraine, sending skilled staff from Grottamare both to train local people in hard engineering and other mechanical skills, and to disseminate participatory principles of public administration. Rossi explained how these participatory envoys work not just with the municipalities in these towns but also with grassroots organisations. His account revealed the usually invisible capillaries through which the democratising currents of international civil society can flow (Alegretti, 2004; Wainwright, 2004a).

The ambiguous consequences of support from global civil society: the case of Guatemala

How should groups in other countries relate to local civil society in order to increase democracy? The well-documented case of Guatemala in the 1990s, following the end of 33 years' war between an insurgent army and a dictatorial government, provides an interesting example of the ambiguous impact of international support for local civil society organisations, including the practical consequences of different definitions of democracy (Howell and Pearce, 2001).The idea of civil society was quickly grasped and applied to local circumstances, especially by the urban movements of Guatemala. Political parties had lost credibility during the dictatorship, and activists wanted focal points other than the guerrilla army for their continuing campaigns for democracy, human rights and social justice. The peace negotiations were only a beginning for achieving these goals. The economic and political elite behind the dictatorship remained virtually intact. The guerrilla army was disbanding and turning itself into a political organisation but without any clear vision of its role. The idea of civil society became a vessel into which people poured a mixture of their utopian hopes and pragmatic needs in response to the political moves of the new government. The Indian groups took a particularly functional attitude: 'If the concept is useful and achieves things, they will adopt it superficially, convincing outsiders that their perspectives are more shared than is the case in reality' (Howell and Pearce, 2001: 15).

Donor priorities (targets, monitoring requirements, timetables) often conflicted with the needs of Guatemalan organisations

Outside support first took the form of solidarity organisations during the years of repression and later funding through both private donation and pressure on international agencies. After decades of war and devastation, local resources were minimal; international funders of local organisations therefore had huge strategic leverage, whether or not they used it consciously. One analyst wrote:

> *Virtually all the organisations participating in the Civil Society Assembly [Asambla de al Sociedad Civil, set up 1994 to bring together all the NGO, social movements and other civil society organisations] were dependent on support from private aid agencies. Without this support many alliances (including indigenous, Indian and Mayan organisations) would not have been able to meet, travel and elaborate proposals. (Biekart, 1999: 271)*

International financial and also political support was undoubtedly of huge benefit in providing the space for civil society to grow. There were problems, however. These revolved around tension between donor assumptions and objectives, and the realities of the social and political problems faced by Guatemalan NGOs, social movements and other organisations. Donor priorities (targets, monitoring requirements, timetables) often conflicted with the needs of Guatemalan organisations to develop their agendas, think through their own strategies and debate their differences while cooperating on common causes and reaching out to vulnerable and excluded groups. Civil society groups in the North and the governmental or intergovernmental donors that they influenced thus contributed to a situation in which organisations in Guatemala City moved away from the grassroots contacts with rural society that they had built during the resistance to the dictatorship. As a result, these urban organisations lost an understanding of the social needs and political dynamics of the rural areas[2].

Limitations to the democratic usefulness of outside support existed at several interconnected levels in Guatemala. This has been revealed by extensive interviews with civil society organisations carried out for the United Nations Development Program by Creative Associates International in 1998. It seems the civil society and governmental donors (both multilateral and bilateral) had timetables and methods insensitive to the working methods of many local groups. Local organisations tended to be engaged in multiple activities rather than single projects. Their priorities were changes they could help to bring about. This didn't mesh comfortably with project cycles. Their multiple engagement, whose rhythm was strongly influenced by local developments and understandings, was often more appropriate to the problems they were facing than to a 'project' approach. Because they needed to ensure that the local organisations they funded were accountable for funds, donors imposed their own particular forms of accountability in a way that took little account of the continuing struggle for democracy and development. There was a strong political debate about the appropriate role of donors and civil society organisations. In this debate, donor and civil society organisations, rather than accepting, and working within, local contours of discussion (thus enabling groups to clarify their strategies and build political cohesiveness), influenced debate to accommodate 'projects'. There was also selective funding, which was divisive in circumstances where cooperation was at a premium. Such funding also created pressure for depoliticisation at a moment when people needed the space collectively to rethink their politics in the aftermath of the civil war. Creative Associates International also found significant differences in motivation and understanding between donors and popular organisations. Interestingly, this was particularly true on issues of democracy. The donors tended to stress work that would make existing political institutions more representative with the highly pragmatic idea of 'making democracy work'. For many Guatemalans, however, the problem went deeper: the existing institutions of democracy were seen as reproducing the inequalities (of wealth, social power and political representation) that they had been resisting. They had a deep distrust of these institutions, feeling that the 'advocacy' that the donors were urging them to engage in would have no serious effect or concerned no issues that really mattered. 'Relatively few advocacy efforts', Creative Associates International concluded, 'are related to the most felt needs of the sectors whose interests Civil Society Organisations claim to represent, such as socio-economic demands, access to land, work and basic services such as health, education, housing etc.' (quoted in Howell and Pearce, 2001: 170).

The experience of Guatemala, a country facing extreme inequalities, illustrates the importance of how democracy is defined. The problem was partly the way that international funders implicitly imposed their definition of democracy on local groups in the conditions of their funding. It was also the narrowness of their understanding of democracy. In such conditions of extreme inequality, defining democracy in terms of the real substance of popular control and political equality – rather than just the formal institutional arrangements of a multiparty political system based on free elections and so forth – becomes vital. Genuine popular control and political equality require more than free elections and the rule of law, more even than basic human rights against the authoritarian tendencies that can lurk behind apparently pristine democratic structures. Real democracy demands a political mechanism that can address the poverty that excludes so many from effective participation. The exclusion of the poor majority empties formal structures of any real content, leading to disillusion, disaffection and conditions that favour a return to authoritarian rule.

The dialectic of international contact and the strengthening of local autonomy: women's organisation in China

China is a one-party state struggling to keep control of a country where the day-to-day control mechanisms are no longer functioning as they used to. The rapid introduction of market reforms has created too great a range of social and economic actors for a single

2 *This analysis is based on the work by Howell and Pearce (2001), whose conclusions draw on both their own research and a survey carried out in 1998 by Creative Associates International for the United Nations Development Program, which involved in-depth interviews with members of civil society organisations.*

Participants of the UN Fourth International Conference on Women

organisation, however octopoid its reach, to oversee. The party, however, through the state, retains its ultimate coercive power. Since the economic reforms began in 1978, people have initiated local civil society organisations, planting them in the cracks opened up through the contradictions facing the state. This process was brutally interrupted by the repression of 1989, when these contradictions burst into the open and the state made efforts to regain control. Local organisations are constantly pushing to expand the openings that were then revealed. International financial support has been important in some contexts, for women's organisations for example, but other organisations – like independent unions – have grown independently of Western support. So, in some areas, there is a degree of dependency comparable to Guatemala. Unlike Guatemala, however, China has a strong tradition of, and self-confidence in, getting the best out of the West for local benefits and according to locally determined agendas. Self-definitions are strong: there is explicit concern not to become 'lackies' of outside donors; concern about who is in control – the donors or local organisations – is explicitly debated. This tradition goes back to the modernisation of the late nineteenth and early twentieth centuries, when China's approach was to get what it could from Western technology but use it for local ends.

The Communist Party's attitude to civil society is contradictory, as is the ambivalence of civil society towards political power. On the one hand, the party encourages a certain contained growth of civil society as a political vent for discontent and also as a source of mediation between itself and society. 'Small government, big society' is its latest slogan. Increasingly, too, the party looks to parts of civil society for welfare provision, especially in areas where private markets will not venture. On the other hand, the party is watchful and repressive of any signs of independence and autonomy, such as local groups making wider connections across the country, or taking up issues beyond their own spheres, especially issues of political reform.

A further twist to the relationship between China and the West, and the repercussions for civil society and democracy, is the Chinese government's need to restore its legitimacy – ultimately for trading purposes – with the West, after the brutal suppression of the democracy movements 15 years ago. It was this cynical imperative that led the Chinese government to agree to host the United Nations Fourth International Conference on Women in Beijing in 1995. The process of preparing this event and the event itself were extremely tense, as could be expected from holding a conference about the rights of half the human race in a country where all democratic (including reproductive) rights of women were being suppressed or were seriously under threat. But the end result has been a significant and lasting growth in independent women's organisations in China and more confidence on the part of the All China Women's Federation (ACWF), the organisation that historically has had a monopoly over the organisation of women, to push for greater autonomy from the Communist Party and the state.

State feminism and women's desire for autonomy

State-derived feminism, of which China is a clear case, has both advanced and constrained the position of women (Howell, 2003a). With women accounting for 21 per cent of all deputies in the National People's Congress, China is near the top of the league of female representation in national legislatures. Conversely, there is not a single woman in the Politburo; and when women do make it to leadership positions, it is almost invariably as deputies and with portfolios with a low political status. The driving force behind women's participation in the public world has been the need to mobilise their energies and their labour for the national tasks of reconstruction, land reform, agricultural collectivisation and industrialisation. This has meant challenging many of the traditions and prejudices that lie behind the long historical subordination of women in China. To help achieve this task, when it gained power in 1949, the Communist Party created the ACWF to mediate between women, the party and state.

The public role of Chinese women has waxed and waned according to the policies and needs of the party. There have been moments when the ACWF played a genuinely emancipatory mobilising role, for example in the 1950s, tackling child marriage, polygamy and other patriarchal traditions, and encouraging women to achieve economic independence and also play a more active public role. In the 1960s, however, the ACWF bent to the will of the party and acquiesced in economic policies that reinforced deep-seated prejudices emphasising women's domestic role and the importance of the family. The same swing from responsiveness to the needs and demands of women to responsiveness to the dictates of the party is evident in recent years. In the late 1980s, the ACWF responded to the economic reforms by setting up new departments addressing the changing needs of women, while demanding greater autonomy from the party and more of a role for women to influence government policy (rather than being a transmission belt solely for the traffic of impulses in the other direction, that is, for the party to convey its message to the female population). A delegate at the 1988 ACWF Congress said: 'The ACWF should be able to manage its own affairs, both according to the constitution and in law' (Howell, 1996: 133). One of the Federation's journals, *Zhongguo Funu*, followed up the congress with debates and imaginative proposals. Then came the 1989 clampdown on dissent and democracy and with it the ACWF's demands for autonomy.

By 1993, new profit-conscious economic reforms presented women with a whole new range of problems, especially at work. Managers began to see women as a burden, with their need for maternity leave, their right to equal pay and so on. There were pressures to take away their statutory rights. They began to face higher unemployment. Health and safety standards collapsed. At the same time, the commercialisation of the economy permeated the sphere of sexuality: prostitution became commonplace in the Special Economic Zones, and sexual harassment at work became an increasing problem. This new and more precarious situation for women gave new life, and presented new dilemmas, to the ACWF, which now came under increasing pressure from its members to prioritise the representation to the party of the interests of women in gender-related policy-making. This led to all sorts of initiatives to represent the different interests of women more effectively, to research their new situations, and to support special measures for women facing discrimination in the workplace. From the standpoint of our concern with civil society and democracy, it led some cadres in the women's federation to express openly the desire for greater autonomy from the party. This began soul-searching essentially about whether the ACWF could wrench itself away from the party state – which paid and appointed its officials – and become a part of civil society's efforts to gain democratic control over the state. It was at this moment that the Chinese government agreed to host the UN Fourth International Conference on Women in 1995.

More than the other organisations set up by the party in 1949 to mediate between the state and society, the ACWF appears torn between the needs of its constituency (it is a huge organisation with branches right down to the village level) and loyalty to the party. Contradictions in official Communist Party policy are perhaps most acute in relation to women. In particular, there is an obvious contradiction between the much-vaunted and occasionally practised principle of gender equality and the suppressed, but no doubt subjectively desired corollary, of personal self-determination and autonomy for women. One reason why the Beijing Women's Conference, and in particular the encounter of Chinese women activists with the new 1970s and 1980s wave of feminism, was so significant is that it gave Chinese women access to a language and a stream of thinking that theorised and valued the subjective dimension of women's liberation.

The Beijing Women's Conference made ACWF's contradictory roles particularly acute. Officially, the ACWF was involved in organising the conference to show the world that China cared about women's rights. The ACWF would, and did, gain from the conference in terms of both prestige and resources, but the most dynamic part of the conference was the NGO Forum also hosted by the ACWF, and the drive and creativity for this came from independent women's organisations and NGOs. *Their* intentions included lobbying and protesting around the governmental meeting, and presenting their arguments about women, including within China.

Beijing and feminist cross-fertilisation

As usual, the ACWF spanned its contradictions. On crunch issues, loyalty to the party prevailed, the most important example being the location of the NGO Forum 50 kilometres outside Beijing, but some ACWF cadres were undoubtedly contaminated by a highly infectious international feminism. One aspect of this, as already mentioned, was the language – though severely restricted by translation – of the subjective dimensions of feminist experience. Another was the subsequent spread of independent women's grassroots organisations and NGOs. The idea of both was strange in China. From the first years of the reform period, the late 1970s, numerous professional organisations, chambers of commerce and learned associations had proliferated, but the idea of bottom-up, grassroots organisations was almost unheard of. Since 1989, moreover, all non-state organisations had had to register with the Ministry of Civil Affairs, which forbade associations to be formed on a gender basis.

In the process of organising the NGOs, the ACWF began to realise what it meant to be an NGO. In a sense, NGO status gave coherence to its bridging position between the state and the mass of women, but it moved it towards a lobbying role on behalf of women rather than a transmission belt for the party. This enhanced its legitimacy as a representative of Chinese women's interests in the international arena. But the ACWF's adoption of this term was more to ease international cooperation with other NGOs than to make a statement about ACWF autonomy from the party. However, it is difficult, by definition, for an organisation to be both a responsive NGO and obedient to a party.

After Beijing, the future of women's organisations no longer depended on the swaying loyalties of the ACWF. Perhaps the most important consequence of the conference was the way that it supported and accelerated the emergence of new, more autonomous women's organisations (Howell, 2003b); Chinese women learned lasting lessons and created ongoing networks. The conference also stimulated research into women's policy issues. In many contexts, this would not be seen as particularly political, but, in a modest way, the plethora of research projects that developed in the wake of the Beijing Women's Conference provided the beginning of a significant challenge to the Communist Party's monopoly on policy. These developments have a significance of their own but they also make it difficult for the ACWF to swing back to the party when under pressure. The ACWF has a cooperative but sometimes tense relationship with independent women's organisations within China that need the ACWF's support to exist in the face of hostile regulations. Interestingly, the feminist cross-fertilisation that occurred both in preparation for Beijing and at the conference also stimulated movements for democracy in other countries. For example, women from Sierra Leone created a network to prepare for Beijing and then played a leading role in the successful campaign to end to military rule.

Stronger women's organisations: what relevance for democracy?

What these developments within civil society – the wrenching of a quasi-state organisation towards greater accountability to civil society – mean for democracy is uncertain. A pessimistic view is that the Chinese government has learned how to play the position of Chinese women as a political card in its international relations, especially with the US. And with the cooperation of ACWF it puts the debate about women into a nationalist perspective, comparing the position of Chinese women with US women, rather than seeking to understand and address gender oppression in China. This would amount to a corporatist relationship between state and civil society, in which a civil society elite (mainly the ACWF and groups they managed to co-opt) influence government policy; but there is no wider participation and no strongly independent public sphere.

Another scenario would be the growth of women's groups at a local level but isolated from each other (there is a prohibition on regional and national organisation across associations) with negligible wider political impact. Certain factors favour this, especially when the position of women's groups is compared with more radical sections of the labour movement, which have been forced to go underground. The party tends to consider women's issues less important than labour issues and the development of autonomous women's initiatives is therefore seen as less threatening. This means that women's organisations can grow stronger unnoticed but that reaction to women's initiatives is less political, even though these initiatives have long-term implications for the power of the party. Perhaps, as a result, women's groups are less conscious of the wider repercussions of their activities. Women's organisations tend not to link their concerns with wider issues of democratic reform, something which labour organisations invariably tend to do. Independent labour organisations appear *anti*-governmental, women's organisations appear *non*-governmental. Some feminists, however, do recognise the link between their work and political reform; as one put it, 'The future of women's organisations is linked to the political democratic process. It depends on political reform. Only then can women's organisations develop. If political reform is limited, then women's organisations cannot develop more' (Howell, 2000: 374).

This leads to a third possible outcome of the process begun in Beijing, in which women's organisations pursue not only their particular campaigns and projects but also, away from the contemptuous eye of the party, develop informal links with each other across issues and regions, and where possible with other social networks, challenging from below the party's 'overview'. This would lead to direct challenges over issues of democracy, but women's organisations, precisely because of the party's male chauvinism, could develop a popular base for democratic rights before the point of confrontation arrives. The international networks of these women's organisations will help protect this process through China's present sensitivity about its international image. Campaigns for democracy that flow from the struggles of women are on particularly high moral ground in such circumstances, so women's organisations are likely to be in a position to develop programmes for political reform flowing directly from their needs as women. This could prepare the path for other movements whose demands are seen by the Chinese government as so threatening that they are denied the opportunity to make the wider connections that would give them some protection.

The World Social Forum: a catalyst for democratic change?

The World Social Forum (WSF) and the social forums born from it – across continents, nations and cities and around a variety of themes – is in one sense no more than a frame for developments in progressive civil society across the world, which are already under way. These include the sometimes unacknowledged, and constantly under relationships of progressive civil society to political power. The social forum process has helped intensify the growth of plural networks of international actors. In its charter, the WSF conceives itself as a 'space' – it makes no claims to represent anyone and does not seek to come to agreements collectively, as a single body. It is a space, however, that has facilitated common action by many of those who use it. Since no human space is ever stable, the shape and character of the forums is permanently contested and changed.

The political context for the momentum behind the formation of the WSF is that the mass of people, especially in the South, has for two decades suffered the battering of unregulated market forces

The political context for the momentum behind the formation of the WSF is that the mass of people, especially in the South, has for two decades suffered the battering of unregulated market forces, and found that the means of finding solutions offered to them by existing, supposedly democratic, political systems are a dead end. In response, a whole variety of new movements, groupings, alliances and initiatives for social justice and democracy emerged, with an increasing need to converge without losing their autonomy and identity. The WSF, and indeed social forums generally, provided an open-ended opportunity to do this. Their potential was reinforced by the initial symbolism of being hosted by the participatory local government of Pôrto Alegre, itself an actor, as we have seen, in an alternative experiment in democracy that stimulates possibilities well beyond the imagination of the traditional left.

The WSF and the democratic power of civil society

From the point of view of civil society's relationship to democracy, the WSF and the international connecting and campaigning that it has helped to stimulate raise four distinct issues. First, the WSF has strengthened the transformative power of civil society. Second, this power is being asserted in order to call governments to account for their acquiescence in the international treaties and

Box 5.2: E-democracy

E-democracy does not simply mean more effective engagement of citizens in the political process. There are as many definitions of e-democracy as there are definitions of traditional democracy, and many more varieties in its application and real-world experiences. Definitions tend to stress the potential of information and communications technologies in a broader democratic process at local, regional, national and increasingly at global levels, in which people interact, deliberate, make decisions and conduct elections. But can e-democracy simply be defined as the use of information and communication technologies (ICTs) by stakeholders in the democratic process?

There is no doubt that ICTs are changing the way people interact, think, communicate, live and ultimately, how they wish to be governed. Some scholars (see Riley and Riley, 2003) have speculated about the potential for the Internet to change the meaning of democracy and create new forms of participation that cannot be envisaged at this time, given the nascent nature of the e-democracy movement. Yet how is, or could, e-democracy be different from 'conventional' or classic notions of democracy, and how will it change the nature of traditional democracy? In a report for the UN's *World Public Sector Report*, Pippa Norris outlines the effects of 'e-governance' on classic theories of democracy:

> *By strengthening government transparency, theories of representative democracies stress that e-governance could improve accountability via the electoral process, allowing citizens to become more informed so that they could evaluate the collective record of the government, the work of particular elected representatives, the contents of parliamentary debates, and the alternative policy proposals of the parties and candidates standing for office. And by facilitating new forms of interaction between citizens and the state, proponents of direct democracy hope that e-governance could channel citizens' voices and priorities more effectively into the public policymaking process. (Norris, 2003: 4)*

Although e-democracy has the potential to make government more effective and more efficient, does it have the potential to engage actively those who would not or cannot participate in the political process through traditional means? A look at current efforts and examples of e-democracy is instructive.

Minnesota E-Democracy is a non-partisan citizen-based organisation with a mission to improve participation in democracy in the state through information networks, in particular the Internet.

> *Minnesota E-Democracy was established in 1994 and created the world's first election-oriented web site. We sponsor election year online partnerships to promote citizen access to election information and interaction. We are known for hosting online candidate debates. In 2002 we launched MyBallot.net, a popular service that allows you to look up who is on your ballot and your polling place location. (www.e-democracy.org)**

Austria is a European leader in the promotion of e-democracy, developing a secure Internet voting system, using national ID cards, which were first tested in May 2003. Among the aims of this e-government initiative is an increase in voter participation among key segments of the population, including professional bodies and chambers of commerce and Austrians living abroad (www.e-voting.at)*.

In Scotland, the Scottish Parliament, established in 1998/9, has developed online petitioning.

> *The Scottish Parliament wished to better support the electronic participation agenda of the Parliament. Therefore they established an e-petitioning system to fit into the normal business of the Public Petitions Committee of the Parliament. The Pubic Petitions Committee website is at www.scottish.parliament.uk/petitions. The e-petitioner tool has the functionality to create petitions; to view/sign petitions; to add background information, to join an integrated discussion forum; and to submit petitions. (Macintosh, 2003: 18)*

The private sector, too, is exploiting the Internet to offer public participation and consultation services to other businesses, the public sector and non-profit sector. Dialogue by Design, a British company, has provided online consultation services for a range of clients, including the Energy Savings Trust, London's Metropolitan Police and Britain's Department of Trade and Industry.

*Dialogue by Design's mission is to help people understand each other better through effective engagement and participation – especially around controversial or complex issues such as sustainable development, social responsibility, human rights, the environment, planning and development. We believe that the Internet is an exceptional tool for expanding dialogue around such issues, and we want to see its potential fully realised. We believe that new technology, well used, can enhance participation and engagement processes – but never replace the need for direct contact between people. (www.dialoguebydesign.net)**

How effective are these various initiatives in encouraging public participation in democratic processes? Based on survey and country case studies, the OECD (2003) has identified a number of key factors that can make online engagement more effective:

1. *Timing*: most examples of online engagement are to be found at the agenda-setting stage of the policy cycle
2. *Tailoring*: a wide range of public bodies are now exploring the use of new ICTs to engage citizens in policy-making; from local governments, to national governments and parliaments as well as those operating at the intergovernmental or international level (for example, the European Commission)
3. *Integration*: experience to date highlights the importance of ensuring the integration of online and traditional methods for citizen engagement in policy-making.

Apart from the question of effectiveness, there are many other issues surrounding e-democracy that require further development. These include:

- The digital divide: how to ensure that e-democracy benefits everyone, not only those people with the technology infrastructure and access
- Two-way flow: how to ensure that e-democracy creates a dialogue between government and citizens, and is not just a one-way channel of communication
- How to ensure that ICTs are not used only for streamlining government bureaucracy
- How to ensure that e-democracy does not create too much 'noise' from citizens, which makes the government less effective.

Useful websites and resources

- The Commonwealth Centre for Electronic Governance: www.electronicgov.net
- Oxford Internet Institute: www.oii.ox.ac.uk
- International Teledemocracy Centre: itc.napier.ac.uk
- Community Informatics Research & Applications Unit: www.cira.org.uk
- IST e-democracy cluster: www.cordis.lu/united_kingdom
- Centre for Democracy and Technology: www.cdt.org
- Multimedia Victoria: www.mmv.vic.gov.au
- National Center for Digital Government: www.ksg.harvard.edu/digitalcenter
- Publicus.net: www.publicus.net
- UK online: www.ukonline.gov.uk
- Office of the e-envoy: www.e-envoy.gov.uk
- European Commission – Your Voice: //europa.eu.int/yourvoice
- IPM: Interactive Policy Making: ipmmarkt.homestead.com
- Commonwealth Centre for Electronic Governance: www.electronicgov.net/
- E-government bulletin: www.headstar.com/egb
- Evaluating Practices and Validating Technologies in E-Democracy (EVE): www.eve.cnrs.fr
- Electronic Democracy European Network: www.edentool.org

Marcus Lam, Center for Civil Society, UCLA

*Websites consulted on 14 July 2004

© JILL TIMMS

Demonstrators at the WSF in Mumbai

deals of free market economics, and their support for US military and political ambitions in the Middle East. Third, these developments are producing a radical, open-ended shift in the relations between civil society and political parties. And fourth, *within* the WSF and the social forums, forms of organisation are being invented to fulfil the forum's aim of facilitating a plural horizontal network of active campaigns. Many questions arise about the sustainability of this process: questions about the obstacles and legacies of more traditional, vertical traditions of the left that these innovations come up against; and questions about whether the WSF process has the depth and resilience to overcome these conflicts and tensions of emphasis and understanding (Corrêa Leite, 2004)

On the first issue of strengthening the transformative power of civil society, the social forum process has strengthened the power of civil society to bring about democratic change, in several ways. First, the forum has progressed from a predominantly Latin American affair, appealing mainly to the organised trade unions, landless movements and progressive intellectuals, to becoming a genuinely open and near-global public space for resistance and alternatives to the neo-liberal world order. The result is that it has given otherwise isolated groups – young people, unemployed, precarious workers, Dalits (the 'untouchables' in the Indian caste system), abandoned rural and urban communities – a boost in collective self-confidence and experience of being part of a wide and potentially powerful movement. Just as the encounter of Chinese women with Western feminism gave independent Chinese women's organisations access to a new language and stream of thinking about self-determination, autonomy and self-organised agency, so encounters within the WSF have enabled traditionally marginalised groups that lack obvious strategic power to move from a consciousness of injustice and oppression to an awareness of feasible connections and directions through which they can achieve change.

While extending the reach of radical civil society, the meetings of the WSF and the process of working together to prepare for them have also strengthened the cohesiveness and strategic thinking of international campaigns and action-oriented research. Although after four annual forums there is a wariness of being or becoming a 'talk shop', there is no doubt the forums have stimulated the growth and spread of a huge variety of campaigning, cultural, solidarity and other networks – including networks of groups working on practical alternatives in, for example, production and agriculture, or public administration. The extraordinary show of organised and politically disenfranchised public opinion seen in the anti-war demonstrations of 15 February 2003 is one sign of the increase in the international cohesiveness and density of progressive civil society. The date was suggested at the European Social Forum in Florence, echoed through innumerable networks, reinforced and spread globally at the third WSF in Pôrto Alegre in January 2003, and on 15 February became a symbol of 'the second superpower', which the first power, the US government, ignores at its peril.

Behind the scenes of these dramatic mobilisations, the No US Bases Campaign provides a good example of the WSF helping to initiate all kinds of sustained cross-border coordinated action. These bases are the points at which the US government becomes physically present across the world, so providing a focal point for calling it and its allies to account. The campaign draws strength from a long tradition of international peace movement collaboration, as well as established local campaigns of base-affected communities. This mixture of local campaigning experience and international networking is crucial to the campaign's success. In particular, the work of creating a global network has been facilitated (not led) by radical

NGOs with extensive experience in this area. The WSF was treated as an important part of a wider process rather than an end in itself. The No US Bases Campaign was the product of two strategic international peace conferences held in May 2003: the Hemispheric Encounter against Militarisation in Chiapas, Mexico, and the Jakarta Peace Consensus in Indonesia. An open coordinating group and email list were established after the Jakarta Conference, and related meetings were held in Cancun and Paris (Reyes and Bouteldja, 2004). This offers a valuable lesson in how the WSF can be used in conjunction with other campaigns and international encounters of the global justice and anti-war movement. Although a thorough mapping of the actions that flow from a meeting of the WSF or another social forum has yet to emerge, this kind of development is central to the potential of the WSF as a new organisational form through which to realise the transformative potential of civil society.

Opening up the political institutions

Where does this development of civic power lead in terms of democracy, or lack of it, in political institutions? This touches on an underlying tension in the 'alter-globalisation' movement between, on the one hand, developing bases of power – including power to organise the means of daily life autonomous from the state, Zapatista-style – and, on the other, directly calling to account politicians and governments or seeking representation, albeit on different terms, within the political system. The WSF process feeds into both approaches and combinations of them.

The impact of the WSF process is easiest to track in relation to transparency – confronting and trying to open up political institutions. Consider the issue of trade and the needs and demands of the economically weaker countries in the South, which was a major motivating factor in the early networks that converged partly through the WSF. A number of very significant NGOs in the South have been working for many years on issues of justice and democracy in trade relations between North and South. Usually, they are both research organisations and, to differing degrees, organisations of popular education with strong connections to mass organisations – trade unions, peasants, social movements of women, young people and so on. They have an ethos of collaboration with these movements, an attentiveness to their needs and a shrewd sense of politics and issues of power. This makes them different from conventional NGOs, which may have good intentions but do not strive for an egalitarian relationship with grassroots organisations and can be naive about power relations. In different ways, all these radical NGOs, along with other organisations, have been campaigning for alternative trade policies to the patterns of trade, which now perpetuate North–South inequalities. This is an important issue of democracy because whether or not there is a market for the products of developing countries is a matter of subsistence or starvation to millions of people. It is also an issue of self-determination: in many areas, people are struggling, through cooperatives, fair trade networks and socially driven financial institutions, to create sustainable and socially just economic relations. They need trade policies that prioritise social equity and environmental sustainability, and this requires, at some point, governmental – or rather inter-governmental – action. And trade is something on which governments, through negotiation, can act – although how governments act is usually decided in secret without even the minimum of accountability to elected parliaments. This was certainly the case in the early years of the WTO and, before that, the General Agreement on Tariffs and Trade (GATT).

RIP: international financial institutions

The achievement of campaigns like Our World is Not for Sale and of the NGOs and movements campaigning through the WSF is that there are now several Southern governments that have been forced to make themselves to some degree accountable to progressive civil society, regarding their negotiations on trade and at the WTO. South Africa has had to move beyond the corporatism of the National Economic Development Labour and Agriculture Council, through which the ANC government negotiated with the unions and business. It has now established a regular consultative council, which precedes meetings of the WTO, to discuss the approach of the South African delegation with a wider constituency of social movements, involving women, young people and other groups not organised through the traditional, national and 'vertical' structures.

Increasingly, African governments have had to admit that, if they want to achieve anything in their negotiations with the US and Europe, they need organised civil society. They need its knowledge of the complexity of the trade agreements (which committed NGOs have researched from every angle); they need links with powerful lobbying NGOs based in Geneva; and they need the campaigning strength that NGOs and social and trade union movements can trigger through their alliances in Europe and the US, aided by the regular meetings of the WSF and other social forums. Recognition of this has meant that, for example, the intergovernmental South and East African Trade Information and Negotiation International asks to meet regularly with radical and independent civil society organisations – not just 'tame' NGOs – to prepare its bargaining positions. This kind of alliance has helped shift the balance of power, slightly – it is important not to exaggerate – towards the South. For instance, the EU and US had to concede in 2002 a long-standing demand from Southern governments for 'special and differential treatment for weaker developing countries'. At the Cancun meeting of the WTO in 2003, an alliance of Southern countries – including South Africa, Kenya, South Korea and Brazil, where there is strong pressure from social movements – blocked the agenda of the US and the EU on agriculture and the privatisation of public services. These are advances for democracy since wider participation has meant both a move towards increased political equality and greater popular control than previously. The ability of elected politicians, for example those of the ANC and other African political parties, to respond to the needs of the people and resist the pressures of the US and the corporate lobby, has been enhanced by these developments.

A further way in which the WSF process has made space for civil society to affect political democracy is as host. In India, the process of organising the forum in Mumbai under the malevolent eye of the chauvinist neo-liberal Bharatiya Janata Party (BJP) had a significant impact, both drawing the attention of the international left and liberal press to the present realities of poverty, fundamentalism and the BJP, and bringing international attention to the struggles of the Indian dispossessed, especially the Dalits. Furthermore, the WSF affected the Indian left: the significant parties to the left of the amorphous Congress Party, the Communist Party of India (CPI) and the Communist Party of India (Marxist) (CPM), were still largely unrepentant of their Stalinist traditions and tended to treat 'movements' as 'their' mass fronts. The necessity of making a political success of the Mumbai WSF brought them closer to Indian social movements and to a respect for the autonomy of these movements. Conversely, the Indian forum persuaded social movements to reconsider the importance of political parties. No general perspective was agreed to guide further cooperation, but the experience of close collaboration strengthened the influence of anti-Stalinist, radically democratic forces of socialist feminism and green politics on the wider left. 'In retrospect', concluded left writer and activist Achin Vanaik, 'Mumbai 2004 might well be identified as the first major collective warning of the shape of things to come' (Vanaik, 2004). The elections in India several months later bore out the truth of this remark more dramatically than Vanaik could have imagined, not because Mumbai had any causal connection to the surprise defeat of the BJP but because Mumbai was an *early sign* of growing anger, self-confidence and self-organisation of the Dalits, whose high turn-out at the election was decisive for the victory of the Congress Party.

The WSF's respect for diversity and plurality is based on a recognition of the fact that these struggles and movements are a source of creativity, insights and power for change

Political parties and civil society: rethinking the relationship

This brings us to the third way in which the WSF influences and throws into relief changing relations between radical civil society and left political parties.

This is a vital issue because the relationship between civil society and democracy hinges on the many different connections between electoral and participatory (not necessarily direct) forms of democracy. Political parties are – in ways yet to be theorised – a vital mediating link between the two levels of democracy.

The emphasis in the WSF is on civil society and its autonomy from political parties and the state. Formally, political parties and state bodies are excluded, though there are signs that they are forming a generally supportive but uneasy relationship with the forum. The PT, as we have seen, provides support through its position in the government of Pôrto Alegre. The Italian Partito Rifondazione Comunista, or its members, played a vital role in organising the European Social Forum in Florence. Similarly, the Indian Communist Party was central to the Coordinating Committee for Mumbai. Indian anti-dam campaigner, Medha Patkar, described the Mumbai WSF's relationship to electoral politics thus:

> *Electoral politicians are not untouchables here, but the WSF is really an expression of people power and non-electoral politics. Non-electoral politicians need to build their strength to challenge elected politicians. Those representing an alternative view of development need to realise the commonality of their ideologies and strategies. (Quoted in Wainwright, 2004b: 32)*

In this way, social forums put into practice the assertion of the women's and ethnic minorities' movements of the 1970s that movements of the oppressed and marginalised need autonomy to develop and identify their own needs, identities and sources of power. Now, as in the 1970s, these movements have a sense not just of particular injustices but also of a need for a wider alternative. The movements that participate in the social forums see themselves as political in the sense of having a full vision of the changes they would like to see, and a comprehensive critique of society as it is. Implicitly and explicitly they challenge the monopoly of the power to achieve change that left political parties have historically presumed is theirs. What has become clear in recent years is that even strong, mass electoral parties cannot adequately defend popular control and political equality against corporate economic power, military apparatuses or bureaucratic state institutions. Movements have grown up in civil society to exert that democratic power precisely where the elected parties failed. The WSF is testimony to a strong desire on the part of radical movements and networks to connect with each other. It is a search for new ways of connecting the universal and the particular, a function which, in the past, belonged to the party. In the traditional notion of the party, the particular became subsumed in the universal: the party programme. The WSF's respect for diversity and plurality is based on a recognition of the fact that these struggles and movements are a source of creativity, insights and power for change. A respect for movements' autonomy at the same time as facilitating their interconnections is fundamental to the WSF.

Autonomy, however, can be the basis of new relationships, and there are tentative signs that this is the case for social movements, and new and old political parties of the left. The experience of the anti-war movement has led to a new self-confidence to act in electoral politics on terms set by radical civil society. We have referred already to the significance of the Spanish elections. In the US, there is a symbolic phenomenon of the League of Pissed Off Voters: young people who are organising support for US Democratic Party presidential candidate, John Kerry, in the swing states, but on their own terms. There are signs, too, across the left that political parties, or significant groups within political parties, are prepared to move beyond the instrumental approach to civil society (the mentality of asking how the party can control it, hegemonise it, lead it) to a recognition of civil society's autonomous sources of power and, as a corollary, an understanding of the position of the party as one actor among many in the process of radical transformation. The WSF and other social forums reflect this development with an increasing number of open debates about the role and relevance of political parties. It retains its determination to grow as an autonomous space, however, and any attempt by political parties to dominate or manipulate its processes is met with stubborn resistance.

Finally, how democratic is the space of the WSF itself? The forum is not a new form of political agency; its founders and those involved in its International Council are consciously determined not to be drawn in that direction. In the vision of WSF founders like the Brazilian radical Catholic, Chico Whitaker, it is 'a laboratory', 'a factory of ideas' or 'an incubator from which new initiatives aiming at the construction of another world can emerge' (Whitaker, 2004: 113). It does not aim to produce common declarations or agreed actions; rather, it nurtures and creates the conditions for many, and increasingly interconnected, actions. Therefore, the democratic principles within it must favour such nurturing.

Like any emergent organisational form, the WSF displays the characteristics of old forms – new approaches struggle with the conservative, inward-looking, self-important habits of the political traditions from whence people come. The WSF and its committees are not meant to be loci of power, yet any participant in the meetings that organise forums can observe intense power struggles over the number, content, length and speakers chosen for the moments in the forum that are seen as most publicly setting the agenda

A creative and influential search is under way into how to dissolve those power centres, rather like the way a massage works on a knot, seeking to get the blood and muscles working across the body. Since the first forum, there has been an uneven move towards the Forum Committees (the International Council and the Organising Committees for different forums) playing more of a role in facilitating consultation processes along cross-national and cross-issue lines, rather than being decision-makers on the content of the agenda. In 2004, this has moved in a radical direction, with the Methodology and Programme Commission (created by the International Council) setting out to create the whole programme through a process of electronic communications, followed by face-to-face discussion between organisations grouped around common 'axes', or areas of concern. This process is more democratic, practising the participatory democracy preached by the WSF Charter. It links organisations to one another, helping the WSF to facilitate '. . . the formulation of alternatives and the construction of common actions'. If it works, it will be achieving a lot more than being a more or less democratically organised mass event; it will be taking practical steps towards solutions to age-old dilemmas about how to achieve effective common action with a diversity of actors; how to create a framework for debate and the development of ideas while meeting the needs of those engaged in action; and how to develop strategy and visions rooted in the experience of those seeking to create new sources of power.

The WSF could be a source of principles for linking universal visions to the convergence or collaboration of particular struggles and campaigns. Idealistic, I'm aware. The proof will be in the practice, both at the next WSF in Pôrto Alegre and on the ground in campaigns across the world.

Concluding comments

If by 'global civil society' we mean non-state organisations that operate across borders, there is no inherent connection between global civil society and democracy. As in Guatemala, civil society organisations can exist in a sphere of their own: meeting Western funders' capacity-building targets but having no roots among the poor and those who have a vested interest in challenging unaccountable power (Howell and Pearce, 2001; Edwards, 2004).

As the Chinese Communist Party intends with women's organisations, and British New Labour with community organisations, well-respected groups in civil society can perform practical functions – running daily welfare services, for example – on terms set by central government without any wider repercussions. In such situations, civil society accepts a contained space, within welfare and within the community, without questioning the wider political framework. Civil society organising can be an escape, playing micro-democracy while the wider democratic institutions burn. In many parts of the US, people spend an admirable amount of time on neighbourhood democracy but, because it is impossible for them to influence federal politics without millions of dollars and they are not part of a powerful national movement, none of this democratic impetus filters upwards, or brings the powerful federal and global institutions downwards. Again, 'tame' civil society organisations, lacking real autonomy, can create an illusion of democracy. There is no doubt, as Ali and Carothers imply, that this has been *part* of the reality in Iraq, where the US-chosen Iraqi Governing Council funded 'civil society' groups to 'promote democracy' at the same time as it cancelled and overrode elections for university posts and city mayors that threatened results that did not please Paul Bremer, administrator of the Coalition Provisional Authority, and the Pentagon.

But this is not the whole story of civil society and democracy. Civil society, however messy and experimental, has always been a necessary precondition for democracy. For democracy to exist, in the sense of movement towards political equity and popular control, there has to be challenging, critical engagement, from autonomous popular bases of power, with the political process. Nowadays, in a globalised world, such critical engagement often seeks and receives empowerment through horizontal cross-border links.

Participatory public administration, whether in Brazil or Italy, in which the power of elected politicians is genuinely augmented by participation, is one example of a source of power to deepen democracy that is rooted in civil society. In participatory budgeting, for example, a public sphere of organised civil society helps, and challenges, elected politicians to achieve popular control over state institutions and increases public bargaining power over the private market. The cross-fertilisation of ideas of self-emancipation to a social group with a strong sense of dignity and equal rights, but a weak sense of its own agency, is potentially another illustration, as we saw with women in China. Such cross-fertilisation may encourage women to use their rights in a self-determining manner. The problem with civil society in Guatemala, influenced by Western donors (sometimes intentionally, sometimes unintentionally), was that it developed no autonomous sources of popular power to challenge the country's economic elite. The potential and need were there, especially among the rural poor and the indigenous people, but the energies of the NGOs and other urban civil society organisations were elsewhere, diverted on to agendas set by international donors.

The WSF illustrates the democratic potential – not yet fully realised – of a horizontal net of connections interlinking civil society across borders. It facilitates a multi-driven process whereby progressive civil society simultaneously maps and resists unaccountable, authoritarian power structures. The established institutions of power may be unified but the resistance comes from many different angles, depending on where the democratic leverage lies. Thus, a multinational corporation exploiting women workers down the chain of sub-contracting is a unified power structure, and is difficult for any conventional political power structure to control, even if it had the will to do so. But such companies can be and are being challenged at many points: in sweatshops and in private homes, where women workers, with the help of women in the community, have organised themselves; and at the supermarket checkout by consumers exposing the companies' policies and using the companies' need for a morally clean brand.

The idea of global civil society as a multiple source of democratic power (latent, not given) can be illustrated through a part of the reality of post-war Iraq, which has unfolded in the early months of 2004. After the invasion, with the Provisional Authority in place, civil society produced all kinds of movements, hastily organised, first to protest at the policies of the Governing Council, then to attempt from outside to assert power over those policies, if only by blocking them. The Union of the Unemployed, formed in the aftermath of hundreds of thousands losing their jobs in Paul Bremer's wholesale dismantling of the Baathist state, organised large demonstrations and demanded jobs. The independent Federation of Iraqi Trade Unions

© JB RUSSELL/PANOS PICTURES

Iraqis protest against the Coalition occupation

organised protest actions and meetings, demanding the right to strike and resisting privatisation. Students took action to stop the occupying forces from coming into the universities, which have traditionally prided themselves on autonomy. They organised in support of those who won elections to positions of university rector, only to be replaced by an appointee of the Governing Council. The mosque, the one institution that Saddam and now the US cannot control, became a focal point for opposition to both regimes. This, of course, is contradictory from a democratic point of view. Iraqi religious leaders are gaining disproportionate influence with serious implications for the rights of women, for example. But Iraq's religious leaders are not all cut from the same cloth. Some are secular-friendly, holding democratic elections and defending the rights of the Kurdish people. Some are even enlightened on the rights of women, who have been especially hard hit by the sanctions and the occupation. Moreover, some Islamic leaders have taken the lead in organising people who rejected the strategy, advocated by other religious leaders, of ending the occupation by cooperating with the occupier. Shia and Sunni religious leaders formed an anti-sectarian front, the Moslem Scholars Committee (MSC). The MSC has organised most of the large demonstrations in Baghdad, encouraging Muslims to unite and pray at each others' mosques, where secular people are also welcome.

The result of these various and contradictory impulses has been a power struggle, a process that neither Carother's nor Ali's cavalier dismissal of civil society as a serious force for democracy would appear to recognise. The refusal of the Iraqis to be fobbed off by promises of democracy in the 'never-never land' of an unspecified future, or by a 'local' transitional government over which, in fact, they have no democratic control has forced the US to abandon (for at least two years) its plans to rule Iraq directly and to reshape its institutions, including its plans to privatise its massive natural and human resources. The Iraqi Governing Council, effectively controlled by Paul Bremer, was discredited and abolished, to give way much sooner than originally planned to the transitional government, custodian of 'full Iraqi sovereignty' until elections scheduled for January 2005. The result is not democracy, because the ambitions of the US government for Iraq and the Middle East mean that the Bush administration is determined to maintain control, by military means. The US government has bowed to the inevitable on social and economic government institutions, while unleashing repressive military force – closing opposition newspapers, shooting at meetings at the mosques and at demonstrations and street protests. As I write, public opinion and organisation is increasingly polarised and increasingly militarised, which presents major obstacles for the development of broadly based sources of civil power.

If the situation in Iraq points to the importance and potential of civil society as a source of power for democracy in even the most unfavourable circumstances, it also points to the limits of that power. A democratic 'civil' sphere locally or nationally can enhance popular control and political equality in a sustained way only where the political party that holds elected office genuinely believes in sharing power with civil society, as in Pôrto Alegre and Grottamare. Where such a belief is lacking, and those in power fear or despise civil society, the sources of power that local civil society can organise bash their heads against a brick wall or find themselves smothered in cotton wool. This brings us back to the importance of international civil society, working with and through local grassroots organisations: the 'second superpower' that was in evidence on 15 February 2003. Already the combined forces of local and global civil society have had a restraining influence on the first superpower. As Noam Chomsky put it:

> *Had the problems of Fallujah, for example, arisen in the 1960s, they would have been resolved by B-52s and mass murder operations on the ground. Today, a more civilized society will not tolerate such measures, providing at least some space for the traditional victims to act to gain authentic independence. (Chomsky, 2004)*

The final achievement of that independence may depend on democratic organisations in local and global civil society transforming electoral democracy, as they began to do with Spanish elections of March 2004, while preserving their distinctive sources of more immediate and popular democratic power. That is the challenge of 2005.

Thanks to Mark Cresswell for additional research and Joyce Wainwright for an ideal setting in which to write.

References

Alegretti, Giovanni (2004) *Between efficiency and local democracy: the challenge of participatory budgeting addresses the European context.* Amsterdam: Transnational Institute.

Ali, Tariq (2002) The Clash of Fundamentalisms: Crusades, Jihads and Modernity. London: Verso Press.

– (2003) *Bush in Babylon: The Recolonisation of Iraq.* London: Verso.

Beetham, David (1999) *Democracy and Human Rights.* Cambridge: Polity Press.

Biekart, Kees (1999) *The Politics of Civil Society Building: European Private Aid Agencies and Democratic Transitions in Central America.* Amsterdam: International Books-Transnational Institute.

Carothers, Thomas (2003) *Is Gradualism Possible? Choosing a Strategy for Promoting Democracy in the Middle East* (Working Paper No. 39). Washington, DC: Carnegie Endowment for International Peace.

– (2004) *Critical Mission: Essays on Democracy.* Washington, DC: Carnegie Endowment for International Peace.

Chomsky, Noam (2004) 'Doctrines and Visions: Who Is to Run The World, and How?' Talk at the University of Oxford, 4 May; the Olaf Palme Lecture. www.chomsky.info/talks/20040604.htm

CIDADE/PMPA (2000) *Research Participatory Budgeting.* Pôrto Alegre.

Corrêa Leite, José (2004) 'WSF (a Brief History): A New Method of Doing Politics', *Transform! Europe: European Network for Alternative Thinking and Political Dialogue,* Newsletter No. 1 (March): 97–107. www.transform.it/newsletter/newsletter01.pdf

Edwards, Michael (2004) *Civil Society.* Cambridge: Polity Press.

Howell, Jude (1996) 'The Struggle for Survival: Prospects for the Women's Federation in Post-Mao China', *World Development* Vol 24 No. 1.

– (2000) 'Organising around women and labour in China: uneasy shadows, uncomfortable alliances.' *Communist and Post Communist Studies* Vol. 33 2000: 355–377.

– (ed.) (2003a) Governance in China. Lanham, MD: Rowman and Littlefield

– and Pearce, Jenny (2001) *Civil Society and Development: A Critical Exploration.* London: Lynne Rienner.

Kaldor, Mary and Vejvoda, Ivan (eds) (2002) Democratization in Central and Eastern Europe. London: Continuum International.

Macintosh, A. (ed.) (2003) *E-Forum E-Democracy Work Group 4 Initial Results* (Version 4: 10 September). www.eu-forum.org/summit/docs/WG4e-democracy-FINAL%20RESULTS.doc

Norris, P. (2003). 'Deepening Democracy through E-Governance.' Draft chapter for the UN *World Public Sector Report 2003.* http://ksghome.harvard.edu/~.pnorris.shorenstein.ksg/Acrobat/World%20Public%20Sector%20Report.pdf

OECD (Organisation for Economic Cooperation and Development) (2003) *Promise and Problems of E-Democracy: Challenges of Online Citizen Engagement.* Paris: OECD. www1.oecd.org/publications/e-book/4204011E.PDF

Öniş, Ziya and Şenses, Fikret (2003) *Rethinking the Emerging Post-Washington Consensus: A Critical Appraisal* (*Working Paper in Economics* 03/09). Ankara: *Economic Research Centre, Middle East Technical University.* www.erc.metu.edu.tr/menu/sayfa.php?icerik=about&lang=eng

Reyes, Oscar and Bouteldja, Naima (2004) 'Networking Activities within the Social Forum Process', *Transform! Europe: European Network for Alternative Thinking and Political Dialogue,* Newsletter No. 1 (March): 125–45. www.transform.it/newsletter/newsletter01.pdf

Riley, T. and Riley, C. (2003) 'E-Governance to E-Democracy: Examining the Evolution', *International Tracking Survey Report '03 Number Five.* Ottawa: Commonwealth Centre for E-Governance and Riley Information Services. www.electronicgov.net/pubs/research_papers/tracking03/IntlTrackRptJune03no.5.doc

Tocqueville, A. (1835/1988) *Democracy in America* (trans. George Lawrence). San Francisco: Perennial Library.

Vanaik, Achin (2004) 'Rendezvous at Mumbai', *New Left Review,* 26: 53–65.

Wainwright, Hilary (2003) *Reclaim the State: Experiments in Popular Democracy.* London: Verso.

– (2004a) 'Local Democracy Italian-style', *Red Pepper,* August.

– (2004b) 'From Mumbai with Hope', *Transform! Europe: European Network for Alternative Thinking and Political Dialogue,* Newsletter No. 1 (March): 31–4. www.transform.it/newsletter/newsletter01.pdf

Whitaker, Chico (2004) 'The WSF As Open Space', in Jai Sen et al. (eds), *The WSF: Challenging Empires.* New Delhi: Viveka Foundation.

PART 3

INFRASTRUCTURE OF GLOBAL CIVIL SOCIETY

CHAPTER 6

THE NEW PIONEERS: THE PEOPLE BEHIND GLOBAL CIVIL SOCIETY

Paola Grenier

My country is the world and my religion is to do good.

(Thomas Paine, *The Rights of Man*, 1791)

This chapter gives an account of the human side of civil society, grounding it in the lives of individuals rather than global issues, which can seem abstract and distant. It tells the stories, albeit briefly, of some of the people who have helped to shape, lead and even define different aspects and issues relating to civil society action. These are the 'pioneers' of global civil society. At the heart of this account are notions of agency and action, of how people influence what can seem to be overwhelming forces, particularly of globalisation and its effects within their countries and communities. Equally central is the diversity of the individuals and what they do: the 27 profiles presented below are eclectic snapshots, painting a picture of the variety of motives, backgrounds, activities, approaches and contexts of global social pioneers. Despite the seemingly idiosyncratic nature of many of the stories, it is possible to identify several common themes and issues, which can shed some light on the nature of global civil society and the actors within it.

This chapter starts by introducing the idea of 'pioneer', drawing inspiration from Lord Beveridge's study (1948) of the people who created and shaped the voluntary sector in the UK in the nineteenth century. It goes on to offer some reflections on the nature of global civil society. This is followed by profiles of individual pioneers, and the chapter concludes with further reflections and analysis.

Inspiration

This is a chapter about exceptional people, of widely different types and origins, and different experience of life. Some found themselves reaching one objective after another in steady progress. Others had moments when all that they had fought for, and the chance of continuing their work, seemed to be lost. (Beveridge, 1948: 185)

Beveridge is generally considered to be a founder of the welfare state in Britain, and yet he also believed profoundly in what he called voluntary action, and what we would today call civil society. In 'A Chapter of Pioneers' he described briefly the lives of a number of individuals who 'had fire in their bellies', who founded new institutions, who blazed new trails, who set an example for others to follow, and so contributed to social progress. As one of the people who shaped post-Second-World-War-Britain, Beveridge was a leader, an astute politician, and a pioneer in his own right. He had a definitive voice and extensive connections, and he wrote from a position of considerable experience and authority. I hope that I draw inspiration from him with due humility.

There are two main reasons why Beveridge's approach is particularly relevant here. The first concerns terminology. A variety of terms are used to label the people of interest here, such as 'civil society leader', 'social activist', 'radical', and 'social entrepreneur'. As 'activist' and 'radical', associated with left-wing progressive visions of social change, have fallen into disuse, (Giddens, 1994: 1), 'social entrepreneur' has become increasingly popular. In many ways, social entrepreneurs are the people of interest here. 'Social entrepreneurship' is a term that is actively promoted by certain organisations and is associated with particular concepts of social change and social action. 'Social entrepreneur' is sometimes applied to leaders and innovators within civil society, who are considered comparable in risk-taking propensity and creativity to business entrepreneurs, even if they do not pursue commercial ends. It is also used to refer to the simultaneous pursuit of financial profit and social or

Box 6.1: Networking and supporting individuals

Many of the organisations that have recently emerged to support individual social entrepreneurs or leaders believe fundamentally that individuals are the drivers of change. They identify and support such individuals by providing a range of funding, learning and networking opportunities. Almost all of these organisations are based in the US or Europe, creating and facilitating extended regional and (often) international networks of individuals. They have been set up and are funded in a variety of ways, by grant-making foundations, rich individuals, and businesses.

The organisations vary in the ways they pursue and realise this idea. One group of networks, emphasises the adoption of business practices and thinking. For example, some associate with a 'venture philanthropy' model, understanding philanthropy in terms of 'investments' (rather than 'donations') that seek a 'social return'. They often refer to the individuals they select as 'social entrepreneurs' – 'individuals who possess the vision, creativity and extraordinary determination of a business entrepreneur, but who devote these qualities to introducing new systemic solutions to societal problems' (Ashoka, URL). These organisations seek to challenge conventional approaches to philanthropy and development by focusing their support and attention on individuals. Interestingly, such a practice does have a long-standing historical precedent in the form of patronage, whereby talented individuals are provided with resources and endorsements, albeit predominantly in culture and the arts. To date, such networks have emphasised the business-like aspects of their work rather than drawing on traditions and experiences in the artistic spheres. There may be potential in the future, as the networks become more established and gain experience, to draw on a wider range of creative approaches and techniques that encompass a broader and more comprehensive vision of social change.

Many organisations provide funding, facilitated networking within the fellowship or membership, and access to other networks. Ashoka, one of the first such networks to be established, envisages itself as 'the world's first global professional association of social entrepreneurs' and invests in people 'with ideas for unprecedented change in their communities' (Ashoka, URL). Avina, which operates largely in Latin America, works with leaders from different sectors, and sees effective cross-sector partnerships as a critical, and hitherto missing, element in development. It therefore strives to build partnerships between sectors through working with individual leaders. *Echoing Green* believes that the entrepreneurial spirit, which has served the US well in terms of economic growth, needs to be nurtured in the pursuit of social change. Interestingly, *Echoing Green* acknowledges that some of the entrepreneurs it supports, fail, but accepts this as part of the risk involved in working with people at the very early stages of the development of their ideas. The Schwab Foundation identifies social entrepreneurs who have already had a significant impact, often internationally, and attempts to promote them to the ranks of the world's business and economic leaders by inviting them to the World Economic Forum. There is a sense of an emerging spectrum of support for people whose ideas and organisations are at different stages of development.

Another group of networks adopts a more developmental approach, typically providing a participatory and targeted programme of learning. These organisations emphasise the complexity and uncertainty of development and social change, and the need for holistic approaches. Synergos works with individuals from grant-making organisations to spread and facilitate the development of best practices in grant-making. LEAD focuses on environmental sustainability, providing training for the leaders admitted to its network in a range of leadership as well as environmental issues. The Development School adopts an open systems perspective and, in contrast to the approaches derived from business practices, believes that certain development skills are unique to social change processes. It emphasises self-reflection, continuous learning and personal integrity. The Africa Leadership Initiative (URL), inspired by the Henry Crown Fellowship in the US, brings together leaders from all sectors to develop a shared vision of the 'good society' and to find ways to 'meld the demands of globalization with local values'.

Box 6.2: **Lord Beveridge**

William Beveridge was born in 1879 in India. The son of a judge, he attended private school and went to Oxford University to study mathematics and classics, and later to the London School of Economics. On leaving university, he embarked on a varied career that included journalism, social work, economics, academia, and the civil service. He was an active social reformer, creating the first network of labour exchanges and the first unemployment insurance scheme. He became director of the London School of Economics in 1919, and, during his 18 years in that post, he oversaw a period of tremendous growth and its establishment as a leading international centre for the social sciences.

In 1941, as a civil servant, he was given the technocratic task of reviewing the administration and coordination of the social insurance schemes that were spread across seven government departments. He carried out that review 'on a scale that no one who appointed him could possibly have envisaged', and his final report, *Social Insurance and Allied Services*, was a rallying call to slay the five giants of 'want, disease, ignorance, squalor and idleness'. This was the Beveridge Report, published in 1942, and the basis for the reforms of the Labour government of 1945 that are credited with the creation of the British welfare state. The report had many opponents, but it achieved extraordinary popular support, and a sense of unity and hope following the horrors of war (Timmins, 1996). Beveridge went on to write *Voluntary Action* in 1948, to promote charitable and philanthropic activity. In 1951, he was one of the founding trustees of the One World Trust, an early example of a global civil society organisation, which is still influential today, promoting a world community and world peace.

environmental goals, such as is found within worker and consumer cooperatives, certain socially motivated businesses, the intermediate labour market, and civil society organisations that use trading activities to achieve their goals. 'Social entrepreneurship' therefore conveys an emphasis on business activities and market-based approaches. While 'social entrepreneur' is a useful term, the focus here is as much on activists, change agents, leaders, and moving spirits: people whose role is to transform directly political structures as well as to generate environmental, economic, and social benefits. The Oxford English Dictionary defines 'pioneer' as 'One who goes before to prepare or open up the way for others to follow; one who begins, or takes part in beginning, some enterprise, course of action.' An older meaning is a foot soldier who clears the way for the main body of the army to follow. These meanings capture much of what is intended here, and in particular the idea that pioneers are leading the way for others to follow at the same time as serving society in general, by testing different routes and determining the best ones. 'Pioneer' is therefore adopted in this chapter as the more inclusive term.

The second reason for drawing inspiration from Beveridge is that he tells the stories of individuals, sometimes in a few lines, sometimes in several pages. He is interested in their idiosyncrasies and the diversity of their experiences and motivations, and somehow their humanity shines through. He does not attempt to systemise or create typologies of the people, and yet is able to draw out themes and common issues. He highlights three necessary factors in the emergence and success of pioneers, and these are still relevant today. First is the significance of the middle class and its relative independence and freedom in terms of its work and how it organises its time. The attributes of middle classes everywhere tend to include access to education and training as professionals, access to broad networks, political voice, self-confidence, and considerable freedom to control their own lives. Second is the importance of motivation, and in many cases of religious belief. Beveridge expressed concern about the decline in religion, and commented that 'there must be something either to revive the religious motive or to do what it did in the hearts and minds of men' (1948: 155). Third is 'the need for material resources to put new ideas into practice; some of the pioneers had fortunes of their own; others had the fortunes of friends at call' (1948: 155). These three factors – middle class attributes, motivations, and resources – are treated in this chapter through the lives of the pioneers presented and again in the conclusion.

Finding the pioneers

To identify those people throughout the world who have made a difference on a variety of social, environmental and, at times, political issues, two main sources were used. First, the network of authors, contributors and advisers to the Global Civil Society Yearbook were contacted for ideas about the pioneers in their fields. The Yearbook covers some of the most salient and pressing issues of global civil society, and has established a strong network of experts and activists in a variety of areas. Second, organisations that recognise and support individuals were contacted directly for their views on the leading people within their networks. In addition, pioneers were sought among individuals who had received awards or been recognised in other ways. This produced hundreds, and potentially thousands, of people from all over the world, working on a wide variety of issues. And yet there is space to profile only a handful of people.

The final process of deciding who would be included was complex and involved a number of factors. Care was taken to identify those people who had initiated or pioneered work that has had a global impact. The emphasis is on contemporary actors rather than historical figures; some are well known, others less so. The final selection reflects the diversity of global civil society in terms of geography, age, ethnicity, gender, and issues of concern. The final choice was entirely my own. There was no attempt to assess or evaluate the people; and the list is not intended to be a definitive one of those who have made the greatest impact, nor of the most important issues. The details about the individuals profiled came from a variety of sources. I interviewed certain people, corresponded with others, and relied on information from websites, reports, organisational documents, speeches, award schemes, press articles and books, including biographies and autobiographies.

Setting the context: global civil society and the space for action

Globalisation is frequently described as 'uneven' or 'unequal', as some parts of the world seem to be more engaged in and in control of the processes of globalisation, and to accrue greater benefits, than others. Similarly, global civil society is also recognised as 'uneven' geographically, with a strong bias towards Western demo-

[illegible] spread of networks and awards

	Ashoka	LEAD	AVINA	Right Livelihood	Goldman	Schwab Awards	Yale Global Leaders
[illegible]	191	270		12	15	9	5
[illegible]	495	567		22	16	20	8
[illegible]		140			4	1	2
Middl[illegible]				5			1
Latin America	584	278	301	13	20	18	7
North America	33	85	10	9	15	20	2
Europe	121	62	13	29	13	8	5
Oceania				2	11	2	1
International				2			
Total	1,424	1,402	324	94	94	78	31

The chart illustrates the geographical coverage of a selection of international networks and awards. Note that some of the network members and award winners overlap, so the figures cannot be added to give numbers in each geographical area. The gaps and concentrations are striking, as is the lack of individual members and award winners in the Middle East and Russia/CIS.

cracies and in particular northwestern Europe (Anheier, Glasius and Kaldor, 2001: 7). It has been acknowledged that issues that are of interest in the West and North are often more likely to become prominent than those initiated in the South (Chandhoke, 2003). In some countries, freedom is very restricted, and so civil society is extremely limited in its scope and ability to connect globally. In other countries, international travel and communication are much more part of normal life. Comparable patterns of unevenness are evident among the pioneers of civil society. The networks of social entrepreneurs, civil society leaders, and award winners are generally based in the North and show significant gaps in coverage, especially in the Middle East, Central Asia and the Caucasus (see Table 6.1).

In spite of the uneven spread of civil society, it has been argued that globalisation in general increases the structural opportunities for action and change:

> *The myriad structural variables that are involved in the globalisation process do not merely constrain actors but also provide them with expanded opportunities for exercising leverage within that process, feeding back into shaping globalisation itself. (Cerny, 2000: 439)*

The search for pioneers reveals that few operate across the globe, yet many more are doing work of global significance or that resonates globally. The starting point is, therefore, those issues that are conceived of as global in some way. Pollution, the destruction of the Amazon rainforest, and holes in the ozone layer are generally understood as global problems, even though they are often manifested locally. Disease, such as the spread of HIV and AIDS, is increasingly understood as a global issue, although the problematic effects are more apparent in some countries than in others (Seckinelgin, 2002). The same goes for human rights, access to medical treatment, economic development, trade, biotechnology, and dams. Often civil society pioneers are critical in the reconceptualisation of issues from the local to global; this is apparent in the influence of environmental campaigners, the women's movement and human rights activists, and is a process that can take several years, even generations. Some changes are facilitated through processes of globalisation; in particular, the development of digital technology and multilateral institutions have helped to create the spaces and means by which information and practices can be shared more rapidly than in the past. Civil society pioneers are divided below into four broad categories by reference to the interconnections between the global and local, and, in particular, to the different ways of achieving a global impact through varying forms of local and global action.

The pioneers

This section tells a series of stories about individuals. The stories are, by their nature, incomplete, and limited by the space available and the accessibility of information. They are a small selection from the enormous breadth of groundbreaking work that takes place.

Just global

Some pioneers act almost from the start at a global level. The ways in which they do so vary and depend on their international position, the nature of their approach, and the way in which opportunities have emerged. George Soros was an international financier before he became an international philanthropist. James Grant was appointed director of UNICEF. It was a platform he actively sought, and where he stayed despite considerable difficulties and obstacles to his work. Craig Kielburger, at the age of 12, had no platform when he started Free the Children, but managed to tap into the energy and interest of a global constituency of children. Anuradha Vittachi's Internet site on UK development agencies was quickly overtaken by the rapid development and globalisation of the web, to which she and her colleagues responded by transforming it into a global network.

M Cherif Bassiouni

NATIONALITY: Egyptian
WORK: international
FIELD: human rights

M. Cherif Bassiouni, who was born in 1937, has followed two complementary paths: as an academic specialising in international criminal law and human rights, and as an expert within various international legal institutions and the United Nations. He studied in France, Switzerland, Egypt and America, and has been a professor of law at DePaul University in the US since 1964, where he is also President of the International Institute of Higher Studies in Criminal Sciences. He is President of the International Institute of Higher Studies in Criminal Sciences, Siracusa, Italy, and also of the Association Internationale de Droit Pénal (AIDP, International Association of Penal Law) in Paris, a worldwide scholarly international criminal justice organisation with more than 3,000 members in 99 countries. He has written extensively, publishing more than 60 books and 200 articles. His writing has not only contributed to his international status but has also been critical in promoting and keeping alive the idea of an international criminal court.

The idea of an international criminal court had been of interest to lawyers and academics for many decades. Two events created opportunities for it to progress from being a dream to something attainable. In 1989, the Prime Minister of Trinidad and Tobago, concerned particularly with drug trafficking, put forward the idea of an international court to the United National General Assembly, and the idea started to be taken seriously within the UN. Shortly after this, during 1992–4, Bassiouni's leadership of the investigations into the human rights violations in the former Yugoslavia contributed to demonstrating that an international court was both effective and workable. Bassiouni was appointed vice chair of the committee responsible for formalising proposals for an international court, and in 1996, was elected chairman of the committee responsible for putting together the draft text of a treaty and statutes. During this period, he also convened informal meetings of NGOs, which took place at the International Institute for the Higher Criminal Sciences in Sicily, and were critical in providing space and time to deliberate complex and controversial issues in detail. The International Criminal Court (ICC) was approved in 1998 and came into being in 2002 as an independent standing court with jurisdiction over genocide, war crimes, and crimes against humanity. In 1999, Bassiouni was nominated for the Nobel Peace Prize as, in the words of the International Scientific and Professional Council of the UN, the 'single most driving force behind the global decision to establish the International Criminal Court'.

- Marlies Glasius, *The International Criminal Court: A Global Civil Society Achievement*. London: Routledge, forthcoming 2005
- Conference on The Establishment and Role of the International Criminal Court, 10 November 2001, University of Cincinnati College of Law, Ohio, USA http://stremedia.uc.edu/law/urban_morgan/2001/seminar_hi_player.html
- UN Press Release, 15 June 1998: 'United Nations Diplomative Conference of Plenipotentiaries on the Establishment of an International Criminal Court'
- DePaul University News Release, 4 March 1999: 'Law Professor M Cherif Bassiouni becomes first DePaul faculty member nominated for Nobel Peace Prize'

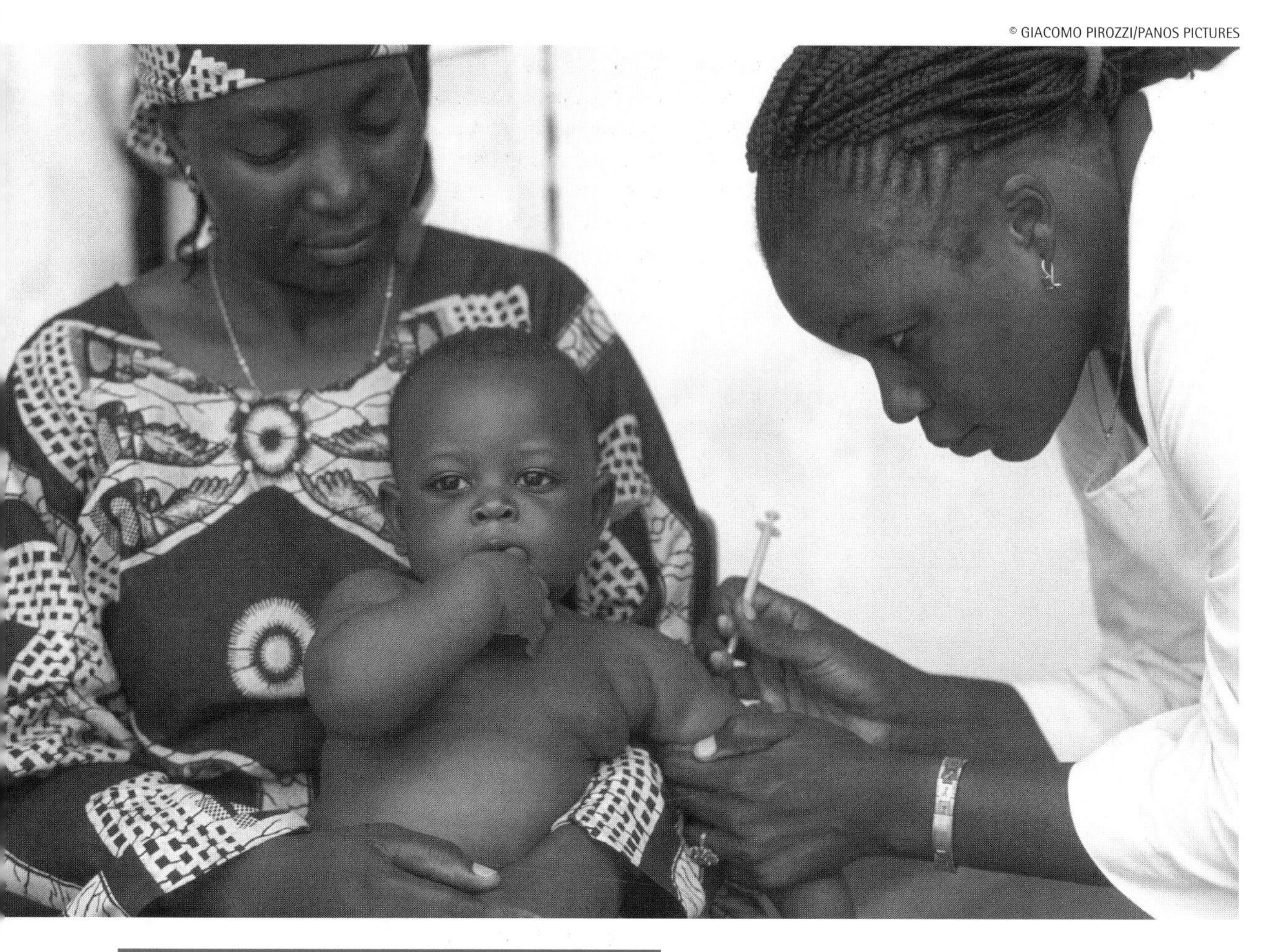

James Grant

NATIONALITY: Canadian/American
WORK: international
FIELD: children and health

James Grant (1922–1995) was born in China. His grandfather had been a medical missionary and his father worked for the Rockefeller Foundation on public health. He was brought up in China and went to university in the US, first in California and then at Harvard Law School. Rather than follow his family tradition and go into medicine, in which his grandfather had felt endlessly frustrated dealing with the medical effects of a range of social and economic problems, Grant decided to go into public service and to try to tackle some of the causes of disease and poverty by working on issues such as land reform, rural development and employment.

He had a successful career in international development, spending much time working in China and India, and in 1980, he was appointed head of the United Nations Children's Fund (UNICEF). His vision was for UNICEF to make a quantum leap in its activities and, rather than focus on a wide range of local projects, he wanted to reach children all over the world. Inspired by the work of Jon Rohde into the causes of death among children, and the fact that the treatments and means existed to prevent such deaths, Grant developed the idea of the 'child survival revolution'. The focus was on low-cost but comprehensive programmes of growth-monitoring, oral rehydration, breast-feeding, and immunisation – otherwise known as GOBI. More precisely, ambitious targets were set, for example, to increase immunisation from 20 per cent to 80 per cent of children in less economically developed countries. He was criticised widely and vigorously, both from within UNICEF and the UN and from outside:

> *In the early and mid-1980s when Jim Grant seemed to be surrounded by nothing but criticism and hostility: his goals were not achievable; they were too 'top down'; he was 'tunnel visioned'; he was 'dealing only with symptoms'. The development establishment, in particular, scorned the simple solutions he espoused. (Adamson, 1995)*

Yet Grant persisted and navigated a course within the establishment and through national governments, even negotiating ceasefires in war zones where they were needed to reach the children. The 80 per cent target of immunisation was reached in 1990, and was a vindication of his vision.

- Richard Jolly (ed), *Jim Grant: UNICEF Visionary* (2001). Written by friends and colleagues of Jim Grant, and distributed by UNICEF
- Peter Adamson, 'Endpiece. A Splendid Torch. Peter Adamson pays tribute to the inspirational life of Jim Grant, the former Executive Director of UNICEF'. *New Internationalist*, No 266, April 1995

Anuradha Vittachi

NATIONALITY: Sri Lankan/British
WORK: international
FIELD: digital technology and media

Anuradha Vittachi was born in Ceylon (now Sri Lanka) in 1947. Her father, Varindra 'Tarzie' Vittachi, editor of the *Ceylon Journal*, was internationally recognised for his journalism in exposing corruption and injustice. When Vittachi was aged 13, the family had to leave Sri Lanka due to political persecution, and settled in the UK. In a speech she made to a Civicus Assembly in 2001, she said:

> *My parents are both journalists, and they used to say, 'Information that's not for transformation is just gossip'. And I owe it to them that I've spent my life struggling against human rights abuses, and also to having had a rather fraught childhood, being saved from being kidnapped.**

Vittachi followed a career in the media, as a film-maker, writer and journalist, with a commitment to making accurate and meaningful information available. For her, a major problem is that most of the media reflect and reinforce power inequalities, based on gender, race, and wealth, rather than pursuing and uncovering the truth. She founded OneWorld.net with Peter Armstrong in January 1995 to help British international NGOs to present themselves and their work on the Internet. The aim was to provide a space for issues and people that do not normally attract media coverage. Their pioneering use of technology attracted first UK and then international attention, and with the rapid expansion of the Internet they started to realise the potential of what they had started. In 1999, OneWorld.net transformed itself into an international organisation, and it is now a network of websites in different countries and in different languages. Its reach has extended far beyond established NGOs. OneWorld.net works directly with local people at grass-roots levels, providing access to information both digitally and in other forms, and working with a wide range of relevant technology, from video-cameras to radio and cheap computers, to help people tell their stories in their own ways.

> *I think we have to develop a completely new kind of bottom-up media whose whole purpose is to amplify the voices of those who are unheard by the mainstream media.***

- OneWorld.net. www.oneworld.net
- www.civicusassembly.org/media/Anuradha%20Vittachi-keynote2001.pdf *
- www.oneworld.net/article/view/51114/1/?PrintableVersion=enabled **

George Soros

NATIONALITY: Hungarian/American
WORK: international
FIELD: philanthropy

George Soros was born to a Jewish family in Hungary in 1930. His father was a lawyer and his mother independently wealthy. During the Second World War, Soros remained in Hungary, posing as the godson of a family friend and government official. His experiences under the Nazi regime and the help that his father provided to escapees were both strong influences on Soros's subsequent philanthropy. Following the Communist takeover in Hungary, Soros left for the UK in 1947. He studied at the London School of Economics, where he was inspired by his philosophy professor Karl Popper and his ideas of 'open society'. At this stage in his life, he lived like many students, with little money and getting by on low-paid part-time work. When he came to realise that he was unlikely to become the great philosopher he dreamt of being, in 1956, with almost no money to his name, he decided to move to America to pursue a career in finance.

Soros went on to become one of the richest people in the world, valued by Forbes at US$7 billion in 2003. He attributes his success to doubting constantly his own judgement and the excitement and sense of achievement he feels when he finds out he is wrong. He has devoted much of his time to criticising global capitalism and engaging in a mission to bring 'open society' and democracy to countries with repressive and authoritarian regimes. He started in 1979 by financing black students to attend university in South Africa; and in the early 1980s, he financed photocopiers in Hungary to enable the sharing of information, ensuring support for dissident movements by striking a deal with the government whereby everyone, not just officials, would have access to the copiers. He donates approximately US$400 million annually to the Open Society Institute and the network of national and regional Soros Foundations. The foundations operate in more than 50 countries, including the US, Africa, Southeast Asia, and central and eastern Europe. He stands out from other philanthropists in his explicit commitment to 'open society', which underpins his work, as well as in establishing foundations that are autonomous, even though many are dependent on annual grants from Soros. He is considered a controversial and paradoxical figure, whose financial successes and engagement with capitalist markets are often held up against his philanthropy and philosophical commitment to open society and to challenging neo-liberalism.

- George Soros, *Soros on Soros: Ahead of the Curve*. New York: John Wiley & Sons, 1995
- George Soros, *The Crisis of Global Capitalism*. London: Little, Brown and Company, 1998
- Neil Clark, 'NS Profile: George', *New Statesman*, 2 June 2003, p 32
- Open Society Institute. www.soros.org

Ka Hsaw Wa

NATIONALITY: Burmese
WORK: Burma and international
FIELD: environment and human rights

Ka Hsaw Wa is a member of the Karen minority in Burma. Born in 1970, as a student activist he joined the pro-democracy demonstrations in Rangoon on 18 September 1988. During the ensuing crackdown, an estimated 10,000 people were killed, and Ka Hsaw Wa was arrested and tortured by the authorities for three days. He then left the country, but returned at intervals to investigate and document the situation there. He spent time hiding in the borderlands and forests of Burma, witnessing directly how large corporations and the government exploited both the natural resources and the local people, resulting in environmental degradation and extreme human suffering. He recorded the extent and form of human rights abuses taking place, and made the information available to international organisations.

He co-founded EarthRights International (ERI) in 1995 with two American lawyers, focused on bringing together environmental issues and human rights. The initial aim was to stop the Yadana pipeline project in Burma, which was resulting in forced labour and persecution of local people. While it continues to emphasise Burma in its work, ERI's role has expanded internationally. It uses the US legal system to challenge corporations in specific cases of environmental and human rights abuse; it works with indigenous people in the Amazon and Southeast Asia, providing training and information so that they can 'become their own best advocates'; it continues to document and publicise human rights and environmental abuse; and has developed a focus on gender-based abuse and women's rights.

- EarthRights International. www.earthrights.org
  Goldman Environmental Prize winner in 1999. www.goldmanprize.org

Peter Eigen

NATIONALITY: German
WORK: international
FIELD: corruption

Born in 1938, Peter Eigen studied law in Germany and obtained a PhD in 1965. He made his career in international development, working for more than 25 years mainly with the World Bank in Africa and Latin America. Increasingly, people in the Bank were concerned about corruption, and, as a World Bank official, Eigen started to raise the issue of international corruption with his colleagues. There was concern that the ways in which politicians and business people were 'bought off', especially by large corporations, was undermining human rights, the environment, economic development, and, in fact, any serious attempts at international development in many parts of the world. And in most cases such bribery was actually legal. Eigen held a series of meetings, and the decision was reached to set up a small and specialist NGO that would focus on corruption in international business transactions.

Transparency International (TI) was launched in May 1993, by ten people from five countries. Very quickly it attracted international publicity and 'thousands of letters' of support. TI established itself in Berlin, and Eigen anticipated working there part time, having taken early retirement from the World Bank. In fact, it became 'the most demanding task of his career'. While corruption was moving up the agenda of a number of development agencies, there was also considerable opposition from certain national governments and the World Bank. Nevertheless, national chapters started to be established, largely on the initiative of local people, such that by March 2004, there were chapters in 90 countries supported by the International Secretariat in Berlin. TI monitors and publishes reports into a range of different forms of corruption, regularly making international headlines, with the effect that corruption is taken increasingly seriously by international organisations, including the World Bank.

- Transparency International. www.transparency.org

Craig Kielburger

Nationality: Canadian
Work: international
Field: children's rights

When he was 12 years old, Craig Kielburger, who was born in 1983, read a newspaper story about Iqbal Masih, a Pakistani boy, also 12. Iqbal had been a 'bonded worker' and had escaped and spoken out against child labour, and was murdered while riding his bicycle. Kielburger found out as much as he could about child labour and bonded workers, and then got together with some friends to form a group called Free the Children. Their aim was to try and stop the abuse and exploitation of children and also to prove that children themselves could make a difference. They started to produce leaflets and information about child labour, and to write letters to world leaders. After six months, Kielburger was invited to speak at a Labour convention in Toronto, and this proved to be a turning point. Following his speech, the union members present donated CAN$150,000 to help build a rehabilitation centre in India.

Since then, Kielburger has travelled around the world, meeting children and political leaders in Asia, Latin America and Africa. Free the Children has supported projects in 35 countries, building 375 primary schools and providing medical supplies. It also speaks out and leads campaigns against child labour and sexual exploitation of children, and provides leadership training and opportunities for children to take action and express themselves. There are Free the Children chapters in Germany, China, Japan and Brazil.

- Free the Children. www.freethechildren.org

Global potential from local success

Some pioneers have developed local models or approaches that have then spread, and in which they themselves have been engaged in the globalisation of the ideas. The ways in which they have done this vary, although all of them work with a wide range of partners and have been able to cede control over the ensuing development, allowing their original ideas and visions to take on lives of their own. Cicely Saunders had the foresight to include a research arm as part of the first hospice that helped to create a body of knowledge about the new medical field, and provided a hub for international interest. Jeroo Billimoria has moved from working in India to developing helplines for children internationally. Oded Grajew has founded several organisations and developed a range of approaches to support ethical and responsible business. Medha Patkar remains committed to the people in the Narmada Valley, but has also informed global debates on the social, environmental and economic effects of dam developments.

Cicely Saunders

Nationality: British
Work: UK and international
Field: health

Cicely Saunders, who was born in 1918, took a break in her education at Oxford University in 1940, during the Second World War, to become a student nurse in London. After injuring her back, she had to leave nursing, but completed her degree and then went on to become a medical social worker. In this role she met and cared for David Tasma, a Polish refugee. His friendship and death in 1948 had a profound effect on her. He left her £500 with the words, 'I'll be a window in your Home', referring to their conversations about providing better care and conditions for people who are close to the end of their lives.

She decided to study medicine, and retrained and qualified as a doctor in her late 30s. She then determined to set up a modern hospice and spent eight years fundraising, promoting her ideas and refining her thinking. In 1967, St Christopher's Hospice in south London opened to patients, the first hospice dedicated to caring for people who were dying. Saunders linked clinical care with teaching and research, and this has helped to establish palliative care as a medical field in its own right. She was motivated and supported by a strong Christian faith and, although initially she saw hospices as Christian organisations, she quickly realised that a secular approach was more appropriate. She has promoted hospices internationally through travelling and speaking, with the result that hospices have been established throughout the world.

- Wesley J. Smith, 'Harsh Medicine', Chapter 1 in *Culture of Death*. San Francisco: Encounter Books, 2000, pp 1–23
- David Clark, 'Foreword', in Cicely Saunders, *Watch With Me: Inspiration for a Life in Hospice Care*. Sheffield, UK: Mortal Press, 2003

Garth Japhet

NATIONALITY: South African
WORK: Africa
FIELD: health

Garth Japhet was born in apartheid South Africa in 1963. His father is Jewish and his mother English, and with their international experiences and liberal approach, Garth was brought up with an acute sense of the injustices of apartheid. At the same time, he came to realise the power of the media in creating social norms and contributing to the maintenance of the regime. He remembers his school days as troubled; he was often unhappy and disruptive. As he grew up, this influenced him to channel his energies and determination into something more productive. Initially, he planned to follow his father's profession and become a lawyer, but he then decided that medicine offered more opportunities to make a difference. He trained as a doctor, but after qualifying, he became increasingly frustrated with the fact that people in townships often needed better and more accessible information rather than medicine.

He realised that, if he was to reach a wide audience, he would need to use the popular media rather than the more traditional forms of health education. He created Soul City, a soap opera that brings together an engaging and populist storyline with a wide range of health and development messages. Soul City is consistently one of the most popular television shows. It is part of a comprehensive initiative that includes outreach work, policy development, and training, and also uses radio and other forms of media. For example, Soul Buddyz, which targets 8–12-year-olds, brings together television drama, radio and printed materials to address issues of racism, HIV and AIDS, children's rights, and substance misuse. Soul City is active in nine other African countries, and has been built into a strong 'social brand', which can act as a platform for the development of a range of projects and initiatives, responding to needs as they change.

- Soul City: www.soulcity.org.za
- Personal communication

Medha Patkar

NATIONALITY: Indian
WORK: Gujarat and international
FIELD: dams

After graduating in social sciences, Medha Patkar moved to the Narmada Valley in the 1980s. The Narmada Valley was the site for a proposed World Bank development of hundreds of interlocking dams that would supply water for agriculture, drinking, and industry to four states in India. Arundhati Roy, the best-selling author, referred to dams in India as 'the temples of modern development', which are justified with an 'irrational passion' as being for the greater good of society (Roy, 2000). Medha Patkar has been one of the forces behind the Narmada Bachao Andolan (NBA), a movement of local villagers, farmers, tribal people and Dalits (untouchables), based on Gandhian principles of non-violence and civil disobedience, raising awareness of the plans for the dam development and assessing its potential impact. NBA argued that the development was set to displace hundreds of thousands of people and to destroy the local environment, without a clear guarantee of any benefits in terms of improved access to water. As a result of the NBA's high profile and persistent campaigning, the World Bank commissioned an independent review in 1992. The review found that the NBA was largely correct in its analysis, and the development was halted.

In the light of the breakdown in relationships between local people and dam developers, exemplified by experiences in the Narmada Valley, the World Bank established the World Commission on Dams in 1997 to review dam developments internationally, with Medha Patkar as one of the 12 commissioners. It published *Dams and Development* in 2000 with a series of recommendations, alternative plans, and proposals for good practice. The NBA reinforced its international influence when Arundhati Roy wrote the essay *The Greater Common Good* in 1999,

© KAREN ROBINSON/PANOS PICTURES

'Not moving but drowning': women protesters in the Narmada Valley

condemning the Narmada Valley development. However, and in spite of the temporary pause and the international influence of the NBA, the development in the Narmada Valley has continued, and the NBA has become increasingly strident. Patkar has continued to campaign, putting her life at risk through fasting and the 'not moving but drowning' protests, where people stood in the rising water until it started to recede.

- Right Livelihood Award Winner in 1991. www.rightlivelihood.org
- Catherine Clyne and Samantha Knowlden, 'Not Moving but Drowning: Satyagraha and the Narmada Dam', Satya, 2000. www.satyamag.com/april00/namard.html
- World Commission on Dams. www.dams.org

Oded Grajew

NATIONALITY: Brazilian
WORK: Brazil
FIELD: ethical commerce and social reform

Oded Grajew, who was born in 1947, studied electrical engineering at the University of São Paulo, and then gained a postgraduate business qualification. He mixed engineering and business to set up Grow Jogos and Brinquedos, a company which specialised in making toys and games for adults and teenagers. As a leading businessman in Brazil, he became increasingly interested in the relationship between democracy, ethics and commerce. In 1989, he helped to found Pensamento Nacional das Bases Empresariais (PNBE); which seeks to raise issues of social justice amongst business leaders. In 1990, he became President of ABRINQ (Brazilian Association of Toy Manufacturers), and demonstrated his commitment to prioritising the eradication of child labour by setting up the Foundation for Children's Rights. By 2000, the foundation was supporting a range of programmes reaching more than one million children. In 1998, he founded and became director of the Ethos Institute for Business Social Responsibility, an association that has attracted a wide membership base among Brazilian businesses.

Grajew's work and position put him in touch with individuals and movements internationally who were attempting to challenge the dominant neo-liberal economic model. During the 1990s, the multilateral summits and the World Economic Forum (WEF) of economic and political leaders held annually at Davos became focal points for protests. The idea of an alternative parallel summit focusing on social needs started to be discussed in Brazil, and, in particular, in relation to Pôrte Alegre, which was recognised internationally as a model of participatory government. Translating the idea from a local to an international level, Grajew was one of the first proponents and architects of the World Social Forum (WSF). The WSF takes place at the same time as the WEF and aims to show that 'another world is possible'. In 2001, its first year, the forum attracted 20,000 people from 117 countries; in 2003 there were more than 100,000 people from 150 countries. There are now social forums at local, national and regional levels.

- Speaker Biography of Oded Grajew, at Annual Bank Conference on Development Economics (ABCDE), 24–6 June, 2002, Oslo, Norway. http://wbln0018.worldbank.org/EURVP/web.nsf/0/18468e07bba72e55c1256bde005d40b0?OpenDocument
- World Social Forum. www.forumsocialmundial.org.br
- Francisco Whitaker, 'World Social Forum: origins and aims', translated by Peter Lenny, 22 June 2002. www.forumsocialmundial.org.br/main.asp?id_menu=2_1&cd_language=2>

Jeroo Billimoria

Nationality: Indian
Work: India and internationally
Field: children

Jeroo Billimoria's mother was a social worker and her father an accountant; both had a strong sense of social responsibility. Born in 1965, Billimoria remembers her childhood as happy, accompanying her mother, playing on the streets, and no doubt being exposed to some of the extreme poverty that exists in India. Her father died when she was 18, and she remembers her surprise that 'there were so many people he had helped that we as a family did not know'. She joined the Tata Institute of Social Science in Mumbai, and travelled to the US for study visits. It was the two years she spent at the Coalition for Homeless in New York that planted the seeds of the idea for a telephone support service for children.

Billimoria started to lobby for a helpline in 1993, and, having gained support, set up Childline in 1996. The Childline network is accessible to children who are lost, abused or in any way in need, through a free phone number. It provides access to a rich support network, including medical help, counselling, education, shelter and so on. In each location where it works, extensive research and outreach has been undertaken to understand local needs and resources. Having stood down as director of Childline in 2002, she is now based in Amsterdam, working to support and initiate the development of helplines for children internationally.

- Schwab Foundation profile. www.schwabfound.org
- David Bornstein, 'Ten-Nine-Eight-Childline!', in *How to Change the World*. New York: Oxford University Press, 2004
- Personal communication

David Green

Nationality: American
Work: international
Field: health

Born in 1956, David Green is one of triplets, and his father is a college professor. He studied at the University of Michigan, where his interest in helping people was prompted by a course in religious mysticism. He pursued postgraduate studies at the School of Public Health. At the same time, he started to work for the SEVA Foundation, which provided donated lenses for use in cataract operations in India and Nepal. Cataract is one of the most common causes of blindness in developing countries, affecting an estimated 40 million people. When the supply of donated lenses dried up in the 1980s, Green decided that the way forward was to start manufacturing lenses. Apart from ensuring a supply of lenses, this would also enable them to control the quality. In 1992, Green set up Aurolab, a non-profit lens factory, in India, with donated funds and investments from the SEVA Foundation. The factory is based next to and supplies the Aravind hospital, SEVA's key partner in India, where Dr Venkataswamy has pioneered cataract surgery en masse. Aravind Hospital charges patients what they can afford, so many pay nothing, and are effectively subsidised by payments made by the better-off. This has enabled the hospital to be self-financing. Green has worked with partners to bring this approach to Nepal, Egypt, Malawi, Guatemala and El Salvador.

By 2003, Aurolab was making 700,000 lenses a year, charging US$4 a lens (compared with the US$100 charged by major manufacturers), supplying customers in 85 countries, and making a profit that is invested in new product development and expansion. It produces ten per cent of the world market in intraocular lenses. Aurolab does not produce the lenses at a lower cost but, because it controls production and distribution, it can keep the price affordable and demonstrate that selling into poorer mass markets can be financially viable. Aurolab is part of a larger organisation set up by Green, known as Project Impact. He has applied the same thinking to hearing aids, which are now being produced for US$45, compared with the commercial price of US$1,500, to start to meet the needs of the estimated 125 million people in developing countries who would benefit from hearing aids. He is also searching for ways of producing affordable drugs to treat HIV and AIDS.

- Brian Dumaine, 'Two ways to help the Third World', Fortune, 27 October 2003, p 187
- Kris Herbst, 'Compassionate Manufacturing: Doing Business with the Poor', *Changemakers Journal*, January 2003
- Jane Black, 'Technology with Social Skills', *Business Week Online*, 19 August 2003

Mercedes 'Mimi' Doretti

Nationality: Argentinian
Work: initially Argentina, now international
Field: human rights

Born in 1958, Mercedes Doretti studied anthropology in Buenos Aires under Dr Clyde Snow, an American forensic anthropologist, who had helped to excavate the graves of some of the many people who 'disappeared' under the Argentinian dictatorship of 1976–83. She began to work alongside him. Then, along with a group of students, she founded Equipo Argentino de Antropologia Forense (EAAF) in 1984, the first forensic organisation focused on investigating human rights abuses. Its work not only exposes the extent of human rights violations but also provides families with much-wanted information about the fates of their members. Since 1986, the organisation has worked in more than 30 countries internationally, in Europe, Africa, Asia, and Latin America carrying out investigations, and working with and training local forensic scientists.

- Forefront, a network of leading human rights defenders internationally. www.forefrontleaders.org
- Argentine Forensic Anthropology Team. www.eaaf.org

Local but not parochial

Some local initiatives do not lend themselves to becoming global movements, but are nevertheless critical components of a global response: for example, Kabuye's work on reconciliation in Rwanda, and Strzmieczny's contribution to the processes of democratisation in Poland through civic education. Such pioneers are personally committed to action in a particular context, and their work is entwined with the people and the place. Some are from the country in which they work, such as Mechai Virvaidya in Thailand and Shirin Ebadi in Iran; others are foreigners who have come to love and be part of the country, such as Annalena Tonelli in Somalia and Tetsu Nakamura along the Pakistan–Afghanistan border. In spite of their local focus, they are connected internationally and draw on international resources, such as funding, information and support networks.

Mechai Virvaidya

Nationality: Thai
Work: Thailand
Field: health and social and economic development

Mechai Virvaidya, who was born in 1941, is from a prestigious family in Thailand – his grandfather was physician to the queen. He was born to a Scottish mother and Thai father, both of whom were doctors. A significant influence on Virvaidya was his mother's 'deep humanitarian compassion'; she worked not only with expatriates and the rich but also with poor people. He was educated in Thailand and Australia, attending Melbourne University to study economics and history. He sees himself as both British and Thai, both Christian and Buddhist.

On returning to Thailand, he embarked on a career in economic development. This took an unusual turn as he found himself taking on, and enjoying, a public role as a journalist, radio presenter, and star of a popular twice-weekly soap opera. In his main work he was increasingly convinced that traditional forms of economic development were not effective. Having identified the high birth rate as one of the most serious problems in rural communities, he decided to establish an NGO, Community-Based Family-Planning Services (CBFPS). He began to distribute condoms and birth control pills to local villages, working with the villagers themselves. He had an extraordinary ability to create publicity, often in highly gimmicky ways, but undoubtedly effective: for example, by providing free vasectomies on the king's birthday and holding condom balloon blowing contests. He became so personally associated with the work that in Thailand condoms have became known as *mechai*. Since then, his focus has broadened, and CBFPS became the Population and Community Development Association (PDA). When the first cases of HIV and AIDS were reported in Thailand in the late 1980s, Virvaidya was well placed to initiate some of the most effective campaigns to prevent its spread. He has become a leading international expert and activist on HIV and AIDS issues.

- Ramon Magsaysay Award, award winner in 1994. www.rmaf.org.ph

Rose Kabuye

NATIONALITY: Rwandan
WORK: Rwanda
FIELD: peace

Rose Kabuye was born in 1961 and brought up in a Ugandan refugee camp when her parents fled Rwanda because of violence. Having finished her university education in 1985, Rose Kabuye went to join the guerrilla army, the Rwandan Patriotic Front:

> *When I joined the army, I joined for a purpose – to fight for my rights, the rights of my children, and the rights of all children. Through fighting, we did achieve those rights.*

She has gone on to be mayor of Kigali and was an MP for two years, and has achieved positions of power in Rwandan society that are almost unique for a woman. As a lieutenant-colonel and the highest-ranking female officer in the Rwandan army, Kabuye now devotes her time to promoting the rights of women and their equal position in society, and in peace-building not only between the Hutu and Tutsi tribes but also between Rwandans and Congolese. She has pioneered working with women as peace activists, providing training and bringing them closer to the processes of policy-making and peace negotiations. She has also participated in international delegations and has been inspired by different experiences of conflict resolution and the role of women in Israel and Palestine, Sri Lanka, Bosnia and Russia.

- Women Waging Peace. www.womenwagingpeace.net/content/articles/0270a.html

Wan Yanhai

NATIONALITY: Chinese
WORK: China
FIELD: health and human rights

Born in 1963, Wan Yanhai qualified as a doctor in 1988, having attended Shanghai's Fudan University School of Medicine. He joined the National Health Education Institute, which proved to be the starting point for his work in raising public awareness and knowledge of HIV and AIDS in China. First, he set up a national telephone hotline providing information on HIV and AIDS, and carried out research into HIV and AIDS. He then established Men's World, a health promotion group for gay men, hosted a gay-rights talk show, and organised outreach programmes providing information on HIV and AIDS. In 1993, his operations were suppressed by the Chinese authorities, the various activities he had initiated were closed down, and he was dismissed from his job. Undeterred, in 1994, Wan set up the AIDS Action Project, which uses the Internet to spread information about HIV and AIDS as widely as possible within China. He has also used the Internet to provide information about homosexuality. He has sought and gained considerable international support, including various awards and academic fellowships to the US, giving him access to a wealth of ideas and knowledge not readily available in China. One of his key messages is that HIV and AIDS is a human rights issue as much as a health issue, with prostitutes, gay people and AIDS orphans experiencing extreme discrimination, as do those who are poor and without access to basic information. His work has prompted fierce criticism from the Chinese authorities, and this was especially the case when he publicised the events surrounding the infection of an estimated one million people in Henan province with HIV and AIDS or hepatitis due to faulty blood-collection practices. As a result, in 2002, his organisation was closed down, he was accused of revealing state secrets, and he was imprisoned. This prompted significant international pressure for his release, and he was let out after a month. Wan is continuing to work to ensure that

HIV and AIDS in China is taken seriously, not only within China but also internationally.

- Award for Action on HIV/AIDS and Human Rights, 2002 International Recipient, Canadian HIV/Aids Legal Network. www.aidslaw.ca/Maincontent/awards/internationalrecipient.htm
- Daniel C. Tsang, 'China's First Homegrown Gay and AIDS Activist, Wan Yan Hai', *San Jose Mercury News*, 9 July 2000. www.commondreams.org/views/070900-103.htm
- Fulbright New Century Scholar Program. www.cies.org/NCS/ncs_ywan.htm#biography

Annalena Tonelli

NATIONALITY: Italian
WORK: Somalia, Kenya and Africa
FIELD: health and human rights

Annalena Tonelli (1943–2003) was born in Forli, the second of five children. Her father was an economist and expert on cooperatives. She trained as a lawyer, but never intended to stay in Italy. She left Italy in 1969 for Africa, inspired by Charles de Foucauld, a Franciscan priest who lived in north Africa, working with local people until he was killed in 1916. This inspired her to follow a spiritual path, based on religious motivations, to live and work with people born into extreme poverty. She moved to Kenya, where she became a teacher and then a health worker, spending most of her time treating ethnic Somalians with tuberculosis (TB). She found her home in Somalia and lived through the civil war and famine of 1991–5 that devastated the country and its people, risking her life to help survivors and smuggle out information to the international community. As a white Christian woman living among Muslims, she came to be loved and admired by many Somali people.

Tonelli established a hospital in Somalia to control and treat TB. Following success with new forms of treatment, she worked with the World Health Organisation to establish protocols for people with TB throughout Africa. Support for the hospital and the work she carried out there came largely from friends and family in Forli rather than from international aid organisations. Her work extended to other areas, including setting up a school for disabled children, treating people with HIV and AIDS, and, perhaps most controversially, trying to find ways to stop female genital mutilation. She helped to set up teams of local people, made up of both men and women, which would pass on information and provide those who were carrying out the circumcisions with funding and support to set up alternative businesses. In June 2003, Annalena Tonelli received the Nansen Refugee Award for her work in Somalia, hoping that the publicity and recognition would raise international awareness of the situation in Somalia. She was shot dead on 5 October 2003, outside the hospital she had founded.

- UNHCR. www.unhcr.org
- Maggie Black, 'Disarming the women who harm girls', *Guardian Weekly*, 12–18 February 2004, p 26
- David Brown, 'The Healing Heart of Annalena Tonelli. Humanitarian Gave Her Life to Helping Others', *Washington Post*, 8 October 2003, p C01

Jacek Strzmieczny

NATIONALITY: Polish
WORK: Poland and international
FIELD: education

Jacek Strzmieczny was born in 1950 and educated under the socialist regime in Poland. As a student he found the system oppressive and cruel, and in particular saw adults as stupid and harsh. He rebelled, fought, and regularly had to repeat the classes he had failed. Even though his parents tended to side with the 'adults' against him, he was inspired by his father, who had always been concerned with broader social issues and had taken a stand by not joining the Communist Party. Strzmieczny joined the student rebellion in 1968, and was active in the left wing of the dissident movement during the 1970s and 1980s. In particular, he was influenced by Jacek Kuron, an activist who had set up a Communist youth organisation, but had then rebelled against the regime to become one of the leading dissidents in Poland. Through Kuron, Strzmieczny came to believe that the way to transform systems was to change the way people think rather than to change the structures.

He was determined 'not to be like other adults' and not to let anyone else suffer as he had. He persevered with his own education, qualifying and practising as a school psychologist, and in 1984 gaining a PhD in education. He worked with young people, and set up the first pre-school education centres in Poland. The political changes that led to the first largely free democratic elections of 1989 represented an opportunity for significant transformation in Poland. In 1989, he took a job in the Ministry of Education, becoming director of teacher training. The opportunity for change had also captured the imagination of many international agencies and donors and, in 1991, he started a project in partnership with the University of Ohio in the US, called Education for Democratic Citizenship in Poland. It then became clear that it would be more effective to work outside government, and in 1994, he set up the Civic Education Project (CEP). CEP focuses on working with local governments on teacher training and curricula development to encourage civic understanding and responsibility, in the belief that these are essential to the democratisation process in Poland. A challenge for CEP has been to expand its work from relatively small-scale projects with local governments to influencing schools and educational policies at the national level. After almost a decade of lobbying by CEP, the government introduced civic education into the national curriculum in 1999. CEP now works with more than 5,000 schools and provides training, teaching materials and a range of projects focused on improving the quality of schools and fostering student engagement.

- Ashoka profile. www.ashoka.org
- Schwab Foundation profile. www.schwabfound.org
- Steve Owad, 'Guiding Polish Students along Democracy's Road', *Changemakers*, September 1998 www.changemakers.net/journal/98sept/owad.cfm
- Written materials from Civic Education Project. www.cep.org.pl
- Personal communication

Shirin Ebadi

NATIONALITY: Iranian
WORK: Iran
FIELD: Human rights

Born in 1947, Shirin Ebadi graduated from the University of Tehran as a lawyer, and became Iran's first female judge in 1975. The 1979 Islamic Revolution, led by Ayatollah Khomeini, resulted in changes to the legal rights and position of women in society. One of the effects was that women could no longer be judges and Ebadi was forced to resign.

She reverted to an academic role at Tehran University and published several articles and books on children, women, and refugee rights. She took on an advocacy role, campaigning for changes in the law, particularly for children and women, and founded the Association for Support of Children's Rights. She has also continued to work as a lawyer, and has taken on high-profile and controversial cases, defending individual dissidents and others oppressed by the political regime. In 2000, together with human rights lawyer Mohsen Rahami, Ebadi was banned from practising law. They had videotaped the confession of one of the perpetrators of violence against pro-reform gatherings, implicating well-known establishment figures. Along with a number of other dissidents, often women, she has contributed to prising open a somewhat fragile space for public debate and the pursuit of equality and human rights, in a country where struggles between modernising and traditional forces are acutely felt.

She was awarded the Nobel Peace Prize in 2003, the first time the award has been made either to an Iranian or to a Muslim woman. She is hailed by some as belonging to a secular reform movement in Iran, as she believes in the rule of law and appeared without a headscarf in Paris, and by others as belonging to the Islamic reform movement, because she asserts her faith and belief that human rights and Islam are compatible.

- Nobel Peace Prize, winner in 2003. www.nobel.se/peace/laureates/2003
- 'Iranian activist wins Nobel prize', BBC News UK edition, 10 October 2003. http://news.bbc.co.uk/1/hi/world/middle_east/3180302.stm
- 'Shirin Ebadi: 2003 Nobel Peace Prize Winner', 10 October 2003. www.farsinet.com/shirin_ebadi/
- 'Shorn of dignity and equality', *The Economist*, 16 October 2003

Abdurrazack 'Zachie' Achmat

NATIONALITY: South African
WORK: South Africa
FIELD: HIV and AIDS and human rights

Zachie Achmat was born in Johannesburg in 1962, and was raised in a Muslim community in Cape Town. His family life was unstable and, at times, violent. He was rebellious and defiant as a child; at the age of 14 he became one of the leaders of the 1976 anti-apartheid school campaign, attempting to burn down his school when laws were passed requiring black children to learn Afrikaans. He was arrested and detained several times, and had to drop out of school. In 1980, he went underground, where he continued as a youth leader within the African National

© GISELE WOLFOHN/PANOS PICTURES

Zachie Achmat and others campaigning for access to affordable anti-retrovirals

Congress (ANC), gaining considerable experience in organising political action.

Following the political changes in South Africa, Achmat started to study at university and helped to found the National Coalition for Gay and Lesbian Equality (NCGLE). He was diagnosed HIV-positive in 1990, publicly disclosing the diagnosis in 1997. He became one of the leaders and the public face of the South African-based Treatment Action Campaign (TAC), which was established in 1998 to campaign for access to affordable drugs for people with HIV and AIDS. Recognition of and treatment for people with HIV and AIDS became highly politicised in South Africa, in part because of the sheer number of people infected and dying, but also because of the government's stand disputing the link between HIV and AIDS and the effectiveness of antiretroviral drug treatments. Zachie Achmat has personified the campaign by refusing to take drugs himself until they became available and affordable to ordinary South Africans. His 'pharmaceutical fast' was publicised through a 2002 film 'It's My Life', which portrays the way he combined campaigning work with managing his erratic health and emotional state, and is 'a moving testament of an individual's extraordinary courage and a searing indictment of government intransigence'*.

While TAC's campaigns have been based on principles of civil disobedience, their actions have been seen at times as aggressive and defiant. TAC has pursued legal cases against the pharmaceutical companies and officially charged government ministers with manslaughter for blocking the supply of drugs. It has organised the mass mobilisation of people aimed at disrupting everyday activities, and has constantly courted both local and international media in order to raise awareness and gain broader support. At the same time, TAC has collaborated with many other national and international organisations, including NGOs, the churches, science and medical professionals, for example to reform trade rules that would create opportunities for producing cheaper drugs. At the end of 2003, following a series of successes by TAC and other campaigns, drugs became more cheaply available in South Africa, and Zachie Achmat started a course of treatment. Nevertheless, at the time of writing, access to treatment is very limited and progress is slow.

- It's My Life: a film by Brian Tilley, 2002. www.frif.com/new2002/mlife.html
- Biography of Adurrazack (Zackie) Achmat. www.frif.com/new2002/mlife2.html

- Derek Ingram, 'Commonwealth Update', in *Round Table. The Commonwealth Journal of International Affairs*, 370, July 2003, pp 333–62
- Ginger Thomas, 'In Grip of AIDS, South African Cries for Equity', *New York Times*, 10 May 2003
- It's My Life film synopsis. www.dayzero.co.za/steps/films/films_52/itsmylife.htm *

Tetsu Nakamura

Nationality: Japanese
Work: Afghanistan/Pakistan
Field: health and human rights

Tetsu Nakamura was born in Fukuoka City in Japan in 1946. He studied medicine and started to practise as a doctor in Japan in 1973. He also had a passion for mountain climbing which took him to the mountainous regions of Afghanistan. He fell in love with the country and the people, and in 1984, decided to volunteer at the hospital in Peshawar, in northwest Pakistan near the Afghan border.

Following the Soviet invasion of the country, he decided to stay, initially working in the hospital's leprosy unit then helping Afghan refugees fleeing across the border to Pakistan. After 1989, and the withdrawal of the Soviet forces, he provided medical aid within Afghanistan. He continued to do so after the Taliban took power, by which time many of the development programmes that had begun so enthusiastically were departing. He spent some time raising awareness of the problems facing Afghanistan, writing and speaking in Japan. He does not depend on international developing funding but prefers to rely on the Peshawar-kai foundation in Japan, which raises funds privately for his work. He built a hospital in Peshawar in 1998 as a base for fieldwork. It has four satellite clinics, which provide medical services to more than 150,000 patients a year, including advanced treatment and reconstructive surgery for people with leprosy. The problems of war have been compounded by global warming and reduced snow fall. This contributed to a severe drought in 2000, which affected approximately 60 million people in central Asia and beyond, and is estimated to have killed 90 per cent of Afghani livestock. Nakamura then started to work on irrigation projects in Afghanistan, using landmines to sink over 900 wells through otherwise impenetrable rock. Since the fall of the Taliban in 2002, he has been supporting local people in agricultural production so that they can make a living without reverting to growing poppies and feeding the drugs trade. At a time of increasing public wariness of Muslims, he presents positive images of Afghans as an Islamic people, based on his friendships and experiences:

> *I do not deny my original 'humanitarian motivation' to save the people, although I now realise the more important fact that we, ourselves, have been helped by this activity.*

- Ramon Magsaysay Awards, award winner in 2003. www.rmaf.org.ph

Local meaning from global ideas

These pioneers have taken an idea or approach that already exists, and have adapted it in particularly effective ways to local needs. The innovative nature of their work means that they are further shaping the form and potential of existing global platforms. Examples of this include M D Mistry, who has developed forms of participatory budgetary analysis that have been influential across India and internationally; Bishop Samual Ruiz Garcia, who was inspired by liberation theology to stand up for indigenous peoples in Mexico; and Arzu Abdullayeva, who has worked through the Helsinki Citizen's Assembly to initiate reconciliation and peace-building between Armenia and Azerbaijan.

Arzu Abdullayeva

Nationality: Azeri
Work: Azerbaijan Republic
Field: human rights

Arzu Abdullayeva was born on 23 March 1954 in Baku, Azerbaijan. She studied history and languages in Azerbaijan. She is deputy chair of the Socialist Democratic Party of Azerbaijan, was chairwoman of the Azerbaijan National Committee of the Helsinki Citizens Assembly (HCA) between 1992 and 2000, and became co-chair of HCA International in 2000. The HCA was formed in 1990 and is a forum where individuals and organisations can share ideas and develop strategies to promote peace and human rights as a collective and inclusive expression of civil society. Branches exist in most European countries.

In December 1991, representatives from the HCAs of Azerbaijan and Armenia issued a call for peace from Nagorno Karabach. This is an area of entrenched conflict, which had experienced war since 1988 over territory that lies within the Azerbaijani Republic but in which a majority of about 75 per cent ethnic Armenians live. Following this show of solidarity, the HCAs of Armenia, Azerbaijan and Georgia initiated the Transcaucasia Dialogue movement, aimed at broadening engagement between people throughout the three countries to establish mutual trust and respect. A tangible result of this cross-border cooperation was HCA involvement in the exchange of over 500 prisoners of war between Azerbaijan and Armenia. In 1992, Anahit Baiandur (Armenia) and Arzu Abdullayeva were jointly awarded the Olof Palme Peace Award for their work in bringing this about. In 1994, a ceasefire was negotiated, which is still in force. Nevertheless, the situation is recognised as unstable and critically important for the development of the region as a whole. The HCA continues to play a key role in fostering peace, for example through civic education and information programmes. In 2000, the HCA General Assembly took place in Baku, where Armenian representative were guaranteed safety by the President of Azerbaijan.

- Helsinki Citizen's Assembly of Vanadzor. www.hcav.am Women Waging Peace. www.womenwagingpeace.net/content/conflict_areas/armenazer.asp#women
- Transcend. www.transcend.org

M D Mistry

NATIONALITY: Indian
WORK: Gujarat, India and internationally
FIELD: socio-economic development

Mistry was a professor of geography and an active trade unionist in Gujarat. He founded Developing Initiatives for Social and Human Action (DISHA) in 1985. DISHA was set up as a mass movement, focusing on mobilising some of the eight million of the poorest and most discriminated against people in Gujarat: Dalits (untouchables), forest workers, tribal women collecting tendu-leaf, and other casual labourers. It is engaged in a wide range of activities, including trades unions, cooperatives, and special interest groups at community, village and state levels.

By 1992, despite government assurance of significant investment, little had been done to improve the lot of the tribal people. Mistry and others in DISHA started to look at government budgets in order to determine the real levels of expenditure. However, it proved impossible to determine expenditures on social programmes from the budgets provided by the government. They then drew on support and expertise about budgetary analysis from Oxfam and specialists in the US. The way to gain a true picture was to re-enter all the figures into a computer system, recode them, and then analyse funds allocated and expenditures to determine how much was actually being spent and on what. These time- and labour-consuming tasks proved to be invaluable not simply in providing people with knowledge but also as an empowering process. Budgetary analysis has proved to be a critical tool for Dalits and tribal people in challenging and engaging with government, and as such has also been influential in reducing power differentials between local people, civil society, and government. DISHA's budgetary analysis and briefings are highly regarded and used extensively by government officials and the media. The methods have been replicated in 12 other states of India, and, in 2000, an umbrella organisation was formed called People's Budget Information and Analysis Service (BIAS) to analyse the national government's budget. DISHA's methods have been promoted internationally as part of a movement in participatory approaches to budgeting.

- DISHA. www.disha-india.org
- M D Mistry, June 1999, Change Exchange journal for Advocacy Institute alumni. www.advocacy.org
- Mihir R Bhatt, Alternative Budget Analysis: DISHA's Experience. Gujarat, India: Civil Society and Governance Project, Foundation for Public Interest, 2000

Paul Rice

NATIONALITY: American
WORK: US
FIELD: trade

Paul Rice was born in 1960. As a student of economics and politics at Yale University in the early 1980s, he was interested in the political context of land reform and was drawn to Nicaragua, which had just gone through the left-wing Sandinista revolution. He went for a year or two, fell in love with the country, and stayed for 11 years. He worked within the cooperative movement, but when the Sandinista government lost power in 1990, support for co-ops dried up. He realised that to continue working with co-ops he would have to take the initiative, and helped to found the coffee co-op, PRODECOOP. It became extremely successful, selling through the fair-trade markets pioneered in the Netherlands by the Max Havelaar brand and by development organisations such as Oxfam. For Rice this was transformational, as he directly experienced the impact of enterprise development as a way of increasing the influence of poor and marginalised coffee farmers in a globalised market. He went on to work with coffee co-ops throughout Latin America and Asia.

Rice came to see the 'market' as not necessarily the enemy but as a tool for change, which he believes can be used by poor communities to gain economic power and thereby greater political voice. In 1994, he returned to the US to study for an MBA. He set up TransFair in the US in 1998 to create more equitable trade and to open up the US as a significant new market for farmers in developing countries. TransFair does this by supporting the development of fair trade in the US through certification and labelling. Coffee, in particular, has been a critical market as the commodity price plummeted in 2000 and farmers found themselves increasingly impoverished. TransFair has played an important role in bringing new retailers to fair trade, and saw imports of fair trade coffee increase by 46 per cent between 2001 and 2002. It now works with bananas and other fresh fruit, tea and chocolate.

- TransFair USA. www.transfairusa.org
- Schwab Foundation. www.schwabfound.org
- Personal communication

Roshaneh Zafar

NATIONALITY: Pakistani
WORK: Pakistan
FIELD: economic development

Roshaneh Zafar was born in Lahore in 1967 to a wealthy family. As a young woman in Pakistan she was influenced by the economic disparity around her and felt passionately about women's rights:

> *I remember one day when I was coming back from school and found out that my mother, along with other female activists, was in jail because she had taken part in a demonstration against the military government regarding the anti-women laws that had been introduced.*

Zafar went to study in the US, gained a Masters degree in development economics from Yale University, and started to work for the World Bank. In 1993, she attended a conference on women and economic development, and by chance sat down next to Muhammad Yunus, who had founded the Grameen Bank in Bangladesh which had pioneered micro-credit as a means of economic and social development. A year later, she left the World Bank,

© ROBERTO BRANCOLINI/PANOS

Zaptistas march in Chiapas, Mexico

frustrated by her lack of contact with women on the ground. She let Yunus know, and he immediately invited her to visit the Grameen Bank in Bangladesh and sent her the plane ticket.

> *I think the chance meeting I had with Professor Yunus of the Grameen Bank really changed my life and provided me a window of opportunity where I could practically do something about poverty and women's empowerment.*

Luck, or what Beveridge called 'providence', was clearly at play.

In 1996, she founded the Kashf Foundation as an action research project to assess and understand better the role of micro-finance in a Pakistani context. Now it provides a range of financial products, including loans, savings and insurance geared to the needs of poor women, with a strong emphasis on systemising repayment and credit management. Working with small groups of up to 25 women has proved to be an effective way for women to express themselves and to gain more control over their lives beyond their families. An evaluation reported significant benefits in economic position as well as individual self-confidence. In 2001, Kashf had five branches and 5,000 clients. Two years later, towards the end of 2003, there were 30 branches and 50,000 clients. It is considered an especially successful adaptation of micro-finance, and Zafar was one of the speakers at the opening plenary of the World Economic Forum, 2004, alongside president Obasanjo of Nigeria, James Wolfensohn of the World Bank, and Carly Fiorini, chief executive of Hewlett-Packard.

- Schwab Foundation. www.schwabfound.org
- Kashf Foundation. www.kashf.org
- Enterprise Development Impact Assessment Information Service, Case notes of Kashf Foundation, compiled by Sarah Mosedale, 2001
- Personal communication

Samuel Ruiz Garcia

Nationality: Mexican
Work: Mexico, Chiapas
Field: human rights

Samuel Ruiz Garcia was born in Irapuato, Mexico, in 1924. He studied at the seminary of Leon in Guanajuato, and then in Rome where he was awarded a PhD in theology and scripture. He was ordained as a priest in 1949, returned to Leon in 1952, and was appointed Bishop of San Cristóbal de las Casas in Chiapas, Mexico, in 1959. As Bishop he quickly became aware of the extent of discrimination and poverty experienced by the indigenous peoples of Chiapas. He was strongly influenced by his participation in the Second Vatican Council in 1962–5, and the ensuing meetings of Latin American theologians who developed ideas of 'liberation theology'. Liberation theology places greater emphasis on the embodiment of a Christian message relevant to local contexts than on evangelism and traditional missionary work. He learned the local languages and in 1974, organised the National Indigenous Congress. This brought together indigenous peoples, providing opportunities for a more powerful collective voice within the country and for collaboration. He went on to found Fray Bartolome de las Casas in 1988 to address human rights abuses in Chiapas. In 1992, he helped to set up SICSAL (Secretariado Internacional Cristiano de Solidaridad con los Pueblos de América Latina, 'Oscar A Romero') to promote solidarity and international understanding of indigenous peoples throughout Latin America.

In 1994, armed conflict broke out between the Zapatista National Liberation Army and the Mexican army as global trade rules threatened the livelihoods of local farmers. Ruiz was appointed mediator in peace talks with the government, gaining the trust and respect of the Zapatista, a role that he played until 1998. He resigned as bishop in 1999, when he reached 75 years of age, but continues to be active in promoting peace internationally. During his time as bishop he was physically attacked several times, nominated for the Nobel Peace Prize three times, and subjected to numerous calls for his resignation from the Church and from the Mexican government. In an interview in 1998 he said:

> *The so called 'Indian problem' is an international problem. The situation of the indigenous peoples varies across the continent but has many points of contact with the Chiapas situation. A volcano erupts where the layers of earth are thinner, but the volcanic activity remains underneath.**

- Rev. Samuel Ruiz Garcia to receive nineteenth Niwano Peace Prize', 22 February 2002. www.npf.or.jp/npf/dnews19e.html
- Quote from Sergio Munoz, 'Samuel Ruiz mediating for peace and social justice in Chiapas, Mexico', *Los Angeles Times*, 10 May 1998 *

Conclusions

More time and space could be spent telling the stories of the pioneers of global civil society, but the task now is to pull together some of what can be learned and shared. In the concluding paragraphs three areas are explored. First, it is suggested that the pioneers are 'rooted cosmopolitans' whose role is primarily connecting the local and the global (Tarrow, 2002). Second, I argue that the processes of change that pioneers initiate are grounded in the anomalies and contradictions between institutions. These anomalies are often most acutely and problematically experienced at the edges of those institutions, and therefore by groups of people who have little power and few resources, and are often marginalised from (and by) the mainstream. Third are some reflections on what motivates and gives strength to the pioneers in carrying out their transformational work.

Both local and global

Global civil society pioneers manage to be both local and global at the same time. To refer to the epigraph by Thomas Paine at the start of this chapter, their country is often not just 'the world' but also a place more like home. Certainly, many of the pioneers are cosmopolitan in having a global perspective and sensitivity, but they are not the 'cosmopolitan upper class' criticised by Rorty as an elite with no sense of community with the majority of people in the world (Rorty, 1998: 85). I suggest that the pioneers are best thought of as what Tarrow has termed 'rooted cosmopolitans' (Tarrow, 2002). In other words, what distinguishes them is not so much their ability to operate at a global level but rather their capacity to connect local and global opportunity structures to pursue their causes. As such, they are rooted in a locality, but are engaged with transnational networks and international structures.

For many of the pioneers, childhood and upbringing provided international exposure and experience. Often it is a combination of having travelled or lived abroad, having parents or family who are from different countries, or being educated abroad. Grant was an American born in China; Vittachi was born in Sri Lanka and brought up in Britain; Soros was born in Hungary, educated in Britain and went to work in America; Virvaidya has Scottish and Thai parents; Japhet was brought up in a liberal-minded, internationally oriented family in apartheid South Africa. This exposes some of them to places that inspire and capture their hearts, as with Rice, who is American but considers his home to be Nicaragua, or Tonelli, an Italian who found her home in Somalia. Such international exposure often arises from a somewhat privileged upbringing and could lead to an elitist perspective on the world. In the case of the pioneers, however, it provides them with an insight into and experience of how certain peoples and issues are marginalised. Equally, such experiences help the pioneers locate themselves and their place within a global context, sensing a reality in the interconnectedness that globalisation represents, and understanding the nature and potential of those connections.

It is in bridging and connecting the local and the global that Tarrow (2002) argues 'rooted cosmopolitans' make their contribution. This is evident in the stories of the pioneers. Wan has actively sought international connections in order to broaden his perspective and gain support for his work in China. Patkar remains committed to the Narmada Valley, and has also connected globally with others campaigning against dams. Soros created an international network of local foundations. Bassiouni managed an extraordinarily complex web of connections between NGOs, the UN, and an international legal community. OneWorld.net, under the leadership of Vittachi and Armstrong, was transformed from a UK-based web service to a global one, not by becoming homogeneous but rather by creating a network of local sites that are grounded in specific contexts. However, many people other than leading figures in civil society fill such bridging roles in their daily lives, and the process of globalisation involves more and more people living and working across national boundaries. What distinguishes pioneers is that they create connections that are transformational, generating opportunities for people who are otherwise marginalised and ignored.

Transformational processes

It is often the case that systems and institutions exist not because they are effective but rather because they are embedded in traditions and upheld by vested interests and a more general sense of familiarity and comfort. The pioneers presented have identified where there are problems with existing institutions, where there is injustice and where systems are failing people. They have then gone to where the trouble is and have stayed with it (Spinosa, Flores, and Dreyfus, 1997). Often the pioneers have spent a long time developing an understanding of what needs to change and strategies for initiating that change. The sorts of problems they then tackle can be thought of as systemic paradoxes, as disharmonies or anomalies between different institutions and practices (Friedland and Alford, 1991). Within these anomalies lie opportunities for change: for example, where the

Intertwined spheres: pioneers can access networks of support and resources

universal nature of human rights is widely accepted but women or indigenous peoples are denied such rights, such as Ebadi experiences in Iran or Ruiz Garcia in his work in Mexico; or where the medical knowledge and treatments exist but are not being made available, such as the situation in South Africa that Achmat is attempting to tackle; or where business is promoted as creating wealth and prosperity for a country but results in child labour and huge economic inequalities, which Grajew is addressing in Brazil. Iniquities and injustices may be apparent to many people, but often it takes a pioneering individual to articulate them in ways that attract support and create momentum for change.

Civil society pioneers depend on a range of techniques that give them impact, legitimacy and influence. They demonstrate the effectiveness of new approaches by setting up organisations and initiating products and services. Some of these act as models that can be adapted and replicated, such as Zafar did with the Grameen Bank, or Billimoria is doing by fostering the establishment of Childline services internationally. Often these initiatives are local but supported through international connections. Others are global or embedded in international transactions, such as finance and trade. Transparency International was set up by Eigen to deal with corruption in financial dealings between countries. Fair trade, by its very nature, requires international action; and by launching it in the US, Rice has opened up a large potential market. Often such initiatives operate as networks and are less focused on developing replicable models than on the nature of the relationships and interactions. Many pioneers influence existing institutions by raising awareness, providing evidence and information, and engaging in dialogue and negotiation. Saunders not only set up the first hospice but carried out research and set up a hub for information. Nakamura has devoted considerable time to informing people in Japan about Afghanistan. Wan has prioritised providing information on HIV and AIDS in China as widely as possible. Virvaidya and Japhet have both used popular media to influence attitudes and behaviours around public health. The impact of some pioneers is through the provision of a space and enabling people to have a voice. Ruiz Garcia has persisted in setting up forums and organisations with indigenous peoples; Kielburger with children; Mistry with marginalised groups in India; Tonelli with ethnic Somalians with TB.

The nature of the obstacles and the extent of the resistance to the new ideas and practices vary. In some cases, ideas and new institutions are adopted relatively quickly. Hospices, for example, were quickly taken up in other countries, and may reflect a widely shared desire to preserve the dignity of people who are dying. Similarly, Transparency International was more popular than anticipated, and the disparity between promoting development and condoning, or at least colluding with, corruption had become untenable. In some cases, the resistance takes more of a bureaucratic form, as with Strzmieczny in reforming education systems in Poland. Yet civil society often challenges powerful people and institutions, and pioneering work can involve danger and violence.

Certainly, civil society does not necessarily lie within the law, nor should it, and Fries (2003) points to the often antagonistic relationship between legal systems and civil society. Even if acting outside of the law, most of the pioneers are explicitly committed to using peaceful means to pursue their ends. Several have been inspired by Gandhi and principles of non-violence and civil disobedience, and Gandhi's influence is felt across the globe. Often, peaceful means are inherent in pioneers' work, such as Abdullayeva's in building peaceful relationships between people in Armenia and Azerbaijan.

Direct action and various forms of civil disobedience are more controversial, as they can cause serious disruption; Achmat and the TAC have organised marches and demonstrations, obstructing daily life for many people. Of course, pioneering activities are, by their nature, controversial and disruptive. And, at times, the boundaries between civil disobedience and extreme disruption, and between self-defence and violence are blurred and difficult to judge, especially without direct and detailed knowledge of the situation. Rose Kabuye, in Rwanda, was part of a resistance army challenging oppression in order to gain freedom and basic rights. For her, such violence was necessary then, although it no longer is, and now her energy is devoted to resolving conflicts and building peace. Similarly, it is one thing to hail Nelson Mandela and his achievements now; it was another to applaud him in the 1960s when he led a violent arm of the African National Congress. For others, it may mean standing alongside and working with people who are violent. The Zapatista National Liberation Army used violence in the Chiapas region of Mexico in order to assert its position and gain influence that it felt was denied through other channels. Ruiz Garcia, constant in his support for indigenous peoples, was able to engage with the complexity of their position, and understood the long-standing history of repression and violence to which they had been subjected, without himself promoting violent action. He focused on mediation and arguing for justice; rather than condemning the Zapatistas, he gained their respect, although he was often judged as collaborating with them. Where Arendt (1969) has criticised force as a means of gaining power, as it destroys what is in place but never legitimises a new authority, Ruiz Garcia comments :

> *The Zapatistas never tried to gain power as the other guerrilla movements did. What they were trying to do was to shake up the sociopolitical conscience of the citizens of this country and ask them to participate in creating a transitional government until a more democratic government was in place. (Quoted in Munoz, 1998)*

More often, however, violence is apparent in the circumstances within which the pioneers are operating and in responses and attempts of others to silence them. The personal risks that many pioneers take, including imprisonment and torture, are evident, especially for those in undemocratic countries with dictatorial regimes. While international recognition can help, it is certainly no guarantor of safety. For example, Tonelli had worked for 33 years in Somalia and Kenya and was murdered only months after receiving a prestigious award for her work with refugees. Similarly, Wa in Burma and Nakamura in Afghanistan and Pakistan have risked their lives, if only by staying put during war or famine, in order to tackle contentious issues. These acts are compelling and require extraordinary commitment and courage.

Transformational capacities

In looking at how people effect change in a globalising world, Cerny (2000) refers to those with a 'transformational actor orientation' without indicating what might make them transformational. Here, the capacities of the pioneers are considered in terms of their leadership abilities, education, financial and other resources, and motivation. These echo Beveridge's identification of middle-class attributes, religious or other motivation, and

'Rooted cosmopolitans': pioneers can connect the local and the global

access to resources, among the British pioneers.

By definition, pioneers demonstrate forms of leadership by leading people directly in organisational settings or social movements, by passing on expertise, or simply by their example (Gardner, 1997). Popular understandings of leadership tend to focus on the personality and attributes of leaders as individuals, where leaders possess certain personal qualities that can be identified, even if with some difficulty. For many this is encapsulated in Weber's notion of the charismatic leader whose authority comes not from his or her position in a hierarchy but rather from charisma and personality. However, in spite of the many academic and theoretical positions that have focused on the characteristics of individuals as leaders, research has consistently failed to identify core personality traits (Yukl, 1989; Chell, Howarth, and Brearly, 1991; Wheatley, 1994; Hesselbein, Goldsmith, and Beckhard, 1996). There is growing recognition theoretically of the variety of types and styles of leadership, and of the complexity of the interplay between leaders, followers, the cultural and institutional context, organisational factors, and the ideas, strategies and responses being enacted (Grint, 2000). Certainly, the research for this chapter showed a great diversity in abilities, skills, aims, and general style among the pioneers: from Tonelli, who avoided almost all publicity in her work on health issues in Africa, to Virvaidya, also working on health issues, who seems to court the media at every turn. While this diversity reflects differences in individual temperaments, attitudes and personality, it is also indicative of the varying needs and contexts within which pioneers work, and the different responses that are therefore called forth.

While common personality traits and leadership styles are elusive, it is striking that many of the pioneers are educated and from middle-class backgrounds. Many have attended university, some have PhDs. Several have professional families backgrounds – parents who were doctors, lawyers, business people or academics – and most, though not all, could be considered middle class, notwithstanding variations in the size and location of the middle classes among countries and regions. It could be argued that a good education and a relatively

Box 6.3: Alfred Nobel's will and the creation of the Nobel Prize

Alfred Nobel was born in Sweden in 1833, and moved to Russia with his family at the age of nine. His father was an engineer and business entrepreneur whose interests included arms manufacture. Alfred had an excellent private education, and at the age of 17 was fluent in five languages as well as having a keen interest in poetry, philosophy, chemistry and physics. He joined the family business and proved to be both an adept entrepreneur and a prolific inventor. He invented dynamite, and took out more than 300 other patents. Factories spread through 20 countries, and he exported munitions and other products worldwide, from Australia to the US. He had homes in several countries, and was officially resident in none. He never married and was something of a solitary figure, retaining his passion for literature and philosophy, and spending much time reading and writing.

Nobel is remembered not as a leading industrialist and inventor but as the founder of the Nobel Prize. He died in Italy in 1896, and in his will he prescribed the establishment of five awards 'to those who, during the preceding year, shall have conferred the greatest benefit to mankind' in physics, chemistry, medicine, literature and peace. Importantly, the nationality of candidates was not to be a consideration – the awards were meant to be international. Little is known about Nobel's vision or intentions in making this legacy, though much can be inferred from his interests and cosmopolitan life. In particular, the peace prize is thought to have been inspired by Nobel's friendship with Bertha von Suttner, a peace activist who set up peace congresses, published a pacifist journal, and wrote the influential book *Lay Down Your Arms* (1889).

At that time, it was extraordinary to leave a significant bequest for scientific and charitable purposes, to be distributed internationally. Nobel's controversial will was contested by members of his extended family. Some of the press supported it, but significant sections of the media declared it unpatriotic, in violation of inheritance laws, and warranting immediate challenge on moral grounds. The institutions named in the will as the awarding bodies also resisted it. In addition, the will had not been drawn up by lawyers, and was unclear about how the awards should be managed. It took five years of considerable dedication and persistence before the two executors of the will convinced the family and the awarding bodies that the awards should go ahead as Nobel had wished. The first awards were made in 1901, and their influence and prestige are a credit not only to Nobel and his remarkable gift, but also to the people and institutions who made them a reality.

Source: www.nobel.se

privileged upbringing give certain advantages, perspectives and skills that provide credibility in an organisational setting or a global arena: a sense of agency and self-confidence, the ability to speak certain languages such as English, and a familiarity with global processes and international systems. Conversely, while some pioneers do not necessarily have such strong professional family backgrounds, such as Achmat and Kabuye, they have actively pursued educational opportunities. This may have helped them to access some of the benefits of middle-class status that would have become available following the major changes in South Africa and Rwanda.

In fact, many of the pioneers are also professionals, and several seem to act from an ethical stance rooted in their professionalism or the ideals of their discipline, whether that is medicine, law, economics, education or anthropology. Bassiouni and Ebadi are both academics and practise law. Japhet trained as a doctor but was frustrated by his limited capacity to help people from within medicine. Vittachi's training as a journalist and her father's commitment to the profession instilled strong values around seeking out and telling the truth. Some who worked in development, such as Eigen, Zafar and Rice, felt unable to have the sort of impact they wanted within existing structures and therefore decided to set up new and independent organisations. Civil society is, then, not best seen as a distinct organisational or professional sector, but a sphere of activity that reaches into and intertwines with many, if not all, other areas of life – not only business, politics and religion, but also science, academia, culture, medicine, law, and even the armed forces. This gives support to the notion of civil society as a space rather than as a sector or organisational form, permeating society and touching people in all walks of life. It also adds a complexity not apparent when civil society is considered as simply 'between the state and the market' – the most prevalent

Box 6.4: **Davos, world economic leaders, and social entrepreneurs**

At the 2004 Annual Meeting of the World Economic Forum (WEF), there was genuine excitement about social entrepreneurship. Social entrepreneurs attend the WEF as members of the Schwab Foundation for Social Entrepreneurship, which was set up by Klaus and Hilde Schwab as a sister organisation to the World Economic Forum in order to promote social entrepreneurs and their causes more effectively among global decision-makers. This was the third WEF that social entrepreneurs had attended, and there was a strong sense that perceptions were changing. As one social entrepreneur said, 'We discerned a genuine shift in the general perception of social entrepreneurship, moving from the loony fringes toward greater recognition and acceptability as a positive and significant force for economic as well as social and political good'. For its critics, the annual meeting in Davos is a networking opportunity that reinforces existing global inequalities and pays little attention to the implications of globalisation for the grassroots. For social entrepreneurs, Davos provides opportunities to meet with business executives and political leaders, to raise the issues they are working on (such as the environment, fair trade, human rights, and HIV and AIDS), and to start to form collaborative relationships.

'I'm participating as a peer of top business, NGO, political, foundation and religious leaders. This puts us at the table, providing an unequalled opportunity to get our message out. It's a long-term opportunity to influence the world. It also brings us immense credibility. Normally, attending the WEF is something only the very top people in Silicon Valley get to do, so even people at home start to take us more seriously' (Jim Fruchterman, BENETECH (a non-profit organisation based in Silicon Valley, which uses technology to promote human rights and other social causes)*.

Collaboration opportunities were pursued directly, as the Schwab Foundation introduced its social entrepreneurs to relevant business and political leaders. For Garth Japhet, meeting the heads of several international development agencies was important for creating strategic connections and enhancing the potential of his organisation, Soul City, to contribute to a global social policy arena. And for Sergei Kostin, who runs The Way Home homelessness organisation in the Ukraine, a three-minute meeting with the Ukrainian Prime Minister has raised the profile of his organisation and the issue of homelessness in the Ukraine and Russia. He has become more directly involved with policy processes and with parliament, and raised finance for a new project.

The benefits of collaboration were also promoted more widely at a reception within the 2004 WEF, hosted by the Schwab Foundation, Hewlett Packard and Visa, and which attracted more than 200 people. 'We are presented with a powerful opportunity,' said Malcolm Williamson, outgoing CEO of Visa. 'First, we need to recognise social entrepreneurs and how they are launching innovative programmes that have a high impact on tough problems. But, more importantly, we need to mobilise the resources of our companies, governments, and organisations to build partnerships that smash challenges and grow opportunities.' Social entrepreneurs also participated on the plenary sessions and specialist sub-plenaries of the 2004 WEF, as keynote speakers and commentators on education, HIV and AIDS, poverty, and the environment (see the profile of Roshaneh Zafar). The attention at Davos helps to define social entrepreneurs as global leaders in the pursuit of social value.

Attendance by social entrepreneurs at Davos is still in a formative stage, but there are indications that it is a useful and expanding platform. Decision-makers have begun to listen. As geopolitical risks grow, so does the demand for creative approaches that build sustainable organisational structures to provide public and private goods. Social entrepreneurs can demonstrate effective approaches and act as catalysts in advancing global civil society agendas. Davos is one opportunity, albeit an important one, for social entrepreneurs to diffuse their innovations and generate momentum and interest behind social, economic and political changes, which do take account of the grassroots.

Maximilian Martin, Head of Research, Schwab Foundation for Social Entrepreneurship, and Paola Grenier

* Quotation is taken from personal communication with Jim Fruchterman.

'The Schwab Foundation in Davos, January 21–25, 2004', *Perspectives*, 2nd issue of the periodical published by the Schwab Foundation and available for download at the Schwab website. www.schwabfound.org

understanding of civil society (Anheier, Glasius and Kaldor, 2001: 13).

Intertwined with professional ethics are often religious, spiritual or personal values. Many are motivated by a deep-seated sense of justice, and, for some, this comes from religious beliefs, such as Saunders, who founded the hospice movement. For others, it comes from family values and actions that impressed them as children. Japhet talks about the environment created by his family that made him aware of the injustices of apartheid. Similarly, Zafar, Billimoria, Strzmieczny and Soros all cite family values that nurtured a desire to help others and make a difference.

What is striking is that many have thought about and are able to articulate, even if not fully, a kind of personal philosophy and set of values that are deeply felt. Soros, perhaps, stands out as having built his philanthropy on the theory of 'open society', which he also writes about and promotes. Grant believed that 'to be able to relieve suffering and not to do so was a grossly immoral act' (Jolly, 2001: 42). His favourite quotation, which seems like a mantra for his life, was from George Bernard Shaw:

> *I am of the opinion that my life belongs to the whole community and as long as I live it is my privilege to do for it whatever I can. Life is no brief candle to me. It is a sort of splendid torch which I have got hold of for the moment, and I want to make it burn as brightly as possible before handing it on to future generations.*

At the age of 12, Kielburger believed that children could make a difference in the world, and a part of Free the Children's mission is to 'free children and young people from the idea that they are powerless to bring about positive social change and to improve the lives of their peers' (Free the Children, URL). But it is not only having a set of beliefs, or a profound philosophy of life that distinguishes the pioneers: it is that they act on it. Strzmieczny not only believed that no one should suffer as he had done as a child, he devoted his life to that end. Pioneers gain strength and have impact in part from knowing and living their convictions.

However, personal skills and strong motives are not enough of themselves; resources are necessary for visions to become reality. Beveridge mentioned that pioneers had 'fortunes of their own' or 'the fortunes of friends at their call'. Certainly, some draw significantly on funds raised through friends and family; Tonelli and Nakamura resourced their work in this way rather than depending on institutional funding. A few finance themselves, such as Soros. Most, however, draw on a wide range of resources – funding, expertise, knowledge and volunteers – both locally and internationally. In accessing such resources, pioneers make substantial use of networks locally, within their own fields, and internationally. The existing networks and infrastructures of global civil society, such as the International Red Cross and Red Crescent, Save the Children, Médecins sans Frontières, as well as international donors, are important support structures. For example, Oxfam was a key source of expertise for Mistry in the development of participatory budgetary analysis. The Ford Foundation is mentioned several times as having been an early and critical funder, for example, in the cases of OneWorld.net, Transparency International, and the World Social Forum. However, funding is not always the most important resource.

For many pioneers, gaining a profile and legitimacy is of ongoing importance. International award schemes can help with credibility, funding, improved morale, and access to a global arena. In recent years, there has been a flourishing of international awards, with the Nobel Prize, which was established in 1901, still the most prestigious and internationally renowned. The creation of award schemes reflects the growing recognition of the importance of global civil action and a desire to be associated with it. A number of new network organisations are emerging, such as Ashoka, Avina and Echoing Green, which specifically promote and support individuals, be they social entrepreneurs, human rights activists, or civil society leaders. These networks are playing a significant role in supporting the work of pioneers at the global level, providing them with access to resources they would otherwise struggle to reach, as well as helping them to move in international circles and understand better their own work within a global context. Access to the World Economic Forum at Davos is seen as one of the main benefits of being selected as a Schwab social entrepreneur, not only in opening doors but also in conferring credibility and thereby facilitating the development of productive relationships. It will be important to ensure that such networks foster 'rooted cosmopolitans' and not an elite that is detached from local realities, which is a problem in the arena of international aid and development. It will be interesting to chart the influence of these emerging networks, the ways in which they create opportunities for a broad range of pioneers to reach a global platform, and perhaps help to even up the benefits of globalisation.

Table 6.2: International networks of civil society leaders

Organisation	Year set up	Aims	Size
Transnational Institute	1974	'An international network of activist-scholars committed to critical analyses of the global problems of today and tomorrow'	25 current fellows
Ashoka	1980	'...to develop the profession of social entrepreneurship around the world'	1,424 fellows
The Advocacy Institute	1985	'...works to make social justice leadership strategic, effective, and sustainable in pursuit of a just world'	700 fellows
Echoing Green	1987/8	'...to spark social change by identifying, investing and supporting the world's most exceptional emerging leaders and the organizations they launch'	371 fellows
LEAD	1991	'...to create, strengthen and support networks of people and institutions promoting change towards sustainable development – development that is economically sound, environmentally responsible and socially equitable'	1,402 fellows
Avina	1994	'...works in partnership with civil society and business leaders in their initiatives toward sustainable development in Ibero-America'	324 partners
Henry Crown Fellowship Program	1997	'...seeks to develop our next generation of community-spirited leaders, providing them with the tools necessary to meet the challenges of corporate and civic leadership in the 21st century'	137 fellows
Synergos Senior Fellows Program	1999	'To make sustained inroads against poverty, foundations need organizational and human skill development, connections to support networks, and access to best practices.'	66
Development School	1999/ 2000	'a university without walls building skills without edges', rooted in critical self-reflection, and engagement with the complexity and unpredictability of social development'	18 graduates
Schwab Foundation for Social Entrepreneurs	2000/1	'...a global platform to promote social entrepreneurship as a key element to advance societies and address social problems in an innovative and effective manner'	78 members
Joel L Fleishman Fellows in Civil Society, Duke University	2002	Improving the capacity of non-profit leaders to play significant public policy roles	12 fellows
Yale World Fellows Program	2002	'...to build a global network of emerging leaders.' Aimed at outstanding mid-career professionals	31 fellows
African Leadership Initiative	2003	'...to develop motivated, effective and responsible young leaders across Africa who are capable of guiding their countries as they struggle to align the demands of globalization with local visions of "a good society"'	89 fellows

Note: The information presented here was taken from organisational websites and in some cases from the organisations directly, and reflects their positions at March 2004. It is not a comprehensive list of such networks.

Geographical coverage	Support provided	Base country	Website
International (fellowship lasts three years)	Emphasis is on the contribution that fellows can make in cooperating to analyse and address global problems	Netherlands	www.tni.org
48 countries (North and Latin America, Asia, Africa, Central Europe)	Funding for three years. Membership of Ashoka fellowship. Access to a range of specialist support and networks	US	ww.ashoka.org
50 countries (international)	Intensive and tailored training in advocacy and leadership to carefully selected groups of fellows. Membership of fellowship	US	www.advocacy.org
30 countries (international, though predominantly US)	Funding for two years. Technical assistance. Membership of Echoing Green fellowship	US	www.echoinggreen.org
more than 70 countries (international)	Leadership training in sustainable development. Membership of a network	UK	www.lead.org
20 countries, all Spanish/ Portuguese-speaking	Funding and support. Facilitates partnerships between civil society and business organisations	Switzerland	www.avina.net
13 countries (predominantly US)	Leadership development programme spread over a two-year period emphasising community service. Involves people from all sectors	US	www.aspeninstitute.org/ index.asp?bid=403
24 countries in current group	Structured programme of mutual learning for grant-makers and foundations	US	www.synergos.org/ programs/fellows.htm
Currently central and eastern Europe, expanding to South Africa and UK	Structured programme of learning and reflection, offering a postgraduate qualification, and opportunities for ongoing dialogue	London	www.development-school.org
30 countries (international)	Membership of network of Schwab social entrepreneurs. Participation in annual summit of social entrepreneurs. Invitation to WEF for three years	Switzerland	www.schwabfound.org
8 countries	Funding and support to attend Duke University to carry out a four-week research project	US	www.pubpol.duke.edu/ centers/civil/index.html
27 countries (international, but *not* including the US)	Year-long study and networking programme	US	www.yale.edu/ worldfellows
First phase took place in South Africa, Ghana, East Africa, Mozambique, plus a pilot in South Africa	Training and seminars, over three years. Intends to develop leadership and facilitate supportive networks	USA/East Africa/ Mozambique/ Ghana/South Africa	www.africaleadership.net

Table 6.3: International awards

Award Set up Based Area covered	Purpose	Founding details	Number of recipients	Award given (US$)	Website
Nobel Peace Prize 1901 Norway International	For the person who has 'conferred the greatest benefit on mankind' during the year	Established in the will of Swedish businessman Alfred Nobel	Over 110 individuals and organisations	10 million Swedish kr (approx $1.3 million)	www.nobel.no www.nobel.se
Nansen Refugee Awards 1955 Switzerland International	To a person or group who excels in supporting refugee causes	Set up in honour of Fridtjof Nansen, the Norwegian explorer, first international refugee official, and Nobel Peace Prize Laureate. Run by United Nations High Commissioner for Refugees	60	$100,000 given annually, plus a medal	www.unhcr.ch/cgi-bin/texis/vtx/home?page=events&id=3fb359bd4
Ramon Magsaysay Award Foundation 1957 Philippines Asia	Honours individuals and organisations in Asia who have achieved distinction in their fields and have helped others generously without anticipating public recognition	Established by the trustees of the Rockefeller Brothers Fund (RBF). Conceived by John D Rockefeller III, the award was created to commemorate President Ramon Magsaysay and to perpetuate his example of integrity in government and pragmatic idealism within a democratic society	15 institutions and 214 individuals (1958–2002)	Six awards in different categories each year. Also facilitates networking between award winners in four areas: rural, urban, education/religion, peace	www.rmaf.org.ph
International Human Rights Award 1968 US International	'To an individual who has made notable contributions to the cause of international human rights'	Founded by the International League for Human Rights	35	One annual award	www.ilhr.org/index.html
Letelier-Moffitt Human Rights Awards 1976 US US and the Americas	Celebrates new heroes of the human rights movement	In memory of Institute for Policy Studies associates, Orlanda Letelier and Ronni Moffit, who were killed by a car bomb detonated by agents of Chilean dictator Augusto Pinochet	57	One US and one international award made annually	www.ips-dc.org/lm-awards/index.htm
Right Livelihood Awards 1980 Sweden International	'For outstanding vision and work on behalf of our planet and its people'	Set up by Jakob van Uexkull, who endowed the award with $1 million from the sale of rare stamps	94	Four annual winners share 2 million Swedish kr (approx $250,000)	www.rightlivelihood.se
International Simón Bolívar Prize 1983 International	'To reward activity of outstanding merit which has contributed to the freedom, independence and dignity of peoples and to the strengthening of solidarity among nations'	United Nations Educational, Scientific and Cultural Organisation (UNESCO) with the government of Venezuela, to commemerate the bicentenery of the birth of Simón Bolívar	12 individuals and organisations	$25,000 awarded every two years	http://portal.unesco.org/culture/en/ev.php@URL_ID=8571&URL_DO=DO_TOPIC&URL_SECTION=201.html

Table 6.3: continued

Award Set up Based Area covered	Purpose	Founding details	Number of recipients	Award given (US$)	Website
Sasakawa Environment Prize 1984 Kenya International	'To individuals who have made outstanding contributions to the protection and management of the environment'	Founded by Ryoicha Sasakawa and the Nippon Foundation. Given by the United Nations Environment Program (UNEP)	19	$200,000 awarded annually	www.unep.org/sasakawa2
Gleitsman Foundation, International Activist Award 1989 US US and International	'Recognizes and encourages leadership in social activism worldwide'	Set up by businessman Alan L Gleitsman to honour individuals who have initiated social change	30 (15 US and 15 International)	Alternate annual awards for US *Citizen Activist* and *International Activist*, of $100,000. Monthly *Award of Achievement*, $500, international (but most in the US)	www.gleitsman.org
Goldman Environmental Prize 1990 US International	To grass roots environmental heroes, 'for their sustained and important efforts to preserve the natural environment'	Established by Richard and Rhoda Goldman to draw attention to the global nature of environmental problems	94	$750,000 plus a bronze sculpture annually to a winner in each of the six continental regions	www.goldmanprize.org
John Humphrey Freedom Award 1992 Canada International (11 countries)	To a non-governmental organisation or an individual from any country or region of the world for exceptional achievement in the promotion of human rights and democratic development	Established by the International Centre for Human Rights and Democratic Development in honour of John Humphrey, a Canadian law professor who prepared the first draft of the Universal Declaration of Human Rights	12	CAN$25,000 plus a speaking tour of Canada	www.ichrdd.ca/frame2.iphtml?language=0&menu=m05&urlpage=nglish/about/brochureHumphrey2001.html
Martin Ennals Award for Human Rights Defenders 1993 Switzerland International (10 countries)	To an individual or organisation who has displayed exceptional courage in combating human rights violations	A collaboration between nine human rights organisations, including Amnesty International and Human Rights Watch, in memory of Martin Ennals, first secretary general of Amnesty International	11	20,000 Swiss francs	www.martinennalsaward.org/en/

Table 6.3: continued

Award Set up Based Area covered	**Purpose**	**Founding details**	**Number of recipients**	**Award given (US$)**	**Website**
Felipa Awards 1994 US International (23 countries)	Honours activists and organisations worldwide that work against discrimination on the basis of sexual orientation, gender identity, and HIV status.	In honour of Felipa de Souza, a Brazilian lesbian tortured by the Portuguese Inquisition in 1591. Run by the International Gay and Lesbian Rights Commission	30	Three-five awards made annually	www.iglhrc.org/site/iglhrc/section.php?id=40
Hilton Humanitarian Prize 1996 US International	'Honors a charitable or non-governmental organization that has made extraordinary contributions toward alleviating human suffering anywhere in the world'	Given by the Conrad N Hilton Foundation	8	$1 million plus a Tiffany sculpture	www.hiltonfoundation.org
Arab Gulf Programme for United Nations Development Organizations (AGFUND) 1999 Saudi Arabia International	'Distinguished efforts aimed at developing and promoting the concepts and dimensions of sustainable human development'	Established by HRH Prince Talal Bin Abdul Aziz to further the work of the AGFUND in supporting sustainable development	15	Gives three prizes annually, totalling $300,000	www.agfund.org/eprize.html
Zayed International Prize for the Environment 2000 United Arab Emirates International	To recognise and promote pioneering contributions in the field of the environment	In recognition and appreciation of the achievements of His Highness Sheikh Zayed Bin Sultan Al Nahyan, President of the United Arab Emirates	5 awards given in 2000	$1 billion every two years, divided among a first, second, and third prize. Each winner also receives a trophy	www.zayedprize.org/
World Awards 2000 Germany International	'Honoring men whose lives are filled with passion for ideals and visions, whose success in their fields helps them help others who have not been as fortunate.' 'First global prize for women whose unique achievements have contributed to a better, more peceful and humane society'	Established by Georg Kindel to promote tolerance and to provide inspiration for others. Originally the World Awards, which were linked to Men's World Day, were for men only. In June 2004, the Women's World Awards were established.		Various categories awarded anually; statuette given	www.worldawards.com
Champions of the Earth 2003 Kenya International	'Outstanding environmental achievers and leaders of the world, who made a significant and recognised contribution, regionally or beyond, to the protection and sustainable management of the Earth's environment and natural resources'	Run by United National Environment Program (UNEP). Originally the Global 500 Roll of Honour, set up in 1987	None as yet (over 700 recipients of Global 500 Roll of Honour)	Six awards to be given annually, starting in 2004	www.unep.org/champions

I am indebted to all the people who are profiled here, and the many more who could have appeared but for whom there was no space. I am grateful to all the people, too many to name, who responded to my requests for suggestions of people to include; to the Schwab Foundation for inviting me to its annual summit of social entrepreneurs; to the people who attended the seminar on 29 October 2003 at the London School of Economics; and to Marlies Glasius and Hakan Seckinelgin for their thoughtful and insightful comments on earlier drafts.

REFERENCES

Adamson, Peter (1995) 'Endpiece. A Splendid Torch. Peter Adamson pays tribute to the inspirational life of Jim Grant, the former Executive Director of UNICEF.' *New Internationalist*, No 266, April.
Anheier, H., Glasius, M. and Kaldor, M. (2001) 'Introducing Global Civil Society', in H. Anheier, M. Glasius, and M. Kaldor (eds), *Global Civil Society 2001*. Oxford: Oxford University Press.
Arendt, H. (1969) *On Violence*. New York: Harcourt, Brace and World.
Ashoka (URL) www.ashoka.org
Beveridge, Lord W. (1948) 'A Chapter of Pioneers', in *Voluntary Action: A Report on Methods of Social Advance*. London: George Allen & Unwin.
Cerny, P. G. (2000) 'Political Agency in a Globalizing World: Toward a Structurational Approach', *European Journal of International Relations*, 6: 435–63.
Chandhoke, N. (2003) 'The Limits of Global Civil Society', in M. Kaldor, H. Anheier, and M. Glasius (eds), *Global Civil Society 2003*. Oxford: Oxford University Press.
Chell, E., Howarth, J. and Brearly, S. (1991) *The Entrepreneurial Personality: Concepts, Cases and Categories*. London: Routledge.
Free the Children (URL) www.freethechildren.org (consulted 26 April 2004)
Friedland, R. and Alford, R.R. (1991) 'Bringing Society Back In: Symbols, Practices, and Institutional Contradictions', in Powell, W.W. and DiMaggio, P.J. (eds.), *The New Institutionalism in Organizational Analysis*. Chicago: University of Chicago Press.
Fries, R. (2003) 'The Legal Environment of Civil Society', in M. Kaldor, H. Anheier, and M. Glasius (eds), *Global Civil Society 2003*. Oxford: Oxford University Press, pp. 221–38.
Gardner, H. (1997) *Leading Minds. An Anatomy of Leadership*. London: HarperCollins.
Giddens, A. (1994) *Beyond Left and Right. The Future of Radical Politics*. Stanford, CA: Stanford University Press.
Grint, K. (2000) *The Arts of Leadership*. Oxford: Oxford University Press.
Hesselbein, F., Goldsmith, M. and Beckhard, R. (eds) (1996) *The Leader of the Future: New Visions, Strategies, and Practices for the Next Era* (Drucker Foundation Future Series). New York: Jossey-Bass Publishers.
Jolly, R. (ed) (2001) *Jim Grant. UNICEF Visionary*. Florence: UNICEF Innocenti Research Centre.
Munoz, S. (1998) 'Samuel Ruiz mediating for peace and social justice in Chiapas, Mexico', *Los Angeles Times*, 10 May.
Rorty, R. (1998) *Achieving Our Country: Leftist though in Twentieth Century America*. Cambridge, MA: Cambridge University Press.
Roy, A. (1999) *The Greater Common Good*. Bombay: India Book Distributor Ltd.
– (2000) 'For the Greater Common Good: The Pen as Tool for Activism. An Interview with Author Arundhati Roy', *Satya*, April. www.satyamag.com/april00/roy.html
Seckinelgin, M.H. (2002) 'Time to stop and think: HIV/AIDS, global civil society, and people's politics', *Global Civil Society 2003*. Oxford: Oxford University Press.
Spinosa, C., Flores, F. and Dreyfus, H.L (1997) *Disclosing New Worlds: Entrepreneurship, Democratic Action, and the Cultivation of Solidarity*. Cambridge, MA: MIT Press.
Tarrow, S. (2002) 'Rooted Cosmopolitans: Transnational Activists in a World of States'. Paper prepared for presentation at the Amsterdam School of Social Research Workshop on Contentious Politics: Identity, Mobilization and Transnational Politics, 6 May.
The Africa Leadership Initiative (URL) www.africaleadership.net
Timmins, N. (1996) *The Five Giants: A Biography of the Welfare State*. London: Fontana Press
Wheatley, M. (1994) *Leadership and the New Science*. San Francisco: Berret-Koehler Publications.
World Commission on Dams (2000) *Dams and Development: A New Framework for Decision-making*. London: Earthscan.
Yukl, G. (1989) 'Managerial Leadership: A Review of Theory and Research', *Journal of Management*, 15(2): 251–89.

Philanthropic Foundations: A New Global Force?

Helmut K Anheier and Siobhan Daly

Introduction

Philanthropic foundations have a long history in most of the world's cultures, reaching back to antiquity. Equally impressive as their longevity has been their expansion in recent decades. During much of the 1980s and 1990s, philanthropy thrived both nationally and internationally. At the beginning of the twenty-first century, there are more foundations holding more assets in more countries than ever before. For example, in 2003, the over 64,000 United States foundations had assets of US$435 billion (Foundation Center, 2004), and the ten largest German foundations alone had assets of about US$20 billion (Anheier, 2003), with significant increases since the early 1990s in each country. Indeed, like the US, Europe experienced a veritable foundation boom; the majority of its estimated 100,000 foundations were created in the last two decades of the twentieth century (Anheier, 2001).

Although most foundations, bounded by their deeds or charters, remain domestic in orientation and activities, they are, as we will see, becoming markedly more involved internationally, as have many corporations and NGOs. The US has, for many decades, been the engine of transnational philanthropy, but foundations in other regions such as Europe and the Asia–Pacific are becoming more active internationally as well[1]. Good examples of the trend include the Ford Foundation in the US, the United Nations Foundation, the Gulbenkian, Mercator and Bosch Foundations in Europe, the Sasakawa Peace Foundation in Japan, the Aga Khan Foundation and George Soros's Open Society network.

Yet little is known about transnational philanthropic foundations in an era of globalisation. Their scale and scope, and above all their distinct role and contribution, if any, have not been systematically explored from a global civil society perspective. This chapter undertakes such an assessment by addressing the following questions:

- What is known about philanthropic foundations operating across borders?
- Are new forms of philanthropy emerging at the global, transnational level alongside the US model of the professional grant-making foundation?
- Does philanthropy have a distinct strategic role in the globalisation process, in particular in relation to global civil society?
- How is the role of foundations affected by the current geopolitical climate and what Kaldor, Anheier and Glasius (2003), and others, have called regressive globalisation?

Behind these seemingly innocent questions lie profound policy dilemmas that have played themselves out domestically in the past, and are now assuming a new quality at the transnational level. But what could possibly be wrong with voluntary donations of private fortunes to benefit the public? Does not philanthropy generate a 'warm inner glow' and an aura of benevolence, as the very name suggests? Who would possibly want to pose nagging questions about the role of philanthropy, particularly in fiscally constrained times?

Even though philanthropic assets are private, they tend to be tax privileged and sometimes even tax exempt, thus, to some extent, substituting for public funds. To justify its tax-privileged treatment, private philanthropy would have to be more efficient or effective than public spending – a topic that has led to heated debates among foundation experts and policy analysts (for example, Anheier and Leat, 2002; Porter and Kramer, 1999; Letts, Ryan and Grossman, 1997; Prewitt, 1999). The core

1 *The establishment of the European Foundation Centre in 1989, of Worldwide Initiatives for Grantmaker Support (WINGS) and Worldwide Initiatives for Grantmaker Support – Community Foundations (WINGS-CF) in the late 1990s, the International Network of Strategic Philanthropy, and the formation of the Asia-Pacific Philanthropy Consortium are indications of this institutionalisation process of global philanthropy.*

argument is whether foundations are better than state action at achieving some kinds of social benefits.

A central consideration is that, in terms of governance, foundations are among the most independent institutions of modern society. They are not subject to market forces or consumer preferences, nor do they have a membership or some electorate to oversee decisions and performance. As a result, critics have stressed the democratic deficit inherent in foundations and likened them to quasi-aristocratic institutions in formally egalitarian societies (W Nielsen, 1972). Conversely, others have suggested that the dual freedom from the market and popular control makes them independent forces of social change and innovation (Anheier and Leat, 2002). The argument here is basically about democracy: are those brought to power in competitive democracies in primary control of the public agenda, and is there room for independent, private action for public benefit by those who can afford it?

Different countries have answered this question differently. Social democratic countries have traditionally sought to limit the realm of foundations, as have countries influenced by the French Jacobin ideals of preventing private interests from interfering in the relationship between the citizen on the one hand and the state as the representative of the republic on the other (Smith and Borgmann, 2001). Liberal countries such as the US and the UK have allocated more space to philanthropy and encouraged the establishment of foundations. Japan, Korea and many countries in the South have traditionally assumed a more controlling approach, although the sometimes adversarial relationship between foundations and governments is everywhere becoming more collaborative.

The democratic deficit of foundations assumes a new quality at the transnational, global level, as does their independence from political control under a weak system of international governance. Foundations can pursue agendas that are different from, or even opposed to, those of national governments; they can fund social movements abroad that are against the interest of both home and host countries; they can implement relief and development programmes over which national governments and international organisations exercise little control. For example, in 2002, the Bill and Melinda Gates Foundation, which funds projects combating malaria, tuberculosis and HIV/AIDS, disbursed nearly US$1.2 billion in grants, more than the total operating budget of the World Health Organization (US$250 million in member-state contributions). Foundations in the field of environmental protection, like the John D and Catherine T MacArthur Foundation in the US or the German *Bundesstiftung Umwelt*, demand more resources than the United Nations Environment Protection Program. Moreover, without the support of foundations, the World Economic Forum, the World Social Forum and similar platforms for global debate might not have been possible.

Thus, foundations are a potentially global force – not as powerful as nation states and transnational corporations, to be sure, but nonetheless independent global actors capable of moving social and political agendas and meeting unmet needs. With this in mind, let us take a closer look at what we mean by 'philanthropy' and 'foundations'.

What is philanthropy? What are foundations?

Philanthropy is a culturally and historically specific concept, and, in the most general of terms, refers to the voluntary use of private assets (finance, real estate, know-how and skills) for the benefit of specific public causes. There are many ways and means of international philanthropy:

- private giving to NGOs that operate across borders, such as Save the Children or OXFAM
- 'friends-of' organisations that collect donations for particular institutions abroad, such as universities or museums
- diaspora organisations that support particular religious and ethnic groups living in different parts of the world, like the United Jewish Appeal in the US
- funding intermediaries, like the Global Fund for Children, which collect contributions and then disburse them as grants to recipient organisations around the world
- donor-advised funds held with financial institutions such as Fidelity or with pooled endowments like the Community Foundation Silicon Valley, which channel assets to charities and similar organisations located abroad
- e-philanthropy and the use of the Internet to distribute funds internationally, such as the Virtual Foundation, founded in 1996 as an online conduit.

However, the term 'philanthropy' is typically applied to philanthropic foundations and similar institutions. They are the main subjects of this chapter, which means that we cannot do justice to some other important forms of philanthropy, like those listed above as well as others[2]. This focus seems justified by the fact that foundations represent one of the main sources of support for global civil society organisations (Pinter, 2001), and have also been the most visible institutions assisting the development of international NGOs, transnational social movements, advocacy coalitions and social forums. At the same time, as we show below, many of the new developments, in particular in the global South, seem to transcend the conventional model of grant-making foundations.

Different interpretations of the term 'philanthropy' are rooted in the history and traditions of particular countries. In the UK, for instance, the terms 'charity' and 'philanthropy' are often used interchangeably, and the latter continues to be associated with Victorian images of upper-class largesse and patronage. By contrast, in the US, from the early twentieth century onwards, 'charity' and 'philanthropy' became distinguishable. In the US, the term 'charity' refers to giving for the purposes of addressing the *symptoms* of an issue or problem, whereas 'philanthropy' refers to giving that seeks to address the *causes* of an issue (Anheier and Leat, 2002).

The distinction between traditional charity and modern philanthropy is perhaps the most important development in the history of large-scale philanthropic foundations over the last 100 years. Historians like Karl and Katz (1987) have shown that the earliest of these new foundations, such as the Carnegie or Rockefeller Foundations, eschewed the more traditional charity approach of directly addressing social and other public problems and aimed at exploring the causes of such problems systematically, with a view to generating long-term solutions for them rather than just alleviating them (Bulmer, 1999; McCarthy, 2003).

US foundations also started to work through third parties to achieve greater multiplier effects through grant-making, thus becoming facilitators rather than operators. The rise of the US foundations in the twentieth century highlights their potential for triggering social change in addressing social problems. However, the service delivery function, which was one of the major raisons d'être of the traditional European foundations (hospitals, schools, and so on) was much less pronounced. In addition, the international presence of the Ford, Gates and Rockefeller Foundations, among others, has further emphasised this particular variant of organised philanthropy in many parts of the world.

The signature characteristics of the early twentieth-century US foundations – the search for the root causes of social problems, professional staff, grant-making, and evolving programme goals in the context of limited governmental responsibilities – came to dominate the world of philanthropy for much of the twentieth century, so much so that the modern foundation is often perceived as a genuinely American invention. The US model has spread to Canada, Europe, Japan, Australia and other parts of the developed world.

However, in the global South, local developments based on the US model remain limited, taking the form of offices representing large Northern-based foundations. This limitation obviously has to do with a lack of local capital in the shape of private assets, but also with weak legal, political and financial systems that offer little incentives for potential philanthropists in developing countries. For these reasons, new developments are taking place in the South that deviate both from the US model of professional philanthropy and from the European model of operating institutions. They are also beginning to shift the meaning of philanthropy away from its elitist connotations (Dulany and Winder, 2001).

Religious teachings and practices shape philanthropy and charity, and all major world religions emphasise both. For example, Islam makes charitable giving a central element of its creed. The paying of *Zakat* is one of the five pillars of Islam, and encouraged the establishment of *Al-Wakfs*, that is, Islamic charitable institutions for religious devotion and education. Yet the link between philanthropy, charity, and religion was nowhere more institutionalised than in Christianity: first, from the fourth century onwards, in the Constantinian system that allowed Catholic parishes to establish their own foundations, and second, after the Reformation, especially within Protestantism, with its emphasis on individualism, proselytising, and public display of religious devotion.

However, throughout much of Christian history, the relationship between philanthropy, religious salvation and 'worldly' affairs caused major theological rifts (Smith and Borgmann, 2001). It is, indeed, closely tied to the Reformation itself, and it is no coincidence that the emergence of the modern foundation in the late nineteenth and early twentieth centuries, while having

2 *However, they would deserve a more careful treatment to do them full justice, and include individual cross-border donations and remittances, as well as the many forms of transnational religious collections and fundraising for political causes of many kinds. To some extent, we also exclude what are called operating foundations, that is, foundations that run their own programmes or institutions (clinics, residential care facilities, universities, and development projects) rather than predominantly making grants to third parties, that is, grantees or recipient organisations.*

© DAYNA BEALY/FORD FOUNDATION

The Ford Foundation building

precursors in England and on the European continent, took place in the US, that is, the country mostly influenced by Protestantism and liberalism. Individual capitalists, guided by religious convictions as well as shrewd market thinking, turned personal fortunes into philanthropic funds. Many, though not all, of those who created US foundations in the early twentieth century were Protestants, although Jewish philanthropy assumed a significant role as well, in particular after the Second World War. Similarly, some of the founders of major European foundations in the twentieth century were Protestants, such as Reinhard Mohn (who founded the Bertelsmann Foundation and whose media empire began as a firm publishing religious and educational books), or J R Rowntree in England (a social reform-minded Quaker).

The professionalisation of philanthropy throughout the latter part of the twentieth century implied also a secularisation, and foundations such as Bertelsmann or Rowntree, despite their pietistic background, appear as secular institutions alongside Ford, Rockefeller or the Pew Charitable Trust. Yet the close link between religion and philanthropy, as well as between certain ideologies and value preferences, continues to be important, be it in the case of Islamic charities operating in Asia; the support for unions and cooperatives by social democratically minded foundations from Scandinavia or the Netherlands in Africa; the pro-market network of foundations supported by George Soros in central and eastern Europe; or the neo-conservative foundations in the US trying to influence the political agenda. In other words, foundations tend to have agendas – religious, humanitarian, political, cultural – that provide the frame for their operations and grant-making.

Definition and types of foundations

The various legal systems define foundations rather differently, and registration, legal practices and oversight regimes vary accordingly (Fries, 2003). Despite these differences, the basic concept of a foundation shares common images: a separate, identifiable asset (the root meaning of the Latin-based 'fund' or 'fond') donated to a particular purpose, usually public in nature (implying the root of 'charity' or 'philanthropy'). In attempting to cut across the diversity of the different definitions, Anheier (2001) proposed the following five characteristics of foundations:

Table 7.1: Types of foundations

Grant-making	Operating	Corporate	Community	Government-sponsored/created
Endowed foundations that engage mainly in grant-making for specified purposes	Foundations that operate their own projects and programmes	Tend to be company-related or company-sponsored foundations. They vary in terms of the links they maintain with the parent company	Grant-making organisations that pool revenue and assets from a variety of sources (individual, corporate and public) for a variety of purposes	Foundations that fit the structural-operational definition of foundation but are either created by public charter or enjoy high degrees of public sector support for either endowment or operating expenditure
Ford Foundation (US), Leverhulme Trust (UK), Volkswagen Stiftung (Germany), Bernard van Leer Foundation (Netherlands), Carlsbergfondet (Denmark)	Russell Sage Foundation (US), Institut Pasteur (France), Pescatore Foundation (Luxembourg), Calouste Gulbenkian Foundation (Portugal)	IBM Foundation (US), Fondation Cartier (France), Agnelli Foundation (Italy)	Worldwide (including southern hemisphere)	Asia Foundation (US), Federal Environmental Foundation (Germany), Fondation de France (France), Government Petroleum Fund (Norway)

- *Asset-based*, financial or otherwise. The foundation must rest on an original deed, typically a charter that gives the entity both purpose and relative permanence as an organisation
- *Private*. Foundations are institutionally separate from government, and are non-governmental in the sense of being structurally separate from public agencies. Therefore, foundations do not exercise governmental authority and are outside direct majoritarian control
- *Self-governing*. Foundations are equipped to control their own activities. Some private foundations are tightly controlled by either governmental agencies or corporations, and function as part of these other institutions, even though they are structurally separate
- *Non-profit-distributing*. Foundations are not to return profits generated by either use of assets or commercial activities to their owners, members, trustees or directors as income. In this sense, commercial goals neither principally nor primarily guide foundations
- *Serving a public purpose*. Foundations should do more than serve the needs of a narrowly defined social group or category, such as members of a family or a closed circle of beneficiaries. Foundations are private assets that serve a public purpose.

Table 7.1 illustrates the basic categories of foundations that underpin the complexity of forms that they assume (Anheier, 2001).

While the definitions and typology set out in Table 7.1 are useful for developed market economies and established democracies, they are less relevant to 'foundations' in the global South, as suggested by the examples given by Dulany and Winder (2001). Indeed, Anheier and Winder (2004) suggest that one of the first insights to be derived from comparative research is that foundations are different in a number of critical respects once we leave the cultural and legal boundaries of the Western-style developed market economies:

- Few foundations are founded by wealthy families or individuals.

- Few have endowments that are large enough to support both their administration and grant-making programmes.
- Most rely on diverse funding from public and private sources, both domestic and international.
- They become conduits of resource and information flows, and are well networked internationally.
- Most operate programmes in addition to giving grants or loans; that is, they are hybrid operating/grant-making foundations.
- They operate within a diversity of philanthropic cultures (US, European, Asian and so on) in addition to local ones.
- They frequently work in less-than-enabling legal and tax environments.

In order to capture more accurately the developing characteristics of these philanthropic institutions, we refer to them as 'foundation-like' organisations (Anheier and Winder, 2004). At the same time, these institutional innovations in the global South have yet to reach the transnational relevance of larger, Northern-based philanthropy, although they are increasingly linked with foundations and NGOs and form part of international networks.

The scale of global philanthropy

There is a lack of comprehensive data on the number, assets and contributions of foundations and foundation-like organisations in global philanthropy. Assessing the funding of civil society globally poses additional difficulties, not least the diverse and underdeveloped nature of existing reporting systems and the frequent use of multiple and indirect funding flows (Anheier and List, 2000; Pinter, 2001: 196).

Studies of international grant-making, published by the US Foundation Center (Renz and Atienza, 2000; 2003) reveal 'record growth' from the mid-1990s onwards. This is attributed to a range of factors, such as a favourable economic climate, patterns of growth in the foundation sector and, in particular, the emergence of 'mega foundations' such as the William and Melinda Gates Foundation, which focuses on international problems like HIV and AIDS, and tuberculosis. The downturn in the economy and the events of September 11, 2001 brought a drop in international giving by foundations. Overall, in relation to patterns of giving by US foundations in 2002–3:

- international giving decreased by 14 per cent in 2002 over 2001
- overall international giving declined 11 per cent to US$2.2 billion in the same period, while giving to overseas recipients increased to US$843 million
- the majority of international funding supported US-based programmes overseas (Foundation Center, 2004).

Despite these declines, in 2002, international giving by US foundations was still US$1.1 billion higher than in 1999 (Renz and Atienza, 2003) and significantly above 1980s and 1970s figures. Although we lack more recent data on the goals and spending of US foundations engaged in international giving, Table 7.2 lists the main foundations active in international grant-making in 2001.

The history and landscape of European foundations differs significantly from the American experience, which partly explains why foundations in Europe have not been as active internationally as US foundations (Smith and Borgmann, 2001). In many European countries, such as France, Greece, Luxembourg and Switzerland, the majority of foundations are operating entities or a mix of operating and grant-making bodies, as in Austria and Belgium (Anheier, 2001: 52). Moreover, patterns of foundation growth that followed the two world wars did not show full signs of recovery until the 1980s, when foundations revived across Europe. This pattern of growth, combined with factors such as an increase in international donor capital, globalisation and the growth of multicultural societies (Pharoah, Brophy and Ross, 2001), have contributed to an increase in international giving among European foundations, in particular in Sweden, the UK, Germany and the Netherlands.

Initiatives such as Europe in the World (EiTW) indicate how the situation in Europe is changing. EiTW seeks to encourage collaboration among funders (not exclusively foundations) in support of global development. The majority of foundations that act as EiTW partners are registered in European countries (EiTW, URL). These foundations vary in their traditional interest in international giving and/or programmes. Typically, the list of grants and beneficiaries of the Compagnia di San Paolo demonstrates a key focus on local, regional and national interests rather than international endeavours. Similarly, the Luso-American Foundation has traditionally been committed to encouraging cooperation between Portugal and the US in the areas of business, education, technology and culture.

By contrast, for some European foundations, international giving is an integral part of their activities. For

Table 7.2: Top 15 US foundations in international giving, 2001

Foundation name	Fdn Type	State	International grants (US$)	No of intl grants	Primary international focus areas
Ford Foundation	GM	NY	616,294,425	1,798	Seeks to strengthen democratic values, and reduce poverty and injustice, promote international cooperation, and advance human achievement through programmes in asset-building and community development; education, media, arts and culture; and peace and social justice
Bill and Melinda Gates Foundation	GM	WA	528,152,573	80	Supports efforts to increase global health equity through infectious disease prevention, vaccine research, and reproductive and child health programmes; and funds libraries worldwide
David and Lucille Packard Foundation	GM	CA	118,844,212	302	Supports family planning and reproductive health services and environmental conservation
John D and Catherine T MacArthur Foundation	GM	IL	94,431,868	250	Seeks to promote international peace and security, healthy ecosystems, reproductive health and human rights
Rockefeller Foundation	GM	NY	86,003,829	527	Seeks to improve the lives of poor people worldwide through programmes in the areas of food security, creativity and culture, global health equity, and global inclusion
William and Flora Hewlett Foundation	GM	CA	66,174,000	214	Supports programmes in the areas of population and reproductive health, conflict resolution, and US–Latin American relations
Starr Foundation	GM	NY	53,227,000	120	Supports higher education and international student exchanges, global health, cultural exchanges, and international relations
Freeman Foundation	GM	NY	51,851,350	181	Supports international exchange programmes, fellowships, and international studies, with a focus on Asia
Andrew W Mellon Foundation	GM	NY	44,961,181	145	Supports conservation and environmental programmes in Latin America and South Africa; and higher education in South Africa
Carnegie Corporation of New York	GM	NY	44,914,700	122	Supports higher education and library development in former British Commonwealth countries in Sub-Saharan Africa and South Africa; and international peace and security
W K Kellogg Foundation	GM	MI	32,789,453	175	Supports programmes in the areas of health, food systems and rural development, youth and education, and philanthropy and voluntarism, with a focus on Latin America, the Caribbean, and Southern Africa
C S Mott Foundation	GM	MI	31,696,789	257	Supports the strengthening of civil society globally and the protection of the global environment
Pew Charitable Trusts	GM	PA	26,137,000	21	Supports efforts to protect the global environment
Open Society Institute	OP	NY	24,957,249	221	Promotes and opens societies through support for civil society, education, media, public health, and human rights
Harry and Jeanette Weinberg Foundation	GM	MD	16,918,052	26	Supports charitable-giving organisations that benefit disadvantaged members of the community

GM = grant-making foundation; OP = operating foundation

Source: Renz and Atienza (2003). Based on a sample of grants of US$10,000 or more from 1,007 larger foundations

Table 7.3: Foundations in the southern hemisphere: patterns of growth,1980–2000

Country	No of foundations 1980	No of foundations 2000	% with endowment 2000	Type of foundation Private %	Corporate %
Brazil	16	31	16.1	38.7	61.3
Ecuador	6	21	60	71	29
Mexico	25	74	64	77	23
Philippines	22	56	41	64	36
Indonesia	9	25	32	84	16
Thailand	6	28	n/a	70.4	29.6

Note: Private foundations include those founded by religious groups of leaders, government departments or agencies and civil society NGO leaders

Source: Dulany and Winder (2001: 3). Data is from research by Synergos Institute, in conjunction with partner organisations in each country; the Mexico study is in draft form – numbers are not final

example, through its Justice and Peace Programme, the Barrow Cadbury Trust has underscored the promotion of civil society in Northern Ireland and the Middle East as key priorities. Grants made in relation to this programme for 2003 amounted to £726,000 (Barrow Cadbury Trust, 2003). The King Baudouin Foundation has developed a programme of international activities that range from support for projects to combat HIV and AIDS in central Africa to addressing child and youth poverty in southeast Europe (King Baudouin Foundation, 2002). The projects in which European foundations are involved as part of EiTW provide some insight into the international activities of foundations in Europe. Moreover, we begin to see the growing importance of international giving for European foundations that may traditionally have been oriented mainly towards domestic giving (see also Table 7.5).

As discussed earlier, the landscape of foundations in the global South differs in many ways from that of their Northern counterparts. Nonetheless, as Table 7.3 demonstrates, Dulany and Winder (2001) identify clear patterns of growth in foundations in the southern hemisphere.

What is more, international giving does feature as a key priority for some prominent Japanese and Australian foundations. In Australia, for instance, the Fred Hollows Foundation, which aims to provide quality eye care for people in developing countries and indigenous Australians, had expenses of AU$2,371,302 for overseas projects in 2001 (Fred Hollows Foundation, 2002). In Japan, the Nippon Foundation (URL), for example, engages in 'overseas cooperative assistance' as one of its main activities. In 2002, its international spending amounted to ¥5.4 billion (US$45 million). Similarly, grant-making by the Toyota Foundation (URL) focuses on Southeast Asia. In 2002, it spent US$248,360 on its regional exchange programme; spending on programmes for 2003 included US$522,000 on the South Asian National Research Programme and US$223,809 on training in research skills. Calculating the figures for total international giving by Japanese foundations is that much more difficult because the law embraces foundations and associations in one group as 'public benefit corporations', 353 of which are involved in 'international relations' as a field of activity (Itoh, 2003: 157; 178).

Funding priorities

Where and what do foundations fund? The dangers of overestimating the economic and cultural importance of US foundations have been noted previously in the literature (Anheier and Toepler, 1999). The larger US foundations have clearly played a role in determining the priorities for international giving by US foundations generally. For example, health and education, respectively the key focus areas for the Bill and Melinda Gates Foundation and the Ford Foundation, account for the largest proportion of international grant-making, as illustrated by Figure 7.1.

International giving by US foundations does not always take place on such a massive scale. The Synergos Institute's (URL) database of US foundations operating in Latin America reveals variations in the size of grants, ranging from grants of US$500 by the Daniele Agostino Foundation Inc to awards of up to US$11 million by the Ford Foundation. Nonetheless, the targets of foundation-giving follow the patterns identified above, with health and education the main priorities for US foundations.

Figure 7.1: Priorities of US international funders in 2001

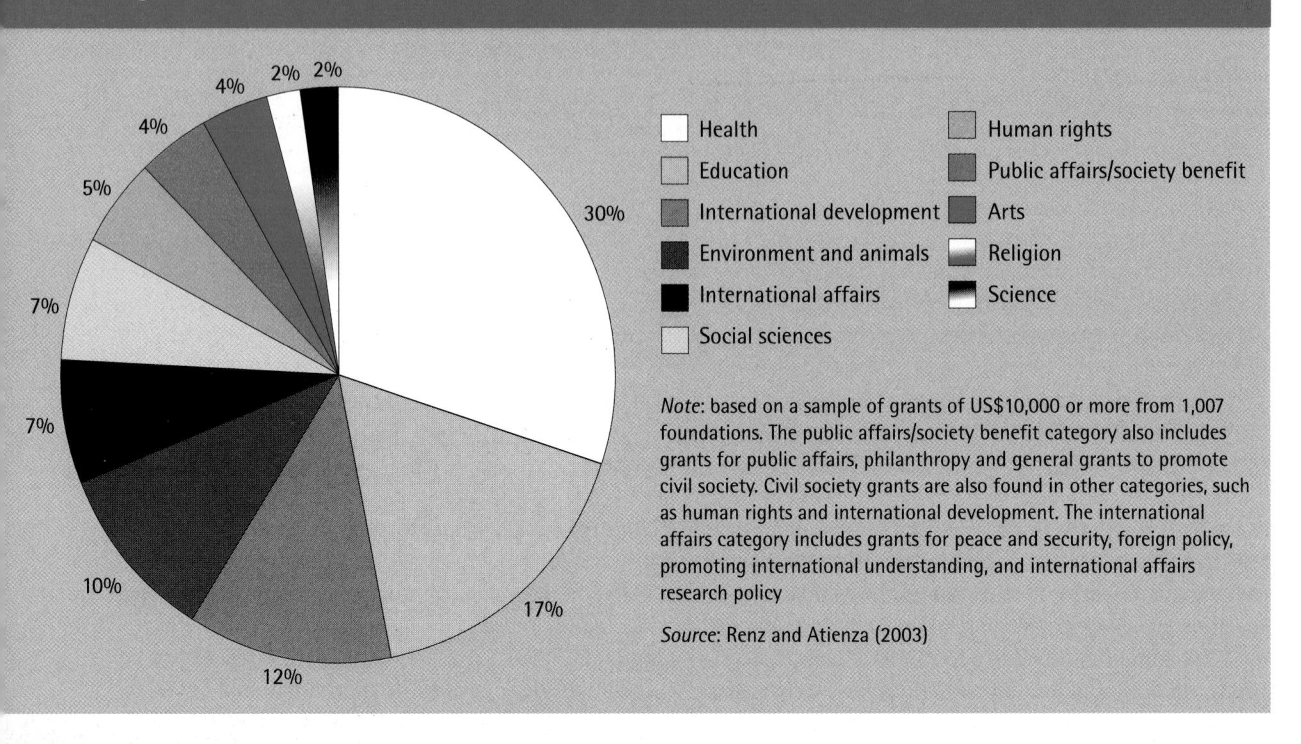

Note: based on a sample of grants of US$10,000 or more from 1,007 foundations. The public affairs/society benefit category also includes grants for public affairs, philanthropy and general grants to promote civil society. Civil society grants are also found in other categories, such as human rights and international development. The international affairs category includes grants for peace and security, foreign policy, promoting international understanding, and international affairs research policy

Source: Renz and Atienza (2003)

Table 7.4: Regional distribution of UK foundation grants abroad

Region	% of total grants value
Eastern and central Europe	16
Other Europe	17
Israel	15
Other Asia	15
South Africa	9
Other Africa	9
Pacific	1

Source: Pharoah, Brophy and Ross (2001: 593)

European foundations have also sought to establish a more global presence in recent years. Although international giving in the early 1990s focused mainly on central and eastern Europe, by the mid-1990s the interest of foundations had turned to South Africa, Asia and western Europe, and by the turn of the twenty-first century to Mediterranean countries (Pharoah, Brophy and Ross, 2001: 594). These trends are represented in Table 7.4, which illustrates the destination of international giving by trusts and foundations in the UK that was estimated to amount to £98 million in 2001 (Pharoah, Brophy and Ross, 2001: 593).

European foundations have sought to establish a more global presence via their involvement in other areas, notably Sub-Saharan Africa, as Table 7.5 demonstrates. Despite the variances between European and US foundations in the scale of philanthropic giving, the dominant focus of the activities of foundations across the globe remains on health, education, culture and the environment.

US foundations emerge clearly as the protagonists of global philanthropy, although European foundations, and to a much lesser extent Japanese foundations, have become more prominent since the end of the cold war.

Table 7.5: **European foundations active in Sub-Saharan Africa: geographic and programme focus**

Foundation	Programme theme/focus	Countries
Fondation de France	Solidarity, health, culture, environment, charitable organisations	Vary, depending on initiative
Volkswagen Stiftung	Research, education	Vary, depending on initiative
Bernard van Leer Foundation	Young children	Mozambique, Namibia, Kenya, Nigeria, South Africa, and Zimbabwe
Fundaçao Calouste Gulbenkian	Public health and human development, education, visual arts, music, science, preservation of Portuguese heritage	Portuguese-speaking countries
Fundaçao Luso-Americana Para o Desenvolvimento	Education, science and technology, culture, environment, public administration, economic and social development, corporate sector outreach	Portuguese-speaking countries
Fundació 'La Caixa'	Social projects, science and environment, education, culture	Ethiopia, Mozambique, Angola, Malawi, and Sudan
Pro Victimis Foundation	Victims of natural or man-made disasters	Not specified
Allavida	Provision of resources: funding, skills and information, to help communities meet their own objectives	Include Kenya, Uganda, and Tanzania
Shell Foundation Uganda	Sustainable energy, sustainable communities, promoting youth enterprise	Include Ethiopia, Ghana, Kenya, Nigeria, and South Africa

Source: European Foundation Centre (2003)

The bulk of international giving is embedded in a relatively small number of large foundations. Although US and European foundations have traditionally been focused on domestic concerns, there are clear signs that international giving is being increasingly recognised as a priority for foundations. Nonetheless, substantial differences of scale remain between US and European foundations and between foundations in the northern and southern hemispheres. In the next section, we turn our attention to the various forms and approaches that this philanthropy assumes on a global scale.

The new philanthropy

The increasing scale of global philanthropy is, in many ways, a response to the prevalence of issues, problems and events that require foundations to think about how they can make an impact beyond their own domestic contexts. However, the international role of philanthropy does not follow a single pattern or approach. Through the International Network on Strategic Philanthropy (INSP), it is possible to identify emerging trends in philanthropy worldwide (Anheier and Simmons, 2004). These include:

- the identification by foundations of strategic areas of intervention around global problems with local manifestations
- the role of philanthropy in addressing private and public sector deficiencies at transnational level, that is, situations where foundations can address problems caused by government or market failures
- the formation of transnational advocacy coalitions
- the role of philanthropy in the UN system
- the role of foundations in 'weak' or 'failed' states, in particular in post-conflict scenarios.

The INSP also provides us with a series of case studies on which we can draw for illustrating the wide range of emerging forms of international philanthropy they represent.

© MORRIS CARPENTER/PANOS PICTURES

Togolese Irene D'Almeida opened her shop with assistance from a microfinance project, supported by the Ford Foundation

Global problems with local manifestations

Philanthropy is emerging as a salient force in addressing problems that have both global and local dimensions. These problems include environmental issues, which have formed the focus of grant-making by foundations such as the MacArthur Foundation, and health issues, such as Rotary International's commitment to the eradication of polio (D Nielsen, 2004). In this regard, HIV and AIDS constitutes one of the world's most serious health problems. It manifests itself on a local level in countries worldwide, but needs to be addressed on a global scale. Through its Global Health Programme, the Bill and Melinda Gates Foundation has identified the prevention of HIV and AIDS as a key priority. Of the US$3.6 billion in grants awarded to its global health programme since 1994, over US$1 billion has been allocated to the search for vaccines for HIV and AIDS, and malaria. The foundation also supports the expansion of access to existing approaches, such as contraceptives, the treatment of sexually transmitted diseases and voluntary counselling and HIV testing (Bill and Melinda Gates Foundation, URL).

Beyond its capacity to commit extensive resources to its global health programme, the Gates Foundation's strategy of promoting cooperation between relevant actors has enabled it to maximise its effectiveness as a private autonomous entity. In its search for vaccines for malaria and HIV, the foundation has earmarked funding for alliances of members of academia, public institutions and private enterprises. In addition, it attaches particular importance to education and advocacy in order to bring its work and the problems it seeks to address to the attention of governments and other potential donors worldwide. For instance, it has been a key funder of the Global Fund to fight AIDS, Tuberculosis and Malaria, which is a partnership of governments, civil society, the private sector and affected communities (Global Fund, URL).

The Gates Foundation's independence and resources have together enabled it to commit itself to the prevention of HIV and AIDS in the long term. For example, it has committed US$750 million to the Global Alliance for Vaccines and Immunizations (GAVI), which aims to ensure that when new vaccines are developed, the structures are in place to direct them to those most in need. This ability to engage in such forward thinking and to maintain its commitment throughout the failures and successes of such a project has been fundamental to the Gates Foundation's support for the search for a HIV and AIDS vaccine. Although by no means typical among foundations, the Gates Foundation does illustrate the potential for philanthropy to address problems that manifest themselves on a global and local scale.

Addressing private and public sector deficiencies at transnational level

Oliviero and Simmons (2004) argue that global philanthropy has adopted three main strategies in addressing private and public sector deficiencies at the transnational level. First, new organisations may be created at the local, national or global level. Second, emphasis may be placed on building cross-sectoral coalitions between funders, civil society organisations, business and government. Finally, the coordination of strategy among philanthropic organisations may be essential to the success of a project. Transparency International (TI) is a good example of how philanthropy has sought to address worldwide problems relating to transparency and corruption. Although TI cites the support of the Ford Foundation and the Rowntree and Nuffield Trusts as instrumental to its creation, Oliviero and Simmons (2004) also stress how the demand for more transparent and non-corrupt practices came from communities of citizens rather than solely from top-down philanthropic initiatives. Berlin serves as the base for coordinating data on the identification and tracking of corruption in governments worldwide (for example, via the Corruption Perceptions Index). However, TI has established national chapters in more than 90 countries. The impact of TI has been substantial, forcing governments and the World Bank to implement effective anti-corruption programmes. The increase in transparent practices globally also enables funders to put their grant-making to more effective use. As well as illustrating how philanthropy seeks to address problems via the creation of new organisations, TI also demonstrates how cooperation and coordination between a range of actors, including philanthropic foundations, national governments and international organisations, may be vital to the success of a project. This requires philanthropic foundations to avoid a 'one size fits all' approach in philanthropy and to tailor their strategies and approach as circumstances dictate.

Health educators in Botswana raising awareness about HIV and AIDS, a priority area for some foundations

The formation of advocacy coalitions

The role of the Funders Network on Trade and Globalisation (FNTG), and specifically its role in the World Social Forum (WSF), shows how, and to what effect, networks of funders interact with global civil society. Caruso (2004) argues that in recent years, foundations have cultivated relations with global civil society in order to help address the negative effects of globalisation. Through research, the FNTG seeks to understand trends and the impact of globalisation, and particularly the likely implications for global philanthropy.

FNTG is not only a network of funders but also a community of more than 200 civil society organisations globally. Thus, it serves as a centre for information exchange and coordination between funders and civil society organisations. The WSF has provided the ideal platform for the FNTG to encourage its funder members to engage directly with the diversity of opinions and approaches often represented by their own grantees at the WSF.

Nonetheless, there are controversial issues. For example, foundations hold substantial investments on the global capital market, which is considered responsible for many of the social and economic imbalances that global civil society seeks to address. Overall, however, cooperation between global civil society actors and philanthropic foundations has more advantages than disadvantages. In particular, cooperation between the

WSF and the FNTG has alerted funders to the need to be involved on a global as well as a national level and has provided an opportunity for global civil society actors to develop key partnerships and to share expertise and ideas with the key players in global philanthropy.

The origins and operations of the United Nations Foundation

The United Nations Foundation (UNF), which engages with and directly supports the UN, marks a new departure for foundations, which have tended to be characterised as being engaged in 'doing what governments do not do' (Toepler and Mard, 2004). The UNF was set up in 1998 to channel a US$1 billion donation by Ted Turner to the UN. The UNF's vision is based on the belief that a strong UN is fundamental to addressing prevalent global challenges. Its four priorities are (a) children's health, (b) the environment, (c) peace, security and human rights, and (d) women and population. Under these broad headings, the UNF has awarded grants to diverse projects ranging from educating the public about the role of the UN to rebuilding Iraq's legal and public healthcare systems. The grant-making process involves both the selected foundation board and the UN Secretariat.

The United Nations Fund for International Partnership (UNFIP) was created to enable the UNF to give direct financial support to specific UN agencies. Four Programme Framework Groups (PFGs) reflect the priorities of the UNF and are made up of representatives from UN agencies, academia and NGOs with the ability to determine the key priorities for each programme framework. Overall, as Toepler and Mard (2004) note, programme selection is a 'joint venture' between the PFGs, the UNFIP and the UNF. Furthermore, the UNF's sister organisation, the Better World Fund, has been instrumental in lobbying and advocacy activities that aim to promote the role of the UN. Although the UNF remains constrained in its decision-making and has been less successful in attracting donors than expected, it has played a salient part in promoting the role of the UN and in encouraging cooperation between UN agencies, as well as between the UN and outside actors in addressing the global challenges of today.

'Weak' or 'failed' states, and post-conflict scenarios

International organisations such as the UN, the EU and large NGOs normally have an important role to play in post-conflict situations by providing humanitarian aid or ensuring that countries comply with peace agreements. Leschenko's case study (2004) of two foundations' role in post-conflict situations underlines how philanthropic foundations also contribute to the development of democratic societies following the end of a conflict. She focuses on the work of the Charles Stewart Mott Foundation and the Soros Foundation Network (SFN) in southeastern Europe, an area that has experienced major ethnic conflict since the end of the cold war. Although a wholesale transfer of foundation experiences in the southeastern context to other areas may not be possible, three salient lessons may be learned from the experience of the SFN and the Mott Foundation that are pertinent to the work of other foundations operating in post-conflict situations (Leschenko, 2004):

- *Mobilisation of local interests and organisations.* A key task for foundations has been to encourage local NGOs to be less reliant on assistance and to cultivate 'good governance' within them. The Mott Foundation opened local offices whereas the SFN created a network of Open Society Foundations, registered as local organisations in specific countries (for example, the Open Society Fund, Bosnia and Herzegovina). The challenge for foundations has been to find a balance between helping local NGOs to develop strategies and imposing their expertise as the only option(s) for them
- *Long-term support.* The commitment of foundations in the long term is fundamental in post-conflict scenarios. This forms part of a strategy of building the capacity of local NGOs for the long term, through measures such as training and the sharing of responsibilities between foundations and local organisations
- *Cooperation and partnership.* In addition to cooperating with local individuals and organisations, foundations work with governments in post-conflict situations. For example, the Mott Foundation supported the training of mid-level officials and other influential professionals in the management of conflicts. The SFN has chosen, where possible, to be more involved in the policy process, such as the commitment of the Open Society Institute, Croatia, to cooperation with the Croation government in policy areas such as education, culture and the decentralisation of public administration. Finally, cooperation with other international entities has also been central to the strategies of both the SFN and the Mott

Foundation. For example, the Balkan Trust for Democracy was created as a result of partnership between the German Marshall Fund, USAID and the Mott Foundation.

What role for global philanthropy?

So far we have looked at the role of foundations very much from a programmatic policy perspective. What broader theoretical arguments can be made for foundations in the context of globalisation? How could we describe their role and the specific challenges involved, in particular, the weakening of national governments in tackling transnational economic and environmental problems; the greater disparity between rich and poor countries; and weaknesses in the functioning of the international political system? What contribution could private wealth make to solving these public problems?

Exclusive reliance on state provision for the wide range of welfare, educational, and cultural services would violate the neo-liberal ideological precept of limited government (Prewitt, 1999)

Many arguments addressing similar questions at the domestic level are derived from the US (Anheier and Leat, 2002), and may need to be modified for our purposes here. Under the new policy doctrine of neo-liberalism, it is argued that foundations exist to provide an alternative to some kinds of state responsibilities. Exclusive reliance on state provision for the wide range of welfare, educational, and cultural services would violate the neo-liberal ideological precept of limited government (Prewitt, 1999: 2).

The most common explanations for the formation of foundations focus on their alleged virtues in providing sources of innovation, redistribution, and policy change; acting as an alternative to the state; providing for those 'beyond' market and state; and adopting a longer-term perspective than is possible for governments, driven as they are by electoral timetables and political expediency (Prewitt, 1999; Anheier and Toepler, 1999; Anheier and Leat, 2002). But what could this reasoning mean at the global level? Certainly, foundations do not have the resources to become global instruments funding private service delivery, be it in higher education, social services, environment or economic development. Given their limited resources, foundations can ultimately play only a secondary, supplementary role (Anheier and Daly, forthcoming). This is not to say that foundations cannot play critical roles, whether as social innovators by funding pilot projects and reacting to special needs, or by building partnerships among civil society organisations and coalitions across sectors, as the above examples have shown.

Indeed, the new forms of global philanthropy we set out in the previous section, however briefly, enhance our understanding of what role(s) foundations can play internationally. The emerging forms of global philanthropy reveal a certain profile that fits foundations operating internationally:

- A need is identified that for whatever reason other actors lack the resources or the interest to meet, and for which international foundations can provide or leverage resources commensurate with the problem at hand
- An existing or potential community or coalition of individuals and organisations is selected to implement the programme locally, and as part of a networked approach transnationally is also pertinent to the success of a philanthropic endeavour
- The foundation places emphasis on the collection, analysis and sharing of information across different project sites. Foundations may assume a role as the 'honest broker' among the different parties by supplying information and offering knowledge as well as financial resources (Then, 2004)
- Foundations and other international philanthropic organisations need to set and insist on clear goals and benchmarks when necessary and easily agreed. But they also need to be willing to take risks in supporting medium- to long-term efforts where there is great uncertainty about likely results.

Overall, we see that, in many ways, the roles of foundations as an alternative to the state (whether in complementing or substituting) and as a source of innovation, redistribution and policy change are mirrored at the international level. Moreover, foundations are facing calls both nationally and internationally to adopt a more strategic approach to their operations. At the national level, this is rooted in new roles emerging for foundations, particularly in Europe with the 'rolling back' of welfare states (Anheier and Daly, forthcoming).

Philanthropy is increasingly being seen to have a salient role to play in these changing policy contexts (Schuyt, 2001). However, while many foundations have been content at the national level to pursue their own agendas, international philanthropy typically requires foundations to cooperate with a range of different actors, from governments to other funders and local actors who are often responsible for implementing programmes. More often than not, this also requires an ability to take risks and make longer-term commitments.

A potentially global role requires foundations to identify areas of support and intervention that have some leverage and capacity for scaling up characteristics of the projects described in the previous section. At the same time, it makes foundations vulnerable politically, as many of the areas are neglected by government or business. This was the case with the role of foundations in conflict resolution and in social justice more generally. And if major political parties and most governments have abandoned social justice as a domestic and international policy objective and refuse to take it seriously at global levels, who other than foundations and the advocacy coalitions they support could bring the issue back to the policy agenda? Put differently, the more foundations step in to compensate for state and market failures, the more they will reveal a theory of change that guides their actions either implicitly or explicitly – and the more they will become subject to political criticism.

Yet the very fact that foundations can operate outside the political system of parties, national government and international organisations gives them considerable independence or 'space' for taking advantage of opportunities to support causes that are either bypassed by or unwelcome to mainstream politics. Such causes would include those of ethnic, religious, or cultural minorities, the socially excluded, or any other disadvantaged group that finds it hard to be heard by, and to gain access to, political institutions. Support for 'unpopular causes' on both sides of the political spectrum, as Anheier and Leat (2002) have noticed, has not gone without criticism. One major criticism is that foundations, both domestic and international, are perhaps among the most unaccountable organisations in democratic societies. Foundations are organisations without shareholders, voters, or customers – and their 'clients' are highly unlikely to criticise them. By contrast, as global actors, foundations can create and provide spaces of independence in autocratic societies, and become a source of stability in failed states and conflict scenarios. For these reasons, foundations face complex accountability challenges that can differ across political and cultural regions. In other words, being relatively unaccountable in one sense requires a different kind of accountability in another to ensure the long-term legitimacy of foundations in politicised global arenas.

However, irrespective of such criticism, foundations can maintain a global role only if they can operate and grow in an enabling legal and political environment, nationally as well as internationally. For much of the 1980s and 1990s, such an environment was in place and consolidating and expanding at the same time. It was essential to the growth of philanthropy and its success in a range of fields, some of which we have reviewed in this chapter. Yet the tragic events of September 11, 2001, and their political aftermath could pose a serious threat to the continued role of global philanthropy.

The impact of September 11, 2001

After September 11, 2001, the US Treasury, the EU and the Financial Action Task Force (FATF) of the OECD intensified their demand for greater scrutiny of non-profit organisations, including foundations, with a view to ensuring that philanthropic funds were neither diverted to, nor ultimately used for, the financing of terrorist organisations[3].

Of course, there is a long history of transnational flows of resources, monetary and in kind, to support various political activities, including terrorism. Examples include funds collected by Irish communities in New York or Boston to support the Irish Republican Army; funds collected by Jewish communities to support settlements on the West Bank; European money to aid Palestinian groups on the West Bank; West German assistance to dissident groups in central and eastern Europe via Protestant and Catholic church organisations during the cold war; or European and US funds finding their way to clandestine organisations in apartheid South Africa. Yet they rarely, if at all, involved philanthropic flows.

Legislation and guidelines issued by the US government in response to the terrorist attacks on September 11, and the subsequent declaration of a 'war on terror' by President Bush radically changed the policy debate about transnational philanthropy, which came to be viewed with suspicion by the US Treasury, regardless of the actual evidence (see OBM Watch, 2004, and Anheier and Daly, 2004, for an overview of the debate). The key responses

3 *For a fuller analysis, see Anheier and Daly (2004).*

included the 'Anti-Terrorist Financing Guidelines: Voluntary Best Practices for US-based Charities', issued in November 2002 by the US Department of the Treasury under the Patriot Act. This measure was seen as a first step towards putting in place detailed and more stringent regulations governing the operation of financial institutions, including foundations.

In many ways, the guidelines reflect broader concerns in the philanthropic community about the accountability of foundations, the transparency of financial practices, and the monitoring of the impact of funding. However, the guidelines have proved controversial on several grounds. The Council of Foundations (2003), the main representative body of foundations in the US, argued that the administrative costs of complying with the guidelines far outweighed the risk of international grants being susceptible to interference by terrorist organisations. Moreover, Barnett Baron (2004) argues that they are extremely vague on what constitutes 'best practices' for international grant-making. They place onerous responsibilities on grantees, many of which are based in developing countries, to gather information that is often not readily accessible because of the poorly regulated legal and fiscal environments in which organisations function. This, in turn, encourages mistrust between the grantor and the grantee.

Combating the use of non-profit organisations for financing terrorism has taken on international salience through the work of the FATF. The eight 'Special Recommendations' issued by the FATF in October 2001 include a special provision on non-profit organisations:

> *Countries should review the adequacy of laws and regulations that relate to entities that can be abused for the financing of terrorism. Non-profit organizations are particularly vulnerable, and countries should ensure that they cannot be misused:*
>
> *i. by terrorist organizations as legitimate entities;*
> *ii. to exploit legitimate entities as conduits for terrorist financing, including for the purpose of escaping asset freezing measures; and*
> *iii. to conceal or obscure the clandestine diversion of funds intended for legitimate purposes to terrorist organisations. (FATF, 2001)*

The work of the FATF has had an important impact on the measures undertaken and the proposals made by the EU and the Council of Europe. As in the US, efforts to prevent the financing of terrorism focus on creating an appropriate regulatory environment and improving the transparency and monitoring of non-profit organisations[4]. However, unlike the US, where foundations have been vocal in their opposition to the proposed voluntary guidelines, the response of European foundations has been muted.

The main argument here is that the post-9/11 response to a known problem has been one of top-down policy-making with the aim of policing rather than enabling global philanthropy. Policy measures that are being discussed disregard the transnational character of global philanthropy and try to impose cold war-like regulations on a phenomenon that, like terrorism itself, has long escaped efficient and effective policing within the boundaries of national jurisdiction. Yet, unlike terrorism, philanthropy is a fragile social phenomenon. Although we lack empirical evidence of the impact of these guidelines, it is clear that they will have the most serious implications for the countries, groups and causes that are most in need of the kind of support that foundations are best equipped to offer.

Moreover, the guidelines reduce global philanthropic giving to a black-and-white issue, thereby ignoring the grey areas in which foundations sometimes find themselves involved. In Sri Lanka, for instance, US foundations supply books and materials to schools and libraries that are located in areas controlled by the Tamil Tigers, a known terrorist organisation. The delivery of these materials requires the permission of local organisations under their control (Baron, 2004). This sort of activity places US foundations in a position where they 'associate' with a terrorist organisation, even though they are not engaged in directly financing it.

There are even wider implications. Bach (2002) argues that the events of September 11, 2001, underscored the dangers posed by weak or failed states – dangers not adequately identified by philanthropic foundations working in these areas. According to Bach, foundations should take on a greater role in issues of security and law enforcement, as well as the protection of rights – fields they have traditionally shunned but which the changed geopolitical environment may require them to consider. There is some evidence that this is occurring, with some foundations allotting funding to projects that reflect the impact of 9/11, such as the prevention of international bio-terrorism, supporting conflict-

4 *Documentation of the EU position on this issue can be found in Commission of the European Communities (2003). The European Council (2004) reaffirmed the EU's support for the improved regulation of non-profit organisations to prevent their use for financing terrorism.*

resolution initiatives, or providing relief assistance and the protection of human rights for Afghanis (Renz and Atienza, 2003).

Conclusion

Global philanthropy has expanded and become a supporter of civil society organisations in many parts of the world. The leadership shown by US foundations in international philanthropy in the past is now enhanced by new 'mega-foundations' like the Bill and Melinda Gates Foundation or the Soros Foundation Network. European and Japanese foundations have also increasingly looked for ways to engage in international grant-making, particularly via cooperation with other foundations through initiatives such as Europe in the World or the Asia-Pacific Philanthropy Consortium. Although philanthropy in the global South shows clear patterns of growth, in many countries it faces obstacles, including legal and fiscal ones, that have yet to be overcome.

Transnational philanthropy has been and can remain a major force for improving the lives of millions of people worldwide, in particular in regions that are underdeveloped economically and are socially and politically fragile. As new forms of philanthropy have emerged, foundations and foundation-like organisations have shown themselves to be catalysts for change and cooperation. Foundations are private institutions, with considerable resources which, through the roles they fulfil, find themselves embroiled in contentious policy areas, particularly at the transnational, global level. The potential for contention is enhanced by the frequent divergence in underlying motivations and implicit or explicit political agendas between foundations and governments.

Yet it is precisely the freedom to have views, objectives and programmes that differ from state and corporate interests, and to support causes that others find inopportune or unimportant, that provides that bedrock for the special roles foundations can play, domestically as well as at the transnational level. Not surprisingly, as we have argued, not all governments and not all political parties agree with what foundations do and stand for.

At the domestic level in the US, this lack of agreement takes the form of political struggles between 'liberal' foundations such as Ford, Pew or Mott and 'conservative' foundations such as the Philanthropy Roundtable, and finds its expression in US Senate hearings about non-profit and foundation practices (US Senate Committee on Finance, 2004). At the international level, the agendas of most (though not all) foundations would bring them into conflict with what Kaldor, Anheier and Glasius (2003) identify as 'regressive' globalisation, because foundations are typically reformist actors seeking to humanise globalisation. They do so, as we have seen, by taking up topics neglected by others, most prominently perhaps the renewed emphasis on global social justice and the efforts to provide healthcare to the millions infected with the AIDS virus in Sub-Saharan Africa.

At the same time, most foundations operating at the transnational level are what Peter Berger (1997) called the 'Faculty Club', representing an intellectual, learned response to globalisation, largely on a reform course by trying to 'tame' and 'humanise' the process, and influenced by the tradition of US philanthropy as a systematic approach to social problems. However, this brings foundations into political-cultural conflict with other attitudes to globalisation: the 'Davos culture' of the international business community that seeks to enhance economic globalisation while neglecting its consequences; the 'McWorld culture' of unreflecting consumerism and the levelling effect popular US culture has on many indigenous and local cultures elsewhere; and, increasingly, the culture of religious revival and the activities of Christian and Islamic groups in proselytising and gaining greater influence.

Berger (1997) has argued that the religious revivalists are on a collision course with the Davos culture and the McWorld culture, and that the Faculty Club is antagonistic towards all three. If this is so, then global philanthropy and the global civil society it seeks to build and support would find themselves, at least, in a latent conflict with the other cultural and political forces driving globalisation. Of course, philanthropy is diverse and includes many voices and political preferences. But, in a highly politicised world, we suggest that, as an institution as well as individually, philanthropy can meet the challenges posed by other globalisation cultures if it is clear about its roles, goals and limitations, and, in particular, aware of the underlying theories of change that drive its choices and activities at the global level.

We would like to thank the participants of the Yearbook's authors' meeting and Volker Then for thoughtful comments and suggestions on an earlier draft of this chapter. Laurie Spivak and Marcus Lam also provided valuable input.

REFERENCES

Anheier, Helmut K. (2003) 'Das Stiftungswesen in Zahlen: Eine sozial-oeknomische Strukturbeschreibung deutscher Stiftungen', in Bertelsmann Stiftung (ed), *Handbuch Stiftungen.* Wiesbaden: Gabler.

— (2001) 'Foundations in Europe: A Comparative Perspective', in Andreas Schlüter, Volker Then, and Peter Walkenhorst (eds), *Foundations in Europe.* London: Directory of Social Change.

— and Daly, S. (2004) 'The Future of Global Philanthropy and Anti-Terrorism Measures: Perspectives from Europe'. Paper presented at the Annual General Assembly of the European Foundation Centre, Athens, 30 May–1 June.

— (forthcoming) *Foundations: Roles and Visions.* London: Routledge.

— and Leat, Diana (2002) *From Charity to Creativity: Philanthropic Foundations in the 21st Century.* Stroud, UK: Comedia.

— and List, Regina (eds) (2000) *Cross-border Philanthropy: An Exploratory Study of International Giving in the United Kingdom, United States, Germany and Japan.* Baltimore, MD: Institute for Policy Studies, Johns Hopkins University; London: Centre for Civil Society.

— and Simmons, Adele (eds) (2004) *The Role of Philanthropy in Globalisation.* Working paper for the International Network on Strategic Philanthropy. Gütersloh: Bertlesmann Foundation.

— and Toepler, Stefan (1999) 'Philanthropic Foundations: An International Perspective', in Helmut K. Anheier and Stefan Toepler (eds), *Private Funds and Public Purpose: Philanthropic Foundations in International Perspectives.* New York: Plenum Publishers.

— and Winder, David (2004). 'Introduction', in Helmut K. Anheier and David Winder (eds), *Innovations in Strategic Philanthropy – Comparative Lessons from Africa, Asia, Central and Eastern Europe and Latin America.* Working paper for the International Network on Strategic Philanthropy. Gütersloh: Bertlesmann Foundation.

Bach, Robert L. (2002) 'New Priorities for Philanthropy', *Ethics and International Affairs*, 16(2): 20–6. www.cceia.org

Baron, Barnett (2004) 'Deterring Donors: Anti-Terrorist Financing Rules and American Philanthropy', *International Journal of Not-for-Profit Law*, 6(2). www.icnl.org/journal/vol6iss2/ar_baron.htm

Barrow Cadbury Trust (2003) *Annual Report 2003.* London: Barrow Cadbury Trust. barrowcadbury.org.uk (consulted 2 April 2004).

Berger, Peter L. (1997) 'Four Faces of Global Culture', *The National Interest*, 40 (Fall): 23–9.

Bill and Melinda Gates Foundation (URL) www.gatesfoundation.org (consulted 20 May 2004).

Bulmer, Martin (1999) 'The History of Foundations in the United Kingdom and the United States: Philanthropic Foundations in Industrial Society', in Helmut K. Anheier and Stefan Toepler (eds), *Private Funds and Public Purpose: Philanthropic Foundations in International Perspectives* New York: Plenum Publishers.

Caruso, Giuseppe (2004) 'Philanthropy and Networks in Global Civil Society', in Helmut K. Anheier and Adele Simmons (eds), *The Role of Philanthropy in Globalisation.* Working Paper for the International Network on Strategic Philanthropy. Gütersloh: Bertlesmann Foundation.

Commission of the European Communities (2003) *Actions to Combat the Financing of Terrorism.* Commission Staff Working Paper SEC (2003) 414). Brussels: Commission of the European Communities, 28 March.

Council of Foundations (2003) 'Comments on US Department of the Treasury Anti-Terrorist Financing Guidelines: Voluntary Best Practice for US-Based Charities'. www.usig.org/Treasury%20Comments_06.03.pdf

Dulany, Peggy and Winder, David (2001). 'The Status of and Trends in Private Philanthropy in the Southern Hemisphere'. A Discussion Paper for the Executive Session on the Future of Philanthropy of the International Network on Strategic Philanthropy. www.synergos.org

EiTW (Europe in the World) (URL) www.europeintheworld.info (consulted 16 March 2004).

European Council (2004) 'Declaration on Combating Terrorism'. Brussels: European Council, 25 March.

European Foundation Centre (2003) 'EFC Foundation and Corporate Members Active in Sub-Saharan Africa'. www.efc.be/ftp/private/IC/03AfricaFunders.pdf

FATF (Financial Action Task Force) (2001) 'Financial Action Task Force on Money Laundering: Special Recommendations on Terrorist Financing'. www1.oecd.org/fatf/pdf/SRecTF_en.pdf

Foundation Center (2004) *Foundation Giving Trends.* New York: Foundation Center.

Fred Hollows Foundation (2002) *Annual Report.* www.hollows.org

Fries, Richard (2003) 'The Legal Environment of Civil Society', in Mary Kaldor, Helmut K. Anheier and Marlies Glasius (eds), *Global Civil Society 2003.* Oxford: Oxford University Press.

Global Fund (URL) www.theglobalfund.org (consulted 20 May 2004).

Itoh, Satoko (2003) 'Japan'. Paper presented at the Asia-Pacific Philanthropy Consortium Conference on Governance, Organizational Effectiveness and the Nonprofit Sector, Manila, 5–7 September.

Kaldor, Mary, Helmut K. Anheier and Marlies Glasius (eds) (2003) *Global Civil Society 2003.* Oxford: Oxford University Press.

(2003) 'Global Civil Society in an Age of Regressive Globalization', in Mary Kaldor, Helmut Anheier and Marlies Glasius (eds), *Global Civil Society 2003*. Oxford: Oxford University Press.

Karl, B. and Katz, S. (1987) 'Foundations and the Ruling Class', *Daedalus*, 116(1): 1–40.

King Baudouin Foundation (2002). *Annual Report 2002*. www.kbs-frb.be

Leschenko, N. (2004) 'Philanthropy in Post-Conflict Societies', in Helmut K. Anheier and Adele Simmons (eds), *The Role of Philanthropy in Globalisation*. Working paper for the International Network on Strategic Philanthropy. Gütersloh: Bertlesmann Foundation.

Letts, C., Ryan, W. and Grossman, A. (1997) 'Virtuous Capital: What Foundations can Learn from Venture Capitalists', *Harvard Business Review*, 97 (March/April): 36–41.

McCarthy, Kathleen D. (2003) *American Creed: Philanthropy and the Rise of Civil Society, 1700–1865*. Chicago: Chicago University Press.

Nielsen, Dan (2004) 'The Global and Local Dimension', in Helmut K. Anheier and Adele Simmons (eds), *The Role of Philanthropy in Globalisation*. Working paper for the International Network on Strategic Philanthropy. Gütersloh: Bertlesmann Foundation.

Nielsen, Waldemar (1972) *The Big Foundations*. New York: Columbia University Press.

Nippon Foundation (URL) www.nippon-foundation.org.jp (consulted 24 March 2004).

OBM Watch (2004) www.ombwatch.org/article/articleprint/2148/-1/213

Oliviero, Melanie and Simmons, Adele (2004) 'The Role of Philanthropy in Globalisation', in Helmut K. Anheier and Adele Simmons (eds), *The Role of Philanthropy in Globalisation*. Working paper for the International Network on Strategic Philanthropy. Gütersloh: Bertlesmann Foundation.

Pharoah, Cathy, Brophy, Michael and Ross, Paddy (2001) 'Promoting International Philanthropy through Foundations', in Andreas Schlüter, Volker Then and Peter Walkenhorst (eds), *Foundations in Europe*. London: Directory of Social Change.

Pinter, Frances (2001) 'Funding Global Civil Society Organisations', in Helmut K. Anheier, Marlies Glasius and Mary Kaldor (eds), *Global Civil Society 2001*. Oxford: Oxford University Press.

Porter, M. and Kramer, M. (1999) 'Philanthropy's New Agenda: Creating Value', *Harvard Business Review*, 77(6): 121–30.

Prewitt, K. (1999) 'The Importance of Foundations in an Open Society', in Bertelsmann Foundation (ed), *The Future of Foundations in an Open Society*. Gütersloh: Bertelsmann Foundation Publishers.

Renz, Loren and Atienza, Josefina (2000) *International Grantmaking II: An Update on US Foundation Trends*. New York: Foundation Center.

(2003) *International Grantmaking Update*. New York: Foundation Center.

Schuyt, Theo N (2001) 'Foundations in Europe: The Historical Context Philanthropy and the Diversification of the Western European "Welfare State" Model', *European Journal of Social Work*, 4(1): 39–44.

Smith, James Allen and Borgmann, Karsten (2001) 'Foundations in Europe: The Historical Context', in Andreas Schlüter, Volker Then, and Peter Walkenhorst (eds), *Foundations in Europe*. London: Directory of Social Change.

Synergos Institute (URL) www.synergos.org (consulted 16 March 2004).

Then, V. (2004) 'What Market Are We Really In? Foundation Strategies Revisited' (manuscript). Gütersloh: Bertlesmann Foundation.

Toepler, Stefan and Mard, Natascha (2004) 'The Role of Philanthropy in the United Nations System', in Helmut K. Anheier and Adele Simmons (eds), *The Role of Philanthropy in an Era of Globalisation*. Working paper for the International Network on Strategic Philanthropy. Gütersloh: Bertlesmann Foundation.

Toyota Foundation (URL) www.toyotafound.or.jp (consulted 24 March 2004).

US Senate Committee on Finance (2004) 'Grassley Plans Hearing on Charitable Giving Problems, Best Practices'. http://finance.senate.gov/press/Gpress/2004/prg060104a.pdf

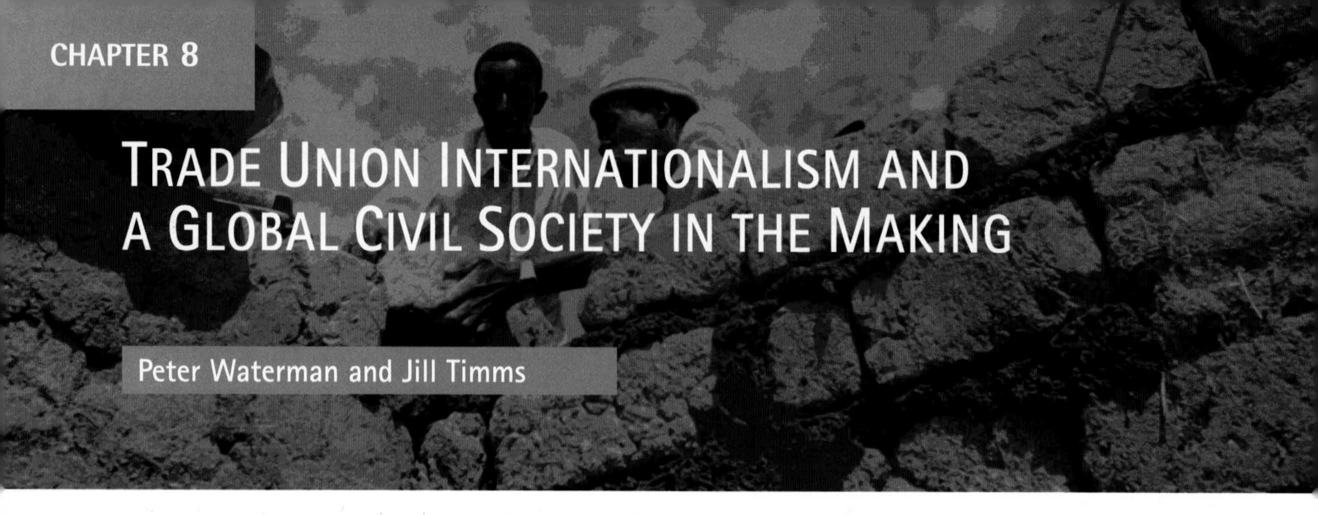

Trade Union Internationalism and a Global Civil Society in the Making

Peter Waterman and Jill Timms

Introduction

Two events, held in January 2004, suggest major ways in which the international trade union movement is trying to respond to the shock of globalisation. The question is whether union participation at these two very different events, one at the fourth World Social Forum (WSF4) in Mumbai, India, and the other at the International Labour Organisation's (ILO) Training Centre in Turin, Italy, represents competing or complementary ways of expressing internationalism in the era of globalisation.

In Mumbai, thousands of people set out their stalls, organised rallies and marches, and held meetings from mass plenaries to intimate workshops. Representing a myriad of different causes and organisations, including trade unionists from the world over, they participated in a huge range of extra-curricular activities, from concerts, plays and dances to fancy dress and face painting. Many meetings were held in makeshift rooms crafted from tarpaulin, ropes and branches, with intermittent electricity for lighting and fans. And at the end of the long, hot days, many people slept in tents. But however basic the facilities and however chaotic the events, nothing could dampen the excitement, passion and sense of challenge that characterised this vibrant gathering. By contrast, the meeting at the ILO's centre in Turin was a very business-like affair. Intended to found a Global Union Research Network (GURN), the event was highly structured, with trade unionists and labour researchers from 39 countries attending on invitation. Delegates were provided with a detailed pack, including a report setting out the collated responses of participants to the idea of the network, a structured schedule and agenda for the event, and the rules of the centre. There followed a series of meetings and working groups, each of which had preset objectives and was run according to specified procedures. Seating was predetermined by the use of nameplates, and facilities such as PowerPoint and individual microphones were provided. The meeting was characterised by the use of formal procedures: 'Does the Chair think it would be helpful to discuss the follow-up of the proposals in this morning's session?'; 'Mr Chair, can a request for the issue of translation and language to be discussed be noted in the minutes please?' Funding was available for those unable to pay travel expenses; free accommodation and meal vouchers were provided for everyone; and dinner was arranged in a traditional local restaurant.

Do these representations of contemporary labour internationalism conflict or compliment each other? The ILO initiative reveals a more assertive attitude towards globalisation than we have seen from the international trade union organisations over the last decade[1]. The organisers state that 'the growing influence of globalisation and transnational companies on the daily life of workers in most countries increases the demand . . . for a better understanding of the global economy' (GURN, 2003). Formally established at this meeting, GURN is intended to allow trade unions to share information more efficiently, mainly via a resources website, on how globalisation is affecting working lives. But it remains firmly within the confines of traditional international unionism. The idea of GURN is said to have originated on the union side and it is formally independent of the ILO. It was, however, initiated by the ILO's Bureau for Workers' Activities, in cooperation with its International Institute for Labour Studies and then with the International Confederation of Free Trade Unions (ICFTU) and the Trade Union Advisory Committee of the OECD. The six priority areas on which it will focus, in the first

1 *As does a matching international Master's course on global labour policies (ILO, URLa).*

instance, are bilateral and regional trade agreements, migration, corporate governance, international financial institutions and poverty reduction strategy papers, the social and labour impact of multinationals, and global trade union strategies (GURN, URL). With the hypothetical exception of the last, these priorities fall within the traditional limits of a century-old international social partnership between unions, states and capital. It therefore remains to be seen whether GURN will produce any union vision independent of that of the ILO, the oldest of the interstate organisations within the United Nations system.

At WSF4 trade union organisations, national and international, were present in greater numbers and with a higher profile than ever before. A major way in which they revealed their presence was through the programme 'Labour in WSF 2004'. This brought together international trade union organisations and federations and their national affiliates, as well as independent trade unions and labour-supporting NGOs. The programme was intended to address the issues facing workers in both the organised and the unorganised sectors worldwide (Mathew and Shetty, 2003). Eye-catching posters, banners, flags and other materials displaying the 'Labour in WSF 2004' logo and the names of trade unions taking part were strategically displayed throughout the forum site. All this suggests growing international union recognition of not simply the WSF but of the new 'global justice and solidarity movement' (GJ&SM) and the 'global civil society' that the forum is taken to symbolise. When one considers that, up to the mid-1990s, the ICFTU, the major international union organisation, was still resisting identification with international NGOs at the Social Summit of the UN, the increasingly enthusiastic commitment to this new agora must be seen as a turning point.

These two events, with their strikingly different natures, can also be seen to symbolise two historical periods, two phases of capitalist development, two institutional settings – and two 'worldviews' within which trade unions have tried to defend or advance internationally the interests of their members in particular and of wage earners generally. In this chapter we consider, first, the long but little-known history of trade union internationalism, and second, the contemporary structures of the international union organisations. The third section explores the responses of the international unions and wider labour movement to neo-liberal globalisation, and we conclude with some reflections on conceptualisation, communication and political strategy.

History of union internationalism

The present or future significance of trade union internationalism, or its relationship to a 'global civil society in the making', cannot be considered in isolation from its relationship to internationalism more generally, its past eminence and its recent marginalisation.

Whereas in the USA, 'internationalism' is commonly understood as an approach to foreign policy, in Europe and elsewhere, it is generally understood as a left-wing or democratic project for creating relations of solidarity between social classes, popular interests, and progressive identities, independently of, or in opposition to, the state or capital. Internationalism existed before unions or labour movements, and was often independent of the latter. For example, pacifist, feminist, and cultural versions of internationalism were elements of European democratic thought and politics in the eighteenth and nineteenth centuries. But, as the word 'inter*nationalism*' itself indicates, it was also a universalism or cosmopolitanism of the epoch of nation-state building. Although labour and socialist internationalism might have been first expressed in cosmopolitan terms (Tristán, 1843/1967), what later developed were relationships of solidarity between unions that were increasingly identified with nation states, nationalists and nationalisms.

The rise of industrial capitalism in nineteenth-century Europe led to waves of labour and socialist internationalisms. Associated with 'The Manifesto of the Communist Party' of Karl Marx and Friedrich Engels (1848/1935) and with the International Working Men's Association (or First International), which lasted from 1864 to 1872/3, labour and socialist internationalism came to be almost synonymous with the word 'internationalism'. After the 1890s, by allying with, or creating its own, women's, peace, and anti-colonial fronts, labour and socialist internationalism largely hegemonised the word. *Trade union* internationalism, as the most direct international expression of the working-class movement, was seen as the heart of *labour and socialist* internationalism. From the 1890s to the 1960s, it was also the most resilient and best-organised part, and, through its representation in the International Labour Organisation (founded in 1919), the only one with a recognised place within the new interstate sphere.

The history of general labour and specifically union internationalism falls into the following three periods (cf van der Linden, 2003):

BY KIND PERMISSION OF THE PEOPLE'S HISTORY MUSEUM

Emblem of the Operating Society of Bricklayers connecting workers in Rome and London

1. *Early (and largely European) craft and industrial capitalism, c 1830s–70s.* This period saw the development of the labour internationalism of skilled male workers in increasingly large-scale capitalist industries. Labour and socialist internationalisms overlapped not only each other but also more general democratic internationalisms. The most dramatic acts of labour internationalism were often combined with anti-racist, anti-slavery, and anti-authoritarian internationalisms.
2. *The mature industrial-national phase, c 1880s–1970s.* This phase encompassed the industrialising peripheries of metropolitan capitalism. It even included the non-industrialised peripheral countries, which adopted metropolitan ideologies and patterns of unionism. Increasingly, this second phase was characterised by national and international union internationalisms, relations between nationally institutionalised unions, mostly of male industrial workers. Labour and socialist internationalisms tended to prioritise themselves over the 'other' internationalisms, such as those concerned with peace, women, or national independence. But labour, cooperative, and socialist internationalisms were also increasingly separated from each other, often with bitter ideological, strategic, bloc or jurisdictional disputes. The prioritisation, institutionalisation and 'nationalisation' of the various internationalist labour and socialist bodies during this period also led to increasing shrinkage and self-isolation. Union institutionalisation nonetheless permitted the creation of robust national and international organisations. These were ideologically distinct and often incorporated or marginalised (where not repressed) in wartime, but were revived and reshaped as a result of the two world wars and related waves of social and national rebellion and revolution. The unions also established their presence in the interstate sphere through their 25 per cent representation in the ILO. Anti-fascist internationalisms appeared in the 1930s. The period after the Second World War saw increased union corporatism[2], national and international, West, East, and South, and a consequent loss of the vanguard role that labour and unions once played in internationalism more generally.
3. *The beginning of a globalised capitalism, c 1980s–present.* Although proletarianisation and factory industrialisation continue to spread (particularly in China), we observe also widespread deindustrialisation and shifts to the finance, services, tourism, information and entertainment industries, and to new forms of employment and new types of worker in new countries. This period is characterised by a crisis of traditional union internationalism, along with the fragile beginnings of new kinds of labour solidarity. The new labour internationalism encompasses a range of 'post-state-nationalist' relations with or between 'working classes' of all kinds, 'typical' or 'atypical'[3], unionised or not, often in networked form. This is a period of disorientation, flux, and experimentation, in which the traditional union internationalisms and the new international labour networks are in both tension and dialogue.

2 *Here, 'corporatism' is used to refer to the state ideology and practice whereby different major social interests become equal partners in overseeing state and economic development. It therefore contrasts with the individualist bias of liberalism or the class-conflict bias of socialism.*

3 *The increased proportion of casual, temporary and non-waged workers has made 'atypical' an increasingly archaic descriptor.*

Table 8.1: Three periods and types of labour internationalism

Period 1: Early (largely European) craft and industrial capitalism, c 1830s–1870s	
Generic internationals of socialists, unionists, cooperators, and left democrats. London, capital of the major industrialised liberal countries of Europe, is their privileged meeting place	
1844	Democratic Friends of all Nations (London)
1845–6	The Fraternal Democrats (London)
1864–72/3	The International Working Men's Association (First International), combining socialist, unionist and related bodies, associated with Marx and Engels
Period 2: The mature industrial–national phase, c 1880s–1970s, including the European periphery and parts of the (semi-) colonial world	
Separate and structured international organisations of trade unions created, distinguished by nation and craft/industry. Internationals are independent of, but allied to, mostly socialist political internationals	
1913–19	International Federation of Trade Unions, separate but associated with the Socialist or Second International
1901–13/19	The International Secretariat of Trade Union Centres
1889/2002–today	The social-reformist International Trade Secretariats, since 2002 Global Union Federations
1905–today	The (anarcho-syndicalist) Industrial Workers of the World (aka Wobblies)
First World War/Russian Revolution, 1914–1918	
Union internationals clearly represented in, or allied with, competing political/ideological internationals	
1919–39/45	The social-reformist International Federation of Trade Unions
1922–today	International Workers Association (anarcho-syndicalist)
1922–37	The Red International of Labour Unions (Profintern), subordinated to the Communist International
1922/68–today	The International Federation of Christian Trade Unions, since 1968 World Confederation of Labour
1938–61	The Mexican-based Latin American Confederation of Trade Unions (CTAL)
Second World War, rise of Communist and nationalist states/blocs, 1945–1970s	
The internationalisation/regionalisation of union internationalism; internationals often identified with or dependent on particular international blocs	
1945–today	The World Federation of Trade Unions (rises and falls with Communist states)
1948	Trade Union Advisory Committee of what became the Organisation for Economic Cooperation and Development OECD (allied with ICFTU)
1949–today	The International Confederation of Free Trade Unions (Western-oriented and dependent on state funds for much development work)
1961–72	The Nkrumah (Ghanaian)-sponsored All African Trade Union Federation
1973–today	The Organisation of African Trade Union Unity (dependent on the Organisation of African Unity)
1956–today	The International Confederation of Arab Trade Unions (dependent on Arab states)
1973	European Trade Union Confederation (independent of the internationals, heavily dependent on the European Common Market/European Union)
Period 3: The beginning of a globalised capitalism c 1980s–today	
The marked appearance of specialised international/regional labour information, research, communication and support services, as well as alliances beyond the unions, often taking NGO or network form, whether created outside the union internationals, sponsored by, or allied to such (see Table 8.3 for a sample of these)	

BY KIND PERMISSION OF THE WORKING CLASS MOVEMENT LIBRARY

Cover of the World Federation of Trade Unions publication in 1950

The history of trade union internationalism can be considered, schematically, in relationship to these three periods (see Table 8.1). However, Table 8.1 excludes one organisation sometimes conflated with the labour internationals (Castree et al, 2004). This is the International Labour Organisation (previously known as the International Labour Office) which, as earlier suggested, is an *inter-state* body that was created in response to the rising international labour and socialist movement (revolutionary or reformist) in the early twentieth century. The ILO pre-dates the United Nations by a generation, is its only tripartite institution (it represents states, employers and labour), and has exercised considerable ideological hegemony over the movement since its foundation (Alcock, 1971; Harrod, 1977; Wilkinson, 2002). We will return to it.

It has been suggested that the 'late nineteenth century and the early twentieth century . . . labour movement generated its own "civil society"' (Gallin, 2000). One can question the use of the modern notion of 'civil society' to refer to the rich expressions of a young, expanding class movement with its own emancipatory intentions and hegemonic pretensions. Yet labour *did* create its own radical and democratic counter culture, both nationally and internationally (van Holthoon and van der Linden, 1988). Even in its specific Communist incarnation, it had a considerable impact in Europe and worldwide (Mattelart and Siegelaub, 1983).

The history of international unionism could be seen in terms of a heroic–charismatic earlier period, then a routine–bureaucratic period, and finally a slow death. But early labour internationalism had its limitations, and there were achievements in its second phase. Labour particularisms have been in tension with labour universalisms throughout (Forman, 1998; Silverman, 2000). The heroic earlier period was often marked by craft corporatism, nationalism, racism, militarism and imperialism (van Holthoon and van der Linden, 1988).

The achievements of twentieth-century labour internationalism need to be seen in terms of the quasi-universal spread of trade unionism and continuing international demands for labour and democratic rights. Union internationalism has made a significant contribution to the spread of liberal–democratic ideals and practices worldwide. This is no mean achievement compared with past or existing alternatives. And one has to credit the international union movement for its contribution to the establishment, in at least some parts of the capitalist world and, for a limited period, of that utopia of socialist and liberal democracy, the capitalist welfare state (Wahl, 2004).

What seems to have constrained union internationalism throughout the twentieth century was the rise of political, and even financial dependence, for 'regional integration' or 'development cooperation', on states, state-oriented political parties, an interstate organisation (the ILO), and ideologies of international social partnership with capital and/or state. This was a worldwide process in the second half of the century, in the liberal–capitalist West, the state–socialist East, and the national–developmentalist South. Operating within the ideological parameters of capital and/or state not only led to the narrowing of traditional notions of international solidarity but also implied the attrition of any autonomous labour 'worldview', not to mention any project looking beyond the parameters of capitalism. With neo-liberal globalisation, this model of trade union internationalism is in crisis and its existence is widely recognised as being under threat (Hyman, 2004; van der Linden, 2003; Wahl, 2004; Waterman, 2001a).

Box 8.1: Global labour force and trade union membership statistics

The global labour force:

World population of working age (15–64 years)	3.9 billion
Total labour force	3 billion
Female labour force as percentage of total	40.7%
Male labour force as percentage of total	59.3%

Source: Adapted from World Bank (URL), with these latest figures relating to 2002.

Global trade union membership

Statistics on trade union membership are obviously dependent on the information originally gathered, its reliability and comparability. Membership information is often collected by trade unions, which have an incentive to exaggerate their membership numbers. Even where information is collated and endorsed by national labour ministries, accuracy cannot be guaranteed, the statistics available are often dated and even what constitutes a free trade union may be disputed (see Industrial and Labor Relations (URL) for further discussion of these problems). The latest available data on changes in membership by region offered below should therefore be treated with caution:

Trade union membership

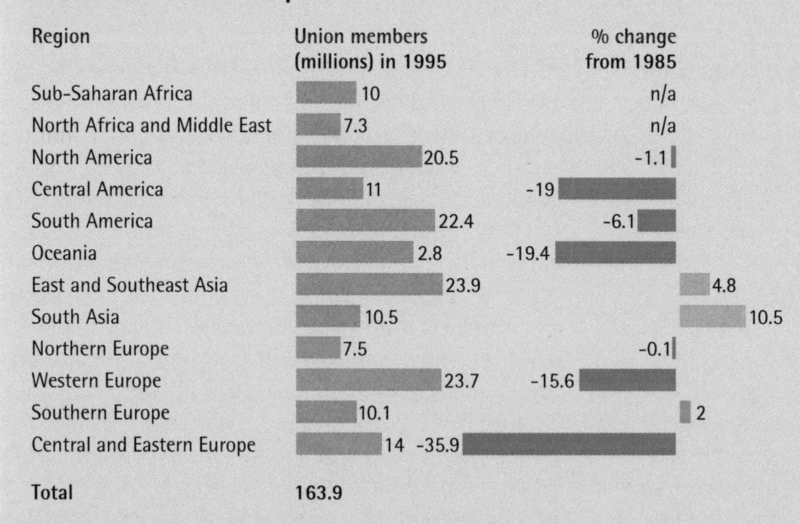

Source: New Internationalist (2001), data originally from ILO (1996)

The best estimate (although already dated) for the number of workers in trade unions worldwide is therefore *164 million*, which represents approximately *one worker in 18.* Note, though, that, mainly for the reasons discussed above, this does not directly correlate with the membership numbers claimed by the global trade union federations.

Structures of international unionism

The global workforce today consists of 3 billion people, of which an estimated 164 million are members of some form of trade union (see Box 8.1). What recent developments have led to this situation? And how do the unions relate to each other?

The major international players

During the latter half of the twentieth century, the international trade union movement was dominated by a small number of organisations, not all of them international (Waterman, 2001a). The best-known are or were: (a) the Communist-controlled World Federation of Trade Unions (WFTU) in Prague, largely denuded of members and influence by the collapse of the

Communist world in 1989 (Waterman, 2001b); (b) the social-reformist ICFTU in Brussels, which has grown as a result of the same process; and (c) the (ex-) Social Christian World Confederation of Labour (WCL), also in Brussels, that has considerable membership in Latin America but a marginal one elsewhere (see Figure 8.1).

The ILO has never had the weight of an institution like the World Trade Organisation (WTO) behind its conventions and standards

Throughout the twentieth century and beyond, the American Federation of Labour-Congress of Industrial Organisations (AFL-CIO) has played a major international role. It has been inspired more by the American variant of social reformism known as 'business unionism' than by social democracy. The AFL-CIO was a major influence within the ICFTU and also a major independent operator. It has acted through corporate and/or state-funded agencies for Asia, Africa and South America, and also engaged in activities in Europe and the Third World in a clandestine or at least low-profile manner (Carew, 1996; Clarke, 1994; Ruiz, 2004). Its work is now carried forward by its Solidarity Centre. In a unique development, the AFL–CIO foreign policy (as we must call it), has been subject to challenge by its California state branch, the largest in the country, representing one in six of AFL–CIO membership, which published a challenging resolution, significantly entitled 'Build Unity and Trust among Workers Worldwide'. After calling for an opening of AFL–CIO books on its contribution to the Pinochet Coup in Chile, 1973, condemning the war in Iraq, and throwing doubt on its dependence on external funding, the resolution calls for the AFL–CIO to henceforth 'fund its international programs and activities, whenever possible, from funds generated directly from its affiliates and their members' (Hirsch 2004). Whilst this resolution might seem overly cautious, no such significant critique has been launched by solidarity activists in Europe, where similar state-dependency pertains.

In addition, there are the oldest international union organisations, those related to specific trades or industries. The most significant are what were once called International Trade Secretariats (ITSs), now reduced in number by mergers (as a consequence of industrial transformation or falling union membership) and renamed Global Union Federations (GUFs). ITSs and GUFs have long considered themselves more unionist and less political than the ICFTU. They have, however, been similarly associated with social reformism and the ICFTU, and are now literally linked to it through the Global Unions (GU) website. Also allied to GU is the Trade Union Advisory Committee of the OECD. A formal structure of regional organisations is affiliated to the international confederations and their related industry-specific federations. But within Europe, there is the independent European Trade Union Confederation (ETUC), both addressed to and dependent on the European Union. Something similar may be emerging in the Common Market of the Southern Cone of Latin America (MERCOSUR). Significant regional union structures also exist in Asia, particularly those of the ICFTU (Greenfield, 1999). And then there are the regional internationals, also dependent on inter-governmental structures, in the Arab world and Africa. Recently, efforts have been made to coordinate the policies and activities of European-international federations and those of Latin America (CIOSL-CMT-CES-ORIT-CLAT, 2004).

How international trade unions operate

Formally speaking, most of the world's trade unions are representative democratic organisations, are controlled by their members, and advance the interests of the working class, generally. They act either defensively for particular categories of workers or more assertively, often by becoming partners or leaders in movements for national liberation, for political and social democracy or for general movements of the poor. However, as acute observers have noted, with the passing of the decades, and not only in the West, they have also become subject to the 'iron law of oligarchy' (Michels, 1915), have themselves become 'managers of discontent' (Mills, 1948/2001; Catalano, 1999), and become involved forms of 'neo-corporatism' at the risk of making themselves irrelevant (Gorz, 1999a). Throughout the twentieth century, at the regional and global levels, these threats to the unions' social presence and impact increased.

Their distance from their base increases such dangers. Despite their considerable differences – involving ideology, industry/occupation, worker constituency, or geographical reach – the international organisations share a number of common characteristics. They are remote from workers on the shop floor, in the office, or in the community, who, indeed, are usually unaware of their existence. They were, and are, marked by their past participation in the Cold War. They tend to reproduce the structure and behaviour of interstate agencies. They were, and are, largely Northern based, led and staffed (see Figure 8.1). They have tended to reduce the complex reality of working people worldwide to a Western model of the unionised (or unionisable) male worker in lifetime employment in a large-scale capitalist or state enterprise. Where they have adapted Western unionism and ILO tripartism in response to the problematic Third World, they have generally adopted the developmentalist ideologies dominant in the North. The 'free' Western internationals have become increasingly dependent on state funding for their 'regional' or 'development' activities, thus taking on the role of state or interstate development agencies. This is not a matter confronted in the otherwise admirable European-based collection on 'Trade Union and NGO Relations in Development and Social Justice' (Eade and Leather 2004; see critique in Waterman 2004b).

Where independent Southern regional organisations have been set up, such as the International Confederation of Arab Trade Unions or the Organisation of African Trade Union Unity, this has often been on the initiative of such states or groups. And such new organisations have, like the Southern states and interstate agencies themselves, tended to reproduce rather than challenge the traditional model and relationships.

The place of the ILO

We have already mentioned the ILO, the interstate body for labour questions, which became part of the UN in 1945–6. The ILO was established after the First World War in an attempt to provide the growing international labour movement with an alternative perspective to that of insurrection (developed by the Russian Revolution of 1917, armed uprisings in Germany and Hungary, and major uprisings in Scotland and elsewhere). The influence of Social Christian doctrine (Pope Leo XIII, 1891) and other such ideologies of reform from above cannot be ruled out. Although described as 'tripartite', the ILO is, of course, an inter-state organisation, in which power is divided between national governments (50 per cent), employers, (25 per cent) and labour (25 per cent). On a liberal–pluralist view, the ILO is an international reflection of the liberal-democratic nation state, with government(s) holding the scales between labour and capital in order to further economic development, social justice and the general interest. A political–economic view might be of an early twentieth-century settlement between capital and the state (75 per cent) on the one hand and labour (25 per cent) on the other. At the same time, however, the ILO, as an interstate bureaucracy, has enjoyed relative autonomy from national and international capital and the nation state, and has created both 'texts and pretexts' (as feminists said about the 1995 World Conference on Women; Vargas,

BY KIND PERMISSION OF NEW INTERNATIONALIST

Cover of New Internationalist magazine, December 2001

2003: 53) for unions to lean on or make use of. (For current standards and campaigns of the ILO, see Table 8.2.)

The ILO has never had the weight of an institution like the World Trade Organisation (WTO) behind its conventions and standards. It does have procedures for inspection and the handling of complaints, but these are inevitably legalistic, complex, and prolonged. If, between the two world wars, the ILO concentrated on social peace in Europe (the heart of labour discontent) after 1945–50 it concentrated on the 'developing countries', the new source of global disorder. The conflict between the 'ideology of the structure' (liberal and/or social democratic) and the 'ideology of the programmes' (developmentalist from the 1960s) has long been noted (Harrod, 1977). In 1969, on its fiftieth anniversary, the ILO was awarded the Nobel Peace Prize. It also launched a huge, expensive – and quite ineffective – World Employment Programme. The man responsible for this declared that 'We frequently had to say that organised labour was [here] an obstacle' (Emmerij, 1988: 119). The 'we' here clearly excludes one of the three parties that the ILO was and is assumed to represent – workers.

Figure 8.1: Contemporary labour organisations and structures

Global Trade Union Organisations	**International Confederation of Free Trade Unions (ICFTU)** www.icftu.org – based in Brussels and claims to represent 150 million workers, including those in: **10 Global Union Federations (GUFs)** Education International (EI) – www.ei-ie.org – based in Brussels International Federation of Chemical Energy, Mine and General Workers (ICEM) – www.icem.org – based in Brussels International Federation of Building and Wood Workers (IFBWW) – www.ifbww.org – based in Geneva International Federation of Journalists (IFJ) – www.ifj.org – based in Brussels International Metalworkers Federation (IMF) – www.imfmetal.org – based in Geneva International Textile, Garment and Leather Workers Federation (ITGLWF) – www.itglwf.org – based in Brussels International Transport Workers Federation (ITF) – www.itf.org.uk – based in London Internatioanl Union of Food, Agriculture, Hotel, Resturant, Catering, Tobacco and Allied Workers (IUF) – www.iuf.org – based in Geneva Public Services International (PSI) – www.world-psi.org – based in Ferney-Voltaire (France) Union Network International (UNI) – www.union-network.org – based in Nyon (Switzerland)	**World Confederation of Labour (WCL)** www.cmt-wcl.org – based in Brussels and claims to represent 30 million workers in: **7 International Trade Federations (ITFs)** International Confederation of Employees in Public Services (INFEDOP) – www.cmt-wcl.org/1cmt-wcl/cmt-en/fip-en/public1.html – based in Brussels International Federation of Trade Unions of Transport Workers (FOIST) – www.cmt-wcl.org/1cmt-wcl/cmt-en/fip-en/transport.html – based in Brussels World Confederation of Teachers (WCT-CSME) – www.wctcsme.org – based in Brussels International Federation of Textile and Clothing (IFTC) – www.cmt-wcl.org/1cmt-wcl/cmt-en/fip-en/fedtextile.htm – based in Brussels World Federation of Industrial Workers (WFIW) – www.cmt-wcl.org/1cmt-wcl/cmt-en/fip-en/fmti1.html – based in Brussels World Federation of Agriculture, Food, Hotel and Allied Workers (WFAFW) – www.acmoti.org/2.WFAFW.FEMTAA.htm – based in Brussels World Federation of Clerical Workers (WFCW) – www.cmt-wcl.org/1cmt-wcl/cmt-en/fip-en/clerical1.html – based in Brussels
International TU Organisations	Examples include: Commonwealth Trade Union Congress (CTUC) www.commonwealthtuc.org Based in London	Trade Union Advisory Council to OECD (TUAC) www.tuac.org Based in Paris
National TU Organisations	Examples include: American federation of Labour – congress of Industrialised Organisations (USA) (AFL-CIO) www.aflcio.org Based in Washington DC	Trade Union Congress (UK) (TUC) www.tuc.org.uk Based in London
Interstate Labour Institution		**International Labour Organisation (ILO)** www.ilo.org – Based in Geneva This is the UN organisation for labour issues made up by: • 50% national governments • 25% employers • 25% labour representatives

World Federation of Trade Unions (WFTU)

www.wftu.cz – based in Prague and claims to represent 67 million workers, including those in:

3 Trade Union Internationals (TUIs)

Trade Union International and Allied Employees (TUI) – www.tradeunionindia.org – based in New Delhi

Trade Union International for Energy, Metal, Chemicals, Oil and Related Industries (TUI-WEMCORI) – www.uis-tui.org – based in Mexico City

Trade Union International of Workers in the Building, Wood, Buildings Materials and Allied Industries (UTIBB) – www.uitbb.org – based in Helsinki

←

European Trade Union Confederation
(ETUC)
www.etuc.org
Based in Brussels

←

Central Única dos Trabalhadores (Brazil)
(CUT)
www.cut.org.br
Based in São Paolo

←

←

Pro-labour activists, NGOs, social movements and networks

Table 8.2: Major programmes of the International Labour Organisation

Campaign or programme	Website
International Labour Standards	http://webfusion.ilo.org/public/db/standards/normes/index.cfm?lang=EN
ILO Declaration on Fundamental Principles and Rights at Work	www.ilo.org/dyn/declaris/DECLARATIONWEB.INDEXPAGE
International Programme on the Elimination of Child Labour (IPEC)	www.ilo.org/public/english/standards/ipec/index.htm
Crisis Response and Reconstruction Programme	www.ilo.org/public/english/employment/recon/crisis/index.htm
Skills, Knowledge and Employability Programme	www.ilo.org/public/english/employment/skills/index.htm
Boosting Employment by Small Enterprise Development (SEED)	www.ilo.org/dyn/empent/empent.portal?p_prog=S
Global Campaign on Social Security and Coverage for All	www.ilo.org/public/english/protection/socsec/pol/campagne/index.htm
Safe Work	www.ilo.org/public/english/protection/safework/index.htm
HIV and AIDS and the World of Work	www.ilo.org/public/english/protection/trav/aids/index.htm
Social Dialogue, Labour Law and Labour Administration (IFP/DIALOGUE)	www.ilo.org/public/english/dialogue/ifpdial/index.htm

Sources: ILO homepage (ILO, URLb) and individual URLs indicated in the table (consulted 25 May 2004)

Labour internationalism under globalisation – within and beyond the unions

The processes of globalisation that started towards the end of the twentieth century have dramatically transformed the world of work. Advances in production, computerisation and transportation allow goods, services and finance to flow easily and rapidly around the world. A globalising neo-liberalism is responsible for the increasing polarisation of the rich and poor (both between and within countries), for dramatic environmental degradation and for the 'race to the bottom' within an economic system that causes exploitation and insecurity for workers on a global scale. Neo-liberal ideologies claim that 'the globalisation of capitalism is an unstoppable juggernaut to which workers can only submit themselves' (Herod, 2001: 104). The impact on the labour movement has, predictably, been dramatic.

Description
Expressions of international tripartite agreements on issues of injustice, hardship, privation, social policy, and human and civil rights
The declaration centres around: • freedom of association and the right to collective bargaining • the elimination of forced and compulsory labour • the abolition of child labour • the elimination of discrimination in the workplace.
A 90-country alliance working to eradicate child labour by strengthening national capacities to address child labour problems and by creating a worldwide movement to combat it
A strategic programme that aims to help understand and overcome employment issues arising from natural disasters, armed conflicts, and economic and financial downturns
Promotes greater investment in the training and skills development of men and women to ensure improved and equal access to decent work
Seeks to create more and better jobs by encouraging the development of small businesses
Treats social security provision as a basic human right and aims to secure it for the entire world's population
Provides policy documents, organises actions and offers resources for the promotion of better health and safety at work
Provides information and advice about HIV/AIDS; campaigns to promote awareness within the workplace and to prevent discrimination against men and women with HIV/AIDS
• Strengthens legal frameworks, institutions, machinery and processes of tripartite and bipartite social dialogue and promotes sound industrial relations at enterprise, national, sectoral and sub-regional levels • Increases the number of member states that base their labour laws and other employment-related legislation on ILO standards and advice, involving a tripartite consultative process • Strengthens labour administrations in their policy-making capacity, responsibility in the implementation of decent work policies and the enforcement of labour law • Assists member states to establish and strengthen labour courts, tribunals and dispute-resolution mechanisms so that individual or collective disputes are dealt with more efficiently, effectively and equitably • Increases participation of social partners in economic and social policy-making in regional or sub-regional groupings and enhances links with relevant international institutions

At the end of the twentieth century, international trade unionism was confronted by a tragic paradox. There were more wage-earners than ever before: 2.9 billion according to the World Bank. The ICFTU/GU, with some 150 million members, covered more countries, unions and workers than ever before. This was due, as suggested, to the incorporation of most of the formerly Communist or national-populist unions. But neo-liberal globalisation implied the simultaneous weakening of traditional unionism's century-old national-industrial base, the shift of that base to countries of the South (particularly China), the undermining of traditional job security and union rights, and the decline or disappearance of support from social-democratic parties, socially-reformist governments and the most powerful interstate agencies. Moreover, the unions were being confronted with a fact that – in their industrial, national or industrial-relations cocoons – they had never previously felt it necessary to face: in this globalising world of labour, only about one in 18 workers was unionised. Finally, with the disappearance of their competitors in Communist or national-populist unions, the ICFTU/GU found itself not only in an alien and hostile world but ideologically disoriented (Maspero, 2000). Previously, it had been able to see itself not only as representing the most advanced union model but as part of the 'free West', opposed to both Communist and national-populist unionism. Now, it found itself left behind by the globalisation of capital and by the decreasing political interest of the international state system. The resulting dilemma of union internationalism was expressed thus by a sympathetic and cautious observer (Hyman, 2004):

> *National and international trade union apparatuses, with their deeply rooted traditions, long-established political and industrial bargaining relationships, and complex internal power dynamics, are both repelled and attracted by the flexibility and spontaneity of alternative modes of intervention in an arena in which unions once claimed exclusive jurisdiction. What were once known as 'new social movements' ... have been able to engage effectively in forms of 'contentious politics'... which most trade union leaders until very recently considered signs of immaturity... In the third century of trade union internationalism, the challenges which are faced are perhaps greater than ever, but there is growing awareness that old recipes for action are inadequate and that new possibilities can be grasped. Thoughtful trade unionists have come to recognise that playing safe is the most risky strategy. The present is either the end of the beginning or the beginning of the end.*

How have the traditional union internationals and the new pro-labour networks been responding recently to globalisation?

The international trade union organisations respond

If the union internationals initially responded in equal measure with disorientation, retreat and (often ineffective) action on a national scale, they are now increasingly raising the old notion of 'social partnership' with capital and state from the national to the global level. This has implied a series of specific campaigns, addressed sometimes directly to multinational corporations, sometimes to the international financial institutions and other promoters of globalisation (the WTO, the World Economic Forum, and so forth).

> *Over the years, the global union federations have established an ongoing social dialogue with a number of multinational enterprises in their sectors or industries' (ICFTU, URL; see also Justice, 2002: 96).*

Three major areas of this union work are international labour standards, codes of conduct and corporate social responsibility policies (Jenkins, Pearson and Seyfang, 2002). The Core Labour Rights set out below are currently represented by a set of those already issued by the ILO, of which only one is actually less than 30 years old:

- the right to form trade unions ('freedom of association')
- the right to effective collective bargaining between workers and management
- freedom from forced or compulsory labour
- an end to child labour
- freedom from discrimination in the workplace.

This list does not, notably, include an explicit right to the international solidarity strike, as called for by the International Centre for Trade Union Rights (Ewing and Sibley, 2000). Directly or indirectly related to this declaration has been the 15-year-plus campaign, most recently within the WTO, for a 'social clause' under which that organisation (initially the General Agreement of Tariffs and Trade, its predecessor) would discriminate against states that did not respect international labour rights. This attempt to get labour rights institutionalised by the very organisation that was promoting 'free trade' at the cost of labour rights and conditions not only failed but provoked much disagreement, as well as forceful criticism within the union movement in the South and among labour specialists (John and Chenoy, 1996; *Working USA*, 2001).

'Global Framework Agreements' between particular GUFs and multinational corporations are another area of union work within the international context (see Box 8.2).

However these agreements do not require internationally enforceable legislation. This is a problem with voluntary 'codes of conduct', which can be difficult to monitor and are often left to underfunded and unaccountable NGOs (Oliviero and Simmons, 2002; Jenkins, Pearson and Seyfang, 2002).

Such voluntary global social contracts have been presented on a slightly more public global stage by union endorsement of the UN's Global Compact. This is another voluntary initiative, aiming to mainstream socially responsible business activities through policy dialogues, learning and local projects. Union support for

Box 8.2: Global framework agreements between trade unions and multinational companies

A global framework agreement is a written document between a global or multinational company and a global trade union federation on behalf of its members. The purpose of the agreement is to formalise a relationship between the company and the union at the global level, similar to those common between local businesses and local unions. The agreement focuses on the international activities of the company (especially how these affect its treatment of employees); it negotiates the expectations and responsibilities of both parties and serves to establish a formal and regular channel of communication between them.

A global framework agreement usually comes about after a number of trade unions in different countries, representing people who work for the same multinational company, form an alliance to approach it. Communications technology makes such alliances increasingly easy to pursue. An actual global framework agreement is presented here as an example; others are available from the sources cited.

CARREFOUR – UNI Union Network International

At the meeting of the Information Committee and the European Committee on Information and Consultation on 27 and 28 November 2000, Carrefour and Union Network International (UNI) agreed that every enterprise needs peace and social consensus in order to develop.

To that end, Carrefour undertakes to monitor jointly with UNI the proper application of ILO conventions 87–98 and 135. Those international standards define:

1. the right of employees to joint a trade union of their choice,
2. the right to collective bargaining,
3. the protection of employees and their representatives against any act of discrimination tending to infringe upon trade union freedom.

Respect for union rights and recognition of fundamental rights are part of the corporate culture of the Carrefour Group.

Carrefour has also condemned child labor in order to prevent slavery and forced labor, and it intends to ensure that the principles established by the ILO are respected by its suppliers.

President of Carrefour Daniel BERNARD
General Secretary of UNI Philip JENNINGS
Head of UNI Commerce Jan FURSTENBORG

A global framework can be beneficial to a multinational company for several reasons. As companies are increasingly expected to report on their social activities as 'good corporate citizens', a framework agreement is a method of demonstrating commitment that goes beyond mere words. It is a signed document and one that allows for the possibility of monitoring.

Such agreements remain voluntary, but they benefit trade unions and workers by opening communications and providing points of leverage when a company is in violation of the agreement or its practices are questionionable. Trade union members, like reporting requirements, can act as monitors. Again, in an era of high-profile scandals and of increasing interest in corporate citizenship, companies do not wish to be seen to be breaking their agreements, which are evidence of the company's attempts to be responsible. Whether the value of the agreements is limited to the present era and whether the agreements themselves are preventing a push for enforceable international regulation remains to be seen.

Sources and further information: ICFTU (URL); Union-Network (URL).

the Global Compact, even though the initiative lacked the power of enforcement or even monitoring, was expressed in a joint UN-ICFTU/GU declaration in 2000:

> *It was agreed that global markets required global rules. The aim should be to enable the benefits of globalisation increasingly to spread to all people by building an effective framework of multilateral rules for a world economy that is being transformed by the globalisation of markets . . . the Global Compact should contribute to this process by helping to build social partnerships of business and labour. (ICFTU, 2000b)*

More recently, we have seen union co-sponsorship of the ILO's World Commission on the Social Dimension of Globalisation (also involving prominent politicians, corporate figures and academics), which has published a report on 'Fair Globalisation: Creating Opportunities for All' (ILO, 2004).

Together, these activities suggest the international union movement is refocusing from states and interstate bodies, seen as the locus of power and regulation, to the multinational corporations, seen as the main actors and regulators of the global economy. While the social-democratic international unions broadly welcome such projects (Justice, 2002), others see in these accords an embrace by UN institutions of the multinationals at the expense of civil society (Judge, 2001). Indeed, there is now an 'Alliance for a Corporate-Free United Nations' (Infact, 2004), although so far it has not won the support of any union, national or international.

While such efforts suggest a reorientation in reaction to globalisation, international trade unions are continuing their historical efforts at union building, in defence of labour rights and in support of workers and unions internationally. Increasingly, this involves new and more assertive language. An exemplar might be the International Transportworkers Federation, whose 2002 Congress was devoted to the theme of 'Globalising Solidarity' (ITWF, 2002). A turning point in its practical solidarity activity is indicated by, on the one hand, its failure to support effectively the Liverpool dock workers during a major lockout in 1995–8 (Waterman, 1997) and its effective support for the Australian dock workers during a related dispute in 1998.

True, much national and international union solidarity activity is carried out under the rubric of 'development cooperation' and financed by the state or interstate organisations. At other times, activity is combined with union-to-union or worker-to-worker solidarity, as with the Irish Congress of Trade Unions (ICTU, URL). It is, however, notable that most of this solidarity activity appears to be on a North–South axis and in a North–South direction. A more holistic and multidirectional notion of labour solidarity is yet to emerge; and even the ICTU website reveals only an implicit recognition of the broader global solidarity movement.

The broader labour and global solidarity movements respond

If the unions were thus responding to the challenge 'from above', they were also responding to that 'from below' or at least 'from the side'. For labour's asserted place as 'by far and away the most democratic institution in every society and certainly the only major democratic international movement' (Spooner, 2004: 27) is being increasingly challenged by the 'new global solidarity movement', fighting on a broader social and ideological terrain, that of 'global civil society'. The 'new social movements' (ecological, women's, anti-war, human rights, indigenous peoples' and so on) have been gathering strength since the 1970s and 1980s, as have numerous international labour networks, concerned with 'atypical' workers, with publications or audiovisuals and labour information, and communication technology. Moreover, since the close of the twentieth century and the beginning of the twenty-first, there has been an explosion of global civil society events, actions, and organisations, such as that represented by the Mumbai WSF (Kaldor, Anheier and Glasius, 2003; Kaldor, 2003; Pianta and Silva, 2003).

These new internationalist labour NGOs, although customarily linked to trade union organisations, differ from them in their origins, 'membership' (if any), constituencies, financing, 'relational form' (networks rather than institutions), and their typical forms of action and expression. They commonly concentrate on a single campaign, aspect of worker life, type of previously unrepresented labour, world area, and type of international labour solidarity activity (such as education or communication). Sometimes they overlap with community movements. Sometimes they are not even identifiable as 'labour oriented' but, rather, take up labour issues as part of a more general set of popular or democratic complaints and demands. A prominent example is international networking between peasants and small farmers (Edelman, 2003). Another is the International Collective in Defence of Fishworkers (Table 8.3; Dietrich and Nayak, 2001). Better-known internationally are those Western-based projects that have

Table 8.3: **Sample list of labour-related international NGOs, networks and groups on the Internet**

INGO	Website
Alianza Continental Social/Hemispheric Social Alliance	www.asc-hsa.org/castellano/site/home.php
Asia Monitor Resource Centre	www.amrc.org.hk/archive.htm
China Labour Bulletin (Hong Kong)	www.china-labour.org.hk/iso/index.adp
China Labor Watch (USA)	www.chinalaborwatch.org
Clean Clothes Campaign	www.cleanclothes.org
Coordinadora de Centrales del Cono Sur/ Coordination of Union Centres of the Southern Cone	www.ccscs.org/index.htm.
E-TradeUnions	www.e-tradeunions.org/home.php
Free the Children: Mobilised Investigation	http://manifestor.org/mi/en/2003/09/72.shtml
Global Labour University	www.global-labour-university.de
Global March Against Child Labour	http://globalmarch.org/index.php
Global Policy Network	www.globalpolicynetwork.org
Global Union Research Network Geneva/Montreal (ILO and Global Unions related)	www.global-unions.org
Instituto del Mundo de Trabajo/World of Labour Institute (Buenos Aires)	www.mundodeltrabajo.org.ar
International Centre for Trade Union Rights	www.ictur.labournet.org
International Collective in Defence of Fishworkers (Chennai, India and Brussels, Belgium)	www.icsf.net/jsp/english/index.jsp
International Dockworkers Council	www.idcdockworkers.org
International Network of Street Newspapers	www.street-papers.org
International Union of Sex Workers	www.iusw.org
International Work Group for Indigenous Affairs	www.iwgia.org/sw617.asp
Labour Behind the Label	www.behindthelabel.org
Labour Start (UK)	www.labourstart.org
Migrants Rights International	www.migrantwatch.org
Mobilised Investigation	http://manifestor.org/mi/en/2003/09/72.shtml
No Border	www.noborder.org/news_index.php
No Sweat (UK)	www.nosweat.org.uk
Open World Conference of Workers	www.owcinfo.org/WHC/index.htm
Peoples' Global Action	www.nadir.org/nadir/initiativ/agp/en
Public World/GAPS	www.publicworld.org/index.htm
Red Latinoamericana de Mujeres Transformando la Economía (Latin American Network of Women Transforming the Economy)	www.movimientos.org/remte/publica.phtml
Reinventing Social Emancipation	www.ces.fe.uc.pt/emancipa/en/
Shack Dwellers International	www.homeless-international.org/ standard_1.asp?category=3&id=275&id=262
Social Movements World Network	www.movsoc.org/htm/who_we_are.htm
Solidar	www.solidar.org
Streetnet International	www.streetnet.org.za
The Commoner: A Web Journal for Other Values	www.commoner.org.uk
This Tuesday: Longs on Migration, Labour, Transnational Organising	www.thistuesday.org
Transnationals Information Exchange-Asia (Kajang, Malaysia)	www.tieasia.org/index2.html
Via Campesina (Peasant Way)	www.viacampesina.org/welcome_english.php3
Web Community of Social Movements	http://movimientos.org
Women in the Informal Economy; Globalizing and Organizing	www.wiego.org/main/
Women Working Worldwide (Manchester, UK)	www.poptel.org.uk/women-ww
Women's Global Strike	http://womenstrike8m.server101.com/English/ shortpost-strikereport.htm

Note: Websites consulted 24 April 2004

addressed themselves energetically and publicly to issues like child labour and sweated labour more generally (Silvey, 2004) and to high-profile attacks on corporations or brands such as McDonald's (Ghigliani, 2003; McSpotlight, URL). Another widespread type of NGO is that which concentrates on labour rights, often linking unions, academics, students and legal professionals, such as the International Centre for Trade Union Rights in the UK (see Table 8.3 for others).

Contrasting the responses

It would be easy to set up a whole series of binary or Manichean oppositions between the old international union organisations and the new labour and social justice movements, and between their responses to globalisation. But perhaps the most significant tensions here are those between the moments of capitalist development at which they appeared; between organisations (representative-democratic membership) and networks (often of self-appointed, often non-worker activists); between the customarily national and frequently cross-national or global constituencies; between 'political-institutional' and 'social-communicational' internationalism; and between implicit references to a traditional 'democracy frame' and references to a growing 'civil society frame'. However, it is not, in practice, possible to identify such characteristics with the union organisation on the one hand, and the labour NGO or social movement network on the other.

In the 1970s or 1980s some of the earlier international labour NGOs or networks, such as Transnationals Information Exchange or Asia Monitor Research Centre, directly challenged the union internationals from, as it were, 'below', 'the Left' and 'the South' (Waterman, 2001a). They certainly opened up new issues and perspectives for the unions, thus having had, at the very least, the impact of pressure groups or of raisers of consciousness for a new kind of labour internationalism. But neo-liberal globalisation in the 1990s had an impact on networks as well as institutions, and many of the NGOs today limit themselves to roles of support or extension, having abandoned any notion of publicly challenging the international unions, or even of initiating public dialogue with them. Conversely, many unions have been taking up activities (towards women, atypical workers) or attitudes (solidarity discourse, openness to other movements) previously highlighted by the networks. Given, further, the increasing presence of unions on major national or international demonstrations against neo-liberal globalisation, the relationship between the unions and the social movements is becoming not only intertwined but interdependent.

Possibly the most dramatic and visible evidence of what is happening is provided by the World Social Forum, mentioned earlier (see Box 8.3). The WSF process has been taken to symbolise the new 'movement of movements' against and beyond neo-liberal globalisation. It is significant that two Brazilian labour organisations were involved in the Organising Committee (later Secretariat) of the Forums held in Porto Alegre, Brazil, during 2001–3. The first was a 'new' union, the Central Trade Union Confederation (CUT), itself critical of the ICFTU (Jakobsen, 2001). The second was the Movement of Landless Rural Workers, an even newer movement, which had its own tensions with CUT and its political arm, the Brazilian Workers' Party (PT). It is significant, finally, that this new internationalist initiative is firmly based in the South.

> **This is a time of dramatic threats to human, or a humane, existence, with devastating wars; overwork that kills and un(der)employment preventing people reaching subsistence levels . . . social polarisation; and the commodification and trafficking of bodies and body parts**

Conclusion

This chapter has been concerned with a quite specific, yet rather complex, matter: the past and present relationship of the international labour movement to democratisation of the social. Such a relationship might have been understood as requiring the overthrow (or at least the radical reform) of capitalism, but is now being thought of as the construction of a global civil society. From yet another perspective, we could say that what we have here been concerned with is the relationship of union internationalism to (a) labour and other internationalisms and (b) 'rethinking social emancipation' (Centro de Estudos Sociais, URL). Let us consider what still needs to be thought and spelt out in terms of conceptualisation, of communication and of political strategy.

Conceptualisation

When the International Transport Workers Federation talks about 'global solidarity', does it have in mind the same idea as when others talk of the 'global solidarity and justice movement'? When the ICFTU talks – as it increasingly does – of 'global civil society', is it referring to the same empirical phenomenon or process, the same desired alternative, as is the latest contributor to the Global Civil Society Yearbook? When the ICFTU says that it is providing the leadership, or must establish leadership, of 'global civil society' (ICFTU, 2000a), is this compatible with anyone else's notion of the latter? Is its aspiration to be simultaneously a partner in industry and a member of civil society (ICFTU, 2002) an internally consistent political project or a contradiction in terms? These are far from academic questions awaiting academic answers. They are the kind of issues the international labour movement has debated in conferences and in print during the 200 years of its existence, and which it will need to continue discussing if it wants to have more than a marginal future.

In the history of labour protest and internationalism, such notions as 'abolition of the wage system', 'a fair day's wage for a fair day's work', 'a socialist world republic' (from a German Communist song of the 1920s), 'the welfare state', 'a proletarian public sphere' (Negt and Kluge, 1972/1983), 'social partnership', even simply 'free trade unionism' have carried varying weight. Sometimes, they have provided the master discourse within which strategy is discussed or is discussable (with denunciation of those who challenge the terms). But this is a time of dramatic threats to human, or a humane, existence, with devastating wars; overwork that kills and un(der)employment preventing people reaching subsistence levels; global warming; widespread hunger here and obesity there; the destruction of social services; social polarisation; and the commodification and trafficking of bodies and body parts. But it is – by the very recognition of such as global problems – also a time of promise, with a worldwide wave of social protest matching or surpassing that of the 1960s–70s.

In giving 'global civil society' meaning for working people worldwide, and in giving social depth to this concept itself, it may be necessary to explore other concepts connected with the world of labour, rights, citizenship and emancipation, and, of course, to consider their relationship with each other and with 'global civil society' itself. Some of these concepts may have been used, if not fully discussed, above; others not. We propose the following concepts, with footnotes for some useful, relevant or at least provocative resources. The concepts are *Work, Solidarity, The Commons, Welfare, Internationalism* and *Utopia*[4]. If these were to be discussed in relationship with 'global civil society', interesting possibilities might appear.

Communication

It was suggested above that the new internationalisms are, in a significant sense, 'communications internationalisms'. This notion has a range of possible meanings.

It can mean that the new internationalisms operate increasingly in social-communicational rather than in political-institutional space – that they work by the spread of information, ideas, son et lumière, dialogue, rather than by occupying positions of (apparent) political influence. This new focus recognises the extent to which powerlessness and empowerment operate culturally.

Characterising the new solidarity movements as communications internationalisms can also mean that they are computer-savvy (in the sense of recognising the low cost, high speed and long reach of information and communication technology) and that unions recognise the need to develop 'countervailing power' to the use of these means by capital and state. But a communications internationalism can also mean that unions increasingly understand the subversive or emancipatory potential of a technology that was developed for quite other purposes, and that, combined with the locally rooted, face-to-face activity of globalisation-affected communities, information and communications technology (ICT) could help make people free (Escobar, 1999).

The labour movement originally became international with an acute awareness of the value of communications and culture, including internationally circulated songs, texts, red flags, May Day, and a whole spectrum of international cultural activities. The increasing incorporation of unions into national polities and bloc alliances was so profound that the labour internationals lost this awareness. They were late, slow and even reluctant to appreciate the possibilities of ICT. Under the impact of other social movements, along with the efforts of often marginal labour ICT projects, this shortcoming is being increasingly overcome (as witness the websites we

4 *For Work, consider Gorz (1999a); for Solidarity, Waterman (2004: 230–8); for The Commons and Welfare,* The Commoner *(2003), Publicworld (URL), Public Services International (URL); for Internationalism, Anderson (2002), Labournet (URL); for Utopia, Panitch and Leys (2000).*

Box 8.3: World Social Forum 4, Mumbai, India, 2004

It was at the WSF4, Mumbai, India, January 2004, that there was the most extensive labour participation, with the high-level involvement of the international trade union bodies (Mathew and Shetty, 2003). As with the WSF3 in Porto Alegre, a World Trade Union Forum was held in Mumbai before the WSF itself began. This was organised jointly by the ETUC, ICFTU and the WCL in collaboration with the ILO. During the WSF4 itself a range of labour-focused events took place, including 22 seminars, a panel, four meetings, a rally, two conferences, eight workshops, a roundtable and a debate. There was a number of marches, up to 6,000-strong, endorsed by some 40 labour organisations. The efforts of the unions represented a significant proportion of the events held during the WSF4, with the union profile being the highest ever. Many of these were part of the 'Labour at WSF 2004' platform, which was coordinated not by a national or international union body, but by the New Delhi-based Centre for Education and Communication, the independent labour NGO that had earlier been responsible for one of the few international labour movement critiques of the 'Social Clause' (John and Chenoy, 1996).

JILL TIMMS

Various messages were promoted during these events, and a significant proportion stressed the fundamental role of trade unions in the global social justice movement. Two examples stand out. First, Juan Somavia, director general of the ILO, used the World Trade Union Forum to remind unions of their vital role in struggling for social justice, for the dignity of work and for the rights of workers across the world. Second, speaking to an audience of 8,000, Guy Ryder, general secretary of the ICFTU, stressed the importance of the ICFTU and the Global Unions working together for global justice, and the significance of their joint presence at the WSF:

> *The trade unions are here, want to be here and have everything to gain from working with civil society who share the same values and visions . . . The unions are internationalists by instinct and practice.*

As well as international activity, a wide range of national and local unions and NGOs, mainly from India, organised smaller events, campaign publicity, marches and information stalls. There was, of course, a particular focus on the labour issues that most strongly affect Indian workers: the impact of globalisation and neo-liberalism in undermining the state sector; the devastation of traditional industries; the plight of unorganised workers in the informal sector; the impact of globalisation on the rural poor, child labour and the status of women in the workplace.

Interviews with Indian labour participants suggest a range of motives for participation:

V Chandra, The New Trade Union Initiative – established in 2002 to coordinate the work of non-party-affiliated unions in India:

We decided to attend the forum, to run an information stall and organise several seminars as a part of our development strategy . . . We have links with trade unions in the USA and South Asia, and for us the World Social Forum is an opportunity to pull together to be able to fight imperialist globalisation and poverty together.

Labour activists at the WSF4

Jason Periera, International Young Christian Workers – one of many international NGOs focusing on labour issues:

We support trade union activities and work on issues of unemployment and migration in India, but we're also part of a worldwide organisation which allows us to coordinate the things we do much wider . . . We have come to the World Social Forum for networking opportunities with similar organisations.

P Suresa, Project Officer – The Dalit Handloom Weavers Welfare Society, a national labour rights group for 'untouchables':

We offer support to workers and particularly campaign to reduce the high suicide rates among weavers and also [against] poverty. We are at the forum to look for international funding.

Thomas Sebastian and Sangam Tripathy, International Transport Workers Federation:

In India, all the main types of transport have their own union, but together they are part of an international union. They have come to the World Social Forum for two main reasons. Firstly, there have already been three WSFs and there was not much of a labour presence at them, so they are here because they wanted there to be more of a presence as labour is a major part of civil society. The second reason is that their own workers are focused on their own local issues and problems and cannot relate [to] or understand how the global problems relate to them. So bringing them here, and reporting back, exposes them to the whole of civil society and helps them to understand how they need to see their struggle as part of a larger one that we have to fight together.

cite and the audio-visuals, PowerPoint and other electronic products increasingly found on them).

Apart from the predictable challenges of reviving or reinventing an international labour culture – such as language, accessibility, training, and funding – another major challenge has to be confronted: the 'culture of networking'. It is difficult for institutions and formal organisations (representative–democratic or not) to overcome the hierarchy, distance, formality and rigidity that is embedded within them, or the fortress mentality (for both defence and attack) that a membership organisation implies. We have not yet found an international union website that has an open 'discussion feature'. This is in contrast with LabourStart (URL), which, while wholly oriented towards the unions, is also independent of them. The lack of feedback and dialogue is in even greater contrast with websites and lists of, or around, the WSF/GJ&SM. These are often primarily concerned with debate, discussion and dialogue. The global justice movement sites may reveal networking *with* or *between* national and international labour organisations, but the generalisation of a networking logic *within* the union movement has a long way to go.

It is difficult for institutions and formal organisations . . . to overcome the hierarchy, distance, formality and rigidity that is embedded within them, or the fortress mentality . . . that a membership organisation implies

Finally, we need to note the relative absence of quite basic *information* concerning labour internationalism. Although the drought in international labour studies of the 1990s is being replaced by something like a flood in the new millennium, the new studies tend to be more about union institutions and their interrelations (with each other, with corporations, with states) than about workers' and solidarity activities or the movements themselves. Case studies of international solidarity actions are so rare that they tend to be repeatedly reproduced, as if the references or cases speak for themselves and do not require critical examination or reinterpretation. There are few comparative, interpretative and movement-oriented studies, even fewer 'in the light of' the WSF/GJ&SM (Aguiton, 2001, is an exception). Nor are such studies much discussed, disseminated or popularised in a manner that might make them available for activists. Finally, we do not actually know the *meaning* for workers of the international organisations with which they are affiliated or the international solidarity campaigns in which they might have been energetically involved. A serious dialogue between labour researchers and commentators, as also between these and the activists, has yet to commence.

Political strategy

One can imagine various scenarios for the future of union internationalism. Indeed, we could project these from five possible identities suggested for unionism in Europe (Hyman, 1999). These are those of the *Guild* (of an occupational elite), of the *Friendly Society* (of individualised workers), of the *Company Union* (a productivity coalition between workers and owners), of the *Social Partner* (a political trade-off between union and state), and of the *Social Movement* (a campaigning unionism seeking mass support). Each of these could have, and often has had, its own internationals and internationalisms. In so far as these are ideal types, we are likely to find, in reality, ambiguous union types and ambiguous internationalisms. It might have been suggested above that union internationalism is today hegemonised by Social Partnership unionism. Yet, in practice, we find varying syntheses of Social Partnership, Company Unionism and Social Movement Unionism.

The growing presence of international unions within the global justice and solidarity movement in general, or the World Social Forum in particular, might suggest a development in the direction of some kind of 'international social movement unionism' (Waterman, 2004a: Appendix 1). However, unlike the Communist International, neither the WSF in particular nor the GJ&SM in general has 21 conditions of membership. So the unions enter this new movement without necessarily abandoning their long-standing traditions of Social Partnership and/or Company Unionism. Moreover, neither the WSF nor the GJ&SM represents some paradise of global solidarity. What they do provide is a new form of international articulation, with 'articulation' referring to both joining together and expression. The new 'joining together' is represented by the centrality of both networking and of the agora – a meeting place of diverse movements and a marketplace of ideas. The new 'expression' is largely shaped by such guiding ideas as 'Another World is Possible!', 'Alternative Globalisation', 'Global Civil Society', and the notion that, given opposition to neo-liberal globalisation, such ideas will find shape through a dialogue and dialectic between class, ideological, social-geographical, gender/sexual, ethnic and other differences.

The presence of the trade unions within this new movement of movements implies the hypothetical possibility not only of adding 100–200 million organised workers to the somewhat inchoate and changing constituency of the GJ&SM, but also of making 'work' as central to the WSF as trade, the environment/ consumption and peace have been in the past. So far, however, work has appeared within the WSF largely in the guise of 'Decent Work', as sponsored originally by an interstate organisation, the ILO. The ILO, the sole interstate institution with unchallenged acceptability to the WSF, incorporated – or even invented – social partnership almost 100 years ago. And, whereas there has been a considerable presence within the WSF of labour's 'others' (female, rural, indigenous, 'atypical', unemployed, migrant labour), and of 'other' ideas about work (cooperatives, the solidarity economy, alternative trade), it cannot be said that there is represented here any such holistic alternative to capitalist work, such as that at least implied by Gorz (1999b).

What the new movement does at least make possible is the emancipation of the unions from two historical, and now archaic, notions of labour internationalism: one that suggested that labour was the privileged bearer of social emancipation and international solidarity, and one that conceived unions in junior partnership with (sections of) national and international capital and (certain) interstate institutions. If, as Hyman (2004) says, playing safe is the riskiest strategy for international labour, the new agora provides the possibility of working out, together with others, a more effective one.

There are, however, no guarantees here. The dialogue or dialectic between the old trade union movement and the new global justice one might just as well witness the infection of the latter by the former, as vice versa. The problematic outcome of such engagements is revealed by the impact of 'second wave' feminism on the trade union movement. After an initial and emancipatory moment, there was, according to Warskett (2001: 230), a loss of energy and direction on both sides. All the activity of the feminists has 'not changed in any fundamental way labour unions' vision of what the workplace, community and society could be'. For this she holds both parties responsible.

What, therefore, seems least likely to occur is some kind of dramatic change of heart – or model – within the international trade union movement. It is difficult to imagine an explicit abandonment of the old social partnership with capital and state for a new one with a global civil society that is still – as all serious commentators add – in the making. Left to its century-old devices, the international trade union organisations are more likely to continue with their present contradictory partnerships – one with capital-and-state, the other with the new movements.

If, however, we address ourselves to the more dynamic party in the relationship, then there is something more to be said. It is this: the new movement needs to supersede the fetishisation of the traditional trade unions, much as it has the state, capital, international relations and political parties (even of the New Left). The new movement already provides space for some expression of that majority of the world's labour force that is beyond either the unions' concerns or their present reach. It also has means of communication (including the kind of presence in the mass media that unions once enjoyed). These resources allow it to approach the base of the international trade union movement – people with little knowledge and less control over those who currently speak or act for them. An energetic address to the increasingly globalised workers of the world – *with* the unions, *through* the unions, *around* the unions, even *despite* the unions – could actually help to reinvent the international labour movement for the century ahead. Those within the unions – from bottom to top – who prefer risk to safety are likely to welcome the challenge.

The authors wish to thank all those who participated in the initial day seminar for this chapter, 'International Labour Organisations and Global Civil Society' held at LSE in October 2003, for their valuable insights, experiences and comments. Jill Timms thanks the labour activists she interviewed in Mumbai at WSF4, and also ACTRAV and the International Institute for Labour Studies at the ILO for her invitation to the GURN meeting in Turin. Finally, we thank Marlies Glasius, Jeffrey Harrod, Dave Hollis, Richard Hyman and Hilary Wainwright for their useful comments and assistance with this chapter.

References

Aguiton, Chistophe (2001) *Le monde nous appartient*. Paris: Plon.

Alcock, Antony (1971) *History of the International Labour Organisation*. London: Macmillan.

Anderson, Perry (2002) 'Internationalism: A Breviary', *New Left Review*, No. 14 (March–April): 5-25.

Anheier, Helmut, Glasius, Marlies and Kaldor, Mary (2001) 'Introducing Global Civil Society', in Helmut Anheier, Marlies Glasius and Mary Kaldor (eds), *Global Civil Society 2001*. Oxford: Oxford University Press.

Carew, Anthony (1996) 'The American Labor Movement in Fizzland: The Free Trade Union Movement and the CIA', *Labor History*, 39: 25–42.

Castree, Noel, Coe, Neal, Ward, Kevin, and Samers, Michael (2004) *Spaces of Work: Global Capitalism and Geographies of Labour*. London: Sage.

Catalano, Ana María (1999) 'The Crisis of Trade Union Representation: New Forms of Social Integration and Autonomy-Construction', in Ronaldo Munck and Peter Waterman (eds), *Labour Worldwide in the Era of Globalisation: Alternative Union Strategies in the New World Order*. Houndmills: Macmillan.

Centro de Estudos Sociais (URL) 'Reinventing social emancipation'. www.ces.fe.uc.pt/emancipa/en/index.html (consulted 30 May 2004).

CIOSL-CMT-CES-ORIT-CLAT. (2004) '2ª. Cumbre Sindical Union Europea – America Latina Y Caribe.(UE/AL-C): Declaración Final' [2nd European-Latin American/Caribbean Union Summit: Final Declaration]. Ciudad de México, 16 de abril de 2004. Brussels: European Trade Union Confederation.

Clarke, Renfrey (1994) 'US Labour "Missionaries" – No Blessing For Russian Workers'. www.nathannewman.org/EDIN/.labor/.files/.internat/.russia.html

Dietrich, Gabriele and Nayak, Nailini (2001) 'Exploring Possibilities of Counter-Hegemonic Globalisation of Fishworkers' Movement in India and its Global Interactions'. Contribution to the Project on Reinventing Social Emancipation, Center of Social Studies, University of Coimbra, Portugal. www.ces.fe.uc.pt/emancipa/research/en/ft/fishworkers.html

Eade, Deborah and Leather, Alan (eds), (2004) 'Trade Union and NGO Relations in Development and Social Justice', *Development in Practice*, Vol. 14, Nos 1–2, pp. 5–285.

Edelman, Marc (2003) 'Transnational Peasant and Farmer Movements and Networks', in Mary Kaldor, Helmut Anheier and Marlies Glasius (eds), *Global Civil Society 2003*. Oxford: Oxford University Press.

Emmerij, Louis (1988) 'The International Labour Organisation as a Development Agency', in Jeffrey Harrod and Nico Schrijver (eds), *The UN Under Attack*, Aldershot: Gower.

Escobar, Arturo (1999) 'Gender, Place and Networks: A Political Ecology of Cyberculture', in Wendy Harcourt (ed), *Women @ Internet: Creating New Cultures in Cyberspace*. London: Zed.

Ewing, Keith and Sibley, Tom (2000) *International Trade Union Rights for the New Millennium*. London: International Centre for Trade Unions Rights and Institute for Employment Rights.

Forman, Michael (1998) *Nationalism and the International Labour Movement: The Idea of the Nation in Socialist and Anarchist Theory*. University Park: Pennsylvania University Press.

Gallin, Dan (2000) 'Civil Society: A Contested Territory'. Paper presented at Euro-WEA Seminar on Workers' Education and Civil Society. Budapest, 16–17 June. www.global-labour.org/civil_society_-_a_contested_territory.htm

Gerassi, John (1971) *The Coming of the New International*. New York: World Publishing Company.

Ghigliani, Pablo (2003) *International Trade Unionism in a Globalising World: A Case Study* [of McDonald's]. Institute of Social Studies, The Hague.

Gorz, Andre (1999a) 'A New Task for the Unions: The Liberation of Time from Work', in Ronaldo Munck and Peter Waterman (eds), *Labour Worldwide in the Era of Globalisation: Alternative Union Strategies in the New World Order*. Houndmills: Macmillan.

– (1999b) *Reclaiming Work: Beyond the Wage-Based Society*. Cambridge: Polity.

Greenfield, G. (1999) 'Democratic Trade Union Responses to Globalisation: A Critique of the ICFTU-APRO's "Asian Monteray Fund" Proposal', paper presented to the Hong Kong Confederation of Trade Unions, September. www.labournet.de/diskussion/gewerkschaft/greenf.html

GURN (Global Union Research Network) (2003) 'Concept Paper on the Global Union Research Network'. Geneva: ACTRAV/ILO.

– (URL) www.gurn.info (consulted 1 April 2004).

Harrod, Jeffrey (1977) 'The Ideology of the International Labour Organisation towards Developing Countries', in *The Impact of International Organisations on Legal and Institutional Change in Developing Countries*. New York: International Legal Center.

Herod, A. (2001) 'Labor Internationalism and the Contradictions of Globalisation', in P. Waterman and J. Wills (eds), *Space, Place and the New Labour Internationalisms*. Oxford: Blackwell.

Hirsch, Fred (2004) 'Build Unity and Trust Among Workers Worldwide', email 17 July 2004.

Hyman, Richard (1999) 'An Emerging Agenda for Trade Unions?'. Paper delivered to an on-line conference on Organised Labour in the 21st Century. Geneva:

International Institute of Labour Studies, International Labour Organisation. www.ilo.org/public/english/bureau/inst/project/network/hyman.htm
– (2004) 'Agitation, Organisation, Diplomacy, Bureaucracy: Trends and Dilemmas in International Trade Unionism', *Labor History*, 45(3).
ICFTU (International Confederation of Free Trade Unions) (2000a) 'Organising International Solidarity'. www.icftu.org/www/english/congress2000/econres2000_V.pdf
– (2000b). Joint UN-ICFTU Statement on the Global Compact. www.icftu.org/displaydocument.asp?Index=991209381&Language=EN (20 January).
– (2002) 'Trade Union Statement to the World Social Forum (Porto Alegre) and the World Economic Forum (New York)'. www.icftu.org/displaydocument.asp?Index=991214585&Language=EN
– (URL) Framework Agreements with Multinational Companies. www.icftu.org/displaydocument.asp?Index=991216332&Language=EN (consulted 20 May 2004).
ICTU (Irish Congress of Trade Unions) (URL) www.ictu.ie (consulted 24 May 2004).
ILO (International Labour Organisation) (1996) *World Employment Report 1996/97*. Geneva: ILO.
– (2002) 'Unprotected Labour: What Role for Unions in the Informal Economy?', *Labour Education* 2002/2, No. 127.
– (2004) A Fair Globalisation: Creating Opportunities for All. www.ilo.org/public/english/wcsdg/docs/report.pdf (launched 24 February 2004).
– (URLa) Master Programme. www.ilo.org/public/english/dialogue/actrav/glp (consulted 20 May 2004).
– (URLb) www.ilo.org (consulted 25 May 2004).
Industrial and Labor Relations (URL) 'Reference question of the month'. www.ilr.cornell.edu/library/research/QuestionOfTheMonth/archive/laborUnionsAcrossTheWorld.html (consulted 25 May 2004).
Infact (2004) Alliance for a Corporate Free UN. www.infactcanada.ca/alliance_for_a_corporate-free_united_Nations.htm (16 January).
Institut Socialiste d'Etudes et de Recherches (1982) *Emancipations nationale et nouvel internationalisme*. Paris: Club Socialiste du Livre.
ITWF (International Transportworkers Federation) (2002) 'Globalising Solidarity: The Popular Movement to Reform the Globalisation Process. Draft Resolution No. 5, ITF Congress, Vancouver'. www.itf.org.uk/congress/2002/pdf/motion_5.pdf
Jakobsen, Kjeld (2001) 'Rethinking the International Confederation of Free Trade Unions and its Inter-American Regional Organisation', in Peter Waterman and Jane Wills (eds), *Place, Space and the New Labour Internationalisms*. Oxford: Blackwell.
Jenkins, Rhys, Pearson, Ruth and Seyfang, Gill (eds) (2002) *Corporate Responsibility and Labour Rights*. London: Earthscan.
John, J. and Chenoy, Auradha (eds) (1996) *Labour, Environment and Globalisation: Social Clause in Multilateral Trade Agreements – A Southern Response*. New Delhi: Centre for Education and Communication.
Judge, Anthony. (2001) '"Globalization": The UN's "Safe Haven" for the World's Marginalized – the Global Compact with Multinational Corporations as the UN's "Final Solution"'. http://laetusinpraesens.org/docs/globcomp.php
Justice, Dwight (2002) 'The International Trade Union Movement and the New Codes of Conduct', in R. Jenkins, R. Pearson, and G. Seyfang, (eds) *Corporate Responsibility and Labour Rights*, London: Earthscan.
Kaldor, M. (2003) *Global Civil Society: An Answer to War*. Cambridge: Polity Press.
–, Anheier, Helmut and Glasius, Marlies (2003) (eds) (2003) *Global Civil Society 2003*. Oxford: Oxford University Press.
Labournet (URL) www.labournet.info/GlobalLabour (consulted 31 May 2004).
Labourstart (URL) www.labourstart.org (consulted 20 May 2004).
Marx, Karl and Engels, Frederick. (1848/1935) 'The Manifesto of the Communist Party', in Karl Marx, *Selected Works*. Moscow: Cooperative Publishing House of Foreign Workers in the USSR.
Maspero, Emilio (2000). *Movimiento de Trabajadores, Siglo XXI*. CLAT. C. www.clat.org/Movimiento%20de%20Trabajadores%20Siglo%20XXI.htm
Mattelart, Armand and Siegelaub, Seth (eds) (1983) *Communication and Class Struggle: 2. Liberation, Socialism*. New York: International General.
Mathew, Babu and Shetty, Rashmi R. (2003) 'Labour in WSF 2004', *Labour File*, 1(6): 5–13.
McSpotlight (URL) The Issues. www.mcspotlight.org/issues/employment/index.html (consulted 20 May 2004).
Michels, Robert (1915) *Political Parties*. London: Jarrold and Sons.
Mills, C. Wright (1948/2001) *The New Men of Power: America's Labour Leaders*. Champaign, ILL: University of Illinois Press.
Negt, Oskar and Kluge, Alexander (1972/1983). 'The Proletarian Public Sphere', in Armand Mattelart and Seth Siegelaub (eds), *Communication and Class Struggle: 2. Liberation, Socialism*. New York: International General.
New Internationalist (2001) 'Trade Unions: The Facts', 341 (December). www.newint.org
Oliviero, M. B. and Simmons, A. (2002) 'Who's Minding the Store? Global Civil Society and Corporate Social Responsibility', in Helmut Anheier, Marlies Glasius and Mary Kaldor (eds), *Global Civil Society 2002*. Oxford: Oxford University Press.
Panitch, Leo and Leys, Colin (2000) 'Rekindling the Socialist Imagination', in Leo Panitch and Colin Leys (eds), *Necessary and Unnecessary Utopias*. London: Merlin and New York: Monthly Review.
Pianta, Mario and Silva, Federico (2003) *Globalisers from Below: A Survey on Global Civil Society Organisations*. Rome: Lunaria.

Pope Leo XIII (1891) 'Rerum Novarum (On Capital and Labour): Encyclical of Pope Leo XIII promulgated on 15 May 1891'. www.ewtn.com/library/ENCYC/L13RERUM.HTM
Public Service International (URL) www.world-psi.org/psi.nsf/6e53a54ebe88ae01c12568270037cc33/40c9637cfa743aa2c125686700158449?OpenDocument (consulted 31 May 2004).
Publicworld (URL) www.publicworld.org (consulted 31 May 2004).
Ruiz, Alberto (2004) 'The Question Remains: What Is the AFL-CIO doing in Venezuela?', Znet. www.zmag.org/content/print_article.cfm?itemID=5074§ionID=45
Silverman, Victor (2000) *Imagining Internationalism in American and British Labour, 1939–49*. Urbana: University of Illinois Press.
Silvey, Rachel, (2004) 'Intervention Symposium: Geographies of Anti-Sweatshop Activism', *Antipode*, 36(2): 191–7.
Spooner, Dave (2004) 'Trade Unions and NGOs: The Need for Cooperation', Development in Practice, 14(1–2): 19–33 (special Issue on 'Trade Union and NGO Relations in Development and Social Justice').
The Commoner (2003) 'What Alternatives? Commons and Communities, Dignity and Freedom', Issue 6 (Winter) www.commoner.org.uk/previous_issues.htm#n6
Tristan, Flora (1843/1967) *L'Union ouvrière* [The Workers' Union]. Paris: Imprimerie Lacour et Maistrasse fils (reprinted by Editions d'Histoire Sociale, Paris, 1967).
Union-Network (URL) www.union-network.org/unimultinationals.nsf/0/67694757a°/c1256eb3002a74e9?OpenDocument&Click (consulted 1 July 2004)
van der Linden, Marcel (2003) 'The ICFTU at the Crossroads: An Historical Interpretation'. Paper delivered to a conference on Labour and New Social Movements in a Globalising World System: The Future of the Past. Linz: September.
van Holthoon, Frits van and van der Linden, Marcel (eds) (1988) Internationalism in the Labour Movement 1830–1940. Leiden: Brill.
Vargas, Virginia (2003) Globalizacion y foro social mundial: Retos de los femininismos en el nuevo mulenio [Globalisation and the world social forum: Challenges for feminists in the new millenium]. Lima: Flora Tristan.
Wahl, Asbjørn (2004) 'The Ideological Legacy of the Social Pact', *Monthly Review*, 55(8). www.monthlyreview.org/0104wahl.htm
Warskett, Rosemary (2001) 'Feminism's Challenge to Unions in the North: Possibilities and Contradictions', in Leo Panitch and Colin Leys (eds), *Socialist Register 2001: Working Classes: Global Realities*. London: Merlin.
Waterman, Peter (1997) 'New Interest in Dockers and Transport Workers: Locally, Nationally, Comparatively, Globally – Some Real and Virtual Resources'. www.labournet.net/docks2/9712/itf1212.htm
– (2001a) *Globalisation, Social Movements and the New Internationalisms*. London: Continuum.
– (2001b) 'A Spectre is Haunting Labour Internationalism, the Spectre of the Ghost of Communism'. www.global-labour.org/prague_1968_the_last_late_short_spring_of_the_wftu.htm
– (2004a) 'Adventures of Emancipatory Labour Strategy as the New Movement Challenges International Unionism', *Journal of World-System Research*, 10(1): 217–54. http://jwsr.ucr.edu/archive/vol10/number1/pdf/jwsr-v10n1-waterman.pdf
– (2004b) 'Trade Unions, NGOs and Global Social Justice: Another Tale to Tell', (forthcoming).
Wilkinson, Rorden (2002) 'Peripheralising Labour: The ILO, WTO and the Completion of the Bretton Woods Project', in Jeffrey Harrod and Robert O'Brien (eds), *Global Unions? Theory and Strategy of Organised Labour in the Global Political Economy*. London: Routledge.
Working USA (2001) 'Labour Rights in the Global Economy' (Special Focus). *WorkingUSA*, 5(1): 3–86.
World Bank (URL) World development indicators database. http://devdata.worldbank.org/external/dgcomp.asp?rmdk=110&smdk=500007&w=0 (consulted 25 May 2004).

PART 4

RECORDS OF GLOBAL CIVIL SOCIETY

NETWORK APPROACHES TO GLOBAL CIVIL SOCIETY

Helmut Anheier and Hagai Katz

Purpose

In this edition of the Yearbook, we explore a different, though complementary, approach to measuring and analysing global civil society. Whereas in 2002 we developed and introduced the Global Civil Society Index, and in 2003 examined aspects of geographical distribution by focusing on the spatial patterns of global civil society, the 2004 methodology chapter looks at the relational aspects of transnational interconnectedness. In other words, our focus is on global civil society as a transnational system of social networks and, methodologically speaking, on analysing global civil society through the lens of network analysis. We are interested in finding out how useful the various approaches and tools of network analysis are for describing, analysing and understanding global civil society.

As with the methodological approaches introduced in previous editions of the Yearbook, using network analysis is an attempt to go beyond the limitations of what Beck (2003), Shaw (2003) and others have labelled 'methodological nationalism', or the tendency of the social sciences to remain in the statistical and conceptual categories of the nation state. This tendency has become a persistent handicap: it equates nation, culture and polity, and ultimately discourages thinking beyond nineteenth- and twentieth-century categories. As an approach, it seems increasingly at odds with the realities of a globalising world.

By contrast, network analysis is promising because it has been little affected by nation-state thinking and national traditions, and therefore facilitates the analysis of non-contiguous social units that traverse the nation state, even regions and continents. As a field, it developed in a systematic way only from the mid-1970s with the publication of two seminal papers (White, Boorman, and Breiger, 1976; Boorman and White, 1976) that laid much of the intellectual and methodological groundwork[1]. It initially emphasised small, local networks rather than the larger, macro-level units like the nation state, and disregarded the statistical systems that dominated conventional social science at that time.

This is not to say that network analysis emerged inherently transnational in scope and with the aspirations of a social science freed of methodological nationalism; rather, its usefulness in analysing transnational phenomenon was unintentional, as its rapid development over the last 25 years was largely confined to an elite of American, European and Australian sociologists who cared about the structure of social relations independent of locale and circumstance. Loosely organised around the Sunbelt Network Conference, they paid little attention to the cultural meanings and contents of social ties; instead, what seemed important was the explanatory power that combinatorics, Boolean algebra, and graph theory could bring to the analysis of complex social structures.

Yet it is precisely this 'acultural' or somewhat 'removed' quality that makes network analysis attractive in examining the relational patterns of global civil society. Since it is based on lower levels of aggregation and is not limited by geography or political units, network analysis is potentially a very promising tool for examining transnational phenomena like global civil society. Put simply, for network analysis it primarily matters whether actors A and B are connected or not, and what their connections with others such as C, D or E might be; the fact that A might be French, B, Nigerian, C, American, D, Japanese and E, German or Israeli matters only secondarily. The structure of relations is key.

Against this background, this chapter explores the utility of network analysis for examining patterns in global connectedness among non-contiguous, multi-site entities, using interpersonal and interorganisational and other network ties as the basic unit of analysis. Given the space limitations of this chapter, we can only

1 *For an introduction and overview, see Wasserman and Faust (1994) and Scott (1999).*

hint at initial results, and we propose to present a fuller analysis in the 2005 edition of the Yearbook. Nonetheless, we hope that the preliminary analyses presented here illustrate the potential contribution network analysis can make to our understanding of global civil society.

Network analysis

Network analysis is not a theory but a set of related approaches, techniques and tools for describing and analysing relationships among individuals, organisations and other social entities. What unites these different approaches is a basic focus on structure. Put differently, network analysis measures social reality not by reference to people's individual attributes (gender, class, age, values, and so on) but by looking at their social relationships, the patterns they form, and their implications for choices and behaviour. Take a hypothetical person such as Akiko Deguchi. Conventional social science would be interested in her nationality (Japanese), gender (female), age (40), marital status (married), number of children (one), education (PhD), occupation (manager), type of field/industry (working for an international NGO), religion (Buddhist) and political orientation (liberal).

Network analysis takes a different starting point: rather than looking at individual attributes, it asks about relational aspects or the social ties Akiko has with others in her daily life, in special settings such as conferences and work situations, or with her friends, professional contacts and the like. Who are her best friends and are they interconnected among themselves? Who are the people she trusts and distrust? With whom does she interact professionally as a manager in a Japanese NGO, and with whom socially? What funding agencies is her organisation in contact with, and what government agencies? Who are her peers in Japan and abroad? What causes does she support? What are her organisational memberships? On what boards does she serve?

For network analysis it is important to know how people (or organisations) are connected and relate to each other, and what structural patterns emerge from such interconnectedness. It is connectedness, not attributes, that is at the focus of network analysis. It is less important for network analysis to know that Akiko is Japanese, female and so on; rather, what matters is the relational patterns she forms and is part of. In conventional social science, her socio-economic background and status, opinions, attitudes and so forth would be at the centre of analytic attention; in network analysis it is how she fits into a wider web of social affiliations between individuals, groups and organisations.

Network analysis is a highly technical field, yet has retained a very straightforward basic intellectual thrust, with three major approaches that take different, though complementary, paths:

- a micro-level view that looks at ego-centered networks and focuses on one particular individual or organisation and its connectedness; analysing Akiko's personal and professional network and their mathematical properties such as reach, density, overlaps, and so on would be an example
- a macro-level perspective that addresses emergent structures among network members; for example, the patterns that can be identified in the relations from not only Akiko's perspective but from those of all her colleagues and friends combined
- hyper-networks that examine network structure generated by combining networks of the same or different kinds. For example, the memberships Akiko and her friends may have in NGOs create links not only between members within the respective organisations but also among the organisations through joint or interlocking memberships, that is, the hyper-network.

We will describe the approach and explore its relevance to global civil society, using a variety of examples. However, before we present them, we have to address one critical question: why analyse global civil society through a social network perspective in the first place?

Why network analysis?

We suggest that network analysis is useful for one basic reason, irrespective of the relatively high level of technical and mathematical knowledge it requires: global civil society is a very relational, 'networky' phenomenon. Indeed, globalisation research is rich in network metaphors, and many connote some notion of connectedness. Examples include Yergin and Stanislav (1998) who use the metaphor of the 'woven world'; Keane (2001: 23–4) who describes global civil society as an 'interconnected and multilayered social space' comprised of 'cross-border networks' and 'chains of interaction' linking the local to the global; Roseneau (1995) who describes global governance as a framework of horizontal relations; and, most notably, Castells' (1996) argument that actors increasingly form meta-networks at the transnational level and create a system of 'decentralised concentration', where a multiplicity of interconnected tasks takes place in different sites.

Since the 1970s, Castells points out, enabling technologies such as telecommunications and the Internet brought about the ascendancy of a 'network society' whose processes occur in a new type of space, which he labels the 'space of flows'. This space, comprising a myriad of exchanges, came to dominate the 'space of places' of territorially defined units of states, regions and neighbourhoods, thanks to its greater flexibility and compatibility with the new logic of network society. Nodes and hubs in this space of flows construct the social organisation of this network society. For Castells, this new space is at the core of the globalisation process – and, for understanding global civil society within the larger process of a shift from 'place' to 'flows', network analysis holds great promise.

Unfortunately, an explicit and systematic focus on network analysis has not been commonplace in global civil society scholarship so far[2]. As Townsend (1999) points out, despite frequent reference to the 'network' character of global civil society as a structured space, global maps of flows and interconnectedness are still missing. For example, Held et al (1999: 17–27) propose that the major contours of global civil society can be described by three related characteristics: *extensity* as the overall spread of the network; *intensity* of the overall density of the network in terms of the number and types of connections involved among the various 'nodes'; and *velocity* of the overall network, as a measure of the frequency with which connections are made or used among network nodes. Yet, like others, these and similar approaches, useful as they are, generally remain metaphorical, and their full descriptive and analytical potentials remain unexploited. In this brief chapter, we want to show the significant potential that network analysis offers for exploring the concepts and theories proposed by Held, Castells and the others just mentioned.

Principles of network analysis

Network analysis is a way of simplifying the complexity of social relations in order to reveal underlying patterns and trends. While this may appear highly abstract, a simple example might help. To anyone standing in the middle of a busy square or intersection in Beijing, Paris, New Delhi or New York, with hundreds of people and many cars, buses, trucks and bicycles going by, individual movements might appear seemingly random. However, if one observes the same movements from an elevated platform – say, the Arc de Triomphe, or from the roof of an adjacent building – patterns, as well as shifts in patterns, become more apparent, and the flow of traffic seems more ordered and, indeed, simpler. Similarly, much of network analysis is about finding the best way of reducing the complexity of social interactions to simpler patterns, and of finding the right 'observation platform'. As highlighted below, there are different ways of doing this.

Let us first return to Akiko to appreciate the challenge network analysis faces and to show its promise. Like most professionals in international NGOs or corporations, Akiko typically knows hundreds of other professionals and individuals with whom she interacts in different kinds of projects, on different levels and in different contexts. These relationships involve supervisory, reporting, collegial, supportive, adversarial, friendship and conflict relations, among many others. If we assume that Akiko has contacts with, say, 500 other people, and that these contacts involve 10 different types of ties (share information, work jointly on project, report to, are friends, acquaintances, and so on), we would potentially have 500 times 10, or 5,000, relations to examine. If we were to include the relations among the 500 others mentioned, we would have to examine 500 times 5,000 data points when limiting ourselves to those mentioned by Akiko, and many more if we were to include those cited not by her but by the others.

Even assuming that we could collect all this information on Akiko's network, how could we then reduce the complexity of these 2,500,000 data points among these 500 people? The answer depends, of course, on what we are looking for in this vast amount of information. Fortunately, network analysis has developed five basic principles or 'conceptual-methodological lenses' for reducing the complexity of social relations to simpler patterns that can be summarised under two general headings: single-mode networks and hyper-networks.

Single-mode networks

This is perhaps the core of most network analysis and emphasises the relations among network 'nodes' (people, organisations) along five principles (Figure M1):

- *Cohesion* emphasises the interconnectedness of social relations and their tendency to form cliques or areas of higher density, that is, a greater

2 *One of the only exceptions is Mario Diani's work; see, for example, his recent edited collection on social movements and networks (Diani and McAdam, 2003).*

Figure M1: Principles of network analysis

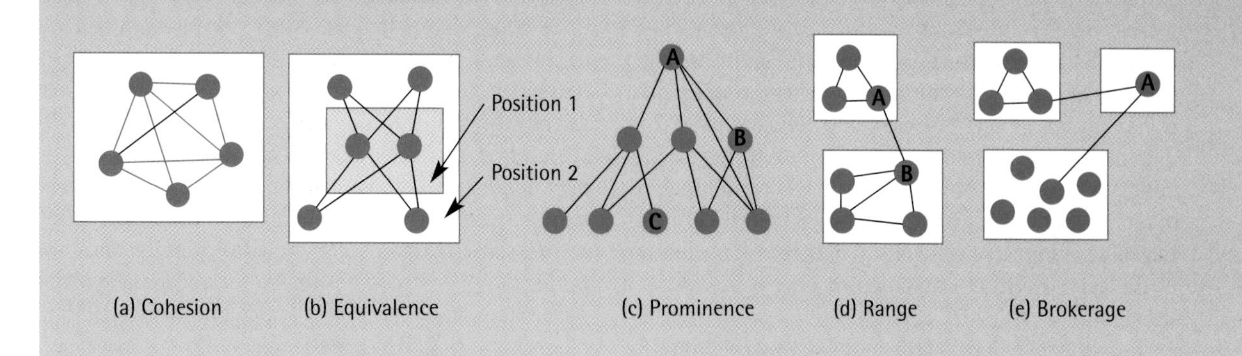

likelihood that links exist. For example, one would look for cohesion in a network among activists to understand the strength of communication ties, the 'bonding' and degree of integration, as suggested in Figure M1(a)

- *Equivalence* emphasises the degree to which members of a network have similar relations with others; if they do, members who occupy a common position can be represented by it, and the complexity of the original structure is thus reduced. In Figure M1(b), note how the two actors in the shaded area have identical relations to all others; in fact, the network can be reduced to two positions: Position 1 comprising actors in the shaded area, and Position 2 comprising those outside. Searching for positions of equivalence is useful for examining reference groups, conflict relations, coalitions, and patterns of homogeneity and diversity in networks
- *Prominence*, indicated by Figure M1(c), refers to positions in networks that originate from being objects of relations with other less or equally prominent contacts (Actors A or B). Conversely, the degree of marginality is a network position based on not being such an object (Actor C). Prominence analysis is useful for analysing formal and informal group structure, leadership formation and power and control relations
- *Range* is basically a bridging phenomenon between two otherwise unconnected networks, as shown in Figure M1(d). While Actors A and B belong to different groups, their mutual relationship provides a structural bridge that can allow for 'flows' between these two networks. Range analysis is important for understanding mobilisation processes and information, resource and innovation flows. For example, advocacy groups located in different countries are typically linked via such bridges. Such bridges linking clusters in sparse networks promote the development of a 'small world' phenomenon, which we examine below
- *Brokerage* is related to range, and refers to a network situation in which one actor (A) sees a structural hole between two groups of actors, which she then tries to connect (Figure M1(e)). Brokerage is the network equivalent of entrepreneurship in markets, and refers to the extent to which actors as entrepreneurs connect and organise networks. The activities of some of the social entrepreneurs presented in Chapter 6 of this edition offer illustrations of this process. Brokerage is important for understanding both the degree of autonomy in a network and its potential for organisation.

Of course, these principles, while highlighting distinct aspects of network structures, complement each other: the extent of range in a network is related to the extent that brokerage is possible; prominence is important for understanding the internal hierarchy of a network, and is also crucial for range: depending on the prominence of bridging actors, the outcomes of range and brokerage can be different. Finally, note that cohesion is a special case of a structurally equivalent position in a wider network: a fully connected circle of friends (cohesive group), for example, in a wider network of relations with lower density would occupy a common position (structural equivalence).

Hyper-networks

Hyper-networks, or two-mode networks, are another and somewhat more complex case. The single-mode networks introduced above require information about direct links among actors. Two-mode networks, however, allow us to deduce ties through coincidental participation in groups or events. Two-mode networks arise from overlapping participation of actors in entities such as boards of directors, or in events such as conferences or demonstrations. For example, two executives serving on the same committee or two organisations participating in the same event are assumed to have a tie between them.

Thus, if we imagine a two-mode network as a matrix, the list of meetings would represent its columns and the list of participating actors its rows. We would observe which actors attend which meetings, and also which meetings are attended by which actors. This creates a 'dual network': we can look at the network of contacts among actors created by their co-participation in various meetings; we can also look at the network of relations among meetings generated by those actors participating in two or more. Examples of two-mode networks in the context of global civil society are organisational memberships in umbrella organisations, interlocking board memberships, people attending various forums, multiple individual memberships in advocacy networks, volunteers donating their time to more than one organisation, and multiple memberships in various UN NGO committees.

Network data

Network data are most often collected using self-reports, normally through surveys or interviews. Actors participating in the network are asked about their connections with other actors as well as about the content and effect of such connections. Link information can be specific, such as cash transfers, or diffuse, such as friendship; it can be unidirectional or mutual; it can have different degrees of intensity or the relationship can be binary, that is, either a relation exists or it does not.

Analysis of social networks places a special burden on data collection. It usually requires that data on the 'complete' network be collected, even though the boundaries of a network can be hard to ascertain. Network sampling is likewise a challenge to more standard statistical methods, as the 'universe' of nodes to be sampled is often difficult to establish and somewhat arbitrary (we are all connected, somehow), and each node requires two pieces of information: how A relates to B and how B relates to A. Obviously, this data challenge is greater for large networks and geographically dispersed relations.

Network studies that use egocentric networks are less demanding, as data are not collected on the entire network but only on one focal node: for example, Akiko as the 'ego' and the ties she has with other actors. If such egos are selected carefully, their egocentric networks can be highly informative and even potentially representative of the larger population (Marsden, 1990). In this sense, Akiko could stand for a larger group of professionals in similar positions, and we would attempt to measure and analyse the 'typical' network structure of Japanese NGO executives.

Networks of global civil society: four examples

Having reviewed some of the basics of network analysis, however briefly, we will now present four examples of network analysis in the context of global civil society, each representing a major strand of analysis.

1. It's a small word after all (for NGOs)

Most of us have experienced the 'small world' phenomenon: during small talk with a participant at some conference, you find out that you unexpectedly share a mutual acquaintance. Perhaps her friend's wife sits on the same committee as the uncle of your daughter's new boyfriend. Or while at a New York meeting you may discover that you share a mutual acquaintance from Nairobi with a person from Jakarta you just encountered. All of a sudden the world feels small. The small-world phenomenon brings together people who are often geographically separate and even temporarily disconnected. Of course, as network analysts remind us, such seemingly unexpected connections are not at all random events but the result of an underlying network structure.

Milgram (1967) decided to examine systematically how 'close' we really are to each other in terms of connectedness. In a famous 1967 study, he tried to see how many intermediaries would connect any two randomly selected persons in the US through personal acquaintance chains. To his astonishment, he found that the average number was 5.5. In other words, on average, every randomly selected pair of US individuals can be connected via a chain with five or six links. Over time, this number was rounded to the 'six degrees of separation' that allegedly exist between every two people. It suggests that, despite the enormous size of the US population, or the world's for that matter, we are nonetheless closely connected through traceable webs of relations, affiliations and acquaintance ties.

But what precisely are 'small worlds'? At a fundamental level, they are a signal that a particular network is making the transition from chaos to order (Barabási, 2002). They are an indication that large networks, despite their overall sparseness, have a high degree of clustering. For example, Akiko's network of 500 individuals is indeed small and hence sparse compared with the potential 110 million ties she could have to Japanese citizens alone, let alone the billions of possible ties globally. Yet it is the clustering and the range or brokerage effects that matter: relatively small and distant clusters are connected by relatively small numbers of bridging actors. Consequently, most nodes in small-world networks may have few links to other nodes, but a minority of well-connected hubs shortens the average path among all (see Figure M1(d)).

The distribution of links that nodes in a small-world network have corresponds to what is called the power law: a very small number of hubs have ties with many other nodes in the network, and a very large number have few ties. If we sort a given network population by the number of ties they have, we find this number declining rapidly, as shown by the hyperbolic curve in Figure M2. This pattern gives rise to the small-world phenomenon.

Small worlds were found in a variety of real-world networks, including technical, natural and social networks (Barabási, 2002). Is global civil society a small world too? To answer this question, we took a random sample of 5,158 international and internationally oriented NGOs, made available to us by the Union of International Associations (URL) (constituting 25 per cent of the total number of NGOs in their database). We found that the distribution of nodal degrees (the number of links each node has) is compliant with the power law: a small number of NGOs has disproportionately large numbers of links with other organisations, whereas the huge majority of nodes have very few links. Figure M2 shows that there is only one organisation that has over 200 links (top left point), one that has over 100 links, and so on. At the other end of the continuum, we find that about 1,500 organisations have no ties at all (bottom right), approximately 1,400 organisations have only one tie to another organisation, about 600 have two ties, and so on.

When we calculate the length of the shortest path between each of the 26.6 million possible pairs among

Figure M2: Distribution of number of links in NGO network

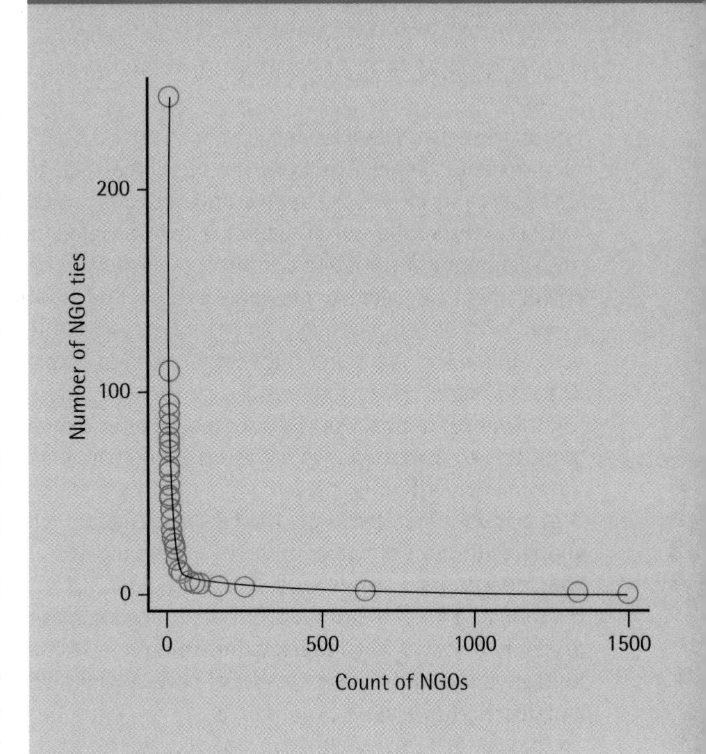

the 5,158 NGOs in our sample, we find that, on average, the two nodes in each pair of nodes in this network are 7.3 links apart. This suggests that, on average, each NGO is 'traceable' through about seven organisations. For example, information, be it important advice or some rumour, needs to go through only seven organisations, on average, to reach the global NGO community. The longest such path between two nodes in this network is 21 links, which is the case for five pairs in our sample.

How small is this small world? Not very, at least at first glance. Of course, the 7.3 steps are at first sight close to Milgram's 'six degrees of separation'. However, the network we are discussing here is, with just over 5,000 nodes, much smaller than Milgram's US population of some 180 million at that time. One the one hand, this is an indication that, organisationally, global civil society networks are still not very structured, even though clusters of higher connectivity are emerging, triggered by the connecting capacity of the few large hubs shown in Figure M2. One the other hand, we have to keep in mind that we are looking at interorganisational networks only, and not at personal ties among NGO staff and members. It seems reasonable to assume that the combined effect of organisational and individual ties could indeed make the world of global civil society a rather small one.

2. Egocentric networks and connectivity: does being Southern mean being more global?

Egocentric networks are less demanding in terms of data requirements[3]. Egocentric networks are often used to study the social environment of individuals and organisations, such as social support networks, amounts of social capital and relations within organisational task environments. Egocentric networks can be studied as single cases or comparatively, as when we look at the composition and structure of personal networks across different actors, as we do here.

The egocentric networks presented for illustration purposes in M3 were created not directly by researching the two organisations portrayed but rather by extracting their relations from the larger NGO data-set mentioned above. Both cases are prominent NGOs, one located in Switzerland and dealing with NGO–government relations (02474), the other a Christian development organisation with headquarters in Ethiopia (03548). Both have almost the same number of network links (28 and 26, respectively).

The fact that one is 'Northern' and the other 'Southern' reveals both similarities and differences in structure and composition. First, in the Swiss organisation's network there is only one organisation not from the North, and 18 of the remaining 27 organisations are also from Switzerland (most probably from Geneva). The Ethiopian organisation's network includes organisations from eight different countries, most of them Northern, too (eight from the UK, eight from the US, and only two organisations from developing countries), making the pattern more global in its geographic dispersion.

So does a Southern location make NGOs more transnational, more global in outreach? By looking at the structure of the two networks, we learn that, in both cases, links between the focal NGO and its 'alters' tend to be mutual, and that links between alters are sparse, as shown in Figure M3. Moreover, inter-alter links are mostly local and always between Northern NGOs. Thus, the two egocentric networks suggest not only that NGO networks tend to be sparse and Northern centered but also that Northern NGOs appear to be more mutually interconnected, even when the focal organisation is a Southern one. Surprisingly, despite the overall sparse network, we find that four organisations link the two ego-networks (126, 3056, 3272 and 4680), which are all Northern and all religious. In other words, while NGO networks reach into developing countries, they are denser and more elaborate in the North. By implication, being Southern makes NGOs more global in the sense that their peripheral position requires them to seek links to better-connected organisations in the North.

3. When things go wrong: blockmodel analysis

Blockmodel analysis can be a powerful tool for understanding underlying relationships in complex networks; it is also a very demanding approach in terms of data requirement and analysis, and therefore a time-consuming exercise. Blockmodels represent a simplification of a network, and are based on the principle of structural equivalence as shown in Figure M1(b). People or organisations in similar positions in a network are grouped into blocks and are treated as 'joint actors' in a reduced network. The relationships between the blocks are then analysed, revealing structures and relationships between network groups and roles rather than individual actors. At present, we have no current blockmodel analysis of global civil society aspects, but we hope to present one in the 2005 edition of the Yearbook. To illustrate its utility, however, we will make use of two cases conducted by one of the authors and reported in Anheier and Romo (1999).

In two African countries, Nigeria and Senegal, local and international NGOs decided to form a common umbrella organisation with three stated purposes: to share information domestically as well as with international funders; to encourage cooperation; and to act as a formal voice and negotiation body with government. In each case, a permanent administrative body would perform these functions, and in each case, a task force was entrusted to organise an initial membership meeting to set the creation of the organisation in motion. In Nigeria, after an initially positive and energetic mobilisation among the 60 NGOs involved, consensus soon turned to series of negotiations, leading to the emergence of complex and shifting alliances among participants, and ultimately to a prolonged period of disarray, with various factions trying to create competing umbrella organisations. In Senegal, the creation involved much less mobilisation of the local NGO community, but it was swift and relatively well-organised; yet it initially had little impact.

3 *'One good sitting' is usually enough to 'reconstruct' the egocentric network for an individual, but in an organisation it is important to gather information from more than one informant due to the effects of hierarchy and specialisation.*

Figure M3(a): Egocentric network of Swiss NGO-government relations organisation (O2474)

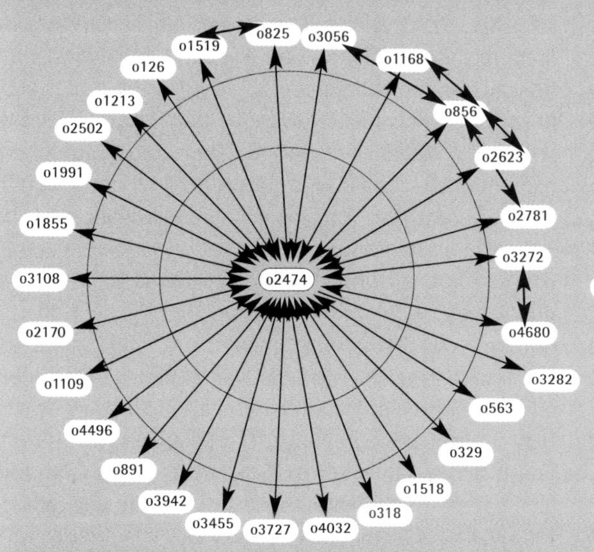

Figure M3(b): Egocentric network of Ethiopian Christian development (O3548)

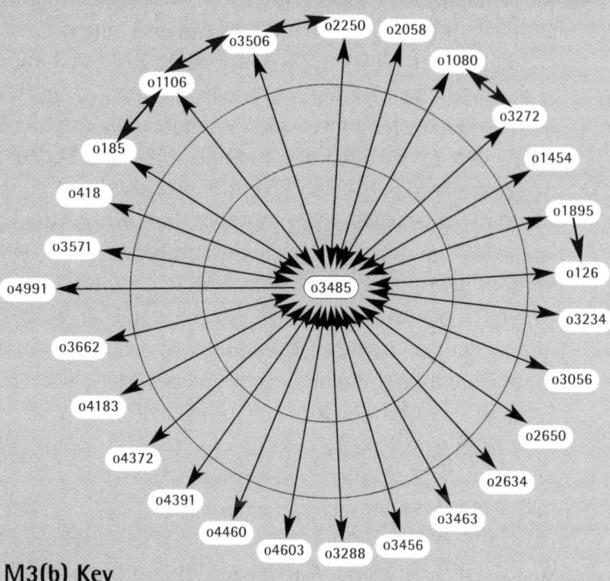

M3(a) Key

Label	Region	Subject
126	N America	Welfare, religious
318	N America	Humanitarian, religious
329	W Europe	Peace
563	W Europe	Economic development
825	W Europe	Child rights
856	W Europe	Women, religious
891	W Europe	Conflict resolution
1109	W Europe	Literary
1168	W Europe	Peace, feminist
1213	W Europe	Motor sports
1518	W Europe	NGO coordination
1519	N America	Mental health
1855	Africa	Economic development
1991	N America	Economic development
2170	W Europe	Refugees
2502	W Europe	Travel
2623	W Europe	Social rights
2781	W Europe	Education, religious
3056	W Europe	Mission, religious
3108	W Europe	Economic research
3272	N America	Religious
3282	W Europe	Development
3455	W Europe	Religious
3727	W Europe	University
3942	N America	Food security
4032	W Europe	Health rights
4496	W Europe	Development
4680	W Europe	Vocational, religious

M3(b) Key

Label	Region	Subject
126	N America	Welfare, religious
185	W Europe	Elder rights
418	W Europe	Child rights
1106	W Europe	Family & child rights
1454	W Europe	Economic development
1895	N America	Development, religious
2058	W Europe	Medical
2250	W Europe	Women's rights
2634	N America	Mission, religious
2650	W Europe	Development
3056	W Europe	Religious
3234	W Europe	Disabled
3272	N America	Mission, religious
3288	W Europe	Child & family rights
3456	W Europe	Voluntary association
3463	Africa	Development
3506	W Europe	Child rights, religious
3571	N America	Pediatric medicine
3662	N America	Food security
4183	N America	Food security
4372	N America	Environment
4391	W Europe	Food security
4460	N America	Medicine
4603	W Europe	Reproductive medicine
4680	W Europe	Vocational, religious
4991	East Asia	Development

The blockmodels tell us much about why these umbrella organisations turned out so differently: in essence, they replicated structural patterns that are typical for the wider society in which they operated. In the Nigerian case (NADA), it was the emergence of highly ambivalent relations of trust and distrust, support and conflict among NGOs; in Senegal (SADA), the dominance of a patron–client relationship between larger and smaller NGOs and between those based in urban areas and those in the vast rural hinterland. The only dissent in Senegal came from 'progressive' social entrepreneurs operating in the Sahel, who were critical of the Islamic authorities in the region and saw the umbrella organisation as yet another instrument of control.

Tables M1 and M2 show only the end results of a more detailed analysis that looks at the relational patterns among these organisations, using ten different types of ties, grouped into two broad classes:

- *support* (for example, cooperate, share information, have same opinion about consortium, vote for)
- *conflict* (for example, decline cooperation, have different opinion, seek to exclude from consortium, dispute actions).

With this information as input in matrix form, blockmodel analysis seeks to reduce the relational structure to a simpler one by trying to identify structurally equivalent groups, that is, NGOs that find themselves in similar relational patterns with others. Once these groups are found, the matrices are rearranged and then further simplified by binarising the matrix using the median block density as the cut-off point, yielding what are called image matrices in Tables M1 and M2. In other words, using the Nigerian case as an example, we reduced the 60 times 60 times 10 data points (that is, 10 types of ties among 60 NGOs), or 36,000, to 36 relationships between blocks as shown in each of Table M1(a) and M1(b). The assumption is that a simpler representation also reveals underlying relational patterns.

In the Nigerian case (Table M1(a)), support relations are much less pronounced than in Senegal (Table M2(a)), which shows solid support across positions. By contrast, conflict relations are more pronounced in Nigeria, and virtually absent in Senegal (Tables M1(b) and M2(b)). In fact, Block 4, which consists of the disenchanted social entrepreneurs from the Sahel, were relatively isolated in the sense that their conflict ties remained unreciprocated. The Nigerian structure is strikingly different: here those who support each other also oppose each other, as the frequent overlap on '1s' in Tables M1(a) and M1(b) demonstrate.

In NADA, Blocks 4, 5 and 6 are in an uneasy coalition united against Block 3, whereas the other blocks are splitting their support among Blocks 3, 4, 5, and 6. In addition, Block 3 reveals internal conflict among its members. Anheier and Romo (1999: 226) suggest that this pattern is characteristic of 'tournament structures', in which small contestant groups align and realign, and struggle with each other for the support of other constituencies, albeit without ultimately succeeding in gaining control or forming sustainable coalitions. The structural patterns suggest a situation of relatively free competition, with no elite or coalition able to achieve popular endorsement from the membership at large. The outcome was a state of stalemate and finally failure.

From a structural perspective, members of Blocks 3 and 5 in particular found themselves in positions where they supported their opponents and opposed their allies, and it became difficult to distinguish friend from foe. This pattern is indicated by the signature element of failure, the stalemate triad, replicated in Figure M4: support and conflict relations overlap, creating high levels of 'structural ambiguity' in a network.

By contrast, the Senegalese consortium developed a congruence structure with hierarchical tendencies: a relatively large group of uninvolved NGOs (Block 1) from rural areas, which had nothing to lose but could potentially gain from the consortium, next to well-connected international Dakar-based NGOs (as patrons, in Block 6) with the Senegalese client NGOs in the other blocks (except Block 4, the Sahel-based social entrepreneurs). As a result, the umbrella organisation basically mirrored the already existing structure, which explains why the consortium ended up having little impact, at least initially.

4. World Social Forum events: hyper-networks

We demonstrate the usefulness of two-mode networks by looking at NGO participation in self-organised events during the World Social Forum (WSF) held in Mumbai, India, in January 2004. The central Indian organising committee organised most forum events (panels, conferences, and so on), while 35 events were organised independently, addressing a wide range of issues from trade and water to AIDS and peace (see Table M3). One hundred and sixty-one organisations were involved in these independent events, and ten participated in two or more. This overlap creates a two-mode network of events and organisations.

Table M1: Blockmodel matrices of NADA

Table M1(a): Conflict image matrix: NADA

	Blk 1	Blk 2	Blk 3	Blk 4	Blk 5	Blk 6
Blk 1	–	–	–	–	–	–
Blk 2	–	–	–	–	–	–
Blk 3	1	1	–	1	1	1
Blk 4	1	–	–	–	–	–
Blk 5	1	–	1	1	–	–
Blk 6	1	–	1	–	–	–

Table M1(b): Support image matrix: NADA

	Blk 1	Blk 2	Blk 3	Blk 4	Blk 5	Blk 6
Blk 1	–	–	–	–	–	–
Blk 2	–	–	–	1	1	1
Blk 3	–	–	1	–	–	–
Blk 4	1	1	1	1	1	1
Blk 5	–	–	–	–	1	1
Blk 6	–	1	1	1	1	1

Table M2: Blockmodel matrices of SADA

Table M2(a): Conflict image matrix: SADA

	Blk 1	Blk 2	Blk 3	Blk 4	Blk 5	Blk 6
Blk 1	–	–	–	–	–	–
Blk 2	–	–	–	–	–	–
Blk 3	–	–	–	–	–	–
Blk 4	1	1	1	1	1	1
Blk 5	–	–	–	–	–	–
Blk 6	1	–	1	–	–	–

Table M2(b): Support image matrix: SADA

	Blk 1	Blk 2	Blk 3	Blk 4	Blk 5	Blk 6
Blk 1	–	–	–	–	–	–
Blk 2	1	1	1	1	1	1
Blk 3	1	1	1	1	1	1
Blk 4	1	1	1	1	1	1
Blk 5	1	1	1	1	1	1
Blk 6	–	1	–	1	1	1

How to read blockmodel image matrices

The presence of a '1' in a matrix cell indicates the existence of the particular type of link between the involved blocks. For example, in Table M2(a) block 4 organisations perceive their relationship with block 1 organisations as conflictual. This is shown in the '1' that appears in the cell at the intersection between block 4 (row) and block 1 (column). This conflictual sentiment is not reciprocated, since in the intersection between block 1 (row) and block 4 (column) in Table M2(a) there is no '1'.

Figure M4: Stalemate relations

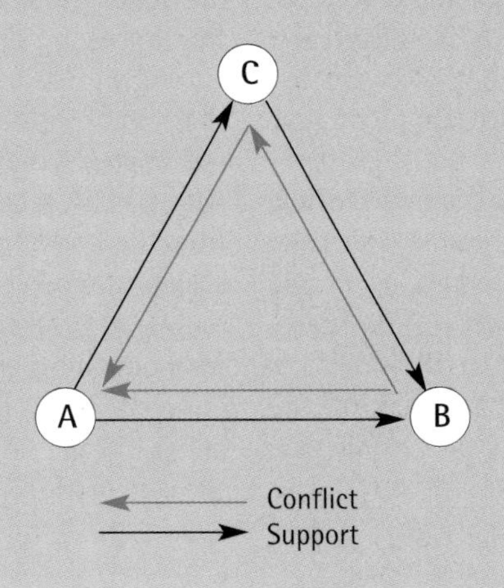

Table M3: Topics and issues of self-organised events, Mumbai World Social Forum, 2004

Issue	Abbreviation	Count
Trade	Trade	5
Accountability	Account	1
Discrimination	Discrim	4
HIV/AIDS	AIDS	1
Peace	Peace	4
Children's Rights	Child	1
Globalisation	Glob	3
Governance	Govern	1
Activism	Activism	2
NGO Networks	Networks	1
Democracy	Democ	2
Sex Workers	Sex	1
Development	Develop	2
Socialism	Socialism	1
Human Rights	HR	2
Water	Water	1
Indigenous People	Indig	2
Women	Women	1
Grand Total		**35**

Note: For a full list, see www.wsfindia.org/event2004/selforg.php

From the two-mode network we generated two one-mode networks: a network of organisations in which co-participation in an event translates into an inter-organisational tie; and a network of events in which common participants link events to each other. We see this analysis as an illustration of the 'structured space for debate' and deliberation in global civil society. Such an analysis can lead to the identification of coalitions that cross between standard 'disciplinary' boundaries, and can show how issues are perceived and connected in an emerging global public sphere. It can also reveal which issues are more and which ones less central in such discourse, and reveal the dynamics of how issues connect.

We conducted a closeness-centrality analysis[4] of the events, to distinguish central from marginal issues and to reveal the link structure between issues, using two network analysis programmes: *UCINET 6* (Borgatti, Everett and Freeman, 2002) and *Visone* (Brandes and Wagner, 2003). Because of the sparseness of the network, the conclusion here can be taken only as a demonstration of the potential this mode of analysis has to offer.

As can be seen in Figure M5, overlapping NGO participation connected only a few events; the resulting network is rather fragmented, consisting of three smaller networks. Interestingly, these networks vary considerably in terms of the issues they link, and no obvious pattern seems to emerge, except for the relative salience of 'trade' as an issue in the network. The make-up of the three small networks gives rise to two possible conclusions. One is that no strong differentiation of interconnected issues currently exists in global civil society discourse, a finding that can be indicative of its early phase of development, as complex systems tend to become more differentiated over time. A second possible conclusion can be drawn from the fragmented nature of the network: global civil society discourse is comprised of many disconnected smaller networks, which may have little communication with one another even though they may share similar interests, and remain fragmented even when they are present in the same place and at the same time, as was the case in Mumbai.

4 *Closeness centrality may be defined as the total distance in terms of network links of a given node from all other nodes.*

Figure M5: Closeness-centrality graph of World Social Forum events

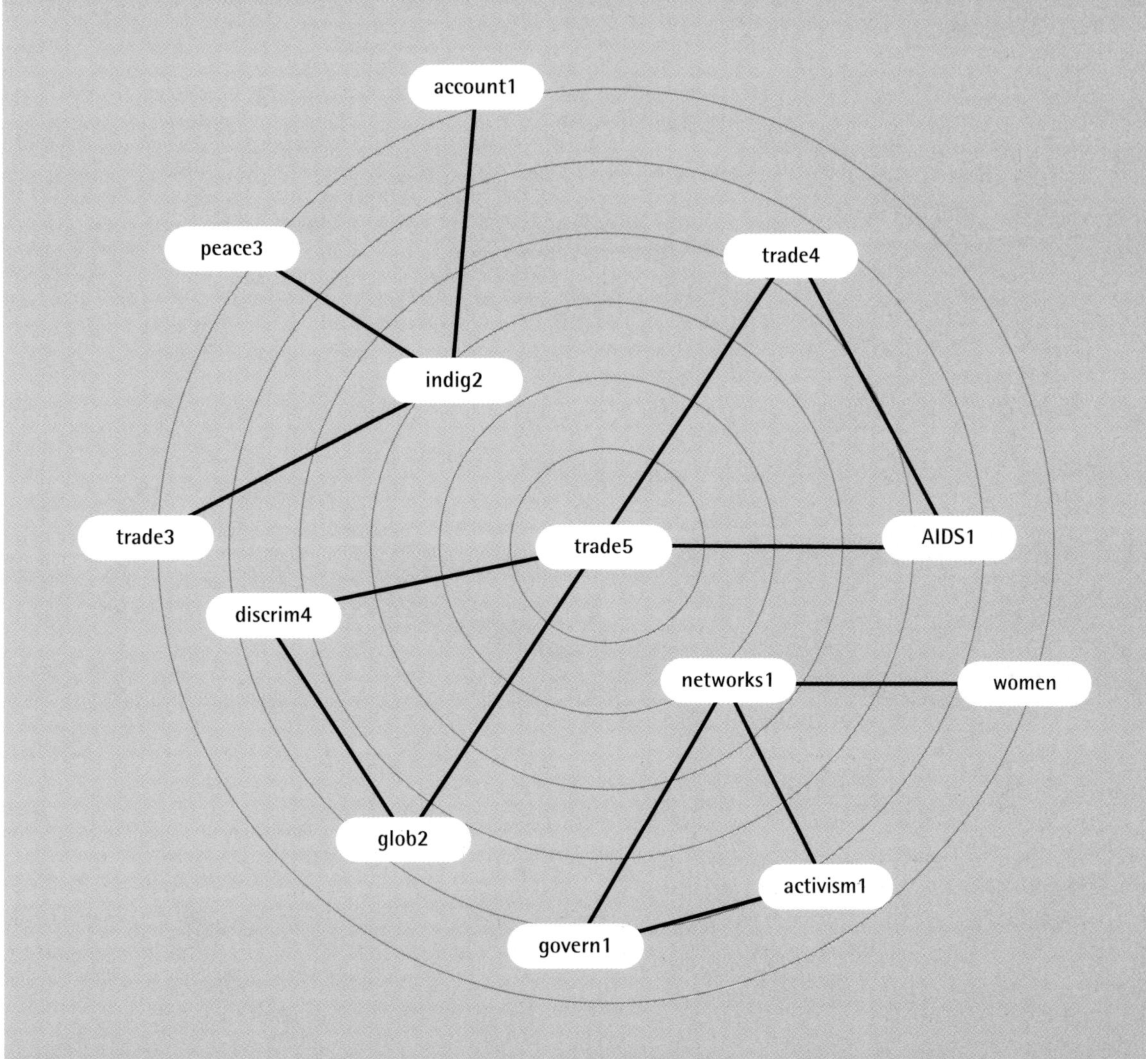

Figure M6: Betweenness centrality of participant organisations in World Social Forum events

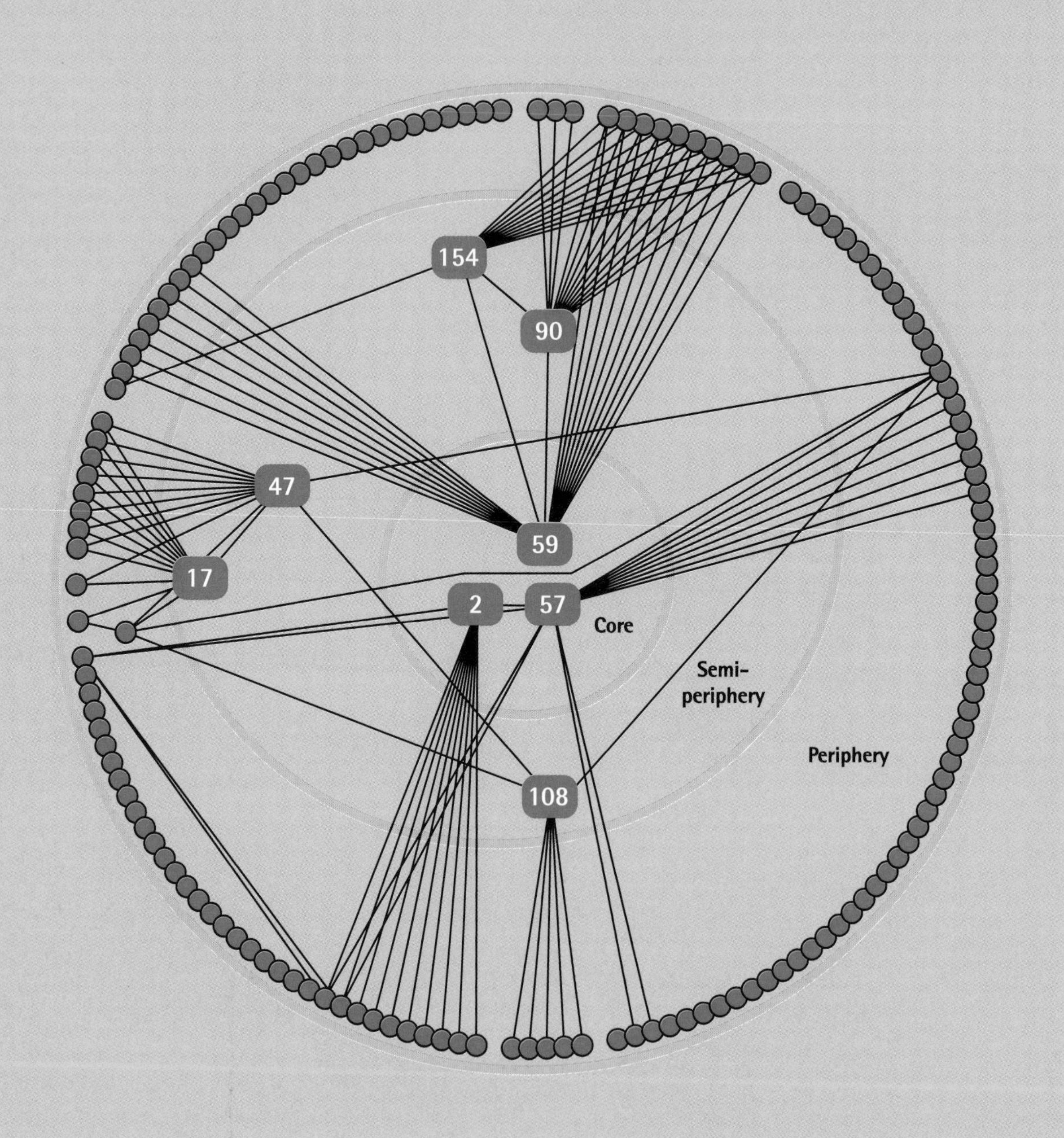

Table M4: Central organisations in World Social Forum events (betweenness centrality)

INNER CIRCLE

2 ActionAid
www.actionaid.org.uk — UK, global level
'ActionAid is a unique partnership of people who are fighting for a better world – a world without poverty. As one of the UK's largest development agencies, we work in more than 40 countries in Africa, Asia, Latin America and the Caribbean, listening to, learning from and working in partnership with over nine million of the world's poorest people.'

57 Focus on the Global South
www.focusweb.org — Thailand, global level
'. . . aims to consciously and consistently articulate, link and develop greater coherence between local community-based and national, regional and global paradigms of change. Focus on the Global South strives to create a distinct and cogent link between development at the grassroots and the "macro" levels.'

59 Friends of the Earth
www.foe.org — Netherlands/US, global level
'Friends of the Earth defends the environment and champions a healthy and just world.'

INTERMEDIATE CIRCLE

47 Development Alternatives with Women for a New Era (DAWN)
www.dawn.org.fj — Fiji, global level
'DAWN is a network of women scholars and activists from the economic South who engage in feminist research and analysis of the global environment and are committed to working for economic justice, gender justice and democracy. DAWN works globally and regionally in Africa, Asia, the Caribbean, Latin America and the Pacific on the themes of the Political Economy of Globalisation; Political Restructuring and Social Transformation; Sustainable Livelihoods; and Sexual and Reproductive Health and Rights, in partnership with other global NGOs and networks.'

17 Articulación Feminista Marcosur
www.mujeresdelsur.org.uy — Uruguay, global level
Feminist organisation interested in promotion of democracy

90 Liberal Association for Movement of People (LAMP)
www.cafonline.org/cafindia/india/ngopage.cfm?charitynumber=LAMP%201%20WB1 — India, national level
'LAMP is a national-level voluntary organisation working for the sustainable development of the socio-economically backward, culturally oppressed, politically underprivileged and disadvantaged group of people of both rural and urban India; issues focussed are street children, sustainable development and income-generation programmes.'

108 National Network of Autonomous Women's Groups (NNAWG) — India, national level
Feminist organisation promoting women's rights and women organising in India

154 Vasudhaiva Kutumbakam (The Earth is a Family)
www.demokratiafoorumi.fi/vk-brochure.html — India/Finland, global level
'Vasudhaiva Kutumbakam, a coalition for Comprehensive Democracy, is about furthering, strengthening and deepening "democracy" simultaneously in economic, social, political, cultural, gender and ecological dimensions of life, from local to global levels.'

Numbers refer to node numbering in figure M6

An analysis of interorganisational links can proceed from the two-mode network of events and NGOs. A one-mode network of organisational links was extracted from the two-mode network, in which participation in the same event was interpreted as disclosing a tie between two organisations. Again, the resulting network was sparse, indicating that global civil society is not very interconnected. An analysis of 'betweenness centrality' reveals, in addition, the structure of the organisational network that emanates from participation patterns in WSF events. This structure indicates that global civil society is bifurcated between a small core of well-connected organisations and a vast multitude of organisations that are very much isolated from their counterparts (see Figure M6). Interestingly, not all of the organisations in the core are interconnected. The result is a network that is fragmented into two main components.

Betweenness centrality can be loosely explained as brokerage: it measures the extent to which a node's presence facilitates connectivity in the network. Hence, the higher the betweenness centrality of a node, the higher its contribution to the network's overall connectivity. Betweenness centrality is particularly important in diffusion and collaboration contexts. In the context of global civil society, an NGO's importance increases if it enables communication between other NGOs. It then allows communication and innovation to flow from one region of the network to another, and it can serve as a broker that enables making connections and establishing coalitions between otherwise disjointed NGOs.

From Figure M6, participating organisations can be arranged in three groups based on their relative betweenness: the inner circle that consists of three organisations, an intermediate circle that includes five more organisations, and the remaining organisations on the outskirts. The split of global civil society into core and periphery has already been observed by Anheier and Katz (2003); in that analysis of the geospatial patterns of global civil society, we pointed out that international NGOs are distributed unevenly between developed and developing countries. It would be interesting to test that conclusion here. For this purpose, we looked at the individual organisations in the inner and intermediate circles in order to characterise them more specifically.

Table M4 lists the identities of the organisations in the inner and intermediate circles. It is apparent that organisations in the well-connected parts of the network operate mostly at the global level. The two national organisations are both Indian, which can be attributed to the 'home advantage'. Moreover, organisations in the inner circle tend to be generalists that define their goals widely and have a mix of objectives; they are also more likely to be from developed nations than organisations in the semi-periphery. The fact that Southern NGOs are relatively absent from the inner circle is indeed indicative of global civil society networks more widely, and suggests the presence of underlying hierarchies and dominance relations. The relative importance of local organisations hints at the potential contribution that locating events such as the World Social Forum in developing countries can have on the integration of southern NGOs in the global networks of civil society.

Conclusion

This chapter can do little more than illustrate the potential of network analysis for understanding global civil society. For what range of purposes do we think network analysis could be useful? In closing, we suggest the following substantive areas for further exploration:

- the signature characteristics of personal and organisational egocentric networks and how they facilitate action and goal-attainment in global civil society contexts
- the patterns of communication flows, mobilisation processes, and the diffusion of ideas and innovations through global connectedness; the patterns and dynamics of global civil society as a space of flows, as suggested by Castells (1996)
- the macro-structure of global civil society in terms of Held et al's (1999) conceptions of extensity, intensity and velocity – where are centres, peripheral and semi-peripheral regions located, and how do different structural positions relate to each other?
- the relationship between the macro-structure of global civil society, the global economy, and the global geopolitical system
- the constitution of global public spheres through hyper-network structures and patterns of inclusion and exclusion.

Of course, there may be other areas as well that are worth exploring. While there certainly are data and technical and analytic challenges involved, the potential that such analyses have for enhancing our understanding of global civil society is formidable. We hope to have shown the potential network analysis has for overcoming the legacy of methodological nationalism,

References

Anheier, H. K. and Katz, H. (2003) 'Mapping Global Civil Society', in Mary Kaldor, Helmut Anheier and Marlies Glasius (eds), *Global Civil Society 2003*. Oxford: Oxford University Press.

– and Romo, F. P. (1999) 'Stalemate: A Study of Structural Failure', in H. K. Anheier (ed), *When Things Go Wrong: Organizational Failures and Breakdowns*. Thousand Oaks, CA: Sage.

Barabási, A.-L. (2002) *Linked: The New Science of Networks*. Cambridge, MA: Perseus.

Beck, U. (2003) 'The Analysis of Global Inequality: From National to Cosmopolitan Perspective', in Mary Kaldor, Helmut Anheier and Marlies Glasius (eds), *Global Civil Society 2003*. Oxford: Oxford University Press.

Boorman, S. A. and White, H. C. (1976) 'Social Structure from Multiple Networks. II. Role Structures', *The American Journal of Sociology*, 81(6): 1384–446.

Borgatti, S. P., Everett, M. G. and Freeman, L. C. (2002) *Ucinet for Windows: Software for Social Network Analysis*. Harvard, MA: Analytic Technologies.

Brandes, U. and Wagner, D. (2003) 'Visone – Analysis and Visualization of Social Networks', in M. Jünger and P. Mutzel (eds), *Graph Drawing Software*. New York: Springer-Verlag.

Castells, M. (1996) *The Rise of Network Society*. Oxford: Blackwell.

Diani, M. and McAdam, D. (eds) (2003) *Social Movements and Networks: Relational Approaches to Collective Action*. Oxford: Oxford University Press.

Held, D., McGrew, A., Goldblatt, D. and Perraton, J. (1999) *Global Transformations*. Cambridge: Polity Press.

Keane, J. (2001) 'Global Civil Society?' in Helmut Anheier, Marlies Glasius and Mary Kaldor (eds), *Global Civil Society 2001*. Oxford: Oxford University Press.

Marsden, P.V. (1990) 'Network Data and Measurement', *Annual Review of Sociology*, 16: 435–63.

Milgram, S. (1967) 'The Small World Problem', *Psychology Today*, 1(1): 60–7.

Roseneau, J.N. (1995) 'Governance and Democracy in a Globalizing World', in D. Archibugi, D. Held and M. Kohler (eds), *Re-imagining Political Community: Studies in Cosmopolitan Democracy*. Cambridge: Polity.

Scott, J. (1999) *Social Network Analysis: A Handbook*. Thousand Oaks: Sage.

Shaw, M. (2003) 'The Global Transformation of the Social Sciences', in Mary Kaldor, Helmut Anheier and Marlies Glasius (eds), *Global Civil Society 2003*. Oxford: Oxford University Press.

Townsend, J. G. (1999) 'Are Non-governmental Organizations Working in Development a Transnational Community?', *Journal of International Development*, 11(4): 613–23.

Union of International Associations (URL) www.uia.org

White, H. C., Boorman, S. A. and Breiger, R. L. (1976) 'Social Structure from Multiple Networks. I. Blockmodels of Roles and Positions', *The American Journal of Sociology*, 81(4): 730–80.

Wasserman, S. and Faust, K. (1994) *Social Network Analysis*. Cambridge: Cambridge University Press.

Yergin, D. A. and Stanislav, J. (1998) *The Commanding Heights: The Battle between Government and the Marketplace that is Remaking the Modern World*. New York: Simon and Schuster.

The last sentence on page 220 should read:

We hope to have shown the potential network analysis has for overcoming the legacy of methodological nationalism, and for allowing us to undertake a systematic study of global connectedness.

Note on data

Relation to data programme *Global Civil Society 2003*

We have updated the information presented in the 2003 edition of the Yearbook wherever possible. Those indicators repeated from the 2003 data programme represent more recent or updated figures. In order to facilitate comparisons, country data are grouped by income and region, using World Bank classifications.

We have added new indicators where we judge them to be valuable, sometimes representing a departure from those presented last year. Such indicators are found in our records on media and communication, social justice, corruption, environment, tolerance, and attitudes towards globalisation. In these records we present data on international telecommunications and personal computers, net primary school enrolment ratio and the ratio of girls to boys in primary education, control of corruption, ratification of environmental conservation treaties, and tolerance toward immigrants and ethnic minorities. This year we include three new records: trafficking in persons, political rights and civil liberties, and attitudes towards Americanisation. Thus we introduce the following data sources to the Yearbook:

- Freedom House (www.freedomhouse.org)
- the Pew Research Centre for the People and the Press (www.people-press.org)
- the Trafficking in Persons Report, issued by the US Department of State's Office of the Under Secretary for Global Affairs, Office to Monitor and Combat Trafficking in Persons (www.state.gov/g/tip/rls/tiprpt/2003)
- the World Bank Institute's Governance project (www.worldbank.org/wbi/governance/pubs/govmatters3.htm)
- Environmental Treaties and Resource Indicators (ENTRI) project of the Centre for International Earth Science Information Network (CIESIN) in Earth Institute at Columbia University (http://sedac.ciesin.columbia.edu/entri/index.jsp)

We continue using graphical formats for presentation of the data. Selected indicators in the tables are illustrated on world maps pages 336–44. In addition, we present a network diagram for the record on world trade. The diagram should be interpreted by reference to node size and position, and line thickness. Each node in the diagram represents a (labelled) region, while lines represent flows. Node size is determined by *degree centrality* in the network, which is determined by the sum of its inflows and outflows. The location of nodes in the diagram is determined by *eigenvector centrality*: regions that are more central in the network (transfer more flows to and from them, and are connected to other highly connected regions) are closer to the centre. Also the higher the volume of flows between regions, the closer these regions are to each other. Line width reflects flow volumes: thicker lines indicate greater flows.

With some elements of last year's data programme we have not been able to obtain updated or equivalent data for this edition of the Yearbook. Thus, we have decided not to reproduce the data on students abroad, daily newspapers, human rights violations, international organisation leaders, value attached to democracy, confidence in institutions, participation in political action, and membership and volunteering. All data from previous Yearbooks remain available on our website at www.lse.ac.uk/depts/global/yearbook/yearbook.htm

Sources and explanatory notes

Brief references to sources are found at the end of each record. All major terms used in the records are briefly defined in the Glossary. As will become clear, comparative information is not available for some countries and variables. A blank entry indicates that the data are not available, not comparable, or otherwise of insufficient quality to warrant reporting. To improve readability of the data and to facilitate interpretation, each record is preceded by a brief description of the information presented and points to some of the key findings.

Time periods

Dependent on data availability, data are reported for 1993 and 2003 or the closest years possible.

Countries

Countries in these tables are independent states with currently more than 100,000 inhabitants according to the most recent population estimates. Short or conventional country names are used. It is not the intention of the editors to take a position with regard to the political or diplomatic implications of geographical names or continental groupings used.

China, Hong Kong, Macao, Taiwan, and Tibet

Hong Kong became a Special Administrative Region (SAR) of China in 1997 after formal transfer from the UK. Macao became a SAR of China in 1999 after formal transfer from Portugal. Data for China before these dates do not include Hong Kong and Macao; thereafter they do unless otherwise stated. Tibet was annexed by the People's Republic of China in 1949. Data for Tibet are included in those for China and Tibet. Taiwan became the home of Chinese nationalists fleeing Communist rule on the mainland and claims separate status from the People's Republic of China. No data are given for Taiwan, which is not recognised by the United Nations as an independent country.

Czechoslovakia

Czechoslovakia ceased to exist (in UN terms) on 31 December 1992. Its successor states, the Czech Republic and the Slovak Republic, became UN members in 1993. Figures predating 1993 are given for the Czech Republic and Slovakia separately where possible, or otherwise not at all.

Ethiopia and Eritrea

Eritrea became independent from Ethiopia in 1993. Data for Ethiopia until 1993 include Eritrea, later data do not.

Germany

The Federal Republic of Germany and the German Democratic Republic were unified in 1990. Data for 1990 and 1991 include both unless otherwise indicated.

Indonesia and East Timor

The Indonesian occupation of East Timor ended in late 1999. After a transitional period under the authority of the United Nations, East Timor became independent on 20 May 2002. Data are presented for Indonesia and East Timor together unless otherwise indicated. All data for Indonesia also include Irian Jaya (West Papua), the status of which has been in dispute since the 1960s.

Israel and the Occupied Territories

Data for Israel generally include both the Occupied Territories and territories administered by the Palestinian Authority. In Records 14–19 they include territories identified by INGOs as 'Palestine', 'Cisjordania', 'Gaza', 'Jerusalem', and 'West Bank'.

Morocco and the Western Sahara

The Western Sahara (formerly Spanish Sahara) was annexed by Morocco in the 1970s. Unless otherwise stated, data are amalgamated for 'Morocco and the Western Sahara'.

Yugoslavia and Serbia & Montenegro

The Socialist Federal Republic of Yugoslavia dissolved in 1991 into Bosnia and Herzegovina, the Republic of Croatia, the Republic of Slovenia, the former Yugoslav Republic of Macedonia, and the Federal Republic of Yugoslavia. In February 2003 the Federal Republic of Yugoslavia was renamed Serbia and Montenegro, reflecting the implementation of constitutional change to a looser federation of its two republics. For ease of presentation, the name 'Serbia and Montenegro' is used throughout these records, where the 'Federal Republic of Yugoslavia' would have applied pre-2003. Wherever possible, including for 1990, data are given separately for Serbia & Montenegro and the other constituent states of the former Yugoslavia.

USSR

The Union of Soviet Socialist Republics (USSR) dissolved in 1991 into Armenia, Azerbaijan, Belarus, Georgia, Kazakhstan, Kyrgyzstan, Republic of Moldova, Russian Federation, Tajikistan, Turkmenistan, Ukraine, and Uzbekistan. 1990 and 1991 data for the Russian Federation refer only to the Russian Federation, except where they are indicated to relate to the USSR.

Aggregations

Where possible we present data for groups of countries (by region and economy) as well as for individual countries. These groups are generally classified according to World Bank definitions. The aggregations are weighted differently depending on information availability. To give an example, in R1 we present figures for trade as a percentage of GDP. The aggregate figure for South Asia is calculated as the sum of trade for Afghanistan, Bangladesh, Bhutan, India, Maldives, Nepal, Pakistan and Sri Lanka, divided by the sum of GDP for those countries, and multiplied by 100 to generate a percentage, ie

Trade as % GDP for South Asia =

$$\frac{\text{Afghan trade + Bangladeshi trade +}}{\text{Afghan GDP + Bangladeshi GDP + ...}} \times 100$$

Most aggregate figures given are calculated in this way. By contrast, in R23 the aggregates we present are simple averages, and are marked as such. For example, with '% favouring American ideas', to calculate the aggregate figure for South Asia we sum the percentages in Bangladesh, India and Pakistan, and divide this figure by the number of countries in this region (three), ie

Average % favouring American ideas for South Asia =

$$\frac{\text{\% favouring American ideas in Bangladesh + India + Pakistan}}{\text{Number of countries for which data is available in South Asia}}$$

Each country's contribution to the regional or world figure is given equal weight under this method of aggregation.

Record 1 Global economy

The first table contains data on the globalisation of domestic economies. It shows total trade, foreign direct investment (FDI), and receipts of official development aid, presented as a percentage of GDP. It also includes information on changes over time between 1991 and 2001 (trade and aid) and between 1992 and 2002 (FDI), with the use of the latest figures available. We try to show the extent to which national economies are parts of an emerging global economy, and where economic growth or contraction has been most pronounced over the last decade in this respect. The table shows significant increases in trade and direct investments between 1991 and 2001 for most countries, and decreases in official development aid for many countries, contrasted with increases in aid in middle- and low-income economies in Europe and Central Asia.

	Trade			**Official development aid***			**Foreign direct investment**					
	Total trade in % GDP		% change	Aid (% of GNI)		% change	Inward FDI stock in % GDP		% change	Outward FDI stock in % GDP		% change
Country	1991	2001	1991–2001	1991	2001	1991–2001	1992	2002	1992–2002	1992	2002	1992–2002
East Asia & Pacific												
Low income economies												
Cambodia	25.5	114.5	349	5.6	12.4	123	3.6	41.0	1,049	*0.1*	0.1	*-50*
Indonesia	49.9	77.1	55	1.7	1.1	-34	30.3	32.2	6	0.1	1.5	2,029
Korea, Dem. Rep.							5.1	10.0	95			
Laos	38.2			13.7	14.6	6	2.4	29.4	1,114	0.0	11.2	112,200
Mongolia	174.9	148.7	-15		20.5		1.2	27.8	2,238			
Myanmar	4.4						1.1	37.2	3,248			
Papua New Guinea	94.4			10.9	7.2	-34	34.4	70.0	103	5.0	22.3	344
Solomon Islands	*119.6*			15.9	20.0	25	37.4	32.0	-14	*0.0*	0.0	*0*
Vietnam	66.9	111.5	67	2.5	4.4	73	*11.2*	50.3	347			
Middle income economies												
China**	35.5	49.2	39	0.5	0.1	-76	9.6	36.2	276	1.8	2.9	62
Fiji	116.3	*131.6*	*13*	3.1	1.5	-50	34.0	64.7	90	3.4		
Malaysia	159.3	214.3	35	0.6	0.0	-95	28.5	59.4	108	6.3	21.2	235
Micronesia	118.4			0.2	56.9	22,985						
Philippines	62.2	95.5	54	2.3	0.8	-67	7.6	15.0	99	0.3	1.8	552
Samoa		*114.2*		35.1	17.7	-49	14.7	21.7	48			
Thailand	78.5	125.7	60	0.7	0.2	-67	11.0	23.9	118	0.6	2.1	240
Tonga	73.1			13.9	14.8	6	1.8	16.6	851	0.1	0.8	1,283
Vanuatu	109.9			30.4	14.6	-52	85.1	170.3	100			
High income economies												
Australia	34.3	*45.6*	*33*				24.2	32.3	33	11.0	22.9	107
Brunei							0.7	108.8	15,220	0.0	3.3	16,450
Japan	18.3	20.3	11				0.4	1.5	263	6.5	8.3	27
Korea, Rep.	57.7	82.2	42	0.0			2.2	9.2	319	1.4	9.1	548
New Caledonia	49.5			11.7	*13.1*	*12*	2.7	4.7	71			
New Zealand	55.9	*71.8*	*29*				31.0	50.3	62	15.5	12.9	-17
Singapore							73.8	142.7	93	22.0	82.0	273
Europe & Central Asia												
Low income economies												
Armenia	100.9	71.5	-29	0.1	9.7	10,850	*0.0*	27.8	*92,600*		2.2	
Azerbaijan	86.9	80.6	-7		4.2			86.4			15.4	
Georgia	58.9	61.8	5	0.0	9.0		0.6	*19.9*	*3,268*			
Kyrgyzstan	72.0	73.7	2	*1.1*	12.9	*1,025*	1.0	25.9	*2,465*		2.8	

Record 1 continued

Country	Trade			Official development aid*			Foreign direct investment					
	Total trade in % GDP		% change	Aid (% of GNI)		% change	Inward FDI stock in % GDP		% change	Outward FDI stock in % GDP		% change
	1991	2001	1991–2001	1991	2001	1991-2001	1992	2002	1992–2002	1992	2002	1992–2002
Moldova	66.4	124.4	87	*0.3*	7.5	*2,094*	3.4	45.0	1,219		1.2	
Tajikistan	65.4	139.6	113	*0.5*	15.5	*3,323*	0.4	14.8	4,117			
Ukraine	50.1	109.3	118	0.4	1.4	214	1.4	12.9	851	*0.2*	0.4	*54*
Uzbekistan	74.4	55.7	-25		1.4		0.4	13.8	3,426			
Middle income economies												
Albania	34.8	60.8	75	29.7	6.3	-79	2.8	21.0	644	2.8	1.8	-35
Belarus	70.3	137.1	95	0.5	0.3	-38	0.2	8.7	5,720		*0.1*	
Bosnia & Herzegovina		*81.3*			12.7			15.8		*0.1*	0.8	*850*
Bulgaria	82.6	118.9	44	3.2	2.6	-19	2.0	25.0	1,137	1.1	0.8	-27
Croatia	163.8	103.2	-37	*0.0*	0.6		1.2	28.4	2,191	6.6	5.0	-24
Czech Republic	98.5	143.7	46	*0.4*	0.6	*30*	*9.8*	64.3	*557*	*0.5*	2.5	*381*
Estonia	*114.6*	185.0	*61*	0.3	1.3	412	2.6	65.9	2,445	1.4	10.5	657
Hungary	66.5	123.3	85	2.0	0.8	-58	9.2	38.2	315	0.6	7.3	1,108
Kazakhstan	*149.3*	96.0	*-36*	0.4	0.7	102	4.9	62.9	1,176		1.9	
Latvia	60.7	98.2	62	0.0	1.4		12.9	32.4	151	26.8	0.8	-97
Lithuania	50.7	107.3	112	0.0	1.1	4,069	5.6	28.9	420		0.4	
Macedonia	48.8	97.9	101		7.3			23.9			0.1	
Poland	49.0	59.8	22	3.4	0.5	-84	1.6	24.0	1,383	0.1	0.7	467
Romania	39.1	75.1	92	1.1	1.6	48	0.5	20.5	4,086	0.3	0.4	13
Russian Federation	26.3	59.9	128	0.1	0.4	255	0.3	6.5	2,000	0.5	5.2	900
Serbia & Montenegro		68.4			11.3		0.7	20.2	2,907			
Slovakia	95.6	156.5	64	1.1	0.8	-23	*3.2*	43.2	*1,270*	*0.9*	1.7	*99*
Slovenia	157.8	120.5	-24		0.7		6.3	23.1	267	2.2	4.9	117
Turkey	30.5	65.8	116	1.1	0.1	-89	8.0	8.3	3	0.8	1.8	126
Turkmenistan		93.7			1.2		*1.7*	25.5	*1,419*			
High income economies												
Austria	77.5	104.8	35				5.9	20.6	250	3.6	19.5	440
Belgium & Luxembourg***	140.8	176.6	25				31.4	*82.5*	*162*	23.1	*73.5*	*218*
Cyprus	104.2			0.7	0.5	-20	19.4	47.7	146	0.5	7.2	1,239
Denmark	68.5	84.8	24				9.8	41.7	327	11.1	43.4	291
Finland	44.9	72.0	60				3.4	27.0	696	7.9	52.8	570
France	43.5	54.3	25				9.5	28.3	198	11.6	46.0	296
Germany	52.8	68.0	29				6.4	22.7	253	8.5	29.1	244
Greece	44.2	*57.9*	*31*				8.0	9.1	14	3.0	5.3	78
Iceland	64.6	81.4	26				1.8	10.0	463	1.4	12.3	774
Ireland	110.8	175.9	59				69.0	128.9	87	22.4	29.9	34
Italy	37.1	54.9	48				3.9	10.7	171	5.8	16.4	185
Netherlands	104.7	124.8	19				22.3	75.1	238	36.2	85.0	135
Norway	72.6	*77.1*	*6*				10.8	17.4	61	9.3	20.0	114
Portugal	67.2	72.9	9				15.3	*36.1*	137	2.1	*26.3*	1,151
Spain	35.9	61.3	71				14.3	33.4	133	3.7	33.1	804

Record 1 continued

	Trade			Official development aid*			Foreign direct investment					
	Total trade in % GDP		% change	Aid (% of GNI)		% change	Inward FDI stock in % GDP		% change	Outward FDI stock in % GDP		% change
Country	1991	2001	1991–2001	1991	2001	1991–2001	1992	2002	1992–2002	1992	2002	1992–2002
Sweden	54.4	87.0	60				5.5	46.0	734	19.2	60.5	216
Switzerland	68.6	86.6	26				13.6	44.2	226	30.6	111.3	264
United Kingdom	47.4	56.4	19				16.1	40.8	153	20.7	66.1	219
Latin America & Caribbean												
Low income economies												
Haiti	57.9	45.9	-21	6.0	4.4	-26	7.6	7.2	-6		0.1	
Nicaragua	74.3			72.3			11.1	67.8	512	*0.0*	0.7	*6,700*
Middle income economies												
Argentina	13.8	21.6	57	0.1	0.1	-61	7.1	75.3	957	3.2	19.0	492
Barbados	97.6	100.0	3	0.1	0.0	-93	12.2	13.8	14	1.6	1.8	9
Belize	122.9	129.2	5	5.2	2.9	-44	22.0	43.2	97	0.8	7.7	924
Bolivia	48.4	42.8	-12	9.9	9.4	-5	21.6	81.9	280	0.2	0.4	110
Brazil	16.6	27.4	65	0.0	0.1		10.2	52.2	409	11.1	11.8	6
Chile	61.8	67.3	9	0.4	0.1	-76	27.0	69.7	159	1.7	20.2	1,090
Colombia	35.3	38.4	9	0.3	0.5	64	7.9	24.0	203	1.0	4.7	369
Costa Rica	70.7	86.4	22	2.6	0.0	-99	21.6	37.3	73	0.6	1.0	51
Cuba		*33.9*					0.1	0.3	162			
Dominican Republic	63.6	56.0	-12	0.9	0.5	-44	10.2	34.1	235	*0.1*	0.4	*282*
Ecuador	61.1	58.1	-5	0.1	0.9	847	15.6	39.5	153		1.1	
El Salvador	47.7	71.8	50	5.7	1.7	-69	4.2	17.1	303	0.9	0.3	-70
Grenada	102.4	128.9	26	7.1	3.1	-56	43.1	100.2	133	0.1	0.2	109
Guatemala	39.5	46.0	16	2.1	1.1	-49	18.4	21.2	15		0.2	
Guyana	257.4	206.2	-20	56.4	15.9	-72	54.6	120.0	120	*0.4*	*0.0*	*-98*
Honduras	70.7	93.1	32	10.5	10.8	3	14.1	27.8	97			
Jamaica	101.0	97.3	-4	4.3	0.7	-83	31.9	56.7	78	3.5	11.2	217
Mexico	35.6	57.0	60	0.1	0.0	-86	9.8	24.2	146	1.5	2.0	30
Panama	64.9	57.5	-11	1.7	0.2	-86	36.9	65.1	76	76.3	69.1	-9
Paraguay	68.4	64.7	-5	2.4	0.9	-62	*9.4*	12.2	*29*	*2.1*	3.0	*43*
Peru	26.7	33.0	24	2.8	0.9	-69	4.2	22.1	429	0.3	1.3	276
St. Lucia	153.3	109.2	-29	5.8	2.6	-55	87.3	119.4	37	0.1	0.1	-54
St. Vincent & the Grenadines	132.7	109.8	-17	7.9	2.6	-67	30.0	146.4	388	0.3	0.2	-36
Suriname	39.0	153.7	294	12.5	3.4	-73						
Trinidad & Tobago	75.7	94.5	25	0.4			45.3	87.6	93	0.4	6.6	1,545
Uruguay	38.6	38.7	0	0.5	0.1	-82	8.1	*13.1*	61	1.4	*2.3*	60
Venezuela	57.6	39.8	-31	0.1	0.0	-34	7.9	33.6	325	4.3	7.2	70
High income economies												
Bahamas				0.1	*0.1*	*12*	18.4	37.6	104	19.3	27.6	43
Middle East & North Africa												
Low income economies												
Yemen	49.3	76.7	55	6.0	5.0	-17	20.5	13.3	-35	0.1	0.1	-38
Middle income economies												
Algeria	52.7	58.3	11	0.8	0.3	-56	3.1	10.5	245	0.5	0.8	63
Djibouti		*107.4*			9.4		*2.3*	6.8	*194*			
Egypt	63.6	40.3	-37	13.7	1.3	-91	28.1	24.1	-14	0.6	0.8	47

Record 1 continued

Country	Trade: Total trade in % GDP		% change	Official development aid*: Aid (% of GNI)		% change	Foreign direct investment: Inward FDI stock in % GDP		% change	Outward FDI stock in % GDP		% change
	1991	2001	1991–2001	1991	2001	1991-2001	1992	2002	1992–2002	1992	2002	1992–2002
Iran	38.9	49.6	28	*0.1*	0.1	*17*	0.2	2.4	1,239		5.0	
Jordan	142.2	113.2	-20	24.5	4.9	-80	12.0	26.0	116	0.7		
Lebanon	97.4	57.9	-41	2.7	1.4	-50	1.3	9.4	609	1.0	2.4	134
Libya	64.6	*51.0*	*-21*							2.0	7.2	262
Malta	185.0	180.1	-3	0.8	0.0	-94	21.2	74.4	251	1.0	5.4	424
Morocco	53.9	66.8	24	4.6	1.6	-66	5.8	26.9	361	1.9	2.3	21
Oman	86.9			0.1	0.0	-92	17.4	12.6	-28	0.1	0.1	57
Saudi Arabia	86.0	66.4	-23	0.0	0.0		18.3	13.4	-27	1.1	1.1	4
Syria	56.5	69.0	22	3.0	0.8	-73	3.4	9.6	180			
Tunisia	85.7	99.2	16	2.8	2.0	-30	54.5	66.4	22	0.2	0.2	20
High income economies												
Bahrain	180.6	139.9	-23	0.9	0.2	-74	42.9	72.9	70	17.3	25.2	46
Israel & Occupied Territories****	75.3	*192.2*	*155*	3.0	*19.9*	*559*	6.6	29.0	343	3.2	10.5	230
Kuwait	142.6	92.2	-35	0.0	0.0		*0.3*	1.1	*340*	23.6	4.6	-80
Qatar				0.0			*2.0*	14.7	633		2.1	
United Arab Emirates	113.8			0.0			2.5	2.0	-22	0.3	4.4	1,417
North America												
High income economies												
Canada	51.3	82.5	61				19.0	30.4	60	15.4	37.6	145
United States	20.6	*26.2*	*27*				6.8	12.9	91	8.0	14.4	79
South Asia												
Low income economies												
Afghanistan							0.1	0.2	220			
Bangladesh	18.9	36.9	95	5.9	2.1	-65	0.5	2.4	392	0.0	0.1	500
Bhutan	74.7	66.5	-11	28.2	12.6	-55	*0.9*	0.7	*-20*			
India	17.2	27.2	58	1.0	0.4	-66	0.8	5.1	566	0.1	0.5	355
Nepal	34.9	54.4	56	11.4	6.7	-41	0.5	2.3	349			
Pakistan	35.6	37.4	5	3.1	3.4	9	5.4	10.2	87	0.7	0.9	39
Middle income economies												
Maldives	*88.5*	158.0	*79*	15.3	4.3	-72	15.4	22.6	46			
Sri Lanka	65.3	80.6	23	10.1	2.1	-80	9.0	16.6	85	0.2	0.6	293
Sub-Saharan Africa												
Low income economies												
Angola	57.3	136.7	138	2.8	3.4	20	34.2	98.3	188			
Benin	43.6	43.1	-1	14.4	11.6	-19	22.0	25.1	14	0.1	2.2	1,855
Burkina Faso	38.7	35.9	-7	15.1	15.7	4	2.1	6.3	198	0.2	1.0	395
Burundi	38.4	24.7	-36	22.3	19.3	-14	2.9	6.8	134	*0.0*	0.3	*1,350*
Cameroon	34.6	61.0	76	4.4	4.9	11	9.3	15.7	69	1.8	2.9	61
Central African Republic	34.9	27.0	-23	12.6	7.9	-37	5.6	9.9	77	1.9	4.0	116
Chad	36.3	67.0	84	14.1	11.3	-20	15.7	78.4	399	3.8	4.1	6
Comoros	55.3	44.7	-19	24.6	12.4	-49	6.8	10.5	55	0.6	0.7	8
Congo, Dem. Rep.	44.5	34.5	-22	5.7	5.3	-8	6.8	11.9	74			

Record 1 continued

Country	Trade			Official development aid*			Foreign direct investment					
	Total trade in % GDP		% change	Aid (% of GNI)		% change	Inward FDI stock in % GDP		% change	Outward FDI stock in % GDP		% change
	1991	2001	1991–2001	1991	2001	1991-2001	1992	2002	1992–2002	1992	2002	1992–2002
Congo, Rep.	92.1	132.7	44	5.9	3.8	-35	*20.8*	69.5	*234*			
Côte d'Ivoire	57.0	69.5	22	6.9	1.9	-73	9.5	31.3	229	2.4	5.8	141
Equatorial Guinea	126.1			51.2	2.9	-94	47.1	92.8	97	0.3	0.1	-56
Eritrea	*59.7*	97.3	*63*		40.9			49.1				
Ethiopia	18.6	46.6	150	11.6	17.5	51	2.4	17.3	636		8.5	
Gambia	138.6	125.9	-9	33.3	13.3	-60	46.1	74.9	62	7.0	13.2	88
Ghana	42.5	122.7	189	13.6	12.6	-7	5.6	26.4	373		7.8	
Guinea	46.2	56.3	22	13.3	9.2	-31	3.9	9.4	142		0.4	
Guinea-Bissau	47.8	114.3	139	47.8	32.0	-33	7.0	22.0	214			
Kenya	56.4	60.6	7	12.1	4.0	-67	8.7	9.3	8	1.2	2.9	135
Lesotho	145.5	119.5	-18	11.7	5.5	-53	11.9	53.4	349	0.1	0.1	0
Liberia							253.2	288.8	14	122.0	155.2	27
Madagascar	44.8	60.3	35	18.3	7.8	-58	4.7	10.1	112	0.0	0.1	125
Malawi	52.6	64.0	22	25.5	23.4	-8	9.0	8.4	-6		1.1	
Mali	52.8	73.8	40	18.7	13.9	-26	0.6	21.9	3,557	0.8	4.8	499
Mauritania	96.3	88.7	-8	20.4	26.6	30	5.7	11.3	101	0.2	0.3	17
Mozambique	49.6	72.5	46	46.6	28.2	-39	4.8	44.8	828	0.0	0.0	100
Niger	32.8	41.7	27	16.3	12.9	-21	15.1	21.0	39	4.2	6.5	56
Nigeria	68.6	84.3	23	1.1	0.5	-55	29.6	42.4	43	10.0	8.5	-14
Rwanda	25.4	35.2	39	19.0	17.3	-9	10.9	14.6	34		0.3	
São Tomé & Principe	96.5	124.2	29	101.4	90.6	-11	0.9	20.2	2,142			
Senegal	56.3	67.3	20	12.0	9.2	-23	4.5	18.6	312	1.4	2.9	114
Sierra Leone	46.4	54.4	17	14.5	45.8	217	0.1	3.4	2,945			
Somalia	*47.5*			*59.1*				0.2				
Sudan		29.3		8.2	1.5	-81	0.8	19.4	2,231			
Tanzania	43.9	39.9	-9	22.6	13.3	-41	2.3	25.0	998			
Togo	75.0	82.4	10	12.7	3.8	-70	15.4	47.0	206	2.0	8.6	332
Uganda	29.4	37.3	27	20.4	14.1	-31	0.3	30.0	10,241	0.0	4.2	10,375
Zambia	71.9	64.4	-10	29.5	10.7	-64	34.3	70.0	104			
Zimbabwe	51.1	42.5	-17	4.7	1.8	-62	2.2	5.8	168	1.5	1.3	-16
Middle income economies												
Botswana	99.6	85.5	-14	3.3	0.6	-82	31.3	38.5	23	11.2	22.2	98
Cape Verde	52.5	82.9	58	29.8	13.6	-54	1.5	30.4	1,890	0.8	0.8	9
Gabon	80.5	101.1	26	3.0	0.2	-92	22.9			3.7	5.5	50
Mauritius	132.2	125.8	-5	2.4	0.5	-80	6.3	15.6	146	1.8	2.8	62
Namibia	112.7	119.9	6	6.6	3.4	-48	70.2	*34.1*	*-52*	2.7	*0.2*	*-93*
South Africa	39.9	52.7	32		0.4		8.8	48.9	459	14.6	27.6	89
Swaziland	165.3	150.1	-9	5.7	2.3	-60	45.0	54.6	21	5.1	13.5	166

Record 1 continued	Trade			Official development aid		
	Total trade in % GDP		% change	Aid in % GNI		% change
Region	1991	2001	1991–2001	1991	2001	1991–2001
Low income	36.1	50.9	41	3.9	2.4	-38
Middle income	40.4	57.3	42	0.8	0.4	-49
Low & middle income	39.8	56.3	42	1.6	0.9	-42
East Asia & Pacific	52.7	77.2	46	1.0	0.5	-57
Europe & Central Asia	44.9	78.8	75	0.8	1.0	31
Latin America & Caribbean	25.7	35.9	40	0.4	0.3	-24
Middle East & North Africa	66.7	60.3	-10	2.6	0.7	-72
South Asia	21.5	31.2	45	2.2	1.0	-57
Sub-Saharan Africa	50.3	62.2	24	6.2	4.6	-25
High income	37.8	*48.2*	*28*	0.0	0.0	
World	38.1	57.0	49	0.3	0.2	-38

Where data for a particular year are not available, figures are taken from the year before or after as an estimate. These figures, and estimates based on them, are presented in italics.

* Official development aid includes both official development assistance and official aid.
** China excludes Hong Kong and Macao.
*** FDI data are not supplied for Belgium and Luxembourg individually; figures for FDI for Belgium and Luxembourg together are therefore estimates calculated by LSE and are not attributable to the World Bank.
**** Separate data for Israel and the occupied territories (The Palestinian Authority) are only available for 2001. For reason of comparability data are presented in one figure.

Sources: World Development Indicators 2003, WDI Online, World Bank; UNCTAD Foreign Direct Investment database, www.unctad.org/Templates/Page.asp?intItemID=1923&lang=1

Record 2 Global trade

This record shows the unevenness of economic globalisation as measured by trade flows. The network graph offers a simplified and consolidated view of trade flows among major world regions for 2001. The graph should be interpreted by reference to the thickness of the lines between regions (indicating volumes of trade), the position of the regions (spatial centrality reflecting a central position in the trading system), and the size of the regions (reflecting total trade flows into and out of each region). There is a clear distinction between core, semi-periphery and periphery in the world trade system. Thus the US, EU, East Asia, and Japan occupy the most central positions within this network, with the greatest amounts of trade flowing between the EU and the US. Europe and Central Asia, and the Middle East and North Africa are at the semi-periphery, and Sub-Saharan Africa and South Asia are at the outer periphery.

The accompanying table illustrates a general trend of increased overall centralisation in the network of world trade between 2000 and 2001 (calculated on the basis of the gap between the most centralised and least centralised nodes in the network). This means that trade is becoming more concentrated in the rich regions. A growing share of world trade is channelled between the US, the EU, and East Asia and the Pacific. European and Central Asian countries are becoming more central, while Japan's and South Asia's centrality has declined (centrality in the global trade network is determined not only by a particular region's share of total world trade but also the 'strength' of the regions it trades with).

Direction of flow (export region → import region)*	Amount of trade in % world trade** 2001
East Asia & Pacific → Europe & Central Asia	0.2
East Asia & Pacific → European Union	1.4
East Asia & Pacific → Japan	1.4
East Asia & Pacific → Latin America & Caribbean	0.2
East Asia & Pacific → Middle East & North Africa	0.1
East Asia & Pacific → South Asia	0.2
East Asia & Pacific → Sub-Saharan Africa	0.1
East Asia & Pacific → United States	1.7
Within East Asia & Pacific	0.8
Europe & Central Asia → East Asia & Pacific	0.1
Europe & Central Asia → European Union	2.5
Europe & Central Asia → Japan	0.1
Europe & Central Asia → Middle East & North Africa	0.1
Europe & Central Asia → United States	0.2
Within Europe & Central Asia	1.3
European Union → East Asia & Pacific	0.8
European Union → Europe & Central Asia	2.8
European Union → Japan	0.7
European Union → Latin America & Caribbean	0.9
European Union → Middle East & North Africa	0.9
European Union → South Asia	0.2
European Union → Sub-Saharan Africa	0.5
European Union → United States	3.5
Within European Union	22.9
Japan → East Asia & Pacific	1.2
Japan → Europe & Central Asia	0.1
Japan → European Union	1.1
Japan → Latin America & Caribbean	0.3
Japan → Middle East & North Africa	0.1
Japan → South Asia	0.1
Japan → Sub-Saharan Africa	0.1
Japan → United States	2.0
Latin America & Caribbean → East Asia & Pacific	0.1
Latin America & Caribbean → Europe & Central Asia	0.1
Latin America & Caribbean → European Union	0.7
Latin America & Caribbean → Japan	0.1
Latin America & Caribbean → Middle East & North Africa	0.1
Latin America & Caribbean → United States	3.3
Within Latin America & Caribbean	0.9
Middle East & North Africa → East Asia & Pacific	0.2
Middle East & North Africa → Europe & Central Asia	0.1
Middle East & North Africa → European Union	0.9
Middle East & North Africa → Japan	0.3
Middle East & North Africa → South Asia	0.1
Middle East & North Africa → Sub-Saharan Africa	0.1
Middle East & North Africa → United States	0.4
Within Middle East & North Africa	0.1
South Asia → East Asia & Pacific	0.1
South Asia → European Union	0.3
South Asia → United States	0.3
Within South Asia	0.1
Sub-Saharan Africa → East Asia & Pacific	0.1
Sub-Saharan Africa → European Union	0.5
Sub-Saharan Africa → United States	0.3
Within Sub-Saharan Africa	0.2

Record 2 continued

Direction of flow (export region → import region)*	Amount of trade in % world trade** 2001
United States → East Asia & Pacific	0.7
United States → Europe & Central Asia	0.2
United States → European Union	2.6
United States → Japan	0.9
United States → Latin America & Caribbean	2.6
United States → Middle East & North Africa	0.2
United States → South Asia	0.1
United States → Sub-Saharan Africa	0.1

* European Union countries: Austria, Belgium, Denmark, Finland, France, Germany, Greece, Ireland, Italy, Luxembourg, The Netherlands, Portugal, Spain, Sweden, United Kingdom. All other regions represented in the diagram comprise the countries listed in Record 1.
** Only flows amounting to at least 0.1% of total world trade are included in this table. Flows not associated with a region are also excluded from the table. Figures do not therefore sum to 100%.

Source: World Bank, World Development Indicators 2003: table 6.2. Direction and growth of merchandise trade; Direction of trade (% of world trade), 2001.

Record 2 continued

Changes in trade network centrality, 2000–2001

Node	Region	Network centrality 2000	2001	Change in centrality (% change) 2000–2001
AF	Sub-Saharan Africa	7.7	8.0	3
SA	South Asia	9.5	8.0	-16
LA	Latin America & Caribbean	9.5	9.7	2
CA	Europe & Central Asia	9.5	10.5	11
MA	Middle East & North Africa	12.0	11.6	-3
JP	Japan	13.0	12.3	-5
EA	East Asia & Pacific	13.0	13.3	3
EU	European Union	13.0	13.3	3
US	United States	13.0	13.3	3
Network centralisation		2.1	2.5	19

AF Sub-Saharan Africa
CA Europe & Central Asia
EA East Asia & Pacific
EU European Union
JP Japan
LA Latin America & Caribbean
MA Middle East & North Africa
SA South Asia
US United States

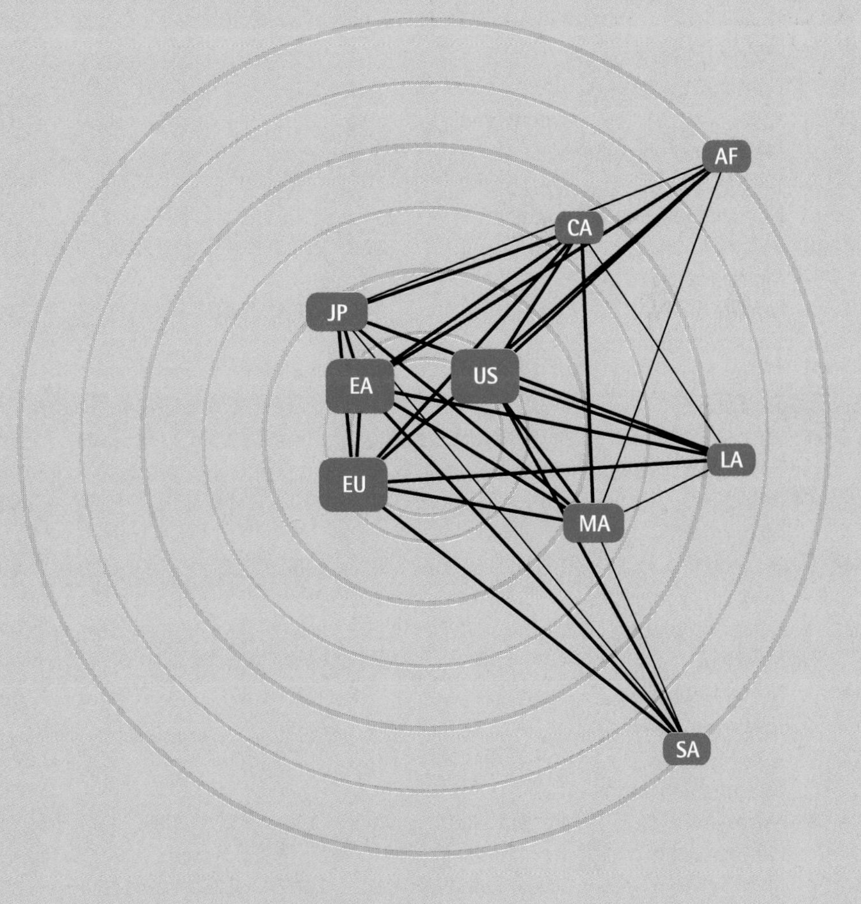

Record 3 Transnationality of top 100 transnational corporations (TNCs)

This record suggests the importance of TNCs, and the globalised economy they create, as a major reference point for the development of global civil society—from the growing numbers and influence of highly mobile groups of managers and professionals working for TNCs to activists protesting against certain corporate practices and cultures. The names and global headquarter countries for the 100 largest non-financial corporations are listed, alongside figures on their sizes and foreign shares of assets, sales, and employment for 2001. TNCs are listed in order of degree of transnationality, with the most transnational companies at the top, where higher index numbers (and lower rank numbers) indicate an overall greater extent of transnationality. The table shows that the majority of large TNCs are located in North America and Western Europe, with a few in South-East Asia and only one in Latin America.

Ranking by Transnationality Index (TNI)*				US $ billions and number of employees, 2001									
				Assets			Sales			Employment			
2001	2000	Corporation & Industry	Country	Foreign	Total	% Foreign	Foreign	Total	% Foreign	Foreign	Total	% Foreign	TNI* (%)
1	-	NTL Incorporated Telecommunications	United States	16.8	16.8	99.9	3.7	3.7	100.0	19,178	19,200	99.9	99.9
2	2	Thomson Corporation Printing & publishing	Canada	17.8	18.4	96.8	7.1	7.2	97.9	43,338	44,000	98.5	97.7
3	3	ABB Machinery & equipment	Switzerland	30.6	32.3	94.7	18.9	19.4	97.4	148,486	156,865	94.7	95.6
4	-	Holcim AG Non-metallic mineral products	Switzerland	15.0	16.1	93.3	7.5	8.2	91.2	44,613	47,362	94.2	92.9
5	18	Roche Group Pharmaceuticals	Switzerland	22.8	25.3	90.1	17.2	17.5	98.2	55,451	63,717	87.0	91.8
6	-	Lafarge SA Construction materials	France	24.9	26.5	94.0	10.5	12.3	85.8	73,940	82,892	89.2	89.7
7	10	Philips Electronics Electrical & electronic equipment	Netherlands	29.4	34.1	86.3	27.6	29.0	95.2	157,661	188,643	83.6	88.4
8	21	WPP Group Plc Business services	United Kingdom	12.0	14.4	83.5	27.9	30.3	92.0	43,690	50,487	86.5	87.4
9	25	Pearson Plc Media	United Kingdom	10.9	11.6	94.0	5.2	6.1	84.2	23,291	29,027	80.2	86.2
10	19	Diageo Plc Food & beverages	United Kingdom	19.7	26.3	75.1	13.7	16.0	85.8	59,868	62,124	96.4	85.8
11	11	News Corporation Media	Australia	35.7	40.0	89.1	13.9	15.1	92.0	24,700	33,800	73.1	84.7
12	-	Nortel Networks Telecommunications	Canada	17.5	21.1	82.7	16.6	17.5	94.6	38,800	52,600	73.8	83.7
13	15	Vodafone Telecommunications	United Kingdom	187.8	207.5	90.5	24.6	32.7	75.1	56,430	67,178	84.0	83.2
14	9	Astrazeneca Plc Pharmaceuticals	United Kingdom	12.8	18.0	71.0	15.5	16.5	94.1	42,400	52,600	80.6	81.9
15	24	BP Petroleum	United Kingdom	111.2	141.2	78.8	141.2	175.4	80.5	90,500	110,150	82.2	80.5
16	17	Danone Groupe SA Food & beverages	France	11.4	15.1	75.5	10.0	13.0	76.7	88,285	100,560	87.8	80.0

Record 3 continued

Ranking by TNI*				US $ billions and number of employees, 2001									
				Assets			Sales			Employment			
2001	2000	Corporation & Industry	Country	Foreign	Total	% Foreign	Foreign	Total	% Foreign	Foreign	Total	% Foreign	TNI* (%)
17	22	Stora Enso Oy Paper	Finland	13.5	18.2	74.0	11.4	12.1	94.3	29,221	44,275	66.0	78.1
18	23	Suez Electricity, gas & water	France	69.3	79.3	87.5	29.9	38.0	78.8	128,750	188,050	68.5	78.2
19	-	Reed Elsevier Publishing & printing	Netherlands/ United Kingdom	12.3	14.3	86.3	4.9	6.6	73.5	25,500	34,600	73.7	77.8
20	4	Nestlé SA Food & beverages	Switzerland	33.1	55.8	59.2	34.7	50.7	68.4	223,324	229,765	97.2	75.0
21	62	TotalFinaElf Petroleum	France	70.0	78.5	89.2	74.6	94.4	79.1	69,037	122,025	56.6	74.9
22	28	Volvo AB Motor vehicles	Sweden	15.9	24.4	65.1	17.0	18.3	92.8	47,463	72,031	65.9	74.6
23	-	Nokia Telecommunications	Finland	12.6	19.9	63.4	27.6	28.0	98.5	35,470	57,716	61.5	74.5
24	50	AES Corporation Electricity, gas & water	United States	23.9	36.7	65.1	5.8	9.3	62.3	35,000	38,000	92.1	73.2
25	8	Anglo American Mining & quarrying	United Kingdom	15.8	25.5	62.1	13.5	19.3	70.1	175,000	204,000	85.8	72.7
26	-	BHP Billiton Group Mining & quarrying	Australia	19.9	29.6	67.3	14.8	17.8	83.4	33,070	51,037	64.8	71.8
27	33	Compagnie De Saint-Gobain SA Construction materials	France	20.0	28.5	70.1	19.1	27.2	70.1	130,000	173,329	75.0	71.7
28	-	National Grid Transco Electricity, gas & water	United Kingdom	19.1	24.8	76.8	3.8	6.3	60.7	10,154	13,236	76.7	71.4
29	53	GlaxoSmithkline Plc Pharmaceuticals	United Kingdom	20.3	31.8	63.9	27.3	29.7	92.0	60,962	107,470	56.7	70.9
30	40	Cemex S.A. Construction materials	Mexico	12.6	16.3	77.7	4.4	6.7	65.2	17,449	25,519	68.4	70.4
31	36	Cable & Wireless Plc Telecommunications	United Kingdom	16.7	23.3	71.6	5.0	8.5	58.5	27,750	35,561	78.0	69.4
32	27	Coca-Cola Company Food & beverages	United States	17.1	22.4	76.1	12.6	20.1	62.5	26,147	38,341	68.2	68.9
33	14	Royal Ahold NV Retail	Netherlands	20.0	28.6	69.9	40.2	59.7	67.3	183,851	270,739	67.9	68.4
34	5	British American Tobacco Plc Tobacco	United Kingdom	10.4	16.4	63.1	11.6	17.4	66.9	59,358	81,425	72.9	67.7
35	49	Unilever Diversified	United Kingdom/ Netherlands	30.5	46.9	65.1	28.7	46.8	61.3	204,000	279,000	73.1	66.5
36	42	Vivendi Universal Diversified	France	91.1	123.2	74.0	29.7	51.4	57.7	256,725	381,504	67.3	66.3

Ranking by TNI*				US $ billions and number of employees, 2001									
				Assets			Sales			Employment			
2001	2000	Corporation & Industry	Country	Foreign	Total	% Foreign	Foreign	Total	% Foreign	Foreign	Total	% Foreign	TNI* (%)
37	-	Singtel Ltd. Telecommunications	Singapore	15.6	19.1	81.6	1.4	4.1	33.6	17,574	21,535	81.6	65.6
38	52	Hutchison Whampoa Limited Diversified	Hong Kong, China	41.0	55.3	74.1	6.1	11.4	53.4	53,478	77,253	69.2	65.6
39	30	Exxonmobil Corporation Petroleum	United States	89.4	143.2	62.5	145.8	209.4	69.6	61,148	97,900	62.5	64.8
40	56	Aventis SA Pharmaceuticals	France	26.4	34.8	75.9	13.4	20.6	65.0	47,968	91,729	52.3	64.4
41	-	LVMH Moët-Hennessy Louis Vuitton SA Luxury goods	France	10.2	21.1	48.3	8.9	11.0	81.2	34,095	53,795	63.4	64.3
42	26	Alcatel Machinery & equipment	France	17.4	32.4	53.6	15.8	22.7	69.5	68,191	99,314	68.7	63.9
43	-	Bertelsmann Media	Germany	12.8	21.0	60.7	11.8	17.0	69.6	48,426	80,296	60.3	63.5
44	43	Honda Motor Co Ltd Motor vehicles	Japan	35.3	52.1	67.7	40.1	56.0	71.6	59,000	120,600	48.9	62.8
45	41	Carrefour SA Retail	France	29.3	41.2	71.3	31.5	62.3	50.6	235,894	358,501	65.8	62.6
46	1	Rio Tinto Plc Mining & quarrying	United Kingdom/ Australia	10.9	19.6	55.3	6.1	10.4	58.0	26,384	36,141	73.0	62.1
47	80	Toyota Motor Corporation Motor vehicles	Japan	68.4	144.8	47.2	59.9	108.8	55.0	186,911	246,702	75.8	59.3
48	46	Royal Dutch/ Shell Group Petroleum	United Kingdom/ Netherlands	73.5	111.5	65.9	73.0	135.2	54.0	52,109	89,939	57.9	59.3
49	39	McDonald's Corporation Restaurants	United States	12.8	22.5	56.6	8.5	14.9	57.4	251,023	395,000	63.6	59.2
50	-	Ericsson LM Telecommunications	Sweden	9.7	24.1	40.4	17.5	22.4	77.8	47,870	85,198	56.2	58.1
51	23	Volkswagen Group Motor vehicles	Germany	47.5	92.5	51.3	57.4	79.4	72.3	157,579	324,413	48.6	57.4
52	55	Telefonica SA Telecommunications	Spain	48.1	77.0	62.5	14.3	27.8	51.5	93,517	161,527	57.9	57.3
53	48	Sony Corporation Electrical & electronic equipment	Japan	26.9	61.4	43.9	38.6	57.6	67.0	99,300	168,000	59.1	56.7
54	37	BASF AG Chemicals	Germany	20.9	32.7	63.9	17.1	29.1	58.7	41,606	92,545	45.0	55.9

Record 3 continued

Ranking by TNI* 2001	2000	Corporation & Industry	Country	Assets Foreign	Assets Total	Assets % Foreign	Sales Foreign	Sales Total	Sales % Foreign	Employment Foreign	Employment Total	Employment % Foreign	TNI* (%)
				US $ billions and number of employees, 2001									
55	67	Conoco Inc. Petroleum	United States	19.4	27.9	69.5	17.5	38.7	45.3	10,362	20,033	51.7	55.5
56	-	Amerada Hess Corporation Petroleum	United States	10.7	15.4	69.8	3.6	13.4	26.8	7,560	10,838	69.8	55.4
57	93	ChevronTexaco Corp. Petroleum	United States	44.9	77.6	57.9	57.7	104.4	55.2	35,569	67,569	52.6	55.3
58	31	Bayer AG Pharmaceuticals/chemicals	Germany	20.3	32.8	61.8	15.8	27.1	58.1	52,300	116,900	44.7	54.9
59	-	Pinault-Printemps Redoute SA Retail	France	18.3	31.0	59.0	13.6	24.9	54.7	54,231	107,571	50.4	54.7
60	51	BMW AG Motor vehicles	Germany	29.9	45.4	65.8	25.3	34.5	73.4	23,338	97,275	24.0	54.4
61	58	Hewlett-Packard Electrical & electronic equipment	United States	17.0	32.6	52.2	26.4	45.2	58.4	44,992	86,200	52.2	54.2
62	69	Motorola Inc Telecommunications	United States	18.1	33.4	54.2	16.1	30.0	53.5	57,720	111,000	52.0	53.2
63	47	Fiat Spa Motor vehicles	Italy	48.7	89.3	54.6	24.9	52.0	47.8	103,565	198,764	52.1	51.5
64	63	LG Electronics Inc. Electrical & electronic equipment	Korea, Rep.	11.6	20.3	56.9	10.0	22.5	44.4	21,017	42,512	49.4	50.3
65	57	IBM Electrical & electronic equipment	United States	32.8	88.3	37.1	50.7	85.9	59.0	173,969	319,876	54.4	50.2
66	61	Dow Chemical Company Pharmaceuticals/chemicals	United States	14.5	35.5	40.9	16.1	27.8	57.8	26,161	52,689	49.7	49.4
67	-	Scottish Power Electricity, gas and water	United Kingdom	13.2	23.3	56.7	4.5	9.1	49.9	6,349	15,758	40.3	49.0
68	59	Pfizer Inc Pharmaceuticals	United States	18.2	39.2	46.4	12.3	32.3	38.2	54,000	90,000	60.0	48.2
69	87	Repsol YPF SA Petroleum	Spain	27.0	45.6	59.3	13.8	39.1	35.1	16,455	35,452	46.4	47.0
70	66	Nissan Motor Co Ltd Motor vehicles	Japan	24.4	54.1	45.1	29.1	47.1	61.7	37,417	125,099	29.9	45.6
71	-	Thyssenkrupp AG Metal & metal products	Germany	14.0	31.6	44.4	15.4	33.8	45.7	88,221	193,516	45.6	45.2
72	79	Texas Utilities Company Electricity, gas and water	United States	18.0	42.3	42.5	13.5	27.9	48.5	7,869	18,301	43.0	44.7
73	60	Procter & Gamble Diversified	United States	17.3	40.8	42.5	19.0	40.2	47.3	43,381	102,000	42.5	44.1

Record 3 continued

Ranking by TNI* 2001	2000	Corporation & Industry	Country	Assets Foreign	Assets Total	Assets % Foreign	Sales Foreign	Sales Total	Sales % Foreign	Employment Foreign	Employment Total	Employment % Foreign	TNI* (%)
				US $ billions and number of employees, 2001									
74	78	Matsushita Electric Industrial Co Ltd Electrical & electronic equipment	Japan	15.7	57.2	27.5	26.8	52.3	51.3	142,984	267,196	53.5	44.1
75	74	ENI Group Petroleum	Italy	29.9	55.6	53.9	19.4	43.9	44.3	26,570	80,178	33.1	43.8
76	54	Renault SA Motor vehicles	France	15.4	44.4	34.8	19.8	32.6	60.8	48,826	140,417	34.8	43.5
77	-	MMO2 Telecommunications	United Kingdom	16.7	31.6	53.0	2.1	6.1	33.6	6,366	15,116	42.1	42.9
78	-	Du Pont (E.I.) De Nemours Pharmaceuticals/chemicals	United States	15.5	40.3	38.5	12.7	24.7	51.2	30,441	79,000	38.5	42.8
79	-	Alcoa Metal & metal products	United States	10.0	28.4	35.1	7.9	22.9	34.4	72,500	129,000	56.2	41.9
80	-	Abbott Laboratories Pharmaceuticals	United States	10.3	23.3	44.2	6.0	16.3	37.1	31,537	71,426	44.2	41.8
81	86	RWE Group Electricity, gas and water	Germany	32.8	81.0	40.5	23.2	58.0	39.9	65,609	155,634	42.2	40.8
82	-	Deutsche Telekom AG Telecommunications	Germany	90.7	145.8	62.2	11.8	43.3	27.3	78,722	257,058	30.6	40.0
83	73	General Electric Electrical & electronic equipment	United States	180.0	495.2	36.4	39.9	125.9	31.7	152,000	310,000	49.0	39.0
84	70	Johnson & Johnson Pharmaceuticals	United States	10.9	38.5	28.3	12.8	33.0	38.8	50,645	101,800	49.7	38.9
85	85	Ford Motor Company Motor vehicles	United States	81.2	276.5	29.4	53.0	162.4	32.6	188,919	354,431	53.3	38.4
86	77	E.On Electricity, gas & water	Germany	34.0	87.8	38.7	22.7	71.4	31.8	64,285	151,953	42.3	37.6
87	84	General Motors Motor vehicles	United States	75.4	324.0	23.3	45.3	177.3	25.5	148,000	365,000	40.5	29.8
88	90	Mitsubishi Corporation Motor vehicles	Japan	16.6	61.1	27.1	15.8	100.6	15.7	18,779	44,034	42.6	28.5
89	-	International Paper Company Paper	United States	9.5	37.2	25.7	5.8	26.4	22.0	37,000	100,000	37.0	28.2
90	94	Philip Morris Companies Inc Diversified	United States	19.3	85.0	22.8	33.9	89.9	37.7	39,831	175,000	22.8	27.8
91	-	Electricité De France Electricity, gas & water	France	28.1	120.1	23.4	12.5	36.5	34.2	38,066	162,491	23.4	27.0

Record 3 continued

Ranking by TNI*				US $ billions and number of employees, 2001									
				Assets			Sales			Employment			
2001	2000	Corporation & Industry	Country	Foreign	Total	% Foreign	Foreign	Total	% Foreign	Foreign	Total	% Foreign	TNI* (%)
92	81	Merck & Co Pharmaceuticals	United States	10.8	44.0	24.4	7.8	47.7	16.4	27,700	78,100	35.5	25.4
93	99	Mirant Corp. Electricity, gas and water	United States	9.7	22.8	42.8	5.0	31.5	15.7	1,600	10,000	16.0	24.8
94	89	Mitsui & Co Ltd Wholesale trade	Japan	14.7	50.0	29.5	25.6	96.2	26.6	6,308	36,116	17.5	24.5
95	91	Wal-Mart Stores Retail	United States	26.3	83.5	31.5	35.5	217.8	16.3	303,000	1,383,000	21.9	23.2
96	96	Deutsche Post AG Transport and storage	Germany	20.8	138.8	15.0	9.8	29.9	32.9	52,680	276,235	19.1	22.3
97	93	DaimlerChrysler AG Motor vehicles	Germany/ United States	25.8	183.8	14.0	43.6	137.1	31.8	76,441	372,470	20.5	22.1
98	95	Hitachi Ltd Electrical & electronic equipment	Japan	12.8	70.4	18.1	14.1	60.8	23.3	72,849	321,517	22.7	21.4
99	-	Bell Canada Enterprises Telecommunications	Canada	9.9	34.2	29.0	2.1	14.0	14.7	11,250	75,000	15.0	19.6
100	100	Verizon Communications Telecommunications	United States	10.2	170.8	5.9	2.5	67.2	3.8	10,012	250,309	4.0	4.6

*TNI = Transnationality Index (average of the ratios of foreign to total assets, sales and employment).

List includes non-financial TNCs only.
Definitions of 'foreign' are not straightforward for some TNCs; see notes accompanying this information in World Investment Report for more details.

Source: UNCTAD, World Investment Report 2003: FDI Policies for Development: National and International Perspectives, Annex table A.I.1. The world's top 100 non-financial TNCs, ranked by foreign assets, 2001, pp. 187–188, www.unctad.org/en/docs/wir2003annexes_en.pdf

Record 4 Trafficking in persons

One of the major vehicles and consequences of globalisation is the flow of people across national boundaries. One such flow, albeit a negative aspect of globalisation, is trafficking of people. Trafficking is defined as 'the recruitment, harbouring, transportation, provision, or obtaining of a person for labour or services, through the use of force, fraud or coercion for the purpose of subjection to involuntary servitude, peonage, debt bondage, or slavery'. While no accurate quantitative data exists (the US government estimates up to 900,000 people are trafficked annually worldwide), the US State Department does issue a report that provides a qualitative assessment of the forms and scope of trafficking by country. In the table below, a country is designated 'yes' if the report lists it as an origin of trafficking, as a transit country for trafficked people, or as a destination for trafficking. The report also identifies countries where internal trafficking exists. The table reveals that low- and middle-income economies, especially in Africa, Latin America and Eastern Europe, are the main sources of trafficking, while high-income economies are usually destinations of trafficking.

	International trafficking			Internal trafficking
Country	**Source**	**Transit**	**Destination**	
East Asia & Pacific				
Low income economies				
Cambodia	yes		yes	yes
Indonesia	yes	yes	yes	yes
Korea, Dem. Rep.				
Laos	yes			
Mongolia				
Myanmar				
Papua New Guinea				
Solomon Islands				
Vietnam	yes	yes	yes	
Middle income economies				
China & Tibet*				
Fiji				
Malaysia	yes	yes	yes	
Philippines	yes	yes	yes	yes
Samoa				
Thailand	yes	yes	yes	
Tonga				
Vanuatu				
High income economies				
Australia				
Brunei			yes	
Korea, Rep.				
Japan			yes	
New Zealand				
Singapore				
Europe & Central Asia				
Low income economies				
Armenia	yes			
Azerbaijan				
Georgia	yes			
Kyrgyztan				
Moldova				
Tajikistan	yes		yes	

Record 4 continued

Country	International trafficking Source	Transit	Destination	Internal trafficking
Ukraine	yes			yes
Uzbekistan	yes	yes		
Middle income economies				
Albania	yes	yes		
Belarus	yes	yes		
Bosnia & Herzegovina				
Bulgaria	yes	yes		
Croatia	yes	yes	yes	
Czech Republic	yes	yes	yes	yes
Estonia	yes			yes
Hungary	yes	yes		
Kazakhstan	yes	yes	yes	yes
Latvia	yes	yes		yes
Lithuania	yes	yes	yes	
Macedonia		yes	yes	
Poland	yes	yes	yes	yes
Romania	yes	yes		
Russian Federation				
Serbia & Montenegro	yes	yes	yes	
Slovakia				
Slovenia	yes	yes	yes	
Turkey		yes	yes	
Turkmenistan				
High income economies				
Austria		yes	yes	
Belgium		yes	yes	
Cyprus				
Denmark		yes	yes	
Finland		yes	yes	
France		yes	yes	
Germany		yes	yes	
Greece		yes	yes	
Iceland				
Ireland				
Italy		yes	yes	
Luxembourg				
Netherlands				
Norway			yes	
Portugal			yes	yes
Spain		yes	yes	
Sweden			yes	
Switzerland		yes	yes	
United Kingdom		yes	yes	
Latin America & Caribbean				
Low income economies				
Haiti	yes	yes	yes	yes
Nicaragua	yes	yes		

Record 4 continued

Country	International trafficking			Internal trafficking
	Source	Transit	Destination	
Middle income economies				
Argentina				
Barbados				
Belize			yes	
Bolivia	yes	yes		yes
Brazil	yes			yes
Chile				
Colombia	yes			yes
Costa Rica			yes	yes
Cuba				yes
Dominican Republic	yes	yes	yes	yes
Ecuador				
El Salvador	yes	yes	yes	yes
Guatemala	yes	yes	yes	yes
Guyana				
Honduras	yes	yes		yes
Jamaica		yes		yes
Mexico	yes	yes		yes
Panama				
Paraguay				
Peru				
St. Lucia				
Suriname		yes	yes	
Trinidad & Tobago				
Uruguay				
Venezuela	yes	yes	yes	yes
High income economies				
Bahamas				
Middle East & North Africa				
Low income economies				
Yemen				
Middle income economies				
Algeria				
Djibouti				
Egypt				
Iran				
Iraq				
Jordan				
Lebanon			yes	
Libya				
Malta				
Morocco	yes	yes		yes
Oman				
Saudi Arabia			yes	
Syria				
Tunisia				
High income economies				
Bahrain			yes	

Record 4 continued

Country	International trafficking			Internal trafficking
	Source	Transit	Destination	
Israel			yes	
Kuwait			yes	
Qatar			yes	
United Arab Emirates			yes	
North America				
High income economies				
Canada		yes	yes	
United States				
South Asia				
Low income economies				
Afghanistan				
Bangladesh	yes	yes		yes
Bhutan				
India	yes	yes	yes	yes
Nepal	yes			yes
Pakistan	yes	yes	yes	yes
Middle income economies				
Maldives				
Sri Lanka	yes		yes	yes
Sub-Saharan Africa				
Low income economies				
Angola	yes	yes		yes
Benin	yes	yes	yes	
Burkina Faso	yes	yes	yes	yes
Burundi	yes		yes	yes
Cameroon	yes	yes	yes	yes
Central African Republic				
Chad				
Comoros				
Congo, Rep.				
Congo, Dem. Rep.				
Côte d'Ivoire				
Equatorial Guinea		yes	yes	
Eritrea				
Ethiopia	yes			yes
Gambia				
Ghana	yes	yes	yes	yes
Guinea				
Guinea-Bissau				
Kenya	yes	yes		
Lesotho				
Liberia	yes		yes	yes
Madagascar				
Malawi	yes	yes		yes
Mali	yes	yes		yes
Mauritania				
Mozambique	yes			yes
Niger	yes	yes	yes	yes

Record 4 continued

Country	International trafficking			Internal trafficking
	Source	Transit	Destination	
Nigeria	yes	yes	yes	yes
Rwanda	yes			yes
São Tomé & Principe				
Senegal	yes	yes		
Sierra Leone	yes			yes
Somalia				
Sudan	yes		yes	yes
Tanzania	yes		yes	yes
Togo	yes		yes	yes
Uganda	yes			
Zambia	yes		yes	yes
Zimbabwe	yes	yes		yes
Middle income economies				
Botswana				
Cape Verde				
Gabon			yes	
Mauritius	yes			
Namibia				
South Africa		yes	yes	yes
Swaziland				

Lack of data for a country does not necessarily mean that it does not have a trafficking problem, but rather it may be that credible information regarding trafficking is not available. Hence, missing data should be treated with caution.

*China & Tibet excludes Hong Kong and Macao.

Source: US Department of State, (June 2003). Victims of Trafficking and Violence Protection Act of 2000: Trafficking in Persons Report, 2003. Office of the Under Secretary for Global Affairs, Office to Monitor and Combat Trafficking in Persons, Publication 11057, www.state.gov/g/tip/rls/tiprpt/2003

Record 5 Air travel and international tourism

Air travel facilitates global activism and creates economic as well as social ties. International tourism is certainly a measure of globalisation; it can be a point of contact between people from different regions and cultures. The table contains data on air transport and international tourism for 1991 and 2001, including the percentage change during this time period. The table shows general growth throughout the world in international travel, with exceptional growth in outbound tourism in low- and middle-income countries in Asia and Europe.

	Air tranport Passengers carried					International tourism Inbound tourists					Outbound tourists				
	1991		2001			1991		2001			1991		2001		
Country	Total (1000s)	Per capita	Total (1000s)	Per capita	% change in total 1991–2001	Total (1000s)	Per capita	Total (1000s)	Per capita	% change in total 1991–2001	Total (1000s)	Per capita	Total (1000s)	Per capita	% change in total 1991–2001
East Asia & Pacific															
Low income economies															
Cambodia			*125*	*0.01*		25	0.00	605	0.05	2,320					
Indonesia	10,402	0.05	10,397	0.05	0	2,570	0.01	5,154	0.02	101	797	0.00			
Korea, Dem. Rep.	223	0.01	79	0.00	-65	116	0.01								
Laos	115	0.03	211	0.04	83	17	0.00	173	0.03	918					
Mongolia	616	0.27	255	0.10	-59	147	0.06	166	0.06	13					
Myanmar	319	0.01	398	0.01	25	22	0.00	205	0.00	832					
Papua New Guinea	911	0.23	1,188	0.24	30	37	0.01	54	0.01	46	49	0.01	38	0.01	-22
Solomon Islands	69	0.20	81	0.17	17	11	0.03								
Vietnam	198	0.00	3,427	0.04	1,631	300	0.00	1,599	0.02	433					
Middle income economies															
China	19,520	0.02	72,661	0.06	272	12,464	0.01	33,167	0.03	166	2,134	0.00	12,133	0.01	469
Fiji	414	0.56	613	0.73	48	259	0.35	348	0.41	34	65	0.09	85	0.10	31
Malaysia	11,837	0.66	16,107	0.72	36	5,847	0.33	12,775	0.57	118	16,802	0.94	36,248	1.63	116
Philippines	5,438	0.08	5,652	0.07	4	951	0.01	1,797	0.02	89	1,269	0.02	1,787	0.02	41
Samoa			174	0.97		39	0.23	88	0.49	126					
Thailand	7,709	0.14	17,662	0.28	129	5,087	0.09	10,133	0.16	99	1,014	0.02	2,044	0.03	102
Tonga	35	0.38	57	0.54	64	22	0.24	32	0.31	45					
Vanuatu	53	0.34	98	0.51	84	40	0.25	53	0.27	33	9	0.06	12	0.06	33
High income economies															
Australia	21,860	1.27	33,477	1.73	53	2,370	0.14	4,856	0.25	105	2,099	0.12	3,443	0.18	64
Brunei	307	1.15	1,008	2.93	228	344	1.29	*984*	*2.86*	*186*	246	0.93			
Korea, Rep.	16,908	0.39	33,710	0.71	99	3,196	0.07	5,147	0.11	61	1,856	0.04	6,084	0.13	228
Japan	78,720	0.64	107,824	0.85	37	3,533	0.03	4,772	0.04	35	10,634	0.09	16,216	0.13	52
New Zealand	5,371	1.58	11,467	2.97	114	963	0.28	1,909	0.49	98	779	0.23	1,287	0.33	65
Singapore	7,746	2.50	16,374	3.81	111	4,913	1.59	6,726	1.56	37	1,607	0.52	4,363	1.01	171
Europe & Central Asia															
Low income economies															
Armenia			369	0.11		*15*	*0.00*	123	0.04	*720*			110	0.03	
Azerbaijan	*1,455*	*0.20*	544	0.07	*-63*	*77*	*0.01*	767	0.10	*896*			1,130	0.15	
Georgia			111	0.02				302	0.06				306	0.06	
Kyrgyztan			192	0.04											

Record 5 continued

Country	Air tranport Passengers carried 1991 Total (1000s)	1991 Per capita	2001 Total (1000s)	2001 Per capita	% change in total 1991–2001	International tourism Inbound tourists 1991 Total (1000s)	1991 Per capita	2001 Total (1000s)	2001 Per capita	% change in total 1991–2001	Outbound tourists 1991 Total (1000s)	1991 Per capita	2001 Total (1000s)	2001 Per capita	% change in total 1991–2001
Moldova	571	0.13	120	0.03	-79	226	0.05	16	0.00	-93	148	0.03	30	0.01	-80
Tajikistan			274	0.04				4	0.00				3	0.00	
Ukraine	4,906	0.09	986	0.02	-80			5,791	0.12				9,410	0.19	
Uzbekistan	4,033	0.19	2,256	0.09	-44			345	0.01				183	0.01	
Middle income economies															
Albania			146	0.04		13	0.00	34	0.01	162					
Belarus			222	0.02				61	0.01				1,386	0.13	
Bosnia & Herzegovina			65	0.02				139	0.04						
Bulgaria	646	0.07	234	0.03	-64	1,410	0.16	3,186	0.41	126	2,045	0.23	2,730	0.35	33
Croatia	113	0.02	1,063	0.25	837	1,346	0.30	6,544	1.51	386					
Czech Republic	837	0.08	2,566	0.25	206	7,565	0.73	5,194	0.51		30,660	2.98			
Estonia	146	0.09	277	0.19	89	372	0.24	1,320	0.93	255	80	0.05	1,658	1.16	1,973
Hungary	911	0.09	2,075	0.21	128	3,042	0.29	3,070	0.30	1	14,317	1.38	11,167	1.10	-22
Kazakhstan	5,273	0.31	501	0.03	-90			1,845	0.11				2,294	0.14	
Latvia	66	0.02	255	0.11	289			591	0.25				2,697	1.13	
Lithuania	557	0.15	304	0.08	-45	780	0.21	1,271	0.35	63			3,390	0.94	
Macedonia			316	0.15		294	0.15	99	0.05						
Poland	1,051	0.03	2,670	0.07	154	11,350	0.30	15,000	0.39	32	20,754	0.54	53,122	1.38	156
Romania	1,149	0.05	1,139	0.05	-1	3,000	0.13	3,300	0.15	10	9,096	0.40	6,408	0.29	-30
Russian Federation	128,761	0.87	20,301	0.14	-84	3,009	0.02	7,400	0.05	146	4,150	0.03	17,939	0.12	332
Serbia & Montenegro	1,888	0.19	1,117	0.10	-41	379	0.04	351	0.03	-7					
Slovakia			43	0.01		623	0.12	1,219	0.23	96	188	0.04	373	0.07	98
Slovenia	188	0.10	690	0.36	266	250	0.13	1,219	0.63	388			2,055	1.06	
Turkey	3,160	0.06	10,604	0.16	236	5,158	0.09	10,784	0.16	109	2,771	0.05	4,856	0.07	75
Turkmenistan			1,407	0.31											
High income economies															
Austria	2,606	0.33	6,550	0.81	151	19,092	2.44	18,180	2.24	-5	8,527	1.09	4,207	0.52	-51
Belgium	3,018	0.30	8,489	0.82	181	4,928	0.49	6,452	0.63	31	3,835	0.38	6,570	0.64	71
Cyprus	820	1.18	1,503	1.97	83	1,385	2.00	2,697	3.54	95	241	0.35	470	0.62	95
Denmark	4,582	0.89	6,382	1.19	39	2,053	0.40	2,028	0.38	-1	3,929	0.76	4,841	0.90	23
Finland	3,999	0.80	6,698	1.29	67	1,457	0.29	2,826	0.55	94	4,465	0.89	5,824	1.12	30
France	33,128	0.58	50,477	0.85	52	55,041	0.96	75,202	1.26	37	17,280	0.30	19,265	0.32	11
Germany	24,830	0.31	56,389	0.69	127	15,648	0.20	17,861	0.22	14	56,261	0.70	76,400	0.93	36
Greece	4,937	0.48	8,430	0.80	71	8,036	0.78	14,057	1.33	75	1,547	0.15			
Iceland	773	3.01	1,358	4.89	76	143	0.56	303	1.09	112	149	0.58	283	1.02	90
Ireland	4,765	1.35	15,451	4.03	224	3,571	1.01	6,353	1.66	78	1,762	0.50	4,216	1.10	139
Italy	18,847	0.33	31,031	0.54	65	25,878	0.46	39,563	0.68	53	16,152	0.28	22,421	0.39	39

Record 5 continued

Country	Air transport Passengers carried 1991 Total (1000s)	1991 Per capita	2001 Total (1000s)	2001 Per capita	% change in total 1991–2001	International tourism Inbound tourists 1991 Total (1000s)	1991 Per capita	2001 Total (1000s)	2001 Per capita	% change in total 1991–2001	Outbound tourists 1991 Total (1000s)	1991 Per capita	2001 Total (1000s)	2001 Per capita	% change in total 1991–2001
Luxembourg	406	1.05	886	1.99	118	861	2.22	829	1.86	-4			261	0.59	
Netherlands	8,893	0.59	20,073	1.25	126	5,842	0.39	9,500	0.59	63	9,400	0.62	14,220	0.89	51
Norway	8,857	2.08	14,556	3.22	64	2,114	0.50	3,073	0.68	45	384	0.09			
Portugal	3,572	0.36	6,651	0.66	86	8,657	0.87	12,167	1.21	41	218	0.02			
Spain	20,945	0.53	41,470	1.03	98	34,181	0.87	50,094	1.25	47	19,405	0.49	4,139	0.10	-79
Sweden	9,827	1.13	13,123	1.47	34	1,443	0.17	7,431	0.83	415	10,191	1.18	10,500	1.17	3
Switzerland	7,974	1.15	16,915	2.31	112	12,600	1.82	10,800	1.48	-14	9,771	1.41	11,554	1.58	18
United Kingdom	42,861	0.74	70,318	1.18	64	17,125	0.30	22,835	0.38	33	30,808	0.53	58,281	0.98	89
Latin America & Caribbean															
Low income economies															
Haiti						119	0.02	142	0.02	19					
Nicaragua	130	0.03	*61*	*0.01*	*-53*	146	0.04	483	0.10	231	189	0.05	499	0.10	164
Middle income economies															
Argentina	4,546	0.14	5,809	0.15	28	1,708	0.05	2,620	0.07	53	3,154	0.09	4,762	0.13	51
Barbados						394	1.49	507	1.84	29					
Belize						87	0.44	196	0.77	125					
Bolivia	1,200	0.18	1,557	0.19	30	206	0.03	308	0.04	50	229	0.03	240	0.03	5
Brazil	19,153	0.12	34,286	0.19	79	1,228	0.01	4,773	0.03	289	1,307	0.01	2,269	0.01	74
Chile	1,406	0.11	5,316	0.35	278	1,349	0.10	1,723	0.11	28	739	0.06	1,608	0.10	118
Colombia	5,540	0.17	9,604	0.24	73	857	0.03	616	0.02	-28	814	0.02	1,382	0.03	70
Costa Rica	508	0.16	738	0.20	45	505	0.16	1,131	0.30	124	189	0.06	*353*	*0.09*	*87*
Cuba	831	0.08	882	0.08	6	418	0.04	1,736	0.16	315	*12*	*0.00*	*56*	*0.01*	*367*
Dominican Republic	264	0.04				1,181	0.16	2,882	0.34	144	137	0.02	*364*	*0.04*	*166*
Ecuador	752	0.07	1,285	0.10	71	365	0.03	641	0.05	76	198	0.02	562	0.04	184
El Salvador	577	0.11	1,692	0.27	193	199	0.04	735	0.12	269	495	0.10	933	0.15	88
Guatemala	165	0.02				513	0.05	835	0.06	63	291	0.03	579	0.04	99
Guyana	112	0.15	48	0.07	-57	73	0.10	95	0.14	30					
Honduras	447	0.09				226	0.05	518	0.08	129	189	0.04	279	0.04	48
Jamaica	894	0.36	1,946	0.73	118	1,007	0.41	1,277	0.48	27					
Mexico	14,901	0.17	20,173	0.20	35	16,067	0.19	19,810	0.20	23	7,713	0.09	12,075	0.12	57
Panama	343	0.14	1,115	0.39	225	277	0.11	519	0.18	87	160	0.07	200	0.07	25
Paraguay	309	0.07	281	0.05	-9	361	0.08	279	0.05	-23	*264*	*0.06*	157	0.03	*-41*
Peru	1,491	0.07	1,844	0.07	24	232	0.01	797	0.03	244	377	0.02	661	0.02	75
St. Lucia						158	1.12	250	1.58	58					
Suriname	150	0.38	203	0.47	35	67	0.17	*58*	*0.13*	*-13*	*55*	*0.14*			
Trinidad & Tobago	1,345	1.13	1,388	1.24	3	220	0.18	383	0.34	74	242	0.20			
Uruguay	318	0.10	559	0.17	75	1,510	0.48	1,892	0.56	25			531	0.16	

Country	Air tranport Passengers carried					International tourism Inbound tourists					Outbound tourists				
	1991		2001			1991		2001			1991		2001		
	Total (1000s)	Per capita	Total (1000s)	Per capita	% change in total 1991–2001	Total (1000s)	Per capita	Total (1000s)	Per capita	% change in total 1991–2001	Total (1000s)	Per capita	Total (1000s)	Per capita	% change in total 1991–2001
Venezuela	6,795	0.34	6,334	0.26	-7	598	0.03	584	0.02	*-2*	425	0.02	933	0.04	120
High income economies															
Bahamas	1,090	4.19	1,626	5.55	49	1,427	5.48	1,538	5.26	8					
Middle East & North Africa															
Low income economies															
Yemen	541	0.04	841	0.05	56	44	0.00	76	0.00	73					
Middle income economies															
Algeria	3,385	0.13	3,419	0.11	1	1,193	0.05	901	0.03	-24	3,056	0.12	1,190	0.04	-61
Djibouti	131	0.35				33	0.09								
Egypt	2,595	0.04	4,389	0.06	69	2,112	0.04	4,357	0.06	106	2,102	0.04	3,074	0.04	46
Iran	5,538	0.09	9,533	0.14	72	212	0.00	1,402	0.02	561	1,178	0.02	2,400	0.04	104
Iraq	28	0.00				268	0.02	127	0.01	-53	220	0.01			
Jordan	797	0.22	1,178	0.23	48	437	0.12	1,478	0.29	238	859	0.24	1,755	0.34	104
Lebanon	536	0.17	816	0.22	52	*210*	*0.07*	837	0.23	*299*					
Libya	1,884	0.44	583	0.11	-69	90	0.02	*174*	*0.03*	*93*	290	0.07			
Malta	649	1.79	1,340	3.40	107	895	2.47	1,180	2.99	32	115	0.32	179	0.45	56
Morocco	1,430	0.06	3,681	0.12	157	4,162	0.16	4,223	0.14	1	1,243	0.05	1,887	0.06	52
Oman	958	0.52	1,980	0.76	107	161	0.09	562	0.21	249					
Saudi Arabia	9,409	0.59	12,836	0.56	36	2,094	0.13	6,727	0.30	221					
Syria	661	0.05	761	0.05	15	622	0.05	1,318	0.08	112	996	0.08	3,492	0.21	251
Tunisia	1,201	0.14	1,926	0.20	60	3,224	0.39	5,387	0.56	67	2,084	0.25	1,669	0.17	-20
High income economies															
Bahrain	876	1.70	1,250	1.94	43	1,674	3.25	2,789	4.32	67	*147*	*0.29*			
Israel	2,048	0.43	3,990	0.67	95	943	0.20	1,196	0.20	27	1,017	0.21	3,562	0.60	250
Kuwait	840	0.88	2,085	1.02	148	4	0.00	73	0.04	1,725	*195*	*0.20*			
Qatar	876	1.74	2,778	3.61	217	143	0.28	76	0.10	-47					
United Arab Emirates	2,042	1.02	7,676	3.19	276	717	0.36	4,134	1.72	477					
North America															
High income economies															
Canada	16,587	0.59	24,204	0.77	46	14,912	0.53	19,679	0.62	32	21,937	0.78	18,359	0.58	-16
United States	452,016	1.78	619,838	2.17	37	42,674	0.17	44,898	0.16	5	41,566	0.16	57,963	0.20	39
South Asia															
Low income economies															
Afghanistan	212	0.01	*150*	*0.01*	*-29*	*8*	*0.00*								
Bangladesh	1,021	0.01	1,450	0.01	42	113	0.00	207	0.00	83	474	0.00	1,075	0.01	127
Bhutan	8	0.00	35	0.02	339	2	0.00	6	0.00	200					
India	10,717	0.01	17,419	0.02	63	1,678	0.00	2,537	0.00	51	1,943	0.00	4,067	0.00	109
Nepal	634	0.03	641	0.03	1	293	0.01	361	0.01	23	106	0.01	200	0.01	89
Pakistan	5,198	0.04	6,012	0.04	16	438	0.00	500	0.00	14					

Record 5 continued

Country	Air tranport Passengers carried					International tourism Inbound tourists					Outbound tourists				
	1991		2001			1991		2001			1991		2001		
	Total (1000s)	Per capita	Total (1000s)	Per capita	% change in total 1991–2001	Total (1000s)	Per capita	Total (1000s)	Per capita	% change in total 1991–2001	Total (1000s)	Per capita	Total (1000s)	Per capita	% change in total 1991–2001
Middle income economies															
Maldives	9	0.04	56	0.18	498	196	0.87	461	1.48	135	24	0.11	41	0.13	71
Sri Lanka	893	0.05	1,718	0.09	92	318	0.02	337	0.02	6	310	0.02	505	0.03	63
Sub-Saharan Africa															
Low income economies															
Angola	456	0.06	193	0.02	-58	55	0.01	67	0.01	22					
Benin	66	0.01	46	0.01	-30	117	0.02	88	0.01						
Burkina Faso	127	0.01	100	0.01	-21	80	0.01	128	0.01	60					
Burundi	8	0.00				125	0.02	36	0.01	-71	27	0.01	35	0.01	30
Cameroon	357	0.03	247	0.02	-31	84	0.01	221	0.01	163					
Central African Republic	120	0.04	46	0.01	-61	8	0.00								
Chad	83	0.01	46	0.01	-44	21	0.00	57	0.01	171	*24*	*0.00*	39	0.00	*63*
Comoros	26	0.06				17	0.04	*24*	*0.04*	*41*					
Congo, Dem. Rep.	150	0.00	95	0.00	-37	33	0.00	*103*	*0.00*	*212*					
Congo, Rep.	229	0.10	*128*	*0.04*	*-44*	33	0.01	*19*	*0.01*	*-42*					
Côte d'Ivoire	178	0.01	46	0.00	-74	200	0.02				2	0.00			
Equatorial Guinea	14	0.04													
Eritrea						*169*	*0.05*	113	0.03	*-33*					
Ethiopia	636	0.01	1,028	0.02	62	82	0.00	148	0.00	80	86	0.00			
Gambia						66	0.07	75	0.05	14					
Ghana	192	0.01	301	0.02	57	172	0.01	439	0.02	155					
Guinea	42	0.01	*61*	*0.01*	*45*			38	0.00						
Guinea-Bissau	21	0.02						8	0.01						
Kenya	760	0.03	1,418	0.05	87	805	0.03	841	0.03	4	220	0.01			
Lesotho	56	0.03	*1*	*0.00*	*-98*	182	0.11								
Liberia	32	0.02													
Madagascar	314	0.03	566	0.04	80	35	0.00	170	0.01	386	33	0.00			
Malawi	120	0.01	113	0.01	-6	127	0.01	266	0.02	109					
Mali	66	0.01	46	0.00	-30	38	0.00	89	0.01	134					
Mauritania	213	0.10	156	0.06	-27			*30*	*0.01*						
Mozambique	283	0.02	264	0.01	-7										
Niger	66	0.01	46	0.00	-30	16	0.00	52	0.00	225	15	0.00			
Nigeria	930	0.01	529	0.00	-43	214	0.00	831	0.01	288	*56*	*0.00*			
Rwanda	10	0.00						113	0.02						
São Tomé & Principe	22	0.18	35	0.21	57	3	0.02	8	0.05	167					
Senegal	138	0.02	176	0.02	27	234	0.03	396	0.04	69					
Sierra Leone	*17*	*0.00*	14	0.00	*-16*	96	0.02	24	0.00	-75			20	0.00	
Somalia	46	0.01				*46*	*0.01*								

Country	Air tranport Passengers carried 1991 Total (1000s)	1991 Per capita	2001 Total (1000s)	2001 Per capita	% change in total 1991–2001	International tourism Inbound tourists 1991 Total (1000s)	1991 Per capita	2001 Total (1000s)	2001 Per capita	% change in total 1991–2001	Outbound tourists 1991 Total (1000s)	1991 Per capita	2001 Total (1000s)	2001 Per capita	% change in total 1991–2001
Sudan	363	0.01	415	0.01	14	16	0.00	50	0.00	213	219	0.01			
Tanzania	290	0.01	175	0.01	-40	187	0.01	501	0.01	168	308	0.01			
Togo	66	0.02	46	0.01	-30	65	0.02	57	0.01	-12					
Uganda	26	0.00	41	0.00	54	69	0.00	205	0.01	197			*152*	*0.01*	
Zambia	293	0.04	49	0.00	-83	171	0.02	492	0.05	188					
Zimbabwe	740	0.07	308	0.02	-58	667	0.06	2,068	0.17	210	352	0.03			
Middle income economies															
Botswana	102	0.08	170	0.11	66	592	0.44	1,049	0.66	77	257	0.19			
Cape Verde	96	0.27	243	0.60	153	20	0.06	115	0.28	475					
Gabon	436	0.45	374	0.30	-14	128	0.13	169	0.13	32	*161*	*0.17*			
Mauritius	525	0.48	1,002	0.84	91	301	0.28	660	0.55	119	86	0.08	161	0.14	87
Namibia	455	0.31	215	0.12	-53	213	0.15	670	0.36	215					
South Africa	4,819	0.13	7,948	0.19	65	1,710	0.05	5,908	0.14	245	677	0.02	3,733	0.09	451
Swaziland	59	0.06	90	0.08	51	264	0.29	283	0.25	7					

Region	International tourism Inbound tourists 1991 Total (1000s)	1991 Per capita	2001 Total (1000s)	2001 Per capita	% change in total 1991–2001	Outbound tourists 1991 Total (1000s)	1991 Per capita	2001 Total (1000s)	2001 Per capita	% change in total 1991–2001
Low income	11,073	0.01	22,914	0.01	107			*11,027*	*0.52*	
Middle income	115,769	0.05	206,435	0.08	78	150,403	0.06	273,535	0.10	82
Low & middle income										
East Asia & Pacific	28,711	0.02	67,815	0.04	136	24,324	0.01	61,131	0.03	151
Europe & Central Asia	43,763	0.09	71,430	0.15	63	*87,991*	0.19	183,289	0.39	108
Latin America & Caribbean	29,943	0.07	45,612	0.09	52	17,667	0.04	29,057	0.06	64
Middle East & North Africa	14,952	0.06	26,209	0.08	75	16,002	0.06	21,501	0.07	34
South Asia	3,096	0.00	4,494	0.00	45	3,261	0.00	6,721	0.00	106
Sub-Saharan Africa	8,134	0.02	18,388	0.03	126			*495*	*0.16*	
High income	317,013	0.35	434,986	0.45	37	223,403	0.25	347,966	0.36	56
World	452,465	0.08	674,985	0.11	49	400,769	0.07	691,330	0.11	73

Data on inbound and outbound tourists refer to numbers of arrivals and departures, not numbers of people.

Where data for a particular year are not available, figures are taken from the year before or after as an estimate. These figures, and estimates based on them, are presented in italics.

Per capita estimates (aggregate and individual country level) are calculated using total midyear country population figures from the US Bureau of the Census International Data Base.

Sources: World Bank, World Development Indicators 2003 (WDI-Online); US Census Bureau, Population Division, International Programs Center, International Data Base (IDB), www.census.gov/ipc/www/idbsprd.html

Record 6 Media and communication

Communications and news are major facilitators of globalisation, as well as of dissent against it. This record offers an indication of people's exposure to media, as well as their local and transnational communication with each other. The data show ownership of television sets and cable TV subscribers, telephone communication infrastructure, volume of cellular and international telephone communications and ownership of personal computers and Internet access, all for the latest available year and with a time comparison where feasible.

The table shows that exposure to news has grown throughout the globe. Communication also generally increased, but international communication has declined in some low- and middle-income nations. Data on computer and Internet use reveal the 'digital divide' between developed nations and the rest of the world.

	Television sets per 1000 people			Cable television subscribers per 1000 people			Main telephone lines per 1000 people			Cellular mobile telephone subscribers per 1000 people			International telecom, outgoing traffic (minutes per subscriber)			Personal Computers per 1000 people	Internet users per 1000 people
Country	1991	2001	% change 1991–2001	1996	2001	% change 1996–2001	1992	2002	% change 1992–2002	1997	2002	% change 1997–2002	1992	2002	% change 1992–2002	2002	2002
East Asia & Pacific																	
Low income economies																	
Cambodia	7.8	7.6	-3				0.4	2.6	492	3.2	27.6	764		278.4		2.0	2.2
Indonesia	71.8	153.0	113		0.3		9.0	36.5	307	4.5	55.2	1,113	13.4			11.9	37.7
Korea, Dem. Rep.	16.5	55.9	239				23.3	21.1	-9	0.0	0.0		326.0	393.9	21		
Laos	6.5	51.9	703				1.9	11.2	486	1.0	10.0	885	2.8	64.8	2,174	3.3	2.7
Mongolia	32.6	72.1	121	3.6	16.5	363	32.5	52.7	62	0.9	88.9	10,046	24.5	26.6	9	28.4	20.6
Myanmar	3.1	7.5	143				2.3	7.0	199	0.2	1.0	412	153.2	*259.9*	*70*	5.1	0.5
Papua New Guinea	2.3	20.8	796		4.2		9.1	11.7	29	0.8	2.7	233	190.0	51.6	-73	58.7	13.7
Solomon Islands	*5.9*	27.8	*367*				15.3	14.9	-3	1.7	2.2	32	58.3	*209.5*	*259*	40.5	5.0
Vietnam	41.3	186.3	351				2.2	48.4	2,098	2.1	23.4	1,017	153.4	81.0	-47	9.8	18.5
Middle income economies																	
China	170.9	312.3	83	36.1	68.6	90	9.7	166.9	1,623	10.6	160.9	1,421	55.4	*6.9*	-87	27.6	46.0
Fiji	15.2	116.9	667				66.6	119.0	79	6.6	109.7	1,561	85.7	172.2	*101*	48.8	61.0
Malaysia	148.6	201.8	36	3.3		-100	111.5	190.4	71	92.3	376.8	308	390.2	*300.1*	-23	146.8	319.7
Philippines	64.3	172.6	168	6.4	30.6	376	10.4	41.7	302	18.6	191.3	931	*583.1*			27.7	44.0
Samoa	86.8	145.6	68	1.3	0.3	-79	39.9	56.9	43	4.5	15.0	235	270.4	577.6	114	6.7	22.2
Thailand	145.1	300.4	107	6.5	2.5	-62	32.1	105.0	227	37.5	260.4	594	183.5	*164.3*	*-10*	39.8	77.6
Tonga	*10.4*	60.7	*484*				57.0	112.9	98	1.2	33.8	2,653		64.4		20.2	29.2
Vanuatu	9.2	12.2	32				23.1	32.7	42	1.2	24.2	1,970		131.6		14.8	34.6
High income economies																	
Australia	543.6	730.8	34	17.3	72.2	318	471.0	538.6	14	246.3	639.8	160	78.7	*214.6*	*173*	565.1	481.7
Brunei	238.0	628.7	164		70.2		179.6	255.7	42	146.6	*400.6*	*173*	453.9	*288.3*	*-36*	76.7	102.3
Korea, Rep.	208.6	363.3	74	148.2	132.0	-11	355.6	488.6	37	152.5	679.5	346	3.2	46.4	1,363	555.8	551.9
Japan	624.2	730.6	17	100.4	167.0	66	463.5	558.3	20	303.3	636.5	110	1.8	63.2	3,423	382.2	448.9
New Zealand	441.0	557.5	26	0.8	7.1	777	440.4	448.1	2	152.7	621.7	307	153.6	123.8	-19	413.8	484.4
Singapore	330.1	300.2	-9	15.7	73.1	366	361.7	462.9	28	223.7	795.6	256	327.2	*799.5*	*144*	622.0	504.4

Record 6 continued

Country	Television sets per 1000 people			Cable television subscribers per 1000 people			Main telephone lines per 1000 people			Cellular mobile telephone subscribers per 1000 people			International telecom, outgoing traffic (minutes per subscriber)			Personal Computers per 1000 people	Internet users per 1000 people
	1991	2001	% change 1991–2001	1996	2001	% change 1996–2001	1992	2002	% change 1992–2002	1997	2002	% change 1997–2002	1992	2002	% change 1992–2002	2002	2002
Europe & Central Asia																	
Low income economies																	
Armenia	207.1	228.8	10		1.2		157.4	142.8	-9	1.3	18.9	1,335		66.7		15.8	15.8
Azerbaijan	207.8	312.9	51	0.1	0.6	775	85.0	113.5	34	5.2	106.9	1,939		35.2		0.0	36.9
Georgia	219.8	354.3	61	2.4	5.3	118	105.1	131.4	25	5.5	102.1	1,750	115.4	189.6	64	31.6	14.9
Kyrgyzstan	20.2	48.6	140		2.6		75.4	77.5	3	0.0	10.4		146.1	172.5	18	12.7	29.8
Moldova	285.3	296.1	4	8.3	11.3	37	117.5	160.7	37	0.5	76.9	15,113	156.8	*226.2*	*44*	17.5	34.1
Tajikistan	183.2	356.7	95		*0.1*		47.9	37.3	-22	0.1	2.1	3,761	233.7	*284.3*	*22*	0.0	0.5
Ukraine	329.2	*455.8*	*38*	*15.7*	29.8	*90*	145.3	216.1	49	1.1	83.8	7,366	142.6	166.1	16	19.0	18.0
Uzbekistan	182.1	280.3	54		3.0		71.6	66.5	-7	0.7	7.4	910	720.8			0.0	10.9
Middle income economies																	
Albania	90.0	*155.1*	*72*		*2.3*		14.2	71.4	403	1.1	276.3	26,006	815.4	281.8	-65	11.7	3.9
Belarus	270.6	361.8	34		65.5		170.4	299.4	76	0.8	46.7	5,668		81.1		0.0	81.6
Bosnia & Herzegovina	88.0	*116.4*	*32*		*19.4*		140.4	236.7	69	2.4	196.3	8,152	*0.8*	*106.1*	*14,042*		26.2
Bulgaria	251.7	*453.0*	*80*	16.7	92.6	453	274.0	367.7	34	8.4	333.0	3,853	34.7	47.7	38	51.9	80.8
Croatia	220.5	*292.9*	*33*	*11.0*	*38.0*	*246*	202.0	417.2	107	26.8	535.0	1,894	110.4	197.7	79	173.8	180.4
Czech Republic	339.7	538.0	58	60.4	94.4	56	176.2	362.3	106	51.1	848.8	1,561	85.0	106.7	26	177.4	256.3
Estonia	351.1	468.5	33	12.9	97.9	657	219.7	350.6	60	98.9	650.2	557	132.3	217.3	64	210.3	327.7
Hungary	419.1	474.9	13	140.0	159.7	14	124.9	361.2	189	69.4	676.0	874	38.1	15.9	-58	108.4	157.6
Kazakhstan	223.2	338.0	51		6.6		88.5	130.4	47	0.7	64.3	9,340	187.1	*178.0*	*-5*	0.0	15.7
Latvia	379.3	839.6	121	*48.5*	116.1	*139*	248.9	301.1	21	31.1	393.8	1,167	28.9	*148.6*	*414*	171.7	133.1
Lithuania	335.2	449.6	34	34.5	65.5	90	224.2	270.3	21	44.6	475.3	965	158.9	108.5	-32	109.7	144.4
Macedonia	180.3	*281.6*	*56*				160.6	271.3	69	6.2	177.0	2,749	225.2	*434.7*	*93*	0.0	48.4
Poland	269.4	421.9	57	71.4	90.6	27	102.6	*295.1*	*188*	21.0	362.6	1,626	491.8	1323.0	169	105.6	230.0
Romania	194.9	*379.0*	*94*	103.9	120.6	16	112.8	194.4	72	8.9	235.7	2,547	492.3	*1421.5*	*189*	83.0	83.0
Russian Federation	366.9	*537.7*	*47*	78.5	42.9	-45	154.1	242.2	57	3.3	120.1	3,552	2362.3	4873.6	106	88.7	40.9
Serbia & Montenegro	173.2	*282.0*	*63*				179.6	232.6	30	8.2	256.6	3,026	371.2	1019.6	175	27.1	59.7
Slovakia	284.4	409.0	44	83.7	135.4	62	154.6	268.2	74	37.1	543.6	1,363	64.1	117.1	83	180.4	
Slovenia	289.7	365.9	26	110.8	160.4	45	247.7	506.1	104	47.2	835.3	1,671	53.2	68.3	29	300.6	375.8
Turkey	253.5	319.2	26	7.7	13.7	78	161.1	281.2	74	25.8	347.5	1,249	616.0	1732.0	181	44.6	72.8
Turkmenistan	200.0	182.0	-9				61.7	77.1	25	0.6	1.7	199	110.2	257.9	134	0.0	1.7
High income economies																	
Austria	474.6	621.4	31	103.0	127.2	24	439.2	488.8	11	143.7	786.2	447	205.8	312.4	52	369.3	409.4
Belgium	451.0	543.2	20	360.1	370.0	3	425.8	494.4	16	95.6	785.6	722	213.7	352.7	65	241.4	328.3
Cyprus	326.9	386.3	18				483.0	688.0	42	141.7	584.4	312	293.2	520.0	77	269.9	293.7
Denmark	536.3	859.0	60	236.1	201.4	-15	581.9	688.6	18	273.7	833.2	204	141.3	214.1	52	576.8	512.8
Finland	497.1	677.6	36	164.2	192.5	17	542.4	523.5	-4	420.2	867.4	106	81.4	138.6	70	441.7	508.9
France	556.6	631.9	14	36.8	54.6	48	525.9	568.9	8	99.9	647.0	547	161.9	*347.7*	*115*	347.1	313.8
Germany	503.0	637.4	27	203.6	246.2	21	437.4	650.9	49	100.9	727.5	621	149.1	212.6	43	431.3	411.9

Record 6 continued

Country	Television sets per 1000 people			Cable television subscribers per 1000 people			Main telephone lines per 1000 people			Cellular mobile telephone subscribers per 1000 people			International telecom, outgoing traffic (minutes per subscriber)			Personal Computers per 1000 people	Internet users per 1000 people
	1991	2001	% change 1991–2001	1996	2001	% change 1996–2001	1992	2002	% change 1992–2002	1997	2002	% change 1997–2002	1992	2002	% change 1992–2002	2002	2002
Greece	194.9	519.1	166				435.7	491.3	13	89.1	845.4	849		*556.9*		81.7	154.7
Iceland	412.2	*508.9*	*23*	4.4	*4.6*	*4*	534.1	652.8	22	239.6	906.0	278	76.6	37.3	-51	451.4	647.9
Ireland	297.8	394.6	33	147.5	160.2	9	313.9	502.4	60	148.9	763.2	413	62.1	*168.5*	*171*	420.8	270.9
Italy	428.2	*493.9*	*15*	0.3	1.4	427	417.0	480.7	15	204.6	938.7	359	22.3	37.1	67	230.7	352.4
Luxembourg	542.5	671.2	24	98.7	314.0	218	525.4	796.8	52	159.6	1060.5	564	70.4	115.5	64	594.2	370.0
Netherlands	484.4	552.6	14	372.6	392.4	5	487.2	617.7	27	109.7	744.7	579	124.5	546.7	339	466.6	506.3
Norway	422.3	884.2	109	151.3	185.4	22	527.7	734.4	39	379.5	843.6	122	148.5	*120.3*	*-19*	528.3	502.6
Portugal	186.5	413.4	122	17.3	108.3	527	305.1	421.3	38	151.3	825.2	445	20.4	50.3	146	134.9	193.5
Spain	401.3	564.0	41	11.2	14.5	30	353.6	506.2	43	110.3	824.2	647	147.1	384.3	161	196.0	156.3
Sweden	466.2	965.2	107	214.8	224.5	4	682.1	735.7	8	358.2	888.9	148	50.4	72.9	45	621.3	573.1
Switzerland	399.1	552.1	38	341.9	368.7	8	603.3	744.2	23	147.0	789.3	437	78.2	51.6	-34	708.7	351.0
United Kingdom	432.4	950.5	120	35.2	64.1	82	457.0	590.6	29	149.8	840.7	461		36.2		405.7	423.1
Latin America & Caribbean																	
Low income economies																	
Haiti	4.7	6.0	29		4.8		6.7	15.7	135	0.0	16.9		205.1	285.2	39	0.0	9.6
Nicaragua	65.2	122.6	88	7.6	*10.8*	*44*	13.7	32.0	133	1.7	37.8	2,128	1036.2			27.9	16.8
Middle income economies																	
Argentina	262.1	325.8	24	154.2	162.9	6	109.1	218.8	101	45.7	177.6	289	35.3	53.3	51	82.0	112.0
Barbados	263.6	328.0	24				309.3	494.4	60	30.1	*198.0*	*557*	287.4	*624.7*	*117*	104.1	111.5
Belize	153.1	182.5	19				127.7	123.7	-3	11.5	204.5	1,683	202.6	369.1	82	127.0	118.6
Bolivia	111.5	*120.6*	*8*	2.8	*9.7*	*252*	32.4	67.6	109	15.2	104.6	587	69.8	69.3	-1	22.8	32.4
Brazil	213.5	349.2	64	11.8	13.8	17	72.6	223.2	208	28.5	200.6	605	14.2	20.8	46	74.8	82.2
Chile	210.2	494.3	135	37.3	46.0	23	94.8	230.4	143	28.0	428.3	1,428	49.8	78.9	58	119.3	237.5
Colombia	106.5	286.4	169	4.5	*13.6*	*203*	77.5	179.4	131	31.6	106.2	236	33.2	*40.1*	*21*	49.3	46.2
Costa Rica	224.7	*231.2*	*3*	14.7			108.9	250.5	130	17.8	111.0	524	101.0	124.7	23	197.2	193.1
Cuba	161.8	251.0	55				31.0	*51.1*	*65*	0.3	1.6	484	15.9	*65.0*	*309*	31.8	10.7
Dominican Republic	84.0			16.0			64.2	110.4	72	17.7	206.6	1,066	145.2	244.9	69	0.0	36.4
Ecuador	86.7	225.2	160	6.8	33.8	394	49.5	110.2	123	10.6	120.6	1,038	53.8	*47.7*	*-11*	31.1	41.6
El Salvador	127.3	232.8	83	*34.2*	*49.7*	*45*	32.2	103.4	221	6.8	137.6	1,931	324.3	*242.6*	-25	25.2	46.5
Guatemala	53.6	145.5	171	24.4			22.9	70.5	207	6.1	131.5	2,054	99.3			14.4	33.3
Guyana	38.6	97.7	153				35.0	91.5	162	1.7	99.3	5,887	185.1	*228.7*	24	27.3	142.2
Honduras	73.2	122.4	67	7.7	*8.0*	*4*	19.3	48.1	149	2.3	48.7	1,994	142.9	65.5	-54	13.6	25.2
Jamaica	134.4	373.6	178	73.9			69.6	169.7	144	26.3	534.8	1,935	165.7	294.1	77	53.7	229.2
Mexico	145.2	282.0	94	15.3	24.8	62	75.4	146.7	94	18.2	254.5	1,296	142.6	123.7	-13	82.0	98.5
Panama	168.0	193.9	15	*11.4*			97.5	122.0	25	6.8	189.5	2,682	52.7	82.0	55	38.3	41.4
Paraguay	57.7	*218.3*	*278*	8.1	21.3	164	28.3	47.3	67	16.6	288.3	1,640	54.0	*73.1*	*35*	34.6	17.3
Peru	97.7	149.5	53	4.2	16.7	296	27.3	66.0	141	17.3	86.2	398	71.6	124.2	74	43.0	93.5
St. Lucia	195.0	296.0	52	*49.1*			149.7	319.5	113	10.8	89.5	725	190.5	336.1	76	150.0	82.4
Suriname	136.0	261.4	92	6.1	4.5	-25	106.4	163.5	54	5.5	225.2	4,017	42.9	*89.9*	*110*	45.5	41.6
Trinidad & Tobago	332.5	345.4	4				150.1	249.8	66	13.5	278.1	1,966	115.5	*124.7*	*8*	79.5	106.0
Uruguay	417.7	*530.4*	*27*	62.4	*125.9*	*102*	157.2	279.6	78	30.6	192.6	530	52.4	17.1	-67	110.1	119.0
Venezuela	166.8	186.1	12	8.8	39.5	349	89.6	112.7	26	46.7	256.4	450	153.6	155.3	1	60.9	50.6

Record 6 continued

Country	Television sets per 1000 people			Cable television subscribers per 1000 people			Main telephone lines per 1000 people			Cellular mobile telephone subscribers per 1000 people			International telecom, outgoing traffic (minutes per subscriber)			Personal Computers per 1000 people	Internet users per 1000 people
	1991	2001	% change 1991–2001	1996	2001	% change 1996–2001	1992	2002	% change 1992–2002	1997	2002	% change 1997–2002	1992	2002	% change 1992–2002	2002	2002
High income economies																	
Bahamas	227.0	247.6	9				291.1	405.6	39	21.3	390.3	1,733	497.4	*545.8*	*10*	0.0	192.3
Middle East & North Africa																	
Low income economies																	
Yemen	273.4	281.5	3				11.5	27.8	142	0.7	21.1	2,738	0.0	0.0		7.4	5.1
Middle income economies																	
Algeria	74.1	113.5	53				36.6	61.0	66	0.6	12.8	2,034	122.6	*111.3*	*-9*	7.7	16.0
Djibouti	43.5	77.6	78	15.3			12.6	15.4	23	0.3	22.9	6,636	703.6	563.0	-20	15.2	6.9
Egypt	123.5	230.8	87				36.6	110.4	201	1.1	66.8	6,064	36.3	36.1	0	16.6	28.2
Iran	67.2	170.9	154				52.9	186.6	253	3.9	33.5	753	266.5	706.3	165	75.0	48.5
Iraq	72.9	*82.8*	*14*				37.6	27.8	-26	0.0	0.8		84.9	385.1	354		1.0
Jordan	132.7	177.2	34	0.1	*0.3*	*106*	72.4	126.6	75	9.8	228.9	2,238	107.8	*74.8*	*-31*	37.5	57.7
Lebanon	346.7	356.7	3	0.4	29.9	7,572	153.8	198.8	29	118.9	227.0	91	508.9	*867.6*	*70*	80.5	117.1
Libya	98.8	*137.4*	*39*				48.4	*118.3*	*144*	1.8	12.6	600	4.5	36.2	703	23.4	22.5
Malta	332.2	566.2	70	137.7	229.8	67	414.5	523.4	26	46.7	699.1	1,398	645.5	*394.3*	*-39*	255.1	209.3
Morocco	144.9	166.7	15				25.6	38.0	49	2.7	209.1	7,627	699.1	499.1	-29	23.6	23.6
Oman	629.6	550.9	-12				68.3	83.9	23	25.5	171.5	571	592.2	*401.6*	*-32*	37.4	66.4
Saudi Arabia	247.9	264.6	7		*0.3*		92.6	143.9	55	17.0	217.2	1,175	179.3	*392.8*	*119*	136.7	61.5
Syria	61.5	172.2	180				39.6	123.2	211	0.0	23.5		502.4	349.4	-30	19.4	12.9
Tunisia	150.3	206.8	38				44.2	117.4	166	0.8	51.5	6,101	*4.9*	36.3	*647*	30.7	51.7
High income economies																	
Bahrain	423.2	430.5	2	*5.5*	11.8	*116*	216.1	263.1	22	99.3	583.3	487	608.3	1136.5	87	160.4	247.5
Israel	262.0	330.4	26	166.7	183.9	10	345.9	467.2	35	283.2	954.5	237	332.7	310.2	-7	242.6	301.4
Kuwait	333.7	417.6	25				194.6	203.8	5	106.1	519.0	389	95.1	*137.8*	*45*	120.6	105.8
Qatar	398.0	868.9	118	40.6	56.3	39	206.8	289.4	40	76.4	438.0	473	239.8	*245.3*	*2*	178.2	114.8
United Arab Emirates	138.9	251.6	81				241.0	313.5	30	130.0	696.1	436	62.2	*87.3*	*40*	119.9	337.0
North America																	
High income economies																	
Canada	632.0	690.6	9	273.0	252.9	-7	588.6	635.5	8	146.7	377.2	157	134.7	254.0	89	487.0	512.8
United States	774.4	937.5	21	241.4	256.2	6	562.3	645.8	15	204.0	488.1	139		*416.4*		658.9	551.4
South Asia																	
Low income economies																	
Afghanistan	8.9	14.2	59				1.8	1.4	-20	0.0	0.5		16.5				0.0
Bangladesh	8.8	50.3	475		*27.0*		2.0	5.1	153	0.2	8.1	3,740	53.2	*77.1*	*45*	3.4	1.5
Bhutan		26.7			13.5		5.6	28.4	410	0.0	0.0		*181.7*	*353.2*	*94*	14.5	14.5
India	34.8	82.8	138	18.1	38.9	115	7.7	39.8	415	0.9	12.2	1,219	43.8	21.3	-51	7.2	15.9
Nepal	2.2	8.5	292	0.2			3.6	14.1	288	0.0	0.9		204.3	*375.7*	*84*	3.7	3.4
Pakistan	29.4	150.2	411	0.1	*0.2*	*201*	10.4	25.0	140	1.0	8.5	714	107.2	103.9	-3	4.2	10.3
Middle income economies																	
Maldives	40.1	119.1	197				37.8	102.0	170	5.1	149.1	2,838	128.8	210.6	64	71.2	53.4
Sri Lanka	45.0	117.4	161		0.3		8.0	46.6	481	6.4	49.2	666	216.5	208.2	-4	13.2	10.6

Country	Television sets per 1000 people			Cable television subscribers per 1000 people			Main telephone lines per 1000 people			Cellular mobile telephone subscribers per 1000 people			International telecom, outgoing traffic (minutes per subscriber)			Personal Computers per 1000 people	Internet users per 1000 people
	1991	2001	% change 1991–2001	1996	2001	% change 1996–2001	1992	2002	% change 1992–2002	1997	2002	% change 1997–2002	1992	2002	% change 1992–2002	2002	2002
Sub-Saharan Africa																	
Low income economies																	
Angola	6.2	52.5	749		*0.9*		4.9	6.1	24	0.6	9.3	1,430	186.3	403.5	117	1.9	2.9
Benin	11.1	11.5	4				3.2	9.2	187	0.7	32.2	4,230	183.9	*294.5*	*60*	2.2	7.4
Burkina Faso	5.4	12.9	139				2.1	5.4	154	0.1	7.5	5,187	123.3	307.0	149	1.6	2.1
Burundi	1.0	29.2	2,850				2.3	3.2	40	0.1	7.4	7,509	148.3	126.8	-15	0.7	1.2
Cameroon	23.5	74.6	217				4.5	7.0	56	0.3	42.7	14,064	320.1	*208.4*	*-35*	5.7	3.8
Central African Republic	4.7	5.8	25				2.0	2.3	15	0.4	3.2	694	262.9	466.1	77	2.0	1.3
Chad	1.3	1.8	34				0.7	1.5	110	0.0	4.3		398.6	*363.0*	*-9*	1.7	1.9
Comoros	2.8	3.7	33				7.6	13.5	78	0.0	0.0		382.8	373.0	-3	5.5	4.2
Congo, Dem. Rep.	1.1	1.9	79				0.9	0.2	-79	0.2	10.6	5,642				0.0	0.9
Congo, Rep.	6.1	12.9	111				7.6	6.7	-12	*0.4*	67.2	*17,832*	280.4			3.9	1.5
Côte d'Ivoire	59.9	61.2	2				6.6	20.4	208	2.6	62.3	2,288	254.7	203.8	-20	9.3	5.5
Equatorial Guinea	8.3			*0.0*			3.5	17.4	397	0.7	63.4	8,771	359.3	*623.2*	*73*	6.9	3.6
Eritrea		39.3					3.9	9.0	129	0.0	0.0		39.4	124.7	217	2.5	2.3
Ethiopia	2.7	5.7	113				2.5	5.3	108	0.0	0.7		79.0	36.4	-54	1.5	0.7
Gambia	*0.5*	15.0	*2,881*				14.0	28.0	99	4.1	72.9	1,698		*108.2*		14.3	18.2
Ghana	20.0	52.6	162		0.3		3.0	12.7	323	1.2	20.7	1,654	66.5	158.4	138	3.8	7.8
Guinea	6.9	47.1	587				1.7	3.4	99	0.4	11.8	2,892	434.6	234.3	-46	5.5	4.6
Guinea-Bissau		35.9					6.4	8.9	40	0.0	0.0		422.1			0.0	4.0
Kenya	17.1	26.0	52		0.5		8.9	10.3	16	0.3	41.5	16,497	*6.1*			6.4	12.5
Lesotho	6.2	32.4	424				6.1	13.2	115	1.7	42.5	2,472	142.2	*68.5*	-52	0.0	9.7
Liberia	18.4	*25.4*	*38*				1.6	*2.2*	*34*	0.0	*0.6*		739.5	*2,756.0*	*273*		
Madagascar	21.4	25.2	18				3.1	3.7	22	0.3	10.2	3,302	100.9	*144.4*	*43*	4.4	3.5
Malawi		3.9					3.5	7.0	101	0.7	8.2	1,047	270.4	244.9	-9	1.3	2.6
Mali	10.1	19.2	90				1.5	5.3	256	0.3	5.0	1,567	1206.2	155.3	-87	1.4	2.4
Mauritania	16.7	99.4	495				3.3	11.8	260	0.0	92.2		101.6	133.6	32	10.8	3.7
Mozambique	2.9	13.0	347				3.9	4.6	18	0.2	14.0	8,574	151.0	101.6	-33	4.5	2.7
Niger	11.2	9.8	-12				1.2	1.9	54	0.0	1.4	14,053	153.4	164.8	7	0.6	1.3
Nigeria	36.9	102.6	178		0.5		3.2	5.8	82	0.1	13.4	9,302	303.0	728.6	140	7.1	3.5
Rwanda	0.5						2.0	2.8	40	0.0	13.6		158.9	194.9	23	0.0	3.1
São Tomé & Principe		70.0					19.8	41.3	109	0.0	13.1		76.3	122.7	61	0.0	72.8
Senegal	43.9	77.5	77		0.1		7.5	22.3	196	0.8	54.9	6,832	99.9	*336.1*	*237*	19.8	10.4
Sierra Leone	10.3	13.2	28				3.3	4.8	48	0.0	13.4		93.5	105.6	13	0.0	1.6
Somalia	12.3	14.4	17				1.7	9.8	484	0.0	3.4		131.2	*58.0*	*-56*		8.8
Sudan	79.2	385.6	387				2.5	20.6	737	0.1	5.9	4,204	364.3	*481.1*	*32*	6.1	2.6
Tanzania	1.7	44.6	2,508		0.2		3.1	4.7	50	0.7	19.5	2,786	224.4	*217.8*	*-3*	4.2	2.3
Togo	6.3	84.2	1,234				4.1	10.5	158	0.7	34.9	4,927	24.4	34.4	41	30.8	41.0
Uganda	11.2	11.5	3		0.3		1.7	2.2	28	0.2	15.9	6,479	70.9	216.6	206	3.3	4.0

Record 6 continued

Country	Television sets per 1000 people			Cable television subscribers per 1000 people			Main telephone lines per 1000 people			Cellular mobile telephone subscribers per 1000 people			International telecom, outgoing traffic (minutes per subscriber)			Personal Computers per 1000 people	Internet users per 1000 people
	1991	2001	% change 1991–2001	1996	2001	% change 1996–2001	1992	2002	% change 1992–2002	1997	2002	% change 1997–2002	1992	2002	% change 1992–2002	2002	2002
Zambia	31.7	51.0	61		1.2		9.2	8.2	-11	0.5	13.0	2,601	0.0	0.0		7.4	4.9
Zimbabwe	26.8	55.6	108		*2.1*		12.2	24.7	103	0.5	30.3	5,724	0.0	0.0		51.6	43.0
Middle income economies																	
Botswana	15.8	44.0	178				26.8	87.2	225	0.0	241.3		761.9	424.7	-44	40.7	29.7
Cape Verde	2.9	100.7	3,430				32.3	159.9	396	0.0	97.8	198,754	205.8	*134.7*	*-35*	79.7	36.4
Gabon	46.2	*114.2*	*147*	*1.8*	*11.5*	*557*	27.9	24.7	-12	8.3	215.0	2,476	191.4	352.0	84	19.2	19.2
Mauritius	177.8	299.1	68				73.5	270.3	268	37.3	289.1	676		*251.9*		116.5	99.1
Namibia	22.0	77.2	251		16.4		42.1	64.8	54	7.6	80.0	954	428.6			70.9	26.7
South Africa	105.0	159.3	52				93.5	106.6	14	44.5	303.9	582	173.5	480.9	177	72.6	68.2
Swaziland	18.3	31.4	72				17.8	34.0	90	0.0	61.0		0.8	42.1	5,257	24.2	19.4
Region																	
Low income	37	91	147		24		8.1	27.8	242	0.3	12.6	4,080	158.9	*108.5*	*-32*	7.5	10.2
Middle income	183	290	59	34	52	55	50.6	166.7	229	8.4	149.1	1,678	142.6	123.7	-13	45.3	80.1
Low & middle income	117	190	62	27	40	49	31.3	99.8	219	1.7	62.3	3,664	149.8	117.1	-22	28.4	49.7
East Asia & Pacific	141	265	88	33	54	63	11.3	131.2	1,065	2.1	23.8	1,037	188.5	44.5	-76	26.3	43.7
Europe & Central Asia	290	*407*	*40*	59	46	-23	140.6	228.0	62	5.5	196.3	3,457	30.9	64.6	109	73.4	87.1
Latin America & Caribbean	168	289	72	24	34	42	70.3	168.4	139	11.2	126.0	1,030	146.1	172.5	18	67.4	91.7
Middle East & North Africa	125	200	61				44.8	107.3	139	1.8	51.5	2,760	147.8	212.9	44	38.2	36.6
South Asia	31	84	173	15	37	142	7.3	33.8	364	0.6	8.3	1,361	53.2	68.3	29	6.8	13.7
Sub-Saharan Africa	27	69	156				10.1	15.0	49	0.3	15.9	6,268	216.5	208.2	-4	11.9	16.4
High income	555	735	32	150	174	16	479.4	585.4	22	125.0	697.6	458	205.1	285.2	39	466.9	363.5
World	191	275	45	53	65	24	105.7	175.9	66	7.1	109.7	1,442	153.6	155.3	1	100.8	130.7

Empty cells indicate that data were unavailable. In such instances, where possible, figures are taken from the year before or after as an estimate. These figures, and estimates based on them, are presented in italics.

Sources: World Bank, World Development Indicators 2003 (WDI-Online); International Telecommunications Union (ITU), ICT - Free statistics homepage, www.itu.int/ITU-D/ict/statistics

Record 7 Governance and accountability

The first section of this record presents findings from the second survey of the 2020 Fund's Global Stakeholder Panel. NGO leaders were asked to rate the importance of various ways of achieving an ideal vision of global governance in 2020. Respondents favoured reforming multilateral agencies, such as the World Trade Organisation and the World Bank, and including more representatives from poor communities in international discussions. Including representatives of business in global governance was unpopular in all parts of the world, except North America.

The second part of the record shows a Voice and Accountability Index developed by the World Bank Institute researchers, in their project *Governance Matters*. The Voice and Accountability Index measures the extent to which citizens of a country participate in the selection of government, and the level of independence of the media. The index comprises various indicators from 25 different sources, which measure different aspects of the political process, civil liberties and political rights. Index values are ranked on a 1–100 scale (see www.worldbank.org/wbi/governance/pdf/govmatters3_wber.pdf for more information on index methodology).

High-income countries in Europe and North America and in parts of Latin America score highest in the index. The table shows the change in a country's rank between 1996 and 2002. Almost all of the nations with a five-point decrease in their rank are low- to middle-income economies.

Thinking of how global society can best make the transition from today to the year 2020, please rate the importance of each of the following in getting to your ideal vision of global governance in the year 2020.

	Region							
% responding 'very important' or 'important' with respect to the following:	**Sub Saharan Africa**	**Asia**	**Middle East & North Africa**	**Latin America & Carribean**	**North America**	**Western Europe**	**Eastern Europe**	**Pacific**
Reform the United Nations secretariat and agencies (eg, UNDP, UNEP, ILO)	71	61	84	88	78	66	75	76
Reform multilateral agencies (eg, World Bank, IMF, WTO)	84	80	84	94	87	90	88	69
Include more representatives from poor communities in developing countries in international discussions on economic, environment, and social affairs	94	96	92	95	96	95	94	94
Include leaders of major environmental and social NGOs, and labour unions in international negotiations	88	89	84	89	85	91	93	81
Include leaders of business (local, national and multinational) in international negotiations	52	62	62	47	74	28	45	81

Record 7 continued

	Per capita GDP		
	Low	Medium	High
Reform the United Nations secretariat and agencies (eg, UNDP, UNEP, ILO)	58	72	75
Reform multilateral agencies (eg, World Bank, IMF, WTO)	92	83	81
Include more representatives from poor communities in developing countries in international discussions on economic, environment, and social affairs	92	96	91
Include leaders of major environmental and social NGOs and labour unions in international negotiations	75	89	80
Include leaders of business (local, national and multinational) in international negotiations	50	61	73

For the purposes of this survey, 'governance' is defined as the way in which society ensures that its values and goals govern the actions of its citizens and organisations. It includes government at all levels, the United Nations system, multilateral agencies like the World Bank and IMF, as well as governance systems within civil society and business.

Source: 2020 Fund (2004). What NGO Leaders Want for the Year 2020? Report of the second survey of the 2020 global stakeholder panel, www.2020fund.org/gsp_results.htm

Voice and accountability

Country	Voice and accountability ranking 1996	Voice and accountability ranking 2002	Rank change 1996–2002
East Asia & Pacific			
Low income economies			
Cambodia	27.7	30.3	3
Indonesia	16.2	34.8	19
Korea, Dem. Rep.	0.5	0.0	-1
Laos	17.8	3.5	-14
Mongolia	62.8	63.1	0
Myanmar	1.6	1.5	0
Papua New Guinea	57.6	46.5	-11
Solomon Islands	80.1	60.1	-20
Vietnam	11.5	10.6	-1
Middle income economies			
China*	12.0	10.1	-2
Fiji	49.7	48.5	-1
Malaysia	51.8	42.4	-9
Micronesia	85.9	76.8	-9
Philippines	58.6	54.0	-5
Samoa	70.7	69.7	-1
Thailand	52.9	57.1	4
Tonga	52.4	47.0	-5
Vanuatu	63.9	73.2	9
High income economies			
Australia	99.0	94.4	-5
Austria	91.6	89.9	-2
Brunei	22.5	23.2	1
Japan	81.2	79.3	-2
Korea, Rep.	68.1	67.7	0
New Zealand	96.3	97.0	1
Singapore	63.4	65.7	2
Europe & Central Asia			
Low income economies			
Azerbaijan	18.8	19.2	0
Georgia	33.5	39.9	6
Kyrgyzstan	34.6	19.7	-15
Moldova	44.5	40.9	-4
Tajikistan	6.8	21.2	14
Uzbekistan	7.9	5.1	-3
Middle income economies			
Albania	41.4	49.5	8
Armenia	31.4	36.9	6
Belarus	20.4	7.6	-13
Bosnia & Herzegovina	15.2	43.9	29
Bulgaria	58.1	66.7	9
Croatia	34.0	63.6	30
Czech Republic	79.6	74.7	-5
Estonia	71.2	80.3	9

Record 7 continued

Voice and accountability

Country	Voice and accountability ranking 1996	2002	Rank change 1996–2002
Hungary	79.1	85.4	6
Kazakhstan	20.9	17.7	-3
Latvia	64.9	75.3	10
Lithuania	69.6	73.7	4
Macedonia	50.8	41.9	-9
Poland	76.4	83.3	7
Romania	54.5	61.1	7
Russian Federation	39.8	33.8	-6
Slovakia	62.3	76.3	14
Turkey	38.2	36.4	-2
Turkmenistan	2.1	2.5	0
Ukraine	39.3	27.8	-12
High income economies			
Belgium	93.2	93.4	0
Cyprus	78.0	77.3	-1
Denmark	99.5	100.0	1
Finland	98.4	99.5	1
France	94.8	88.4	-6
Germany	95.8	95.5	0
Greece	75.4	81.3	6
Iceland	92.7	96.5	4
Ireland	93.7	91.9	-2
Italy	82.2	83.8	2
Luxembourg	94.2	92.9	-1
Malta	82.7	88.9	6
Netherlands	96.9	98.0	1
Norway	100.0	98.5	-2
Portugal	90.1	89.4	-1
Slovenia	75.9	82.8	7
Spain	84.8	87.9	3
Sweden	97.4	99.0	2
Switzerland	97.9	97.5	0
United Kingdom	91.1	93.9	3
Latin America & Caribbean			
Low income economies			
Haiti	36.1	15.2	-21
Nicaragua	43.5	52.0	9
Middle income economies			
Argentina	66.5	52.5	-14
Belize	81.7	72.2	-10
Bolivia	56.5	50.0	-7
Brazil	59.7	58.1	-2
Chile	74.9	84.3	9
Colombia	50.3	30.8	-20
Costa Rica	90.6	84.8	-6
Cuba	8.4	3.0	-5

Record 7 continued

Voice and accountability

Country	Voice and accountability ranking 1996	2002	Rank change 1996–2002
Dominican Republic	53.4	56.6	3
Ecuador	55.5	47.5	-8
El Salvador	44.0	51.5	8
Guatemala	28.8	35.4	7
Guyana	73.8	69.2	-5
Honduras	40.3	46.0	6
Jamaica	66.0	65.2	-1
Mexico	42.9	59.6	17
Panama	61.8	64.6	3
Paraguay	38.7	32.3	-6
Peru	27.2	57.6	30
St. Lucia	83.8	79.8	-4
St. Vincent & the Grenadines	84.3	78.8	-6
Suriname	51.3	58.6	7
Trinidad & Tobago	70.2	66.2	-4
Uruguay	71.7	77.8	6
Venezuela	55.0	38.9	-16
High income economies			
Bahamas	83.2	86.9	4
Barbados	86.4	91.4	5
Middle East & North Africa			
Low income economies			
Yemen	23.6	21.7	-2
Middle income economies			
Algeria	15.7	20.2	5
Djibouti	25.7	26.8	1
Egypt	26.7	22.2	-5
Iran	18.3	18.2	0
Iraq	1.0	0.5	-1
Jordan	48.7	38.4	-10
Lebanon	36.6	31.8	-5
Libya	5.2	4.5	-1
Morocco	29.3	40.4	11
Oman	30.4	31.3	1
Saudi Arabia	14.7	9.1	-6
Syria	10.5	5.6	-5
Tunisia	33.0	22.7	-10
High income economies			
Bahrain	23.0	24.7	2
Israel*	80.6	67.2	-13
Kuwait	46.1	41.4	-5
Qatar	24.6	32.8	8
United Arab Emirates	28.3	35.9	8
North America			
High income economies			
Canada	92.1	94.9	3

Voice and accountability

Country	Voice and accountability ranking 1996	2002	Rank change 1996–2002
United States	95.3	90.9	-4
South Asia			
Low income economies			
Afghanistan	3.7	11.1	7
Bangladesh	41.9	29.3	-13
Bhutan	9.4	13.6	4
India	60.7	60.6	0
Nepal	57.1	33.3	-24
Pakistan	22.0	15.7	-6
Middle income economies			
Maldives	21.5	25.3	4
Sri Lanka	45.0	48.0	3
Sub-Saharan Africa			
Low income economies			
Angola	6.3	9.6	3
Benin	69.1	51.0	-18
Burkina Faso	35.6	42.9	7
Burundi	13.1	14.1	1
Cameroon	19.9	16.7	-3
Central African Republic	47.1	23.7	-23
Chad	26.2	20.7	-6
Comoros	49.2	34.3	-15
Congo, Rep.	14.1	16.2	2
Congo, Dem. Rep.	13.6	2.0	-12
Côte d'Ivoire	46.6	11.6	-35
Equatorial Guinea	4.7	8.1	3
Eritrea	17.3	1.0	-16
Ethiopia	30.9	14.6	-16
Gambia	11.0	18.7	8
Ghana	40.8	50.5	10
Guinea	16.8	12.6	-4
Guinea-Bissau	31.9	25.8	-6
Kenya	35.1	28.3	-7
Lesotho	53.9	45.5	-8
Liberia	7.3	6.1	-1
Madagascar	60.2	49.0	-11
Malawi	37.2	29.8	-7
Mali	61.3	55.1	-6
Mauritania	24.1	27.3	3
Mozambique	45.5	43.4	-2
Niger	37.7	44.9	7
Nigeria	4.2	26.3	22
Rwanda	5.8	8.6	3
São Tomé & Principe	72.8	64.1	-9
Senegal	47.6	53.0	5
Sierra Leone	9.9	28.8	19

Record 7 continued

Voice and accountability

Country	Voice and accountability ranking 1996	2002	Rank change 1996–2002
Somalia	0.0	6.6	7
Sudan	2.6	4.0	1
Tanzania	25.1	37.9	13
Togo	19.4	12.1	-7
Uganda	29.8	24.2	-6
Zambia	48.2	39.4	-9
Zimbabwe	42.4	7.1	-35
Middle income economies			
Botswana	68.6	71.2	3
Cape Verde	74.3	61.6	-13
Gabon	32.5	37.4	5
Mauritius	72.3	71.7	-1
Namibia	64.4	59.1	-5
South Africa	67.5	70.7	3
Swaziland	12.6	13.1	1

* China excludes Hong Kong and Macao. Israel excludes the Occupied Territories.

Source: World Bank Institute: Governance Matters III: Governance Indicators for 1996–2002, by D. Kaufmann A. Kraay, and M. Mastruzzi (2003), www.worldbank.org/wbi/governance/pubs/govmatters3.html

Record 8 Ratification of treaties

Global civil society is both dependent on the international rule of law and one of the main actors pushing for the adoption and enforcement of international law. The table indicates which countries have ratified the major human rights, humanitarian, disarmament, and environmental treaties, and in which years, up to 30 April 2004. It shows how many countries have ratified each particular treaty, and how many of the listed treaties each country has ratified. The number of listed treaties ratified by each country since 2000 is also shown. In terms of the number of treaties ratified, it seems that low- and middle-income countries in Europe and Central Asia, Latin America and Africa are catching up with high-income economies. The highest numbers of recent ratifications are of humanitarian and environmental law treaties.

ICESCR – International Covenant on Economic, Social and Cultural Rights (As of 02 November 2003)
ICCPR – International Convenant on Civil and Political Rights (As of 02 November 2003)
ICCPR-OP1 – Optional Protocol to the International Convenant on Civil and Political Rights (As of 02 November 2003)
ICCPR-OP2 – Second Optional Protocol to the International Convenant on Civil and Political Rights (As of 02 November 2003)
CERD – International Convention on the Elimination of all forms of Racial Discrimination (As of 02 November 2003)
CEDAW – Convention on the Elimination of All Forms of Discrimination Against Women (As of 02 November 2003)
CAT – Convention against Torture and Other Cruel, Inhuman or Degrading Treatment or Punishment (As of 02 November 2003)
Gen – Convention on the Prevention and Punishment of the Crime of the Genocide (As of 09 October 2001)
ILO 87 – Freedom of Association and Protection of the Right to Organise Convention (As of 15 April 2004; Latest ratification registered on 9 April 2003)
CSR – Convention relating to the Status of Refugees (As of 05 February 2002)
ICC – Rome Statute on the International Criminal Court (Updated on 4/15/04; Latest ratification registered on 09/05/03)
CWC – Chemical Weapons Convention (As of 30 April 2004)
BWC – Biological Weapons Convention (As of 19 March 2004)
LMC – Convention on the Prohibition of the Use, Stockpiling, Production and Transfer of Anti-Personnel Mines and on their Destruction (As of 19 March 2004)
Geneva – Geneva Conventions (As of 20 May 2003)
Prot 1 – First Additional to the Geneva Conventions (As of 20 May 2003)
Prot 2 – Second Additional Protocol to the Geneva Conventions (As of 20 May 2003)
BC – Basel Convention on the Control of Transboundary Movements of Hazardous Wastes and Their Disposal (As of 15 April 2004; Latest ratification or accession registered on 03 June 2003)
CBD – Convention on Biological Diversity (As of 30 March 2004)
UNFCCC – United Nations Framework Convention on Climate Change (As of 26 February 2004)
KP – Kyoto Protocol to United Nations Framework Convention on Climate Change (As of 15 April 2004)
VCPOL – Vienna Convention for the Protection of Ozone Layer (As of 15 April 2004; Latest ratification or accession registered on 22 December 2003)

	Human Rights											Humanitarian Law						Environmental Law						
Country	**ICESCR**	**ICCPR**	**ICCPR-OP1**	**ICCPR-OP2**	**CERD**	**CEDAW**	**CAT**	**Gen**	**ILO 87**	**CSR**	**ICC**	**CWC**	**BWC**	**LMC**	**Geneva**	**Prot 1**	**Prot2**	**BC**	**CBD**	**UNFCCC**	**KP**	**VCPOL**	**Total**	**Ratified since 2000**
East Asia & Pacific																								
Low income economies																								
Cambodia	92	92			83	92	92	50	99	92	02		83	99	58	98	98	01	95	95	02	01	19	4
Indonesia & East Timor					99	84	98		98			98	92		58			93	94	94		92	11	0
Korea, Dem. Rep.	81	81				01		89					87		57	88			94	94		95	10	1
Laos	00				74	81		50				97	73		56	80	80		96	95	03	98	13	2
Mongolia	74	74	91		69	81	02	67	69		02	95	72		58	95	95	97	93	93	99	96	19	2
Myanmar						97		56	55						92				94	94	03	93	8	1
Papua New Guinea					82	95		82	00	86		94	80		76			95	93	93	02	92	13	2
Solomon Islands	82				82	02				95			81	99	81	88	88		95	94	03	93	13	2
Vietnam	82	82			82	82		81				98	80		57	81		95	94	94	02	94	14	1

Record 8 continued

Country	Human Rights											Humanitarian Law						Environmental Law						
	ICESCR	ICCPR	ICCPR-OP1	ICCPR-OP2	CERD	CEDAW	CAT	Gen	ILO 87	CSR	ICC	CWC	BWC	LMC	Geneva	Prot 1	Prot2	BC	CBD	UNFCCC	KP	VCPOL	Total	Ratified since 2000
Middle income economies																								
China & Tibet	01				81	80	88	83		82		97	84		56	83	83	91	93	93		89	15	1
Fiji					73	95		73	02	72	99	93	73	98	71				93	93	98	89	14	1
Malaysia						95		94				00	91	99	62			93	94	94	02	89	11	2
Philippines	74	86	89		67	81	86	50	53	81		96	73	00	52		86	93	93	94	03	91	19	2
Samoa						92				88	02	02		98	84	84	84	02	94	94	00	92	13	4
Thailand	99	96				85						03	75	98	54			97	04	94	02	89	12	3
Tonga					72			72					76		78	03	03		98	98		98	9	2
Vanuatu						95							90		82	85	85		93	93	01	94	9	1
High income economies																								
Australia	75	80	91	90	75	83	89	49	73	54	02	94	77	99	58	91	91	92	93	92		87	21	1
Brunei												97	91		91	91	91	02				90	7	1
Korea, Rep.	90	90	90		78	84	95	50		92	02	97	87		66	82	82	94	94	93	02	92	19	2
Japan	79	79			95	85	99		65	81		95	82	98	53			93	93	93		88	15	0
New Zealand	78	78	89	90	72	85	89	78		60	00	96	72	99	59	88	88	94	93	93	02	87	21	2
Singapore						95		95				97	75		73			96	95	97		89	9	0
Europe & Central Asia																								
Low income economies																								
Armenia	93	93	93		93	93	93	93		93		94	94		93	93	93	99	93	94	03	99	18	1
Azerbaijan	92	92	01	99	96	95	96	96	92	93		00			93			01	00	95	00	96	17	5
Georgia	94	94	94	99	99	94	94	93	99	99	03	95	96		93	93	93	99	94	94	99	96	21	1
Kyrgyzstan	94	94	95		97	97	97	97	92	96					92	92	92	96	96	00	03	00	17	3
Moldova	93	93			93	94	95	93	96	02		96		00	93	93	93	98	95	95	03	96	18	3
Tajikistan	99	99	99		95	93	95		93	93	00	95		99	93	93	93		97	98		96	17	1
Ukraine	73	73	91		69	81	87	54	56			98	75		54	90	90	99	95	97	04	86	18	1
Uzbekistan	95	95	95		95	95	95	99				96	96		93	93	93	96	95	93	99	93	17	0
Middle income economies																								
Albania	91	91			94	94	94	55	57	92	03	94	92	00	57	93	93	99	94	94		99	19	2
Belarus	73	73	92		69	81	87	54	56	01		96	75	03	54	89	89	99	93	00		86	19	3
Bosnia & Herzegovina	92	93	95	01	93	93	93	92	93	93	02	97	94	98	92	92	92	01	02	00		92	21	5
Bulgaria	70	70	92	99	66	82	86	50	59	93	02	94	72	98	54	89	89	96	96	95	02	90	22	2
Croatia	91	92	95	95	92	92	92	92	91	92	01	95	93	98	92	92	92	94	96	96		91	21	1
Czech Republic	93	93	93		93	93	93	93	93	93		96	93	99	93	93	93	93	93	93	01	93	20	1
Estonia	91	91	91		91	91	91	91	94	97	02	99	93		93	93	93	92	94	94	02	96	20	2
Hungary	74	74	88	94	67	80	87	52	57	89	01	96	72	98	54	89	89	90	94	94	02	88	22	2
Kazakhstan					98	98	98	98	00	99		00			92	92	92	03	94	95		98	14	3
Latvia	92	92	94		92	92	92	92	92	97	02	96	97		91	91	91	92	95	95	02	95	20	2
Lithuania	91	91	91	02	98	94	96	96	94	97	03	98	98	03	96	00	00	99	96	95	03	95	22	6
Macedonia	94	94	94	95	94	94	94	94	91	94	02	97	96	98	93	93	93	97	97	98		94	21	1
Poland	77	77	91		68	80	89	50	57	91	01	95	73		54	91	91	92	96	99	02	90	20	2
Romania	74	74	93	91	70	82	90	50	57	91	02	95	79	00	54	90	90	91	94	94	01	93	22	3
Russian Federation	73	73	91		69	81	87	54	56	93		97	75		54	89	89	95	95	94		86	18	0
Slovakia	93	93	93	99	93	93	93	93	93	93	02	95	93	99	93	93	93	93	94	94	02	93	22	2

Record 8 continued

Country	Human Rights										Humanitarian Law							Environmental Law						
	ICESCR	ICCPR	ICCPR-OP1	ICCPR-OP2	CERD	CEDAW	CAT	Gen	ILO 87	CSR	ICC	CWC	BWC	LMC	Geneva	Prot 1	Prot2	BC	CBD	UNFCCC	KP	VCPOL	Total	Ratified since 2000
Slovenia	92	92	93	94	92	92	93	92	92	92	01	97	92	98	92	92	92	93	96	95	02	92	22	2
Turkey	03	03			02	85	88	50	93	62		97	74	03	54			94	97	04		91	16	5
Turkmenistan	97	97	97	00	94	97	99		97	98		94	96	98	92	92	92	96	96	95	00	93	20	2
Yugoslavia	01	01	01	01	01	82	01	01	00	01		00			01	01	01	00	02	97		92	18	15
High income economies																								
Austria	78	78	87	93	72	82	87	58	50	54	00	95	73	98	53	82	82	93	94	94	02	87	22	2
Belgium	83	83	94	98	75	85	99	51	51	53	00	97	79	98	52	86	86	93	96	96	02	88	22	2
Cyprus	69	69	92	99	67	85	91	82	66	63	02	98	73	03	62	79	96	92	96	97	99	92	22	2
Denmark	72	72	72	94	71	83	87	51	51	52	01	95	73	98	51	82	82	94	93	93	02	88	22	2
Finland	75	75	75	91	70	86	89	59	50	68	00	95	74		55	80	80	91	94	94	02	86	21	2
France	80	80	84		71	83	86	50	51	54	00	95	84	98	51	01	84	91	94	94		87	20	2
Germany	73	73	93	92	69	85	90	54	57	53	00	94	72	98	54	91	91	95	93	93	02	88	22	2
Greece	85	97	97	97	70	83	88	54	62	60	02	94	75	03	56	89	93	94	94	94	02	88	22	3
Iceland	79	79	79	91	67	85	96	49	50	55	00	97	73	99	65	87	87	95	94	93	02	89	22	2
Ireland	89	89	89	93	00	85	02	76	55	56	02	96	72	97	62	99	99	94	96	94	02	88	22	4
Italy	78	78	78	95	76	85	89	52	58	54	99	95	75	99	51	86	86	94	94	94	02	88	22	1
Luxembourg	83	83	83	92	78	89	87	81	58	53	00	97	76	99	53	89	89	94	94	94	02	88	22	2
Netherlands	78	78	78	91	71	91	88	66	50	56	01	95	81	99	54	87	87	93	94	93	02	88	22	2
Norway	72	72	72	91	70	81	86	49	49	53	00	94	73	98	51	81	81	90	93	93	02	86	22	2
Portugal	78	78	83	90	82	80	89	99	77	60	02	96	75	99	61	92	92	94	93	93		88	21	1
Spain	77	77	85	91	68	84	87	68	77	78	00	94	79	99	52	89	89	94	93	93	02	88	22	2
Sweden	71	71	71	90	71	80	86	52	49	54	01	93	76	98	53	79	79	91	93	93	02	86	22	2
Switzerland	92	92		94	94	97	86	00	75	55	01	95	76	98	50	82	82	90	94	93	03	87	21	3
United Kingdom	76	76		99	69	86	88	70	49	54	01	96	75	98	57	98	98	94	94	93	02	87	21	2
Latin America & Caribbean																								
Low income economies																								
Haiti		91			72	81		50	79	84					57				96	96		00	10	1
Nicaragua	80	80	80		78	81		52	67	80		99	75	98	53	99	99	97	95	95	99	93	19	0
Middle income economies																								
Argentina	86	86	86		68	85	86	56	60	61	01	95	79	99	56	86	86	91	94	93	01	90	21	2
Barbados	73	73	73		72	80		80	67		02		73	99	68	90	90	95	93	94	00	92	18	2
Belize		96			01	90	86	98	83	90	00	03	86	98	84	84	84	97	93	94	03	97	19	4
Bolivia	82	82	82		70	90	99		65	82	02	98	75	98	76	83	83	96	94	94	99	94	20	1
Brazil	92	92			68	84	89	52		60	02	96	73	99	57	92	92	92	94	94	02	90	19	2
Chile	72	72	92		71	89	88	53	99	72		96	80	01	50	91	91	92	94	94	02	90	20	2
Colombia	69	69	69	97	81	82	87	59	76	61	02	00	83	00	61	93	95	96	94	95	01	90	22	4
Costa Rica	68	68	68	98	67	86	93	50	60	78	01	96	93	99	69	83	83	95	94	94	02	91	22	2
Cuba					72	80	95	53	52			97	76		54	82	99	94	94	94	02	92	15	1
Dominican Republic	78	78	78		83	82			56	78			73	00	58	94	94	00	96	98	02	93	17	3
Ecuador	69	69	69	93	66	81	88	49	67	55	02	95	75	99	54	79	79	93	93	93	00	90	22	2
El Salvador	79	79	95		79	81	96	50		83		95	91	99	53	78	78	91	94	95	98	92	19	0
Guatemala	88	92	00		83	82	90	50	52	83			73	99	52	87	87	95	95	95	99	87	19	1
Guyana	77	77	93		77	80	88		67			97		03	68	88	88	01	94	94	03	93	17	3

Record 8 continued

Country	Human Rights											Humanitarian Law						Environmental Law						
	ICESCR	ICCPR	ICCPR-OP1	ICCPR-OP2	CERD	CEDAW	CAT	Gen	ILO 87	CSR	ICC	CWC	BWC	LMC	Geneva	Prot 1	Prot2	BC	CBD	UNFCCC	KP	VCPOL	Total	Ratified since 2000
Honduras	81	97			02	83	96	52	56	92	02		79	98	65	95	95	95	95	95	00	93	**19**	**3**
Jamaica	75	75			71	84		68	62	64		00	75	98	64	86	86	03	95	94	99	93	**18**	**2**
Mexico	81	81	02		75	81	86	52	61	00		94	74	98	52	83		91	93	93	00	87	**19**	**3**
Panama	77	77	77	93	67	81	87	50	58	78	02	98	74	98	56	95	95	91	95	95	99	89	**22**	**1**
Paraguay	92	92	95			87	90	01	62	70	01	96	76	98	61	90	90	95	94	94	99	92	**20**	**2**
Peru	78	78	80		71	82	88	60	60	64	01	95	85	98	56	89	89	93	93	93	02	89	**21**	**2**
St. Lucia					90	82			80			97	86	99	81	82	82	93	93	93		93	**13**	**0**
St. Vincent & the Grenadines	81	81	81		81	81	01	81	01	93		02	99	01	81	83	83	96	96	96		96	**19**	**4**
Suriname	76	76	76		84	93			76	78		97	93		76	85	85		96	97		97	**15**	**0**
Trinidad & Tobago	78	78			73	90			63	00	99	97		98	63	01	01	94	96	94	99	89	**17**	**3**
Uruguay	70	70	70	93	68	81	86	67	54	70	02	94	81	01	69	85	85	91	93	94	01	89	**22**	**3**
Venezuela	78	78	78	93	67	83	91	60	82		00	97	78	99	56	98	98	98	94	94		88	**20**	**1**
High income economies																								
Bahamas					75	93		75	01	93			86	98	75	80	80	92	93	94	99	93	**15**	**1**
Middle East & North Africa																								
Low income economies																								
Yemen	87	87			72	84	91	87	76	80		00	79	98	70	90	90	96	96	96		96	**18**	**1**
Middle income economies																								
Algeria	89	89	89		72	96	89	63	62	63		95	01	01	62	89	89	98	95	93		92	**19**	**2**
Djibouti	02	02	02	02		98	02		78	77	02			98	78	91	91	02	94	95	02	99	**18**	**8**
Egypt	82	82			67	81	86	52	57	81					52	92	92	93	94	94		88	**15**	**0**
Iran	75	75			68			56		76		97	73		57			93	96	96		90	**12**	**0**
Iraq	71	71			70	86		59					91		56								**7**	**0**
Jordan	75	75			74	92	91	50			02	97	75	98	51	79	79	89	93	93	03	89	**18**	**2**
Lebanon	72	72			71	97	00	53					75		51	97	97	94	94	94		93	**14**	**1**
Libya	70	70	89		68	89	89	89	00				82		56	78	78	01	01	99		90	**16**	**3**
Malta	90	90	90	94	71	91	90		65	71	02	97	75	01	68	89	89	00	00	94	01	88	**21**	**5**
Morocco & Western Sahara	79	79			70	93	93	58		56		95	02		56			95	95	95	02	95	**15**	**2**
Oman												95	92		74	84	84	95	95	95		99	**9**	**0**
Saudi Arabia					97	00	97	50				96	72		63	87		90		94		93	**11**	**1**
Syria	69	69			69			55	60						53	83		92	96	96		89	**11**	**0**
Tunisia	69	69			67	85	88	56	57	57		97	73	99	57	79	79	95	93	93	03	89	**19**	**1**
High income economies																								
Bahrain					90	02	98	90				97	88		71	86	86	92	96	94		90	**13**	**1**
Israel & Occupied Territiories	91	91			79	91	91	50	57	54					51			94	95	96	04	92	**14**	**1**
Kuwait	96	96			68	94	96	95	61			97	72		67	85	85	93	02	94		92	**16**	**1**
Qatar					76		00					97	75	98	75	88		95	96	96		96	**11**	**1**
United Arab Emirates					74							00			72	83	83	92	00	95		89	**9**	**2**
North America																								
High income economies																								
Canada	76	76	76		70	81	87	52	72	69	00	95	72	97	65	90	90	92	92	92	02	86	**21**	**2**
United States		92			94		94	88				97	75		55					92		86	**9**	**0**

Record 8 continued

Country	ICESCR	ICCPR	ICCPR-OP1	ICCPR-OP2	CERD	CEDAW	CAT	Gen	ILO 87	CSR	ICC	CWC	BWC	LMC	Geneva	Prot 1	Prot2	BC	CBD	UNFCCC	KP	VCPOL	Total	Ratified since 2000
	Human Rights										Humanitarian Law							Environmental Law						
South Asia																								
Low income economies																								
Afghanistan	83	83			83	03	87	56	57		03		75	02	56				02	02			**13**	5
Bangladesh	98	00			79	84	98	98	72			97	85	00	72	80	80	93	94	94	01	90	**18**	3
Bhutan						81							78		91			02	95	95	02		**7**	2
India	79	79			68	93		59				96	74		50			92	94	93	02	91	**13**	1
Nepal	91	91	91	98	71	91	91	69				97			64			96	93	94		94	**14**	0
Pakistan					66	96		57	51			97	74		51			94	94	94		92	**11**	0
Middle income economies																								
Maldives					84	93		84				94	93	00	91	91	91	92	92	92	98	88	**14**	1
Sri Lanka	80	80	97		82	81	94	50	95			94	86		59			92	94	93	02	89	**16**	1
Sub-Saharan Africa																								
Low income economies																								
Angola	92	92	92			86			01	81				02	84	84			98	00		00	**12**	4
Benin	92	92	92			92	92		60	62	02	98	75	98	61	86	86	97	94	94		93	**18**	1
Burkina Faso	99	99	99		74	87	99	65	60	80		97	91	98	61	87	87	99	93	93		89	**19**	0
Burundi	90	90			77	92	93	97	93	63		98			71	93	93	97	97	97	01	97	**17**	1
Cameroon	84	84	84		71	94	86		60	61		96		02	63	84	84	01	94	94	02	89	**18**	3
Central African Republic	81	81	81		71	91			60	62	01			02	66	84	84		95	95		93	**15**	2
Chad	95	95	95		77	95	95		60	81				99	70	97	97		94	94		89	**15**	0
Comoros						94			78					02	85	85	85	94	94	94		94	**10**	1
Congo, Rep.	83	83	83		88	82			60	62	02		78	01	67	83	83		96			94	**15**	2
Congo, Dem. Rep.	76	76	76		76	86	96	62	01	65			75	02	61	82	02	94	94	95		94	**18**	3
Côte d'Ivoire	92	92	97		73	95	95	95	60	61		95		00	61	89	89	94	94	94		93	**18**	1
Equatorial Guinea	87	87	87		02	84	02		01	86		97	89	98	86	86	86	03	94	00	00	88	**19**	6
Eritrea	01	02			01	95			00			00		01	00				96	95			**10**	7
Ethiopia	93	93			76	81	94	49	63	69		96	75		69	94	94	00	94	94		94	**17**	1
Gambia	78	79	88		78	93		78	00	66	02	98	91	02	66	89	89	97	94	94	01	90	**20**	4
Ghana	00	00	00		66	86	00	58	65	63	99	97	75	00	58	78	78	03	94	95	03	89	**21**	7
Guinea	78	78	93		77	82	89	00	59	65	03	97		98	84	84	84	95	93	93	00	92	**20**	3
Guinea-Bissau	92	00				85				76			76	01	74	86	86		95	95		02	**12**	3
Kenya	72	72			01	84	97			66		97	76	01	66	99	99	00	94	94		88	**16**	3
Lesotho	92	92	00		71	95	01	74	66	81	00	94	77	98	68	94	94	00	95	95	00	94	**21**	5
Liberia					76	84		50	62	64				99	54	88	88		00	02	02	96	**13**	3
Madagascar	71	71	71		69	89			60	67				99	63	92	92	99	96	99	03	96	**16**	1
Malawi	93	93	96		96	87	96		99	87	02	98		98	68	91	91	94	94	94	01	91	**19**	2
Mali	74	74	01		74	85	99	74	60	73	00	97	02	98	65	89	89	00	95	94	02	94	**21**	5
Mozambique		93		93	83	97	99	83	96	83		00		98	83	83	02	97	95	95		94	**17**	2
Niger	86	86	86		67	99	98		61	61	02	97	72	99	64	79	79	98	95	95		92	**19**	1
Nigeria	93	93			67	85	01		60	67	01	99	73	01	61	88	88	91	94	94		88	**18**	3
Rwanda	75	75			75	81		75	88	80			75	00	64	84	84		96	98		01	**15**	2
Sao Tome & Principe									92	78		03	79	03	76	96	96		99	99		01	**11**	3

Record 8 continued

Country	Human Rights										Humanitarian Law							Environmental Law						
	ICESCR	ICCPR	ICCPR-OP1	ICCPR-OP2	CERD	CEDAW	CAT	Gen	ILO 87	CSR	ICC	CWC	BWC	LMC	Geneva	Prot 1	Prot2	BC	CBD	UNFCCC	KP	VCPOL	Total	Ratified since 2000
Senegal	78	78	78		72	85	86	83	60	63	99	98	75	98	63	85	85	92	94	94	01	93	21	1
Sierra Leone	96	96	96		67	88	01		61	81	00		76	01	65	86	86		94	95		01	17	4
Somalia	90	90	90		75		90			78					62							01	8	1
Sudan	86	76			77					74		99		03	57				95	93		93	10	1
Tanzania	76	76			72	85		84	00	64	02	98		00	62	83	83	93	96	96	02	93	18	4
Togo	84	84	88		72	83	87	84	60	62		97	76	00	62	84	84		95	95		91	18	1
Uganda	87	95	95		80	85	86	95		76	02	01	92	99	64	91	91	99	93	93	02	88	20	3
Zambia	84	84	84		72	85	98		96	69	02	01		01	66	95	95	94	93	93		90	18	3
Zimbabwe	91	91			91	91		91	03	81		97	90	98	83	92	92		94	92		92	16	1
Middle income economies																								
Botswana		00			74	96	00		97	69	00	98	92	00	68	79	79	98	95	94	03	91	18	5
Cape Verde	93	93	00	00	79	80	92		99			03	77	01	84	95	95	99	95	95		01	18	5
Gabon	83	83			80	83	00	83	60	64	00	00		00	65	80	80		97	98		94	17	4
Mauritius	73	73	73		72	84	92				02	93	72	97	70	82	82	92	92	92	01	92	18	2
Namibia	94	94	94	94	82	92	94	94	95	95	02	95		98	91	94	94	95	97	95	03	93	21	2
South Africa		99	02	02	98	95	98	98	96	96	00	95	75	98	52	95	95	94	95	97	02	90	21	4
Swaziland					69				78	00		96	91	98	73	95	95		94	96		92	12	1
Total States in table	142	145	101	46	157	162	127	129	135	131	82	140	138	123	174	148	142	145	169	170	104	170	2,980	
Total States Parties*	145	148	102	47	165	170	132	132	142	139	87	150	165	131	190	160	155	156	187	188	105	185	3,181	
Ratified since 2000 (States in table)	7	8	10	7	8	5	14	4	14	6	77	19	3	43	2	5	6	21	10	8	89	10		376

* Total States Parties refers to the total number of ratifications for each treaty, including from those countries with populations of less than 100,000 that are not included in this table.

Sources: Office of the UN High Commissioner for Human Rights, www.unhchr.ch/pdf/report.pdf, www.unhchr.ch/html/menu3/b/treaty2ref.htm, www.unhchr.ch/html/menu3/b/treaty1gen.htm; United Nations, www.un.org/law/icc/statute/status.htm; International Criminal Court, www.iccnow.org/countryinfo/worldsigsandratifications.html; International Labour Organization, www.ilo.org/ilolex/cgi-lex/ratifce.pl?C087, Organisation for the Prohibition of Chemical Weapons, www.opcw.org/html/db/members_frameset.html; Federation of American Scientists, www.fas.org/nuke/control/bwc/text/bwcsig.htm; Secretariat, Basel Convention on the Control of Transboundary Movements of Hazardous Wastes and Their Disposal, www.basel.int/ratif/ratif.html; Secretariat, United Nations Framework Convention on Climate Change, unfccc.int/resource/conv/ratlist.pdf, unfccc.int/resource/kpstats.pdf; United Nations Environment Programme, www.unep.org/ozone/Treaties_and_Ratification/2C_ratificationTable.asp; International Committee of the Red Cross, www.icrc.org/eng/party_gc, www.icrc.org/eng/party_cmines; Convention on Biological Diversity, www.biodiv.org/world/parties.asp

Record 9 Social justice

This record illustrates another element of the spread of the international rule of law, namely, the realisation of social and economic rights, or social justice. This record contains indicators of poverty, inequality, and social exclusion. Growing inequality appears to be one of the characteristics of globalisation. It can be seen as inhibiting the emergence of global civil society, but it is also one of global civil society's major causes. Figures are given for 1990 and 2001 unless otherwise indicated. The Human Development Index (HDI) is the first indicator listed. It is a composite index of three separate indicators measuring GDP per capita, educational attainment, and life expectancy at birth. Higher numbers suggest higher levels of development. As further measures of social justice, the table also includes the extent of income inequality revealed by the Gini coefficient, with higher numbers indicating greater inequality; net primary school enrolment ratio (the number of students enrolled in a level of education who are of official school age for that level, as a percentage of the population of official school age for that level); and the ratio of girls to boys in primary education, to indicate gender inequality. HIV/AIDS appears to be having a strong impact: social justice indicators for middle-income countries in parts of South Asia and Sub-Saharan Africa affected by the pandemic show extremely low health, education and equality outcomes.

	Human Development Index (HDI)			GDP per capita, PPP in current international $			Infant mortality rate (% live births)			Life expectancy at birth (years)			Net primary school enrolment ratio (%)			Income inequality (Gini Index)*	Ratio of girls to boys in primary education (%)		
Country	value 1990	value 2001	% change 1990–2001	1990	2001	% change 1990–2001	1990	2001	% change 1990–2001	1990	2001	% change 1990–2001	1990–1991	2000–2001	% change 1990–2001	see note below	1990–1991	2000–2001	% change 1990–2001
East Asia & Pacific																			
Low income economies																			
Cambodia	0.501	0.556	11	980	1,860	90	9.5	9.7	3	50	57	14		95		40.4		86	
Indonesia	0.623	0.682	9	1,952	2,940	51	6.0	3.3	-45	65	66	2	98	92	-6	30.3	95	95	0
Laos	0.404	0.525	30	900	1,620	80	10.6	8.7	-18	69	54	-22		81		37.0	77	83	8
Mongolia	0.657	0.661	1	1,804	1,740	-4	7.3	6.1	-16	63	63	0		89		44.0	100	100	0
Myanmar		0.549			1,027		10.0	7.7	-23	58	57	-1		83			94	97	3
Papua New Guinea	0.479	0.548	14	1,580	2,570	63	8.3	7.0	-16	68	57	-16		84		50.9	80	83	4
Solomon Islands		0.632		1,801	1,910	6	3.0	2.0	-33	64	69	7					80		
Vietnam	0.605	0.688	14		2,070		4.0	3.0	-25	65	69	6		95		36.1		91	
Middle income economies																			
China & Tibet**	0.625	0.721	15	1,394	4,020	188	3.8	3.1	-18	69	71	3	97	93	-4	40.3	86	92	7
Fiji	0.723	0.754	4	3,804	4,850	27	3.5	1.8	-48	67	69	4	101	99	-2			93	
Malaysia	0.722	0.790	9	4,739	8,750	85	1.6	0.8	-49	62	73	18		98		49.2	95	95	0
Philippines	0.716	0.751	5	3,332	3,840	15	3.7	2.9	-22	71	70	-2	98	93	-5	46.1	95	96	1
Samoa	0.666	0.775	16	4,325	6,180	43	2.7	2.0	-26	66	70	5		97			98	91	-7
Thailand	0.713	0.768	8	3,835	6,400	67	3.7	2.4	-35	69	69	1		85		43.2	94	94	0
Tonga							3			69				91			92	87	-5
Vanuatu		0.568		2,445	3,190	30	4.6	3.4	-25	64	68	6		96			89	99	11
High income economies																			
Australia	0.888	0.939	6	17,271	25,370	47	0.8	0.6	-25	77	79	3	99	96	-3	35.2	95	95	0
Brunei		0.872		14,727	19,210	30	0.9	0.6	-36	74	76	3	91					90	
Korea, Rep.	0.815	0.879	8	8,880	15,090	70	1.2	0.5	-59	75	75	0	104	99	-5	31.6	94	89	-5
Japan	0.909	0.932	3	20,183	25,130	25	0.5	0.3	-35	68	81	19	100	101	1	24.9	95	95	0

Country	Human Development Index (HDI) value 1990	value 2001	% change 1990–2001	GDP per capita, PPP in current international $ 1990	2001	% change 1990–2001	Infant mortality rate (% live births) 1990	2001	% change 1990–2001	Life expectancy at birth (years) 1990	2001	% change 1990–2001	Net primary school enrolment ratio (%) 1990–1991	2000–2001	% change 1990–2001	Income inequality (Gini Index)* see note below	Ratio of girls to boys in primary education (%) 1990–1991	2000–2001	% change 1990–2001
New Zealand	0.875	0.917	5	14,190	19,160	35	0.8	0.6	-28	64	78	21	101	99	-2	36.2	94	94	0
Singapore	0.818	0.884	8	12,783	22,680	77	0.7	0.3	-55	74	78	5				42.5	90		
Europe & Central Asia																			
Low income economies																			
Armenia	0.759	0.729	-4	3,565	2,650	-26	1.9	3.1	67	72	72	1		69		37.9		95	
Azerbaijan		0.744		4,591	3,090	-33	2.3	7.4	222	71	72	1		91		36.5	94	96	2
Georgia		0.746		9,101	2,560	-72	1.6	2.4	51	72	73	2		95		38.9	96	95	-1
Kyrgyzstan		0.727		3,608	2,750	-24	3.0	5.2	73	50	68	37		82		29.0	99	95	-4
Moldova	0.759	0.700	-8	5,216	2,150	-59	3.9	2.7	-31	63	69	9		78		36.2	97	96	-1
Tajikistan	0.740	0.677	-9	2,796	1,170	-58	4.1	5.3	30	69	68	-1		103		34.7	96	90	-6
Ukraine	0.795	0.766	-4	6,694	4,350	-35	1.3	1.7	32	70	69	-1		72		29.0	96	95	-1
Uzbekistan	0.731	0.729	0		2,460		3.5	5.2	50	69	69	0				26.8	96		
Middle income economies																			
Albania	0.702	0.735	5	2,843	3,680	29	2.8	2.6	-8	71	73	3		98			93	94	1
Belarus	0.809	0.804	-1	7,031	7,620	8	1.2	1.7	43	71	70	-2		108		30.4		94	
Bosnia & Herzegovina		0.777			5,970		1.5	1.5	-2	71	74	3							
Bulgaria	0.786	0.795	1	5,797	6,890	19	1.5	1.4	-5	71	71	-1	86	94	9	31.9	93	93	0
Croatia	0.797	0.818	3	7,133	9,170	29	1.1	0.7	-35	72	74	3	79			29.0	94	94	0
Czech Republic	0.835	0.861	3		14,720		1.1	0.4	-64	72	75	5		90		25.4	96	94	-2
Estonia		0.833		7,957	10,170	28	1.2	1.1	-11	69	71	2		98		37.6	94	91	-3
Hungary	0.804	0.837	4	9,447	12,340	31	1.5	0.8	-46	78	72	-8	91	90	-1	24.4	95	94	-1
Kazakhstan		0.765		6,095	6,500	7	2.6	6.1	132	57	66	15		89		31.2		95	
Latvia	0.804	0.811	1	8,487	7,730	-9	1.4	1.7	24	68	71	4	83	92	11	32.4	96	94	-2
Lithuania	0.816	0.824	1	8,534	8,470	-1	1.0	0.8	-22	75	72	-4		95		36.3	90	94	4
Macedonia		0.784		5,011	6,110	22	3.2	2.2	-30	53	73	39	94	92	-2	28.2	93	94	1
Poland	0.792	0.841	6	5,684	9,450	66	1.9	0.8	-59	74	74	0	97	98	1	31.6	95	94	-1
Romania	0.777	0.773	-1	6,219	5,830	-6	2.7	1.9	-29	70	71	1	77	93	21	30.3	96	94	-2
Russian Federation	0.824	0.779	-5	10,079	7,100	-30	1.7	1.8	3	69	67	-3				45.6	97	95	-2
Slovakia	0.820	0.836	2	9,028	11,960	32	1.2	0.8	-33	71	73	3		89		25.8		95	
Slovenia	0.845	0.881	4	11,345	17,130	51	0.8	0.4	-52	73	76	4		93		28.4		94	
Turkey	0.686	0.734	7	4,834	5,890	22	5.8	3.6	-38	66	70	6	89			40.0	89	89	0
Turkmenistan		0.748		5,962	4,320	-28	4.5	7.6	68	66	67	1				40.8			
High income economies																			
Austria	0.890	0.929	4	18,664	26,730	43	0.8	0.5	-36	76	78	3	90	91	1		95	94	-1
Belgium	0.896	0.937	5	19,411	25,520	31	0.8	0.5	-37	76	79	3	97	101	4	25.0	97	95	-2
Cyprus	0.845	0.891	5	12,784	21,190		1.1	0.5	-55	77	78	2	87	95	9		93	94	1
Denmark	0.891	0.930	4	19,513	29,000	49	0.8	0.4	-47	75	76	2	98	99	1	24.7	96	95	-1
Finland	0.896	0.930	4	17,797	24,430	37	0.6	0.4	-29	75	78	4	99	100	1	25.6	95	95	0
France	0.897	0.925	3	17,966	23,990	34	0.7	0.4	-45	77	79	3	101	100	-1	32.7	94	94	0
Germany	0.885	0.921	4	18,224	25,350	39	0.7	0.4	-43	75	78	4	84	87	4	38.2		94	

Record 9 continued

Country	Human Development Index (HDI) value 1990	value 2001	% change 1990–2001	GDP per capita, PPP in current international $ 1990	2001	% change 1990–2001	Infant mortality rate (% live births) 1990	2001	% change 1990–2001	Life expectancy at birth (years) 1990	2001	% change 1990–2001	Net primary school enrolment ratio (%) 1990–1991	2000–2001	% change 1990–2001	Income inequality (Gini Index)* see note below	Ratio of girls to boys in primary education (%) 1990–1991	2000–2001	% change 1990–2001
Greece	0.859	0.892	4	11,464	17,440	52	1.0	0.5	-48	77	78	2	94	97	3	35.4	94	94	0
Iceland	0.913	0.942	3	21,343	29,990	41	0.6	0.3	-49	59	80	35		102				94	
Ireland	0.870	0.930	7	12,687	32,410	155	0.8	0.6	-27	76	77	1	91	90	-1	35.9	95	94	-1
Italy	0.879	0.916	4	17,438	24,670	41	0.8	0.4	-51	73	79	7		100		36.0	95	94	-1
Luxembourg	0.884	0.930	5	21,363	53,780	152	0.7	0.5	-32	72	78	9		97		30.8	103	95	-8
Netherlands	0.902	0.938	4	17,407	27,190	56	0.7	0.5	-30	75	78	4	95	100	5	32.6	99	94	-5
Norway	0.901	0.944	5	19,527	29,620	52	0.7	0.4	-42	69	79	14	100	101	1	25.8	95	95	0
Portugal	0.819	0.896	9	11,176	18,150	62	1.1	0.5	-54	75	76	1	102			38.5	91	94	3
Spain	0.876	0.918	5	12,848	20,150	57	0.8	0.4	-47	77	79	3	103	102	-1	32.5	94	94	0
Sweden	0.894	0.941	5	18,284	24,180	32	0.6	0.3	-50	78	80	3	100	102	2	25.0	95	97	2
Switzerland	0.905	0.932	3	24,154	28,100	16	0.7	0.5	-26	77	79	2	84	99	18	33.1	96	95	-1
United Kingdom	0.878	0.930	6	16,706	24,160	45	0.8	0.6	-24	76	78	3	97	99	2	36.0	96	95	-1
Latin America & Caribbean																			
Low income economies																			
Haiti	0.447	0.467	4	1,638	1,860	14	10.2	7.9	-23	65	49	-24	22				93		
Nicaragua	0.592	0.643	9	1,721	2,450		5.1	3.6	-29	45	69	54	72	81	13	60.3	104	98	-6
Middle income economies																			
Argentina	0.808	0.849	5	7,721	11,320	47	2.5	1.6	-37	72	74	3		107				96	
Barbados		0.888		11,252	15,560		1.2	1.2	3	75	77	3	78	105	35			97	
Belize	0.750	0.776	3	3,633	5,690	57	3.5	3.4	-2	72	72	-1	98	100	2		94	94	0
Bolivia	0.597	0.672	13	1,826	2,300	26	8.0	6.0	-25	58	63	9	91	97	7	44.7	90	95	6
Brazil	0.713	0.777	9	5,562	7,360	32	4.8	3.1	-35	66	68	3	86	97	13	60.7		93	
Chile	0.782	0.831	6	4,981	9,190	85	1.6	1.0	-38	74	76	3	88	89	1	57.5	95	94	-1
Colombia	0.724	0.779	8	7,195	7,040	-2	3.0	1.9	-38	68	72	5		89		57.1	111	96	-14
Costa Rica	0.787	0.832	6	5,288	9,460	79	1.5	0.9	-39	75	78	3	86	91	6	45.9	94	93	-1
Cuba		0.806			5,259		1.1	0.7	-35	75	77	2	92	97	5	..	93	91	-2
Dominican Republic	0.677	0.737	9	3,361	7,020	109	5.0	4.1	-18	66	67	1		93		47.4		94	
Ecuador	0.705	0.731	4	2,781	3,280	18	4.5	2.4	-47	67	71	5		99		43.7		97	
El Salvador	0.644	0.719	12	2,969	5,260	77	4.6	3.3	-28	66	70	7	75	81	8	50.8		93	
Guatemala	0.579	0.652	13	2,824	4,400	56	5.6	4.3	-23	44	65	49		84		55.8		88	
Guyana	0.680	0.740	9	2,858	4,690	64	5.9	5.4	-8	53	63	19	93	98	5	44.6	97	95	-2
Honduras	0.615	0.667	8	2,074	2,830	36	5.0	3.1	-38	78	69	-11	89	88	-1	59.0	99	98	-1
Jamaica	0.720	0.757	5	3,261	3,720	14	2.5	1.7	-33	79	76	-4	96	95	-1	37.9	99	96	-3
Mexico	0.761	0.800	5	6,383	8,430	32	3.6	2.4	-34	68	73	7	100	103	3	51.9	94	95	1
Panama	0.747	0.788	5	3,871	5,750	49	2.6	1.9	-27	55	74	35	91	100	10	48.5	92	93	1
Paraguay	0.717	0.751	5	3,922	5,210	33	3.1	2.6	-17	66	71	7	93	92	-1	57.7	93	94	1
Peru	0.704	0.752	7	3,251	4,570	41	5.4	3.0	-44	66	69	6		104		46.2		96	
St Lucia		0.775		4,360	5,260	21	1.9	1.7	-11	71	72	2		100		42.6	95	90	-5
Suriname		0.762		2,508	4,599	83	3.4	2.6	-24	69	71	3		92			96	96	0
Trinidad & Tobago	0.781	0.802	3	6,035	9,100	51	1.8	1.7	-4	71	72	1	91	92	1	40.3	97	95	-2

Record 9 continued

Country	Human Development Index (HDI) value 1990	value 2001	% change 1990–2001	GDP per capita, PPP in current international $ 1990	2001	% change 1990–2001	Infant mortality rate (% live births) 1990	2001	% change 1990–2001	Life expectancy at birth (years) 1990	2001	% change 1990–2001	Net primary school enrolment ratio (%) 1990–1991	2000–2001	% change 1990–2001	Income inequality (Gini Index)* see note below	Ratio of girls to boys in primary education (%) 1990–1991	2000–2001	% change 1990–2001
Uruguay	0.801	0.834	4	6,177	8,400	36	2.1	1.4	-34	73	75	3	91	90	-1	44.8	95	94	-1
Venezuela	0.757	0.775	2	5,050	5,670	12	2.5	1.9	-23	71	74	3	88	88	0	49.1	99	94	-5
High income economies																			
Bahamas	0.822	0.812	-1	14,521	16,270		2.8	1.3	-54	69	67	-3	96	83	-14			93	
Middle East & North Africa																			
Low income economies																			
Yemen	0.399	0.470	18	567	790	39	11.0	7.9	-28	52	59	14		67		33.4		60	
Middle income economies																			
Algeria	0.639	0.704	10	4,502	6,090	35	4.6	3.9	-15	67	69	3	93	98	5	35.3	81	88	9
Djibouti		0.462			2,370		12	10.0	-17	47.8	46	-3	32	33	3		71	75	6
Egypt	0.574	0.648	13	2,509	3,520	40	6.8	3.5	-48	63	68	9		93		34.4	80	89	11
Iran	0.645	0.719	11	3,878	6,000	55	5.4	3.5	-35	61	70	14		74		43.0	86	91	6
Iraq							4.0			75			79	93	18		80	79	-1
Jordan	0.677	0.743	10	3,304	3,870	17	3.0	2.7	-10	68	71	3	66	94	42	36.4	94	95	1
Lebanon	0.680	0.752	11	1,870	4,170	123	3.6	2.8	-23	58	73	27		74				93	
Libya		0.783			7,570		3.3	1.6	-51	71	72	2	97				91	97	7
Malta	0.826	0.856	4	8,742	13,160		0.9	0.5	-45	49	78	59	99	99	0		92	95	3
Morocco & Western Sahara	0.540	0.606	12	2,888	3,600	25	6.6	3.9	-41	43	68	57	58	78	34	39.5	66	84	27
Oman		0.755			12,040		2.2	1.2	-45	59	72	22	70	65	-7		89	93	4
Saudi Arabia	0.706	0.769	9	9,401	13,330		3.2	2.3	-28	69	72	4	59	58	-2		84	92	10
Syria	0.634	0.685	8	2,215	3,280	48	3.9	2.3	-41	66	72	8	98	96	-2		87	89	2
Tunisia	0.646	0.740	15	3,900	6,390	64	3.7	2.1	-44	70	73	3	94	99	5	41.7	85	91	7
High income economies																			
Bahrain		0.839		12,088	16,060		2.3	1.3	-43	71	74	3	99	96	-3		95	96	1
Israel**	0.855	0.905	6	13,450	19,790		1.0	0.6	-39	77	79	2		101		35.5	98	95	-3
Kuwait		0.820		9,952	18,700		1.4	0.9	-34	68	76	12	45	66	47		92	96	4
Qatar		0.826			19,844		2.1	1.1	-48	72	72	-1	87	95	9		91	95	4
United Arab Emirates		0.816		20,204	20,530		2.0	0.8	-60	74	74	1	94	87	-7		93	92	-1
North America																			
High income economies																			
Canada	0.926	0.937	1	20,122	27,130	35	0.7	0.5	-26	77	79	3	97	99	2	31.5	93	95	2
United States	0.914	0.937	3	23,447	34,320	46	0.9	0.7	-26	75	77	2	96	95	-1	40.8	94	95	1
South Asia																			
Low income economies																			
Afghanistan							16.9			42							52		
Bangladesh	0.416	0.502	21	1,004	1,610	60	9.1	5.1	-44	55	61	10	64	89	39	31.8	81	96	19
Bhutan		0.511		882	1,833	108		7.4			63					..		86	
India	0.511	0.590	15	1,400	2,840	103	8.0	6.7	-16	62	63	3				37.8	71	77	8
Nepal	0.416	0.499	20	883	1,310	48	10.1	6.6	-35	77	59	-23		72		36.7	56	79	41

Record 9 continued

Country	Human Development Index (HDI) value 1990	value 2001	% change 1990–2001	GDP per capita, PPP in current international $ 1990	2001	% change 1990–2001	Infant mortality rate (% live births) 1990	2001	% change 1990–2001	Life expectancy at birth (years) 1990	2001	% change 1990–2001	Net primary school enrolment ratio (%) 1990–1991	2000–2001	% change 1990–2001	Income inequality (Gini Index)* see note below	Ratio of girls to boys in primary education (%) 1990–1991	2000–2001	% change 1990–2001
Pakistan	0.442	0.499	13	1,394	1,890	36	11.0	8.4	-24	72	60	-17		66		33.0	48	55	15
Middle income economies																			
Maldives	0.676	0.751	11	3,611	4,798	33	6.0	5.8	-3	45	67	48		99				95	
Sri Lanka	0.697	0.730	5	2,036	3,180	56	1.9	1.7	-8	70	72	3		97		34.4	93	94	1
Sub-Saharan Africa																			
Low income economies																			
Angola		0.377		1,581	2,040	29	13.0	15.4	18	45	40	-12		37			92	88	-4
Benin	0.358	0.411	15	706	980	39	10.4	9.4	-10	52	51	-2	49	70	43		50	68	36
Burkina Faso	0.290	0.330	14	636	1,120	76	11.1	10.4	-6	45	46	1	27	36	33	48.2	62	70	13
Burundi	0.344	0.337	-2	722	690	-4	11.9	11.4	-4	44	40	-7	52	54	4	33.3	84	80	-5
Cameroon	0.513	0.499	-3	1,561	1,680	8	8.1	9.6	19	54	48	-11				47.7	85	86	1
Central African Republic	0.372	0.363	-2	1,060	1,300	23	10.2	11.5	13	48	40	-15	53	55	4	61.3	65	69	6
Chad	0.322	0.376	17	766	1,070	40	11.8	11.7	-1	46	45	-3		58			45	63	40
Comoros	0.502	0.528	5	1,716	1,870	9	8.4	5.9	-30	56	60	8		56			71	85	20
Congo, Dem. Rep.		0.363		1,290	680		8.4	12.9	54	52	41	-21	54	33	-39		74	90	22
Congo, Rep.	0.510	0.502	-2	760	970	28	8.2	8.1	-1	51	49	-5					90	93	3
Côte d'Ivoire	0.415	0.396	-5	1,552	1,490	-4	9.5	10.2	7	50	42	-16	47	64	36	36.7	71	76	7
Equatorial Guinea	0.553	0.664	20	1,052	15,073	1,333	12.1	10.1	-17	47	49	4		72				91	
Eritrea		0.446			1,030		8.1	7.2	-12	49	53	7		41			95	82	-14
Ethiopia	0.297	0.359	21	486	810	67	13.1	11.6	-11	45	46	2		47		48.6	66	68	3
Gambia		0.463		1,488	2,050	38	10.9	9.1	-16	49	54	9	51	69	35	47.8	68	91	34
Ghana	0.506	0.567	12	1,368	2,250	64	6.6	5.7	-14	57	58	1		58		39.6	82	90	10
Guinea		0.425		1,520	1,960	29	12.1	10.9	-10	42	49	15		47		40.3	46	70	52
Guinea-Bissau	0.304	0.373	23	686	970	41	14.5	13.0	-10	64	45	-29		54		47.0		67	
Kenya	0.533	0.489	-8	977	980	0	6.2	7.8	26	66	46	-29		69		44.5	95	98	3
Lesotho	0.574	0.510	-11	1,087	2,420	123	10.2	9.1	-10	45	39	-14	73	78	7	56.0	121	102	-16
Liberia							16.8			68				83				69	
Madagascar	0.434	0.468	8	818	830	1	10.3	8.4	-18	45	53	19		68		46.0	97	96	-1
Malawi	0.362	0.387	7	445	570	28	12.8	11.4	-11	71	39	-45	50	101	102	50.3	82	96	17
Mali	0.312	0.337	8	582	810	39	13.6	14.1	4	75	48	-36	21	43	105	50.5	59	71	20
Mauritania	0.390	0.454	16	1,167	1,990	71	11.2	12.0	7	70	52	-25		64		37.3	73	93	27
Mozambique	0.310	0.356	15	521	1,140	119	15.0	12.5	-17	55	39	-28	47	54	15	39.6	76	77	1
Niger	0.256	0.292	14	738	890	21	15.0	15.6	4	49	46	-7	25	30	20	50.5	57	65	14
Nigeria	0.425	0.463	9	764	850	11	8.6	11.0	27	77	52	-32				50.6	76		
Rwanda	0.346	0.422	22	952	1,250	31	13.2	9.6	-27	40	38	-5	66	97	47	28.9	99	100	1
São Tomé & Principe		0.639			1,317		6.1	5.7	-6	62	69	12						92	
Senegal	0.380	0.430	13	1,199	1,500	25	7.4	7.9	7	50	52	6	48	63	31	41.3	72	87	21
Sierra Leone		0.275		894	470	-47	19.0	18.2	-4	35	35	-2				62.9	70	76	9
Somalia							15.2			42									

Country	Human Development Index (HDI) value 1990	value 2001	% change 1990–2001	GDP per capita, PPP in current international $ 1990	2001	% change 1990–2001	Infant mortality rate (% live births) 1990	2001	% change 1990–2001	Life expectancy at birth (years) 1990	2001	% change 1990–2001	Net primary school enrolment ratio (%) 1990–1991	2000–2001	% change 1990–2001	Income inequality (Gini Index)* see note below	Ratio of girls to boys in primary education (%) 1990–1991	2000–2001	% change 1990–2001
Sudan	0.419	0.503	20	803	1,970	145	9.8	6.5	-33	52	55	6		46			75	82	9
Tanzania	0.422	0.400	-5	453	520	15	11.5	10.4	-9	50	44	-12	51	47	-8	38.2	98	100	2
Togo	0.465	0.501	8	1,400	1,650	18	8.1	7.9	-2	50	50	0	75	92	23		65	79	22
Uganda	0.388	0.489	26	746	1,490	100	10.4	7.9	-24	47	45	-4		109		37.4	80		
Zambia	0.468	0.386	-18	837	780	-7	10.7	11.2	4	49	33	-32		66		52.6		93	
Zimbabwe	0.597	0.496	-17	2,336	2,280	-2	5.2	7.6	47	56	35	-37		80		56.8	99	97	-2
Middle income economies																			
Botswana	0.653	0.614	-6	4,911	7,820	59	5.5	8.0	47	57	45	-21	93	84	-10	63.0	107	99	-7
Cape Verde	0.626	0.727	16	2,926	5,570	90	6.4	2.9	-55	65	70	7		99				96	
Gabon		0.653		5,241	5,990	14	7.2	6.0	-16	52	57	9		88				98	
Mauritius	0.723	0.779	8	5,597	9,860	76	2.0	1.7	-17	71	72	1	95	95	0		98	97	-1
Namibia		0.627		4,411	7,120	61	6.4	5.5	-14	54	47	-12	89	82	-8	70.7	108	100	-7
South Africa	0.714	0.684	-4	8,282	11,290	36	5.5	5.6	2	62	51	-18	103	89	-14	59.3	98	94	-4
Swaziland	0.615	0.547	-11	3,630	4,330	19	7.9	10.6	35	57	38	-33	88	93	6	60.9	99	95	-4

Region	Human Development Index (HDI) value 2001	GDP per capita, PPP in current international $ 2001	Infant mortality rate (% live births) 2001	Life expectancy at birth (years) 2001	Net primary school enrolment ratio (%) 1990-1991	2000-2001	% change 1990-2001
Low income	0.561	2,230	8.0	59.1	69	74	7.2
Middle income	0.744	5,519	3.1	69.8	92	93	1.1
Low & middle income:							
East Asia & the Pacific	0.722	4,233	3.2	69.5	96	93	-3.1
Europe & Central Asia	0.787	6,598	1.8	69.3	88	91	3.4
Latin America & Caribbean	0.777	7,050	2.8	70.3	87	97	11.5
Middle East & North Africa	0.662	5,038	4.9	66.0	73	77	5.5
South Asia	0.582	2,730	6.9	62.8	73	79	8.2
Sub-Saharan Africa	0.468	1,831	10.7	46.5	56	59	5.4
High income	0.927	26,989	0.5	78.1	97	97	0.0
World	0.722	7,376	5.6	66.7	82	84	2.4

* Survey year for Gini index varies by country. 0 represents perfect equality, 100 represents perfect inequality.

** Data for China & Tibet excludes Hong Kong and Macao; Data for Israel excludes the Occupied Territories.

Sources: World Bank, World Development Indicators 2003 (WDI-Online); Human Development Report 2003, Millennium Development Goals: A compact among nations to end human povert, New York: Oxford University Press.

Record 10 Corruption

This record examines the state of the rule of law through the prism of corruption. Corruption not only hinders economic development, it inhibits the formation of trust and social capital. It is therefore likely to be an obstacle to the growth of civil society generally as well as a focus of civil society activism, both locally and globally. The table presents three kinds of indicators of corruption: the Corruption Perceptions Index by Transparency International, and the Institute for Management Development's Bribing and Corruption, and Transparency of Government indices. Since these are relatively new measures, we can compare data only from 2000 and 2003. Scores range between 10, indicating high transparency and the absence of bribery and corruption, and 0, indicating lack of transparency and high levels of perceived corruption and bribery. The Control of Corruption Index is new in this record. It was developed by The World Bank Institute researchers in their project *Governance Matters*. The Control of Corruption Index measures perceptions of corruption, conventionally defined as the exercise of public power for private gain. A higher score in this index represents better control of corruption (a detailed explanation of the index appears in www.worldbank.org/wbi/governance/pdf/govmatters3_wber.pdf). As seen from the table, corruption is closely related to income, as high-income countries tend to score better on all corruption indices in the table. High-income countries also show relative stability in their control of corruption scores. The highest increases and decreases were found among low- and middle-income countries.

	Corruption Perceptions Index		Bribing and corruption		Transparency of government		Control of Corruption Index		
Country	2000	2003	2000	2003	2000	2003	1998	2002	% change 1998-2002
East Asia & Pacific									
Low income economies									
Cambodia							2.7	20.1	17
Indonesia	1.7	1.9	1.3	0.8	5.0	2.1	6.6	6.7	0
Korea, Dem. Rep.							33.9	5.7	-28
Laos							24.6	3.6	-21
Mongolia							54.6	54.1	-1
Myanmar							2.2	2.1	0
Papua New Guinea							24.0	20.6	-3
Vietnam	2.5	2.4					28.4	33.0	5
Middle income economies									
China & Tibet*	3.1	3.4	2.2	2.4	6.3	4.8	57.9	42.3	-16
Malaysia	4.8	5.2	3.2	4.9	6.4	6.3	80.9	68.0	-13
Micronesia							48.6	40.2	-8
Philippines	2.8	2.5	1.6	1.4	3.3	3.6	45.9	37.6	-8
Samoa							48.6	56.2	8
Thailand	3.2	3.3	2.0	2.7	4.3		61.2	53.6	-8
Tonga							48.6	40.2	-8
High income economies									
Australia	8.3	8.8	8.2	8.1	6.9	6.9	93.4	93.8	0
Brunei							66.7	65.5	-1
Fiji							70.5	61.3	-9
Japan	6.4	7.0	5.3	5.6	3.7	3.6	86.9	85.1	-2
Korea, Rep.	4.0	4.3	2.6		3.7		69.9	66.5	-3
New Zealand	9.4	9.5	8.8	9.2	6.6	6.7	97.8	99.0	1
Singapore	9.1	9.4	8.7	8.6	8.4	6.9	97.3	99.5	2
Europe & Central Asia									
Low income economies									
Armenia	2.5	3.0					23.0	30.4	7

Record 10 continued	Corruption Perceptions Index		Bribing and corruption		Transparency of government		Control of Corruption Index		
Country	2000	2003	2000	2003	2000	2003	1998	2002	% change 1998–2002
Azerbaijan	1.5	1.8					5.5	9.8	4
Cyprus							87.4	79.9	-8
Georgia		1.8					27.3	12.4	-15
Kyrgyzstan		2.1					26.2	23.7	-3
Malta							78.7	76.8	-2
Moldova	2.6	2.4					38.3	21.6	-17
Tajikistan							3.8	10.3	7
Ukraine	1.5	2.3					12.0	17.5	6
Uzbekistan	2.4	2.4					7.7	11.9	4
Middle income economies									
Albania		2.5					9.8	23.2	13
Belarus	4.1	4.2					29.5	26.8	-3
Bosnia & Herzegovina							45.4	34.5	-11
Bulgaria	3.5	3.9					39.9	52.6	13
Croatia	3.7	3.7					46.4	63.9	18
Czech Republic	4.3	3.9	1.8	2.5	3.2	4.3	73.2	68.6	-5
Estonia	5.7	5.5		4.9		6.0	76.5	74.2	-2
Hungary	5.2	4.8	3.3	2.8	5.2	5.0	79.8	73.7	-6
Kazakhstan	3.0	2.4					13.1	10.8	-2
Latvia	3.4	3.8					61.7	60.8	-1
Lithuania	4.1	4.7					67.8	64.4	-3
Macedonia		2.3					48.1	29.4	-19
Poland	4.1	3.6	2.9	1.3	3.4	2.8	77.0	69.1	-8
Romania	2.9	2.8		1.5		4.1	44.3	45.4	1
Russian Federation	2.1	2.7	1.9	1.3	2.5	2.8	26.8	21.1	-6
Serbia & Montenegro	1.3	2.3					8.2	26.3	18
Slovakia	3.5	3.7		1.7		5.1	62.8	64.9	2
Slovenia	5.5	5.9	3.7	4.3	3.1	4.3	82.5	80.4	-2
Turkey	3.8	3.1	2.6	2.4	6.0	3.7	65.6	43.8	-22
Turkmenistan							3.3	4.6	1
High income economies									
Austria	7.7	8.0	6.7	7.8	5.3	6.1	91.8	93.3	2
Belgium	6.1	7.6	5.0	5.7	5.9	4.9	86.3	91.2	5
Denmark	9.8	9.5	9.2	9.5	5.5	7.0	99.5	98.5	-1
Finland	10.0	9.7	9.5	9.6	7.6	8.1	98.9	100.0	1
France	6.7	6.9	5.0	6.1	5.8	5.8	90.7	89.2	-2
Germany	7.6	7.7	5.4	6.6	4.5	4.0	94.0	92.8	-1
Greece	4.9	4.3	2.4	2.6	5.5	3.4	83.1	73.2	-10
Iceland	9.1	9.6	8.5	9.0	6.8	7.2	95.1	97.4	2
Ireland	7.2	7.5	6.5	5.0	7.5	5.8	92.3	91.8	-1
Italy	4.6	5.3	2.8	3.5	3.8	3.7	84.7	76.3	-8
Luxembourg	8.6	8.7	7.2	6.6	6.9	6.7	92.9	95.4	3
Netherlands	8.9	8.9	7.8	7.2	7.3	5.8	96.2	96.4	0
Norway	9.1	8.8	8.3	7.7	5.3	6.6	95.6	94.8	-1
Portugal	6.4	6.6	4.3	3.7	5.4	5.6	89.1	88.1	-1
Spain	7.0	6.9	5.3	5.8	6.9	5.7	89.6	89.7	0
Sweden	9.4	9.3	8.4	8.1	4.2	6.1	98.4	97.9	-1

Record 10 continued	Corruption Perceptions Index		Bribing and corruption		Transparency of government		Control of Corruption Index		
Country	2000	2003	2000	2003	2000	2003	1998	2002	% change 1998–2002
Switzerland	8.6	8.8	7.5	7.5	6.1	6.8	100.0	96.9	-3
United Kingdom	8.7	8.7	7.6	7.6	5.8	5.2	94.5	94.3	0
Latin America & Caribbean									
Low income economies									
Antigua & Barbuda								77.8	
Barbados								85.6	
Haiti		1.5					13.7	0.5	-13
Nicaragua		2.6					25.7	39.7	14
Middle income economies									
Argentina	3.5	2.5	1.5	0.7	5.2	0.8	59.6	27.8	-32
Belize							48.6	50.0	1
Bolivia	2.7	2.3					42.1	25.3	-17
Brazil	3.9	3.9	2.6	2.6	5.3	5.4	68.9	56.7	-12
Chile	7.4	7.4	6.3	4.9	5.6	5.2	85.8	90.7	5
Colombia	3.2	3.7	1.6	2.9	5.0	6.9	30.6	38.7	8
Costa Rica	5.4	4.3					80.3	79.4	-1
Cuba							53.6	55.2	2
Dominican Republic		3.3					37.7	43.3	6
Ecuador	2.6	2.2					19.1	14.4	-5
El Salvador	4.1	3.7					47.5	36.6	-11
Grenada							63.4	74.7	11
Guatemala		2.4					23.5	30.9	7
Guyana							55.2	38.1	-17
Honduras		2.3					21.9	27.3	5
Jamaica		3.8					55.7	39.2	-17
Mexico	3.3	3.6	2.1	2.2	5.5	5.1	41.0	52.1	11
Panama		3.4					54.1	51.0	-3
Paraguay		1.6					9.3	4.1	-5
Peru	4.4	3.7					58.5	51.5	-7
St. Kitts & Nevis							63.4	69.6	6
St. Lucia							63.4	69.6	6
St. Vincent & The Grenadines							63.4	69.6	6
Suriname							66.7	62.4	-4
Trinidad & Tobago		4.6					69.4	57.2	-12
Uruguay		5.5					74.9	75.8	1
Venezuela	2.7	2.4	1.4	0.9	2.4	0.8	21.3	18.6	-3
High income economies									
Bahamas							78.7	88.7	10
Middle East & North Africa									
Low income economies									
Yemen							32.8	32.0	-1
Middle income economies									
Algeria							25.1	31.4	6
Djibouti							15.8	28.4	13
Egypt	3.1	3.3					56.3	47.9	-8
Iran							27.9	44.3	16
Iraq							1.6	1.0	-1

Record 10 continued	Corruption Perceptions Index		Bribing and corruption		Transparency of government		Control of Corruption Index		
Country	2000	2003	2000	2003	2000	2003	1998	2002	% change 1998–2002
Jordan	4.6	4.6		4.9		5.4	71.6	59.3	-12
Lebanon							47.0	45.9	-1
Libya							10.9	24.7	14
Morocco	4.7	3.3					62.3	58.2	-4
Oman							83.6	82.5	-1
Saudi Arabia							72.7	72.7	0
Syria							31.7	47.4	16
Tunisia	5.2	4.9					68.3	67.0	-1
High income economies									
Bahrain							73.8	82.0	8
Israel	6.6	7.0	6.0	5.8	5.5	4.8	88.0	83.5	-5
Kuwait							85.2	83.0	-2
Qatar							82.0	81.4	-1
United Arab Emirates							81.4	84.0	3
North America									
High income economies									
Canada	9.2	8.7	8.3	7.8	6.9	5.9	96.7	95.9	-1
United States	7.8	7.5	6.8	6.5	6.2	6.0	91.3	92.3	1
South Asia									
Low income economies									
Afghanistan								2.6	
Bangladesh		1.3					43.7	7.7	-36
Bhutan							75.4	80.9	6
India	2.8	2.8	1.5	1.6	5.0	3.8	60.1	49.5	-11
Nepal							30.1	46.9	17
Pakistan		2.5					20.2	29.9	10
Middle income economies									
Maldives							34.4	59.8	25
Sri Lanka		3.4					57.4	54.6	-3
Sub-Saharan Africa									
Low income economies									
Angola	1.7	1.8					4.9	7.2	2
Benin							19.7	34.0	14
Burkina Faso	3						38.8	57.7	19
Burundi							15.8	12.9	-3
Cameroon	2.0	1.8					4.4	8.8	4
Central African Republic							34.4	12.9	-22
Chad							14.2	12.9	-1
Comoros							15.8	28.4	13
Congo, Dem. Rep.								1.5	
Congo, Rep.							7.1	18.0	11
Côte d'Ivoire	2.7	2.1					44.8	22.7	-22
Equatorial Guinea							15.8	0.0	-16
Eritrea							75.4	60.3	-15
Ethiopia	3.2	2.5					56.8	44.8	-12
Gambia							40.4	24.2	-16
Ghana	3.5	3.3					43.2	42.8	0

Record 10 continued

Country	Corruption Perceptions Index		Bribing and corruption		Transparency of government		Control of Corruption Index		
	2000	2003	2000	2003	2000	2003	1998	2002	% change 1998–2002
Guinea							14.8	35.6	21
Guinea-Bissau							32.2	33.5	1
Kenya	2.1	1.9					10.4	11.3	1
Lesotho							66.1	48.5	-18
Liberia							0.5	16.5	16
Madagascar		2.6					15.3	61.9	47
Malawi	4.1	2.8					39.3	19.6	-20
Mali							31.1	46.4	15
Mauritania							48.6	63.4	15
Mozambique	2.2	2.7					18.6	14.9	-4
Niger							12.6	8.2	-4
Nigeria	1.2	1.4					6.0	3.1	-3
Rwanda							34.4	35.1	1
São Tomé & Principe							15.8	50.0	34
Senegal	3.5	3.2					41.5	53.1	12
Sierra Leone							22.4	25.8	3
Somalia							0.5	5.2	5
Sudan							20.8	9.3	-12
Tanzania	2.5	2.5					8.7	15.5	7
Togo							42.6	32.5	-10
Uganda	2.3	2.2					29.0	19.1	-10
Zambia	3.4	2.5					33.3	17.0	-16
Zimbabwe	3.0	2.3					60.7	6.2	-55
Middle income economies									
Botswana	6.0	5.7					78.1	75.3	-3
Cape Verde							48.6	66.0	17
Gabon							11.5	36.1	25
Mauritius	4.7	4.4					71.0	72.2	1
Namibia	5.4	4.7					72.1	62.9	-9
South Africa	5.0	4.4	2.7	3.2	6.0	5.6	74.3	67.5	-7
Swaziland							59.0	49.0	-10

*China & Tibet excludes Hong Kong and Macao.

Sources: Transparency International, 2000 Corruption Perceptions Index, www.transparency.org/cpi/2000/cpi2000.html; Transparency International, 2003 Corruption Perceptions Index, www.globalcorruptionreport.org/download/gcr2004/12_Corruption_research_I.pdf (Table 10.1: Corruption Perceptions Index 2003); International Institute for Management Development (2000), The World Competitiveness Yearbook 1999, Institute for Management Development, Lausanne, Switzerland; International Institute for Management Development (2003), Tables 2.3.14 'Transparency' and 2.3.17 'Bribing and Corruption', The World Competitiveness Yearbook 2002, Institute for Management Development, Lausanne, Switzerland; World Bank Institute: Governance Matters III: Governance Indicators for 1996–2002, by D. Kaufmann A. Kraay, and M. Mastruzzi, 2003, www.worldbank.org/wbi/governance/pubs/govmatters3.html

Record 11 Refugee populations and flows

This record shows two dimensions of the refugee problem: if a country 'generates' many refugees or internally displaced persons (IDPs), it can be assumed that there is little respect for the international rule of law in that country. On the other hand, countries that host many refugees can be considered as extending international hospitality and bearing the associated financial burden. The table presents data on refugee populations, both in total counts and per 1,000 inhabitants for 1992 and 2002. In addition, the table provides information on inflows and outflows of refugees during 2002, as well as estimates of IDPs. Negative inflow for a country indicates that there are fewer refugees in that country at the end of the year than at the beginning, while negative outflow indicates that the number of refugees originating from that country decreased over the year. Refugees are numerous in current and recent conflict areas such as the Balkans, Central Africa, and Central America, among others. Some Western European countries appear as major recipients of refugees, refugees representing more than one per cent of their populations.

	Refugee populations*						IDP Populations			Refugeee Flows**	
	Total (1000s)			per 1000 inhabitants			Total (1000s)			2002 (1000s)	
Country of asylum	**1992**	**2002**	**% change**	**1992**	**2002**	**% change**	**2001**	**2002**	**% change**	**Inflow**	**Outflow**
East Asia & Pacific											
Low income economies											
Cambodia		0.2			0.0					0.2	-1.3
Indonesia & East Timor	3.5	28.6	717	0.0	0.1	588				-45.0	-44.1
Papua New Guinea	6.7	4.9	-26	1.7	1.0	-43					
Vietnam	16.3	15.9	-2	0.2	0.2	-16					-5.4
Middle income economies											
China & Tibet	288.1	297.3	3	0.2	0.2	-6				2.0	7.7
Malaysia	11.4	50.6	344	0.6	2.2	259				0.1	
Philippines	6.7	0.1	-98	0.1	0.0	-99				0.0	0.0
Thailand	63.6	112.6	77	1.1	1.8	58				1.9	
High income economies											
Australia	49.8	55.1	11	2.8	2.8	-1					
Korea, Rep.	0.1	0.0	-83	0.0	0.0	-84				0.0	
Japan	6.7	2.7	-60	0.1	0.0	-61				-0.5	
New Zealand	17.3	5.3	-70	5.0	1.3	-73					
Singapore	0.1	0.0	-98	0.0	0.0	-99					
Europe & Central Asia											
Low income economies											
Armenia	300.0	247.6	-17	87.0	74.3	-15				-16.8	1.3
Azerbaijan	246.0	0.5	-100	33.2	0.1	-100	573.0	577.2	1	0.1	-15.9
Georgia		4.2			0.8		264.2	261.6	-1	-3.7	-3.1
Kyrgyzstan	*21.2*	7.7	*-175*	*4.7*	1.6	*-193*				-1.6	0.2
Moldova		0.2			0.0		1.0	1.0	0	0.0	1.0
Tajikistan	3.0	3.4	15	0.5	0.5	-5				-11.9	6.9
Ukraine		3.0			0.1					0.0	5.0
Uzbekistan	*8.0*	44.9	*82*	*0.4*	1.8	*79*				5.4	0.5
Middle income economies											
Albania	3.0	0.0	-99	0.9	0.0	-99				-0.3	0.9
Belarus		0.6			0.1					0.0	0.3
Bosnia & Herzegovina		28.0			7.1		438.3	367.5	-16	-4.7	-54.8

Record 11 continued

Country of asylum	Refugee populations* Total (1000s)			Refugee populations* per 1000 inhabitants			IDP Populations Total (1000s)			Refugeee Flows** 2002 (1000s)	
	1992	2002	% change	1992	2002	% change	2001	2002	% change	Inflow	Outflow
Bulgaria	0.2	3.7	1,729	0.0	0.5	1,967				0.7	-0.2
Croatia	403.0	8.4	-98	90.9	1.9	-98	23.4	17.1	-27	-13.5	-19.0
Czech Republic	9.4	1.3	-86	0.9	0.1	-86				0.1	0.1
Hungary	32.4	6.1	-81	3.1	0.6	-81				1.4	0.1
Kazakhstan	*5.0*	20.6	*76*	*0.3*	1.2	*76*				1.1	0.1
Latvia		0.0			0.0					0.0	0.0
Lithuania		0.4			0.1					0.1	
Macedonia	32.0	2.8	-91	16.6	1.4	-92	16.4	9.4	-42	-1.5	-7.3
Poland	2.7	1.6	-41	0.1	0.0	-41				0.3	-0.1
Romania	0.5	1.9	271	0.0	0.1	278				0.1	-0.8
Russian Federation		15.0			0.1		443.3	371.2	-16	-3.0	2.3
Serbia & Montenegro	516.4	354.4	-31	50.5	33.3	-34	263.6	261.8	-1	-45.9	1.7
Slovenia	74.1	0.4	-99	39.2	0.2	-99				-2.0	-0.1
Turkey	28.5	3.3	-88	0.5	0.0	-90				-0.2	-0.9
Turkmenistan	*15.4*	13.7	*-12*	*4.0*	2.9	*-37*				-0.3	0.0
High income economies											
Austria	62.4	14.1	-77	7.9	1.7	-78				-0.3	
Belgium	24.3	12.6	-48	2.4	1.2	-50				0.3	
Cyprus	0.1	0.2	73	0.1	0.2	59				0.1	
Denmark	39.1	73.6	88	7.6	13.7	81				0.3	
Finland	6.0	12.4	106	1.2	2.4	100				-0.2	
France	156.5	102.2	-35	2.7	1.7	-37				-29.4	
Germany	1,236.0	903.0	-27	15.3	11.0	-28					-0.1
Greece	8.5	2.8	-67	0.8	0.3	-68				0.1	
Iceland	0.2	0.2	3	0.8	0.7	-4				0.0	
Ireland	0.5	5.4	976	0.1	1.4	887				1.8	
Italy	9.3	8.6	-8	0.2	0.1	-10					
Luxembourg	2.2	1.2	-45	5.6	2.7	-52					
Netherlands	29.7	148.4	400	2.0	9.2	370				-3.6	
Norway	29.8	50.4	69	7.0	11.1	60				0.3	
Portugal	1.8	0.5	-74	0.2	0.0	-75				0.0	
Spain	4.0	6.8	70	0.1	0.2	67				0.0	
Sweden	131.1	142.2	8	15.0	15.9	6				-4.3	
Switzerland	51.9	64.4	24	7.4	8.8	18				5.9	
United Kingdom	47.8	159.2	233	0.8	2.7	222				10.7	
Latin America & Caribbean											
Low income economies											
Nicaragua	14.5	0.3	-98	3.7	0.1	-98					-0.4
Middle income economies											
Argentina	11.5	2.4	-79	0.3	0.1	-81				0.0	0.1
Belize	20.4	1.0	-95	101.7	4.0	-96				-0.1	
Bolivia	0.5	0.4	-30	0.1	0.0	-43				0.0	
Brazil	5.4	3.2	-41	0.0	0.0	-49				0.3	0.0
Chile	0.1	0.4	313	0.0	0.0	262				0.0	-0.2

	Refugee populations*						IDP Populations			Refugeee Flows**	
	Total (1000s)			per 1000 inhabitants			Total (1000s)			2002 (1000s)	
Country of asylum	1992	2002	% change	1992	2002	% change	2001	2002	% change	Inflow	Outflow
Colombia	0.5	0.2	-59	0.0	0.0	-66	720.0	950.0	32	0.0	12.4
Costa Rica	114.4	12.4	-89	36.1	3.2	-91				4.3	
Cuba	5.1	1.0	-80	0.5	0.1	-81				0.0	-1.3
Ecuador	0.2	3.4	1,609	0.0	0.3	1,275				1.7	0.0
El Salvador	19.9	0.1	-100	3.8	0.0	-100				0.0	-0.5
Guatemala	222.9	0.7	-100	21.8	0.1	-100				0.0	-2.8
Honduras	100.3	0.0	-100	20.0	0.0	-100				0.0	-0.1
Mexico	361.0	13.0	-96	4.1	0.1	-97				-2.5	0.1
Panama	1.0	1.6	57	0.4	0.5	34				0.1	
Peru	0.6	0.7	15	0.0	0.0	-6				0.0	-0.4
Suriname	0.1	0.0	-100	0.2	0.0	-100					
Uruguay	0.1	0.1	-1	0.0	0.0	-8				0.0	
Venezuela	2.0	0.1	-97	0.1	0.0	-98				0.0	-0.1
Middle East & North Africa											
Low income economies											
Yemen	59.7	82.8	39	4.5	4.4	-1				13.3	-0.7
Middle income economies											
Algeria	219.3	169.2	-23	8.3	5.2	-36				-0.2	-0.2
Djibouti	28.0	21.7	-22	72.9	48.5	-33				-1.4	0.0
Egypt	5.5	80.5	1,364	0.1	1.1	1,086				73.3	0.3
Iran	4,150.7	1,306.6	-69	68.3	19.3	-72				-561.4	-8.1
Iraq	115.0	134.2	17	6.4	5.6	-13				6.0	-180.6
Jordan	0.3	1.2	300	0.1	0.2	191				0.1	0.0
Lebanon	6.0	2.8	-53	1.9	0.8	-59				0.0	-1.6
Libya	*1.2*	11.7	*90*	*0.3*	2.2	*87*				0.0	0.1
Morocco	0.3	2.1	609	0.0	0.1	487				0.0	0.0
Saudi Arabia	28.7	245.3	755	1.7	10.4	507				0.0	
Syria	6.3	2.9	-54	0.5	0.2	-64				-0.4	-0.2
Tunisia	0.1	0.1	2	0.0	0.0	-11				0.0	0.1
High income economies											
Israel		4.2			0.7					0.0	79.6
Kuwait	44.9	1.5	-97	31.7	0.7	-98				0.3	0.0
United Arab Emirates	*0.4*	0.2	*-145*	*0.2*	0.1	*-193*				-0.4	
North America											
High income economies											
Canada	183.7	130.0	-29	6.4	4.1	-37				0.7	
United States	580.0	485.2	-16	2.3	1.7	-25				-30.7	
South Asia											
Low income economies											
Afghanistan	60.0	0.0	-100	3.6	0.0	-100	1,200.0	665.2	-45		-1,353.6
Bangladesh	245.2	22.0	-91	2.2	0.2	-92				-0.1	-0.4
India	258.4	168.9	-35	0.3	0.2	-45				-0.7	0.2
Nepal	75.4	132.4	76	3.7	5.1	38				1.5	0.2
Pakistan	1,629.2	1,227.4	-25	13.7	8.3	-39				-971.4	1.2

Record 11 continued

	Refugee populations*						IDP Populations			Refugeee Flows**	
	Total (1000s)			per 1000 inhabitants			Total (1000s)			2002 (1000s)	
Country of asylum	1992	2002	% change	1992	2002	% change	2001	2002	% change	Inflow	Outflow
Middle income economies											
Sri Lanka	0.0	0.0		0.0	0.0		683.3	447.1	-35	0.0	-5.2
Sub-Saharan Africa											
Low income economies											
Angola	11.0	12.3	11	1.3	1.2	-11	202.0	188.7	-7		-38.4
Benin	0.3	5.0	1,574	0.1	0.7	1,118				0.2	
Burkina Faso	5.7	0.5	-92	0.6	0.0	-94					
Burundi	271.7	40.5	-85	49.6	6.8	-86	20.0	100.0	400	12.6	20.2
Cameroon	42.2	58.3	38	3.4	3.8	10				17.1	1.2
Central African Republic	19.0	50.7	167	6.4	14.0	118				1.5	-3.4
Chad	0.1	33.5	33,355	0.0	3.7	23,926				20.3	1.0
Congo, Dem. Rep.	391.1	333.0	-15	9.6	6.0	-37	3.5	9.0	160	-29.0	21.5
Congo, Rep.	3.4	109.2	3,112	1.4	37.6	2,502				-9.9	2.7
Côte d'Ivoire	174.1	44.7	-74	13.6	2.7	-80		100.0		-81.5	22.1
Eritrea		3.6			0.8					1.3	-17.8
Ethiopia	431.8	132.9	-69	8.4	2.0	-76				-19.6	-4.6
Gambia	3.6	12.1	237	3.5	8.3	140					0.0
Ghana	12.1	33.5	177	0.7	1.7	124				21.7	-0.2
Guinea	478.5	182.2	-62	68.5	20.7	-70				3.7	0.7
Guinea-Bissau	12.2	7.6	-37	11.6	5.7	-51				-0.1	0.0
Kenya	402.2	233.7	-42	15.8	7.5	-53				-5.6	0.3
Lesotho	0.1	0.0	-100	0.1	0.0	-100				0.0	
Liberia	100.0	65.0	-35	50.4	19.9	-60	196.1	304.1	55	10.2	29.6
Madagascar		0.0			0.0					0.0	
Malawi	1,058.5	2.2	-100	107.2	0.2	-100				-4.0	
Mali	13.1	9.1	-31	1.5	0.8	-47				0.7	0.0
Mauritania	37.5	0.4	-99	17.7	0.1	-99				0.0	0.2
Mozambique	0.3	0.2	-31	0.0	0.0	-50					
Niger	3.7	0.3	-92	0.5	0.0	-94				0.2	0.0
Nigeria	4.8	7.4	53	0.0	0.1	15				0.2	17.2
Rwanda	25.2	30.9	22	3.4	4.0	17				-3.9	-9.8
Senegal	71.6	20.7	-71	9.2	2.0	-78				0.0	0.0
Sierra Leone	5.9	63.5	976	1.4	11.4	726				52.7	-41.2
Somalia	0.5	0.2	-60	0.1	0.0	-69				0.0	-11.8
Sudan	725.9	328.2	-55	25.7	8.8	-66				-19.7	15.0
Tanzania	292.1	689.4	136	10.8	19.5	81				42.5	0.1
Togo	3.4	12.3	262	0.9	2.3	171				0.0	0.4
Uganda	196.3	217.3	11	10.6	8.7	-18				17.6	-0.2
Zambia	142.1	246.8	74	17.2	24.3	41				-37.4	
Zimbabwe	237.7	9.4	-96	22.2	0.8	-97				0.7	2.7
Middle income economies											
Botswana	0.5	2.8	461	0.4	1.8	392				-0.8	
Gabon	0.3	13.5	4,391	0.3	10.5	3,341				-2.1	
Namibia	0.2	21.7	10,726	0.1	11.4	8,408				-9.2	-1.0
South Africa	*250.0*	23.3	*-971*	*6.5*	0.5	*-1,083*				4.7	
Swaziland	55.6	0.7	-99	57.8	0.6	-99				0.0	

Record 11 continued

	Refugee populations*						IDP Populations			Refugee Flows**	
	Total (1000s)			per 1000 inhabitants			Total (1000s)			2002 (1000s)	
Region	1992	2002	% change	1992	2002	% change	2001	2002	% change	Inflow	Outflow
East Asia & Pacific	470.3	573.4	18	12.0	9.7	-23				-41.4	-43.1
Europe & Central Asia	*3,542.0*	2,481.6	*-43*	*410.0*	213.8	*-92*	2,023.1	1,866.8	-8	-114.7	-82.0
Latin America & Caribbean	880.5	41.0	-2,046	192.9	8.6	-2,134	720.0	950.0	24	3.9	6.8
Middle East & North Africa	*4,666.4*	2,067.0	*-126*	*196.7*	99.5	*-98*				-470.7	-111.4
North America	763.7	615.1	-24	8.7	5.8	-51				-30.0	
South Asia	2,268.2	1,550.8	-46	23.5	13.8	-71	1,883.3	1,112.2	-69	-970.7	-1,357.6
Sub-Saharan Africa	*5,484.3*	3,058.3	*-79*	*538.3*	251.2	*-114*	421.6	701.8	40	-15.0	6.6

Empty cells indicate that the value is below 100, zero or not available.

* The figures for refugee populations are as of end of year.
** Figures for inflow and outflow of refugees were obtained by netting the populations of refugees reported in the beginning of 2002 and at the end of 2002 for the country of asylum, in the case of inflow, and for the country of origin in the case of outflow.

Inflows and outflows based on primae facie arrivals and individually recognised refugees. IDPs refer to internally displaced persons of concern to/assisted by UNHCR at end of 2002.
When data for a specific year were not available, data for an adjacent year were substituted. These data and estimates based on them are presented in italics.
Per capita calculations were made by us, using population data from US Census Bureau International Database, www.census.gov/ipc/www/idbsprd.html

Sources: World Development Indicators 2002 (WDI-Online); UNHCR Statstics Online, www.unhcr.ch/cgi-bin/texis/vtx/goto?page=statistics; UNHCR Statistical Yearbook 2001 (compressed in a Zip file), www.unhcr.ch/static/statistical_yearbook/2001/pdfall.zip; US Census Bureau International Database, www.census.gov/ipc/www/idbsprd.html

Record 12 Peacekeeping

A country's preparedness to contribute part of its armed forces to peacekeeping duties in foreign conflicts can be seen as a commitment to the international rule of law. This record reports the ratio of peacekeeping forces to total military personnel, comparing numbers of military personnel (for 2001, the latest available data) with the total number of forces per country committed to peacekeeping (as of February 2004).

Country	Total military personnel 2001	Peacekeeping forces as of Feb 2004*	Peacekeeping forces per 1000 military personnel
East Asia & Pacific			
Low income economies			
Cambodia	140,000		
Indonesia & East Timor	297,000	205	0.1
Korea, Dem. Rep.	1,082,000		
Laos	29,100		
Mongolia	9,100	5	0.2
Myanmar	344,000		
Papua New Guinea	4,400		
Vietnam	484,000		
Middle income economies			
China & Tibet	2,310,000	337	0.0
Fiji	3,500	191	49.5
Malaysia	100,500	75	0.7
Philippines	107,000	198	0.6
Thailand	306,000	58	1.8
High income economies			
Australia	50,700	325	13.2
Brunei	5,900		
Korea, Rep.	683,000	42	0.7
Japan	239,800	408	2.7
New Zealand	9,200	17	1.9
Singapore	60,500	3	4.2
Europe & Central Asia			
Low income economies			
Armenia	42,000		
Azerbaijan	72,100		
Georgia	16,800		
Kyrgyzstan	9,000	2	0.1
Moldova	8,200	3	
Tajikistan	6,000		
Ukraine	303,800	1,129	3.1
Uzbekistan	52,000		
Middle income economies			
Albania	27,000	3	0.1
Belarus	82,900		
Bosnia & Herzegovina	24,000	14	0.4
Bulgaria	77,300	8	0.1
Croatia	58,300	27	0.3
Czech Republic	53,600	22	0.3

Record 12 continued

Country	Total military personnel 2001	Peacekeeping forces as of Feb 2004*	Peacekeeping forces per 1000 military personnel
Estonia	4,500	2	0.1
Hungary	33,800	137	2.7
Kazakhstan	64,000		
Latvia	6,500		
Lithuania	12,200		
Macedonia	*16,000*		
Poland	206,000	612	2.7
Romania	103,000	43	0.2
Russian Federation	977,100	203	0.2
Serbia & Montenegro	105,500	10	0.0
Slovakia	33,000	499	13.9
Slovenia	7,600	2	0.3
Turkey	515,100	6	0.0
Turkmenistan	17,500		
High income economies			
Austria	34,600	390	8.1
Belgium	39,400	14	0.3
Cyprus	10,000		
Denmark	21,400	36	1.4
Finland	32,300	229	1.3
France	273,700	245	0.5
Germany	308,400	25	0.1
Greece	159,200	9	0.1
Ireland	10,500	471	15.1
Italy	230,400	115	0.3
Luxembourg	900		
Netherlands	50,400	13	0.2
Norway	26,700	19	0.7
Portugal	43,600	520	9.1
Spain	143,500	10	0.1
Sweden	33,900	175	0.6
Switzerland	26,800	20	0.5
United Kingdom	211,400	455	2.1
Latin America & Caribbean			
Low income economies			
Nicaragua	16,000		
Middle income economies			
Argentina	70,100	405	4.8
Belize	1,100		
Bolivia	31,500	221	6.5
Brazil	287,600	73	0.3
Chile	87,500	6	0.1
Colombia	158,000		
Costa Rica	*10,000*		
Cuba	46,000		
Dominican Republic	24,500		
Ecuador	59,500	4	

Country	Total military personnel 2001	Peacekeeping forces as of Feb 2004*	Peacekeeping forces per 1000 military personnel
El Salvador	16,800	5	0.3
Guatemala	31,400		
Guyana	1,600		
Honduras	8,300	12	0.4
Jamaica	2,800		
Mexico	192,800		
Panama	*12,000*		
Paraguay	18,600	34	1.4
Peru	100,000	13	0.0
Suriname	2,000		
Trinidad & Tobago	2,700		
Uruguay	23,900	1,879	66.5
Venezuela	82,300		0.0
Middle East & North Africa			
Low income economies			
Yemen	54,000		
Middle income economies			
Algeria	124,000	19	0.2
Djibouti	9,600		
Egypt	443,000	56	0.2
Iran	513,000	3	0.0
Iraq	424,000		
Jordan	100,200	1,273	11.2
Lebanon	71,800		
Libya	76,000		
Malta	2,100		
Morocco & Western Sahara	198,500	830	3.2
Oman	43,400		
Saudi Arabia	201,200		
Syria	321,000		
Tunisia	35,000	504	8.2
High income economies			
Bahrain	11,000		
Israel & Occupied Territories	163,500		
Kuwait	15,500		
Qatar	12,300		
United Arab Emirates	65,000		
North America			
High income economies			
Canada	56,800	218	3.6
United States	1,367,700	23	0.0
South Asia			
Low income economies			
Afghanistan			
Bangladesh	137,000	6,333	37.4
Bhutan	*8,000*		

Record 12 continued

Country	Total military personnel 2001	Peacekeeping forces as of Feb 2004*	Peacekeeping forces per 1000 military personnel
India	1,263,000	2,572	2.0
Nepal	46,000	2,120	24.1
Pakistan	620,000	6,649	6.7
Middle income economies			
Maldives			
Sri Lanka	121,000	4	0.0
Sub-Saharan Africa			
Low income economies			
Angola	130,500		
Benin	4,800	299	2.8
Burkina Faso	10,000	12	1.3
Burundi	45,500		
Cameroon	22,100	3	0.2
Central African Republic	3,200		
Chad	30,400		
Congo, Rep.	81,400		
Côte d'Ivoire	13,900		
Equatorial Guinea	1,300		
Eritrea	171,900		
Ethiopia	252,500		
Gambia	800	178	17.0
Ghana	7,000	2,229	282.3
Guinea	9,700	17	66.1
Guinea-Bissau	9,300	649	
Kenya	24,400	1,776	63.9
Lesotho	2,000		
Liberia	15,000		
Madagascar	13,500		2.3
Malawi	5,300		3.4
Mali	7,400		
Mozambique	11,000	4	0.3
Niger	5,300	24	2.8
Nigeria	78,500	3,303	42.3
Rwanda	70,000		
São Tomé & Principe	*1,000*		
Senegal	9,800	758	35.1
Sierra Leone	6,000		
Sudan	117,000		
Tanzania	27,000		0.6
Togo	9,500	151	
Uganda	55,000		
Zambia	21,600	874	41.0
Zimbabwe	39,000		
Middle income economies			
Botswana	9,000		
Cape Verde	1,200		

Record 12 continued

Country	Total military personnel 2001	Peacekeeping forces as of Feb 2004*	Peacekeeping forces per 1000 military personnel
Gabon	4,700		
Mauritius	*1,000*		
Namibia	9,000	866	0.3
South Africa	61,500	1,454	2.1
Swaziland	*3,000*		
Total	**20,050,200**	**43,185**	

Military personnel data in italics are from 1998.
* Peacekeeping forces here comprise military observers and troops

Country of mission	Name of mission
Democratic Republic of Congo	MONUC
East Timor	UNTAET
India/Pakistan	UNMOGIP
Bosnia and Herzegovina	UNMIBIH
Cyprus	UNFICIP
Georgia	UNIMIG
Kosovo	UNMIK
Golan Heights	UNDOF
Iraq/Kuwait	UNOKOM
Lebanon	UNIFIL
Middle East	UNTSO

Sources: US Department of State, Bureau of Arms Control, World Military Expenditures and Arms Transfers 1998; US Department of State, Annual Report on Military Expenditures, 1999; United Nations, Department of Peacekeeping Operations, www.un.org/Depts/dpko/dpko/contributors/index.htm ; International Institute for Strategic Studies, London: The Military Balance 2001/2. Oxford: Oxford University Press, Table 26 International comparisons of defense expenditure and military manpower, 1985, 2000 and 2001.

Record 13 Environment

This record gives an indication of the extent to which countries protect or harm the global environment, with the use of the latest data available. It is now generally agreed that carbon dioxide emissions are a major contributor to the problem of global warming: a large volume of emissions can therefore be considered as an infringement of the environmental element of the international rule of law. It is difficult to evaluate emissions' indicators at the country level, since per capita figures may favour populous countries, while per unit of income measures may favour high-income countries (we use purchasing power parity [PPP], which represents the relative value of currencies based on what those currencies will buy in their nation of origin). We therefore present both in the table, for comparison purposes.

Consumption of renewable energy is an indicator of the efforts made by societies to develop alternative, more environmental friendly, energy sources . The number of environmental conservation treaties ratified/signed is an indicator of a country's commitment to international norms of environmental conservation. The entries in the table indicate the number of environmental conservation treaties signed by each country out of a list of 220 treaties generally pertaining to environmental conservation, from the list maintained by the Environmental Treaties and Resource Indicators (ENTRI) project (see table note for a list of treaty categories considered for this table; for a detailed list of treaties included see www.sedac.ciesin.columbia.edu/entri/treatySearch.jsp, updated as of September 2000).

	Carbon dioxide emissions						Consumption of renewable energy per 100,000 population (1000 metric tons of oil equivalent)			Number of ratified or signed environmental conservation treaties*			
	metric tons per capita			kg per PPP $ of GDP									
Country	1990	1999	% change 1990–1999	1990	1999	% change 1990–1999	1990	1999	% change 1990–1999	Party	Signatory	% party or signatory	% party or signatory since 1995
East Asia & Pacific													
Low income economies										2	3	4	5
Cambodia										17	2	8.6	36.8
Indonesia	35.6	43.0	21	188	174.1	-7	22.5	22.6	1	19	5	10.9	12.5
Korea, Dem. Rep.	85.4	86.9	2				18.4	13.1	-29	10	3	5.9	15.4
Laos										11	0	5.0	36.4
Mongolia										13	0	5.9	53.8
Myanmar	9.1	16.7	84	102.3	89.7		23.7	23.1	-3	13	0	5.9	38.5
Papua New Guinea										25	3	12.7	28.6
Solomon Islands										27	2	13.2	27.6
Vietnam	17.4	24.8	43				29.1	30.4	4	15	0	6.8	6.7
Middle income economies													
China	65.6	66.0	1	1,249.10	442.3	-65	18.4	18.3	-1	28	1	13.2	27.6
Fiji										23	3	11.8	30.8
Malaysia	56.6	56.7	0	362	321.5	-11	14.0	14.6	5	22	1	10.5	26.1
Philippines	33.1	38.9	18	106.3	122.2	15	23.4	24.5	5	20	5	11.4	16.0
Samoa										17	2	8.6	42.1
Thailand	44	52.9	20	159	249.9	57	27.3	22.9	-16	21	3	10.9	33.3
Tonga										12	2	6.4	42.9
Vanuatu										8	8	7.3	12.5
High income economies													
Australia	70.9	71.2	0	419.5	352.3	-16	29.8	34.9	17	52	3	25.0	10.9
Brunei	54.2	55.8	3				7.1	5.6	-22	7	2	4.1	33.3
Korea, Rep.	60.8	54.1	-11				1.3	1.3	4	30	1	14.1	29.0

Record 13 continued

Country	Carbon dioxide emissions: metric tons per capita 1990	1999	% change 1990–1999	Carbon dioxide emissions: kg per PPP $ of GDP 1990	1999	% change 1990–1999	Consumption of renewable energy per 100,000 population (1000 metric tons of oil equivalent) 1990	1999	% change 1990–1999	Number of ratified or signed environmental conservation treaties*: Party	Signatory	% party or signatory	% party or signatory since 1995
Japan	57.1	53.7	-6	233.8	259.4	11	12.6	12.5	-1	41	3	20.0	27.3
New Zealand	39.2	40.2	3	409.4			146.6	146.4	0	43	6	22.3	14.3
Singapore	62.2	56.0	-10	130.1	82.4	-37	0.0	0.0		6	1	3.2	14.3
Europe & Central Asia													
Low income economies													
Armenia		38.3			384.4			3.4		11	1	5.5	41.7
Azerbaijan		63.0			653.3			1.7		4	1	2.3	60.0
Georgia		48.7			304.7			13.0		14	3	7.7	58.8
Kyrgyzstan		46.1								6	0	2.7	66.7
Moldova		55.7						1.5		11	4	6.8	53.3
Tajikistan		40.8						21.0		8	0	3.6	62.5
Ukraine		61.0			1,725.60			2.6		25	7	14.5	53.1
Uzbekistan		56.8			1,422.70			2.0		10	0	4.5	70.0
Middle income economies													
Albania	58.4	33.5	-43	585.5	138.3	-76	18.7	14.8	-21	20	5	11.4	44.0
Belarus		57.0			255.4			7.7		13	5	8.2	16.7
Bosnia & Herzegovina		63.3						8.5		14	2	7.3	31.3
Bulgaria	63.1	57.4	-9	500.7	924.2	85	3.8	8.1	117	42	7	22.3	36.7
Croatia		55.8						19.2		27	4	14.1	51.6
Czech Republic							1.2	6.4		34	5	17.7	56.4
Estonia		77.0			315			36.5		21	2	10.5	26.1
Hungary	56.7	54.6	-4	392.3			3.6	3.4	-4	37	5	19.1	23.8
Kazakhstan		77.1			1,359.80			4.0		8	1	4.1	33.3
Latvia		42.4			290.8			48.1		22	3	11.4	60.0
Lithuania		39.4			250.9			17.1		17	4	9.5	57.1
Macedonia		78.3						16.3		17	0	7.7	70.6
Poland	83.4	79.3	-5	350.5	389.4	11	4.1	9.7	134	53	10	28.6	23.8
Romania	65.6	56.8	-13	733.6	389.3	-47	6.9	19.6	183	39	9	21.8	35.4
Russian Federation		58.9			530.2		13.5	12.8	-6	64	4	30.9	8.8
Serbia & Montenegro		74.7					17.1	12.5	-27	26	2	12.7	7.1
Slovakia	61	52.3		844.4	818		6.2	8.6	38	33	3	16.4	38.9
Slovenia		55.1						27.8		33	10	19.5	51.2
Turkey	62.7	62.1	-1	320.4	397.5	24	16.6	15.6	-6	27	8	15.9	20.0
Turkmenistan		59.3						0.0		8	0	3.6	100.0
High income economies													
Austria	54	50.9	-6	249.7	213.6	-14	70.4	80.8	15	47	15	28.2	25.8
Belgium	52.4	48.4	-8	440.1	466.2	6	2.4	3.9	67	74	15	40.5	15.7
Cyprus	60.4	61.6	2	303.1			0.9	5.9	557	26	5	14.1	35.5
Denmark	66.5	63.4	-5	169.9	128.1	-25	15.1	22.2	47	86	9	43.2	16.8
Finland	44.2	41.4	-6	437.4	348.6	-20	102.5	140.5	37	65	8	33.2	20.5

Country	Carbon dioxide emissions: metric tons per capita 1990	1999	% change 1990–1999	Carbon dioxide emissions: kg per PPP $ of GDP 1990	1999	% change 1990–1999	Consumption of renewable energy per 100,000 population (1000 metric tons of oil equivalent) 1990	1999	% change 1990–1999	Number of ratified or signed environmental conservation treaties*: Party	Signatory	% party or signatory	% party or signatory since 1995
France	38.5	33.8	-12	226.6	224	-1	23.6	27.5	16	93	29	55.5	20.5
Germany	64.9	58.2		281.9	218.4		4.9	4.6	-6	91	20	50.5	19.8
Greece	75.7	72.4	-4	296.7	253.4	-15	6.8	13.7	101	48	15	28.6	28.6
Iceland	22.8	15.5	-32	261.4			520.2	819.7	58	33	13	20.9	23.9
Ireland	73.4	68.2	-7	259.5	142.6	-45	1.7	6.8	300	44	17	27.7	21.3
Italy	62.5	59.4	-5	231.3	217	-6	9.8	14.4	48	74	16	40.9	21.1
Luxembourg	69.9	51.3	-27	1,435.10	431.8	-70	1.6	5.7	263	43	18	27.7	21.3
Netherlands	56.2	53.7	-4	386.9	336.7	-13	1.3	2.9	130	89	9	44.5	17.3
Norway	31.7	33.3	5	202.7	164.1	-19	267.5	263.2	-2	80	6	39.1	17.4
Portugal	58.1	61.8	6	235.4	236.6	1	19.7	18.3	-7	63	13	34.5	19.7
Spain	55.8	54.8	-2	236.2	223.3	-5	13.9	14.9	7	81	8	40.5	19.1
Sweden	24.8	22.5	-9	197.2			132.4	160.6	21	83	6	40.5	19.1
Switzerland	39.2	35.7	-9				44.7	56.8	27	52	19	32.3	32.4
United Kingdom	64.2	55.5	-14	226.1	205.3	-9	1.6	3.7	128	88	14	46.4	17.6
Latin America & Caribbean													
Low income economies													
Haiti	14.2	16.0	13	77.8	175.6	126	20.6	22.3	8	13	2	6.8	26.7
Nicaragua	19.7	30.4	54	143.8	79.7	-45	40.6	30.7	-24	13	7	9.1	25.0
Middle income economies													
Argentina	55.3	54.0	-2	169.1	173.6	3	9.9	13.1	31	30	8	17.3	15.8
Barbados										14	2	7.3	25.0
Belize										15	4	8.6	26.3
Bolivia	45.7	51.4	12	224.9	304.2	35	13.0	12.5	-4	18	8	11.8	30.8
Brazil	36.2	40.6	12	157.9	267	69	39.3	39.4	0	36	2	17.3	26.3
Chile	53.7	55.6	4	207	241.8	17	27.0	35.2	30	32	4	16.4	13.9
Colombia	46.6	48.1	3	175.4	293.8	68	24.9	20.9	-16	19	8	12.3	22.2
Costa Rica	33.1	36.7	11	138.7	80.3	-42	34.1	36.3	6	20	5	11.4	20.0
Cuba	45.9	54.3	18		759.7		53.0	25.7	-52	18	6	10.9	8.3
Dominican Republic							14.6	18.1		14	4	8.2	16.7
Ecuador	49	52.8	8	186.5	196.3	5	14.6	16.2	11	21	4	11.4	20.0
El Salvador	22	31.7	44	118.9	149.8	26	33.8	35.6	5	14	3	7.7	23.5
Guatemala	20	32.7	64	146.8	170.5	16	31.9	26.3	-18	19	4	10.5	21.7
Guyana										14	3	7.7	23.5
Honduras	21.5	31.5	47	257.8	245.8	-5	35.6	30.1	-16	13	4	7.7	41.2
Jamaica	62.5	58.1	-7	159.1	275.4	73	18.6	24.3	30	17	5	10.0	31.8
Mexico	57.1	57.4	1	440.2	271.3	-38	16.4	15.9	-3	25	4	13.2	13.8
Panama	42.6	49.0	15	328.3	357	9	24.9	25.2	1	23	8	14.1	32.3
Paraguay	15.3	23.0	50	34.2	48.2	41	108.1	123.9	15	19	2	9.5	38.1
Peru	38.3	38.6	1	161.5	214.3	33	22.4	22.1	-1	27	3	13.6	23.3
St. Lucia										12	3	6.8	26.7

Country	Carbon dioxide emissions: metric tons per capita 1990	Carbon dioxide emissions: metric tons per capita 1999	Carbon dioxide emissions: metric tons per capita % change 1990–1999	Carbon dioxide emissions: kg per PPP $ of GDP 1990	Carbon dioxide emissions: kg per PPP $ of GDP 1999	Carbon dioxide emissions: kg per PPP $ of GDP % change 1990–1999	Consumption of renewable energy per 100,000 population (1000 metric tons of oil equivalent) 1990	Consumption of renewable energy per 100,000 population (1000 metric tons of oil equivalent) 1999	Consumption of renewable energy per 100,000 population (1000 metric tons of oil equivalent) % change 1990–1999	Number of ratified or signed environmental conservation treaties*: Party	Number of ratified or signed environmental conservation treaties*: Signatory	Number of ratified or signed environmental conservation treaties*: % party or signatory	Number of ratified or signed environmental conservation treaties*: % party or signatory since 1995
Suriname										15	3	8.2	33.3
Trinidad & Tobago	50.4	46.5	-8				4.1	2.8	-31	19	4	10.5	26.1
Uruguay	41.7	50.1	20	98.5	143	45	37.7	29.1	-23	24	8	14.5	15.6
Venezuela	56.9	53.7	-6	538.1	719.8	34	19.2	24.8	29	27	1	12.7	28.6
High income economies													
Bahamas										11	2	5.9	46.2
Middle East & North Africa													
Low income economies													
Yemen	66.2	65.3		199	97.4		0.6	0.5	-27	13	0	5.9	30.8
Middle income economies													
Algeria	57.7	57.6	0	76.5	63.3	-17	0.2	0.5	109	21	3	10.9	25.0
Djibouti										8	3	5.0	18.2
Egypt	61.5	59.2	-4	612.1	447.8	-27	3.4	3.8	12	27	4	14.1	16.1
Iran	64.3	60.7	-6				2.1	1.9	-12	9	13	10.0	9.1
Iraq	62.9	67.2	7				1.4	0.3	-75	6	2	3.6	0.0
Jordan	63.8	65.6	3	408.6	427.3	5	1.9	1.4	-24	17	1	8.2	50.0
Lebanon	66.2	68.1	3		728.9		4.6	4.6	-1	13	4	7.7	23.5
Libya	56.1	80.7	44				3.0	2.7	-10	12	4	7.3	12.5
Malta	70.9	60.7	-14				0.0	0.0		16	7	10.5	21.7
Morocco	66.4	67.4	2	157.3	176.5	12	1.7	1.7	-1	24	12	16.4	22.2
Oman	56.8	59.5	5	156.4			0.0	0.0		10	0	4.5	20.0
Saudi Arabia	60.5	60.9	1	277.5			0.0	0.0	-86	12	0	5.5	33.3
Syria	64.2	63.6	-1				3.9	4.7	21	11	3	6.4	28.6
Tunisia	53.7	52.0	-3	308.1	244.9	-21	12.7	13.0	3	26	7	15.0	24.2
High income economies													
Bahrain	50.4	52.4	4	1439.4			0.0	0.0		8	0	3.6	25.0
Israel	69.7	72.2	4				8.0	9.5	19	19	3	10.0	22.7
Kuwait	59.5	64.2	8	795.8			0.0	0.0		7	2	4.1	0.0
Qatar	51.4	53.3	4				0.0	0.0	0	6	1	3.2	42.9
United Arab Emirates	57.8	57.0	-1	837.2			0.0	0.0		6	2	3.6	0.0
North America													
High income economies													
Canada	48.1	48.3	0	365.8			121.1	131.1	8	47	11	26.4	13.8
United States	60.1	58.8	-2				15.0	38.7	158	60	11	32.3	11.3
South Asia													
Low income economies													
Afghanistan										8	6	6.4	0.0
Bangladesh	26.5	35.1	32	167.6	186.5	11	6.3	5.9	-7	16	4	9.1	20.0
Bhutan										3	1	1.8	25.0
India	39.3	44.9	14	517.3	360.4	-30	21.6	20.8	-4	32	1	15.0	18.2

Record 13 continued

Country	Carbon dioxide emissions: metric tons per capita 1990	1999	% change 1990–1999	Carbon dioxide emissions: kg per PPP $ of GDP 1990	1999	% change 1990–1999	Consumption of renewable energy per 100,000 population (1000 metric tons of oil equivalent) 1990	1999	% change 1990–1999	Number of ratified or signed environmental conservation treaties*: Party	Signatory	% party or signatory	% party or signatory since 1995
Nepal	3.5	8.9	154	80.4	171.4	113	30.0	29.2	-3	13	4	7.7	11.8
Pakistan	34	36.8	8	489.8	466.7	-5	17.6	17.8	1	23	8	14.1	12.9
Middle income economies													
Maldives										6	3	4.1	33.3
Sri Lanka	17.2	29.7	73	47.6	115.6	143	24.4	23.9	-2	20	5	11.4	12.0
Sub-Saharan Africa													
Low income economies													
Angola	16.4	15.1	-8	401	185	-54	54.5	56.0	3	7	3	4.5	20.0
Benin	3.5	14.3	309	61.6	192.9	213	33.6	24.3	-28	18	5	10.5	21.7
Burkina Faso										22	5	12.3	11.1
Burundi										7	5	5.5	16.7
Cameroon	13	10.1	-22	36.3	43.8	21	34.6	35.7	3	18	8	11.8	11.5
Central African Republic										8	4	5.5	8.3
Chad										14	4	8.2	22.2
Comoros										8	2	4.5	10.0
Congo, Rep.	8.3	4.0	-52				34.6	21.0	-39	13	8	9.5	23.8
Congo, Dem. Rep.							27.6	27.3	-1	12	7	8.6	10.5
Côte d'Ivoire	16.6	18.5	11	130.4	112.3	-14	27.7	27.2	-2	24	7	14.1	29.0
Equatorial Guinea										14	3	7.7	17.6
Eritrea	..	21.6		..	51.6			11.1		5	0	2.3	20.0
Ethiopia				169.8	186.4	10				10	7	7.7	11.8
Gambia										11	5	7.3	25.0
Ghana	11.9	14.7	24	123.2	53.1	-57	28.5	28.9	1	19	8	12.3	11.1
Guinea										24	3	12.3	18.5
Guinea-Bissau										10	4	6.4	35.7
Kenya	12.5	12.4	-1	296.8	288.1	-3	42.9	40.7	-5	22	4	11.8	15.4
Lesotho										10	6	7.3	31.3
Liberia										11	11	10.0	0.0
Madagascar										16	7	10.5	17.4
Malawi										17	4	9.5	14.3
Mali										21	2	10.5	17.4
Mauritania										13	9	10.0	31.8
Mozambique	3.3	3.7	12	87.7	25.7	-71	53.9	40.7	-24	11	3	6.4	35.7
Niger										23	3	11.8	15.4
Nigeria	12.9	10.5	-19	159.6	265.3	66	61.5	60.5	-2	25	2	12.3	3.7
Rwanda										8	4	5.5	16.7
São Tomé & Principe										8	3	5.0	36.4
Senegal	23.4	26.5	13	131.2	181.9	39	18.4	17.6	-4	31	2	15.0	21.2
Sierra Leone										16	5	9.5	4.8
Somalia										6	4	4.5	0.0

Record 13 continued

Country	Carbon dioxide emissions: metric tons per capita			Carbon dioxide emissions: kg per PPP $ of GDP			Consumption of renewable energy per 100,000 population (1000 metric tons of oil equivalent)			Number of ratified or signed environmental conservation treaties*			
	1990	1999	% change 1990–1999	1990	1999	% change 1990–1999	1990	1999	% change 1990–1999	Party	Signatory	% party or signatory	% party or signatory since 1995
Sudan	12.3	8.4	-32		265.6		33.0	39.7	20	16	6	10.0	22.7
Tanzania	3.9	3.5	-10	153.6	137.7	-10	45.9	43.3	-6	15	5	9.1	30.0
Togo	12.9	15.3	19	129.2	255.6	98	21.0	20.7	-1	21	4	11.4	40.0
Uganda										20	6	11.8	19.2
Zambia	11.2	7.3	-35	318.1	387.3	22	57.9	59.2	2	16	4	9.1	20.0
Zimbabwe	38.2	32.1	-16	544.6	311.2	-43	49.8	47.7	-4	15	3	8.2	16.7
Middle income economies													
Botswana										12	5	7.7	29.4
Cape Verde										11	5	7.3	25.0
Gabon	21.5	22.1	3	80.3	132	64	85.6	80.7	-6	16	8	10.9	33.3
Mauritius										23	3	11.8	15.4
Namibia		47.8			12.1			15.1		14	2	7.3	43.8
South Africa	76.2	75.7	-1	520.9	508	-2	28.7	29.8	4	38	3	18.6	31.7
Swaziland													

* Includes 220 treaties in the following categories: Animal species protection – management; environmental conservation (general); fishing – management -use of harvestable fish; forest conservation – management – exploitation; hunting – management -use of harvestable species; marine resources conservation – management; natural resources and nature conservation; plant species protection – management; renewable energy sources and energy conservation; soil conservation – management; water resources conservation – management.

Sources: World Development Indicators 2002, WDI Online; International Energy Agency (IEA), 2001. CO2 Emissions from Fossil Fuel Combustion (2001 Edition), available online through EarthTrends: earthtrends.wri.org/text/theme6vars.htm
Environmental Treaties and Resource Indicators (ENTRI) project of The Center for International Earth Science Information Network (CIESIN), Earth Institute, Columbia University, sedac.ciesin.columbia.edu/entri/index.jsp

Record 14 Number of NGOs in countries and cities

The first table gives the total number of secretariats (headquarters) of international non-governmental organisations (INGOs) and internationally oriented NGOs in a given country for 1993 and 2003. These are the principal secretariats of the organisation. Secondary (including regional) secretariats are not included. The table also indicates the number of secretariats per million of the population, that is, 'organisational density', and the expansion or contraction in the number of secretariats by country over the time period. The second part of the record shows in which cities the secretariats are primarily based, for 2002 and 2003. It includes only cities that had at least 50 INGO secretariats located in them in 2003. There has been growth in the number of NGOs worldwide, particularly in low- and middle-income countries in Asia. Yet most NGOs are in the developed world. Only eight of the 43 top NGO cities are in the global South.

Secretariats in countries

Country	Number of secretariats 1993	Organisational density per million of population 1993	Number of secretariats 2003	Organisational density per million of population 2003	Absolute growth % 1993–2003	Density growth % 1993–2003
East Asia & Pacific						
Low income economies						
Cambodia	0	0.0	8	0.6		
Indonesia	30	0.2	46	0.2	53	29
Korea, Dem. Rep.	0	0.0	1	0.0		
Laos	0	0.0	1	0.2		
Mongolia	2	0.9	3	1.1	50	30
Myanmar	0	0.0	2	0.0		
Papua New Guinea	2	0.5	4	0.8	100	56
Solomon Islands	4	11.2	1	2.0	-75	-82
Vietnam	1	0.0	3	0.0	200	158
Middle income economies						
China & Tibet*	26	0.0	32	0.0	23	12
Fiji	19	25.3	28	32.7	47	29
Malaysia	53	2.9	83	3.7	57	27
Philippines	89	1.3	118	1.4	33	7
Samoa	0	0.0	3	16.8		
Thailand	50	0.9	104	1.6	108	85
Tonga	4	43.4	2	18.8	-50	-57
Vanuatu	3	18.6	1	5.1	-67	-73
High income economies						
Australia	184	10.5	364	18.6	98	77
Brunei	2	7.3	6	17.1	200	134
Korea, Rep.	43	1.0	61	1.3	42	30
Japan	158	1.3	264	2.1	67	63
New Zealand	28	8.1	55	14.1	96	73
Singapore	50	15.7	83	18.6	66	19
Europe & Central Asia						
Low income economies						
Armenia	0	0.0	1	0.3		
Azerbaijan	0	0.0	2	0.3		
Georgia	0	0.0	4	0.8		
Kyrgyzstan	1	0.2	3	0.6	200	182
Moldova	0	0.0	1	0.2		

Record 14 continued

Secretariats in countries Country	Number of secretariats 1993	Organisational density per million of population	Number of secretariats 2003	Organisational density per million of population	Absolute growth % 1993–2003	Density growth % 1993–2003
Tajikistan	0	0.0	0	0.0		
Ukraine	2	0.0	14	0.3	600	651
Uzbekistan	0	0.0	5	0.2		
Middle income economies						
Albania	1	0.3	1	0.3	0	-5
Belarus	2	0.2	2	0.2	0	0
Bosnia & Herzegovina	1	0.2	1	0.3	0	12
Bulgaria	27	3.1	34	4.4	26	42
Croatia	8	1.8	15	3.4	88	89
Czech Republic	39	3.8	47	4.6	21	21
Estonia	1	0.6	5	3.5	400	446
Hungary	40	3.9	64	6.3	60	64
Kazakhstan	1	0.1	5	0.3	400	407
Latvia	0	0.0	14	5.9		
Lithuania	1	0.3	5	1.4	400	415
Macedonia	0	0.0	4	1.9	0	0
Poland	30	0.8	47	1.2	57	56
Romania	11	0.5	14	0.6	27	30
Russian Federation	42	0.3	84	0.6	100	105
Serbia & Montenegro	0	0.0	11	1.0		
Slovakia	4	0.8	12	2.2	200	194
Slovenia	8	4.2	17	8.8	113	108
Turkey	15	0.3	40	0.6	167	130
Turkmenistan	0	0.0	0	0.0		
High income economies						
Austria	148	18.7	272	33.4	84	79
Belgium	1,484	147.7	1855	179.9	25	22
Cyprus	6	8.5	17	22.2	183	161
Denmark	220	42.5	246	45.8	12	8
Finland	99	19.6	141	27.2	42	38
France	1,334	23.3	1405	23.4	5	1
Germany	637	7.9	987	12.0	55	52
Greece	38	3.7	94	8.9	147	141
Iceland	12	46.3	18	64.4	50	39
Ireland	44	12.4	62	16.0	41	29
Italy	412	7.2	544	9.4	32	30
Luxembourg	45	114.6	43	95.4	-4	-17
Netherlands	523	34.5	817	50.7	56	47
Norway	132	30.8	176	38.8	33	26
Portugal	36	3.6	66	6.5	83	80
Spain	131	3.3	301	7.5	130	126
Sweden	255	29.2	331	37.0	30	26
Switzerland	593	84.8	717	97.4	21	15
United Kingdom	1,272	22.0	1923	32.1	51	46

Record 14 continued

Secretariats in countries Country	Number of secretariats 1993	Organisational density per million of population 1993	Number of secretariats 2003	Organisational density per million of population 2003	Absolute growth % 1993-2003	Density growth % 1993-2003
Latin America & Caribbean						
Low income economies						
Haiti	1	0.2	0	0.0		
Nicaragua	12	3.0	14	2.8	17	-8
Middle income economies						
Argentina	96	2.8	137	3.6	43	26
Barbados	27	101.9	23	83.3	-15	-18
Belize	0	0.0	1	3.8	0	0
Bolivia	2	0.3	9	1.1	350	267
Brazil	67	0.4	101	0.6	51	31
Chile	61	4.5	51	3.3	-16	-27
Colombia	41	1.2	45	1.1	10	-8
Costa Rica	46	14.5	61	15.9	33	10
Cuba	20	1.9	23	2.0	15	10
Dominican Republic	7	1.0	7	0.8	0	-15
Ecuador	19	1.8	28	2.1	47	19
El Salvador	9	1.7	10	1.6	11	-8
Guatemala	13	1.3	15	1.1	15	-13
Guyana	3	4.1	11	15.7	267	284
Honduras	0	0.0	13	2.0		
Jamaica	16	6.4	17	6.3	6	-1
Mexico	63	0.7	101	1.0	60	38
Panama	16	6.5	21	7.2	31	11
Paraguay	6	1.3	6	1.0	0	-24
Peru	52	2.3	51	1.8	-2	-19
St. Lucia	3	21.1	2	12.5	-33	-41
St. Vincent & the Grenadines	2	18.5	5	43.0	150	132
Suriname	0	0.0	1	2.3	0	0
Trinidad & Tobago	22	18.6	42	37.8	91	103
Uruguay	38	12.1	45	13.3	18	10
Venezuela	72	3.6	55	2.3	-24	-36
High income economies						
Bahamas	0	0.0	6	20.3		
Middle East & North Africa						
Low income economies						
Yemen	0	0.0	0	0.0		
Middle income economies						
Algeria	11	0.4	12	0.4	9	-10
Djibouti	0	0.0	0	0.0		
Egypt	58	1.0	64	0.9	10	-11
Iran	1	0.0	9	0.1	800	710
Iraq	20	1.1	9	0.4	-55	-67
Jordan	18	4.7	28	5.3	56	13

Record 14 continued

Secretariats in countries	Number of secretariats	Organisational density per million of population	Number of secretariats	Organisational density per million of population	Absolute growth %	Density growth %
Country	1993		2003		1993-2003	1993-2003
Lebanon	13	4.0	33	9.0	154	122
Libya	14	3.2	4	0.7	-71	-77
Malta	14	38.3	20	50.3	43	31
Morocco & Western Sahara	17	0.7	17	0.5	0	-17
Oman	1	0.5	1	0.4	0	-29
Saudi Arabia	22	1.3	20	0.9	-9	-35
Syria	15	1.1	9	0.5	-40	-54
Tunisia	27	3.2	31	3.2	15	0
High income economies						
Bahrain	2	3.8	4	6.1	100	61
Israel & Occupied Territories*	71	10.1	98	10.4	38	3
Kuwait	10	7.1	8	3.8	-20	-46
Qatar	3	5.7	0	0.0	-100	-100
United Arab Emirates	3	1.5	7	2.9	133	95
North America						
High income economies						
Canada	305	10.7	462	14.5	51	35
United States	1,978	7.7	3305	11.5	67	49
South Asia						
Low income economies						
Afghanistan	0	0.0	0	0.0		
Bangladesh	14	0.1	24	0.2	71	44
Bhutan	0	0.0	0	0.0	0	0
India	129	0.1	191	0.2	48	25
Nepal	8	0.4	24	0.9	200	136
Pakistan	26	0.2	27	0.2	4	-16
Middle income economies						
Maldives	0	0.0	0	0.0		
Sri Lanka	13	0.7	22	1.1	69	52
Sub-Saharan Africa						
Low income economies						
Angola	1	0.1	2	0.2	100	61
Benin	10	2.0	20	2.9	100	46
Burkina Faso	12	1.2	20	1.6	67	25
Burundi	0	0.0	1	0.2		
Cameroon	19	1.5	25	1.6	32	5
Central African Republic	3	1.0	0	0.0		
Chad	1	0.2	0	0.0		
Comoros	0	0.0	1	1.6		
Congo, Rep.	10	4.2	2	0.7	-80	-84
Congo, Dem. Rep.	9	0.2	5	0.1	-44	-59
Côte d'Ivoire	30	2.3	25	1.5	-17	-36

Record 14 continued

Secretariats in countries	Number of secretariats	Organisational density per million of population	Number of secretariats	Organisational density per million of population	Absolute growth %	Density growth %
Country	1993		2003		1993–2003	1993–2003
Equatorial Guinea	0	0.0	0	0.0		
Eritrea	0	0.0	0	0.0		
Ethiopia	17	0.3	15	0.2	-12	-30
Gambia	2	1.9	5	3.4	150	78
Ghana	25	1.5	36	1.8	44	16
Guinea	1	0.1	2	0.2	100	59
Guinea-Bissau	1	1.0	0	0.0		
Kenya	104	4.1	122	3.9	17	-4
Lesotho	4	2.3	4	2.2	0	-6
Liberia	1	0.5	0	0.0		
Madagascar	2	0.2	2	0.1	0	-26
Malawi	4	0.4	3	0.3	-25	-35
Mali	6	0.7	10	0.9	67	26
Mauritania	2	0.9	1	0.4	-50	-63
Mozambique	1	0.1	4	0.2	300	187
Niger	5	0.6	1	0.1	-80	-85
Nigeria	61	0.6	64	0.5	5	-21
Rwanda	3	0.4	3	0.4	0	-4
Senegal	59	7.5	59	5.7	0	-24
Sierra Leone	4	0.9	3	0.5	-25	-42
Somalia	0	0.0	0	0.0	0	0
Sudan	8	0.3	10	0.3	25	-5
Tanzania	15	0.6	19	0.5	27	-3
Togo	9	2.3	22	4.2	144	83
Uganda	5	0.3	24	1.0	380	257
Zambia	11	1.3	13	1.3	18	-4
Zimbabwe	30	2.8	39	3.1	30	12
Middle income economies						
Botswana	4	2.9	12	7.6	200	163
Cape Verde	0	0.0	0	0.0		
Gabon	2	2.0	4	3.1	100	53
Mauritius	5	4.6	16	13.3	220	192
Namibia	0	0.0	3	1.6		
South Africa	36	0.9	140	3.3	289	252
Swaziland	3	3.1	2	1.7	-33	-44

Record 14 continued

Number of secretariats						
	Number of secretariats	Organisational density per million of population	Number of secretariats	Organisational density per million of population	Absolute growth %	Density growth %
Region	1993		2003		1993-2003	1993-2003
Low income	705	0.3	926	0.4	31	8
Middle income	1,428	0.6	2,087	0.8	46	32
Low & middle income						
East Asia & the Pacific	283	0.2	440	0.2	55	39
Europe & Central Asia	226	0.5	435	0.9	92	90
Latin America & Caribbean	692	1.5	874	1.6	26	8
Middle East & North Africa	217	0.8	237	0.8	9	-11
South Asia	190	0.2	288	0.2	52	26
Sub-Saharan Africa	525	1.0	739	1.1	41	10
High income	10,414	11.5	14,939	15.4	43	34
World	12,547	2.3	17,952	2.9	43	25

* The number of secretariats have been given as for China & Tibet and Israel & Occupied Territories as geographical units. There are, however, no secretariats in either Tibet or the Occupied Territories. Data for China & Tibet excludes Hong Kong and Macao.

Per capita figures were calculated using total midyear population figures, US Census Bureau International database.
Regional sums include countries that were not included in the table above.

Source: © Union of International Associations, Yearbook of International Organizations: Guide to Civil Society Networks, 1994 and 2004; US Bureau of the Census International Data Base, April 2004. United States Department of Commerce. IDB Data Access - spreadsheet, www.census.gov/ipc/www/idbsprd.html

Record 14 continued

Secretariats in cities

City	Country	Number of secretariats 2002	2003	% Change 2002–2003
Amsterdam	Netherlands	152	173	14
Athens	Greece	60	56	-7
Bangkok	Thailand	80	82	3
Barcelona	Spain	73	72	-1
Berlin	Germany	113	108	-4
Berne	Switzerland	42	51	21
Bonn	Germany	78	81	4
Brussels	Belgium	1,420	1,428	1
Budapest	Hungary	45	52	16
Buenos Aires	Argentina	110	120	9
Copenhagen	Denmark	114	119	4
Dakar	Senegal	53	56	6
Frankfurt Main	Germany	57	57	0
Geneva	Switzerland	276	298	8
The Hague	Netherlands	98	96	-2
Helsinki	Finland	62	70	13
Kuala Lumpur	Malaysia	48	54	13
Lausanne	Switzerland	68	72	6
London	United Kingdom	781	810	4
Madrid	Spain	143	138	-3
Mexico City	Mexico	78	71	-9
Milan	Italy	82	82	0
Montreal	Canada	86	90	5
Moscow	Russian Federation	70	69	-1
Munich	Germany	61	63	3
Nairobi	Kenya	110	113	3
New Delhi	India	74	77	4
New York NY	United States	355	353	-1
Oslo	Norway	96	96	0
Ottawa	Canada	65	72	11
Oxford	United Kingdom	46	53	15
Paris	France	706	701	-1
Rome	Italy	210	216	3
San Francisco CA	United States	63	69	10
Singapore	Singapore	80	82	3
Stockholm	Sweden	135	132	-2
Strasbourg	France	59	55	-7
Tokyo	Japan	160	155	-3
Toronto	Canada	70	66	-6
Utrecht	Netherlands	83	81	-2
Vienna	Austria	194	200	3
Washington DC	United States	461	437	-5
Zurich	Switzerland	77	82	6

This table lists only cities with 50 or more INGO headquarters in 2003.

Source: © Union of International Associations, Yearbook of International Organizations: Guide to Civil Society Networks, 2003 and 2004. Data have been restructured from more comprehensive country and organisation coverage in the Yearbook of International Organizations.

Record 15 Country participation in INGOs

This record indicates the extent to which INGOs have organisational and individual members in each country, for 1993 and 2003. Data are for INGOs only; no information is available for internationally oriented NGOs. 'Membership' has a specific meaning here: whether an INGO has a million members or a single member in a given country, this is counted as one membership. So a count of 100 for a country means that 100 INGOs each have at least one member or member organisation in that country. The table also offers data on membership density for each country, expressed as the number of memberships in INGOs per million of the population, for the same years, and presents the percentage growth during the decade. Membership of NGOs has grown considerably in the last decade, around the world, yet the majority are still in developed nations. Nonetheless, the highest growth rates in organisational presence were in Eastern Europe and Central Asia.

Country	Number of organisation memberships	Membership density per million of population	Number of organisation memberships	Membership density per million of population	Absolute growth %	Density growth %
	1993		2003		1993–2003	1993–2003
East Asia & Pacific						
Low income economies						
Cambodia	110	10.9	404	31.3	267	187
East Timor	6	7.5	52	54.6	767	624
Indonesia	1,379	7.1	1,943	8.4	41	19
Korea, Dem. Rep.	223	10.8	271	12.2	22	13
Laos	118	26.5	273	47.3	131	78
Mongolia	160	69.2	471	176.1	194	155
Myanmar	301	7.7	425	10.1	41	30
Papua New Guinea	589	146.4	684	132.2	16	-10
Solomon Islands	216	602.2	279	563.9	29	-6
Vietnam	387	5.6	930	11.5	140	107
Middle income economies						
China & Tibet *	1,380	1.2	2,415	1.9	75	60
Fiji	499	665.1	659	769.5	32	16
Malaysia	1,398	76.3	2,033	89.7	45	18
Micronesia	51	444.7	111	1,027.1	118	131
Philippines	1,548	23.0	2,114	25.5	37	11
Samoa	224	1,287.3	327	1,830.6	46	42
Thailand	1,358	23.9	2,003	31.5	47	31
Tonga	188	2,041.4	267	2,515.6	42	23
Vanuatu	185	1,146.2	282	1,437.5	52	25
High income economies						
Australia	2,781	159.1	4,029	206.1	45	30
Brunei	235	858.6	345	983.2	47	15
Japan	2,733	22.0	3,863	30.4	41	38
Korea, Rep.	1,468	33.5	2,335	48.7	59	45
New Caledonia	101	575.1	130	625.4	29	9
New Zealand	1,886	548.6	2,679	685.5	42	25
Singapore	1,251	393.5	1,921	431.4	54	10
Europe & Central Asia						
Low income economies						
Azerbaijan	47	6.3	446	57.2	849	802

Record 15 continued

Country	Number of organisation memberships 1993	Membership density per million of population 1993	Number of organisation memberships 2003	Membership density per million of population 2003	Absolute growth % 1993–2003	Density growth % 1993–2003
Georgia	112	20.5	766	154.4	584	654
Kyrgyzstan	25	5.5	305	63.2	1,120	1,047
Moldova	59	13.3	556	125.4	842	845
Tajikistan	23	4.1	216	32.1	839	683
Uzbekistan	54	2.5	415	16.2	669	550
Middle income economies						
Albania	201	60.4	851	242.6	323	301
Armenia	73	21.2	578	173.6	692	720
Belarus	125	12.1	829	80.2	563	561
Bosnia & Herzegovina	69	15.6	684	172.5	891	1,007
Bulgaria	1,306	150.8	2,268	296.0	74	96
Croatia	374	84.4	2,069	471.2	453	458
Czech Republic			3,460	337.4		
Estonia	367	237.5	1,673	1,181.8	356	398
Hungary	2,166	209.3	3,630	360.0	68	72
Kazakhstan	62	3.7	556	33.2	797	810
Latvia	263	100.0	1,456	615.3	454	515
Lithuania	319	86.1	1,606	446.0	403	418
Macedonia	12	6.2	781	380.1	6,408	6,010
Poland	2,247	58.6	3,768	97.6	68	67
Romania	1,269	55.7	2,549	113.8	101	104
Russia	1,377	9.3	3,284	22.7	138	144
Serbia & Montenegro	1,682	164.4	1,803	169.2	7	3
Slovakia			2,226	411.5		
Turkey	1,498	25.7	2,500	37.1	67	44
Turkmenistan	28	7.3	163	34.8	482	378
Ukraine	238	4.6	1,731	35.8	627	681
High income economies						
Austria	3,162	399.5	4,741	581.8	50	46
Belgium	4,295	427.5	5,841	566.4	36	32
Cyprus	854	1,207.4	1,421	1,851.9	66	53
Denmark	3,747	724.6	5,010	932.1	34	29
Finland	3,134	621.7	4,733	911.4	51	47
France	4,847	84.5	6,755	112.7	39	33
Germany	4,707	58.4	6,652	80.8	41	38
Greece	2,606	252.4	3,854	363.5	48	44
Iceland	1,267	4,891.7	1,775	6,353.3	40	30
Ireland	2,528	710.6	3,790	977.0	50	37
Italy	4,364	76.8	6,085	105.0	39	37
Luxembourg	1,725	4,394.3	2,167	4,807.2	26	9
Malta	725	1,981.4	1,209	3,041.5	67	54
Netherlands	4,308	283.9	6,005	372.5	39	31
Norway	3,181	742.1	4,478	987.3	41	33
Portugal	2,889	291.4	4,206	417.1	46	43
Slovenia	386	204.1	2,169	1,122.1	462	450

Record 15 continued

Country	Number of organisation memberships 1993	Membership density per million of population 1993	Number of organisation memberships 2003	Membership density per million of population 2003	Absolute growth % 1993–2003	Density growth % 1993–2003
Spain	4,014	101.5	5,782	144.0	44	42
Sweden	3,675	421.5	5,413	604.5	47	43
Switzerland	3,780	540.4	5,357	727.7	42	35
United Kingdom	4,554	78.7	6,509	108.6	43	38
Latin America & Caribbean						
Low income economies						
Haiti	509	81.1	607	82.0	19	1
Nicaragua	602	152.5	805	160.2	34	5
Middle income economies						
Argentina	2,176	64.1	3,031	79.1	39	23
Belize	318	1,584.9	383	1,473.4	20	-7
Bolivia	934	135.5	1,216	144.0	30	6
Brazil	2,396	15.4	3,365	18.7	40	22
Chile	1,628	119.9	2,247	145.0	38	21
Colombia	1,514	44.3	2,045	49.9	35	13
Costa Rica	1,122	353.6	1,422	370.8	27	5
Cuba	704	65.7	1,096	97.6	56	49
Dominican Republic	779	106.0	986	114.7	27	8
Ecuador	1,029	95.1	1,371	102.0	33	7
El Salvador	640	121.3	886	139.4	38	15
Guadeloupe	88	226.7	98	224.9	11	-1
Guatemala	858	84.0	1,090	80.5	27	-4
Guyana	451	615.8	492	703.3	9	14
Honduras	651	130.0	825	126.6	27	-3
Jamaica	803	320.5	898	335.1	12	5
Martinique	88	230.5	101	239.2	15	4
Mexico	2,098	23.8	2,900	28.3	38	19
Panama	889	358.5	1,075	368.1	21	3
Paraguay	737	164.4	980	166.5	33	1
Peru	1,383	60.1	1,833	65.6	33	9
St. Lucia	287	2,015.4	340	2,123.1	18	5
St. Vincent & the Grenadines	226	2,090.8	268	2,302.5	19	10
Suriname	297	737.1	342	788.6	15	7
Trinidad & Tobago	691	583.5	814	732.3	18	26
Uruguay	1,203	382.0	1,609	475.1	34	24
Venezuela	1,531	75.5	1,918	79.0	25	5
High income economies						
Bahamas	433	1,639.6	515	1,745.0	19	6
Barbados	531	2,004.3	644	2,331.8	21	16
Middle East & North Africa						
Low income economies						
Yemen	252	18.9	352	18.8	40	0
Middle income economies						
Algeria	849	32.0	1,069	33.1	26	4

Record 15 continued

Country	Number of organisation memberships 1993	Membership density per million of population 1993	Number of organisation memberships 2003	Membership density per million of population 2003	Absolute growth % 1993–2003	Density growth % 1993–2003
Djibouti	184	479.0	226	505.1	23	5
Egypt	1,510	25.4	2,005	27.3	33	8
Iran	734	12.1	992	14.7	35	22
Iraq	557	31.2	527	22.0	-5	-30
Jordan	690	178.4	983	185.2	42	4
Lebanon	734	228.0	1,083	294.5	48	29
Libya	400	91.6	471	87.7	18	-4
Morocco & Western Sahara	1,072	41.2	1,382	44.0	29	7
Oman	254	132.6	394	145.2	55	9
Saudi Arabia	788	47.2	1,105	47.0	40	0
Syria	500	37.8	620	36.1	24	-4
Tunisia	973	114.2	1,255	127.9	29	12
High income economies						
Bahrain	348	657.2	491	748.0	41	14
Israel & Occupied Territories	2,221	315.4	3,449	366.2	55	16
Kuwait	633	446.4	775	367.0	22	-18
Qatar	237	447.7	371	467.6	57	4
United Arab Emirates	452	220.6	790	323.0	75	46
North America						
High income economies						
Canada	3,141	110.1	4,394	137.7	40	25
United States	3,615	14.1	5,225	18.2	44	29
South Asia						
Low income economies						
Afghanistan	155	9.3	162	5.8	5	-38
Bangladesh	849	7.5	1,192	8.8	40	18
Bhutan	94	56.2	139	66.4	48	18
India	2,354	2.7	3,219	3.1	37	15
Nepal	531	26.1	877	33.9	65	30
Pakistan	1,143	9.6	1,606	10.9	41	13
Middle income economies						
Maldives	86	370.6	159	496.6	85	34
Sri Lanka	1,094	62.2	1,354	69.2	24	11
Sub-Saharan Africa						
Low income economies						
Angola	334	39.4	469	44.4	40	13
Benin	509	102.3	722	105.6	42	3
Burkina Faso	506	52.2	691	53.6	37	3
Burundi	365	66.6	484	81.1	33	22
Cameroon	776	63.0	1,082	70.1	39	11
Central African Republic	323	109.0	396	109.3	23	0

Record 15 continued

Country	Number of organisation memberships 1993	Membership density per million of population 1993	Number of organisation memberships 2003	Membership density per million of population 2003	Absolute growth % 1993–2003	Density growth % 1993–2003
Chad	292	45.3	397	44.3	36	-2
Comoros	125	275.1	167	271.8	34	-1
Congo, Dem. Rep.	780	19.2	868	15.8	11	-18
Congo, Rep.	466	197.8	553	190.2	19	-4
Côte d'Ivoire	803	62.9	993	59.8	24	-5
Equatorial Guinea	116	299.2	161	323.2	39	8
Eritrea	6	1.7	182	42.3	2,933	2,435
Ethiopia	601	11.6	766	11.7	27	1
Gambia	404	389.8	482	331.1	19	-15
Ghana	968	59.5	1,245	61.7	29	4
Guinea	357	51.1	502	56.9	41	11
Guinea-Bissau	171	162.7	246	184.5	44	13
Kenya	1,276	50.0	1,639	52.5	28	5
Lesotho	403	231.6	499	268.6	24	16
Liberia	450	226.7	420	128.8	-7	-43
Madagascar	574	47.0	700	42.5	22	-10
Malawi	492	49.8	656	57.6	33	16
Mali	472	55.1	639	56.5	35	3
Mauritania	310	146.3	422	149.2	36	2
Mozambique	402	30.6	639	34.9	59	14
Niger	371	46.0	488	45.4	32	-1
Nigeria	1,399	14.2	1,655	12.7	18	-11
Rwanda	415	56.6	515	67.2	24	19
São Tomé & Principe	79	627.4	121	710.2	53	13
Senegal	935	119.6	1,097	106.4	17	-11
Sierra Leone	557	130.4	601	108.0	8	-17
Somalia	259	42.5	223	28.8	-14	-32
Sudan	671	23.8	743	20.0	11	-16
Tanzania	846	31.2	1,113	31.5	32	1
Togo	552	139.0	686	129.4	24	-7
Uganda	712	38.5	1,047	42.1	47	9
Zambia	777	94.0	938	92.4	21	-2
Zimbabwe	1,028	95.8	1,339	107.4	30	12
Middle income economies						
Botswana	473	341.7	689	436.2	46	28
Cape Verde	154	425.8	241	589.6	56	38
Gabon	399	404.3	487	378.0	22	-6
Mauritius	664	605.7	811	675.7	22	12
Namibia	333	223.4	670	353.2	101	58
South Africa	1,686	43.6	2,941	68.9	74	58
Swaziland	373	387.5	464	403.4	24	4

Record 15 continued

Region	Number of organisation memberships 1993	Membership density per million of population 1993	Number of organisation memberships 2003	Membership density per million of population 2003	Absolute growth % 1993–2003	Density growth % 1993–2003
Low income	31,288	15.2	44,120	17.7	41	16
Middle income	64,193	25.8	104,446	37.8	63	46
Low and middle income						
East Asia & Pacific	10,869	6.6	16,806	9.1	55	38
Europe & Central Asia	15,992	34.0	41,111	86.3	157	154
Latin America & Caribbean	27,502	60.4	36,151	67.9	31	12
Middle East & North Africa	9,497	37.1	12,464	39.5	31	7
South Asia	6,306	5.4	8,708	6.3	38	15
Sub-Saharan Africa	25,306	47.1	33,321	48.5	32	3
High income	92,900	102.7	134,285	138.5	45	35
World	188,381	34.6	282,851	45.4	50	31

* China & Tibet excludes Hong Kong and Macao.
Regional sums include data from countries that weren't included in the table above.
Per capita figures were calculated using total midyear population figures, US Census Bureau International database.

Sources: © Union of International Associations, Yearbook of International Organizations: Guide to Civil Society Networks, Brussels 1994 and 2004; US Bureau of the Census International Data Base. (April 2004). United States Department of Commerce, www.census.gov/ipc/www/idbsprd.html

Record 16 Links between international organisations

This table indicates different aspects of the inter-organisational network that links international and internationally oriented NGOs to each other and to international governmental organisations (IGOs). It indicates the number of citations, or references, made by either NGOs or IGOs to any other international organisation (whether NGO or IGO). Examples of citations would be (1) '. . . founded under the auspices of "X"' . . , (2) ' . . . financed by annual subventions from "X", "Y" and "Z" . . ', (3) ' . . . consultative relations with "X"'. The number of links is shown for 1993 and 2003, in addition to a percentage growth figure. The networks of linkages between international organisations are becoming denser, particularly when membership and funding is considered. More organisations participate in these networks, and their overall density is increasing.

Citations NGO to IGO & NGO; IGO to IGO & NGO

Paragraph	1993	2003	% change	
Founded				
NGOs	3,167	5,096	61	The citing organisation cites another organisation as having had some role in its founding or establishment.
IGOs	2,469	3,539	43	
Total	**5,636**	**8,635**	**53**	
Structure				
NGOs	970	1,766	82	The citing organisation has a structural link with another organisation, for instance as sister organisation or parent and subsidiary organisation.
IGOs	1,376	1,999	45	
Total	**2,346**	**3,765**	**60**	
Staff				
NGOs	0	4		The citing organisation shares, or is provided with, key staff with the other organisation it cites.
IGOs	72	121	68	
Total	**72**	**125**	**74**	
Finances				
NGOs	878	3,048	247	There is a financial link between the citing organisation and another organisation.
IGOs	269	598	122	
Total	**1,147**	**3,646**	**218**	
Activities				
NGOs	2,339	2,433	4	The citing organisation cites another organisation as having a role in its activities, for instance joint activities, or activities aimed at the cited organisation.
IGOs	2,260	4,189	85	
Total	**4,599**	**6,622**	**44**	
Publications				
NGOs	10	21	110	The citing organisation cites another organisation as having a role in its publications, for instance joint publications, or publications about the cited organisation.
IGOs	31	32	3	
Total	**41**	**53**	**29**	
Members				
NGOs	6,292	13,531	115	There is a membership link between the citing organisation and another organisation, for instance because one of them is a federation of organisations, or coordinating body of which the other is a member.
IGOs	630	1,247	98	
Total	**6,922**	**14,778**	**113**	

Record 16 continued

Citations NGO to IGO & NGO; IGO to IGO & NGO

Paragraph	1993	2003	% change	
Consultative Status				
NGOs	3,117	3,343	7	The citing organisation has consultative status with another organisation. This mainly concerns NGOs having such a status with IGOs.
IGOs	5	5	0	
Total	**3,122**	**3,348**	**7**	
IGO Relations				
NGOs	8,439	15,443	83	The citing organisation has some other form of relation with an IGO.
IGOs	11,510	15,707	36	
Total	**19,949**	**31,150**	**56**	
NGO Relations				
NGOs	25,818	46,922	82	The citing organisation has some other form of relation with an NGO.
IGOs	11,250	13,305	18	
Total	**37,068**	**60,227**	**62**	
Total number of organisations cited				
NGOs	12,759	18,333	44	
IGOs	1,736	1,938	12	
Total	**14,495**	**20,271**	**40**	
Total number of citations				
NGOs	51,039	91,607	79	
IGOs	29,875	40,742	36	
Total	**80,914**	**132,349**	**64**	
Average number of citations				
NGOs	4.0	5.0	25	
IGOs	17.2	21.0	22	
Total	**5.6**	**6.5**	**17**	

Source: © Union of International Associations, Yearbook of International Organizations: Guide to Civil Society Networks, 1994 and 2004. Data have been restructured from more comprehensive country and organisation coverage in the Yearbook of International Organizations.

Record 17 Meetings of international organisations (IGOs and INGOs)

Following the International Classification of Non-profit Organisations (ICNPO), this record presents data on international meetings according to the country in which events were held, and their purposes. These include meetings organised by INGOs, internationally oriented NGOs and IGOs, and other significant international meetings recorded by the Union of International Associations. Most meetings are recorded as having several purposes. In the first table, the number of meetings held in each country in 2003 is shown in absolute figures and as a percentage of all meetings recorded that year. The second table shows the number of meetings ('hits' in the meetings database) held for a particular purpose in each country in 2003, as a percentage of the total number of meetings for that purpose.

Meetings are concentrated in the developed world – two-thirds of the total number of meetings recorded took place in developed countries in Europe, North America, and East Asia and the Pacific. Conferences focused on education and environment tended to be slightly more evenly dispersed between the North and the South.

Country	No of meetings	% of total meetings
	2003	
East Asia & Pacific		
Low income economies		
Cambodia	12	0.1
Indonesia	39	0.4
Laos	4	0.0
Myanmar	2	0.0
Vietnam	28	0.3
Middle income economies		
China & Tibet*	104	0.9
Fiji	3	0.0
Malaysia	64	0.6
Philippines	43	0.4
Samoa	2	0.0
Thailand	93	0.8
High income economies		
Australia	342	3.1
Brunei	6	0.1
Korea, Rep.	166	1.5
Japan	292	2.7
New Zealand	63	0.6
Singapore	148	1.3
Europe & Central Asia		
Low income economies		
Azerbaijan	7	0.1
Georgia	2	0.0
Kyrgyzstan	7	0.1
Moldova	2	0.0
Ukraine	29	0.3
Uzbekistan	3	0.0
Middle income economies		
Belarus	6	0.1
Bosnia & Herzegovina	9	0.1
Bulgaria	34	0.3
Croatia	56	0.5

Country	No of meetings	% of total meetings
	2003	
Czech Republic	92	0.8
Estonia	19	0.2
Hungary	116	1.1
Kazakhstan	6	0.1
Latvia	26	0.2
Lithuania	18	0.2
Macedonia	6	0.1
Poland	129	1.2
Romania	32	0.3
Russian Federation	117	1.1
Slovakia	24	0.2
Slovenia	43	0.4
Turkey	81	0.7
High income economies		
Austria	291	2.6
Belgium	373	3.4
Cyprus	16	0.1
Denmark	176	1.6
Finland	230	2.1
France	798	7.3
Germany	581	5.3
Greece	124	1.1
Iceland	15	0.1
Ireland	78	0.7
Italy	513	4.7
Luxembourg	23	0.2
Netherlands	318	2.9
Norway	131	1.2
Portugal	123	1.1
Spain	397	3.6
Sweden	224	2.0
Switzerland	352	3.2
United Kingdom	568	5.2

Record 17 continued

Country	No of meetings	% of total meetings
	2003	
Latin America & Caribbean		
Low income economies		
Nicaragua	5	0.0
Middle income economies		
Argentina	99	0.9
Barbados	8	0.1
Belize	2	0.0
Bolivia	13	0.1
Brazil	119	1.1
Chile	40	0.4
Colombia	29	0.3
Costa Rica	21	0.2
Cuba	57	0.5
Dominican Republic	15	0.1
Ecuador	17	0.2
El Salvador	13	0.1
Guatemala	13	0.1
Guyana	4	0.0
Honduras	3	0.0
Jamaica	12	0.1
Mexico	87	0.8
Panama	14	0.1
Peru	19	0.2
St. Lucia	3	0.0
Trinidad & Tobago	12	0.1
Uruguay	19	0.2
Venezuela	22	0.2
High income economies		
Bahamas	9	0.1
Middle East & North Africa		
Middle income economies		
Algeria	15	0.1
Egypt	62	0.6
Iran	4	0.0
Iraq	2	0.0
Jordan	13	0.1
Lebanon	27	0.2
Libya	4	0.0
Malta	11	0.1
Morocco & Western Sahara	42	0.4
Oman	3	0.0
Saudi Arabia	13	0.1
Syria	11	0.1
Tunisia	18	0.2
High income economies		
Bahrain	10	0.1
Israel & Occupied Territories	67	0.6
Kuwait	6	0.1
Qatar	3	0.0
United Arab Emirates	23	0.2
North America		
High income economies		
Canada	279	2.5
United States	1,384	12.6
South Asia		
Low income economies		
Bangladesh	2	0.0
India	101	0.9
Nepal	14	0.1
Pakistan	10	0.1
Middle income economies		
Sri Lanka	10	0.1
Sub-Saharan Africa		
Low income economies		
Angola	1	0.0
Benin	9	0.1
Burkina Faso	10	0.1
Cameroon	15	0.1
Congo, Dem. Rep.	2	0.0
Ethiopia	3	0.0
Gambia	2	0.0
Ghana	13	0.1
Guinea	2	0.0
Kenya	32	0.3
Lesotho	1	0.0
Madagascar	2	0.0
Malawi	3	0.0
Mali	6	0.1
Mozambique	5	0.0
Nigeria	17	0.2
Senegal	15	0.1
Sudan	2	0.0
Tanzania	20	0.2
Togo	3	0.0
Uganda	11	0.1
Zambia	12	0.1
Zimbabwe	16	0.1

Record 17 continued

Country	No of meetings	% of total meetings
	2003	
Middle income economies		
Botswana	9	0.1
Gabon	4	0.0
Mauritius	4	0.0
Namibia	4	0.0
South Africa	108	1.0
Swaziland	3	0.0
Total meetings in sample**	**10,729**	**97.5**

*Does not include Hong Kong and Macao.
**Some countries in the UIA database are not listed in this table (see Note on Data). The second column therefore does not sum to 100%.

Source: © Union of International Associations, Yearbook of International Organizations:Guide to Civil Society Networks, Brussels 2004.

Record 17 continued

Purposes of meetings for selected countries*

2003 Country % of hits per purpose	Culture & recreation	Education	Research	Health	Social development	Environment	Economic development	Law, policy & advocacy	Religion	Defence	Politics	Hits per country**	country % of all hits for year
East Asia & Pacific													
Low income economies													
Indonesia	0.6	1.0	0.7	0.1	0.5	1.1	1.2	1.3	3.0	0.0	1.3	363	0.9
Vietnam	0.3	0.4	0.4	0.2	0.1	0.5	0.6	0.5			1.0	173	0.4
Middle income economies													
China & Tibet***	1.0	1.3	1.2	0.8	0.7	1.9	1.5	0.8	0.3	0.9	1.0	457	1.2
Malaysia	0.8	1.3	0.8	0.6	0.9	1.3	1.2	1.1	1.5		0.9	378	1.0
Philippines	0.3	0.6	0.4	1.1	0.9	2.0	0.5	0.6		0.5	0.2	228	0.6
Thailand	1.3	2.1	1.1	0.9	1.7	1.4	1.9	2.2	2.3	0.5	1.4	602	1.5
High income economies													
Australia	3.5	3.4	3.2	4.0	2.8	3.0	2.8	1.9	3.2	1.8	1.9	1,137	2.9
Korea, Rep.	1.5	1.8	1.8	0.9	1.5	2.1	1.7	1.1	1.7	1.4	1.4	628	1.6
Japan	2.4	2.1	4.0	1.9	2.1	3.6	2.8	1.8	0.5	2.3	2.5	1,131	2.9
Singapore	1.4	1.5	1.3	1.4	1.1	1.2	1.7	0.8	0.2		1.2	517	1.3
Europe & Central Asia													
Low income economies													
Kyrgyzstan	0.1	0.1	0.1				0.1	0.2		2.3	0.0	29	0.1
Middle income economies													
Croatia	2.1	0.3	0.4	0.5	0.5	0.3	0.4	0.3	0.8	0.9	0.2	186	0.5
Hungary	1.3	1.4	1.1	1.4	1.0	1.6	1.1	0.9	1.3	2.7	0.8	444	1.1
Latvia	0.5	0.7	0.2		0.3	0.2	0.4	0.3		0.5	1.2	135	0.3
Poland	1.3	1.2	1.5	0.8	0.8	0.7	1.5	0.6	0.8		0.7	472	1.2
Russian Federation	1.1	0.8	1.5	0.3	1.6	0.9	1.2	2.2	0.3	2.3	1.7	539	1.4
Turkey	0.6	1.5	0.7	1.4	0.9	0.9	0.7	1.1	0.0	0.5	1.0	327	0.8
Ukraine	0.2	0.3	0.5	0.6	0.4	0.3	0.4	0.4	0.3	1.4	0.6	171	0.4
High income economies													
Austria	3.3	3.6	3.2	2.9	3.5	2.3	3.0	3.9	2.5	3.7	5.4	1,319	3.4
Belgium	1.6	3.6	2.5	2.9	5.6	4.3	4.3	5.2	2.5	8.7	6.8	1,515	3.9
Denmark	2.3	2.2	1.6	2.7	1.6	1.8	1.5	1.3	0.3	0.5	1.3	624	1.6
Finland	3.4	3.4	2.1	2.7	2.8	3.0	2.1	1.5	0.2	0.9	1.7	864	2.2
France	14.2	8.1	8.2	9.1	10.1	7.6	7.5	11.7	7.0	8.7	11.4	3,528	9.0
Germany	5.2	6.9	5.7	6.1	5.4	6.8	5.6	4.6	6.5	3.2	4.5	2,156	5.5
Greece	2.0	1.0	1.5	1.3	1.1	2.1	1.2	1.2	0.2	1.8	1.4	522	1.3
Ireland	1.2	1.7	0.4	0.6	0.9	0.3	0.8	0.7	1.0	0.5	0.2	264	0.7
Italy	4.1	4.4	6.4	7.6	3.7	6.3	6.0	4.2	7.8	5.0	3.2	2,170	5.5
Netherlands	2.6	4.3	3.1	2.3	3.1	1.9	3.4	2.9	3.0	4.1	3.2	1,215	3.1
Norway	0.9	1.4	1.2	1.6	1.2	1.7	1.2	0.5			0.9	442	1.1
Portugal	1.7	2.6	1.1	1.5	1.2	1.0	1.4	1.4	0.2		1.1	501	1.3
Spain	3.9	3.7	3.7	4.2	3.6	3.9	4.6	4.0	1.8	4.6	2.4	1,515	3.9
Sweden	1.2	2.8	1.9	3.0	2.2	2.1	1.6	2.6	0.5	2.3	3.7	821	2.1
Switzerland	4.4	1.9	2.9	5.4	8.8	4.1	5.6	9.1	11.1	13.2	5.8	2,067	5.3
United Kingdom	4.9	5.0	5.3	6.3	4.2	4.7	4.9	3.4	11.3	5.9	4.5	1,938	5.0

Purposes of meetings for selected countries*

2003 Country % of hits per purpose	Culture & recreation	Education	Research	Health	Social development	Environment	Economic development	Law, policy & advocacy	Religion	Defence	Politics	Hits per country**	country % of all hits for year
Latin America & Caribbean													
Middle income economies													
Argentina	1.3	0.8	1.0	1.7	1.2	0.9	1.1	1.0	0.5		0.9	416	1.1
Brazil	0.8	1.0	1.3	0.9	1.2	1.3	1.1	1.0	1.3	0.5	1.0	439	1.1
Costa Rica		0.3	0.2	0.2	0.3	1.2	0.4	0.3			0.5	120	0.3
Jamaica	0.1	0.3	0.0	0.1	0.3		0.1	0.3	0.2		0.2	54	0.1
Mexico	1.0	1.8	0.8	1.6	0.8	1.4	0.8	1.3	0.2	0.9	0.6	361	0.9
St. Vincent & the Grenadines									1.3			8	0.0
Middle East & North Africa													
Middle income economies													
Egypt	0.3	0.9	0.7	0.8	0.8	0.8	1.0	0.8	0.8	0.5	1.5	331	0.8
High income economies													
Israel & Occupied Territories****	0.2	0.2	0.8	1.2	0.5	0.6	0.3	0.7	1.2		0.2	227	0.6
North America													
High income economies													
Canada	3.4	2.9	2.9	3.0	2.5	2.6	2.6	2.3	2.0	1.8	3.2	1,070	2.7
United States	13.6	9.3	18.0	10.5	11.6	10.9	13.4	11.2	16.4	12.3	12.1	5,518	14.1
South Asia													
Low income economies													
India	0.7	2.0	1.1	1.1	1.4	1.1	1.1	1.3	3.0	1.4	1.1	456	1.2
Sub-Saharan Africa													
Low income economies													
Zimbabwe		0.2	0.1	0.3	1.2	0.2	0.3	1.1	0.8		0.3	153	0.4
Middle income economies													
South Africa	1.5	2.1	1.2	1.3	1.2	1.9	1.6	2.1	0.3	1.8	1.9	583	1.5

* Covers only countries that had 1% of all international meetings in at least one of the categories. Empty cells indicate that the share of meetings was below 0.05%.
** One 'hit' is recorded for each meeting purpose: multi-purpose meetings may therefore generate several hits.
*** Excludes Hong Kong and Macao
****All hits recorded here are for Israel; total for the Occupied Territories is zero.

Source: © Union of International Associations, Yearbook of International Organizations: Guide to Civil Society Networks, Brussels 2004.

Record 18 NGOs by purpose

Following the International Classification of Non-profit Organisations (ICNPO), this record presents data on the purposes of activities of international and internationally oriented NGOs by country. The classification does not report actual activities or expenditures but is based on statements of intent. The first column gives the percentage of each purpose type in relation to the total number of NGOs in that country for 2003. The second column gives the percentage change from 2002 to 2003. The summary table shows the overall rate of growth or decline for each purpose over the last year. This summary is not comparable to the similar table in *Global Civil Society 2003*. The 2003 table reported the number of all international organisations (NGOs and IGOs) by purpose, while the 2004 table reports the number of NGOs by purpose only.

Country declines in number of specific types of meetings were more frequent in the fields of religion, environment and health. However, only in the field of politics did the total overall global number of meetings decline.

Country	Culture & Recreation		Education		Research		Health		Social development		Environment		Economic development infrastructure		Law, policy and advocacy		Religion		Defence		Politics	
	% country total 2003	% change 2002-2003	% country total 2003	% change 2002-2003	% country total 2003	% change 2002-2003	% country total 2003	% change 2002-2003	% country total 2003	% change 2002-2003	% country total 2003	% change 2002-2003	% country total 2003	% change 2002-2003	% country total 2003	% change 2002-2003	% country total 2003	% change 2002-2003	% country total 2003	% change 2002-2003	% country total 2003	% change 2002-2003
East Asia & Pacific																						
Low income economies																						
Indonesia	0.8		1.5	100.0	26.9	29.6	1.5	-33.3	9.2	-14.3	7.7	0.0	42.3	77.4	4.6	-40.0	2.3	-25.0	0.0		3.1	-20.0
Middle income economies																						
China & Tibet*	6.1	-25.0	10.1	66.7	30.3	7.1	3.0	50.0	5.1	25.0	3.0	0.0	23.2	21.1	8.1	60.0	0.0	0.0	1.0	0.0	10.1	25.0
Fiji	12.2	120.0	7.8	-22.2	10.0	-18.2	6.7	0.0	8.9	60.0	3.3	-25.0	24.4	37.5	8.9	60.0	13.3	-20.0	0.0		4.4	0.0
Malaysia	7.6	18.8	3.2	60.0	18.8	-7.8	4.4	-26.7	10.0	0.0	4.0	-9.1	27.2	-1.4	15.2	35.7	6.4	60.0	0.0		3.2	33.3
Philippines	2.1	125.0	5.8	8.7	15.9	19.3	5.6	50.0	12.1	-3.7	4.9	-16.0	25.2	9.1	17.5	31.6	5.1	15.8	0.5	100.0	5.1	22.2
Thailand	1.6	66.7	5.6	12.5	21.1	-5.6	4.7	-11.8	13.4	-4.4	6.8	-4.3	20.5	10.0	18.3	7.3	4.3	-6.7	0.0		3.7	-14.3
High income economies																						
Australia	6.7	4.6	6.4	12.1	28.4	-1.0	6.6	9.8	9.5	-1.0	2.5	-16.7	21.1	5.4	9.9	6.4	4.1	46.4	0.3	0.0	4.5	-6.1
Japan	7.5	26.1	5.8	12.5	21.8	-7.1	4.0	3.3	8.9	1.5	3.7	-9.4	25.3	8.3	12.0	3.3	3.0	9.5	1.0	60.0	6.8	-17.2
Korea, Rep.	11.8	20.0	5.9	28.6	30.7	23.7	5.9	12.5	8.5	8.3	2.0	0.0	13.7	10.5	9.8	36.4	5.2	14.3	1.3	0.0	5.2	0.0
New Zealand	9.6	45.5	4.2	250.0	22.3	23.3	4.2	-22.2	11.4	18.8	3.6	50.0	19.3	60.0	7.2	20.0	6.0	25.0	1.2	100.0	10.8	12.5
Singapore	7.4	12.5	11.1	28.6	25.4	-6.1	7.8	-17.4	8.2	17.6	1.6	0.0	21.3	15.6	9.8	50.0	3.3	-20.0	0.4		3.7	50.0
Europe & Central Asia																						
Middle income economies																						
Bulgaria	11.8	-12.5	6.7	33.3	20.2	20.0	5.0	20.0	7.6	0.0	1.7	-50.0	30.3	5.9	2.5	200.0	3.4	-33.3	4.2	0.0	6.7	14.3
Czech Republic	6.3	50.0	5.6	0.0	28.2	-9.1	8.5	-7.7	12.7	-25.0	4.9	75.0	15.5	-4.3	10.6	-16.7	2.1	-50.0	0.0		5.6	-20.0
Hungary	12.2	8.0	7.7	41.7	25.8	-6.6	5.4	140.0	6.3	40.0	2.3	-16.7	20.4	12.5	10.0	29.4	1.4	-50.0	0.5	0.0	8.1	0.0
Poland	8.2	-20.0	4.1	100.0	26.7	-13.3	4.1	50.0	8.9	18.2	4.1	50.0	21.9	6.7	13.0	137.5	0.7		0.0		8.2	33.3
Romania	13.6	80.0	13.6	0.0	18.2	33.3	9.1	0.0	10.6	250.0	0.0		7.6	150.0	18.2	140.0	0.0		0.0		9.1	50.0
Russian Federation	4.6	-7.7	12.0	14.8	22.4	-13.4	2.3	50.0	10.4	12.5	3.9	-16.7	14.3	-15.9	15.8	2.5	2.3	-25.0	1.9	66.7	10.0	-10.3
Turkey	1.7	100.0	5.0	0.0	38.0	17.9	5.0	0.0	7.4	28.6	3.3	100.0	21.5	-7.1	5.8	-30.0	5.0	0.0	0.8		6.6	0.0
Ukraine	3.6	100.0	7.3	0.0	25.5	0.0	1.8	-66.7	12.7	-12.5	5.5	0.0	25.5	-6.7	5.5	-25.0	3.6	100.0	0.0	-100.0	9.1	-28.6

Record 18 continued

Country	Culture & Recreation		Education		Research		Health		Social development		Environment		Economic development infrastructure		Law, policy and advocacy		Religion		Defence		Politics	
	% country total 2003	% change 2002-2003	% country total 2003	% change 2002-2003	% country total 2003	% change 2002-2003	% country total 2003	% change 2002-2003	% country total 2003	% change 2002-2003	% country total 2003	% change 2002-2003	% country total 2003	% change 2002-2003	% country total 2003	% change 2002-2003	% country total 2003	% change 2002-2003	% country total 2003	% change 2002-2003	% country total 2003	% change 2002-2003
High income economies																						
Austria	6.4	-5.0	4.9	-8.3	27.1	10.6	3.7	26.9	9.2	0.0	1.9	21.4	24.4	3.8	12.9	9.5	1.7	0.0	0.9	14.3	6.9	-17.6
Belgium	4.8	2.8	4.8	0.0	17.1	-8.0	4.8	-1.7	11.7	-4.1	2.8	-6.6	36.3	-5.9	10.3	-6.5	2.7	0.6	0.6	-5.4	4.1	2.0
Denmark	7.7	22.4	5.6	7.3	24.1	0.5	7.1	-8.3	12.3	20.0	3.5	17.4	25.7	12.4	7.7	0.0	2.2	-15.0	0.1	-50.0	4.0	29.2
Finland	7.2	33.3	8.7	11.4	24.2	-4.4	5.4	-31.4	9.6	7.5	2.9	30.0	24.7	37.5	9.9	15.8	4.3	26.7	0.2		2.9	30.0
France	10.0	8.0	5.4	0.4	21.2	-1.0	3.8	-6.8	10.1	-3.8	2.8	-0.7	28.0	0.9	10.8	-0.4	3.1	-4.3	0.7	27.6	4.1	-8.9
Germany	7.1	0.5	5.4	7.6	21.9	2.4	5.6	-2.2	9.4	2.8	2.8	12.8	26.7	4.1	11.3	7.6	4.4	5.3	0.9	12.5	4.6	-11.0
Greece	11.3	6.5	6.1	12.5	18.8	-6.8	5.8	6.3	8.9	23.8	4.4	8.3	14.7	13.2	13.3	8.3	5.1	36.4	2.7	33.3	8.9	8.3
Iceland	4.5	50.0	4.5	50.0	34.3	43.8	0.0	-100.0	7.5	66.7	4.5	200.0	20.9	100.0	13.4	50.0	4.5	0.0	3.0	0.0	3.0	-60.0
Ireland	4.8	12.5	9.7	50.0	17.7	10.0	9.7	-10.0	12.9	-25.0	2.7	-16.7	22.6	5.0	14.0	13.0	1.6	0.0	1.1	100.0	3.2	-33.3
Italy	7.1	10.0	4.6	2.4	23.2	2.4	4.5	-7.7	10.1	5.0	2.6	11.6	23.0	5.9	10.8	-2.4	9.1	6.3	0.8	50.0	4.3	-1.2
Luxembourg	9.9	-7.1	3.8	-16.7	9.2	-7.7	6.9	80.0	13.0	0.0	2.3	0.0	28.2	2.8	13.7	63.6	4.6	-14.3	0.8	0.0	7.6	11.1
Netherlands	6.6	-9.6	6.3	-7.5	24.2	-0.3	6.1	-1.9	10.0	-7.9	3.4	-8.5	26.5	-3.8	10.5	-9.2	2.3	-16.9	0.6	-30.4	3.4	-9.4
Norway	6.3	6.5	6.4	0.0	23.5	0.8	5.7	20.0	8.0	-4.5	3.4	0.0	23.9	15.6	12.9	11.5	4.7	78.6	0.6	-25.0	4.7	-10.7
Portugal	9.2	-30.8	10.8	31.3	23.1	9.8	3.6	-22.2	11.8	9.5	2.1	0.0	23.6	-6.1	5.6	-26.7	5.1	25.0	0.0		5.1	-23.1
Spain	7.7	-3.8	6.3	6.9	23.0	0.0	6.1	-1.6	10.3	-10.5	2.8	-12.5	24.7	-3.9	11.8	4.5	1.1	-15.4	0.6	-25.0	5.6	-5.2
Sweden	6.7	0.0	5.0	-3.8	24.7	4.7	6.7	6.3	10.9	0.9	3.1	6.9	26.3	4.8	9.5	3.3	2.4	0.0	0.9	-25.0	3.6	-5.3
Switzerland	7.7	-6.9	3.8	-4.9	17.2	7.7	5.8	26.1	12.8	5.7	2.2	16.0	25.7	-2.8	13.9	7.4	6.0	-7.7	0.8	33.3	4.2	-14.2
United Kingdom	5.2	2.2	4.5	2.2	21.2	-0.5	5.3	1.9	11.6	1.4	3.3	10.1	27.1	3.4	11.8	7.3	5.3	6.8	1.0	-11.1	3.6	-10.0
Latin America & Caribbean																						
Low income economies																						
Nicaragua	3.6	0.0	1.8	0.0	27.3	15.4	1.8	0.0	9.1	0.0	3.6	-33.3	38.2	10.5	10.9	100.0	0.0		1.8		1.8	-50.0
Middle income economies																						
Argentina	4.9	17.6	5.3	22.2	25.7	15.2	6.6	8.0	9.7	-14.9	2.2	28.6	25.2	2.0	8.5	-23.9	6.8	55.6	0.0		5.1	-12.5
Barbados	6.9	0.0	6.9	200.0	8.0	75.0	1.1	0.0	9.2	100.0	3.4	0.0	37.9	37.5	8.0	16.7	13.8	20.0	1.1	0.0	3.4	50.0
Brazil	5.2	7.1	3.8	-21.4	28.5	12.2	4.1	-14.3	10.7	0.0	2.7	14.3	23.7	25.5	12.0	9.4	3.8	10.0	0.0	0.0	5.5	-15.8
Chile	1.6	50.0	5.3	42.9	24.5	21.1	4.8	28.6	16.5	6.9	6.4	20.0	19.1	-7.7	12.2	35.3	3.7	16.7	1.1	0.0	4.8	125.0
Colombia	3.7	25.0	13.2	0.0	15.4	-30.0	8.8	33.3	10.3	-6.7	1.5	-33.3	19.1	-23.5	10.3	0.0	12.5	41.7	0.0		5.1	0.0
Costa Rica	2.0	100.0	8.3	-10.5	18.0	12.1	1.5	50.0	12.7	-13.3	4.9	0.0	26.8	1.9	16.1	6.5	2.9	200.0	0.5		6.3	0.0
Cuba	5.4	-20.0	9.5	0.0	17.6	-13.3	1.4	0.0	13.5	-9.1	0.0	-100.0	27.0	-23.1	14.9	-15.4	0.0	-100.0	0.0		10.8	-27.3
Ecuador	0.0		6.3	14.3	14.8	0.0	0.8	-50.0	12.5	14.3	3.1	33.3	26.6	21.4	17.2	-4.3	7.8	42.9	1.6	0.0	9.4	0.0
Guatemala	4.0	0.0	8.0	-20.0	24.0	50.0	2.0		12.0	0.0	2.0		28.0	0.0	10.0	-28.6	4.0	-33.3	0.0		6.0	200.0
Jamaica	3.2	0.0	17.7	22.2	19.4	20.0	6.5	33.3	6.5	-33.3	1.6	0.0	21.0	8.3	8.1	66.7	9.7	-33.3	0.0		6.5	0.0
Mexico	5.9	-10.0	10.5	3.2	21.0	-19.0	7.9	-11.1	8.9	-18.2	3.0	-40.0	23.0	-4.1	11.1	3.0	2.3	16.7	0.0	0.0	6.6	-20.0
Panama	7.5	25.0	4.5	0.0	19.4	44.4	0.0		16.4	83.3	0.0		31.3	23.5	13.4	12.5	0.0		0.0		7.5	25.0
Peru	1.4	-75.0	7.8	10.0	18.4	-3.7	4.3	20.0	8.5	-20.0	5.7	-27.3	31.2	-6.4	17.0	-7.7	0.0		0.0		5.7	-20.0

Record 18 continued

Country	Culture & Recreation		Education		Research		Health		Social development		Environment		Economic development infrastructure		Law, policy and advocacy		Religion		Defence		Politics	
	% country total 2003	% change 2002-2003	% country total 2003	% change 2002-2003	% country total 2003	% change 2002-2003	% country total 2003	% change 2002-2003	% country total 2003	% change 2002-2003	% country total 2003	% change 2002-2003	% country total 2003	% change 2002-2003	% country total 2003	% change 2002-2003	% country total 2003	% change 2002-2003	% country total 2003	% change 2002-2003	% country total 2003	% change 2002-2003
Trinidad & Tobago	1.5	0.0	4.4	0.0	26.7	-7.7	3.7	150.0	23.7	3.2	5.9	33.3	20.0	-6.9	5.9	14.3	6.7	28.6	0.0		1.5	-33.3
Uruguay	3.1	-37.5	4.3	16.7	34.2	17.0	2.5	-42.9	9.3	-16.7	6.8	37.5	19.3	10.7	16.1	4.0	1.2	-33.3	0.0		3.1	0.0
Venezuela	8.6	7.1	9.2	-11.1	20.7	-18.2	4.0	-22.2	16.7	-19.4	1.1	0.0	23.6	-14.6	10.9	-13.6	1.1	-33.3	0.6	0.0	3.4	-33.3
Middle East & North Africa																						
Middle income economies																						
Egypt	6.3	-6.3	5.1	33.3	18.6	57.1	3.8	0.0	12.2	-3.3	3.4	-27.3	24.1	5.6	15.6	19.4	5.5	18.2	0.0		5.5	18.2
Jordan	4.3	0.0	12.8	20.0	21.3	25.0	3.2	-40.0	6.4	50.0	2.1	-33.3	35.1	13.8	8.5	33.3	2.1	100.0	0.0		4.3	0.0
Lebanon	4.6	-28.6	6.5	40.0	14.8	-5.9	8.3	50.0	9.3	25.0	1.9	100.0	30.6	0.0	3.7	-42.9	15.7	54.5	0.9	0.0	3.7	0.0
Malta	6.7	0.0	6.7	-14.3	30.3	35.0	0.0		10.1	-25.0	6.7	0.0	13.5	-14.3	14.6	-35.0	5.6	-28.6	0.0		5.6	-54.5
Saudi Arabia	12.7	-10.0	4.2	50.0	8.5	0.0	5.6	-42.9	11.3	33.3	1.4		16.9	-33.3	8.5	-14.3	26.8	5.6	1.4	0.0	2.8	0.0
Tunisia	4.5	-16.7	5.4	20.0	21.4	41.2	1.8	100.0	10.7	9.1	0.0		31.3	40.0	17.9	42.9	0.9	0.0	1.8	100.0	4.5	0.0
High income economies																						
Israel **	7.3	26.3	4.8	100.0	11.8	5.4	2.1	40.0	8.5	75.0	0.9	0.0	15.4	10.9	21.8	9.1	16.6	3.8	0.9	50.0	10.0	17.9
North America																						
High income economies																						
Canada	7.1	2.9	6.3	6.7	18.8	-6.6	5.3	2.6	11.6	4.8	2.3	-16.7	22.8	8.9	14.2	8.6	5.0	19.0	0.7	0.0	6.0	-12.6
United States	4.7	7.9	5.1	6.8	21.6	8.2	5.1	8.5	11.3	8.7	2.9	6.5	22.1	5.8	13.2	13.9	7.5	6.9	0.9	18.5	5.6	-10.3
South Asia																						
Low income economies																						
Bangladesh	5.2	25.0	4.1	-20.0	8.2	14.3	6.2	20.0	12.4	0.0	2.1	0.0	28.9	0.0	25.8	-3.8	4.1	0.0	1.0	0.0	2.1	-50.0
India	5.2	78.9	6.1	14.3	19.4	-5.9	4.1	-6.9	10.9	10.8	2.4	0.0	20.9	-2.1	18.4	9.0	7.9	33.3	0.2		4.6	-3.2
Nepal	1.1		2.3	100.0	18.2	33.3	1.1	0.0	10.2	12.5	6.8	20.0	23.9	-12.5	22.7	11.1	8.0	600.0	1.1	0.0	4.5	0.0
Pakistan	5.6	-16.7	3.4	50.0	12.4	22.2	0.0	-100.0	14.6	30.0	2.2	0.0	29.2	18.2	14.6	18.2	13.5	-33.3	0.0		4.5	-20.0
Sri Lanka	3.0	0.0	9.0	-14.3	9.0	-25.0	7.5	-16.7	17.9	50.0	1.5	0.0	20.9	-26.3	16.4	-38.9	6.0	300.0	3.0	100.0	6.0	-20.0
Sub-Shahran Africa																						
Low income economies																						
Benin	3.8	0.0	6.3	25.0	7.5	-33.3	6.3	-58.3	13.8	0.0	3.8	0.0	28.8	-20.7	17.5	-6.7	7.5	500.0	1.3	0.0	3.8	-25.0
Burkina Faso	3.4	0.0	3.4	0.0	31.0	28.6	0.0		12.1	75.0	5.2	50.0	34.5	0.0	6.9	-20.0	0.0	-100.0	1.7	0.0	1.7	0.0
Cameroon	12.1	33.3	7.1	75.0	14.1	40.0	3.0	200.0	12.1	33.3	6.1	0.0	24.2	-11.1	9.1	-10.0	9.1	50.0	0.0		3.0	200.0
Côte d'Ivoire	7.2	-33.3	9.9	10.0	20.7	53.3	3.6	33.3	8.1	50.0	6.3	250.0	22.5	8.7	10.8	20.0	8.1	28.6	0.0		2.7	200.0
Ethiopia	1.1		2.1	0.0	25.3	14.3	3.2	50.0	11.6	22.2	1.1	0.0	27.4	73.3	18.9	200.0	3.2	-40.0	3.2	50.0	3.2	50.0
Ghana	8.1	0.0	5.7	-30.0	13.8	41.7	1.6	-50.0	12.2	-6.3	2.4	0.0	20.3	-7.4	15.4	18.8	14.6	5.9	0.0		5.7	0.0
Kenya	1.0	25.0	5.5	-6.9	23.7	-0.9	2.4	-14.3	13.1	14.3	7.8	5.6	24.3	9.2	10.4	37.8	10.0	11.4	0.0		1.8	28.6
Nigeria	7.2	7.7	9.7	11.8	19.5	-22.4	10.3	17.6	9.7	0.0	4.1	-33.3	19.5	-2.6	14.4	3.7	3.1	-40.0	1.0	0.0	1.5	-57.1
Senegal	7.0	7.7	5.5	-8.3	15.6	-16.2	0.0	-100.0	12.1	4.3	4.0	0.0	35.7	-2.7	17.1	-2.9	0.5	-66.7	0.5	0.0	2.0	-33.3
Tanzania	1.8		9.1	0.0	23.6	30.0	9.1	25.0	14.5	-11.1	1.8	0.0	16.4	-30.8	20.0	37.5	1.8	-75.0	0.0		1.8	0.0

Country	Culture & Recreation		Education		Research		Health		Social development		Environment		Economic development infrastructure		Law, policy and advocacy		Religion		Defence		Politics	
	% country total 2003	% change 2002–2003	% country total 2003	% change 2002–2003	% country total 2003	% change 2002–2003	% country total 2003	% change 2002–2003	% country total 2003	% change 2002–2003	% country total 2003	% change 2002–2003	% country total 2003	% change 2002–2003	% country total 2003	% change 2002–2003	% country total 2003	% change 2002–2003	% country total 2003	% change 2002–2003	% country total 2003	% change 2002–2003
Togo	3.8	50.0	2.5	0.0	11.4	50.0	1.3	0.0	17.7	0.0	2.5	-33.3	38.0	20.0	16.5	8.3	2.5	-33.3	0.0		3.8	-40.0
Uganda	1.2	-50.0	4.8	0.0	21.4	20.0	3.6	50.0	15.5	-7.1	8.3	-12.5	25.0	40.0	13.1	0.0	2.4	-33.3	1.2		3.6	
Zimbabwe	3.1	-33.3	6.9	-10.0	21.4	40.0	3.8	0.0	13.0	-15.0	3.8	0.0	25.2	0.0	10.7	-22.2	8.4	0.0	0.0		3.8	-16.7
Middle income economies																						
Mauritius	4.0	-33.3	4.0	0.0	18.0	12.5	2.0		12.0	-25.0	2.0	0.0	40.0	-4.8	12.0	200.0	2.0	-66.7	0.0		4.0	-33.3
South Africa	8.6	13.3	5.1	25.0	22.0	1.2	4.8	-9.5	7.1	-12.5	3.8	0.0	24.5	-4.0	6.1	-4.0	14.4	14.0	0.5		3.3	-7.1

* China & Tibet excludes Macao and Hong Kong.

** Israel excludes the occupied territories.

This table includes only countries that had at least 50 incidences in the total count of NGO purposes.

Overall growth rate of number of International NGOs by purpose

Purpose	2002	2003	% change 2002–2003
Culture and Recreation	3,531	3,666	3.8
Education	3,077	3,212	4.4
Research	12,161	12,387	1.9
Health	2,869	2,925	2.0
Social Development	6,303	6,434	2.1
Environment	1,740	1,781	2.4
Economic Development, Infrastructure	14,880	15,221	2.3
Law, Policy and Advocacy	6,713	7,090	5.6
Religion	2,945	3,082	4.7
Defence	394	425	7.9
Politics	2,983	2,780	-6.8
Totals	**57,596**	**59,003**	**2.4**

Source: © Union of International Associations, Yearbook of International Organizations: Guide to Civil Society Networks, 2004. Data have been restructured from more comprehensive country and organisation coverage in the Yearbook of International Organisations.

Record 19 Employment, volunteering and revenue of NGOs

For a selected number of countries that participated in the Johns Hopkins Comparative Nonprofit Sector Project, this record presents employment and volunteering figures (first table), and revenue structure (second table), for non-profit organisations operating primarily at the international level. These include prominent international humanitarian and relief organisations as well as INGOs in the field of development. They also include associations promoting international understanding, exchange, and friendship. The first part of the revenue table shows the percentages in terms of cash flow, while the second accounts also for the financial value of volunteer input.

The data show that, in general, INGOs comprise a very small share of the non-profit sector, their funding sources vary greatly, and no single pattern is found within regions.

Employment and volunteering

1995/1996/1997	INGOs		Total non-profit sector		INGOs as % of total nonprofit sector		
Country	number of paid FTE workers	number of FTE volunteers	number of paid FTE workers	number of FTE volunteers	in % of paid employment	in % of volunteers	in % of paid employment and volunteers
Argentina	5,201	7	464,214	391,043	1.1	0.0	0.6
Australia	919	1,227	415,651	218,352	0.2	0.6	0.3
Austria	1,110		150,425	40,686	0.7		0.6
Belgium	594	1,018	358,853	100,686	0.2	1.0	0.4
Brazil	4,182		1,128,387	335,098	0.4		0.3
Colombia	181	22	286,861	90,756	0.1	0.0	0.1
Czech Republic	814	816	78,200	45,400	1.0	1.8	1.3
Egypt			611,888	17,335			
Finland	160	367	66,043	77,030	0.2	0.5	0.4
France	17,403	30,986	974,867	1,114,816	1.8	2.8	2.3
Germany	9,750	28,510	1,480,850	1,211,474	0.7	2.4	1.4
Hungary	342	226	45,101	10,187	0.8	2.2	1.0
India			2,655,400	3,379,600			
Ireland	370	234	125,584	33,690	0.3	0.7	0.4
Israel	98		147,166	32,405	0.1		0.1
Italy	1,400	4,625	580,109	430,130	0.2	1.1	0.6
Japan	7,693	37,785	2,287,993	850,264	0.3	4.4	1.4
Kenya			177,075	113,873			
Korea, Rep.			513,820	188,703			
Mexico			93,809	47,215			
Morocco			74,514	83,364			
Netherlands	3,860	8,644	669,122	425,554	0.6	2.0	1.1
Norway	1,066	3,635	66,243	115,229	1.6	3.2	2.6
Pakistan			264,251	212,324			
Peru	3		129,826	80,144	0.0		0.0
Philippines	1,259	593	207,025	337,694	0.6	0.2	0.3
Poland	884	637	122,944	33,126	0.7	1.9	1.0
Romania	485	2,828	37,974	49,417	1.3	5.7	3.8
Slovakia	138	68	18,888	7,233	0.7	0.9	0.8
South Africa	113	149	328,327	316,995	0.0	0.0	0.0
Spain	9,380	9,794	475,179	253,599	2.0	3.9	2.6
Sweden	2,224	5,625	82,559	260,300	2.7	2.2	2.3

Employment and volunteering

1995/1996/1997	INGOs		Total non-profit sector		INGOs as % of total nonprofit sector		
Country	number of paid FTE workers	number of FTE volunteers	number of paid FTE workers	number of FTE volunteers	in % of paid employment	in % of volunteers	in % of paid employment and volunteers
Tanzania	3,534	9,236	82,192	249,381	4.3	3.7	3.9
Uganda	437	114	94,084	137,097	0.5	0.1	0.2
United Kingdom	53,726	7,298	1,473,443	1,664,003	3.6	0.4	1.9
United States		45,026	8,555,980	7,246,856		0.6	

Revenue structure of INGOs

1995/1996/1997	Cash revenue only			Cash and volunteer input		
Country	Public sector payments %	Private giving %	Private fees and charges %	Public sector payments %	Private giving %	Private fees and charges %
Argentina	100			100		
Australia	30	70		26	74	
Austria	40	55	5	40	55	5
Belgium	33	58	9	28	64	8
Brazil			100			100
Colombia		99	1		99	1
Czech Republic	37	52	11	23	70	7
Finland	30	8	61	14	58	28
France	43	40	17	16	78	6
Germany	51	41	8	15	83	2
Hungary	66	14	20	64	17	19
Ireland	24	76		22	78	
Israel	23	51	26	23	51	26
Italy	35	35	30	27	49	24
Japan	19	27	54	5	82	14
Netherlands	45	35	20	35	50	15
Norway	35	24	41	25	46	29
Peru		3	97		3	97
Poland	19	36	45	19	38	44
Romania	47	31	22	8	88	4
Slovakia	22	21	57	22	24	55
Spain	56	36	8	32	63	5
Sweden	49	37	14	36	53	10
Tanzania	31	22	48	14	63	22
Uganda		93	7		95	5
United Kingdom	40	33	27	38	36	26

Source: Johns Hopkins Comparative Nonprofit Sector Project.

Record 20 Political rights and civil liberties

This is a new record for the Yearbook. It presents an index of political rights and civil liberties, developed by Freedom House. Political rights and civil liberties are an indicator of the levels of democracy in countries around the world. Freedom House defines these as 'real-world rights and freedoms enjoyed by individuals, as a result of actions by both state and non-governmental actors, and are based on the Universal Declaration of Human Rights' (for details on the methodology used by Freedom House in producing these indices, see www.freedomhouse.org/research/freeworld/2003/methodology.htm). Scores range from one, the lowest degree of freedom, to seven, the highest. The combined average rating is a simple average of the two indices, also represented in the bar charts.

High-income European countries scores the highest on this index, followed by Latin American and Caribbean nations and by the middle-income countries in Europe and Central Asia. The deepest deficits in democracy are found in most Arab nations and in many Sub-Saharan African nations.

Country	Political Rights Index 2004	Civil Liberties Index 2004	Combined average ratings value
East Asia & Pacific			
Low income economies			
Cambodia	2	3	2.5
East Timor	5	5	5
Indonesia	5	4	4.5
Korea, Dem. Rep.	1	1	1
Laos	1	2	1.5
Mongolia	6	6	6
Myanmar	1	1	1
Papua New Guinea	5	5	5
Vietnam	1	2	1.5
Middle income economies			
China*	1	2	1.5
Fiji	4	5	4.5
Malaysia	3	4	3.5
Philippines	6	5	5.5
Thailand	6	5	5.5
High income economies			
Australia	7	7	7
Brunei	2	3	2.5
Korea, Rep.	6	6	6
Japan	7	6	6.5
New Zealand	7	7	7
Singapore	3	4	3.5
Europe & Central Asia			
Low income economies			
Armenia	4	4	4
Azerbaijan	2	3	2.5
Georgia	4	4	4
Kyrgyzstan	2	3	2.5
Moldova	5	4	4.5
Tajikistan	2	3	2.5

Record 20 continued

Country	Political Rights Index 2004	Civil Liberties Index 2004	Combined average ratings value	bar chart (0–7)
Ukraine	4	4	4	
Uzbekistan	1	2	1.5	
Middle income economies				
Albania	5	5	5	
Belarus	2	2	2	
Bosnia & Herzegovina	4	4	4	
Bulgaria	7	6	6.5	
Croatia	6	6	6	
Czech Republic	7	6	6.5	
Estonia	7	6	6.5	
Hungary	7	6	6.5	
Kazakhstan	2	3	2.5	
Latvia	7	6	6.5	
Lithuania	7	6	6.5	
Macedonia	5	5	5	
Poland	7	6	6.5	
Romania	6	6	6	
Russian Federation	3	3	3	
Serbia & Montenegro	5	6	5.5	
Slovakia	7	6	6.5	
Slovenia	7	7	7	
Turkey	5	4	4.5	
Turkmenistan	1	1	1	
High income economies				
Austria	7	7	7	
Belgium	7	7	7	
Cyprus	7	7	7	
Denmark	7	7	7	
Finland	7	7	7	
France	7	7	7	
Germany	7	7	7	
Greece	7	6	6.5	
Ireland	7	7	7	
Italy	7	7	7	
Luxembourg	7	7	7	
Netherlands	7	7	7	
Norway	7	7	7	
Portugal	7	7	7	
Spain	7	7	7	
Sweden	7	7	7	
Switzerland	7	7	7	
United Kingdom*	7	7	7	

Record 20 continued

Country	Political Rights Index 2004	Civil Liberties Index 2004	Combined average ratings value
Latin America & Caribbean			
Low income economies			
Nicaragua	5	5	5
Middle income economies			
Argentina	6	6	6
Belize	7	6	6.5
Bolivia	5	5	5
Brazil	6	5	5.5
Chile	7	7	7
Colombia	4	4	4
Costa Rica	7	6	6.5
Cuba	1	1	1
Dominican Republic	5	6	5.5
Ecuador	5	5	5
El Salvador	6	5	5.5
Guatemala	4	4	4
Guyana	6	6	6
Honduras	5	5	5
Jamaica	6	5	5.5
Mexico	6	6	6
Panama	7	6	6.5
Paraguay	5	5	5
Peru	6	5	5.5
Suriname	7	6	6.5
Trinidad & Tobago	5	5	5
Uruguay	7	7	7
Venezuela	5	4	4.5
Middle East & North Africa			
Low income economies			
Yemen	3	3	3
Middle income economies			
Algeria	2	3	2.5
Djibouti	3	3	3
Egypt	2	2	2
Iran	2	2	2
Iraq	1	3	2
Jordan	3	3	3
Lebanon	2	3	2.5
Libya	1	1	1
Malta	7	7	7
Morocco & Western Sahara	3	3	3
Oman	2	3	2.5
Saudi Arabia	1	1	1

Record 20 continued

Country	Political Rights Index 2004	Civil Liberties Index 2004	Combined average ratings value	bar chart (0–7)
Syria	1	1	1	
Tunisia	2	3	2.5	
High income economies				
Bahrain	3	3	3	
Israel & Occupied Territories	7	5	6	
Kuwait	4	3	3.5	
Qatar	2	2	2	
United Arab Emirates	2	2	2	
North America				
High income economies				
Canada	7	7	7	
United States	7	7	7	
South Asia				
Low income economies				
Afghanistan	2	2	2	
Bangladesh	4	4	4	
Bhutan	2	3	2.5	
India	6	5	5.5	
Nepal	3	4	3.5	
Pakistan	2	3	2.5	
Middle income economies				
Maldives	2	3	2.5	
Sri Lanka	5	5	5	
Sub-Saharan Africa				
Low income economies				
Angola	2	3	2.5	
Benin	6	6	6	
Burkina Faso	4	4	4	
Burundi	3	3	3	
Cameroon	2	2	2	
Central African Republic	1	3	2	
Chad	2	3	2.5	
Congo, Dem. Rep.	2	2	2	
Congo, Rep.	3	4	3.5	
Côte d'Ivoire	2	3	2.5	
Equatorial Guinea	1	2	1.5	
Eritrea	1	2	1.5	
Ethiopia	3	3	3	
Gambia	4	4	4	
Ghana	6	6	6	
Guinea	2	3	2.5	
Guinea-Bissau	2	4	3	
Kenya	5	5	5	

Record 20 continued

Country	Political Rights Index 2004	Civil Liberties Index 2004	Combined average ratings value
Lesotho	6	5	5.5
Liberia	2	2	2
Madagascar	5	5	5
Malawi	5	4	4.5
Mali	6	6	6
Mozambique	5	4	4.5
Niger	4	4	4
Nigeria	4	4	4
Rwanda	2	3	2.5
São Tomé & Principe	6	6	6
Senegal	6	5	5.5
Sierra Leone	4	5	4.5
Sudan	1	1	1
Tanzania	4	5	4.5
Togo	2	3	2.5
Uganda	3	4	3.5
Zambia	4	4	4
Zimbabwe	2	2	2
Middle income economies			
Botswana	6	6	6
Cape Verde	7	7	7
Gabon	3	4	3.5
Mauritius	7	6	6.5
Namibia	6	5	5.5
South Africa	7	6	6.5
Swaziland	1	3	2

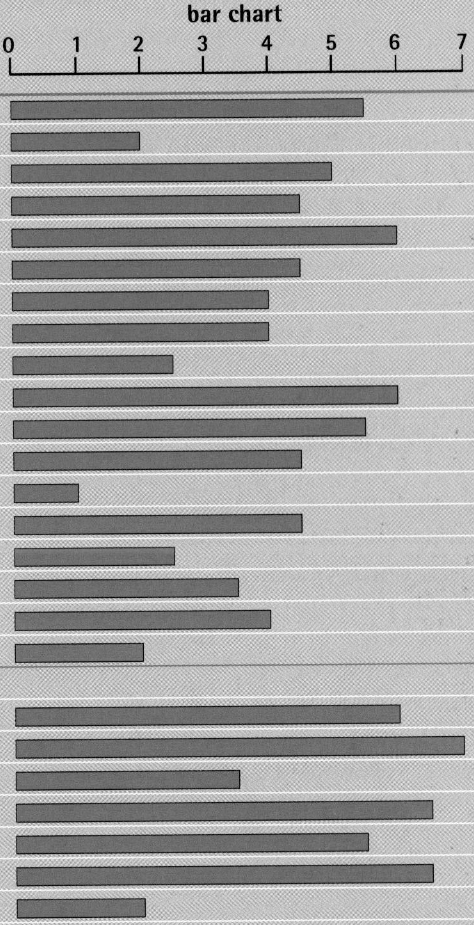

bar chart: 0 1 2 3 4 5 6 7

* China excludes Tibet, Hong Kong and Macao; United Kingdom excludes Northern Ireland.

Source: Freedom House: Freedom in the World 2004: Global Freedom Gains Amid Terror and Uncertainty, www.freedomhouse.org/research/survey2004.htm

Record 21 Tolerance

This record shows attitudes towards immigrants and minority ethnic groups in the population as an indicator of tolerance. It draws on the survey *Views of a Changing World 2003*, by the Pew Research Centre for the People and the Press, as part of its Global Attitudes Project. The table indicates the percentage of people who responded positively ('very good', 'somewhat good') or negatively ('very bad', 'somewhat bad') to the following questions:

- What kind of influence is the following group having on the way things are going in your country?
  - Is the influence of immigrants very good, somewhat good, somewhat bad or very bad?
  - Is the influence of ethnic group (applicable ethnic group to respondent's country) very good, somewhat good, somewhat bad or very bad?

Intolerance of immigrants is pronounced worldwide for, in two-thirds of the countries for which there is data, a majority displayed unfavourable attitudes towards immigrants. This is most notable in Europe. Conversely, in more than two-thirds of the countries a majority displayed favourable attitudes towards their local ethnic minority.

in % respondents per country	Immigrants			Ethnic minority		
Country	**Positive**	**Negative**	**Don't know/refused**	**Positive**	**Negative**	**Don't know/refused**
East Asia & Pacific						
Low income economies						
Indonesia	41	45	14	51	45	4
Vietnam	50	39	11			
Middle income economies						
China*	43	34	23			
Philippines	63	32	5	32	62	6
High income economies						
Japan	30	55	15	49	40	11
Korea, Rep.	40	39	22			
Europe & Central Asia						
Low income economies						
Uzbekistan	22	38	40	75	9	15
Middle income economies						
Bulgaria	42	24	35	42	16	42
Czech Republic	17	79	5	69	18	13
Poland	24	45	31	33	33	33
Russian Federation	13	59	28	5	82	13
Slovakia	25	69	5	85	11	4
Turkey	25	54	21	31	52	17
Ukraine	30	47	23	61	27	12
High income economies						
France	46	50	4	43	51	6
Germany	35	60	4	47	41	12
Italy	25	67	8	14	80	6
United Kingdom	37	50	14	63	26	11
Latin America & Caribbean						
Middle income economies						
Argentina	33	41	26			
Bolivia	41	52	7	62	30	8
Brazil	47	32	21			
Guatemala	35	58	7	64	28	8
Honduras	51	42	7	69	18	13
Mexico	42	43	15	66	16	18

Record 21 continued

in % respondents per country	Immigrants			Ethnic minority		
Country	Positive	Negative	Don't know/refused	Positive	Negative	Don't know/refused
Peru	41	37	22	42	37	22
Venezuela	38	58	4	31	64	3
Middle East & North Africa						
Middle income economies						
Jordan	31	63	6			
Lebanon	51	43	5			
North America						
High income economies						
Canada	77	18	6	75	14	11
United States	49	43	8	73	17	10
South Asia						
Low income economies						
Bangladesh	33	32	35	49	30	21
India	33	31	36	0	0	
Pakistan	13	27	60	11	36	53
Sub-Saharan Africa						
Low income economies						
Angola	34	51	15	47	23	30
Ghana	47	41	12	54	20	26
Côte d'Ivoire	45	54	1	55	45	0
Kenya	36	54	10			
Mali	55	39	5	47	45	8
Nigeria	59	36	5	63	34	4
Senegal	55	41	4	4	93	3
Tanzania	30	41	29			
Uganda	49	41	10	64	30	7
Middle income economies						
South Africa	28	67	5	70	26	4

For Angola, Bolivia, Brazil, China, Guatemala, Honduras, India, Indonesia, Côte d'Ivoire, Mali, Pakistan, Senegal, Venezuela and Vietnam data is based on predominantly urban samples. For all other countries data is based on national samples.
For the United States, Pakistan, Nigeria, and Uganda, respondents were requested to consider two ethnic minority groups. The data presented for these countries is an average of responses for these two groups.

* China excludes Tibet, Hong Kong and Macao.

Source: The Pew Research Center For The People & The Press: Views of a Changing World, 2003. Pew Global Attitudes Project, people-press.org/reports/display.php3?ReportID=185, questions 35g, 35h.

Record 22 Attitudes towards globalisation

This record presents public attitudes towards globalisation, as captured in *Views of a Changing World 2003*, a survey by the Pew Research Centre for the People and the Press. It shows the percentage of people who responded positively ('very good', 'somewhat good') or negatively ('very bad', 'somewhat bad') to the following questions:

- What do you think about the growing trade and business ties between your country and other countries?
- What about faster communication and greater travel between the people of your country and people in other countries?
- What about the way movies, TV and music from different parts of the world are now available in your country?
- What about the different products that are now available from different parts of the world?
- All in all, how do you feel about the world becoming more connected through greater economic trade and faster communication?
- Is the influence of anti-globalisation protestors very good, somewhat good, somewhat bad or very bad in your country?

Except for rare occurrences, globalisation supporters outnumber opponents. However, in many countries, particularly in Latin America and the Caribbean, opponents were numerous, beyond the global average.

Attitudes towards international connectivity

in % respondents per country	Trade ties			Communications and travel ties			Media imports (movies, TV, music)			Consumer goods imports			Overall international ties			Attitudes towards anti-globalisation protestors		
Country	Positive	Negative	Don't know/ refused	Positive	Negative	Don't know/ refused	Positive	Negative	Don't know/ refused	Positive	Negative	Don't know/ refused	Positive	Negative	Don't know/ refused	Positive	Negative	Don't know/ refused
East Asia & Pacific																		
Low income economies																		
Indonesia	87	10	3	86	11	3	74	26	0	88	10	2	90	8	2	20	31	49
Vietnam	98	1	1	99	1	0	87	11	2	94	4	2	97	0	3	23	34	44
Middle income economies																		
China*	90	3	6	93	2	5	90	6	4	89	7	4	90	2	8			
Philippines	83	13	4	88	8	3	75	22	3	74	21	4	84	10	5	54	32	15
High income economies																		
Japan	72	22	6	92	5	3	91	5	4	83	14	3	91	5	3	17	29	55
Korea, Rep.	90	7	3	94	4	2	78	19	3	69	30	1	92	6	2	21	19	61
Europe & Central Asia																		
Low income economies																		
Uzbekistan	97	3	0	91	6	2	71	28	1	68	31	1	96	3	1	5	19	76
Middle income economies																		
Bulgaria	89	6	5	90	3	6	84	10	5	81	14	5	79	6	15	16	15	69
Czech Republic	84	14	3	95	4	1	87	13	1	88	11	1	96	3	1	18	72	11
Poland	78	15	7	90	6	4	82	12	5	70	26	4	79	10	12	21	34	45
Russian Federation	88	7	4	85	6	8	54	40	5	77	19	3	89	3	8	9	24	66
Slovakia	86	12	1	94	6	0	79	20	1	65	34	1	94	5	1	32	58	10
Turkey	82	12	6	86	8	6	78	15	7	84	11	5	80	11	9	29	27	44
Ukraine	93	6	1	92	6	2	70	28	0	57	43	0	87	10	3	20	23	56

Record 22 continued

Attitudes towards international connectivity

in % respondents per country	Trade ties			Communications and travel ties			Media imports (movies, TV, music)			Consumer goods imports			Overall international ties			Attitudes towards anti-globalisation protestors		
Country	Positive	Negative	Don't know/ refused	Positive	Negative	Don't know/ refused	Positive	Negative	Don't know/ refused	Positive	Negative	Don't know/ refused	Positive	Negative	Don't know/ refused	Positive	Negative	Don't know/ refused
High income economies																		
France	88	11	1	98	1	0	91	8	1	91	9	0	94	5	1	44	52	5
Germany	91	8	1	91	8	1	86	11	3	86	13	1	92	7	1	34	55	10
Italy	79	13	8	89	6	5	78	14	7	78	19	4	85	9	6	27	54	20
United Kingdom	87	9	3	94	4	1	87	8	4	94	5	1	92	6	3	39	43	19
Latin America & Caribbean																		
Middle income economies																		
Argentina	60	31	9	78	14	9	76	17	7	55	38	7	75	15	11	24	31	45
Bolivia	77	19	5	76	18	6	52	46	2	53	44	3	79	16	4	47	32	21
Brazil	73	18	9	85	8	7	78	18	4	73	23	4	79	12	8	31	39	30
Guatemala	83	14	2	90	9	2	72	25	2	90	9	1	89	8	3	44	38	18
Honduras	93	6	1	94	3	3	73	26	1	95	4	1	92	4	4	46	17	37
Mexico	79	13	8	85	8	8	75	18	7	76	17	7	85	7	8	37	28	35
Peru	83	13	4	86	8	6	63	30	7	68	26	6	88	5	7	28	20	52
Venezuela	86	12	1	89	9	1	88	11	0	92	7	1	92	6	1	34	42	24
Middle East & North Africa																		
Middle income economies																		
Egypt	67	15	19	69	15	15	56	36	8	60	31	9	66	17	17			
Jordan	52	48	0	54	46	0	51	49	0	60	40	0	57	42	1	23	57	20
Lebanon	83	14	3	92	7	1	81	18	1	82	18	0	83	14	2	24	40	36
North America																		
High income economies																		
Canada	86	12	3	93	6	2	90	8	2	93	6	1	92	7	1	39	50	11
United States	78	18	4	84	14	2	78	15	7	81	16	3	88	9	3	30	49	21
South Asia																		
Low income economies																		
Bangladesh	84	9	7	89	5	6	51	47	2	73	25	2	83	4	13	22	21	57
India	69	7	23	73	5	22	60	23	17	67	14	19	69	7	24	24	19	57
Pakistan	78	2	20	71	4	25	26	55	19	57	22	21	62	6	32	9	12	79
Sub-Saharan Africa																		
Low income economies																		
Angola	89	6	5	91	7	3	79	18	3	71	26	3	83	12	5	27	32	42
Ghana	88	5	8	89	4	7	73	21	6	92	6	2	90	2	7	36	18	46
Côte d'Ivoire	96	4	0	93	7	0	95	6	0	93	7	0	96	4	0	43	36	21
Kenya	90	5	5	96	1	3	66	29	6	83	15	2	94	4	2	21	45	34
Mali	95	3	2	93	5	2	77	22	1	84	15	1	88	7	4	20	16	64
Nigeria	95	3	2	96	3	1	90	8	2	94	5	1	94	3	3	28	42	30

Attitudes towards international connectivity

in % respondents per country	Trade ties			Communications and travel ties			Media imports (movies, TV, music)			Consumer goods imports			Overall international ties			Attitudes towards anti-globalisation protestors		
Country	Positive	Negative	Don't know/ refused	Positive	Negative	Don't know/ refused	Positive	Negative	Don't know/ refused	Positive	Negative	Don't know/ refused	Positive	Negative	Don't know/ refused	Positive	Negative	Don't know/ refused
Senegal	98	1	0	97	2	0	62	37	0	81	19	0	96	4	0	22	52	26
Tanzania	82	7	11	86	4	9	72	19	9	88	7	5	44	6	50	20	17	63
Uganda	95	4	1	96	3	1	78	18	4	94	5	1	94	4	2	22	37	41
Middle income economies																		
South Africa	88	9	3	92	6	2	83	15	2	83	13	4	86	9	5	44	32	24

For Angola, Bolivia, Brazil, China, Guatemala, Honduras, India, Indonesia, Côte d'Ivoire, Mali, Pakistan, Senegal, Venezuela and Vietnam data is based on predominantly urban samples. For all other countries data is based on national samples.

*China excludes Tibet, Hong Kong and Macao.

Source: The Pew Research Center For The People & The Press: Views of a Changing World, 2003. Pew Global Attitudes Project, people-press.org/reports/display.php3?ReportID=185, questions 24 through 28, 35m.

Record 23 Attitudes favouring Americanisation

For many people and organisations around the globe, the United States has become synonymous with globalisation, even imperialism. Hence, favourable attitudes towards American customs and policies can be seen as an indicator of support for globalisation, and unfavourable attitudes are often a cause of the emergence of global civil society. As part of the Pew Global Attitudes Project 2002, respondents were asked their attitudes towards American values and culture. This table shows the percentage of respondents in each country who favour American values and culture, as gauged by the following four questions, which were included in the survey, *How Global Publics View: Their Lives, Their Countries, The World, America:*

- Which of the following phrases comes closer to your view? It's good that American ideas and customs are spreading here, OR it's bad that American ideas and customs are spreading here.
- And which of these comes closer to your view? I like American ideas about democracy, OR I dislike American ideas about democracy.
- Which comes closer to describing your view? I like American ways of doing business, OR I dislike American ways of doing business.
- Which is closer to describing your view? I like American music, movies and television, OR I dislike American music, movies and television.

In the summary table, regional averages were calculated based only on countries included in this table. Low-income countries in general, and particularly Sub-Saharan African nations, scored highest in favour of American values and culture. High-income countries generally were in favour of American values and culture, with the exception of American business style.

in % respondents in favour, per country Country	Favouring American ideas	Favouring American democracy	Favouring American business style	Favouring American cultural products
East Asia & Pacific				
Low income				
Indonesia	20	52	54	59
Vietnam	33	68	45	45
Middle income				
China*	0	0	36	55
Philippines	58	69	73	70
High income				
Japan	49	62	40	74
Korea, Rep.	30	58	59	53
Europe & Central Asia				
Low income				
Uzbekistan	33	65	76	51
Middle income				
Bulgaria	36	50	50	64
Czech republic	34	64	44	59
Poland	31	51	46	70
Russia	16	28	41	42
Slovakia	34	54	52	58
Turkey	11	33	27	44
Ukraine	35	53	58	55
High income				
France	25	42	23	66
Germany	28	47	32	66

Record 23 continued

in % respondents in favour, per country Country	Favouring American ideas	Favouring American democracy	Favouring American business style	Favouring American cultural products
Italy	29	45	39	63
United Kingdom	39	43	37	76
Latin America & Caribbean				
Middle income				
Argentina	16	29	29	52
Bolivia	22	27	32	39
Brazil	30	35	34	69
Guatemala	40	59	63	70
Honduras	44	58	67	71
Mexico	22	41	44	60
Peru	37	47	47	46
Venezuela	44	67	64	78
Middle East & North Africa				
Middle income				
Egypt	6	0	34	33
Jordan	13	29	44	30
Lebanon	26	49	65	65
North America				
High income				
Canada	37	50	34	77
United States	79	70	63	48
South Asia				
Low income				
Bangladesh	14	31	21	20
India	24	36	50	24
Pakistan	2	9	14	4
Sub-Saharan Africa				
Low income				
Angola	33	51	41	81
Ghana	47	80	70	59
Côte d'Ivoire	69	78	76	84
Kenya	40	87	78	50
Mali	35	55	48	56
Nigeria	64	86	85	76
Senegal	34	65	49	63
Tanzania	18	43	47	41
Uganda	50	67	66	57
Middle income				
South Africa	43	53	60	71

Record 23 continued

In average % respondents in favour** Region	Favouring American ideas	Favouring American democracy	Favouring American business style	Favouring American cultural products
Low income	34	58	55	51
Middle income	28	43	48	57
Low and middle income	31	49	51	55
East Asia & Pacific	28	47	52	57
Europe & Central Asia	29	50	49	55
Latin America & Caribbean	32	45	48	61
Middle East & North Africa	15	26	48	43
South Asia	13	25	28	16
Sub-Saharan Africa	43	67	62	64
High income	40	52	41	65
World	33	50	49	57

For Angola, Bolivia, Brazil, China, Guatemala, Honduras, India, Indonesia, Côte d'Ivoire, Mali, Pakistan, Senegal, Venezuela and Vietnam data is based on predominantly urban samples. For all other countries data is based on national samples.

* China excludes Tibet, Hong Kong and Macao.

** Unweighted averages.

Source: The Pew Research Center for the People and the Press, The Pew Global Attitudes Project, 2002. What the World Thinks in 2002: How Global Publics View: Their Lives, Their Countries, The World, America, www.people-press.org/reports/display.php3?ReportID=165, Questions 67-70, www.people-press.org/reports/pdf/165topline.pdf, pp. T54-T57.

Maps

Hagai Katz

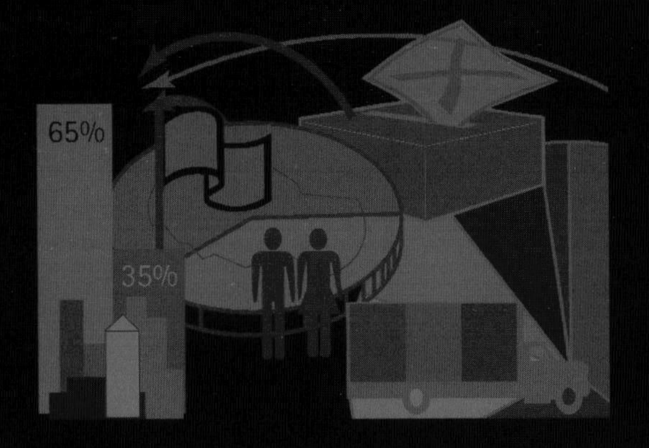

The maps that follow present an up-to-date picture of three key drivers of globalisation: economic globalisation, international rule of law and global civil society. They are intended to give an impression of overall trends; more specific details are available in the data programme.

For the sake of clarity, we have selected a limited number of indicators for each of the four maps. Data used in the maps were derived primarily from Records in this Yearbook, as listed in the map notes (page 344). Other sources of data used are also listed in the notes.

In each map Europe has been exaggerated for the purpose of clarity and readability. Map shapes (continents, countries, world cities and capitals) were derived from ESRI data and Maps CD volume 2003, Environmental Systems Research Institute (ESRI), Redlands, CA.

Maps designed by Derek Power

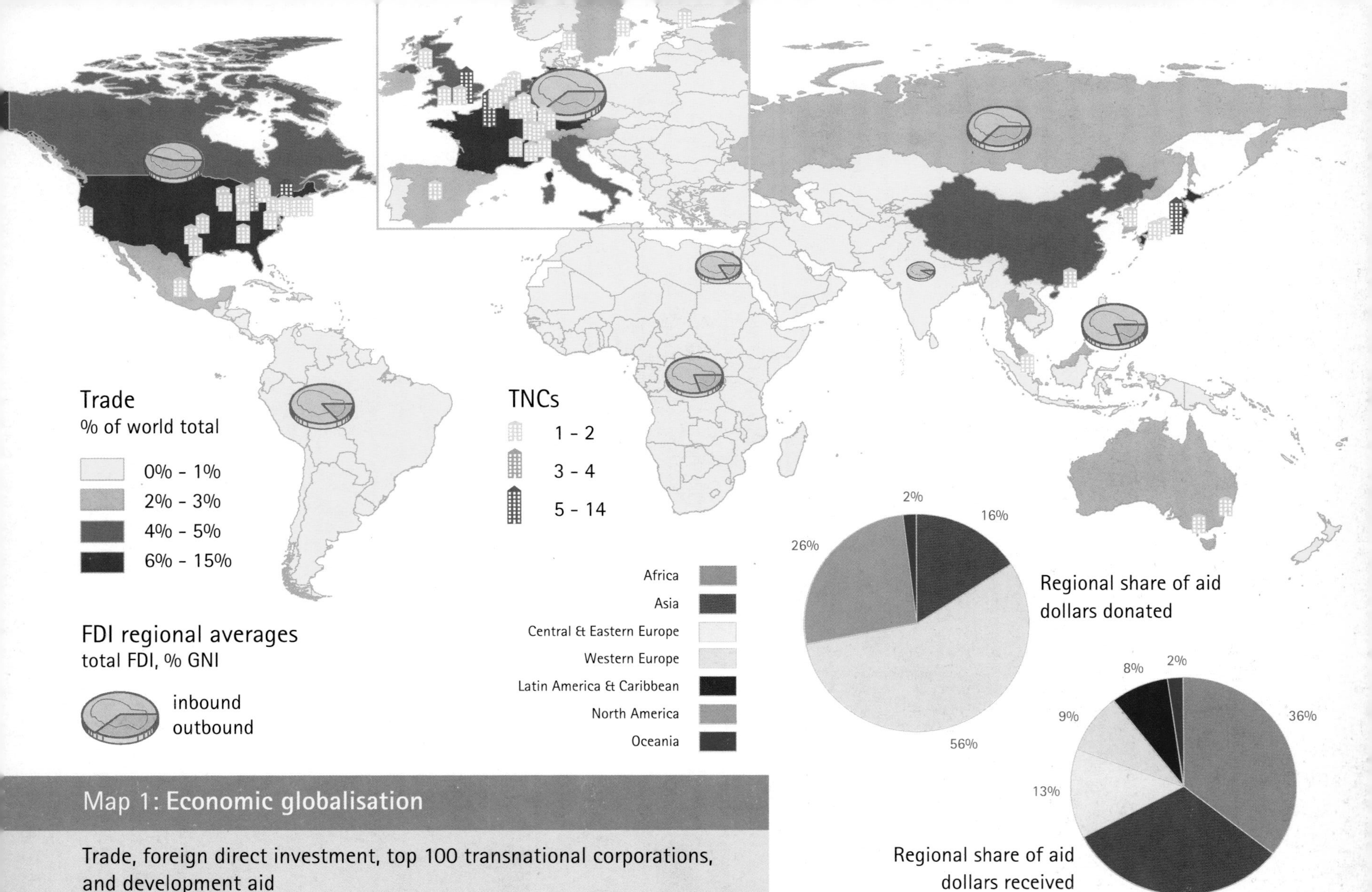

Map 1: Economic globalisation

Trade, foreign direct investment, top 100 transnational corporations, and development aid

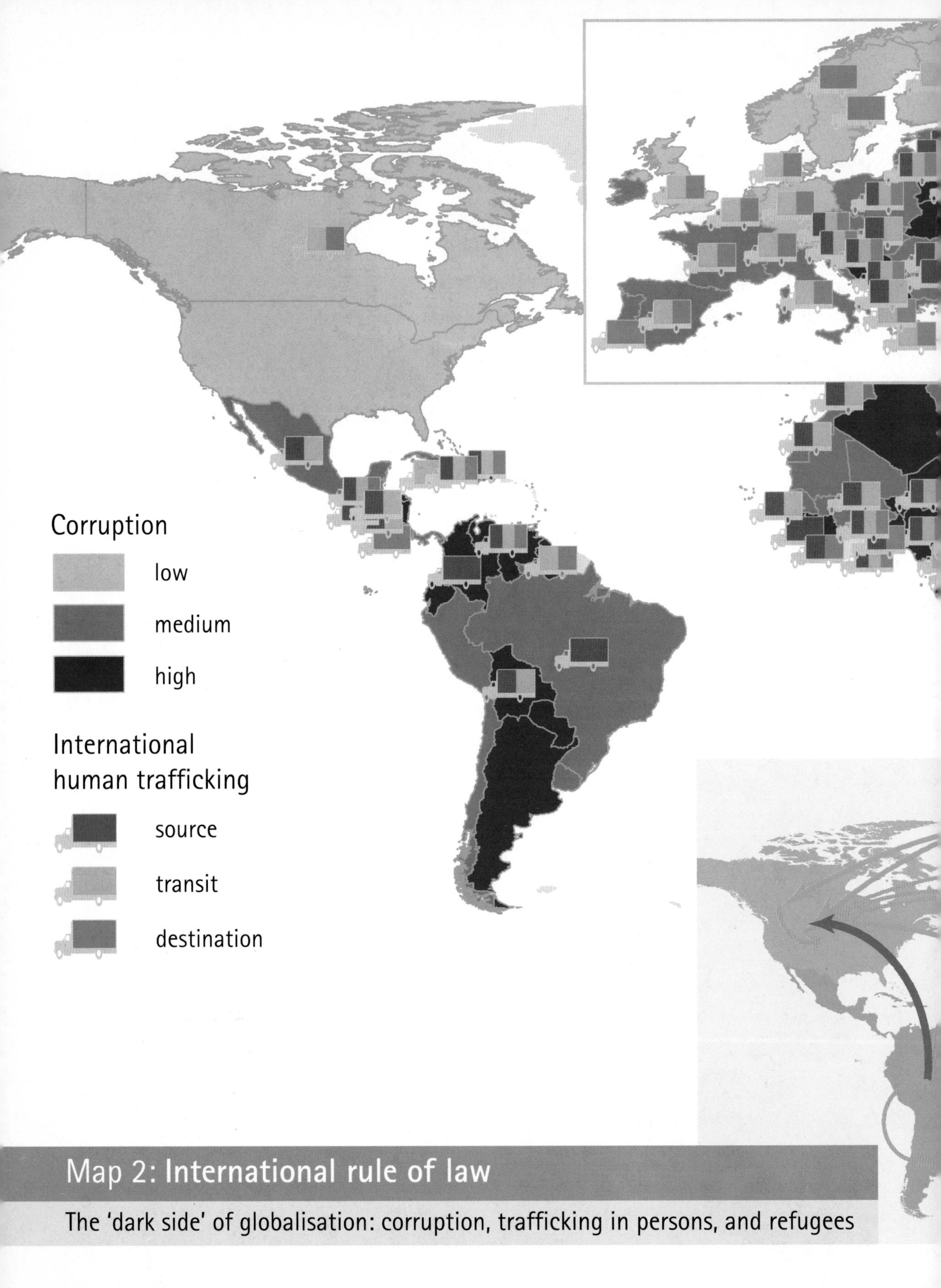

Map 2: International rule of law

The 'dark side' of globalisation: corruption, trafficking in persons, and refugees

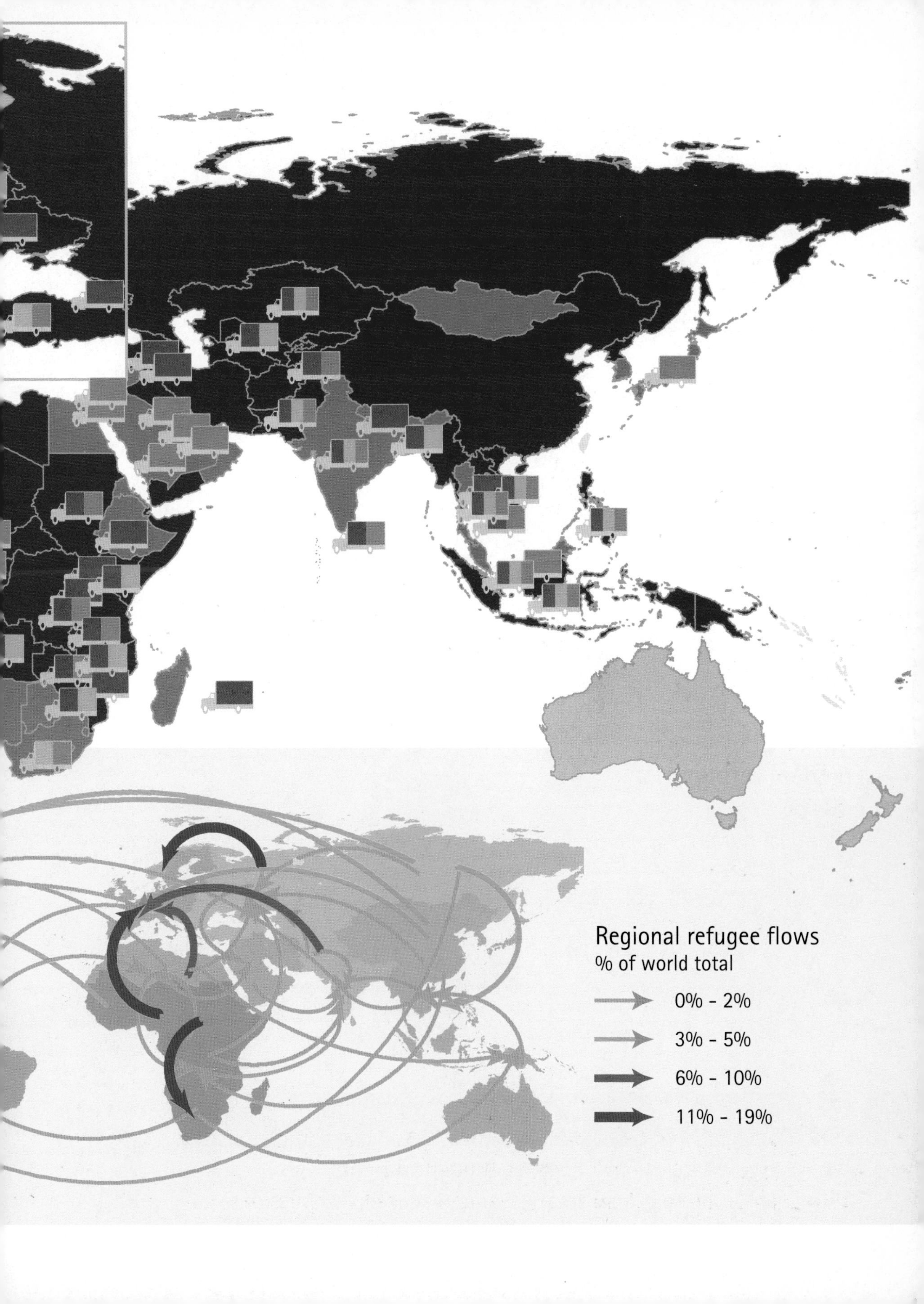
Regional refugee flows
% of world total
0% - 2%
3% - 5%
6% - 10%
11% - 19%

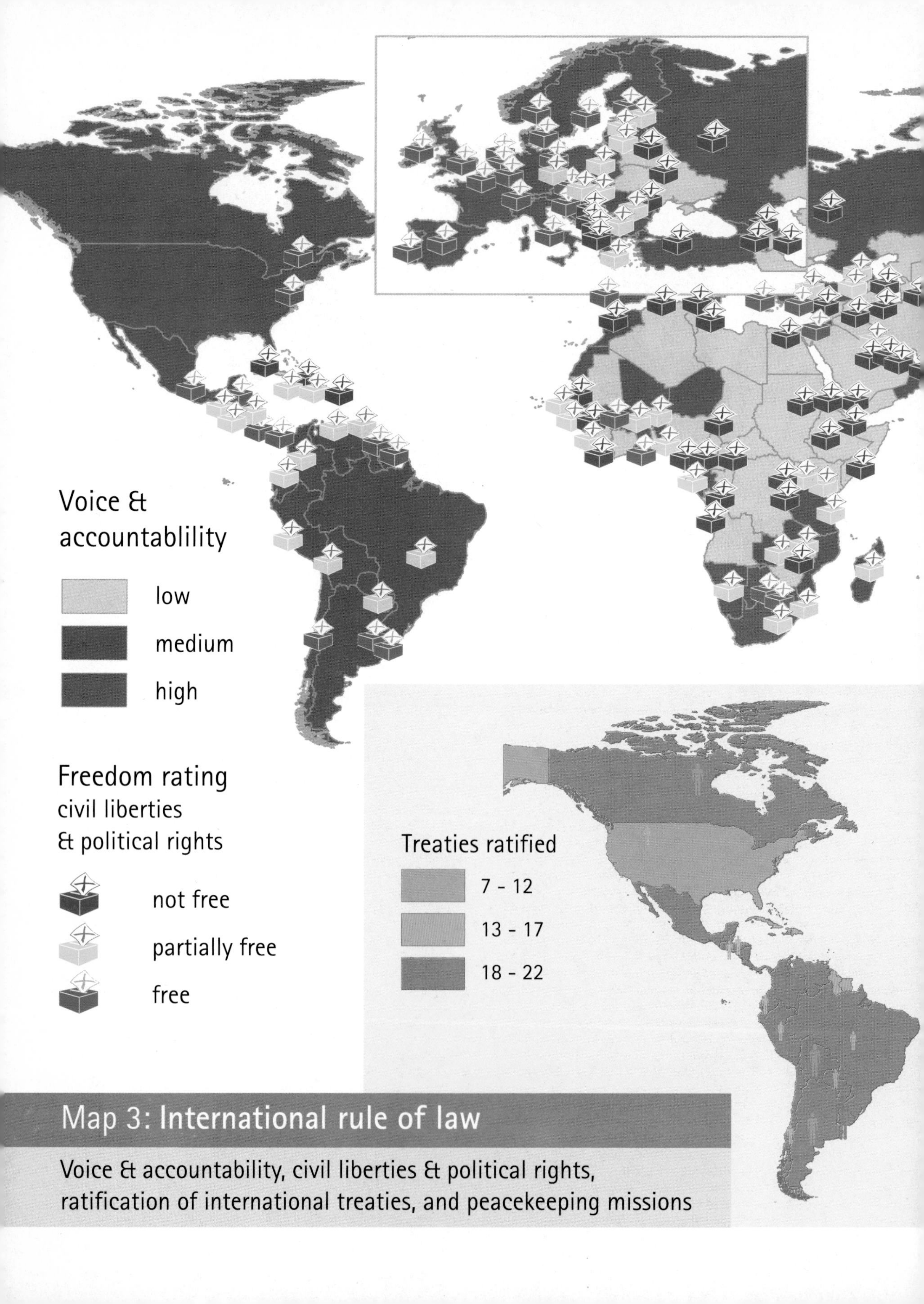

Map 3: International rule of law

Voice & accountability, civil liberties & political rights, ratification of international treaties, and peacekeeping missions

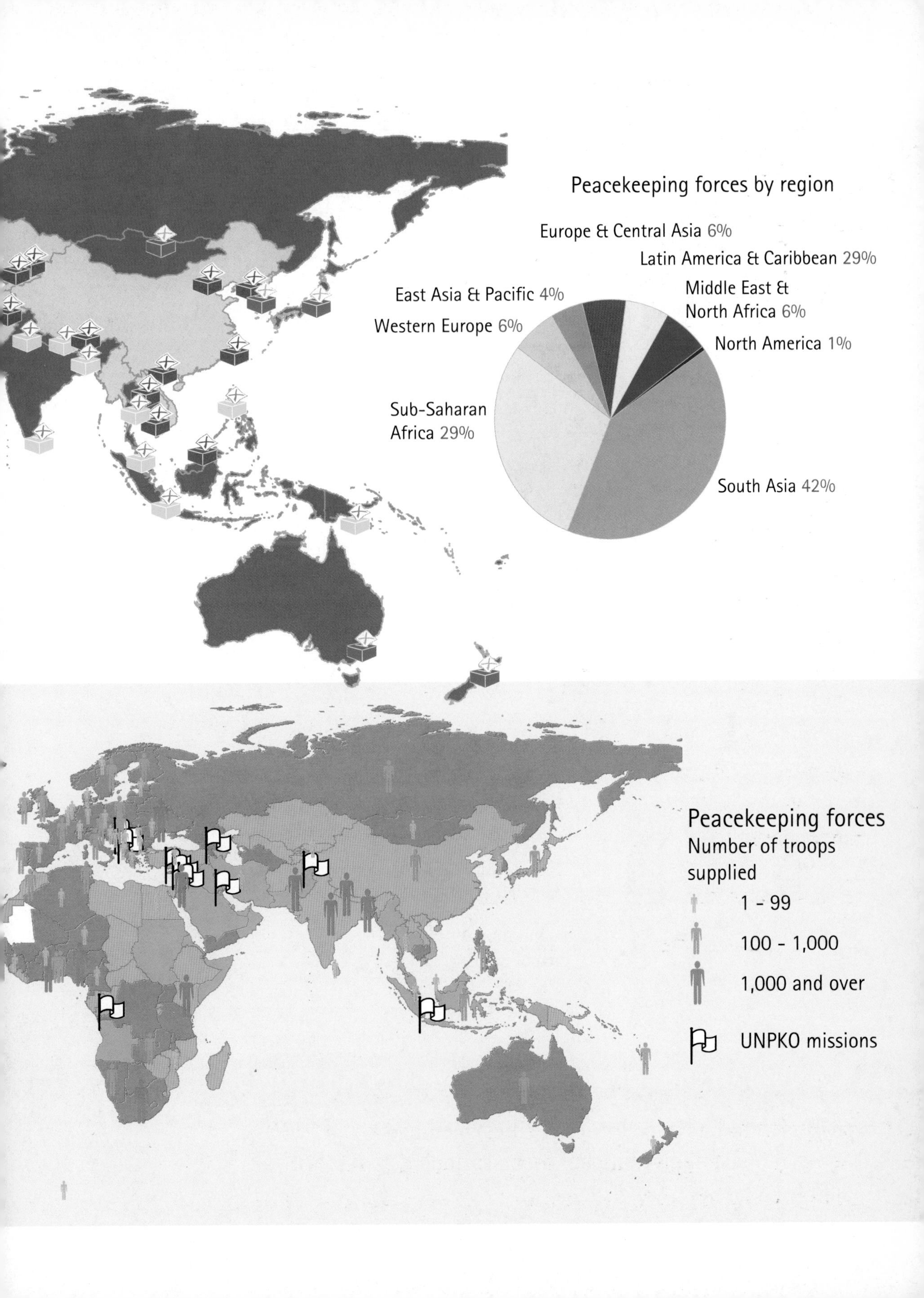
Peacekeeping forces by region
Europe & Central Asia 6%
Latin America & Caribbean 29%
East Asia & Pacific 4%
Middle East &
North Africa 6%
Western Europe 6%
North America 1%
Sub-Saharan
Africa 29%
South Asia 42%
Peacekeeping forces
Number of troops
supplied
1 - 99
100 - 1,000
1,000 and over
UNPKO missions

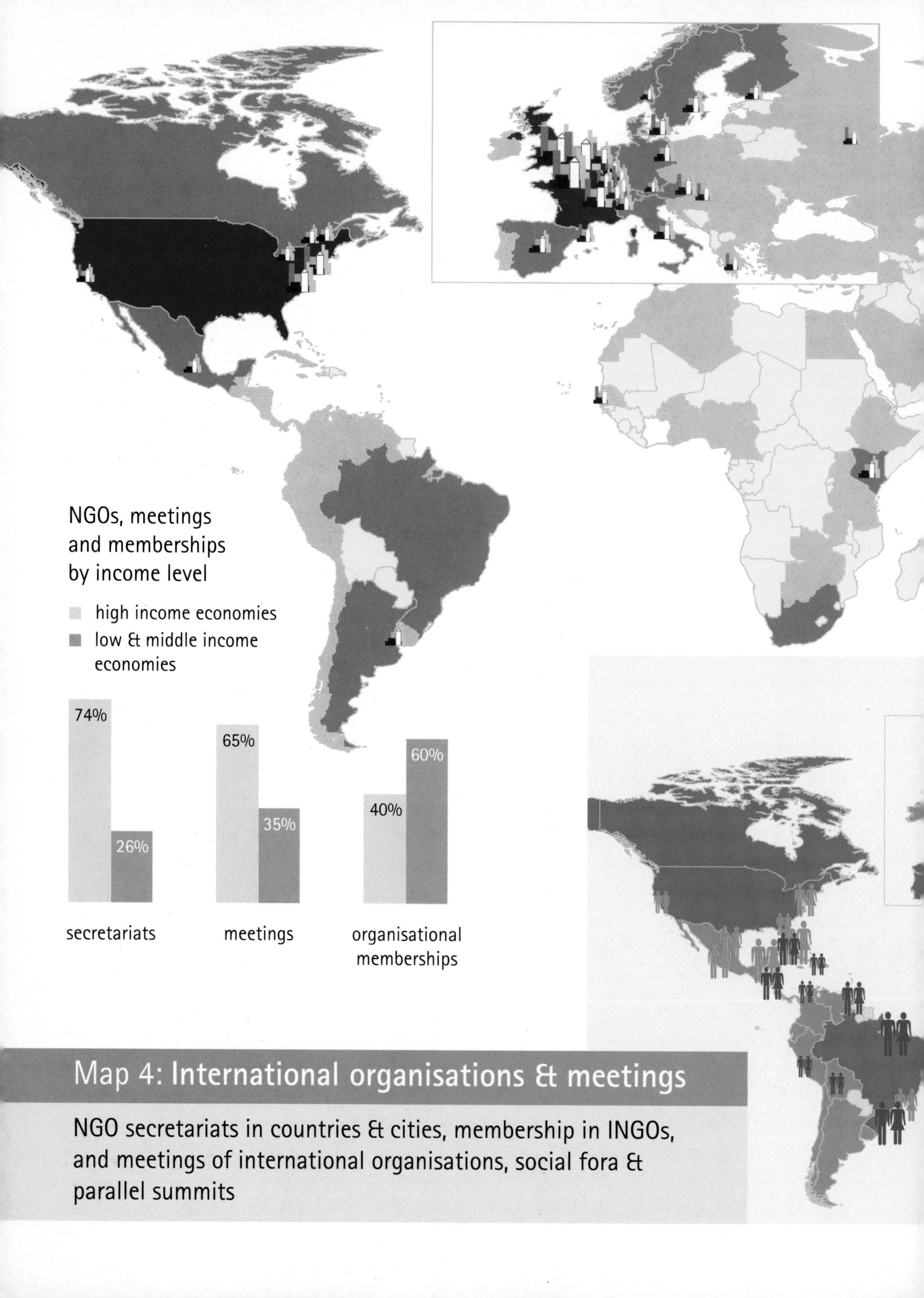

Map 4: International organisations & meetings

NGO secretariats in countries & cities, membership in INGOs, and meetings of international organisations, social fora & parallel summits

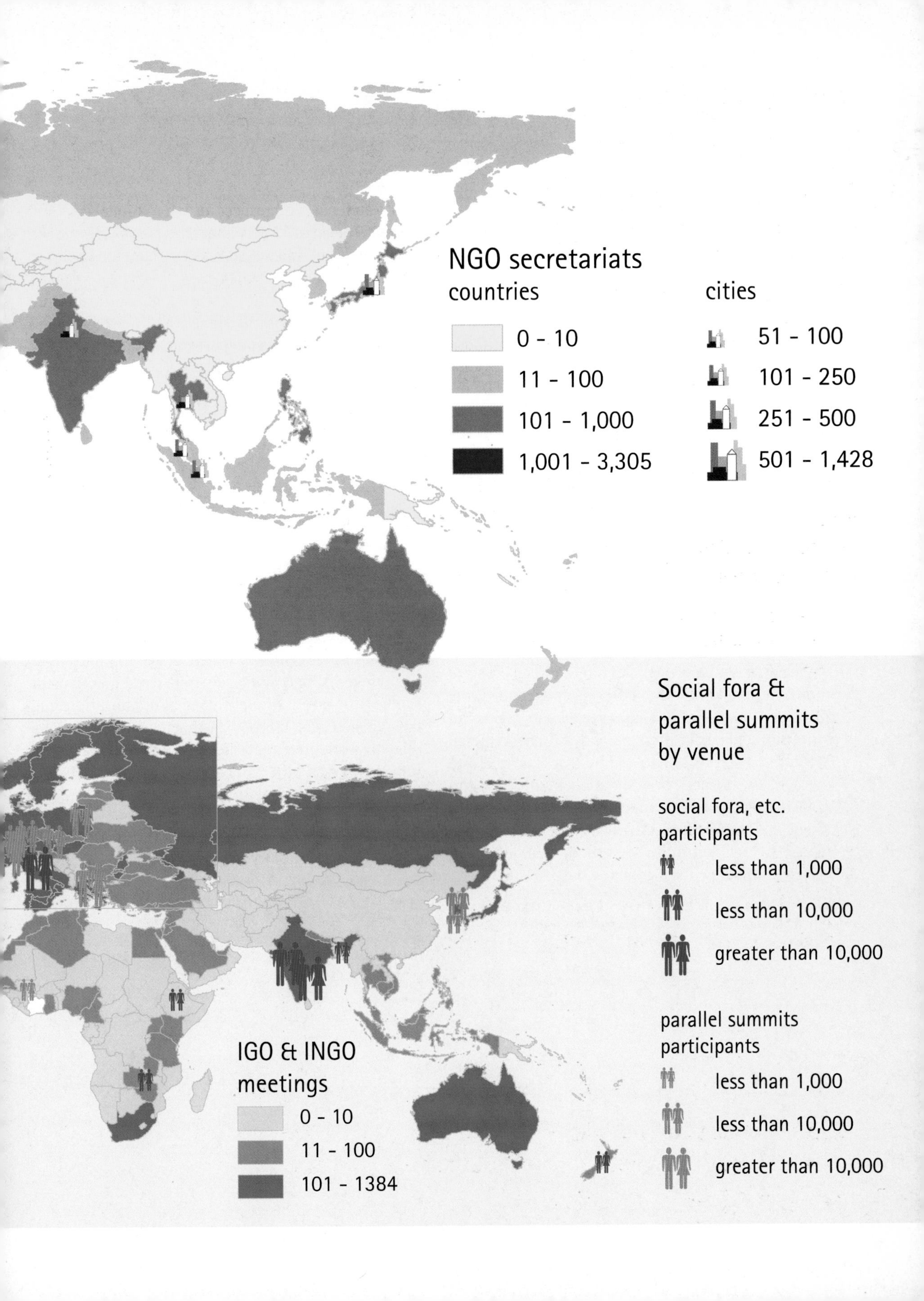
NGO secretariats
countries
0 - 10
11 - 100
101 - 1,000
1,001 - 3,305
cities
51 - 100
101 - 250
251 - 500
501 - 1,428
Social fora &
parallel summits
by venue
social fora, etc.
participants
less than 1,000
less than 10,000
greater than 10,000
parallel summits
participants
less than 1,000
less than 10,000
greater than 10,000
IGO & INGO
meetings
0 - 10
11 - 100
101 - 1384

Map notes

Map 1

This map focuses on economic globalisation. It reveals the bifurcation of the world into North and South, and the rising economic power of China. Foreign direct investment (FDI) flows reveal that developed nations tend to have a more balanced FDI portfolio between in- and outbound FDI. FDI data is summarised by regions, defined according to World Bank classifications. The size of the coin symbol represents the regional average of total sum of in- and outbound FDI per region as share of gross national income (GNI). Pink and blue slices represent outbound and inbound FDI, respectively. Transnational corporations (TNCs) are placed in the map according to the location of their headquarters.

Sources: Record 1 Global economy; Record 3 Transnationality of top 100 transnational corporations (TNCs); the location of TNCs headquarters was obtained from corporate websites; OECD Aid Statistics <www.oecd.org/department/0,2688,en_2649_34447_1_1_1_1_1,00.html>

Map 2

This map focuses on breaches of international laws and norms. It highlights the differences between the developed and developing worlds in terms of corruption, human trafficking and refugees. Human trafficking, which is symbolised by trucks coloured to indicate source, transit or destination countries, seems to flow from eastern Europe and Africa to western Europe and the Middle East. Africa and eastern Europe appear to be important sources of refugees, and western Europe the most common destination.

Sources: Record 4 Trafficking in Persons; Record 10 Corruption; UNHCR Statstics Online <www.unhcr.ch/cgibin/texis/vtx/goto?page=statistics>

Map 3

This map focuses on respect for international laws and norms. The map shows that citizens of developed countries have a greater ability to exercise their political rights and civil liberties than people in many developing nations. Commitment to international norms is more evenly spread around the globe when viewed through the prism of peacekeeping efforts and ratification of international treaties.

Sources: Record 7 Governance and accountability; Record 8 Ratification of treaties; Record 12 Peacekeeping; Record 20 Political rights and civil liberties.

Map 4

This map portrays the spread of global civil society through NGOs, their members and their events. NGOs appear to be concentrated mostly in North America and western Europe, with secondary concentrations in some developing countries. In the secondary map, NGO meetings are slightly more evenly dispersed. For example, social fora are more often held in southern nations. In the secondary map, 'parallel summits' refer to the events held alongside ministerial meetings or summits of international financial organisations (eg IMF,WB, WTO, G8, WEF, EU, FTAA, etc); and 'social fora' refer to world, regional, thematic and national social fora, as well as other global civil society events, for example People Global Action meetings.

Sources: Record 14 Numbers of NGOs in countries and cities; Record 15 Country participation in INGOs; Record 17 Meetings of international organisations (IGOs and INGOs); Mario Pianta and Federico Silva, *Global Civil Society Actions: a Survey of Events and Organisations*, GLOBI Research Report, Rome, 2004 (Events are reviewed in Mario Pianta, Federico Silva and Duccio Zola, *Global Civil Society Events: Parallel Summits, Social Fora, Global Days of Action*, Global Civil Society 2004/2005 www.lse.ac.uk/Depts/global/Yearbook)

Glossary of terms

Bribing and corruption. This indicator is taken from the survey of business executives that forms part of the Institute for Management Development's World Competitiveness Yearbook. Respondents are asked to what extent bribing and corruption exist in the economy.

Control of Corruption Index. This index measures perceptions of corruption, conventionally defined as the exercise of public power for private gain, and perceived as a failure of governance. A higher score in this index represents better control of corruption. The index is comprised of a range of measures from various sources, from the frequency of 'additional payments to get things done', through the effects of corruption on the business environment, to measuring 'grand corruption' in the political arena – the tendency to engage in 'state capture.'

Corruption Perceptions Index (CPI). This measures corruption in the public sector and defines corruption as the abuse of public office for private gain. The CPI makes no effort to reflect private sector fraud. The index is based on surveys compiled by Transparency International from other organisations that tend to ask questions about the misuse of public power for private benefits, with a focus, for example, on bribing of public officials, taking kickbacks in public procurement, or embezzling public funds, etc. Surveys consulted:

- Economist Intelligence Unit (Country Risk Service and Country Forecasts)
- Gallup International (50th Anniversary Survey)
- Institute for Management Development (World Competitiveness Yearbook)
- Political & Economic Risk Consultancy (Asian Intelligence Issue)
- Political Risk Services (International Country Risk Guide)
- World Development Report (private sector survey by the World Bank)
- World Economic Forum & Harvard Institute for International Development (Global Competitiveness Survey).

Consumption of renewable energy per capita. Energy consumption is the amount of energy consumed by each country, divided by its population estimate. Energy consumption means the total amount of primary energy consumed from all energy sources, including losses through transportation, friction, heat, and other inefficiencies. Specifically, consumption equals indigenous production plus imports, minus exports, plus stock changes, minus international marine bunkers. The values presented are calculated by the International Energy Agency (IEA) using an energy balance methodology based on the calorific content of energy commodities. The indicator in our record is a summary of two IEA indicators: energy consumption by source: renewables (excluding hydroelectric); and energy consumption by source: hydroelectric. Renewables excluding hydroelectric includes energy from primary solid biomass, thermal solar, photovoltaic solar, wind, biogas, liquid biomass, tide, wave, and ocean. Hydroelectric includes the energy content of the electricity produced in hydro-power plants. Hydro output excludes output from pumped storage.

Emissions. Emissions refer to the release of greenhouse gases and/or their precursors, and aerosols into the atmosphere over a specified area and period of time.

Environmental conservation treaties. Our record includes 220 treaties in the following categories: animal species protection/management; environmental conservation (general); fishing, management/use of harvestable fish; forest conservation, management/exploitation; hunting, management/use of harvestable species; marine resources conservation/management; natural resources and nature conservation; plant species protection/management; renewable energy sources and energy conservation; soil conservation/management; water resources conservation/management.

Foreign direct investment (FDI). Investment to acquire a lasting management interest (10 per cent or more of voting stock) in an enterprise operating in an economy other than that of the investor. It is the sum of equity capital, reinvestment of earnings, other long-term capital, and short-term capital as shown in the balance of payments. FDI stock is the value of the share of capital and reserves (including retained profits) attributable to enterprises based outside the domestic economy, plus the net indebtedness of domestic affiliates to the parent enterprise. UNCTAD FDI stock data are frequently estimated by accumulating FDI *flows* over a period of time, or adding flows to an FDI *stock* that has been obtained for a particular year.

Full-time equivalent employment. Indicates total employment in terms of full-time jobs. Part-time employment is converted into full-time jobs and added to the number of full-time jobs, based on country-specific conventions.

Gross domestic product (GDP). Total domestic expenditure of a country, minus imports, plus exports of goods and services.

GDP per capita, PPP. GDP per capita based on purchasing power parity (PPP). GDP PPP is gross domestic product converted to international dollars using purchasing power parity rates. An international dollar has the same purchasing power over GDP as the US dollar in the United States. Data are in current international dollars.

Gini index. Measures the extent to which the distribution of income (or, in some cases, consumption expenditures) among individuals or households within an economy deviates from a perfectly equal distribution. A Lorenz curve plots the cumulative percentages of total income received against the cumulative number of recipients, starting with the poorest individual or household. The Gini index measures the area between the Lorenz curve and a hypothetical line of absolute equality, expressed as a percentage of the maximum area under the line. Thus, a Gini index of zero represents perfect equality, while an index of 100 implies perfect inequality.

Gross national income (GNI). Formerly known as gross national product or GNP. The sum of value added by all resident producers, plus any product taxes (less subsidies) not included in the valuation of output, plus net receipts of primary income (compensation of employees and property income) from abroad.

Human Development Index (HDI). A composite index based on three indicators: longevity, as measured by life expectancy at birth; educational attainment, as measured by a combination of adult literacy (two-thirds weight) and the combined gross primary, secondary, and tertiary enrolment ratio (one-third weight); and standard of living, as measured by GDP per capita (PPP US$).

Infant mortality rate. The probability of dying between birth and exactly one year of age times 1,000.

Internally displaced persons (IDPs). Individuals or groups of people who have been forced to flee their homes to escape armed conflict, generalised violence, human rights abuses, or natural or man-made disasters, *and* have remained within the borders of their home country.

International NGOs. These are currently active, autonomous non-profit making organisations with operations or activities in at least three countries (or members with voting rights in at least three countries), a formal structure with election of governing officers from several member countries and some continuity of activities. Notably excluded are obviously national or bilateral organisations, informal social movements and ad hoc bodies, and international business enterprises, investment houses or cartels and other obvious profit making bodies. Irrelevant are size, importance, degree of activity, financial strength, political or ideological position, field of interest or activity, location of headquarters and language.

Internationally oriented NGOs. These are national, currently active, autonomous, non-profit making organisations with various forms of international activity or concern such as research, peace, development or relief. They may also include national bodies which have relations with international organisations, where these international organisations list them in conjunction with truly international bodies. They may also be organisations which appear from their titles to be international. This criterion includes organisations having consultative status with United Nations and other intergovernmental organisations.

International telecom. Outgoing traffic refers to the telephone traffic, measured in minutes per subscriber, either line or cellular mobile, that originated in the country with a destination outside the country.

Main telephone lines. Telephone lines connecting a customer's equipment to the public telephone network.

Meetings. These are meetings organised or sponsored by 'international organisations' (INGOs, internationally oriented NGOs and IGOs) that appear in the Union of International Associations' *Yearbook of International Organizations*, and other meetings of significant international character. Excluded are purely national meetings, as well as those of an essentially religious, didactic, political, commercial or sporting nature and meetings with strictly limited participation, such as those of subsidiary (internal) statutory bodies, committees, groups of experts etc, and corporate and incentive meetings.

Merchandise trade. Includes all trade in goods. Trade in services is excluded.

Multidimensional scaling (MDS). A multivariate data analysis method, MDS encompasses a collection of methods that show the underlying structure of relations between entities by providing a geometrical representation of them. In MDS the relation between a pair of entities on a set of traits (variables) is translated into a proximity measure, and a selected algorithm reduces the number of dimensions in the data to a two- or three-dimensional diagram. For example, in the Introduction of this Yearbook we illustrate how countries are related to each other in terms of four variables, in a graphical plot with two dimensions. Countries most similar to each other will be placed in close proximity on the plot, while countries very dissimilar from each other will be far apart. For further reading see Bartholomew, David J., Fiona Steele, Irini Moustaki and Jane I. Galbraith (2002). *The analysis and interpretation of multivariate data for social scientists.* London: Chapman & Hall/CRC. For a brief overview online see: www.mathpsyc.uni-bonn.de/doc/delbeke/delbeke.htm#0>

Net primary school enrolment ratio. An indicator of the level of education in countries, listing the number of students enrolled in a level of education that are of official school age for that level, as a percentage of the population of official school age for that level.

Network. Interpersonal or inter-organisational ties that reflect structural or legal relations, information flows and other exchanges. Network analysis seeks to identify and explain patterns in complex networks, and how these influence behaviour.

Official development assistance (ODA). Official development assistance and net official aid record the actual international transfer by the donor of financial resources or of goods or services valued at the cost to the donor, minus any repayments of loan principal during the same period. ODA data are comprised of disbursements of loans made on concessional terms (net of repayments of principal) and grants by official agencies of the members of the Development Assistance Committee (DAC) of the OECD, by multilateral institutions, and by certain Arab countries to promote economic development and welfare in recipient economies listed as 'developing' by DAC. Loans with a grant element of at least 25 per cent are included in ODA, as are technical cooperation and assistance.

Passengers carried. Air passengers carried include both domestic and international aircraft passengers.

Peacekeeping forces. Military personnel and civilian police serving in United Nations peacekeeping missions.

Political rights and civil liberties. An indicator of the levels of democracy in countries around the world. Real-world rights and freedoms enjoyed by individuals, as a result of actions by both state and non-governmental actors, are based on the Universal Declaration of Human Rights. Scores range from one, the lowest degree of freedom, to seven, the highest (we modified them from the original index scores which are reversed, for the sake of clarity).

Public sector or government. All branches of the government, including the executive, judicial, and administrative and regulatory activities of federal, state, local, or regional political entities; the terms 'government' and 'public sector' are used synonymously.

Public sector payments. Include grants and contracts, ie. direct contributions by the government to the organisation in support of specific activities and programmes; statutory transfers, ie. contributions by the government, as mandated by law, to provide general support to an organisation in carrying out its public programmes; and third-party payments, ie. indirect government payments reimbursing an organisation for services rendered to individuals (eg. health insurance, 'vouchers', or payments for day care).

Private giving. Includes foundation giving, including grants from grant-making foundations, operating foundations, and community foundations; business or corporate donations, which includes giving directly by businesses or giving by business or corporate foundations; and individual giving, ie. direct contributions by individuals and contributions through 'federated fund-raising' campaigns.

Private fees and charges (or 'programme fees'). These include four types of business or commercial income: fees for service, dues (eg. membership charges), proceeds from sales of products, and investment income.

Refugee. As defined by the UN High Commissioner for Refugees, a person is a refugee if she/he qualifies under the Arrangements of 12 May 1926 and 30 June 1928 or under the Conventions of 28 October 1933 and 10 February 1938, the Protocol of 14 September 1939 or the Constitution of the International Refugee Organisation. For further information see www.unhcr.ch/cgi-bin/texis/vtx/home

Transnationality Index (TNI). The average of three ratios: a corporation's foreign assets to total assets, foreign sales to total sales, and foreign employment to total employment.

Transparency of government. This indicator is taken from the survey of business executives which forms part of the Institute for Management Development's World Competitiveness Yearbook. Respondents are asked to what extent their government communicates its policy intentions clearly and publicly.

Total military personnel. Active duty military personnel, including paramilitary forces if those forces resemble regular units in their organisation, equipment, training, or mission.

Total trade. The sum of the market value of imports and exports of goods and services.

Tourists. Visitors who travel to a country other than that where they have their usual residence for a period not exceeding 12 months and whose main purpose in visiting is other than an activity remunerated from within the country visited.

Voice and Accountability. An index comprised of a number of indicators measuring various aspects of the political process, civil liberties and political rights. These indicators measure the extent to which citizens of a country are able to participate in the selection of their government, as well as the independence of the media to monitor those in authority and hold them accountable for their actions.

Volunteer input. Calculated by converting the total volunteer hours into full-time equivalent employment, multiplied by the average wage for the group, industry, or the economy as a whole.

CHRONOLOGY OF GLOBAL CIVIL SOCIETY EVENTS

Compiled by Jill Timms

Contributors: Brian Appelbe, Uri Avnery, Marcelo Batalha, Reine C. Borja, Thierry Brugvin, Joabe Cavalcanti, Hyo-Je Cho, Andrew Davey, Bernard Dreano, Nenad Durdevic, Mary Fischer, Louise Fraser, Iulian Gavril, Nihad Gohar, Anil Gupta, Martin J Gurch, Stuart Hodkinson, Vicky Holland, Zafarullah Khan, Yung Law, Silke Lechner, Maritza Lopez-Quintana, Mukul Mundy, Otilia Mihai, Nuria Molina, Richard Nagle, Alejandro Natal, Beatriz Martin Nieto, Katarina Sehm Patomaki, Mario Pianta, Asthriesslav Rocuts, Marjanie Roose, Thomas Ruddy, Florent Schaeffer, Robert Sommers, Toralf Staud, Vanessa Tang, Kate Townsend, Caroline Walker, Aled Williams.

Introduction to the chronology

This section of the Yearbook provides an alternative type of record to the tables and statistics in the data programme. The purpose of the chronology is to offer an account of diverse global civil society activities and landmark events. This year it covers a longer time span than in previous Yearbooks, extending from January 2003 to the end of April 2004, and includes events whose theme, participation or outcome are judged to have been significant. Our criteria for inclusion continue to be refined, as global civil society develops. Often records of global civil society activity are limited to available statistics of NGO activity, membership, funding and so forth, which restricts information to a particular type of civil society organisation and to certain sources. This chronology takes a different approach, seeking to prioritise events that are not reported in the mainstream media, that occur worldwide rather than only in the West, and that fall under a broad definition of global civil society activity. To achieve this we rely on a network of correspondents around the world, who report on events and activity within their countries and regions (see the next section for information on how you could contribute).

The chronology presented here is not a comprehensive list of every global civil society action or event. Indeed, as the number of events increase each year, we are able to include a selection of the most significant, and those most under-represented in standard indicators of global civil society. Space constraints and the welcome growth of activity mean we are continually refining the criteria for inclusion; nonetheless the chronology provides an insight into the depth and range of actions, and indicates the types of activity perceived as most significant by our correspondents. For example, this year's chronology highlights the proliferation of social forums, regional and thematic, although space limitations prevent us from covering them all. An extended version of the chronology is on our website, www.lse.ac.uk/depts/global/yearbook. We are keen to use the data creatively and, with your assistance, we hope to develop its collection, collation and presentation in order to ensure that this alternative record continues to help our understanding of global civil society.

Invitation to contribute to the Global Civil Society Yearbook

The contributions of our team of Global Civil Society correspondents provide the basis for this chronology, and to each we again offer our thanks. Each year we expand the team, and this has allowed us to include entries from over 70 countries, even in this edited version. The Yearbook always includes an invitation to readers to join the team, and this year we are particularly interested in your feedback as we embark on a development programme.

In return, each contributor has the opportunity to influence the project, is acknowledged in the Yearbook as a Global Civil Society correspondent, receives a complimentary copy and, of course, our thanks. We contact correspondents on a regular basis for information about events and actions taking place in their country, sphere of activity or region. This year, in particular, we would also welcome feedback on the past and present chronologies, details of how you use the data, other information that you would find useful, or ideas for further development. If you would like more information about being a Global Civil Society correspondent, or to offer feedback, please contact us via the website mentioned above. We look forward to hearing from you and receiving your contribution to this important project.

Global Civil Society events, January 2003–April 2004

January 2003

2–7 January The First Asian Social Forum is held in Hyderabad, India. Fifteen thousand people take part in over 300 seminars, workshops and other events – the first time that the social forum process has occurred in this region and on this scale. There are organisational and technical difficulties, and the events are mainly India-centric, which is not helped by problems with visas, especially for Pakistani delegates, but organisers view this as a learning process.

5–9 January In Addis Ababa, Ethiopia, the Second African Social Forum takes place, involving people and organisations from 40 countries. The forum discusses how the African Social Forum has strengthened since the last meeting. There is a consensus that African unity and social integration are fundamental and that civil society action is needed to work towards these, especially against the adoption by the African Union of the New Partnership for Africa's Development (NEPAD) as the paradigm for the continent's development.

6 January In Bahrain, a sit-in of 70 women at the Ministry of Justice calls for a unified civil-status law, the right to housing, the raising of the marriage age to 22 for both women and men, and women's right to divorce.

10 January Protests in San Francisco mark the deadline for the registration process imposed by the Immigration and Naturalization Service (INS) on US temporary residents from 20 countries. Protesters say that there have been arrests and interrogations of hundreds of people who have complied with the order to give their fingerprints, names and other details. This applies to all men aged 16 years and above who were born in Afghanistan, Algeria, Bahrain, Eritrea, Lebanon, Morocco, North Korea, Oman, Qatar, Somalia, Tunisia, United Arab Emirates and Yemen. The protests are organised by a multitude of ethnic and religious groups.

11–12 January In Rabat, Morocco, the NGO Initiative to Support Iraq coordinates a sit-in at the UN headquarters. This is followed by a mass march of 10,000 people in solidarity with Iraq and Palestine, involving over 50 trade unions, political parties and NGOs.

16–19 January The Second Pan-Amazonic Social Forum takes place in Belem, Brazil, bringing together a wide range of people and focusing on environmental issues and preparations for the Third World Social Forum.

18 January The weekly Wednesday rally of former 'comfort women', who were forced to serve as sexual slaves for Japanese soldiers during the Second World War, marks its 11th anniversary in front of the Japanese embassy in downtown Seoul. A dozen comfort women, along with civic activists and supporters, stage the 540th rally to call for an official apology and compensation from the Japanese government.

21–23 January The first Global Assembly of Peasant Farmers' Organisations takes place in Porto Alegre as groups gather there in preparation for the Third World Social Forum. This is organised by Via Campesina.

23–28 January The Third World Social Forum takes place in Porto Alegre, Brazil, attended by 100,000 people attend from 123 countries, making it the largest social forum to date. A quarter of participants are young people. Highlights include the speech of the new Brazilian president, Luiz Inacio Lula da Silva (known as Lula), witnessed 50,000 people, and the controversial visit by Venezuelan president Hugo Chavez, whose rally was kept separate from the official forum in keeping with the WSF commitment to remaining non-governmental.

24 January Following pressure and boycott campaigns from a range of international civil society organisations, Nestle drops its $6m claim against the Ethiopian government.

31 January In Grenoble, France, 8,000 protesters demonstrate against the arrest of ten activists

charged with destroying genetically modified plants.

February 2003

13 February The Korean Truth Committee on the Vietnam War, a civil society group, announces the opening of a citizen-funded peace park to pay tribute to victims of the Vietnam War. Finance for the Han-Viet Peace Park in Vietnam has been collected by a range of organisations to repent for the atrocities allegedly committed by Korean soldiers during the Vietnam War. More than 100,000 South Koreans helped raise 150 million Korean Won. A 20-member Korean delegation and about 500 Vietnamese officials and citizens attend the opening ceremony.

15 February This is claimed to be a global day of mobilisation against the war in Iraq. One of the largest demonstrations takes place in Barcelona, with two million people besieging the city centre to protest the war and also the environmental damage caused by the Prestige oil tanker, which sank off northern Spain in 2002. In Dublin up to 100,000 people march to voice their opposition to military action against Iraq. Numerous smaller protests are held in cities and towns throughout Ireland. In Berlin, 500,000 people protest, including some ministers of the federal government, making this the biggest demonstrations in Germany since the Second World War. Throughout France protests are held, including a 600,000-strong march in Paris.

17–18 February In Bolivia a strike organised by the country's largest union, Central Bolivian Workers Union, ends in riots, with at least 33 dead.

19 February Rallies are staged simultaneously in 11 cities, including Seoul, Tokyo, Osaka and Vancouver, to protest against the imprisonment of North Korean defectors detained in China. The NGO Exodus 21 coordinates this action and the protest in front of the Chinese consulate in the Republic of Korea.

20 February In Venezuela, the strike leader and prominent entrepreneur, Carlos Fernandez, is placed under house arrest to await trial on charges of rebellion, treason and sabotage, after his involvement in the organisation of protests that resulted in a two-month strike, which forced the suspension of oil exports.

23 February One million people take part in demonstrations in Madrid, under the banner 'Never Again', to protest against the environmental catastrophe created by the sinking of the Prestige oil tanker. A system of volunteers cleans the coastline on a daily basis and plans to continue doing so until the end of the year.

24–25 February Due to deteriorating social conditions and government privatisation plans in Algeria, thousands of workers from many sectors agree to a national strike.

26 February A Korean NGO, the People's Solidarity for Participatory Democracy (PSPD), announces its intention to file a lawsuit against Microsoft, the US software giant, to seek reparation for damage caused by an Internet attack on 15 January.

28 February Over 30 University of Chicago students and 20 day labourers from Union Latina participate in a one-day hunger strike outside the University of Chicago's Taco Bell restaurant, in solidarity with farm workers on hunger strike outside Taco Bell headquarters in Irvine, California. The strike, organised by the Anti-Sweatshop Coalition, is in response to the annual hunger strike of farm workers representing the Coalition of Immokalee Workers, which wants Taco Bell to take responsibility for the sweatshop conditions in the Florida fields where its tomatoes are picked.

March 2003

8 March Protests throughout the world take place on International Women's Day. In Italy, traditional celebrations include the giving of fragrant and long-lasting mimosa flowers, symbols of peace and light, to mothers, sisters, daughters, wives and friends. Women in many countries mark the day by protesting peacefully against the war in Iraq.

10 March The Initiative for the Protection of Women's Rights (IDPF) reveals that seven out of ten Moroccan women suffer from domestic violence, and half of them do not report it.

10 March The Landless Movement and other agricultural social movements set up a camp in front of Monsanto's research buildings in the city of Uberlândia, Minas Gerais, Brazil. Under the tag 'Brazil Free of Transgenic Organisms', the camp lasts for six months.

13–15 March ATTAC Germany organises protests against privatisation and the General Agreement on Trade in Services (GATS) in 50 German cities. In

Göttingen, symbolic shares of public sector properties, such as bridges, are distributed to passers-by; in Munich the *Stachus* (public space) is temporarily privatised; and in Marburg protesters chain themselves to the fountain in the market square shouting 'Water belongs to all.'

16–23 March At the Third World Water Forum in Japan, US$180 billion is pledged to cut by half the number of people without access to drinking water and sanitation. International civil society groups argue that the pledge is motivated by self-interest – construction companies will profit from the ensuing work.

17 March In Bahrain, the Arab National Conference launches a large-scale campaign to consolidate the international forces against the war in Iraq. The campaign includes gratitude messages to France, Germany and Turkey, as well as letters to Security Council members praising anti-war efforts and denouncing those governments that support the war.

18 March In Cuba, 26 independent journalists who had established two underground publications, are imprisoned, an action unprecedented in the 44 years of Castro's rule. The international NGO, Reporters Without Borders, mounts a worldwide petition to campaign for their immediate release.

20 March Despite strong civil society protests internationally, the US-led war to topple Iraqi president Saddam Hussein officially starts when American missiles are launched against targets in Baghdad. Around the world, anti-war activities are stepped-up.

30 March A concert for peace is held in Barcelona, bringing out 40,000 people to peacefully proclaim their opposition to the war in Iraq.

April 2003

4–5 April The Third International Citizens Meeting is organised by the UNESCO Chair on Peace and Human Rights and the City Council in Barcelona, under the title 'Towards a new form of citizenship: alternatives to single discourse.'

5–6 April The First Hungarian Social Forum is held in Miskolc, northeastern Hungary. Discussions include the role of Hungarian soldiers in the Iraq war and initiatives to encourage the development of social forums throughout eastern Europe.

7 April In Oakland, California, local police fire non-lethal bullets, sandbags and concussion grenades against some 500 anti-war protesters who assemble by the Port of Oakland. One of the activist groups involved is the San Francisco-based Direct Action to Stop the War. The protesters assemble at the port because one of the nearby shipping companies is handling war supplies.

12 April In Rome, 300,000 people demonstrate against the war in Iraq, an action organised by the Italian Stop the War, in cooperation with international peace groups.

18 April In Srinagar, Kashmir, 20,000 people gather at a rally to hear Indian prime minister Atal Bihari Vajpayee speak of the possibility of peace with Pakistan. This is seen, at least in part, to be a result of civil society pressure for the resumption of peace talks. Both countries also agree to play cricket after a gap of 15 years.

22 April In the Algerian city of Tiziozo, the largest tribal region, 10,000 people come out to the streets: the nation is divided between defenders of the Arabic- and French-speaking traditions. The protest is sparked by a dispute over which alphabet will be used – the Arabic or Latin – to write the Berber language, which became a national language the previous year.

25–27 April The Uppsala Social Forum takes place, the fourth social forum in Sweden to date, with 3,000 participants from 63 organisations. The possibility of establishing a Nordic regional forum is discussed.

May 2003

1 May International Labour Day becomes a platform for anti-war protests. This includes Athens, where 7,000 protesters gather, some burning American flags outside the US embassy. In Berlin, large protests eventually end in riots against the well-prepared police. In Britain, protests are peaceful in spite of the heavy policing, indicating that trouble has been expected. In Bulgaria, 5,000 protesters call for the resignation of the government because of its failure to improve the economy. China is forced to cancel its celebrations, which are among the largest national Labour Day events in the world, due to the SARS virus. In Cyprus, Greek and Turkish residents celebrate May Day together for the first time in 30 years. Throughout Russia rallies are held calling for an increase in wages and

student stipends, and for better social provision. In Turkey, demonstrators clash with police, causing riots in the capital, Istanbul.

6 May Lawyers representing 30,000 rainforest people in Ecuador file a suit against Chevron Texaco, claiming that the company has destroyed their homeland by dumping huge quantities of toxic waste and crude oil over a 20-year period.

6–9 May In San Cristobal de las Casas, Chiapas, Mexico, delegates from 28 countries meet to express their will to maintain their autonomy and to defend their territories and resources. They also celebrate the resistance experiences in Latin America and the Caribbean, such as the expulsion of US Marines from Vieques. They stress the need for peace, social justice and the demilitarisation of the region, and emphasise the need to draw more attention to human rights issues in the area. The meeting was organised by the Call of the Excluded, Movement for the Peoples of the Americas, Jubilee Americas, Non-violence International and the Chiapaneca Network Against Neo-liberalism.

7–9 May The Stockholm Social Forum and the Skane Social Forum take place.

10 May The Belgium Social Forum is held in Brussels.

11–12 May In Mexico, meetings are held by groups against the Free Trade Area of the Americas (FTAA) and the World Trade Organisation (WTO) to coordinate the civil society actions planned to coincide with the WTO summit, which is to be held in Cancun in September.

22 May Former Sudanese president Major Sawar Addahab meets with the wife of John Garang in Cairo at a brainstorming session that brings Sudanese and Egyptian NGOs together. The meeting was organised by the national NGO Center for Population and Development (NCPD) with the aim of promoting the unity of Arab and African peoples and building trust among local communities. Ninety Sudanese NGOs participated (65 from northern Sudan and 25 from southern Sudan) as well as 45 Egyptian NGOs.

29 May –1 June The Austrian Social Forum is held in Hallein, Salzburg.

June 2003

1–3 June Around 150,000 protesters demonstrate against the meeting of the G8 in Evian.

7–10 June The first-ever Portuguese Social Forum is held in the country's capital, Lisbon.

16 June China admits that small cracks have appeared in the controversial Three Gorges Dam – for which more than 1,200,000 people will eventually have been moved – and which international civil society groups have campaigned against.

16–20 June A thematic social forum, conceived at the Third World Social Forum, is held on Democracy, Human Rights, War and Drug Trafficking. This takes place in Cartagena de Indias, Colombia, a country where more than 270,000 people have died at as a result of the drugs trade since 1991. The forum brings together diverse global civil society groups to discuss these issues, and organises action around the impact of illegal drug trafficking at local and global levels.

20–22 June In Thessaloniki, the first Greece Social Forum is held, which marks the culmination of civil society protests throughout Greece's presidency of the EU. An international protest march is held, joined by people from growing movement of local social forums throughout Greece.

20–25 June At the Ministerial Conference and Expo on Agricultural Science and Technology in Sacramento, California, Trade, Agriculture and Environment Ministers from 180 WTO member states are faced with activists from a variety of organisations including Via Campesina, the Organic Consumers Association, and Biodevastation, which together invited activists from all nations to come to Sacramento and resist corporate domination of the world's food supply.

21–23 June International women's and children's rights groups hold a three-day conference on legal instruments for the prevention of female genital mutilation. Held in Cairo, it brings together representatives from 28 Arab and African countries and includes the Italian Association for Women in Development, No Peace without Justice and the Egyptian National Council for Childhood and Motherhood (NCCM). The conference receives support from the EU Commission and the United Nations Development Program (UNDP). The Grand Imam of al Azhar and a representative of Pope Shenouda attend, as well as the Chair of the UN Commission for the Rights of the Child.

26 June The WTO holds an unofficial mini-ministerial meeting in the Red Sea resort of Sharm al Shaikh.

NGOs, including Greenpeace, are invited to the conference but are not participants in the talks behind closed doors. They are, however, allowed on the premises of the venue.

29 June The first ever gay pride march in India is held in Calcutta.

July 2003

1 July A peaceful protest involving 500,000 people takes place in Hong Kong in opposition to the national security legislation (Article 23 of the Basic Law, the mini-constitution of Hong Kong). Campaigners believe it is a serious threat to freedom of expression and freedom of assembly. As a result, the Hong Kong Special Administrative Region (SAR) government defers the second reading of the bill.

6 July After worldwide controversy between church groups supportive and opposed to the appointment of gay clerics, and involving human and gay rights groups, canon Jeffery John, a gay celibate priest in the Church of England, withdraws his nomination to be appointed the Bishop of Reading, England. He would have been the first openly gay bishop in the Anglican Church. He is later appointed Dean of Reading Cathedral.

15 July Following the campaigns of human rights and civil liberties activists, the Syrian president pardons hundreds of prisoners. He also orders an end to the judicial pursuit of lawyer Haitham al Malih, head of the Syrian Human Rights Organisation, and three of his colleagues, who were to appear before a military court facing charges related to their activities in the field of human rights.

16 July An Internet site is launched for the World Campaign for in-depth Reform of the System of International Institutions, www.reformcampaign.net. The site is intended to collect pledges in support of the Campaign Manifesto, to be submitted at the United Nations General Assembly in 2006, in order to promote reform of the international system.

18 July In Brazil, a judge is seen to support the campaign of activists against homelessness by suspending the eviction of 4,000 members of the Workers Without a Roof Movement, who are squatting on a 20-hectare plot owned by Volkswagen in São Paulo.

21–24 July The Fourth Foro Mesoamericano – Campaign Against the FTAA – takes place in Tegucigalpa, Honduras. Participants focus on strategies to resist and reverse neo-liberal policies.

23 July Trade unions in Colombia call for a worldwide boycott of Coca-Cola's products amid allegations that the company has employed militias to murder nine union members in the past 13 years.

23 July In Juarez City, Chihuahua, 40 Mexican and international NGOs, as well as observers from the UN, meet with the ministers of the Interior and Social Development, the national judicial authorities, the governor and the mayor, to demand an end to the violence against and murder of women and children in the city.

28–30 July During a WTO meeting in Montreal, Quebec, ahead of the organisation's full-scale September 2003 conference in Cancun, hundreds of protesters from across Canada and beyond come to protest, some smashing storefront windows of multinational brands.

August 2003

6 August Demonstrations and protests take place against social security reform in Brasilia, the capital of Brazil. They are attended by 80,000 civil servants, with some protesters breaking windows in an attempt to invade the Government Palace.

9 August In Chicago, Illinois, 1,500 immigrant workers and their allies rally in preparation for the Immigrant Workers Freedom Ride in late September.

9–10 August In Larzac, France, 150,000 people demonstrate against GATS and the genetic modification of food.

20 August Human rights activists mourn the death of the Brazilian diplomat Sergio Vieira de Mello. He was the top UN official in Iraq and UN High Commissioner for Human Rights, and had served in conflict areas worldwide. He died when the UN headquarters in Baghdad was bombed.

23 August In Chicago, Illinois, over 1,000 citizens from 60 organisations gather at Federal Plaza to participate in a rally organised by the Chicago Coalition Against War and Racism (CCAWR). The lobby for an end to the occupation of Iraq and return of troops.

24–26 August In Macedonia, representatives of civil society from both Serb and Albanian communities in Serbia meet as part of a Partnerships for Peace Project, with the aim of initiating dialogue between young leaders and creating a tolerant and democratic atmosphere for the talks.

September 2003

5–7 September In Cancun, Mexico, a Universal Forum for Biodiversity is held to bring together civil society groups in order to consolidate views on trade, property rights and biodiversity. Groups stress their opposition to patents on living beings and to the privatisation of natural resources. They also express their concerns about the violation of indigenous peoples' rights and the impact of free trade on their communities. The forum is promoted mainly by Friends of the Earth, Action Group on Erosion, Technology and Concentration (ETC), Traditional Doctors from Chiapas, and other organisations.

7 September Under the banner 'Take off your hands, Brazil is our land', the ninth Cry of the Excluded protest takes place, with marches organised by a range of social movements throughout Brazil.

8 September Peru's government releases a report by a truth commission on the deaths of more than 69,000 people between 1980 and 2000. The report, which mostly blames a Maoist rebel group, Shining Path, also states that the armed forces and two supposedly democratic governments share responsibility for human rights violations; and that the majority of Peru's powerful political class turned their backs on the suffering and deaths of Peru's Quechua-speaking Indians. Blame is also placed upon Vladimiro Montesinos, head of intelligence under President Alberto Fujimori, for organising torture and disappearances. The report is criticised by those implicated, such as former military chief, Roberto Clemente Noel, who accuses commission members of being Marxists with connections to Shining Path.

8–9 September Civil society groups in Mongolia work with international organisations to host the International Civil Society Forum's Fifth Conference of the New or Restored Democracies. This takes place in Ulaan Baatar, the capital of Mongolia.

8–9 September A thematic Social Forum for Global Social Rights takes place in Buenos Aires, Argentina.

9–15 September In Cancun, Mexico, the International Forum for Indigenous and Campesino takes place. Delegates from at 33 countries join to express their concerns about the increasing impoverishment of the agricultural sector. Delegates from Spain, US, Thailand, Greece, Canada, South Africa, The Philippines, Holland, Portugal, Honduras, Haiti, Mozambique, Dominican Republic, Belgium, Japan, Korea, Panama, Cuba, Brazil, Argentina and Mexico demonstrate their rejection of free trade. The forum is mainly promoted by the National Indigenous Congress of Mexico, The Landless Movement of Brazil, UNORCA de Mexico, The Assembly of the People of Thailand and the National Family Farm Coalition. At the same time, 3,000 peasants representing grassroots organisations worldwide, arrive in Cancun.

10 September In Stockholm, the Swedish Foreign Minister Anna Lindh is assassinated. The perpetrator, Mijailo Mijailovic, a 25-year-old Swede of Serbian origin, stabs her as she shops at a department store in downtown Stockholm. Lindh, well known for her commitment to human rights, freedom and peace, is mourned worldwide.

10–14 September The Fifth Ministerial Meeting of the WTO is held in Cancun, Mexico, surrounded by thousands of civil society activists. For the first time, the WTO allows the participation of civil society groups, which express their serious concerns about globalisation and free trade; and campaign for neglected rural areas. The WTO is also accused of being undemocratic, anti-development and obsolete. Particularly critical are organisations such as 'Our World is Not For Sale', Public Citizen, and the International Forum against Globalisation, as well as Food First, among many others. Parallel to the formal meeting, several direct action groups rail against the police. A Korean peasant leader, Lee Kyung Hae stabs himself to death. His chest is inscribed with 'The WTO kills peasants.'

13 September Following the suicide of Lee Kyung Hae, farmers and civic activists seek to pressure the Korean government to withdraw its representatives from the WTO meeting. Representatives of farming and civic groups warn they will take further 'provocative' actions if the government does not call back its negotiators from the Cancun talks.

Protests supporting this call are held around the world.

14 September The WTO summit in Cancun collapses after a walk-out by African countries. The trade talks see a new group of militant developing countries, led by Brazil, India and China, flexing their negotiating muscles for the first time.

19–21 September The Swiss Social Forum takes place in Friburgo, Switzerland.

20 September The Immigrant Workers Freedom Ride starts across America, bringing joining together trade unions, immigrant civil society groups, and community and student organisations. Modelled on the Freedom Rides of the 1960s civil rights campaigns, immigrants, their families, other workers and their allies board buses from ten major cities to ride across the US, making hundreds of stops along the way, to protest against and draw attention to the injustices of immigration legislation. Activists call for reform of immigration law, the right of immigrants to form unions, have driving licences, and an end to the deportation of Arabs, Muslims and undocumented immigrants. The rides will go to Washington DC to lobby the government and culminate in protests in New York.

25–26 September The Nigerian Women Social Forum takes place in Niamey, Nigeria.

26–28 September The themed Universitarian Social Forum takes place in Asuncion, capital of Paraguay.

October 2003

9–11 October The first Zimbabwe Social Forum takes place in the capital, Harare, described by the organisers as a People's Forum for Peace, Reconstruction and Prosperity. The forum adopts a charter of principles based on 'no to capitalism, no to globalisation and no to any form of domination.'

9–12 October The Fifth Assembly of the Peoples' United Nations on 'Europe and the world: the role and responsibilities of Europe in the world', is organised by Tavola della Pace, a coalition of hundreds of civil society groups. Two hundred and fifty representatives of global civil society, from 150 countries, meet for three days with 400 Italian participants. The event ends in a 15-mile march from Perugia to Assisi, with 500,000 people protesting against the war in Iraq, and for a different European policy.

10–12 October The Second Uruguayan Social Forum takes place in Montevideo.

17 October In Bolivia, Carlos Mesa, a political unknown, takes over the presidency after a month-long revolt by the country's Indian majority. The former president and a key US ally, Gonzalo Sanchez de Lozada, flees in the wake of violent protests against the American-backed drive to wipe out crops of the staple coca leaf, and against plans to export natural gas to the US. An estimated 74 people are believed to have been killed in this period.

17–19 October This weekend an array of social forums take place around the world. The Second Sao Joao Social Forum takes place in Sao Joao del Rei, Brazil. The Alberta Social Forum takes place in Edmonton, Alberta, Canada. The Majorca Social Forum takes place in Palma, Majorca. The First Irish Social Forum takes place in Dublin, Ireland.

23 October Hundreds of Saudis participate in a demonstration to mark the opening of the kingdom's first human rights conference, and the proclamation by the Saudi government that it would hold its first legislative elections.

31 October–2 November The Norwegian Social Forum takes place in Oslo and simultaneously the Denmark Social Forum takes place in Copenhagen.

November 2003

1 November In Berlin, a broad coalition of left-wing groups, trade unions and ATTAC mobilise more than 100,000 people for a demonstration against the welfare reforms of the German federal government.

4–5 November Students in universities all over Germany launch 'strikes.' Over a period of weeks they organise demonstrations and seize academic and governmental buildings, demanding more money for education.

5–6 November In St Julien, Malta, the fourth Euro-Mediterranean Socio-economic Summit takes place. Trade unionists, employers, farmers, civil rights activists, members of NGOs from Bulgaria, Cyprus, Estonia, Hungary, Israel, Italy, France, Greece, Jordan, Luxembourg, Malta, Palestine, Portugal, Spain, Syria and Turkey, meet in Malta to promote institutions of social dialogue, a greater involvement of civil society in Euro-Mediterranean relations, and a balance between economic progress and social development.

6–9 November The Brazilian Social Forum takes place in Belo Horizonte, Brazil.

7–9 November The Thematic Second Health Social Forum is held in Buenos Aires, Argentina.

9–10 November The African Social Forum takes place in Lusaka, Zambia.

12–16 November The Second European Social Forum takes place in Paris, France. This is held in 130 locations, mainly in the outlying areas of Saint Denis, Bobigny and Ivry. Fifty thousand people register for the event and more than 100,000 take part in the march on the closing day, which is dedicated to peace and opposition to the war in Iraq.

20–23 November The Paraguayan Social Forum takes place in the country's capital, Asuncion.

21–23 November The Aotearoa Social Forum takes place in Wellington, New Zealand.

25–26 November The Regional Forum of Civil Society against Hemispheric Integration meets in Mexico City, attended by 71 civil society organisations from 21 countries of the Americas. They discuss their position vis-à-vis the coming Summit of the Americas, to be held in January 2004, in Monterrey, Mexico. The event is organised by the Mexican Network against Free Trade, Civic Alliance, Canadian Foundation for the Americas, and the Interamerican Network for Democracy, with observers from the governments of Mexico, US and Canada, as well as from the Interamerican Development Bank, the World Bank and the Organisation of American States.

25–27 November The Ivory Coast Social Forum takes place in Abidjan, Ivory Coast.

26–29 November The Central Africa Social Forum is held in the capital city of Bangui.

27–29 November The Global Progressive Forum brings together more than 500 policy makers, leaders and representatives of NGOs, trade unions, businesses and academia from around the world in Brussels. Organised by the Parliamentary Group of the Party of European Socialists and the Socialist International, civil society organisations such as Oxfam International, Third World Network, World Wide Fund for Nature, UBUNTU Forum, Médecins du Monde, and the International Confederation of Free Trade Unions take part. The Forum addresses three main goals: turning globalisation into a peace-building process, making globalisation a sustainable process for present and future generations, and ensuring that globalisation works for all.

28–30 November The Euro-Mediterranean Forum is held in Naples, stressing the importance of paving the way for cultural exchange and a dialogue between cultures. It is attended by 300 representatives of civil society organisations in the Mediterranean region.

December 2003

5 December Civil society organisations, governments, and volunteers celebrate International Volunteer Day (IVD) to recognise the contribution made by volunteers to the strengthening of civil society.

13–14 December Hundreds of Arab and international activists throughout the world meet in Cairo under the slogan 'Yes to resistance in Palestine and Iraq: No to capitalist globalization and US hegemony.'

13–14 December The second Cairo anti-war rally, organised by the International Campaign against Zionist and US Occupation, attracts 1,000 activists. It brings together international figures, political and trade union activists, writers, journalists, artists, and defenders of human rights from Asia, Africa, Latin America, Europe and the United States in a common struggle against imperialism and capitalist globalisation, US hegemony, Zionism and racism, and for a more humane and just alternative.

14 December In Brazil, senator Heloisa Helena, congresswoman Luciana Genro, and congressmen, Joao Batista and Joao Fontes, are expelled from the Partido dos Trabalhadores (PT). Labelled the 'radicals', they are against the neo-liberal reforms promoted by the Brazilian government. Many politicians and civil society activists protest against their expulsion.

16–17 December The Somalian Social Forum takes place in Mogadishu, Somalia.

18–20 December The Senegal Social Forum takes place in Dakar, Senegal.

21 December Civil society institutions affiliated to the African Union meet to discuss the charter of the Economic, Social and Cultural Council of the Union. The meeting is attended by civil society representatives from member countries who have an official consultative relationship with the

Union, as per its charter. The Economic, Social and Cultural Council consists of 50 civil society organisations selected from all member states, in addition to representatives of the economic groups in diaspora.

21 December Many protests are organised in Paris against the government decision to ban the wearing of religious clothing in French state schools, including the Islamic Hijab, Jewish yamulke, and 'excessive' Christian crosses. The controversy draws the attention of civil liberties and religious groups around the world.

22 December Human Rights Watch criticises a peace agreement that gives rebels and soldiers temporary immunity from prosecution for atrocities committed against civilians during Burundi's 10 year civil war (1993–2003), in which more than 200,000 people died.

January 2004

2 January Political parties and civic groups condemn Japanese Prime Minister Junichiro Koizumi's New Year's Day visit to a controversial shrine honouring Japan's war criminals, and demand that the government take a strong stand on the issue.

4–5 January The Social Forum for Another Mali takes place in Bamako, Mali.

9 January The Final Court of Appeal in Hong Kong rules against the Town Planning Board on the Wanchai Reclamation Phase II project because it failed to comply with Section 3 of the Protection of the Harbour Ordinance. This is a major victory for the Society for the Protection of the Harbour and international environmental groups, which have been campaigning together. It is seen as an example of the strength of civil society when it uses legal methods.

12–13 January The Pakistan Social Forum takes place in Lahore, Pakistan.

16–21 January The Fourth World Social Forum is held in Mumbai, India, the first time the event has been hosted outside Porto Alegre. One hundred thousand people from 132 countries register at the event, with strong representation from groups of all backgrounds across India. For the first time an organised counter-event, Mumbai Resistance 2004, is held directly opposite site of the main forum. Mumbai Resistance 2004 is critical of the social forum process.

February 2004

4–8 February The Third Pan-Amazon Social Forum takes place in Ciudad Guayana, Venezuela.

8 February Three South Koreans who returned home after years of captivity in North Korea go to Tokyo to testify before the Japanese parliament. The Citizen's Coalition for Human Rights of Abductees and North Korean Refugees, which helped organise the visit, said the former abductees were invited by Japan as part of a government effort to raise public awareness and support in resolving North Korea's abduction of Japanese citizens.

16 February The Federation of Egyptian Industries hosts the formal launch of the Global Compact – the UN Initiative on Corporate Social Responsibility – in Egypt. Two hundred delegates representing the private sector, academics and civil society groups attend the launch.

28 February Disruptions occur at the shareholders' meeting of Samsung Electronics, where the People's Solidarity for Participatory Democracy, one of the most active shareholders' rights groups in Japan, attend for the first time in three years.

March 2004

4 March After scientist Hwang Woo-suk's breakthrough in cloning human cells was announced in early February, at least ten civil society groups, including the Citizens' Movement for Environmental Justice, join the campaign against Hwang's nomination for a Nobel Peace Prize.

13 March Spontaneous demonstrations take place in Spanish cities and towns, and among Spanish expatriate communities, in protest at the terrorist attacks that devastated the country prior to the general elections.

13 March Seventy thousand people from more than 500 civic organisations gather in Kwanghwamun, South Korea, to demand an annulment of the National Assembly and the impeachment of the President. Similar rallies are witnessed in Kwangju, Pusan, Taegua and other major cities across the country.

17 March Simultaneous demonstrations in seven countries mark South Korean comfort women's 600th Wednesday rally in front of the Japanese Embassy in Seoul. Many Asian comfort women, who were compelled to serve as sex slaves for Japanese soldiers during the Second World War,

and their supporters, gather simultaneously in Japan, Taiwan, the US, Germany, Belgium and Spain.

20 March An international day of action for peace is marked around the world on the anniversary of the start of the war in Iraq. For example, in Italy, a million people participate in a protest organised by the Italian Stop the War committee. There are also several general strikes and large trade union demonstrations. The main theme of the action is a call for troops to be withdrawn and for sovereignty to be returned to the Iraqi people.

21 March In Washington DC a peaceful vigil is held at which the names of all the US military personnel killed in Iraq are read out, together with names symbolising the Iraqi dead. This reading is repeated hundreds of times.

21–25 March 'Acting Together for a Just World', the CIVICUS fifth biennial World Assembly, takes place in Gaborone, Botswana.

April 2004

1 April In Nepal, 50,000 people protest against King Gyanendra on the streets of Kathmandu, calling on him to restore regular democratic processes and parliamentary life, which has been suspended for 18 months. The majority of the protests are peaceful but this marks the start of more than 20 days of demonstrations.

3–4 April The Finnish Social Forum takes place in Helsinki.

7 April Hundreds of protesters, including people from international peace groups, take part in demonstrations against the building of the barrier wall under construction by the Israeli government to keep Palestinians out. If completed, the wall will run for 640km (397 miles) through the West Bank. During the protest campaigners try to prevent construction workers cutting down olive trees to make way for the wall in Bidou, near Jerusalem.

21 April Mordechai Vanunu is released from Ashkelon prison in Israel, where he has been a prisoner since 1986 after he alerted the international press to the existence of Israel's nuclear weapons. Systematic international civil society campaigns, coordinated by the Campaign to Free Vanunu and for a Nuclear Free Middle East, are credited with Vanunu's release.

26 April International environmental activists led by Greenpeace block a shipment of genetically modified (GM) foods in Port Kemble Harbour, New South Wales, Australia, for eight hours.

INDEX

Readers interested in previous editions of the Global Civil Society Yearbook can consult the website of the Centre for the study of Global Governance

http://www.lse.ac.uk/depts/global/yearbook

The contents of *Global Civil Society 2001*, *Global Civil Society 2002*, and *Global Civil Society 2003* are listed overleaf.

Global Civil Society 2003
Contents

PART III
Infrastructure of Global Civil Society

PART IV
Records of Global Civil Society

Global Civil Society 2002

Contents

Global Civil Society 2001
Contents